GACE
003

Early Childhood
Special Education
General Curriculum
Teacher Certification Exam

By: Sharon Wynne, M.S.

XAMonline, INC.

Boston

To obtain permission(s) to use the material from this work for any purpose including workshops or seminars, please submit a written request to:

XAMonline, Inc.
25 First Street Suite 106
Cambridge, MA 02141
Toll Free 1-800-509-4128
Email: info@xamonline.com
Web www.xamonline.com
Fax: 1-617-583-5552

Library of Congress Cataloging-in-Publication Data

Wynne, Sharon A.
    GACE: Early Childhood Education Special Education General Curriculum Teacher Certification
/ Sharon A. Wynne. -1st ed.
    ISBN: 978-1-60787- 065-4
    1. Early Childhood Education Special Education   2. Study Guides.   3. GACE
    4. Teachers' Certification & Licensure.   5. Careers

Disclaimer:
The opinions expressed in this publication are the sole works of XAMonline and were created independently from the National Education Association, Educational Testing Service, or any State Department of Education, National Evaluation Systems or other testing affiliates.

Between the time of publication and printing, state specific standards as well as testing formats and website information may change that is not included in part or in whole within this product. Sample test questions are developed by XAMonline and reflect content similar to that on real tests; however, they are not former tests. XAMonline assembles content that aligns with state standards but makes no claims nor guarantees teacher candidates a passing score. Numerical scores are determined by testing companies such as NES or ETS and then are compared with individual state standards. A passing score varies from state to state.

Printed in the United States of America   œ-1

GACE: Early Childhood Special Education General Curriculum
ISBN: 978-1-60787-065-4

Table of Contents

Great Study and Testing Tips!

What to study in order to prepare for the subject assessments is the focus of this study guide, but equally important is *how* you study.

You can increase your chances of truly mastering the information by taking some simple but effective steps.

Study Tips:

1. <u>**Some foods aid the learning process**</u>. Foods such as milk, nuts, seeds, rice, and oats help your study efforts by releasing natural memory enhancers called CCKs (*cholecystokinin*) composed of *tryptophan*, *choline*, and *phenylalanine*. All of these chemicals enhance the neurotransmitters associated with memory. Before studying, try a light, protein-rich meal of eggs, turkey, and fish. All of these foods release the memory enhancing chemicals. The better the connections, the more you comprehend.

Likewise, before you take a test, stick to a light snack of energy-boosting and relaxing foods. A glass of milk, a piece of fruit, or some peanuts will release various memory-boosting chemicals and help you to relax and focus on the subject at hand.

2. <u>**Learn to take great notes**</u>. A by-product of our modern culture is that we have grown accustomed to getting our information in short doses (e.g., TV news sound bites or newspaper articles styled after USA Today).

Consequently, we've subconsciously trained ourselves to assimilate information in <u>neat little packages</u>. If your notes are scrawled all over the paper, it fragments the flow of the information. Strive for clarity. Newspapers use a standard format to achieve clarity. Your notes can be much clearer through the use of proper formatting. A very effective format is called the <u>*"Cornell Method."*</u>

Take a sheet of loose-leaf lined notebook paper and draw a line all the way down the paper about 1-2" from the left-hand edge.

Draw another line across the width of the paper about 1-2" up from the bottom. Repeat this process on the reverse side of the page.

Look at the highly effective result. You have ample room for notes, a left hand margin for special emphasis items or inserting supplementary data from the textbook, a large area at the bottom for a brief summary, and a little rectangular space for just about anything you want.

3. <u>Get the concept, then the details.</u> Too often we focus on the details and don't gather an understanding of the concept. However, if you simply memorize only dates, places, or names, you may well miss the whole point of the subject.

A key way to understand things is to put them in your own words. If you are working from a textbook, automatically summarize each paragraph in your mind. If you are outlining text, don't simply copy the author's words.

Rephrase them in your own words. You remember your own thoughts and words much better than someone else's, and subconsciously tend to associate the important details with the core concepts.

4. <u>Ask Why?</u> Pull apart written material paragraph by paragraph and don't forget the captions under the illustrations.

Example: If the heading is "Stream Erosion," flip it around to read "Why do streams erode?" Then answer the questions.

If you train your mind to think in a series of questions and answers, not only will you learn more, but it will also help to lessen test anxiety because you are used to answering questions.

5. <u>Read for reinforcement and future needs.</u> Even if you only have 10 minutes, put your notes or a book in your hand. Your mind is similar to a computer; you have to input data in order to have it processed. *By reading, you are creating the neural connections for future retrieval.* The more times you read something, the more you reinforce the learning of ideas.

Even if you don't fully understand something on the first pass, *your mind stores much of the material for later recall.*

6. <u>Relax to learn; go into exile.</u> Our bodies respond to an inner clock called biorhythms. Burning the midnight oil works well for some people, but not everyone.

If possible, set aside a particular place to study that is free of distractions. Shut off the television, cell phone, and pager, and exile your friends and family during your study period.

If you really are bothered by silence, try background music. Light classical music at a low volume has been shown to be particularly effective in aiding concentration. Music that evokes pleasant emotions without lyrics is highly recommended. Try just about anything by Mozart. It relaxes you.

7. <u>Use arrows, not highlighters</u>. At best, it's difficult to read a page full of yellow, pink, blue, and green streaks. Try staring at a neon sign for a while and you'll soon see that the horde of colors obscure the message.

A quick note, a brief dash of color, an underline, or an arrow pointing to a particular passage is much clearer than a horde of highlighted words.

8. <u>Budget your study time</u>. Although you shouldn't ignore any of the material, *allocate your available study time in the same ratio that topics may appear on the test.*

By setting your personal study topics in much the same way that the test will be patterned, you will be better equipped to answer all of the test questions.

Testing Tips:

1. Get smart, play dumb. *Don't read anything into the question.* Don't make an assumption that the test writer is looking for something other than what is asked. Stick to the question as written and don't read extra things into it.

2. Read the question and all the choices *twice* before answering the question. You may miss something by not carefully reading and re-reading both the question and the answers.

If you really don't have a clue as to the right answer, leave it blank on the first time through. Go on to the other questions, as they may provide a clue as to how to answer the skipped questions.

If, later on, you still can't answer the skipped ones . . . *Guess.* The only penalty for guessing is that you *might* get it wrong. Only one thing is certain; if you don't put anything down, you will get it wrong!

3. Turn the question into a statement. Look at the way the questions are worded. The syntax of the question usually provides a clue. Does it seem more familiar as a statement rather than as a question? Does it sound strange?

By turning a question into a statement, you may be able to spot if an answer sounds right, and it may also trigger memories of material you have read.

4. Look for hidden clues. It's actually very difficult to compose multiple-foil (choice) questions without giving away part of the answer in the options presented.

In most multiple-choice questions you can often readily eliminate one or two of the potential answers. This leaves you with only two real possibilities; automatically, your odds go to Fifty-Fifty for very little work.

5. Trust your instincts. For every fact that you have read, you subconsciously retain something of that knowledge. On questions that you aren't really certain about, go with your basic instincts. *Your first impression on how to answer a question is usually correct.*

6. Mark your answers directly on the test booklet. Don't bother trying to fill in the optical scan sheet on the first pass through the test.

Just be very careful not to mismark your answers when you eventually transcribe them to the scan sheet.

7. Watch the clock! You have a set amount of time to answer the questions. Don't get bogged down trying to answer a single question at the expense of ten questions you can more readily answer.

SUBAREA I   READING AND ENGLISH LANGUAGE ARTS

OBJECTIVE 1   UNDERSTAND CONCEPTS OF PRINT, PHONOLOGICAL
                   AWARENESS, AND WORD IDENTIFICATION
                   STRATEGIES, INCLUDING PHONICS

SKILL 1.1   Recognizing developmental stages in learning to write and
             read and how beginning writers and readers learn to apply
             knowledge of the relationship between letters and letter
             combinations of written words and the sounds of spoken
             words

Sequence of Reading and Writing Development[SAW2]

It should be noted that research shows that from the most basic foundation
concepts required to learn the skills, to the stages through which students move
as they learn, reading and writing are two sides of the same coin. Both rely upon
understanding the same metalinguistic principles: the alphabetic principle and
sound-letter associations, the structure of language, and the conventions of
writing. Regardless of the specific system or labels used to describe the stages
of development, reading and writing skills will each follow complementary paths.
In a given child, sometimes reading skills will outpace writing skills, or writing
skills outpace reading skills, but both will follow a similar path and each skill can
be used to assist learning of the other. Specific learning disabilities (to be
discussed later) can, however, impact one (either reading or writing) more
heavily than the other.

The U.S. Department of Education and the National Reading Panel (2000) have
described a research based sequence of typical reading development that begins
at home, and moves through preschool to about grade three, when a child begins
to transition *from learning to read, to reading to learn*. Although children
progress through these stages at different speeds and show strengths and
weaknesses in differing areas, most will move through these stages in this order.
For convenience, brief descriptions of the concurrent stage of writing
development are included.

Age 3-4 through PreK: Developing Print concepts. Children learn that print
has meaning and that meaning does not change with successive readings. They
learn print directionality. In English, this means that books are read from front
(left) to back (right) and that print is read from left to right, and top to bottom.
They learn that pictures are related to print.

During this period, the child's language concepts are also developing. Chief among these is phonological awareness, the awareness of all the sound aspects of spoken language. Most critical for the later development of reading is phonemic awareness, the awareness that spoken words are made up of discrete sounds uttered in a specific order.

This stage's progress is largely determined by whether parents read to their children. Parents generally begin to read to their children when they are between 4 to 8 months old. Significant in the parental reading to a child is the recognition that the print does not change, thus the story does not change. Children begin to mimic the story or "read along" with the parents around 8 months of age. At times the child may even hold the book upside down and repeat the story the parent/guardian has read to them. This shared reading aids a child to recognize letters at an earlier age.

In addition, when children scribble write or use invented spelling during their preschool years, they reveal themselves as detectives of the written word, having watched parents make lists, write thank-you notes, or leave messages. Children show an understanding that print contains a message and they often draw-write to send a message. They may not be able to write many letters, but will begin to draw shapes that resemble letters or use a few known letters (or approximations of letters) in their "writing." This view of the reader/writer assumes that all children have a drive to make meaning out of print and will begin doing it almost on their own if surrounded by a print-rich environment.

Kindergarten-First Grade: Beginning alphabetic concepts. Children learn to manipulate phonemes, or sounds, in words by deleting, adding, or substituting sounds in individual words, and blending those sounds into new words orally. They also begin to understand the alphabetic principle that letters stand for sounds and that words have correct spellings. They can recognize and name most letters of the alphabet and they begin to identify the most common sounds of most letters.

At this stage, they can also recognize high frequency sight words and can begin to decode simple texts. They can make predictions about what is read to them and ask and answer questions about what they read.

Writing at this stage shows the child's emerging understanding of the alphabetic principle and phonics. Writers use very simple oral language structures and use at least some real letters. They may get only the first or first and last letter/sound or only the most noticeable sound(s) in a word when writing. They begin to show an understanding of the one to one correspondence between words in speech and words on the page (i.e., there are spaces between their "words.").

Second: Expanded phonics knowledge and decoding. The child's knowledge of phonics, the sound letter code, improves and he/she can decode both one and two syllable words, and use context (both syntactic and semantic) cues to help decode unfamiliar words. The child can sequence events in a simple story, make brief oral summaries of material read, and begins to understand story elements and main ideas.

The child's writing shows the growing understanding of phonics, and invented spelling becomes more phonetic. Some frequently used words will be spelled correctly. When writing about topics which interest them and with which they have a rich background of information, students can use basic sentence structures with some variation in beginnings, and may begin to try to use "cool" words they encounter in reading or listening. Students begin to attempt to use punctuation and capitalization correctly.

Third Grade: Transition to reading to Learn. Up to this point, children have been engaged in learning to read, in acquiring the many skills necessary to construct meaning from print, and to encode their own ideas in print through writing. Sometime during third grade, children typically acquire sufficient reading ability to use that ability to learn other information from content area texts. The opening page of the Georgia Performance Standards Frameworks for Reading describes this stage:

"Third graders are making the transition from learning to read to reading to learn. They read much more widely on a variety of topics. The third-grade students increase their abilities to read aloud with fluency and comprehension. Third graders read more thoughtfully, discover more details, extract deeper meaning in what they read, and read more complex texts. They enjoy a variety of genres, including fiction and non-fiction texts and poetry.

Third graders are more able to work independently on research projects, making their writing more sophisticated and meaningful. With some guidance, they use all aspects of the writing process in producing their own compositions and reports. They are much more adept at summarizing main points from fiction and non-fiction texts, and they use more abstract skills of synthesis and evaluation in writing.

By the end of the third grade, students are aware of the importance of the conventions of language. Third graders understand the importance of spelling and the importance of correct language.

Third-grade responses to questions are more logically developed as students show evidence of expanding language with increased vocabulary and a wider range of language structures. Third graders are aware of the many registers of language, and they become flexible in their ability to vary language patterns in both speaking and writing. These students are ready to engage in abstract discussions as they respond to text and to life experiences."

Writers at this stage are able to group sentences together by topic into paragraphs and write in a variety of forms (e.g., informational text, reports, poetry, and stories).

Throughout these stages in the development of reading and writing skills, there are a number of critical areas to consider when planning how to help children move through these stages and become proficient readers and writers.
In 2000, the National Reading Panel released its now well-known report on teaching children to read. In a way, this report slightly put to rest the debate between phonics and whole language. It argued, essentially, that word-letter recognition was as important as understanding what the text means. The report's "big 5" critical areas of reading instruction are as follows:

Phonemic Awareness: This is the understanding that words are composed of tiny, individual sounds (phonemes) which must be blended together to make each word. It is the acknowledgement of sounds and words (for example, a child's realization that some words rhyme). Onset and rhyme are two of the skills that might help students learn that the first sound ('buh') in the word "bad" can be changed to the sound "duh" to make it "dad." The key in phonemic awareness is that when you teach it to children, it can be taught with the students' eyes closed. In other words, it's all about sounds, not about ascribing written letters to sounds.

Phonics: As opposed to phonemic awareness, the study of phonics must be done with the eyes open. It is the connection between the sounds and letters on a page. In other words, students who are learning phonics might see the word "bad" and sound each letter out slowly until they recognize that they just said the word.

Comprehension: Comprehension simply means that the reader can ascribe meaning to text. Even though students may be good with phonics and even know what many words on a page mean, some of them are not good with comprehension because they do not know the strategies that would help them to comprehend. For example, students should know that stories often have structures (beginning, middle, and end). They should also know that when they are reading something and it does not make sense, they will need to employ "fix-up" strategies where they go back into the text they have just read and look for clues. Teachers can use many strategies to teach comprehension, including questioning, asking students to paraphrase or summarize, utilizing graphic organizers, and focusing on mental images.

Fluency: Fluency is the ability to read in much the same manner as speaking, with fluidity and smoothness. Students who are fluent readers are more likely to be successful with comprehension, as they are less focused on individual words and more focused on what is actually being read.

Vocabulary: Vocabulary demonstrates the strong ties between oral and written language. Students who are learning to read are just beginning to realize the link between the words they say and the words they read. Increasing vocabulary—whether by listening to others, reading to themselves, or being read to—will help students with both comprehension and fluency.

Methods used to teach these skills are often featured in a "balanced literacy" curriculum that focuses on the use of skills in various instructional contexts. For example, with independent reading, students independently choose books that are at their reading levels; with guided reading, teachers work with small groups of students to help them with their particular reading problems. With whole group reading, the entire class reads the same text, and the teacher incorporates activities to help students learn phonics, comprehension, fluency, and vocabulary. In addition to these components of balanced literacy, teachers incorporate writing so that students can learn the structures of communicating through text.

SKILL 1.2   **Demonstrating knowledge of characteristics and purposes of printed information and developmentally appropriate strategies for promoting students' familiarity with concepts of print**[SAW3]

Development of the Understanding that Print Carries Meaning

This understanding is demonstrated every day in the elementary classroom when a teacher holds up a selected book to read it aloud to the class. The teacher is explicitly and deliberately thinking about how to hold the book, how to focus the class on looking at its cover, where to start reading, and in what direction to begin.

Even in writing the morning message on the board, the teacher is targeting the children by placing the message at its proper place at the top of the board and following it by additional activities and a schedule for the rest of the day. When the teacher challenges children to make posters of items that begin with a single letter by using the items in the classroom, their home, or their general knowledge base, the children are making concrete the understanding that print carries meaning.

Strategies for Promoting Awareness of the Relationship between Spoken and Written Language

- Write down what the children are saying on a chart.
- Highlight and celebrate the meanings and uses of print products found in the classroom. These products include: posters, labels, yellow sticky pad notes, labels on shelves and lockers, calendars, rule signs, and directions.
- Intentionally read big-print and oversized books to teach print conventions such as directionality.
- Practice exercises in reading to others (for K-1-2) through which young children practice how to handle a book: how to turn pages, how to find tops and bottoms of pages, and how to tell the difference between the front and back covers of a book.
- Search and discuss adventures in word awareness and close observation through which children are challenged to identify and talk about the length, appearance, and boundaries of specific words, and the letters which comprise them.
- Have children match oral words to printed words by forming an echo chorus (where children echo the reading) as the teacher reads the story aloud. This often works best with poetry or rhymes.
- Have the children combine, manipulate, switch, and move letters to change words and spelling patterns.
- Work with letter cards to create messages and respond to the messages that they create.

The Role of Environmental Print in Developing Print Awareness

An environmental print book can be created that contains collaged symbols of the labels from, e.g., students' favorite lunch or breakfast foods. Initially, this can be created by the teacher, but later the teacher can ask students to bring in their labels and alphabetically arrange the cut and clipped symbols from the packaging of these foods into the book. Students can then add to the book as they clip and place symbols and logos from additional sources of environmental print.

Newspapers are an excellent and easily available source of environmental print. With food ads, clothing ads, and other child-centered products and personalities, a newspaper lends itself wonderfully to developing print awareness activities. Supermarket circulars and coupons distributed in chain drug stores are also excellent for engaging children in using environmental print as a reading device. What is particularly effective in using environmental print is that it immediately transports all children, including those from an ELL background into print awareness through the familiarity of commercial logos and packaging symbols used on a daily basis.

Development of Book Handling Skills

Have the children identify the front cover, back cover, and title page of a specific book.

Model storytelling by holding the book up and facing the audience so that they can see the illustrations shown to them. Then have them demonstrate the skills for their peers. A modified "show and tell" format

Have children search through the class libraries for special features on the fronts or backs of books as they help return the books to their bins. Have the children display and talk about the special symbols they found.

Review with the children, in an age and grade appropriate format, additional parts of the book as they emerge through the mini-lessons and read alouds. These additional parts of the book can include: title pages, dedication page, foreword, appendix, credits, copyright date, table of contents, etc.

Techniques for Promoting the Ability to Track Print in Connected Texts

Model directionality and one-to-one word matching by pointing to words while using a big book, pocket chart, or poem written out on a chart. As you repeatedly lead the children in this reading, they can follow along and eventually track the print, and also make one-to-one matches on the connected text independently. They can also practice by using a pointer (most children love to use the pointer because then pleasure becomes associated with the reading) or their fingers to follow the words. In general, children will happily vie to be the point person. Even before Vanna White, the joy of "signifying letters" existed and has tremendous appeal for children.

Copy down a brief, familiar rhyme (perhaps from a favorite book or song) and post it in the room at a child's eye level, so the child can independently walk around and read it.

Copy down a brief or familiar rhyme or poem on individual word cards. You can challenge the children in small groups or independently to reassemble and display them on a pocket chart. As children "play" with constructing and reconstructing this pocket chart, they will develop an awareness of directionality, one-on-one matching of print to spoken words, spacing, and punctuation.

Model interactive emergent writing with the class. While discussing and writing down the weather, deliberately ask and have the children suggest where the first word in that report should go: the top or the bottom of the felt board? Will the first letter be upper case or lower case? What goes at the end of the sentence?

Create with the children sing-song repetitions/rules for using capitals, periods, commas, etc. Encourage the children to begin reciting these sing-songs as soon as they identify specific concepts of print in connected texts.

Model for children how, when pointing at words, they can start at the top and move from left to right. Tell the children that if there are more words to the sentence they are reading under the first line of print, they must go back to the left and under the previous line. Young children enjoy practicing this kinesthetic "return sweep." You might want to teach them to identify the need to do this by saying "don't fall asleep at the page" or "time to get to the 'return sweep' stage!!" Post this saying and encourage them to sing-song as they joyously take ownership of their reading.

Have even beginning readers "read" through the text to find letters they recognize in the story. Share some of the text that includes these specific letters to whet their appetite for more reading.

Strategies for Promoting Letter Knowledge and Letter Formation

Engage the children in a "tale trail" game. Use a story they have already heard or read. Ask the children to circle certain letters and then re-read the story, sharing the letters they have circled.

Give the children plenty of opportunities to do letter sorts. Pass out word cards which have the targeted letter on them. Ask the children to come up and display their answers to questions about the letter. As an example, consider the letter "R."

- R as the first letter—rose, rise, ran,
- R as the last letter—car, star, far,
- R with a t after it—start, heart, part, smart
- Two Rs in the middle of a word—carry, sorry, starry

Play "What's in a Name?" Select a student's name. As an example, consider "William." Copy the name down on a sentence strip. Have the children count the number of letters in the name and how many of them appear twice. Allow them to talk about which letter is upper case and which letters are lower case. Have the students chant the name. Then rewrite the name on another sentence strip. Have the strip cut into separate letters and see if someone from the class can put the name back together correctly.

As you read a book with or to the children, ask them to show you specific letters or lower case or upper case letters. Read the text first and encourage as many children as possible to come up and identify the letters. Use a big book and have felt letters available for display as well. If grade-, age-, and developmentally-appropriate, have the children write the letter they identified themselves. (Or, for even more fun, construct the letter using pipe cleaners, craft sticks, or colored markers, using different colors for upper and lower case letters.)

Play "letter leap" with the children and have them look carefully at the room to identify labeled items that begin with a specific letter by "leaping" over to them and placing a large lettered placard next to them. Children who have advanced in letter formation can then be challenged to "leap" through the classroom when called upon to literally "letter" unlabeled objects.

Use of Reading and Writing Strategies for Teaching Letter-Sound Correspondence

Provide children with a sample of a single letter book (or create one from environmental sources, newspapers, coupons, circulars, magazines, or your own text ideas). Make sure that your selected or created sample includes a printed version of the letter in both upper and lower case forms. Make certain that each page contains a picture of something that starts with that specific letter and also has the word for the picture. The book you select or create should be a predictable one in that when the picture is identified, the word can be read.

Once the children have been provided with your sample and have listened to it being read, challenge them to each make a single letter book. It is often best to focus on familiar consonants or the first letter of the child's first name. Use of the first letter of a name invites children to develop a book that tells about themselves and the words that they find. This is an excellent way for the reading workshop aspect of teaching alphabetic principles to complement and enhance the writing workshop.

Encourage children to be active writers and readers by finding words for their book on the classroom word wall, in alphabet books in the special alphabet book bin, and in grade- and age-appropriate pictionaries (dictionaries for younger children that are filled with pictures).

Of course, the richest resource within the reading and writing workshop classroom for teaching and fostering the alphabetic principle lies in the use of alphabet books as anchor books for inspiring students' writing. While young children in grades K-1 will do better with the single letter book authoring activity, children in grades 2 and beyond can truly be inspired and motivated by alphabet books that enhance their own reading, writing, and alphabetic skills. Furthermore, use of these books—which have and are being produced in a variety of formats to enhance social studies, science, and mathematical themes—provides an opportunity for even young children to create a meaningful product that authenticates their content study while enhancing alphabetic skills and, of course, print awareness[SAW4]. Consider selecting an alphabet book that has a particularly inviting concept, art style, or adaptable format within the children's capacity to use as a model.

For example, author Tana Hoban uses actual color photographs of letters in her *26 Letters and 99 Cents*. Children may want to make clay letters or create letter sculptures that develop their own "in style of" alphabet book similar to Hoban's. If nutrition is the science topic, children might want to examine Lois Ehlert's very accessible *Eating the Alphabet: Fruits and Vegetables from A to Z*. This, combined with an examination of the fruits and vegetables in a local store (perhaps a pleasant walk from the school and a quick break from the routine local outing) can yield a wonderful alphabet book on fruits and vegetables that can also include those fruits and vegetables eaten in various cultures (e.g., mangos, plantains, pomegranates, etc).

The alphabet book can also offer the class a chance to work collaboratively within a template created by the teacher. Completion of this collaborative work can be shared with peers in another class and parents. It can also be kept as a model for the following year's class (of course, with the recognition and acceptance of the authors!).

SKILL 1.3 Demonstrating knowledge of phonological awareness (e.g., awareness that spoken words consist of sound units such as syllables) and phonemic awareness (e.g., the ability to perceive and discriminate among the component sounds in words[SAW5])

Phonological Awareness: Flippo (2002) states that phonological awareness "refers to an awareness of *many* aspects of spoken language, including words within sentences, syllables within words, and phonemes within syllables and words…"

Phonological awareness refers to the ability of the reader to recognize the various levels and chunks (syllables, words, etc.) of sound in spoken language. This recognition includes how these sounds can be blended together, segmented (divided up), and manipulated (switched around). This awareness then leads to phonics, a method for teaching children to read. It helps them "sound out words." Development of phonological skills may begin during pre-K years. Indeed, by the age of five, a child who has been exposed to rhyme can recognize a rhyme. Such a child can demonstrate phonological awareness by filling in the missing rhyming word in a familiar rhyme or rhymed picture book.

Phoneme awareness is one part of phonological awareness, and is the understanding that spoken words are composed of tiny, individual sound units, called phonemes. Again, children need to learn to segment, blend, and manipulate the individual sounds in the language in order to be ready to learn to read. Children need a strong background in phonemic awareness in order for phonics instruction (sound-spelling relationships in print) to be effective.

Knowledge of Phonemes

In order to assess and teach phoneme awareness and, subsequently, phonics, a teacher must be familiar with the phonemes of the English language. A **phoneme** is the smallest unit of sound that can distinguish one word from another. The phoneme is said to have mental, physiological, and physical substance: our brains process the sounds; the human speech organs produce the sounds; and the sounds are physical entities that can be recorded and measured. Consider the English words "pat" and "sat," which appear to differ only in their initial consonants. This difference, known as *contrastiveness* or *opposition*, is sufficient to distinguish these words, and therefore the "p" and "s" sounds are said to be different phonemes in English. They sound different, our mouths and tongues move differently to produce them, and we can process the difference mentally. A pair of words, identical except for such a sound, is known as a *minimal pair*, and the two sounds that distinguish each from the other are separate phonemes.

Where no minimal pair can exist to demonstrate that two sounds are distinct, it may be that they are *allophones*. An allophone is a slight variation in a phoneme's sound, a variation not recognized as distinct by a speaker, and not meaningfully different in the language, so these "allophones" are perceived as being the same. An example of this would be the heavy sounding "l" when landed on at the end of a word like "wool," as opposed to the lighter sounding "l" when starting a word like "leaf." This demonstrates allophones of a single phoneme. While it may exist and be measurable, such a difference is unrecognizable and meaningless to the average English speaker. The real value is as a technique for teaching reading and pronunciation. Identifying phonemes for students and applying their use is a step in the process of developing language fluency. American English has 44 phonemes, and they are usually listed like this:

Phoneme	Sound and sample spellings (graphemes)
/A/	a (table), a_e (bake), ai (train), ay (say)
/a/	a (flat)
/b/	b (ball)
/k/	c (cake), k (Key), ck (back)
/d/	d (door)
/E/	e (me), ee (feet), ea (leap), y (baby)
/e/	e (pet), ea (head)
/f/	f (fix), ph (phone)
/g/	g (gas)
/h/	h (hot)
/I/	i (I), i_e (bite), igh (light), y (sky)
/i/	i (sit)
/j/	j (jet), dge (edge), g (gem)
/l/	l (lamp)
/m/	m (map)
/n/	n (no), kn (knock)
/O/	o (okay), o_e (bone), oa (soap), ow (low)
/o/	o (hot)
/p/	p (pie)
/kw/	qu (quick)
/r/	r (road), wr (wrong), er (her), ir (sir), ur (fur)
/s/	s (say), c (cent)
/t/	t (time)
/U/	u (future), u_e (use), ew (few)
/u/	u thumb, a (about)
/v/	v (voice)
/w/	w (wash)
/gz/	x (exam)
/ks/	x (box)
/y/	y (yes)
/z/	z (zoo), s (nose)

/OO/	oo (boot), u (truth), u_e (rude), ew (chew)
/oo/	oo (book), u (put)
/oi/	oi (soil), oy (toy)
/ou/	ou (out), ow (cow)
/aw/	aw (saw), au (caught), al (tall)
/ar/	ar (car)
/sh/	sh (ship), ti (nation), ci (special)
/hw/	wh (white)
/ch/	ch (chest), tch (catch)
/th/	th (thick)
/th/	th (this)
/ng/	ng (sing)
/zh/	s (measure)

The oral production of these phonemes provides kinesthetic feedback that children have unconsciously learned as they learn to speak their language at home. The teacher can use this to help children discriminate among these sounds by calling attention to the different ways we produce the sounds, the differing positions of lips, tongue, and teeth. Children will differ in the amount of help they will need to develop their phoneme awareness. Once children have a good grounding in phoneme awareness, they are ready to study phonics.

Skill 1.5 discusses strategies for helping students develop phonemic and phonological awareness.

SKILL 1.4 Analyzing the significance of phonological and phonemic awareness in reading acquisition

The National Reading Panel's report (2000) on learning to read specifically listed phonemic awareness as one of the five critical skills necessary to learning to read. It also discussed the need for overall phonological awareness. As discussed in the previous section, phonological awareness involves recognizing that spoken words are comprised of a set of smaller units—including syllables and sounds, and phonemic awareness is a specific type of phonological awareness that focuses on the ability to distinguish, manipulate, and blend specific sounds or phonemes *within a given word*. Think of phonological awareness as an umbrella and phonemic awareness as a specific spoke under this umbrella.

Since the ability to distinguish between individual sounds, or phonemes, within words is a prerequisite to association of sounds with letters and manipulating sounds to blend words—a fancy way of saying "reading"—the teaching of phonemic awareness is crucial to emergent literacy (early childhood K-2 reading instruction). Children need a strong background in phonemic awareness in order for phonics instruction (sound-spelling relationships in print) to be effective.

The National Reading Panel (2000) specified six phoneme awareness skills crucial to learning to read:

- Phoneme isolation: recognizing individual sounds (/g/ and /O/ in "go")
- Phoneme identification: Recognizing common sounds in different words (/b/ in boy, bike, and bell)
- Phoneme categorization: recognizing sounds in sequence (bus, bun, rug)
- Phoneme blending: hearing a series of individual phonemes, then blending them into a word (hearing /g/ /O/ and saying "go")
- Phoneme segmentation: separating and counting out the sounds in a word (given "go" saying /g/ and /O/)
- Phoneme deletion: recognizing what would be left if one phoneme is removed (hear "flat" and remove the /f/ sound and state that "lat" would be left)

Phonics deals with printed words and the learning of sound-spelling correlations; that is, learning to assign discrete phonemes to various letters and letter combinations. Children, who have problems with phonics, learning the letter-sound code of English, often have deficits in these phonemic awareness skills. Often, they have not acquired or been exposed to phonemic awareness activities usually fostered at home and in preschool to second grade, such as extensive songs, rhymes and read –alouds. In other cases, the child may have a disability that affects phoneme awareness, and needs more explicit instruction and/or more practice with these skills.

Assessment of Phonological and Phonemic Awareness

These skills can be assessed by having the child listen to the teacher say two words. The child should then be asked to decide if these two words are the same word repeated twice or two different words. When you make this assessment, if you do use two different words, make certain that they only differ by one phoneme, such as /d/ and /g/. Children can be assessed on words that are not real words or that are not familiar to them. The words used can be make-believe. Teachers can maintain ongoing logs and rubrics for assessment throughout the year of Phonemic Awareness for individual children. Such assessments would identify particular stated reading behaviors or performance standards, the date of observation of the child's behavior (in this context, phonemic activity or exercise), and comments.

The rubric or legend for assessing these behaviors might include the following descriptors: demonstrates or exhibits reading behavior consistently, making progress/strides toward this reading behavior, and/or has not yet demonstrated or exhibited this behavior.

Depending on the particular phonological task you are modeling, the performance task might include:

- Saying rhyming words in response to an oral prompt
- Segmenting a word spoken by the teacher into its beginning, middle, and ending sounds (phonemic)
- Correctly counting the number of syllables in a spoken word (phonological)
- Changing or rearranging a syllable orally in a word (e.g., "change the first syllable in the word 'cricket' to /pak/.")(phonological)
- Changing the beginning, middle, or ending sound in a word (e.g., "change the sound at the beginning of the word 'dog' to the /l/ sound"—phonemic, etc).

THE ROLE OF PHONOLOGICAL PROCESSING IN THE READING DEVELOPMENT OF INDIVIDUAL STUDENTS

English Language Learners (ELL)

Children who are raised in homes where English is not the first language and/or standard English is not spoken may have difficulty with hearing the difference between similar sounding words like "send" and "sent." Any child who is not in a home, day care, or preschool environment where English phonology operates may have difficulty perceiving and demonstrating the differences between English language phonemes. In other words, their *phoneme* awareness in terms of the English language will be poor. If children cannot hear the difference between words that sound the same like "grow" and "glow," they will be confused when these words appear in a print context. This confusion is likely to impact their comprehension.

Considerations for teaching phonological processing to ELL children include recognition by the teacher that what works for the English language speaking child from an English language speaking family does not necessarily work with students who speak other primary languages.

Research recommends that ELL children initially learn to read in their first language. It has also been found that a priority for ELL should be learning to speak English before being taught to read English. Research supports oral language development, since it lays the foundation for phonological awareness. All phonological instruction programs must be tailored to the children's learning backgrounds. Rhymes and alliteration introduced to ELL children should be read or shared with them in their first language, if possible. If you do not speak the student's first language, get a paraprofessional or pull out an ELL educator to support your instruction in the first language.

Struggling Readers

Among the causes that make reading a struggle for some children (and adults) is auditory trauma or ear infections that affect the ability to hear speech. Such children need one-on-one support with articulation and perception of different sounds. When a child says a word such as "parrot" incorrectly, repeat it back as a question with the correct pronunciation of the sounds. If the child "gets" the sound correctly after your question, this type of extra support was all that was needed. If the child still has difficulty with pronunciation, it may be necessary to consult with a speech therapist or audiologist. Early identification of medical conditions that affect hearing is crucial to reading development. Therefore, as an educator, you need to make the time to sit with struggling readers and play games such as "same or different" in order to identify those children who may be struggling due to a hearing difficulty.

The most common characteristic among children with language learning disabilities that produce delays in learning to read is weakness in either phonological or phonemic awareness. Many students with reading disabilities will have been diagnosed with some form of Dyslexia. Dyslexia is a language learning disorder that is often based on difficulties with phonological awareness and processing. Common symptoms included difficulty decoding words, poor fluency, poor writing and spelling, and sometimes comprehension difficulties, as well. These difficulties are present in spite of normal intelligence and instructional methods. Pierangelo & Giuliani (2007) describe a variety of types of Dyslexia cited by and most of them have phonemic or phonological weakness as one significant component.

SKILL 1.5   Recognizing developmentally appropriate strategies for promoting students' phonological and phonemic awareness (e.g., identifying rhyming words, segmenting words, blending phonemes)

As discussed in previous sections, phonological awareness is the awareness of numerous principles of sound in the language, including the sounds of words, sentences, syllables, and phonemes. Phonemic awareness is the understanding that words are made up of distinct elements of sound and the ability to manipulate those phonemes.

The key in phonemic and phonological awareness is that they can be taught with the students' eyes closed. In other words, it's all about sounds, not about ascribing written letters to sounds. To be phonemically aware means that the reader and listener can recognize and manipulate specific sounds in **spoken** words. Phonemic awareness deals with sounds in words that are spoken. The majority of both phonological and phonemic awareness tasks, activities, and exercises are therefore ORAL.

Phonemic awareness skills are a subset of phonological awareness skills. Phonological awareness skills that go beyond the single word phonemic awareness skills might include:

- Clapping or tapping out first the words in a sentence, then the syllables in a word (clapping or tapping the individual sounds within a word would be a phonemic awareness task-see below)
- Manipulating and rearranging the syllables in a word
- Rhyming
- Recognizing other smaller words in the bigger word by removing parts of the word (recognizing the word "art" in "smart")
- Phonemic awareness activities, below, are a type of phonological awareness activity

Phoneme Awareness Activities

Blevins (1997) describes the earlier work of theorist Marilyn Jager Adams in designing five types of phoneme awareness tasks that can be used in the classroom. These align well with the International Reading Associations' Reading Panel Report, *Teaching Children to Read* (2002) and its analysis of phoneme awareness skills.

Task 1—the ability to hear rhymes and alliteration—for example, the children listen to a poem, rhyming picture book or song and identify the rhyming words heard.

Task 2—the ability to do oddity tasks (recognize the member of a set that is different [odd] among the group)—for example, the children look at the pictures of a door, a dog, and a cat, and say each word. The teacher asks which starts with a different sound.

Task 3—the ability to orally blend words and split syllables—for example, the children can say the first sound of a word (e.g., /b/) and then the rest of the word (/at/) and then put it together as a single word (bat), as in onsets and rimes.

Task 4—the ability to orally segment words—for example, the ability to count sounds. The children would be asked as a group to count the sounds in "sat" (/s/, /a/, /t/--3 sounds).

Task 5—the ability to do phoneme manipulation tasks—for example, replace the "r" sound in rose with a "n" sound and say "nose."

Other instructional methods that may be effective for teaching phonemic awareness include:

- Clapping the SOUNDS (not syllables) in words. (e.g., "bat" has three sounds, /b/, /a/, /t/)
- Games where students must identify the beginning, middle, or end sound (not letter) of a word (e.g., "Find something that begins with the /t/ sound").
- Games with common nursery rhymes where the students change one sound in several words (e.g., "Jack and Jill went up the hill..." Now change Jack and Jill to begin like 'Mary")
- Using visual cues and movements to help children understand when the speaker goes from one sound to another. This can also be done with colored blocks, a different color for each sound, and children can move their blocks around as the teacher moves the sound around (e.g. starting with three different colored blocks for "cat" and changing the "word" to "tac.")
- Singing familiar songs (e.g., Happy Birthday, Knick Knack Paddy Wack) and replacing key words with words with a different ending or middle sound (oral segmentation).
- Dealing children a deck of picture cards and having them sound out the words for the pictures on their cards or calling for a picture by asking for its first and second sound.
- Onset and rhyme games where children are given a beginning sound and told to blend it with a specific series of endings (e.g., "OK, start with /ch/ and add "eep' then "eet" etc.)
- Games like "I'm going on vacation and I'm taking a (something that begins or ends with a particular phoneme)
- Auditory games and drills during which students recognize and manipulate the sounds of words, separate or segment the sounds of words, take out sounds, blend sounds, add in new sounds, or take apart sound to recombine them in new formations are good ways to foster phonological awareness
- Using kinesthetic feedback, particularly the position of the lips, teeth and tongue, as well as the vibration of the voice box, to identify various phonemes

Consideration for ELL Learners

Given the demographics of our country, which is becoming increasingly pluralistic and has burgeoning numbers of citizens who are from other language backgrounds, the likelihood that you will be teaching at least one, if not more, children who are from a non-native English speaking background (even though they may not be officially classified as ELL students), is at least 75 percent[SAW7]. Therefore, as a conscientious educator, it is important that you understand the special factors involved in supporting their literacy development, including fostering progress in native language literacy as a perquisite for second language (English) reading progress.

Although there are hundreds of phonemes that can be and are produced by the human vocal system, and babies are typically born with the ability to hear and produce all of them, by about a year of age a child's phoneme production has become somewhat restricted to the phonemes characteristic of the language(s) the child hears on a daily basis. Since languages differ in the specific set of phonemes they use, not all English phonemes are present in other languages. If a phoneme is not used in the child's native language, the child learns to ignore it aurally, and does not learn to produce it. Sometimes the phonemes learned in one language actively interfere with learning the phonemes of another.

This means that students from other language groups may never have learned to distinguish some English phonemes that, to a native English speaker, would be obvious and clear. For example, in some languages (e.g., Japanese) there is no distinct phoneme for the sound /r/, so the sounds of /l/ and /r/, which involve similar positioning of tongue and mouth, are easily confused. They have also not learned to produce those phonemes, and they have not learned the system of rules for combining phonemes that are obvious to a native English speaker. These rules are often unstated and unconscious (e.g., in English, you can put the sound /s/ before the sound /l/, but you cannot put the sound /m/ before /l/; you can put the sound /t/ before /r/, but not the sound /t/ before /l/. Most people would not be able to verbalize the rule; they just wouldn't do it).

When teaching phonological and phonemic awareness to ELL students, therefore, it is necessary to begin at the very early stages of phonemic awareness and determine which phonemes are going to be the most difficult for the student.

It is recommended that all teachers of reading—particularly those who are working with ELL students—use meaningful, student-centered, and culture-customized activities. These activities may include: language games, word walls, and poems. Some of these activities might also, if possible, be initiated in the child's first language and then reiterated in English.

Considerations for Struggling Readers

Modern research on the manner in which the brain learns to read an alphabetic language such as English points to deficits in phonological and phonemic awareness as key sources of interference for students who struggle to learn to read. Willis (2008), in her review of neuro-imaging and magneto encephalography research, describes three areas of the brain that must function well *together* in order for the child to learn to decode written symbols and understand their meaning. Readers with weaknesses or with disabilities that produce deficits in any of these areas may struggle to learn critical phonological and phonemic awareness skills. Such readers will need a great deal of support and practice at the phonological awareness level before and while moving on to phonics and other decoding skills. These students may need not only *more practice* with phonological awareness tasks, but also *different kinds of practice.* They may need more emphasis on kinesthetic feedback in producing distinct sounds and more multimedia and hands on activities.

Points to Ponder:

- Phonological awareness is auditory
- It does not involve print
- It must start before children have learned letter-sound correlations
- It is the basis for the successful teaching of phonics and spelling
- It can and must be taught and nurtured

SKILL 1.6 Demonstrating knowledge of phonics skills and their application to decoding unfamiliar words; the use of spelling patterns and syllabication as decoding techniques; and structural analysis (e.g., identifying prefixes, suffixes, and roots) as a word identification strategy

DECODING

Decoding is both a skill and a process by which the reader translates written symbols (letters of the alphabet) into the words which make up our language. It includes translating letters and combinations of letters into the sounds of our language, as well as using other semantic and syntactic knowledge to translate letters into words and words into sentences. This process and skill is critical to the ability to read. Before meaning can be constructed from printed letters, the letters must be translated (decoded) into words.

Effective word recognition involves the use of multiple cueing systems and readers must learn to use them all in unison, relying on one set more heavily in some situations, and on other cues in other situations. The teacher must not only teach these skills, but help the student learn strategies for determining which skill or combination of skills will be most useful in different situations.

Graphophonemic cues are cues related to the association of phonemes with specific letters or letter combinations. This is the area generally known as **phonics**.

Morphemic cues are cues related to the structure of words, to how words and word parts can be combined to make meaningful words. As noted in earlier sections, a morpheme is the smallest unit of language that conveys meaning and students must learn the rules for making meaningful words in order to use **structural analysis** to aid word recognition.

Syntactic cues are cues related to the system of rules about how morphemes and words can be combined into sentences. Syntactic cues are context cues that also help a child recognize words and their meaning.

Semantic cues are context cues based upon meaning—both individual word meaning and meaning conveyed in sentences, paragraphs, even pictures.

This section will describe phonics skills and structural analysis skills and appropriate methods of instruction for these skills. Section 1.07 will address syntactic and semantic cues and methods for integrating various cuing system in decoding.

PHONICS

The English Language is based on the alphabetic Principle. The **Alphabetic Principle** is the concept that spoken words are represented by specific written symbols (letters), and conversely, that letters stand for specific (if often variable) sounds. The National Children's Reading Foundation points out that the ability to acquire reading skills is hard wired into the brain, but actually acquiring them requires both early exposure to print and explicit instruction. Learning phonics, or the specific letter-sound code for English, is critical to learning to read. Numerous summaries of reading research, including those of the International Reading Association (1997), the National Institute of Child Health and Human Development (2000), the National Reading Panel Report on Teaching Children to Read (2002), and the National Institute for Early Education Research (2006), have documented the importance of phonics as a significant part of any reading program.

Phonics is the letter-sound correspondence in written language. It is also known as the *code* for which letter or letter combinations represent which phonemes in the language. It is the connection between the sounds we say and the letters on the page, and it is absolutely crucial to learning to read. Students must be taught how to produce a correct sound for a letter or letter combination and blend the sounds for several letters together into a recognizable word. Word recognition is taught through grapheme (letter symbol)-phoneme associations (use of graphophonemic cues), with the goal of teaching the student to independently apply these skills to new words. Unlike phoneme awareness activities, phonics instruction requires students to LOOK at what they are doing. It requires coordination of visual and auditory senses. By age five or six, children can typically begin to use phonics to begin to understand the connections between letters, their patterns, vowel sounds (e.g., short vowels or long vowels), and the collective sounds they all make.

The study of phonics is one that involves sound as well as sight. It is defined by the connection between hearing the sounds and seeing the letters on a page. In the beginning stages of phonics, students may use sight to see the word "cat," but they use sound to break the word down to its letter components. It may require slowly speaking each letter before the students recognize that they actually said the word.

Using Phonics to Decode Words in Connected Text

The Alphabetic Principle, mentioned above, is sometimes called Graphophonemic Awareness. This technical reading foundation term details the understanding that written words are composed of patterns of letters that represent the sounds of spoken words. There are basically two parts to the alphabetic principle:

- An understanding that words are made up of letters and that each of these letters or letter combinations has a specific sound
- An understanding that the correspondence between sounds and letters leads to phonological reading. This consists of reading regular and irregular words as well as doing advanced analysis of words.

Since the English language is dependent on the alphabet, being able to recognize and sound out letters is the first step for beginning readers. Simply relying on memorization for word recognition is not feasible as a way for children to learn to recognize words. Therefore, decoding is essential. The most important goal of beginning reading teachers is to teach students to decode text so that they can read fluently and with understanding.

There are four basic features of the alphabetic principle:

- Students need to be able to take spoken words apart and blend different sounds together to make new words (based on phonemic awareness).
- Students need to apply letter sounds to all their reading.
- Teachers need to use a systematic, effective program in order to teach children to read.
- The teaching of the alphabetic principle usually begins in kindergarten.

It is important to keep in mind that some children already know the letters and sounds before they come to school. Others may catch on to this quite quickly; still others need to have one-on-one instruction in order to learn to read.

Models of Phonics Instruction

Phonics refers to instruction in and learning of the letter/sound code of the language. Once the child can discriminate among the various phonemes of the language and manipulate them in verbally presented words, it is necessary to attach those sounds to certain letters and letter combinations. Phonics instruction may be synthetic or analytic.

In the **synthetic** method, letter sounds are learned before the student goes on to blend the sounds to form words. This usually means repeated drills on individual letters or letter combinations and sounds. Once the students can reliably produce a correct sound for a letter or combination of letters, the task of blending them into words begins.

The **analytic** method teaches letter sounds as integral parts of words. Regularly spelled sight words are memorized first, then the sounds in each are mapped out with the teacher's help. This approach is more common in classes using the whole language approach in reading. However, both methods can be used and students with disabilities or limited phoneme awareness backgrounds (e.g., ELL learners) may need at least some practice with a synthetic approach in order to master the code. Many students with severe deficits in phonemic awareness will need long term, intensive instruction in phonics.

The sounds are often taught in the sequence: vowels, consonants, consonant blends at the beginning of words (e.g., bl and dr) and consonant blends at the end of words (e.g., ld and mp), consonant and vowel digraphs (e.g., ch and sh), and diphthongs (e.g., ow and oy). However, some methods that emphasize kinesthetic feedback to help identify sounds will teach consonant pairs first, because they are the most easily distinguished and have the most consistent spellings. In addition, consonant sounds are more easily differentiated *kinesthetically* through the positions of the lips, teeth, and tongue. This provides additional feedback to a child struggling with phoneme awareness preceding the phonics piece. Vowels would then be taught as a group since they are both more difficult to distinguish and have more varied spellings.

Some languages have very consistent grapheme-phoneme relationships. English does not, although the relationship is more consistent than many may think. There are, however, significant variations in the English grapheme-phoneme code. One letter or group of letters can make more than one sound in different contexts, and most phonemes can be represented by a number of different letters. Examination of the phoneme-grapheme chart in Section 1.03 shows that most sounds have multiple spellings. This is particularly true for vowel phonemes, which can have many grapheme representations (e.g., 'i', 'i-e', 'igh', or '-y' for long I). In addition, *digraphs* are multiple letter combinations that represent only one phoneme (e.g., 'ph' or 'f' for /f/, or 'ch' or 'tch' for /ch/). There are also vowel *diphthongs*, a single vowel phoneme that slides or glides from one sound to another in a fluid roll such as the 'ow' sound in 'cow,' or the 'oi' sound in 'boy.'

There are many programs and techniques for teaching phonics, and some children will pick it up more easily than others. However, most will require multiple exposures to specific phonics patterns and a step by step approach to the instruction. This can be accomplished through specifically decodable readers, readers with very controlled letter sound patterns that emphasize one or a family of phonics concepts at a time. Such readers usually include certain high frequency irregular words for practice, as well. This approach can be particularly effective with ELL students or students with decoding disabilities such as Dyslexia, because they may need extensive practice to master the code.

Other students can learn through phonics presented through a whole language or basal reader approach where the phonics portion is included in the "real" literature. Lists of children's picture books that emphasize certain phonics principles are available from many publishers and libraries. Examples of phonics series are *Science Research Associates, Merrill Phonics* and DML's *Cove School Reading Program.*

Professor Uta Frith has done work on the sequence of children's phonic learning. Frith has identified three phases that describe the progression of children's phonic learning from ages four through eight. Whatever model of instruction teachers use, they need to consider each child's stage of development. These are:

Logographic Phase: Children recognize whole words that have significance for them, such as their own names, the names of stores they frequent, or products that their parents buy.

Strategies that nurture development in this phase can include explicit labeling in the classroom using the children's names and the names of classroom objects, components, furniture, and materials. In addition, during snack time and lunch- time, explicit attention and talk can be focused on new brands of foods and drink. This is whole word recognition, often based on context. Toward the end of this phase children start to notice initial letters in words and the sounds that they represent.

Analytic Phase: During this phase, the children make associations between the spelling patterns in the words they know and the new words they encounter. This is the stage at which most phonics instruction occurs. (See below).

Orthographic Phase: In this phase, children recognize words almost automatically. They can rapidly identify an increasing number of words because they know a good deal about the structure of words and how they're spelled. At this stage instruction in other cueing systems will predominate.

Explicit and Implicit Strategies for Teaching Phonics

To best support these phases and the development of emergent and early readers, teachers should focus on elements of phonics learning, which help children analyze words for their letters, spelling patterns, and structural components. The children need to be involved in activities where they can use what they know about words in order to learn new ones. For example, the teacher can build on what the children know to introduce new spelling patterns, vowel combinations, and short and long vowel investigations. The teacher must do this and be aware that these will be reintroduced again and again as needed. Keep in mind that children's learning of phonics and other key components of reading is not linear, but rather falls back to review and then flows forward to build new understandings.

Graphophonemic (phonic) Prompts as Children Read aloud: Teachers can use carefully individualized questions to help a child attend to phonics cues and develop strategies for using them. This involves careful prompting in small group or one-on-one read alouds with the teacher. A good strategy to use in working with individual children is to have them explain how they finally correctly identified a word that was troubling them. Some promptings emphasizing graphophonemic cues include:

- You said (the child's incorrect attempt). Does that match the letters you see?
- If it were the word you just said, (the child's incorrect attempt), what would it have to start with?
- If it were the word you just said (the child's incorrect attempt), what would it have to end with?
- Look at the first letter/s . . . look at the middle letter/s . . . the last letter. . What could it be?
- If you were writing (the child's incorrect attempt), what letter would you write first? What letters would go in the middle?
- What letters would go last?

These prompts can be interwoven with prompts for other cues (e.g., morphemic, syntactic, semantic) described in later sections.

Sorting Words: This activity allows children to focus closely on the specific features of words and begin to understand the basic elements of letter-sound relationships.

Start with monosyllabic words. Choose words that will illustrate whatever phonic principle is the objective for the lesson. Have the children group them by their length, common letters, sound, and/or spelling pattern.

Prepare for the activity by writing ten to fifteen words on oak-tag strips and placing them randomly on the sentence strip holder. These words should come from a book previously shared in the classroom or a language experience chart. Next, begin to sort out the word with the children, perhaps by focusing on where a particular letter appears in a word. While the children sort the place of a particular letter in a given word, they should also be coached (or facilitated) by the teacher to recognize that sometimes a letter in the middle of the word can still be the last sound that we hear, and that some letters at the end of a word are silent (such as "e").

Children should be encouraged to make their own categories for word sorts and to share their own discoveries as they do the word sorts. The children's discoveries should be recorded and posted in the rooms with their names so they have ownership of their phonics learning.

Pre-reading for Beginning Phonics Decoding: First, focus on the particular letter/s that you want the child to investigate. It is good to choose one from a shared text that the children are familiar with. Make certain that the teachers' directions to the children are clear and either direct them to look for a specific letter or listen for sounds.

Next, begin a list of words that meet the task given to the children. Use chart paper to list the words that the children identify. This list can be continued into the next week as long as the children's focus is maintained on the list. This can be done by challenging the children with identifying a specific number of letters or sounds and "daring" them as a class team to go beyond those words or sounds.

Third, continue to add to the list. Remind the children at the beginning of the day of their individual goal to add to the list. Give them an adhesive note (sticky pad sheet) on which each can write down the words found. Then they can attach their newly found words with their names on them to the chart. This provides the children with a sense of ownership and pride in their letter-sounding abilities. During shared reading, discuss the children's proposed additions and have the group decide if these meet the directed category. If all the children agree that they do meet the category, include the words on the chart.

Fourth, do a word sort from all the words generated and have the children put the words into categories that demonstrate similarities and differences. They can be prompted to see if the letter appeared at the beginning of the word, or in the middle of the word. They might also be prompted to see that one sound can have two different letter representations. The children can then "box" the word differences and similarities by drawing colors established in a chart key.

Finally, before the children go off to read, ask them to look for new words in the texts that they can now recognize because of the letter-sound relationships on their chart. During shared reading, make certain that they have time to share the words they were able to decode because of their explorations.

The CVC Phonic Card Game: This game was developed by Jackie Montierth, a computer teacher in South San Diego for use with fifth and sixth grade students. It is a good activity to adapt to the needs of any group with appropriate modifications for age, grade level, and language needs.

To play, the children use the vehicle of the card game to practice and enhance their use of consonants and vowels. Their fluency in this will increase their ability to decode words.

Potential uses beyond whole classroom instruction include use as part of the small group word work component of the reading workshop and as part of cooperative team learning.

This particular strategy is also particularly helpful for grade four and beyond English Language learners who are in a regular English Language classroom setting.

The card game works well because the practice of the content improves transfer as the children continue to improve their reading skills. In addition, the card game format allows "instructional punctuation" using a student-centered high interest exploration.

Card Design: The teacher can use the computer, 5"x 8" index cards, or actual card deck sized oak-tag cards to create a deck. For repeated use and durability, it is recommended that the deck be laminated.

The deck should consist of the following:

44 consonant cards (including the blends)
15 vowel cards (including 3 of each vowel)
5 wild cards (which can be used as any vowel)
6 final "e" cards

The teacher can vary the cards above to include consonant or vowel digraphs and diphthongs in order to provide more advanced instruction.

The design of this project can also focus on particular CVC words that are part of a particular book, topic, theme, or genre format (e.g., study of American history, U.S. Geography, other content area themes). In advance of playing the game, children can also be directed to review the words on the word wall or other words on a word map.

Procedure: The game is best introduced first as part of a mini-lesson in which the teacher reads the rules and a pair of children demonstrates the game step-by-step before the class plays the game for the first time.

Have the children divide into pairs or small groups of no more than four per group. Each group needs one deck of CVC cards.

Have each group choose a dealer. The dealer shuffles the deck of cards. The dealer deals five cards to each player. The remaining cards are placed face down for drawing during the play. One card is turned over to form the discard pile.

Players may not show their cards to the other players.

The first player to the left of the dealer looks at his/her cards and if possible, puts down three cards that make a consonant-vowel-consonant word.

For more points, four cards forming a consonant-vowel-consonant word can be placed down. The player must then say the word and draw the number of cards he or she laid down.

If he or she is unable to form a word, he or she draws a card from either the draw pile or the discard pile. The player then discards one card. All players must have five cards at all times.

The next player to the left now takes his or her turn. That player puts down any cards forming a C-V-C word. That player must then say the word and draw the number of cards that he or she laid down. Should the player not be able to say the word he or she draws from the pile, he or she draws a card from the discard or the draw pile.

The game continues until one or more of the following happens:

1. There are no more cards in the draw pile
2. All players run out of cards.
3. All players cannot form a word

The winner is the player who has laid down the most cards during the game. Players may only lay down words at the beginning of their turn. Proper names may not be counted as words.

Other ways the game may be played: The game can be played with teams of individuals in a small group of four or fewer competing against one another (excellent for special needs or resource room students). It can also be done as a whole class activity where all the students are divided into cooperative teams or small groups that compete against one another. This second approach will work well with a heterogeneous classroom that includes special needs and/or ELL children.

Teachers of ELL learners can do this game in the native language first and then transition it into English, which will facilitate native language reading skills and second language acquisition. They can develop their own appropriate decks to meet the vocabulary needs of their children and to complement the curricula.

Special Considerations for Individual Students

Phonics and the ELL Learner: Research has shown that there is a positive and strong correlation between a child's literacy in his or her native language and his or her learning of English. The degree of native language proficiency and literacy is a strong predictor of English language development. Children who are literate and engaged readers in their native language can better transfer their skills to a second language (e.g., English).

What this means is that educators should not approach the needs of ELL learners in reading in the same manner that they would approach native English speaking students. Those whose families are not from a focused oral literacy and reading culture in the native language will need additional oral language rhymes, read-alouds, and singing as support for reading skills development in both their native and the English language. As mentioned earlier, additional work on the foundations of phonological awareness related to English will be necessary before and during phonics instruction.

Development of Alphabetic Knowledge in Individual Students: Struggling Readers, Students with Disabilities, and Highly Proficient Readers

Researchers Laura M. Justice and Helen K. Ezell of the University of Virginia did a study in 2002 that evaluated alphabetic knowledge and print awareness in pre-school children from low income households. Their research findings offer potential insights for educators who seek to foster the skills and capabilities of all their students.

In their post-testing of children in the experimental group who had participated in shared reading sessions that emphasized a print focus, they found that the at-risk children outperformed their control group peers (other Head Start children) on three measures of print awareness (Words In Print, Print Recognition, and Alphabetic Knowledge).

Other researchers, including Chaney (1994), have demonstrated a statistically significant and inverse relationship between household income and children's performance on measures of print awareness and alphabetic principle.

A study by Lonigan, et al (1999) found that substantial group differences existed on a variety of pre-literacy tasks administered to eighty-five preschool children from lower and middle income households. Measures of print awareness used included environmental print, print and book reading conventions, and alphabet knowledge. Results showed that preschool children from middle income households showed significantly higher levels of skill across all print awareness tasks in comparison with preschoolers from low income households.

Obviously this data highlights the importance of extensive alphabetic knowledge activities and print awareness opportunities for children from low income households in grades K-1 and, when necessary, beyond.

Two other studies undertaken by Ezell and Justice (in the year 2000) suggested that structuring adult-child shared book reading interactions to include an explicit print awareness and alphabetic principle focus resulted in a substantial increase in children's verbal interactions with print.

This work highlights the importance of not only classroom and preschool emphasis on print awareness and alphabetic principle routines, but also the need for teachers to reach out to parents to model for them these shared reading experiences so that family life can parallel the classroom experiences. Many schools currently have parent volunteers and reading buddy programs. Training of these volunteers, particularly in high need, low economic income status communities, is certainly warranted.

Students with disabilities

As discussed earlier, many students who struggle to learn to decode have deficits in phonological and phonemic awareness, and these deficits must be addressed both before and during phonics instruction. Even once these deficits have been addressed, however, some students will struggle with learning the graphophonemic code of phonics. Willis (2008) reviewed research showing that a distinct region of the brain may be involved in learning to connect the visual written symbols (letters) to the phoneme sounds of language. This means some students may be phonemically aware, but struggle to connect written symbols to sounds. Such students will need additional practice and more specialized instruction to make these connections. Hand on activities, kinesthetic feedback, and multimedia based instruction can be helpful to these students.

David J. Chard and Jean Osborn (1999) have reflected on the guidelines necessary for teachers to use in selecting supplemental phonics and word-recognition materials for addressing students with learning disabilities.
They note that an important part of helping children with reading disabilities to figure out the system underlying the printed word is to lead them to understand the alphabetic principle. Children with learning disabilities (LD) particularly benefit from organized instruction that centers on letters, sounds, and the relations between sounds and letters. They also benefit from word-recognition patterns instruction that offers practice with, for example, word families that share similar letter patterns.

Children with learning disabilities also benefit from opportunities to apply what they are learning to the reading and re-reading of stories and other texts. Such texts contain a high portion of words that reflect the letters, sounds, and spelling patterns the children are learning.

For special needs children, a beginning reading program should include the following elements of Alphabetic Knowledge instruction:

- A variety of alphabetic knowledge activities in which the children learn to identify and name both upper and lower case letters
- Games, songs, and other activities that help children to learn to name the letters quickly

- Writing activities that encourage children to practice the letters they are writing
- A sensible sequence of letter introduction that can be adjusted to the needs of the children

See Guide 004 for more information on working with students with disabilities.

Highly Proficient Readers

Sometimes highly proficient readers can be paired as buddy tutors for ELL or special needs classroom members, or they can be used to assist the resource room teacher during their reading time. They can use the CVC game developed by Jacki Montierth to support their peers, and can even modify the game to meet the specific needs of classroom peers. This offers the highly proficient reader the opportunity to do a service learning project while still in elementary school. It also introduces the learner to another dimension of reading, the role of the reader as trainer and recruiter of other peers into the circle of readers and writers!

If the highly proficient readers are so motivated or if their teachers so desire, the peer tutors can also maintain an ongoing reading progress journal for their tutees. This will be a wonderful way to realize the goals of the reading and writing workshop.

STRUCTURAL ANALYSIS IN DECODING AND WORD IDENTIFICATION

As described earlier, morphology is the system of rules for making words, including such things as making plurals, possessives, inflections, etc. Morphemes are the smallest units of language that convey meaning. Free morphemes are morphemes that can stand alone as base or root words, such as 'dog' or 'walk.' Bound morphemes are morphological units that cannot stand alone. They convey or alter meaning when attached to other morphemes, and include such things as affixes, endings, and inflections (e.g. pre-, ed, -s, -ing).

Structural analysis is a process of examining the words in the text for meaningful word units, or morphemes, such as affixes, base words, and inflected endings. There are six word types that are formed and therefore can be analyzed using structural analysis strategies. They include:

1. Common prefixes or suffixes added to a known word ending with a consonant
2. Adding the suffix –ed to words that end with consonants
3. Compound words
4. Adding endings to words that end with the letter e
5. Adding endings to words that end with the letter y
6. Adding affixes to multisyllabic words

When teaching and using structural analysis procedures, teachers should remember to make sound decisions on which to introduce and teach. Keeping in mind the number of primary words in which each affix appears and how similar they are will help the teacher make the instructional process smoother and more valuable to the students.

Adding affixes to words can be started when students are able to read a list of one-syllable words by sight at a rate of approximately 20 words correct per minute. At the primary level, there is a recommended sequence for introducing affixes. The steps in this process are:

- Start by introducing the affix in the letter-sound correspondence format
- Practice the affix in isolation for a few days.
- Provide words for practice which contain the affix (word lists/flash card).
- Move from word lists to passage reading, which includes words with the affix (and some from the word lists/flash cards).

Some teachers choose to directly teach structural analysis, in particular, those who teach by following the phonics-centered approach for reading. Other teachers, who follow the balanced literacy approach, introduce the structural components as part of mini lessons that are focused on the students' reading and writing.

Structural analysis of words as defined by Cooper and Kiger (2009) involves the study of significant word parts. This analysis can help the child with identification, pronunciation, and constructing meaning.

Key Structural Analysis Components (Morphemic elements) Defined

Base Words. These are stand-alone linguistic units (free morphemes) which cannot be deconstructed or broken down into smaller meaningful units. They stand alone as words, and often form the base of other words when affixes or inflections (bound morphemes) are added to them. For example, in the word *retell*, the base word is "tell."

Root Word. This term is often used interchangeably with 'base word' for a free morpheme. However, it can also refer to the word (often from another language) from which another word is developed. The second word can be said to have its "root" in the first, such as *vis* in visor or vision.

Regardless of the term you use to describe them, base words and roots can be illustrated by a tree with roots to display the meaning for children. Children may also want to literally construct root words using cardboard trees to create word family models.

ELL students can construct these models for their native language root-word families, as well for the English language words they are learning. ELL students in the 5th and 6th grade may even appreciate analyzing the different root structures for contrasts and similarities between their native language and English. Learners with special needs can focus in small groups or individually with a paraprofessional on building root-word models.

Contractions. These are shortened forms of two words (one is a verb) in which a letter or letters have been deleted. These deleted letters have been replaced by an apostrophe.

Prefixes. These are beginning units of meaning which can be added (the vocabulary word for this type of structural adding is "affixed") to a base word or root word. They cannot stand alone. They are also sometimes known as "bound morphemes" because they cannot stand alone as a base word. Examples are *re-, un-,* and *mis-*.

Suffixes. These are ending units of meaning which can be "affixed" or added on to the ends of root or base words. Suffixes transform the original meanings of base and root words. Like prefixes, they are also known as "bound morphemes," because they cannot stand alone as words. Examples are *-less, -ful*, and *-tion*.

Compound Words. These occur when two or more base words are connected to form a new word. The meaning of the new word is in some way connected with that of the base words. Examples are *firefighter, newspaper*, and *pigtail*.

Inflectional Endings. These are types of suffixes that impart a new meaning to the base or root word. These endings in particular change the gender, number, tense, or form of the base or root words. Just like other suffixes, these are also termed "bound morphemes." Examples are *–s* or *-ed*.

Word forms: Sometimes a very familiar word can appear as a different part of speech, as in the examples below:

You may have heard that *fraud* involves a criminal misrepresentation, so when it appears as the adjective form *fraudulent* ("He was suspected of fraudulent activities."), you can make an educated guess as to the meaning.

You probably know that something out of date is *obsolete;* therefore, when you read about "built-in *obsolescence,*" you can detect the meaning of the unfamiliar word.

Activities for improving structural analysis

Word Study Group: This is a strategy generally used with children in grades 3-6. It involves the teacher taking time to meet with children in a small group of no more than six children for a word study session. Taberski (2000) suggests that this meeting take place next to a word wall. The children selected for this group are those who need to focus more on Morphemic cues and word parts.

It is important that this not be a formalized traditional reading group that meets at a set time each week or biweekly. Rather the group should be spontaneously formed by the teacher based on the teacher's quick inventory of the selected children's needs at the start of the week. Taberski has templates in her book of *Guided Reading Planning Sheets*. These sheets are essentially targeted word and other skills sheets with her written dated observations of children who are in need of support to develop a given skill.

The teacher should try to meet with this group for at least two consecutive 20-minute periods daily. Over those two meetings, the teacher can model a *Making Words Activity*. Once the teacher has modeled making words the first day, the children would then make their own words. On the second day, the children would "sort" their words.

Other topics for a word study group within the framework of the *Balanced Literacy Approach* that Taberski advocates are: inflectional endings, prefixes and suffixes, and/or common spelling patterns.

Discussion Circles: This is an activity that fits nicely into the balanced literacy lesson format. After the children conclude a particular text, they respond to the book in discussion circles. Among the prompts, the teacher-coach might suggest that the children focus on words of interest they encountered in the text. These can also be words that they heard if the text was read aloud. Children can be asked to look for words that show various structural elements or changes. Through this focus on children's response to words as the center of the discussion circle, peers become more interested in word study.

Banking, Booking, and Filing It: Children can realize the goal of making words their own and exploring word structures through creating concrete objects or displays that demonstrate the words they own. They can maintain their own files of words they have learned and sets of affixes or inflections that can be added to them to change the meaning of each word. Games in which children "play" with the structural elements of words can help them understand and manipulate these elements in their reading and writing.

Write Out Your Words, Write with Your Words. Ownership of words can be demonstrated by having the children use the words in their writings. The children can author a procedural narrative (a step-by-step description) of how they went about their word searches to compile the words they found for any of the activities. If the children are in grades K–1, or if the children are struggling readers and writers, their procedural narratives can be dictated.

Then they can be posted by the teacher. Children can also keep "word wallets" of base words with lists of affixes that can alter the meaning.

Children with special needs may model a word box or wallet on a specific holiday theme, genre, or science/social studies topic with the teacher. Initially this can be done as a whole class. As the children become more confident, they can work with peers or with a paraprofessional to create their own individual or small team/pair word boxes.

Special needs children can create a storyboard with the support of a paraprofessional, their teacher, or a resource specialist. They can also narrate their story of how they all found the words, using a digital recorder.

Knowledge of Greek and Latin Roots That Form English Words. Knowledge of Greek and Latin roots which comprise English words can measurably enhance children's reading skills and can also enrich their writing. Taberski (2000) does not advocate teaching Greek and Latin derivatives in the abstract to young children. However, when she comes across (as is common and natural) specific Greek and Latin roots while reading to children, she uses that opportunity to introduce children to these rich resources. For example, during readings on rodents (a favorite of first and second graders), Taberski draws her class's attention to the fact that beavers gnaw at things with their teeth. She then connects the root *dent* with other words with which the children are familiar. The children then volunteer *dentist, dental, denture.* Taberski begins to place these in a graphic organizer, or word web.

When she has tapped the extent of the children's prior knowledge of *dent* words, she shares with them the fact that *dens/dentis* is the Latin word for teeth. Then she introduces the word *indent,* which she has already previewed with them as part of their conventions of print study. She helps them to see that the *indenting* of the first line of a paragraph can even be related to the *teeth* Latin root in that it looks like a "print" bite was taken out of the paragraph.

Taberski displays the word web in the Word Wall Chart section of her room. The class is encouraged throughout, say, a week's time to look for other words to add to the web. Taberski stresses that for her, as an elementary teacher of reading and writing, the key element of the Greek and Latin word root web activity is the children's coming to understand that if they know what a Greek or Latin word root means, they can use that knowledge to figure out what other words mean. She feels the key concept is to model and demonstrate for children how fun and fascinating Greek and Latin root study can be.

USE OF SYLLABIFICATION AS A WORD IDENTIFICATION STRATEGY

There is controversy in the literature about the efficacy of using syllabification as a means of word identification. Some research (e.g., Glass, 1967) suggests that readers of all ages start with the sounds and only *after* decoding and identifying the word do they determine its syllables. However, many authorities still argue that syllabification techniques can help decode unfamiliar words. It is possible that both are true, that readers sometimes use knowledge of syllables to decode and at other times decode first and break the word into syllables for comprehension afterwards. In any case, understanding the basics of syllabification and methods for teaching it are important in teaching reading.

Some Basic Syllabification Concepts

A **syllable** is a pronounceable segment of a word made up of one or more letters with one (and ONLY one) **vowel sound**. A syllable can have any number of vowel *letters* but only one vowel sound. For example, the word "breathe" has three vowels (2 e's and one a) but only one vowel sound—long 'E'. A vowel diphthong (such as oi, that slides from one sound to another) is considered a single vowel sound, 'boy' has only one syllable. A single vowel can be a syllable all by itself, but a consonant cannot be a syllable without a vowel sound.

There are two basic types of syllables. An **open syllable** ends with a vowel sound (not necessarily a vowel letter), and a **closed syllable** ends with a consonant sound (not necessarily a consonant). The word 'pilot' for example, has two syllables, pi—lot. The first syllable ends with a vowel sound and is open. The second ends with a consonant sound and is closed. As is common, the open syllable is a long vowel sound and the closed one has a short vowel sound.

Pronunciation of the vowels in syllables is strongly influenced by stress and accent. In multiple syllable words, there will usually be one syllable more heavily accented than others. At times there may even be three levels of stress or accent. It is the accented syllable that is most likely to have a regular spelling pattern, whereas vowels in unaccented syllables can be "swallowed" into a schwa—a vowel phoneme in an unaccented syllable that sounds like a soft "uh" and can be represented by any vowel. For this reason, understanding not only syllabification, but also accent and stress, can be useful in identifying unknown words.

There are a number of useful strategies students can use to syllabify and recognize words.

Identifying Syllables in an Unknown Word

In order to use syllabification to identify a word, the student must first identify the syllables in a word. One method for doing this starts with teaching students that each syllable can have only one vowel sound. Then they are taught to look for known vowel spelling patterns in the word and underline each vowel or combination of vowels that commonly makes a vowel sound. For example, in the word 'kitten,' they would underline the 'i' and the 'e' and decide there must be two syllables. For the word, 'teacher,' the student would underline the 'ea' as ONE sound, since they recognize it as a common long E spelling pattern. Likewise, the 'e' in 'er' would be underlined; again, a two syllable word.

Students can also be taught to look for double consonants as clues to the number of syllables.

Students can be taught to look for special endings such as "-tion," "-ing," or "-ture." These are always a separate syllable, and it helps to teach them as units in much the way sight words are taught, so that the student will recognize them in longer words. A good way to do this is to combine it with root word study and use cards or post-its to show what happens to a word when such special endings are added to it.

Identifying Accent and stress

Children must be taught that some syllables are said with more force than others. One way to do this is to provide colored post-its or manipulatives of different colors and have the students lay out a differently colored manipulative for every syllable when the teacher says a word. For the word, "student," two colors are pushed out onto the table. For the word, "vacation" three colors, and so on. Use of Post-its allows the student to write the syllable on a post-it for a modification of this exercise.

Once students can set up the correct number of colors for the number of syllables, stress or accent can be introduced. Having pushed out two post-its for "student," children push forward the one associated with greatest stress. (For 'student' it would be the first one, for 'vacation' the second one, etc.) The teacher may need to exaggerate the stress at first. A variation on this method would be to use colored highlighters to differentially highlight stressed and unstressed syllables in written words. Once the student understands the concept of stress, they can begin to map the sounds in a stressed syllable.

Common syllabic principles such as those below should also be taught.

- The vowel sound of an accented open syllable is usually long.
- The vowel sound in an unaccented syllable, open or closed, is often the schwa, and can be any vowel letter.
- Single vowels in closed syllables are usually short unless affected by another vowel or a letter that makes a long vowel pattern (e.g., -ow for long O).
- If a vowel is followed by a double consonant, the syllable will be divided between the two consonants.
- If a vowel is followed by two different consonants, the syllable may be divided between them unless they form a blend or digraph.
- Affixes are usually separate syllables
- Given a choice, try starting a syllable with a consonant

Once students have mastered some basic tendencies, they can attack an unfamiliar multiple syllable word by going backwards. Students first underline all the vowel patterns they see in order to get an idea how many syllables there are. They then look for special endings and circle those. After that they attempt to form a syllable around each vowel sound using the principles they have learned. They can try several different stress pronunciations until they find one that fits the context in which they find the word.

Strategy - Clap Hands, Count those Syllables as They Come!! (Taberski, 2000)

This is one of the most common syllabification activities and it lays the foundation for using syllabification to identify words. At the start, however, it presupposes that the student *already knows or has heard the word*, so it is *not* initially a method for using syllabification to identify a word. The objective of this activity is for children to understand that every syllable in a polysyllabic word has one vowel sound and can be studied for its spelling patterns in the same way that monosyllabic words are studied for their spelling patterns. Once children understand the basic concept of syllables, they can be taught how to identify syllables in an unfamiliar word.

The easiest way for the K-3 teacher to introduce this activity to the children is to share a familiar poem from the poetry chart (or to write out a familiar poem on a large experiential chart).

First, the teacher reads the poem with the children. As they are reading it aloud, the children clap the beats of the poem, and the teacher uses a colored marker to place a tic (/) above each syllable.

Next, the teacher takes letter cards and selects one of the polysyllabic words from the poem that the children have already "clapped" out.

The children use letter cards to spell the word on the sentence strip holder, or the letter can be placed on a felt board or up against a window on display. Sticky note pads will also work. Together, the children and teacher divide the letters into syllables and place blank letter cards between the syllables. The children identify spelling patterns they know.

Finally, and as part of continued small group syllabification study, the children identify other polysyllabic words they clapped out from the poem. They make up the letter combinations of these words. Then they separate them into syllables with blank letter cards between the syllables.

Children who require special support in syllabification can be encouraged to use plenty of letter cards to create a large chart paper syllabic (in letter cards with spaces) representation of the poem or at least a few lines of the poem. They can be told that this is for use as a teaching tool for others. In this way, they authenticate their study of syllabification with a real product that can actually be referenced by peers.

SKILL 1.7 Applying knowledge of developmentally appropriate instruction and curriculum materials for promoting students' decoding skills and word identification strategies

Please refer to Skill 1.6 for phonics and structural analysis.

In addition to the phonic and structural cues described in the previous section, students must be able to use syntactic and semantic cues to help identify unfamiliar words. They must also be able to monitor their own reading and manage the use of these various cueing systems, moving from one to the other and combining cues as they go in order to decode and read the material. As the student practices the use of these decoding strategies, decoding and word identification become more and more automatic. The proficient reader has developed automaticity in word recognition that no longer requires conscious use of these cues except when reading extremely demanding material.

SYNTACTIC AND SEMANTIC CUES

Syntactic cues

Syntax is the set of rules, commonly known as grammar, which governs how morphemes and words are correctly combined to make sentences. As children learn oral language, they adopt the syntactic and grammatical patterns of the adults around them. They learn that certain words or classes of word *sound right* and others *sound wrong* in various parts of a sentence. However, children whose home language does not reflect standard English grammar, and children with reading disabilities may struggle to learn these rules without very explicit instruction.

Many of the syntactic rules that provide contextual clues to help identify words are based on *word classes* such as parts of speech (e.g., nouns, verbs, adjectives). However, words do not fall into such conceptual categories in fixed, constant ways. A particular word's syntactic class can vary depending upon how it is used in the sentence. The word, *fish* for example, can be a noun in one sentence (e.g., "I like to eat fish."), and a verb in another (e.g., "I like to fish on the lake."). Other syntactic cues depend upon placement in the sentence, or upon related words in a sentence, and this, too, is an abstract concept that means a word can mean one thing in one place and another in a different place, or that different forms of a word should be used in different places. It also means that words that *look* very different can be essentially different forms of the same word (e.g., be, is, are). Children whose oral language development has been different from that of mainstream English, or who have language disabilities, will need extra help to learn how to use syntactic cues.

Semantic cues

Semantic cues are based primarily upon word meanings. Children can deduce the meaning of an unknown word based upon the meaning of the passage as a whole and the sentences immediately around the unknown word, as well.

Illustrations and diagrams can also provide clues to meaning. When the probable meaning of a word is clear, the student can compare the idea or meaning with the letters (phonics cues) and figure out the word. Once again, children with language disabilities may struggle to use this cueing system because it requires pulling information together from different parts of a sentence or paragraph, holding it in working memory, and putting it together to form a conclusion.

Both Syntactic and Semantic cues are *context cues*. That is, their use depends upon understanding the context in which they are found, the part of the sentence, the words before and after, previous (and sometimes succeeding) sentences, etc.

What's the Role/Job? Sometimes it can help if students are given a concrete analogy for understanding why a word can mean one thing in one context and something else in another, or even be a different part of speech in different sentences, and why identifying the word and its meaning may require examining context cues. One way to do this is to get photos (use the internet!) of a selection of actors and actresses in various roles.

- Try to select at least two or three roles for each actor. Select pictures in which the actors' clothes or the settings in which they are photographed provide clear clues to the role (e.g., a pirate movie still, cowboy movie still, etc.).
- Then show a particular actor and ask what he is in the picture (e.g., a pirate). Name the actor and ask how they know he's a pirate (they might note his three corner hat, the ship he is standing on, the flag, etc.).
- Next, show a second photo in a clearly different role, note that it is the same actor and ask what he is in *this* photo (e.g., a cowboy). Ask how they know (e.g., horse, six shooter, cattle, etc.).
- After going through a few of these, discuss how they used the *context* to determine what the actor's *job* was in each photo. They used clothes and setting. Note that in the same way, they can use context (other words in a sentence, other sentences, storyline, plot, illustrations, etc.) to identify a word's *job* (noun, verb, etc.) in the sentence and even its meaning.

An activity such as this can help make these abstract concepts more concrete and kick off other lessons in the use of context cues in word identification and comprehension.

Using Context Cues to identify and understand unfamiliar words

The directed questioning described in Skill 1.06 can be used to help children struggling with the use of syntactic or semantic cues.

When handling syntactic problems, a teacher can use prompts such as:

- You said (child's incorrect attempt). Does that sound right?
- You said (child's incorrect attempt). Can we say it like that?
- Since some children come from backgrounds where incorrect grammar contributes to the problem, say: Would your *teacher* say it that way? Or: Would you say it that way in class?

When handling problems with semantic cues, a teacher can use prompts such as:

- You said (child's word/incorrect attempt). Does that make sense to you? Can it DO that?
- If someone said (repeat the child's attempt), would you know what he or she meant?
- You said (child's incorrect attempt). Would you write that?

Mystery word game: There are a number of strategies for explicitly teaching children how to use context to both identify and determine what a word means. One method is to design a sort of "Mystery Word" game in which sentences with blanks or nonsense words are recorded on colorful cards and set up in a box for students. Students take a card or set of cards and try to figure out what word will fit in the blank. Context clues can be of two types:

Syntax clues are clues related to a parts of speech and grammar; a word's job in the sentence (for example, in "The _____ ran up the wall," the word in the blank would have to be a noun of some sort).

Semantic clues are based on meaning in the sentence and the word (for example, in "My dad drove the _____ to work," the blank would have to be some sort of a vehicle, not a butterfly or feeling).

A set of sentences can be developed that provide increasing context clues to the meaning of the word. An example of a set of cards with increasing clues would be:

- We have a new _____ at our house. (Not much in the way of semantic clues, though syntax dictates it should be a noun; could be a pet, a piece of furniture, a book, a baby, whatever).

- We have a new _____ at our house and it is bigger than the one that broke. (OK, so NOT a baby or a pet…semantic cue based on "broke").
- We have a new _____ at our house and it is bigger than the one that broke so we can put TWO gallons of milk in it at a time (Now, we are probably talking about a refrigerator—semantic cue "gallons of milk").

Children can guess at each word and discuss their guesses with the teacher. The teacher can guide the student to evaluate their guesses and clues and look at both syntactic and semantic context. The object in such lessons is NOT the actual vocabulary, but rather the *strategy* of using context to determine a word's meaning. It doesn't matter what word the child puts in the blank as long as it fits the clues. it is the learning and thinking process that is important.

Of course, in real life reading there will be an unknown word in the sentence and its spelling will offer phonic cues, so if the student has figured out what the word means or what kind of word it is, the student can compare that to the letters and try to come up with a word that fits both. This is not a linear process. The student may go back and forth between the three cueing systems in finding the right word. In the example given above, suppose the word "refrigerator" is in the sentence, but the student cannot figure out that long word. Given the first sentence cue, a number of 'r' words could fit (e.g., rat, relative, ringer, raccoon, rocking chair, etc). The second sentence would eliminate most of those and a new list might start including 'r' words that can break (ringer, rocking chair, etc.). The third sentence might lead to the actual word, "refrigerator."

Such an activity can be modified to include actual vocabulary words necessary for reading once the student has mastered the use of the strategy. Since some students will have more problems with semantic clues, while others will have problems with syntactic clues, such lessons must be individualized for each problem type.

Some strategies to share with children during conferences or as part of shared reading include the following prompts related to combining the cues:

- Look at the beginning letter/s. What sound do you hear?
- What *kind* of word do you need? Can it be a noun or do you need an action word?
- Stop to think about the text or story. What word with this beginning letter would make sense here?
- Look at the book's illustrations. Do they provide you with help in figuring out the new word?
- Think of which word would make sense, sound right, and match the letters that you see. Start the sentence over, making your mouth ready to say that word.
- Skip the word, read to the end of the sentence, and then come back to the word. How does what you've read help you with the word?
- Listen to whether what you are reading makes sense and matches the letters (this is asking the child to self-monitor). If it doesn't make sense, see if you can correct it on your own.
- Look for spelling patterns you know from the spelling pattern wall.
- Look for smaller words you might know within the larger word.
- Think of any place you may have seen this word before in a story read to you or read by you, or where you may have met up with this word before.
- Read on a little, and then return to the part that confused you.

Diagnosing and Assessing Student Decoding and Word identification Strategies

One way to explore the specific difficulty a child is having with word identification is through the use of Oral Running Records. In *On Solid Ground: Strategies for Teaching Reading K-3*, Sharon Taberski (2000) discusses how oral reading records can be used by the K-3 teacher to assess how well children are using cueing systems. She notes that the running record format can also show visual depictions for the teacher of how the child "thinks" as the child reads. The notation of miscues, in particular, shows how a child "walks through" the reading process. They indicate if and in what ways the child may require "guided" support in understanding the words he or she reads aloud (oral language).

Although such running records are usually used for determining the source of phonic decoding errors, careful attention to the incorrect word that a child uses in a sentence can also alert the teacher to whether it is semantic or syntactic cues that are most problematical for the child. For example, In the sentence, "Bobby lived is a big house at the end of the street," if a child says "home" instead of "house," he has the semantics correct and just made a mistake with the visual/phonic decoding. If the child says, "horse" it means he is NOT looking at the semantics of the sentence— nor at the specific letters for phonic cues. If he says "hops," he is missing syntactic cues, as well.

Using Running Records

A Running Record, or Record of Reading Behavior, is a formalized assessment for analyzing miscues when a student reads aloud. It can be combined with basic comprehension questions, as well. It must be administered individually and one on one with a child, so it takes more time than a group assessment of readability. However, it provides not only a very accurate look at the readability of a particular text for a particular child, it also provides detailed information on the cause of a student's errors and the student's efforts to correct them.

While there are various acceptable formats for emergent literacy assessment used throughout the country, the one selected for use here is based on the work of Marie Clay and Kenneth Goodman. These two are key researchers in the close observation and documentations of children's early reading miscues (reading mistakes).

It is important to emphasize that the teacher should not just "take the Record of Reading Behavior" and begin filling it out as the child reads from a random book prior to the beginning of the observation. There are specific steps for taking the record and analyzing its results.

- **Select a text**—If you want to see if the child is reading on instructional level, choose a book that the child has already read. If the purpose of the test is to see whether the child is ready to advance to the next level, choose a book from that level which the child has not yet seen.

- **Introduce the text**—If the book is one that has been read, you do not need to introduce the text, other than by saying the title. But if the book is new to the child, you should briefly share the title and tell the child a bit about the plot and style of the book.

- **Take the record**—Generally, with emergent readers in grades 1-2, there are only 100-150 words in a passage used to take a record. Make certain that the child is seated beside you so that you can see the text as the child reads it.

If desired, you may want to photocopy the text in advance for yourself, so you can make direct notations on your text while the child reads from the book. After you introduce the text, make certain that the child has the chance to read the text independently. Be certain that you do not "teach" or help the child with the text, other than to supply an unknown word that the child requests you to supply. The purpose of the record is to see what the child does on his or her own.

As the child reads the text, you must be certain to record the reading behaviors the child exhibits using the following notations. In taking the record, keep in mind the following:

- Allow enough time for the child to work independently on a problem before telling or supplying the word. If you wait too long, you could run the risk of having the child lose the meaning and his/her interest in the story as he or she tries to identify the unknown word.
- It is recommended that when a child is way off track, you tell him or her to "Try that again" (TTA). If a whole phrase is troubling, put it into square brackets and score it as only one error.

The notation for filling out the Record of Reading behavior involves noting the child's response on the top and the actual text below. There are a number of standard forms available for recording such behavior and many of them have information on recording and analyzing errors, as well as formulae for evaluating responses and readability.

Comprehension Check

This can and should be done by inviting the child to retell the story. This retelling can then be used by you to ask further questions about characters, plot, setting and purpose, which allows you to observe and to record the child's level of comprehension.

Calculating the Reading Level and the Self-correction Rate

Calculating the reading level lets you know if the book is at the level from which the child can read it independently or comfortably with guidance (instructional level), or if the book is at a level where reading it frustrates the child.

Generally, an accuracy score of 95-100% suggests that the child can independently read the text and other books or texts on the same level.

An accuracy score of 90-94% indicates that the text and texts likely will present challenges to the child, but with guidance from you, a tutor or parent, the child will be able to master these texts and enjoy them (instructional level). However, an accuracy score of less than 89% tells you that the material you have selected for the child is too hard for the child to control alone. Such material needs to be shared with the child in a Shared Reading situation or read to the child.

Keeping Score on the Record

Insertions, omissions, substitutions and teacher-told responses all count as errors. Repetitions are not scored as errors. Corrected responses are scored as self-corrections. When analyzing the miscues for purposes of diagnosing decoding problems, look for the *type* of error made. Is the child looking at only some of the letters? Does the child get single letter sounds correct but miss digraphs and diphthongs? Do the errors make sense (semantic cues) even if they are the wrong word? Do the erroneous words *fit the grammar* (syntactic cues) of the sentence? Careful perusal of the running record can give the teacher an excellent view of exactly what cues the child is and is not using. This information can then be used to provide guidance and, if necessary, additional lessons.

Assessment of Decoding Skills Throughout the Year

The teacher will want to maintain individual records of children's reading behaviors demonstrating alphabetic principle/graphophonemic awareness and other decoding skills throughout the year.

For example, the following performance standards might be part of a record template form for each child in grades K-1 and beyond, as needed (depending on ELL or special needs):

- Match all consonant and short vowel sounds
- Read one's own name
- Read one syllable words and high frequency words
- Demonstrate the ability to read and understand that as letters in words change, so do the sounds

- Generate the sounds from all letters, including consonant blends and long vowel patterns, and blend those different sounds into recognizable words
- Read common sight words
- Read common word families
- Recognize and use knowledge of spelling patterns when reading (run/running, hop/hopping)
- Decode (sound out) regular words with more than one syllable (vacation, graduation).
- Recognize regular abbreviations (Feb., Mr., P.S.)
- Uses grade appropriate syntactic knowledge when decoding
- Uses within-sentence semantic cues when decoding.
- Uses surrounding sentences' semantic cues when decoding.
- Uses illustrations' semantic cues when decoding.

Any record kept of an individual child's progress should include each date of observation and some legend or rubric detailing the level of performance, standard acquisition, or mastery. Some teachers use Y for "exhibits the reading behavior consistently," M for "making progress toward the standard," and N for "has not yet exhibited the behavior." Beyond this objective legend for the assessment, the teacher may want and should include any other comments that detail the child's progress in this awareness.

OBJECTIVE 2   UNDERSTAND THE DEVELOPMENT OF VOCABULARY KNOWLEDGE AND SKILLS ACROSS THE CURRICULUM

SKILL 2.1   Recognizing criteria for selecting appropriate words to increase students' vocabulary knowledge (e.g., synonyms, antonyms, words with multiple meanings, idioms, classifications) to increase students' vocabulary[SAW8]

In its 2000 report on teaching children to read, the National Reading Panel identified vocabulary as one of the five critical areas of reading instruction. It defined vocabulary as "the part of comprehension based on the meaning of individual words in context." The term vocabulary, then, refers to the precise meaning of words, particularly meaning in various contexts, and the Panel stated that there is a need for direct vocabulary instruction on specific words.

The selection of specific vocabulary words or categories of words to teach in any given lesson will depend in large part on the developmental level of the students. Burns, et al (2002) pointed out that children acquire vocabulary at a very rapid rate during elementary school years. Early vocabulary development begins with differentiating antonyms, then generalizing (and over generalizing) key words without using more accurate synonyms or related words (calling any machine that moves a car, for example). Later vocabulary development includes understanding multiple meaning words, homonyms, synonyms, and more abstract definitions. Still later, children learn the specialized, often technical vocabulary of various content areas (understanding that the word, "line" has a much different meaning in math than in daily use, for example). Since word meaning is variable and fluid, often depending upon context, vocabulary skills are a key part of any reading instruction.

SUGGESTED CRITERIA FOR SELECTION OF VOCABULARY WORDS

Key words that are useful in a specific text or content area to be taught:

The National Reading Panel specifically includes this as an important criterion for selection, and other researchers agree. Cooper (2009) feels that it is up to the teacher to preview the content area text to identify the main ideas. Then the teacher should compile a list of terms related to the content thrust. These terms and words become part of the key concepts list. Next, the teacher sees which of the key concept words and terms are already defined in the text. These will not require direct teaching. Words for which children have sufficient skills to determine their meaning, through base, root, prefixes or suffixes, also will not require direct teaching. Words that the student cannot be expected to understand through these methods, need to be explicitly taught.

Words that are useful in *many* contexts: The National Reading Panel also states that vocabulary words should include those that will be used by the students in many different contexts, those words most necessary for the students at a given level of development. Classes of words, such as synonyms, antonyms, and multiple meaning words, for example, will be found in all reading and writing contexts and each should be taught *as a class* in addition to instruction in context.

Words selected by or important to the individual child: Since children arrive with widely varying background vocabularies, their vocabulary deficits will also vary. Words that one child already understands will puzzle another. It is often helpful to let each child select those terms in the reading assignment he/she does not understand and use those for vocabulary instruction. Children can also choose further study on words they simply think are "cool" words. This helps to individualize and differentiate vocabulary instruction.

In addition, each child's interests will affect the choice of vocabulary. A child interested in cars, trucks and large machines will need to be familiar with certain terms in order to enjoy reading and writing in that subject area (e.g., engine, motor, excavator, bulldozer), while a child whose interests lie in horses will need a different set of terms (e.g., hock, withers, saddle, cinch).

Words that the child will use frequently when writing: Since writing and reading are closely interrelated, it is important to choose vocabulary words the students will actually use in writing. As above, these may be words related to a favorite subject that they frequently discuss in daily journals or free writing assignments. For example, the child who frequently writes about the Atlanta Braves games in a daily journal, may need to understand words like double (for double play), outfield, pinch hitter, or designated (they do sometimes play American League teams), as well as the specialized meaning for the word "kitchen" in baseball (for a pitch "in his kitchen"), etc.

Vocabulary words chosen for their importance to writing should also include classes of words such as synonyms and antonyms. Since the use of interesting word choices when writing is part of the writing standards, it follows that students will need to be able to choose more interesting synonyms for overused words or use antonyms in compare and contrast writing. See Skill 2.04 for more on this type of vocabulary instruction.

SKILL 2.2   Demonstrating knowledge of developmentally appropriate strategies for promoting and reinforcing students' oral and written vocabulary knowledge[SAW9]

According to Burns, et al (2002), vocabulary develops in humans as they listen to conversation around them as they develop. Therefore, a language rich environment stimulates vocabulary development in children and a language impoverished environment can result in deficits in vocabulary development. In addition, some language disabilities also limit vocabulary acquisition. Such deficits have serious implications for ultimate reading comprehension.

Biemiller (2003) sites research results indicating that the listening vocabulary for a 6th grader who tests at the 25th percentile in reading is equivalent to that attained by the 75th percentile 3rd grader. This deficit in vocabulary presents a formidable challenge for the 6th grader to succeed, not only on reading tests, but also in various content subjects in elementary school and beyond. His research also indicates that those children entering 4th grade with significant vocabulary deficits demonstrate increasing reading comprehension problems. Evidence shows that these children do not catch up, but rather continue to fall behind. The National Reading Panel has put forth the following conclusions about vocabulary instruction as it relates to overall reading comprehension.

- There is a need for direct instruction of vocabulary items required for a specific text.
- Repetition and multiple exposures to vocabulary items are important. Students should be given items that will be likely to appear in many contexts.
- Learning in rich contexts is valuable for vocabulary learning. Vocabulary words should be those that the learner will find useful in many contexts. When vocabulary items are derived from content learning materials, the learner will be better equipped to deal with specific reading matter in content areas.
- Vocabulary tasks should be restructured as necessary. It is important to be certain that students fully understand what is asked of them in the context of reading rather than focusing only on the words to be learned.
- Vocabulary learning is effective when it entails active engagement in learning tasks.
- Computer technology can be used effectively to help teach vocabulary.
- Vocabulary can be acquired through incidental learning. Much of a student's vocabulary will have to be learned in the course of doing things other than explicit vocabulary learning. Repetition, richness of context, and motivation may also add to the efficacy of incidental learning of vocabulary.

- Dependence on a single vocabulary instruction method will not result in optimal learning. Research shows that a variety of methods can be used effectively with emphasis on multimedia aspects of learning, richness of context in which words are to be learned, and the number of exposures to words that learners receive.
- The Panel found that a critical feature of effective classrooms is the instruction of specific words that includes lessons and activities where students apply their vocabulary knowledge and strategies to reading and writing. Included in the activities were discussions where teachers and students talked about words, their features, and strategies for understanding unfamiliar words.

There are many methods for directly and explicitly teaching words. In fact, the Panel found twenty-one methods that have been found effective in research projects. Many emphasize the underlying concept of a word and its connections to other words, such as semantic mapping and diagramming that use graphics. The keyword method uses words and illustrations that highlight salient features of meaning. Visualizing or drawing a picture, either by the student or by the teacher, was found to be effective. Many words cannot be learned in this way, of course, so it should be used as only one method among others. Effective classrooms provide multiple ways for students to learn and interact with words. The Panel also found that computer-assisted activities can have a very positive role in the development of vocabulary. A few such strategies and techniques are mentioned here.

Key Word Instruction: Once a selection of key words for a particular content area assignment is chosen, Cooper (2004) suggests that instruction in key words, which should not be more than two or three key words, can be provided before, during, or after reading. If students have previewed the content area and identified those words they need support with, the instruction should be provided before reading. Instruction can also easily be provided as part of guided reading support. After reading support is indicated, the text offers the children an opportunity to enrich their own vocabularies.

Having children work as a whole class or in small groups on a content-specific dictionary for a topic regularly covered in their grade level social studies, science or mathematics curriculum offers an excellent collaborative opportunity for children to design a dictionary/word resource that can celebrate their own vocabulary learning. Such a resource can then be used with the next year's classes as well.

Word Map Strategies: These strategies can be useful for children both in elementary and secondary school, provided care is taken to adjust the level of complexity to the needs of the students. The target group of children for this strategy includes those who need to improve their independent vocabulary acquisition abilities. The strategy is essentially teacher-directed learning where children are "walked through" the process. The teacher helps the children to identify the type of information that makes a definition. Children are also assisted in using context clues and background understanding to construct meaning.

The *word map graphic organizer* is the tool teachers use to complete this strategy with children. Word map templates are available online from the Houghton Mifflin web site and from *ReadWriteThink*, the web site of the NCTE. The word map helps children to visually represent the elements of a given concept.

The children's literal articulation of the concept can be prompted by three key questions: What is it? What is it like? What are some examples? For instance, the word "oatmeal" might yield a word map with boxes that have the answers to each of the three key questions. What is it? (A hot cereal) What's it like? (Mushy and Salty) What are some examples? (Plain or Apple-Flavored)

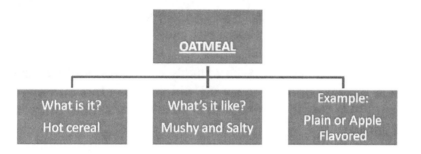

To share this strategy with children, the teacher selects three concepts familiar to the children and shows them the template of a word map with the three questions asked on the map. The teacher then helps the children to fill in at least two word maps with the topic in the top box and the answers in the three question boxes. The children should then independently complete the word map for the third topic. To reinforce the lesson, the teacher has the children select a concept of their own to map either independently or in a small group. As the final task for this first part of the strategy, the children, in teams or individually, write a definition for at least one of the concepts using the key things about it listed on the map. The children share these definitions aloud and talk about how they used the word maps to help them with the definitions.

For the next part of this strategy, the teacher picks an expository text or a textbook the children are already using to study mathematics, science, or social studies. The teacher either locates a short excerpt where a particular concept is defined or uses the content to write original model passages of definition.

After the passages are selected or authored, the teacher duplicates them. Then they are distributed to the children along with blank word map templates. The children will be asked to read each passage and then to complete the word map for the concept in each passage. Finally, the children share the word maps they have developed for each passage, and explain how they used the word in the passage to help them fill out their word map. Lastly, the teacher reminds the children that the three components of the concept—class, description, and example—are just three of the many components for any given concept.

This strategy has assessment potential because the teacher can literally see how the students understand specific concepts by looking at their maps and hearing their explanations. The maps the students develop on their own demonstrate whether they have really understood the concepts in the passages. This strategy serves to ready students for inferring word meanings on their own. By using the word map strategy, children develop concepts of what they need to know to begin to figure out an unknown word on their own. It assists the children in grades 3 and beyond to connect prior knowledge with new knowledge.

This word map strategy can be adapted by the teacher to suit the specific needs and goals of instruction. Illustrations of the concept and the comparisons to other concepts can be included in the word mapping for children grades 5 and beyond. This particular strategy is also one that can be used with a research theme in other content areas.

Hierarchical and Linear Arrays The very complexity of the vocabulary used in this strategy description, may be unnerving for the teacher. Yet this strategy included in the Cooper (2004) literacy instruction is really very simple once it is outlined directly for children.

The term "*hierarchical and linear arrays*" refers to how some words are grouped based on associative meanings. The words may have a "hierarchical" relationship to one another. For instance, the sixth grader is lower in the school hierarchy than the eighth grader. Within an elementary school, the fifth or sixth grader is at the top of the hierarchy and the pre-K or kindergartener is at the bottom of the hierarchy.

Words can have a linear relationship to one another in that they run a spectrum from bad to good. An example for K–3 children might be *pleased–happy–overjoyed*. These relationships can be displayed in horizontal boxes connected with dashes. The following is another way to display hierarchical relationships. Once you get past the seemingly daunting vocabulary words, the arrays turn out to be another excellent graphic organizer tool which can help children "see" how words relate to one another.

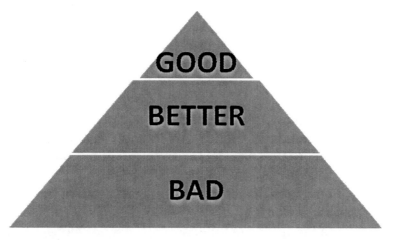

To use this graphic organizer, the teacher should pre-select a group of words from a read-aloud or from the children's writing. Show the children how the array will look using arrows for the linear array and just straight lines for the hierarchy. In fact, invite some children up to draw the straight hierarchy lines as the array is presented. This lets the children have a role in developing even the first hierarchical model.

Create one hierarchy array and one linear array of the pre-selected word with the children. Talk them through filling in (or helping the teacher to fill in) the array. After the children have had their own successful experience with arrays, they can select the words from their independent texts or familiar, previously read favorites to study. They will also need to decide which type of array, hierarchical or linear, is appropriate.

This strategy is best used *after* reading because it will helps children to expand their word banks.

Semantic Feature Analysis: This technique for enhancing vocabulary skills by using semantic cues is based on the research of Johnson and Pearson (1984) and Anders and Bos (1986). It involves young children in setting up a feature analysis grid of various subject content words, which is an outgrowth of their discussion about these words.

For instance, Cooper (2004) includes a sample of a Semantic Features Analysis Grid for Vegetables:

Vegetables	Green	Have Peels	Eat Raw	Seeds
Carrots	-	+	+	-
Cabbage	+	-	+	-

Note the use of the + for yes, - for no, and possible use for + and - if a vegetable like squash could be both green and yellow. Make this grid very accessible for young readers and very easily done by them on their own as part of their independent word analysis.

Teachers of children in grade one and beyond can design their own semantic analysis grids to meet their students' needs and to align with the topics the kids are learning. The steps to create semantic analysis grids are as follows:

- Select a category or class of words (e.g., planets, rodent family members, winter words, weather words).
- Use the left side of the grid to list at least three, if not more, items that fit this category. The number of actual items listed will depend on the age and grade level of the children, three or four items is fine for K-1 and up, while ten to fifteen items may be appropriate for grades 5 and 6.
- Brainstorm with the children, or if better suited to the class, the teacher may list features that the items have in common. As can be noted from the example excerpted from Cooper's *Literacy: Helping Students Construct Meaning* (2009), these common features, such as vegetables' green color, peels and seeds are usually pretty easy to identify.
- Show the children how to insert +, -, and even?, (if they are not certain) notations on the grid. The teacher might also explore with the children the possibility that an item could get both a + and a -. For example, a vegetable like broccoli might be eaten cooked or raw, depending on taste, and squash can be green or yellow.

Whatever the length of the grid when first presented to the children (perhaps as a semantic cue lesson in and of itself tied in to a text being read in class), make certain that the grid as presented and filled out is not the end of the activity. Children can use it as a model for developing their own semantic features grids and share them during the share time with the whole class. Child developed grids can become part of a Word Work center in the classroom or even be published in a Word Study Games book by the class as a whole. Such a publication can be shared with parents during open school week and evening visits and with peer classes.

Vocabulary Instruction for Students with Disabilities

Students with language and reading disabilities may have significant difficulties acquiring, remembering, or using vocabulary correctly. Words are labels for things such as objects, ideas, actions, and relationships among these and other concepts. Word referents range from literal ("dog" stands for a particular animal), to the very abstract ("analogous" stands for a concept concerning the relationship between abstract ideas). In order to properly comprehend and use words correctly, the word must be understood, stored, and retrieved when needed. It may also be necessary to hold a number of words and their referents in working memory while reading a complex passage or composing a sentence with them.

A disability in any of these areas of attaching meaning to a word, storing it, or retrieving and working with it can seriously affect vocabulary development. Children with such disabilities may not acquire vocabulary as efficiently as children without disabilities, even if they *are* in a language rich environment. Children with disabilities may need more explicit instruction, practice with strategies, and accommodations to learn the vocabulary necessary to become good readers and writers.

Most children develop vocabulary skills as they read or are read to by parents and teachers. They hear words and attach meanings to them based on the context in which they hear them. However, children with learning disabilities may not be able to use context without explicit training and practice. Some children will "read" or listen to a passage and be able to parrot back the words, but do not understand what they mean in context. The Mystery word game in Skill 1.07 can be particularly helpful to students with disabilities because it teaches the steps needed to use context to understand vocabulary.

It can also be helpful to make the vocabulary as concrete as possible. Students with language learning disabilities, for example, may have great difficulty understanding definitions and applying them. Providing visual or kinesthetic "backup" to definitions can be very helpful. For example, if you have selected a set of key words to teach for a content area unit, such as the Solar System, you can put the words on colorful cards with the definition on one side and pictures on the other. Even abstract words and action words can sometimes lend themselves to pictorial representation. The internet can be a very helpful source of printable pictures for many concepts and vocabulary words. If you type in "gravity" for example, you will find a number of graphic representations of gravity at different levels, from abstract mathematic images (not appropriate here) to pictures of people standing on the planet with arrows, chains, or hands emerging from the ground holding them down, etc. Children can also draw their own pictures of clues that will help them visualize and remember the definition.

Some vocabulary concepts are easier to act out than to see. A diagram of a planet orbiting the sun can be helpful, as can a spinning top as an illustration of the word, 'rotate'. It is even better, though, to have children, themselves, "orbit" a desk by walking around it in a fixed path while they spin ("rotate") around like a top dong so (be careful to avoid accidents!).

SKILL 2.3   Applying knowledge of how context is used to determine the meaning of unfamiliar words

The National Reading Panel's review of research on vocabulary instruction specifically stated that one of the effective strategies that can be used to enhance vocabulary is to teach students how to use context to understand word meaning. Skill 1.07 described the use of context cues such as syntax and meaning for word identification and those techniques can be modified for use in vocabulary comprehension, as well.

Contextual Redefinition

This strategy helps children use context more effectively by presenting them with sufficient background *before* they begin reading. It models for the children the use of contextual clues to make informed guesses about word meanings.
To apply this strategy as a teacher, first select unfamiliar words for teaching. No more than two or three words should be selected for direct teaching. Write a sentence in which there are sufficient clues supplied for the child to successfully figure out the meaning. Among the types of context clues the teacher can use are: compare/contrast, synonyms, and direct definition.

The next step is to present the words only on chart paper or as letter cards. Have the children pronounce the words. As they pronounce them, challenge them to come up with a definition for each word. After more than one definition is offered, encourage the children to decide as a whole group what the definition is. Write down their agreed upon definition with no comment as to its true meaning.

Share with the children the contexts (sentences written with the words and explicit context clues). Ask that the children read the sentences aloud. Then have them come up with a definition for each word. Make certain not to comment as they present their definitions. Ask that they justify their definitions by making specific references to the context clues in the sentences. As the discussion continues, direct the children's attention to their previously agreed upon definition of the word. Facilitate them in discussing the differences between their guesses about the word when they saw only the word itself and their guesses about the word when they read it in context. Finally, have the children check their use of context skills to correctly define the word by using a dictionary.

This type of direct teaching of word definitions is useful when the children have dictionary skills and the teacher is aware of the fact that there are not sufficient clues about the words in the context to help the students define it. In addition, struggling readers and students from ELL backgrounds may benefit tremendously from being walked through this same process, even though highly proficient and successful readers may apply it automatically.

By using this strategy, the teacher can also "kid watch" and note students' prior knowledge as they guess the word in isolation. The teacher can also actually witness and hear how various students use context skills.

Through their involvement in this strategy, struggling readers gain a feeling of community as they experience the ways in which their struggles and guesses resonate in other peers' responses to the text. They are also getting a chance to be "walked through" this maze of meaning, and are learning how to use context clues in order to navigate it themselves.

Preview in Context

This is a similar direct teaching strategy that allows the teacher to guide the students as they examine words in context prior to reading a passage. Before beginning the strategy, the teacher selects only two or three key concept words. Then the teacher reads carefully to identify passages within the text that evidence strong context clues for the word.

Then the teacher presents the word and the context to the children. As the teacher reads aloud, the children follow along. Once the teacher has finished the read-aloud, the children reread the material silently. After the silent rereading, the children are coached by the teacher on a definition of one of the key words selected for study. This is done through a child-centered discussion. As part of the discussion, the teacher asks questions that can help the children activate their prior knowledge and use the contextual clues to figure out the correct meaning of the selected key words. The teacher makes certain that the definition of the key concept word is finally made by the children.

Next, the teacher helps the children to expand the word's meaning by having them consider the following for the given key concept word: synonyms, antonyms, other contexts, or other kinds of stories/texts where the word might appear. This is the time the children check their responses to the challenge of identifying word synonyms and antonyms by having them go to the thesaurus or the dictionary to confirm their responses. In addition, the children are asked place the synonyms or antonyms they find in their word boxes or word journals. The recording of their findings will guarantee them ownership of the words and deepen their capacity to use contextual clues.

The main point to remember in using this strategy is that it should only be used when the context is strong. It will not work with struggling readers who have less prior knowledge. Through listening to the children's responses as the teacher helps them to define the word and its potential synonyms and antonyms, the teacher can assess students' ability to successfully use context clues. The key to this simple strategy is that it allows the teacher to draw the children out and to learn about their thinking process through their responses. The more talk from the child the better.

Vocabulary Self-Collection

This strategy is one in which children, even on the emergent level from grade 2 and up, can take responsibility for their learning. It is also by definition, a student centered strategy, which demonstrates student ownership of their chosen vocabulary.

To start, ask the children to read a required text or story. Invite them to select one word for the class to study from this text or story. The children can work individually, in teams, or in small groups. The teacher can also do the self-collecting so that this becomes the joint effort of the class community of literate readers. Tell the children that they should select words that particularly interest them or are unique in some way.

After the children have had time to make their selections and to reflect on them, make certain that they have time to share them with their peers as a whole class. When each child shares the word he/she has selected, have them provide a definition for the word. Each word that is given should be listed on a large experiential chart or even in a BIG BOOK format, if that is age and grade appropriate. The teacher should also share the word he/she selected and provide a definition. The teacher's definition and sharing should be somewhere in the middle of the children's recitations.

The dictionary should be used to verify the definitions. When all the definitions have been checked, a final list of child-selected and teacher-selected words should be made.

Once this final list has been compiled, the children can choose to record all or part of the list in their word journals. Some students may record only those words they find interesting. It is up to the teacher at the onset of the vocabulary self-collection activity to decide whether the children have to record all the words on the final list or can eliminate some.

To further enhance this strategy, children, where appropriate to their developmental level, can be encouraged to use their collected words as part of their writings or to record and clip these words as they appear in newspaper stories or online. This type of additional recording demonstrates that the child has truly incorporated the word into his/her reading and writing. It also habituates children to be lifelong readers, writers, and researchers.

Assessment is built into the strategy. As the children select the word for the list, they share how they used contextual clues. Further, as children respond to definitions offered by their peers, their prior knowledge can be assessed.

Knowledge of Common Sayings, Proverbs, and Idioms

Common sayings, idioms, and proverbs may create some misunderstandings among all children, and they are particularly difficult for students with disabilities or those who are learning English as a second language. Common sayings such as: "A bird in the hand is worth two in the bush," may leave a child wondering why that was said and how it was relevant. The lesson below provokes a child to seek understanding from reliable sources on this type of language.

Based on *The Fortune Cookie Strategy (Reissman, 1994).* Distribute a selection of "fortune cookies" to the children. Have them eat the cookies and then draw their attention to the enclosed fortunes. The "fortunes" and the "cookies" can be modified from standard fortune cookies to those made and written by the teacher so as to make them appropriate to the developmental level of the children and the concepts being taught.

First, the teacher will model by reading aloud his/her own fortune. After reading the fortune aloud, the teacher will explain what the fortune means using its vocabulary as a guide. Finally, the teacher may share whether or not the teacher agrees with the statement made in the fortune.

Similarly, children can read their fortunes aloud, explain the saying, and tell whether they agree with the proverb or prediction.

Following this activity, children can be asked to go home and interview their parents or community members to get family proverbs and common sayings.

Once the children return with the sayings and proverbs, they can each share them and explain their meaning. The class as a whole can discuss to what extent these sayings are true for everyone. Proverbs and sayings can become part of a word wall or be included in a special literacy center. The teacher can create fill-in, put-together, and writing activities to go with the proverbs. These activities can be made to tie in to social studies standards for different cultures or subcultures or for language arts such as figurative language.

This strategy also highlights, in a positive way, both the uniqueness and commonality of the family proverbs contributed by children from ELL backgrounds. If possible their proverbs can also be posted in their native languages as well as in English.

SKILL 2.4 **Recognizing ways to help students identify and use references such as dictionaries and thesauri for various purposes (e.g., determining word meanings and pronunciations, finding alternative word choices)**

Dictionaries and thesauruses can expand a student's understanding of even familiar words and are useful for spelling, writing, and reading. Thesauruses can expand children's understanding of specific words and help them understand how different words are related. It is very important to help students become familiar with the use of these reference sources.

Cooper (2004) suggests that the following be kept in mind as the teacher of grades K-6 introduces and then habituates children in what is to be hoped will be a lifelong fascination with the dictionary and with vocabulary acquisition. Requesting or suggesting that children look up a word in the dictionary should be an invitation to a wonderful exploration, not a punishment or busy work that has no reference to their current reading assignment. Do not routinely require children to look up every new word in the dictionary.

In addition, dictionary skills must be taught in all subject areas. Teachers should also consider that teaching vocabulary is not just the teaching of words: rather, it is the teaching of complex concepts, each with histories and connotations.

The teacher as a model

The teacher who keeps a dictionary on her desk and automatically turns to it to answer questions that arise about words (what they mean, how to pronounce them, where they come from, etc.) helps students learn why and how a dictionary is used. The teacher serves as an example of the usefulness of the reference source. The teacher might even make a show of using the dictionary periodically when she already knows a word, just to serve as a demonstration.

Teaching how to find words in the reference

Model the correct way to use the dictionary for children even as late as the third to sixth grade. Many have never been taught proper dictionary skills. The teacher needs to demonstrate to the children that as an adult reader and writer, he/she routinely and happily uses the dictionary and learns new information that makes him or her better at reading and writing.

It is possible to begin dictionary study and use as early as kindergarten, because of the proliferation of lush picture dictionaries that can be introduced at that grade level. Children can not only look at these picture dictionaries, but also begin to make dictionaries of their own at this grade level filled with pictures and beginning words. In early grade levels, use of the dictionary can nicely complement the children's mastery of the alphabet. They should be given whole-class and small-group practice in locating words.

Depending upon the skill level of the students, it may be necessary to lay the conceptual groundwork for finding words, using guide words, etc. For elementary students even a children's dictionary can seem daunting. If it is too much for the students, start by providing words on sticky notes or cards and practice putting them in ABC order. Provide some larger cards with two "guide words" at either end and have children practice putting various words on sticky notes before the guide words, between them or after them. Be sure they realize that a word that goes before them will be on an earlier page and a word that goes after them will be on a following page, etc. This complexity of this task (e.g., different first letters, or same first two letters) task can be modified to suit older or younger children and give them practice with the practical act of simply finding a word.

As the children progress with their phonetic skills, the dictionary can be used to show them phonetic re-spelling using the pronunciation key. In addition, their growing knowledge of alternative spelling patterns for various sounds can be used to help them find words they hear but do not see.

Older children in grades 3 and beyond need explicit teacher demonstrations and practice in the use of guide words. They also need to begin to learn about the hierarchies of various word meanings. In the upper grades, children should also explore using special content dictionaries and glossaries located in the backs of their books.

A variety of "bingo" or "scavenger hunt" games can be constructed or purchased that will help the children practice finding various pieces of information in dictionaries at their developmental level.

Thesaurus use

Like a dictionary, a thesaurus is an excellent resource to use when writing. Students can use a thesaurus to find appropriate synonyms, antonyms, and other related words to enhance their writing. However, it is important for teachers to model and instruct students in using a thesaurus so that students do not simply replace words. Students need to learn about word connotations and the "between the lines" meanings of words to effectively use a thesaurus.

Thesauruses can be used in conjunction with the "word wallets" mentioned earlier. One way to begin is to start with a small group of students. Begin by having an assortment of colorful thesauruses of various types available on the table. Pass out a thesaurus to each child. Differentiation can occur here simply by ensuring that the teacher passes out a thesaurus at each child's ability level. This would allow for a group of mixed ability students.

Have each child look up a generic word. You may have all the children look up the same word or assign the same word to pairs of students. Once they have had time to examine the word in their thesaurus, ask what other word someone found that means the same as their given word. Discuss the various words each child finds. Hold up each kind of thesaurus and note how it is organized. (e.g., "See, Bob's thesaurus has words in a list with one is big letters, then a list of others. Sue's has one word at the side in red and a bunch of others in a box like this," and so on). Discuss how some of the words are just more interesting or "cool" than others. Talk about the different contexts in which you might encounter one of the synonyms, etc. Adjust the complexity of these discussions to the student's level.

Children can construct packets of colorful 3X5 cards, each with a set of word families of synonyms with various connotations for concept words. They can use these to help understand words they find in print, as well as to improve word choice in their own writing. Children put the main word at the top and copy various synonyms onto the card. They can share their words during a brief sharing period each day. homework might consist of bringing in new words they hear or see outside of class or in their various reading activities, checking these out in the dictionary or thesaurus, and sharing the results.

In writing class or whenever students need to write (answering an open response question in a content area, e.g.), refer them to their word wallets or to the Thesaurus in order to improve their word choice and make their writing more interesting.

If students find dictionary and thesaurus activities interesting and fun, they will be more willing to work with and learn about them, and to use them in everyday reading and writing.

OBJECTIVE 3 **UNDERSTAND READING FLUENCY AND STRATEGIES FOR THE COMPREHENSION OF LITERARY AND INFORMATIONAL TEXTS ACROSS THE CURRICULUM**

SKILL 3.1 **Demonstrating knowledge of the concepts of rate, accuracy, expression, and phrasing in reading fluency; factors that affect fluency; and the relationship between reading fluency and comprehension**

In its report on teaching children to read (2000), the National Reading Panel defined fluency; the ability to read with speed, accuracy and proper expression without conscious attention and to handle both word recognition and comprehension simultaneously.

When students practice fluency, they practice reading connected pieces of text. In other words, instead of looking at a word as just a word, they might read a sentence straight through. The point of this is that in order for the student to comprehend what he or she is reading, it is necessary to "fluently" and quickly piece words in a sentence together. If a student is not fluent in reading, he or she sounds each letter or word out slowly and pays more attention to the phonics of each word. A fluent reader, on the other hand, might read a sentence out loud using appropriate intonations. The best way to test for fluency is to have a student read something out loud, preferably a few or more sentences in a row.

Most students just learning to read will probably not be very fluent right away; however, with practice, they will increase their fluency. Even though fluency is not the same as comprehension, it is said that fluency is a good predictor of comprehension. Think about it: If you're focusing too much on sounding out each word, you're not going to be paying attention to the meaning behind them. According to Salvia and Ysseldyke (1998), common oral fluency problems include the following:

- **Omissions**. The student skips individual words or groups of words.
- **Insertions**. The student inserts one or more words into the sentence being orally read.
- **Substitutions**. The student replaces one or more words in the passage by one or more meaningful words.
- **Gross mispronunciation of a word**. The student's pronunciation of a word bears little resemblance to the proper pronunciation.
- **Hesitation.** The student hesitates for two or more seconds before pronouncing a word.
- **Inversions.** The student changes the order of words appearing in a sentence.
- **Transpositions**. Reading words in the wrong order (She away ran instead of she ran away.)

- **Unknown words.** Being unable to pronounce certain words in a reasonable amount of time.
- **Slow choppy reading.** Not recognizing words quickly enough (20 to 30 words per minute)
- **Disregard of punctuation**. The student fails to observe punctuation; for example, may not pause for a comma, stop for a period, or indicate a vocal inflection, a question mark, or an exclamation point.

Accuracy

One of the best ways to evaluate reading fluency is to look at student accuracy. One method of accomplishing this involves keeping running records of students during oral reading. Calculating the reading level lets teachers know if the book is at a level where the child can read it independently or comfortably with guidance, or if the book is at a level where reading it frustrates the child.

As part of the informal assessment of primary grade reading, it is important to record the child's word insertions, omissions, requests for help, and attempts to get the word. In informal assessment, the rate of accuracy can be estimated from the ratio of errors to total words read.

The results of keeping a running record as an informal assessment can be used for teaching based on text accuracy. For example, if a child reads from 95 to 100 percent correctly, the child is ready for independent reading. If the child reads from 92 to 97 percent correctly, the child is ready for guided reading. A score below 92 percent indicates that the child needs a read-aloud or shared reading activity.

Automacity

Fluency in reading is dependent on automatic word identification, which assists the student in achieving comprehension of the material. Even slight difficulties in word identification can significantly increase the time it takes a student to read material, as the difficulties may therefore require re-reading parts or passages of the material and reduce the level of comprehension expected. If the student experiences reading as a constant struggle or an arduous chore, he or she may avoid reading whenever possible and consider it a negative experience. Obviously, the ability to read for comprehension, and learning in general, will suffer if all aspects of reading fluency are not presented to the student as acquirable skills that will be readily accomplished with the appropriate effort.

Automatic reading involves the development of strong orthographic representations, which allows fast and accurate identification of whole words made up of specific letter patterns. Most young students move easily from the use of alphabetic strategies (See Skill 1.0) to the use of orthographic representations that can be accessed automatically.

Initially, word identification is based on the application of phonic word accessibility strategies (letter-sound associations). These strategies are in turn based on the development of phonemic awareness, which is necessary to learn how to relate speech to print. (See Skills 1.3-1.7 for more).

One of the most useful devices for developing automacity in young students is through the visual pattern provided in the six syllable types.

EXAMPLES OF THE SIX SYLLABLE TYPES

- **CLOSED (NOT):** <u>Closed</u> in by a consonant—vowel makes its short sound
- **OPEN (NO):** <u>Ends</u> in a vowel—vowel makes its long sound
- **SILENT "E" (NOTE):** <u>Ends</u> in vowel consonant "e"—vowel makes its long sound
- **VOWEL COMBINATION (NAIL):** <u>Two vowels together</u> make the sound
- **"R" CONTROLLED (BIRD):** <u>Contains</u> a vowel plus "r"—vowel sound is changed
- **CONSONANT "LE" (TABLE):** <u>Applied</u> at the end of a word

These orthographic (letter) patterns signal vowel pronunciation to the reader. Students must be able to apply their knowledge of these patterns to recognize the syllable types, as well as to see these patterns automatically. This will ultimately allow students to read words as wholes. The move from decoding letter symbols and identifying recognizable terms to automatic word recognition is a substantial move toward fluency. A significant aid for helping students move through this phase was developed by Anna Gillingham when she incorporated the Phonetic Word Cards activity into the Orton-Gillingham lesson plan (Gillingham and Stillman, 1997). This activity involves asking the students to practice reading words (and some non-words) on cards as wholes, beginning with simple syllables and moving systematically through the syllable types to complex syllables and two-syllable words. The words should be divided into groups that correspond to the specific sequence of skills being taught.

The students' developments of the elements necessary to attain automacity continually move through stages. One of the next important stages involves the automatic recognition of single graphemes as a step toward the development of the letter patterns that make up words or word parts. English orthography is made up of four basic word types:

- Regular, for reading and spelling (e.g., <u>cat, print</u>)
- Regular, for reading but not for spelling (e.g., <u>float, brain</u> - could be spelled "flote" or "brane," respectively)
- Rule based (e.g., <u>canning</u> - doubling rule, <u>faking</u> - drop e rule)
- Irregular (e.g., <u>beauty</u>)

Students must be taught to recognize all four types of words automatically in order to be effective readers. Repeated practice in pattern recognition is often necessary. Practice techniques for student development can include speed drills in which students read lists of isolated words with contrasting vowel sounds that are signaled by the syllable type. For example, several closed syllable and vowel-consonant-"e" words containing the vowel "a" can be arranged randomly on pages containing about twelve lines and read for one minute. Individual goals are established and charts should be kept of the number of words read correctly in successive sessions. The same word lists are then repeated in sessions until the goal has been achieved for several succeeding sessions. When selecting words for these lists, the use of high-frequency words within a syllable category increases the likelihood of generalization to text reading.

Speed or Rate of Accurate Reading

A student whose reading rate is slow, halting, or inconsistent is exhibiting a lack of reading fluency. According to an article by Mastropieri, Leinart, and Scruggs (1999), some students have developed accurate word pronunciation skills but read at a slow rate. They have not moved to the phase where decoding is automatic, and their limited fluency may affect performance in the following ways:

- They read less text than peers and have less time to remember, review, or comprehend the text
- They expend more cognitive energy than peers trying to identify individual words
- They may be less able to retain text in their memories and less likely to integrate those segments with other parts of the text

The simplest means of determining a student's reading rate is to have the student read aloud from a prescribed passage (which should be at the appropriate reading level for age and grade and contain a specified number of words). The passage should not be too familiar for the student (some will try to memorize or "work out" difficult bits ahead of time), and should not contain more words than can be read comfortably and accurately by a normal reader in one or two minutes. Count only the words pronounced *correctly* on first reading, and divide this word count into elapsed time to determine the student's reading rate. To determine the student's standing and progress, compare this rate with the norm for the class and the average for all students who read fluently at that specific age/grade level.

The following general guidelines can be applied for reading lists of words with a speed drill and a 1-minute timing: 30 correct wpm for first and second grade children; 40 correct wpm for third grade children; 60 correct wpm for mid-third grade; and 80 wpm for students in fourth grade and higher.

Various techniques are useful with students who have acquired some proficiency in decoding skill but whose levels of skill are lower than their oral language abilities. Such techniques have certain, common features:

- Students listen to text as they follow along with the book
- Students follow the print using their fingers as guides
- Reading materials are used that students would be unable to read independently.

Experts recommend that a beginning reading program should incorporate partner reading, practice in reading difficult words prior to reading the text, timings for accuracy and rate, opportunities to hear books read, and opportunities to read to others.

Prosody

Prosody concerns the versification of text and involves such matters as which syllable of a word is accented. As regards fluency, it is that aspect that translates reading into the same experience within the reader's mind as listening. Prosody involves intonation and rhythm through such devices as syllable accent, phrasing, and punctuation.

In their article for *Perspectives* (Winter, 2002), Pamela Hook and Sandra Jones proposed that teachers can begin to develop awareness of the prosodic features of language by introducing a short three-word sentence with each of the three different words underlined for stress (e.g., *He is sick. He is sick. He is sick.*) The teacher can then model the three sentences while discussing the possible meaning for each variation. The students can practice reading them with different stresses until they are fluent. These simple three-word sentences can be modified and expanded to include various verbs, pronouns, and tenses. (e.g., *You are sick. I am sick. They are sick.*) This strategy can also be used while increasing the length of phrases and emphasizing the different meanings (e.g., *Get out of bed. Get out of bed. Get out of bed now.*). Teachers can also practice fluency with common phrases that frequently occur in text.

Prepositional phrases are also good syntactic structures for this type of work (e.g., *on the _____, in the _____, over the _____*). Teachers can pair these printed phrases with oral intonation patterns that include variations of rate, intensity, and pitch. Students can infer the intended meaning as the teacher presents different prosodic variations of a sentence. For example, when speakers want to stress a concept they often slow their rate of speech and may speak in a louder voice (e.g., *Joshua, get-out-of-bed-**NOW!***). Often, the only text marker for this sentence will be the exclamation point (!) but the speaker's intent will affect the manner in which it is delivered.

Practicing oral variations and then mapping the prosodic features onto the text will assist students in making the connection when reading. This strategy can also be used to alert students to the prosodic features present in punctuation marks. In the early stages, using the alphabet helps to focus a student on the punctuation marks without having to deal with meaning. The teacher models for the students and then has them practice the combinations using the correct intonation patterns to fit the punctuation mark (e.g., ABC. DE? FGH! IJKL? or ABCD! EFGHI? KL.). Teachers can then move to simple two-word or three-word sentences. The sentences are punctuated with a period, question mark, and exclamation point, and the differences in meaning that occur with each different punctuation mark (e.g., *Chris hops. Chris hops? Chris hops!*) are discussed. It may help students to point out that the printed words convey the fact that someone named Chris is engaged in the physical activity of hopping, but the intonation patterns get their cue from the punctuation mark. The meaning extracted from an encounter with a punctuation mark is dependent upon the students' ability to project an appropriate intonation pattern onto the printed text.

Keeping the text static while changing the punctuation marks helps students to attend to prosodic patterns. Students who read word-for-word may benefit initially from practicing phrasing with the alphabet rather than words, since letters do not tax the meaning system. This is similar to using the alphabet to teach intonation patterns. To accomplish this task, letters are grouped, an arc is drawn underneath, and students recite the alphabet in chunks (e.g., ABC DE FGH IJK LM NOP QRS TU VW XYZ). Once students understand the concept of phrasing, it is recommended that teachers help students chunk text into syntactic (noun phrases, verb phrases, and prepositional phrases) or meaning units until they are proficient themselves. There are no hard and fast rules for chunking, but syntactic units are most commonly used.

For better readers, teachers can mark the phrasal boundaries with slashes for short passages. Eventually, the slashes will be used only at the beginning of long passages, and students will be asked to continue "phrase reading" even after the marks end. Marking phrases can be done together with students, or those on an independent level may divide passages into phrases themselves.

Comparisons can be made to clarify reasons for differences in phrasing. Another way to encourage students to focus on phrase meaning and prosody (in addition to word identification) is to provide tasks that require them to identify or supply a paraphrase of an original statement.

The Relationship between Reading Fluency and Comprehension

Reading fluency refers to a student's speed, smoothness, and ease of oral reading. Fluent readers read rapidly and smoothly, allowing their minds to focus on comprehension of the text, thereby gaining meaning from the text they read.

Because reading fluency leads to reading comprehension, fluent readers typically enjoy reading more than students who apply all their energy to just sounding out the words. Struggling readers often labor to identify each word on the page, becoming so occupied in the process of identifying words that they are unable to devote any attention to comprehending the text they are reading.

Strategies to Improve Reading Fluency

For students who do not naturally develop their fluency skills, the teacher must provide strategies or activities that help develop them. A few instructional techniques for improving fluency are presented below.

Repeated Oral Readings with Guidance. Repeated reading passages are one of the most effective strategies for increasing oral reading fluency. This can be done individually or in pairs. Tying graphing, paired reading, and repeated oral reading into one time frame within the classroom can provide teachers and students with a specific strategy easily incorporated for a few minutes a day into the classroom routine.

Choral Reading. Choral reading is an effective reading strategy used to increase fluency. Students can read with a group or the teacher to build their fluency. In this strategy, reading should be done at an appropriate pace and with good prosody. For children with language disabilities, this can be very helpful. The choral reading provides a lot of context and modeling that helps improve fluency over time.

Reader's Theater. This strategy helps to bring drama back into the classroom by creating, scripts with different parts for different characters. The students practice the script in small groups for a few days, and then they complete a reading with good fluent reading for their peers. There is no preparation of costumes or set design, but it allows the students to have the practice of reading different parts. Such reading in dramatic form emphasizes prosody and expression. It also means that the child will be reading and rereading the same text, and this, too, is helpful.

Frequent Independent Reading. The more opportunity students have to practice reading, the more fluent they will become. The key is that the reading is on their independent level and the text is enjoyable for the reader. Students need to have some independent reading time daily.

Paired or Buddy Reading. Students are sometimes the best teachers. Paired reading is an opportunity for them to provide effective instruction to their peers. For the struggling readers, this is an excellent strategy to increase reading fluency. Sometimes, students can graph the results of their *words correct per minute* (wcpm) with their student helpers to have a visual representation of their progress. There are different things to consider when pairing students, including: reading level, ability to work together and stay on task, and appropriate materials for both partners to read. In any given pair, one child may be a more accomplished reader than the other, but this should not be a problem. The struggling reader would be reading at their *independent level,* which means that they should be able to read it reasonably well. When the more accomplished reader reads his or her more difficult selection, it also serves as a model for the less accomplished reader.

Instructor modeling. The instructor models fluent reading for the student, and the student follow by re-reading the same passage in imitation. Teachers need to provide examples of good reading, as well as non-examples where the teacher reads "robotically." In this way, students can hear the differences between good oral reading and poor oral reading.

Recorded Books. One way to model correct prosody is to allow students to listen to well-read books on tape or CD. As the students listen and scan the text at the same time, they not only hear the words modeled, they also experience rapidly putting the letter image they *see* with the sound they *hear.* As with instructor modeling, students can re-read passages themselves after hearing them.

While the majority of reading will occur silently in the student's head, it is necessary to take the time to practice reading out loud to ensure students develop this more natural flow of language. Such practice makes it more likely the phrasing and expression will transfer into the silent reading, and this will enhance comprehension, as well. If students are unable to do the task orally, the reading in their head may be just as robotic or choppy which can impact comprehension in a negative manner.

In order to develop fluent readers, knowledgeable teachers should devote substantial instructional time to enhancing the reading fluency of students.

SKILL 3.2   Recognizing the effects of various factors (e.g., prior knowledge, context, vocabulary knowledge, graphic cues) on reading comprehension and identifying strategies (e.g., predicting, rereading, retelling) that facilitate comprehension before, during, and after reading

Conspicuous Strategies

As an instructional priority, conspicuous strategies are a sequence of teaching events and teacher actions used to help students learn new literacy information and relate it to their existing knowledge. Conspicuous strategies can be incorporated in beginning reading instruction to ensure that all learners have basic literacy concepts. For example, during storybook reading, teachers can show students how to recognize the fronts and backs of books, locate titles, or look at pictures and predict the story, rather than assume children will learn this through incidental exposure. Similarly, teachers can teach students a strategy for holding a pencil appropriately or checking the form of their letters against an alphabet sheet on their desks or the classroom wall.

Mediated Scaffolding

Mediated scaffolding can be accomplished in a number of ways to meet the needs of students with diverse literacy experiences. To link oral and written language, for example, teachers may use texts that simulate speech by incorporating oral language patterns or children's writing. Teachers can use daily storybook reading to discuss book-handling skills and directionality concepts that are particularly important for children who are unfamiliar with printed texts. Teachers can also use repeated readings to give students multiple exposures to unfamiliar words, extend opportunities to look at books with predictable patterns, and provide support by modeling the behaviors associated with reading. Teachers can act as *scaffolds* during these storybook reading activities by adjusting their demands (e.g., asking increasingly complex questions or encouraging children to take on portions of the reading) or by reading more complex text as students gain knowledge of beginning literacy components.

Strategic Integration

Many children with diverse literacy experiences have difficulty making connections between old and new information. Strategic integration can be applied to help link old and new learning. For example, in the classroom, strategic integration can be accomplished by providing access to literacy materials in classroom writing centers and libraries. Students should also have opportunities to integrate and extend their literacy knowledge by reading aloud, listening to other students read aloud, and listening to tape recordings and videotapes in reading corners.

Background Knowledge about the Reading Process

All children bring some level of background knowledge (e.g., how to hold a book, awareness of directionality of print) to beginning reading. Teachers can utilize children's background knowledge to help children link their personal literacy experiences with beginning reading instruction, while also closing the gap between those students with rich and those students with impoverished literacy experiences. Activities that draw upon background knowledge include incorporating oral language activities (which discriminate between printed letters and words) into daily read-alouds as well as providing frequent opportunities to re-tell stories, look at books with predictable patterns, write messages with invented spellings, and respond to literature through drawing.

Emergent Literacy

Emergent literacy research examines early literacy knowledge and the contexts and conditions that foster that knowledge. Despite differing viewpoints on the relation between emerging literacy skills and reading acquisition, there is strong support that early childhood exposure to oral and written language is linked to the facility with which children learn to read.

Reading for comprehension of factual material (e.g., content area textbooks, reference books, and newspapers) is closely related to study strategies in the middle/junior high setting. Organized study models, such as the SQ3R method, a technique that makes it possible to learn the content of even large amounts of text (Survey, Question, Read, Recite, and Review Studying), teach students to locate main ideas and supporting details, to recognize sequential order, to distinguish fact from opinion, and to determine cause and effect relationships.

STRATEGIES THAT FACILITATE COMPREHENSION

Prior Knowledge

Prior knowledge can be defined as all of an individual's prior experiences, education, and development that precede his or her entrance into a specific learning situation or his or her attempts to comprehend a specific text. At times, prior knowledge can be erroneous or incomplete. If there are misconceptions in a child's prior knowledge, these must be corrected so that the child's overall comprehension skills can continue to progress. Prior knowledge even at the Kindergarten level includes accumulated positive and negative experiences both in and out of school.

Prior knowledge might range from family travels, watching television, and visiting museums and libraries to visiting hospitals, prisons, and struggling with poverty. Whatever the prior knowledge the child brings to the school setting, the independent reading and writing the child does in school immeasurably expands his or her prior knowledge, hence broadening his or her reading comprehension capabilities.

Literary response skills are also dependent on schemata. Schemata (the plural of schema) are those structures that represent generic concepts stored in the memory. Effective textual comprehension, whether done by adults or children, uses schemata and prior knowledge in addition to the ideas from the printed text for reading comprehension; graphic organizers help to organize this information. In order for the child's prior knowledge to be most useful in helping the child's reading comprehension, that knowledge must be "activated" or brought to the forefront of the child's conscious mind. Many of the comprehension strategies discussed here have a component that helps to activate and/or expand a child's prior knowledge.

Graphic Organizers

Graphic organizers solidify in a chart format a visual relationship among various reading and writing ideas. These ideas include: sequence, timelines, character traits, fact and opinion, main ideas and details, differences, and likenesses (generally done using a VENN DIAGRAM of interlocking circles, KWL Chart, etc.). These charts and formats are essential for providing scaffolding for instruction by activating pertinent prior knowledge.

KWL (Know, Want, Learn) charts are exceptionally useful for reading comprehension, as they outline what children _know_, what they _want_ to know, and what they've _learned_ after reading. Students are asked to activate prior knowledge about a topic and further develop their knowledge about a topic using this organizer. Teachers often opt to display and maintain KWL charts throughout a classroom to continually record pertinent information about students' reading.

When the teacher first introduces the KWL strategy, the children should be allowed sufficient time to brainstorm in response to the first question: what all of them in the class or small group actually know about the topic. The children should have a three-columned KWL worksheet template for their journals, and there should be a chart to record the responses from class or group discussions. Children who are old enough can write under each column in their own journal, and should also help their teacher with notations on the chart. For younger children, the teacher can record ideas on large chart paper for all to share. This strategy involves the children in actually gaining experience in note-taking and in creating a concrete record of new data and information gleaned from the passage about the topic.

Depending on the grade level of the participating children, the teacher may also want to channel them into considering categories of information they hope to find out from the expository passage. For instance, they may be reading a book on animals to find out more about the animal's habitats during the winter or about the animal's mating habits. When children are working on the middle column—what they want to know about the reading—the teacher may want to help them to express it in question format.

When reading and research is complete, children can go back and check what they put in the K column to be sure they were right about what they *thought* they knew. Then they can record new information learned in the L column. It is helpful if this is lined up with the questions in the W column. If there are questions that were *not* answered in the reading, these can be a springboard to additional research.

KWL is a useful tool and can even be introduced as early as second grade with extensive teacher discussion and support. It not only serves to support the child's comprehension of a particular expository text, but also models for children a format for note-taking. In addition, when the teacher wants to introduce report writing, the KWL format provides excellent outlines and question introductions for at least three paragraphs of a report.

Cooper (2004) recommends this strategy for use with thematic units and with reading chapters in required science, social studies, or health text books. In addition to its usefulness with thematic unit study, KWL is wonderful for providing the teacher with a concrete format to assess how well children have absorbed pertinent new knowledge within the passage (by looking at the third L section). Ultimately, it is hoped that students will learn to use this strategy, not only under explicit teacher direction with templates of KWL sheets, but also on their own by informally writing questions they want to find out about in their journals and then going back and answering them after the reading.

Note Taking

Older children should take notes in their reading journals, while younger children and those more in need of explicit teacher support may contribute their ideas and responses as part of the discussion in class. Their responses should be recorded on the experiential chart.

Connecting Texts

The concept of readiness is generally regarded as a developmentally-based phenomenon. Various abilities, whether cognitive, affective, or psychomotor, are perceived to be dependent upon the mastery or development of certain prerequisite skills or abilities. Readiness, then, implies that prior to accomplishing the knowledge, experience, and readiness prerequisites, children should not yet engage in the new task.

Readiness for subject area learning is dependent not only on prior knowledge, but also on affective factors such as interest, motivation, and attitude. These factors are often more influential on student learning than the pre-existing cognitive base.

When texts relate to a student's life or other reading materials or areas of study, they become more meaningful and relevant to students' learning. Students typically enjoy seeing reading material that connects to their lives, other subject areas, and other reading material. This can be particularly important for students from diverse cultures and language groups. If a student's background is significantly different from the target group of the reading material, the student is more likely to struggle with comprehension.

Discussing the Text

Discussion is an activity the children (this activity works well from grades three through six and beyond) usually conduct at the conclusion of a particular text. Among the prompts, the teacher-coach might suggest that the children focus on words of interest they encountered in the text. These can also be words that they heard if the text was read aloud. Children can be asked to share something funny, upsetting, or unusual about the words they have read. Through this focus on children's responses to words as the center of the discussion circle, peers become more interested in word study.

Furthermore, in the current teaching of literacy, reading, writing, thinking, listening, viewing, and discussing are not viewed as separate activities or components of instruction, but rather as simultaneous and interactive elements of reading comprehension.

Questions as guideposts

Generating questions can also motivate and enhance children's comprehension of reading in that they are actively involved in generating their own questions and then answering these questions based on their reading. The following guidelines will help children generate meaningful questions that will trigger constructive reading of expository texts.

First, children should preview the text by reading the titles and subheads. Then they should also look at the illustrations and the pictures. Finally, they should read the first paragraph. These first previews should yield an impressive batch of specific questions.

Next, children should get into their Dr. Seuss mode, and ask themselves a "THINK" question. For younger children, having a "THINK" silly hat in the classroom might be effective, as well, so that the children could actually go over and put it on. Make certain that the children write down the question.

Then, have them read to find important information to answer their "Think" questions. Ask that they write down the answer they found and copy the sentence or sentences where they found the answer. For students with writing difficulties, they can put a numbered post-it on the part of the text that holds the answer or clue. Also, have them consider whether, in light of their further reading through the text, their original questions were good ones or not.

Finally, ask them to be prepared to explain why their original questions were good ones or not. Once the children have answered their original "think" questions, have them generate additional ones, and then find their answers and judge whether these questions were "good" ones in light of the text.

Use of Comprehension Skills Before, During, and After Reading.

Many researchers (e.g., Cooper, 2004, Taberski, 2000) recommend a broad array of comprehension strategies before, during and after reading. The foundation of reading comprehension begins *before* actually "reading" of the text starts. Reading comprehension does not occur in isolation. A child's background information and experiences, the schemata a child has that are relevant to the material being read, provide the framework to which new information can be attached, the context for comprehending what is read. In order to comprehend what is being read, a child must have a vocabulary adequate for the material and at least some prior experience related to the material. In addition, that background and vocabulary must be at the forefront of the child's mind so that it can be used as the child reads. If the child's prior experience with the new material is lacking, it may be necessary to build additional background for the child through pre-reading activities. For this reason, many comprehension strategies begin before reading the text as a whole.

One traditional method designed by Robinson (1961) is often referred to as SQ3R. This method takes the reader through pre-reading, during reading and after reading activities:

- **Survey:** Before reading, the child scans the title, any pictures or illustrations throughout the text, looks at headings or captions, and sometimes reads the first and last paragraphs of a text or section of the text.
- **Question:** As readers survey the material, they ask themselves questions and make predictions about what they are about to read. This can be as simple or as complex as is appropriate for the students' level. Early readers might simply find a question to ask orally or make a prediction about where the story is going. More fluent readers might actually record questions and predictions on a graphic organizer suitable to the story. The reader is, basically, establishing a *purpose* for reading and a framework for organizing and attaching new information.
- **Read:** The student reads the material (silently or aloud) and looks for information that can answer the questions and confirm or reject the predictions already made.
- **Recite:** The reader "recites" answers to his earlier questions or even records those answers if appropriate.
- **Review:** The reader reviews the original survey and questions to see what new information relates to them, to see whether all the questions have been answered, whether new questions have emerged.

Some version of the Survey portion of this strategy is present in most pre-reading strategies. In some cases it is called an "anticipation guide." In this version, the teacher or the students list a set of declarative statements (true or false or unknown) about the subject or story and readers decide whether they agree or disagree. Then during reading (in the Read and Recite portion above) readers adjust their decisions about whether or not they agree with each statement. The traditional KWL chart mentioned earlier is another version of this. In other versions, a more complex web of topics and questions is constructed and answers are entered as the student reads.

Higher Order Predictions

One theory/approach to the teaching of reading that gained currency in the late 1960s and the early 1970s involved asking inferential and critical thinking questions of the reader that would challenge and engage the children in the text. This approach to reading went beyond the literal level of what was stated in the text to an inferential level of using text clues to make predictions, and extended further to a critical level of involving the child in evaluating the text. While asking engaging and thought-provoking questions is still viewed as part of the teaching of reading, it is currently viewed only as one component of the teaching of reading.

Most **during reading** strategies are based on searching for or finding information about the questions or predictions made during pre-reading. These answers can be recorded or simply stated orally during reading. Students who need additional help with these strategies can employ such things as highlighting or post-it arrows to help. For example, a simple list of questions or predictions can be color coded and as the students read they can put a colored post-it arrow on sentences or illustrations that answer one of the color-coded questions. This makes it easy for the student to find the information later and avoids the interruption caused by writing down the information. For some students, writing is easier, and these may record information on a graphic organizer.

In addition to during reading strategies based on opening questions, others may simply be based on self monitoring to determine whether the student understands what has been read. After each paragraph, the student can pause and ask, "Did I understand all those words? Did I get the point? Does it make sense?" Can I put it in my own words? Students can also be taught various "fix-it" strategies for what to do when it does *not* make sense. These might include; rereading the passage, read a little further to see if it is clarified, look at illustrations, figure out unknown words, or ask for help.

After reading strategies usually involve answering the initial questions or purpose for reading, or evaluating what has been learned and how it affects what the reader *thought* he/she knew at the start—modifying the background knowledge or schemata with which the reader approached the text. Such strategies can be as simple as answering questions orally or in print about the material, retelling the sequence of events in stories or chronologically organized text, or more creative responses such as a reader's theatre based on a story or a poster or demonstration regarding facts learned while reading. The primary purpose of post reading strategies is to consolidate the learning, though they sometimes feed into assessment tools, as well. If a KWL chart was used, the student fills in the Learned side of the chart. Or students might come up with additional questions that were not answered in the text, or speculate about what might happen next in a story. Retelling and summarizing are also useful post reading strategies.

Cooper (2004) suggests providing the student with a list of steps to use when reading, for example: My Strategic Reading Guide:

- Do I infer/predict important information, use what I know, think about what may happen, or what I want to learn?
- Identify important information about the story elements.
- Self-question, generate questions and search for the answers.
- Monitor-Ask: Does this make sense to me? Does this help me meet my purpose in reading?
- If lost, what should I do? Try fix-ups: re-read, read further ahead, look at the illustrations, ask for help and think about the words.

- Evaluate what I have read.
- Summarize: Think about how the parts of the stories that I was rereading came together.

Story maps can also provide good post reading activities for chronologically arranged material, particularly fiction.

Storyboard panels, which are used by comic strip artists and by those artists who do advertising campaigns, as well as television and film directors, are perfect for engaging children K-6 in a variety of comprehension strategies before, during, and after reading. They can storyboard the beginning of a story, read aloud, and then storyboard its predicted middle or end. Of course, after they experience or read the actual middle or ending of the story, they can compare and contrast what they produced with its actual structure. They can play familiar literature identification games with a buddy or as part of a center by storyboarding one key scene or characters from a book and challenging a partner or peer to identify the book and characters correctly.

Think Alouds. Thinking aloud is one of the most effective strategies both for teaching comprehension and for working through complex concepts presented in some texts. When using the think-aloud approach, the teacher is simply speaking out loud every thought that would normally be going on silently in her head. As the teacher demonstrates and explains the connections he/she is making while reading, the students begin to understand how the teacher arrived at these connections. Integrating new information with the old information is a valuable skill for students to master. Students can practice their own think alouds by reviewing the questions they have chosen to set a purpose for reading. Creative teacher queries can help students direct their own think alouds as they practice.

Visualization. Visualization is the process of creating a mental picture corresponding to the words on the page. Generally, good readers have a mental image of what they are reading. The phrasing and author's voice provide clear details that allow multiple readers to have the same basic vision. When working with visualization it can sometimes be helpful for students to take the additional step of drawing out the picture as they see it in their mind. Working with the teacher, the students can advance their comprehension even if key concepts are missing. Some techniques for improving students' visualization of what they read include practice in simply verbalizing specific descriptions of pictures or images so other students can visualize them. Discussion of the manner in which the description did or did not match the picture can be very fruitful, too.

Topic and Concluding Sentences. As we teach students to write, we often spend a lot of time focusing on writing paragraphs with topic sentences and concluding sentences. However, we also need to focus on how these same features—topic and concluding sentences—may be used to better understand the text. These parallels can help students better understand what they are reading and also help them develop their writing skills. Understanding that topic sentences tell the main idea of the paragraph, and that concluding sentences restate that idea, can help students' comprehension as well.

Semantic Mapping. Another beneficial tool for students is *semantic mapping.* In semantic mapping, students begin to make the connections between the information they already know about the topic and the new information they are learning. It is typically a more graphic representation of the information, but it is built upon words and ideas. Mapping generally increases knowledge and improves vocabulary development. This is a strategy that can be used to reach all learning styles and therefore is an important one to teach. It is exactly what its name implies—a map of the reading. Just as a road map helps the driver get from point A to point B, so it is for a reading map. It helps the reader maneuver through the information in a meaningful manner. Maps can use words with key ideas connected to smaller chunks of information. They can also use pictures instead of words to help the more visual learner. Adding color to a map can help certain ideas stand out. This can be particularly helpful for students to begin to understand the process of prioritization in skills. Combining words and pictures is probably the most commonly used type of map. Lines are drawn between connecting concepts to show relationships and because the reader is creating it himself or herself, it is meaningful only to them. Maps are individual creations and revolve around the reader's learning and prior knowledge.

SKILL 3.3	Recognizing types and characteristics of literary and informational texts; distinguishing among literal, inferential, and evaluative comprehension; and identifying strategies for promoting students' literal, inferential, and evaluative comprehension

TYPES (GENRES) AND CHARACTERISTICS OF LITERARY AND INFORMATIONAL TEXTS

Fiction vs. Nonfiction

Most literature can be divided into one of two major categories: fiction or nonfiction. Other genre and literary types listed below can typically be found in both fiction and nonfiction.

Fiction is a large category including anything made up or imaginary, not literally true, whether it is fantastic or realistic, and it can overlap with many other genres.

Nonfiction is a large category of material that is factual or true, and it, too, comes in many forms that overlap with other genres.

Students often misunderstand the differences between fiction and nonfiction. They mistakenly believe that stories are always examples of fiction. The simple truth is that stories are both fiction and nonfiction. The primary difference is that fiction is made up by the author and nonfiction is generally true (or an opinion). It is harder for students to understand that nonfiction entails an enormous range of material, from textbooks and true stories to newspaper articles and speeches. Fiction, on the other hand, is fairly simple—made-up stories, novels, etc. However, it is also important for students to understand that authors use their own life experiences to help them create works of fiction.

In understanding fiction, it is important to recognize the artistry in telling a story to convey a point. When students see that an author's choice in a work of fiction is for the purpose of conveying a viewpoint, they can make better sense of the specific details in the work of fiction.

Regardless of the specific content of a work of fiction, the basic text structure is almost always the same: chronological. Fiction stories have a beginning, middle and end. The occasional flashback notwithstanding, they generally start at the beginning of a set of events, then follow them through to the last event. They can generally be organized using story maps or story grammar markers of some sort. These tend to have similar story elements: characters, setting (time and place), a problem, goal or initiating event, a series of events leading to a conclusion or solution.

In comparing fiction to nonfiction, students need to learn about the conventions of each. In fiction, students can generally expect to see plot, characters, setting, and themes. In some nonfiction (e.g., biography, historical accounts) students may see a plot, characters, settings, and themes, arranged in chronological order. However, there are a great many more diverse text structures found in nonfiction, and they will also experience interpretations, opinions, theories, research, and other elements.

In understanding nonfiction, it is important to realize what is truth and what is perspective. Often, a nonfiction writer will present an opinion, and that opinion may be very different from someone's view of the truth. Knowing the difference between the two is very crucial.

Over time, students may begin to see patterns that identify fiction from nonfiction. Oftentimes, the more fanciful or unrealistic a story is, the more likely it is fiction. On the other hand, the saying "truth is stranger than fiction" is reinforced by the outrageous true events that sometimes comprise the basis of nonfiction. Therefore, it is vital for students to have a strong framework of understanding for the literary conventions that separate the two genres.

Other Genres and Literary Types

Allegory: A story in verse or prose with characters representing virtues and vices. There are two meanings, symbolic and literal. John Bunyan's *The Pilgrim's Progress* is the most renowned of this genre.

Ballad: An *in medias res* (Latin for "in the middle of things") story told or sung, usually in verse and accompanied by music. Literary devices found in ballads include the refrain, or repeated section, and incremental repetition, or anaphora, for effect. The earliest forms were anonymous folk ballads. Later forms include Coleridge's Romantic masterpiece, "The Rime of the Ancient Mariner." This genre can overlap heavily with the poetry genre.

Biography/Autobiography: A form of nonfiction that informs about the real events in the lives of real people, such as inventors, explorers, scientists, political and religious leaders, social reformers, artists, sports figures, doctors, teachers, writers, and war heroes, etc. Biographies are written by someone about another person. In autobiographies the authors are writing about their own lives.

Drama: Plays – comedy, modern, or tragedy -- typically conducted in multiple acts. Traditionalists and neoclassicists adhere to Aristotle's unities of time, place, and action. Plot development is advanced through dialogue. Literary devices include asides, soliloquies, and the chorus representation of public opinion. William Shakespeare is considered by many to be the greatest of all dramatists/playwrights. Other notable dramaturges include: Ibsen, Williams, Miller, Shaw, Stoppard, Racine, Moliére, Sophocles, Aeschylus, Euripides, and Aristophanes. Drama can be fiction or nonfiction and the subject matter can fall into many other categories (e.g., historical fiction, science fiction, biography).

Epic: A long poem usually of book length reflecting values inherent in the generative society. Epic devices include an invocation to a Muse for inspiration, an overall purpose for writing, a universal setting, a protagonist and antagonist who possess supernatural strength and acumen, and the interventions of a God or the gods. Among the most notable are: Homer's *Iliad* and *Odyssey*, Virgil's *Aeneid*, Milton's *Paradise Lost*, Spenser's *The Fairie Queene*, Barrett Browning's *Aurora Leigh*, and Pope's mock-epic, *The Rape of the Lock*.

Epistle: A letter that is not always originally intended for public distribution, but due to the fame of the sender and/or recipient, becomes public domain. For example, the apostle Paul wrote epistles that were later placed in the Bible. This genre is sometimes imitated by authors in fiction work (e.g., Bram Stoker's *Dracula*, or Cleary's *Dear Mr. Henshaw*).

Essay: Typically a limited length prose work focusing on a topic and propounding a definite point-of-view through an authoritative tone. Great essayists include Carlyle, Lamb, DeQuincy, Emerson, and Montaigne, who is credited with defining this genre.

Fantasy: A form of fiction in which at least one of the basic elements of fiction--characters, setting, or plot--is impossible. Many of the themes found in these stories are similar to those in traditional literature. The stories often start out based in reality, which makes it easier for the reader to suspend disbelief and enter worlds of unreality.

Historical Fiction: A form of fiction in which the story takes place in a real historical setting. Though characters and events are primarily fiction, the setting is as close to the real historical setting as possible. Often real events and real historical figures are woven into the story. Such fiction often follows fictional, but realistic characters as they experience real historical events.

Informational Books: A form of nonfiction intended to inform the reader about some topic. They can be found in a wide range of formats covering diverse topics. See Skill 3.05 for more on this genre.

Novel: The longest form of fictional prose containing a variety of characterizations, settings, local color, and regionalism. Most have complex plots, expanded descriptions, and attention to detail. Some of the great novelists include Austen, the Brontës, Twain, Tolstoy, Hugo, Hardy, Dickens, Hawthorne, Forster, and Flaubert.

Poetry: a genre where the message usually involves characteristics such a rhyme, rhythm, sensory and nature imagery, colorful language such as simile and metaphor, although the only requirement is rhythm. Sub-genres include fixed types of literature such as the: sonnet, elegy, ode, pastoral, and villanelle. Unfixed types of literature include blank verse and dramatic monologue. Poetry can be fiction such as the poems of Shel Silverstein, or nonfiction, such as *Spiders Spin Webs* by Yvonne Winer. Epic poetry such as *The Midnight Ride of Paul Revere* or *Hiawatha* may also fall into a traditional or historical literature classification.

Realistic Fiction: A type of fiction in which the basic elements—characters, setting, and plot—are all possible. Characters are fictional, but just like "real" people. The setting is a modern, real world setting, and events are plausible. This type of fiction stands in contrast to fantasy, in which such elements are impossible.

Romance: A highly imaginative tale set in a fantastical realm dealing with the conflicts between heroes and villains and/or monsters. "The Knight's Tale" from Chaucer's Canterbury Tales, *Sir Gawain and the Green Knight*, and Keats' "The Eve of St. Agnes" are prime examples.

Science Fiction: Robots, spacecraft, mystery, and civilizations from other planets or ages often appear in these stories. Most presume advances in science on other planets or in a future time.

Short Story: Typically a terse narrative, with less developmental background about characters, but which may still include description, point-of-view, and tone. Poe emphasized that a successful short story should create one focused impact. Considered among the great short story writers are: Hemingway, Faulkner, Twain, Joyce, Jackson, O'Connor, de Maupassant, Saki, Poe, and Pushkin.

Traditional Literature—Several types of literature including folktales, fables, fairy tales, myths and legends, all forms that were handed down, orally from generation to generation in various cultures. Many have no identifiable author, though many authors may have rewritten and modified the original tales over the years.

Fable: A form of Traditional Literature, usually a terse tale offering up a moral or exemplum. Often, these are precautionary tales meant to teach a lesson, or moral. Chaucer's "The Nun's Priest's Tale" is a fine example of a bête fabliau (beast fable) in which animals speak and act characteristically human, illustrating human foibles.

Folktales/Fairy Tales: A type of traditional literature characterized by adventures of animals or humans and the supernatural. The hero is usually on a quest and is aided by other-worldly helpers. More often than not, the story focuses on good and evil and reward and punishment.

Legend: A traditional narrative or collection of related narratives, popularly regarded as historically factual but actually a mixture of fact and fiction, often related to myths. Many legends have a core of reality and involve a real person or event that has been transformed into a fictionalized account over the years.

Myth: Stories that are more or less universally shared within a culture to explain its history and traditions. Myths are often considered true in their own societies. The subject matter usually "explains" the origins of creation, a people, or some event or aspect of the world.

Tall Tales: These are traditional tales that are fantastic and set in a real setting in which people or creatures do impossible things. Examples: *Paul Bunyan*, *John Henry* and *Pecos Bill*. These are purposely-exaggerated accounts of individuals with superhuman strength.

DISTINGUISHING AMONG LITERAL, INFERENTIAL, AND EVALUATIVE COMPREHENSION

Comprehension involves understanding what is read regardless of purpose or thinking skills employed. Comprehension can be delineated into categories of differentiated skills. Benjamin Bloom's taxonomy includes: knowledge, comprehension, application, analysis, synthesis and evaluation. Thomas Barrett suggests that comprehension categories be classified as: literal meaning, reorganization, inference, evaluation and appreciation. In both lists, difficulty increases as you move up the list (i.e., "knowledge" and "literal meaning" are the easiest to comprehend, and "evaluation" and "appreciation" are the most difficult).

Literal Comprehension

Literal comprehension is the understanding of the basic facts of a given passage. This level of comprehension is the priority for the reader so that he or she can maintain coherence and a general understanding of what is being read. *Literal Comprehension* focuses on ideas and information that are explicitly stated in the details of the reading selection. It can require either recognition or recall. Recognition is typically less cognitively demanding than recall because it does not involve as much memory.

Recognition requires the student to locate or identify ideas or information explicitly stated in the reading selection. Using the story of *Goldilocks and the Three Bears,* recognition of literal information might include such things as:

- Recognition of setting: Where did the three bears live?
- Recognition of main ideas: Why did the three bears go out for a walk? Note that a 'why' question is only a literal question IF the answer is clearly stated in the text. If the reader must pull clues together from different parts of the text or use their own background knowledge or judgment, it would be an inference question.
- Recognition of sequence: What did Goldilocks try first in the house? Whose porridge did Goldilocks taste first?
- Recognition of comparisons: Whose porridge was too hot? Too cold? Just right?

- Recognition of cause-and-effect relationships: Why didn't Papa Bear's and Mama Bear's chairs break into pieces like Baby Bear's chair? Again, such a question would be literal ONLY IF the cause and effect relationship is clearly made in the text, and would be inferential if the student needs to combine clues or use information from outside the text.
- Recognition of character traits: Which words in the text can you find that describe Goldilocks?

In any of the above cases, the teacher may provide the answers herself, or she may state the answer without the question and have the child show her in the pictures, or read in the text, the part of the story pertaining to her statement. The objective is to test the child's literal comprehension and not his memory.

Recall of literal material requires the student to produce from memory ideas and information explicitly stated in the reading selection.

- Recall of details: What were the names of the three bears?
- Recall of main ideas: Why did Goldilocks go into the bears' house?
- Recall of a sequence: In order, name the things belonging to the three bears that Goldilocks tried.
- Recall of comparisons: Whose bed was too hard? Too soft? Just right?
- Recall of cause-and-effect relationships: Why did Goldilocks go to sleep in Baby Bear's bed?
- Recall of character traits: What words in the story described each of the three bears?

Inferential Comprehension

Inferential comprehension is the ability to create or infer a hypothesis for a given statement based on collected facts and information. Research suggests that students must mentally "highlight" relevant information they might need later in order to relate and connect ideas from the passage. Understandings of concepts such as syntax, morphology, discourse, and pragmatics are all needed for students to effectively make inferences while reading.

Inferential Comprehension is demonstrated by the student when he "uses the ideas and information explicitly stated in the selection, his intuition, and his personal experiences as a basis for conjectures and hypotheses," according to Barrett (cited in Ekwall & Shanker, 1983, p. 67). It often requires that the student *combine information*, either pulling together information from different parts of the text or pulling together text information and combining it with his/her own background information or information from some other source. It is, therefore, a much more complex cognitive task than literal comprehension. It requires at least some selection and evaluation in order to determine what information is relevant to the conclusion and what is not relevant. Using the *Goldilocks and the Three* Bears story again, sample inferential questions might include:

- Inferring supporting details: Why do you think Goldilocks found Baby Bear's things to be just right?
- Inferring main ideas: What did the bear family learn about leaving their house unlocked?
- Inferring sequence: At what point did the bears discover that someone was in their house? (assuming this was not explicitly stated in the story).
- Inferring comparisons: Compare the furniture mentioned in the story. Which was adult size and which was a child's size?
- Inferring cause-and-effect relationships: What made the bears suspect that someone was in their house?
- Inferring character traits: Which of the bears was the most irritated by Goldilocks' intrusion? What kind of person is Goldilocks?
- Predicting outcomes: Do you think Goldilocks ever went back to visit the bears' house again? Or do you think she ever went uninvited to anyone's house again, and why or why not?
- Interpreting figurative language: What did the author mean when he wrote, "The tress in the deep forest howled a sad song in the wind?"

It is often necessary to explicitly teach children the differences between these types of comprehension. Familiar nursery rhymes such as Goldilocks and the Three Bears or The Three Little Pigs can be adapted for this purpose. Children can be taught that some facts are *right there on the page* (literal comprehension). For example, the first pig used straw, the second sticks, and the third bricks. The teacher can demonstrate it is possible to point to a specific sentence that provides the information. Highlighters and post-it arrows can provide concrete evidence that the information is right in the text.

Children can be shown that other information will be right in the text, but will be scattered and it will be necessary to pull it together. For example, how did the wolf change his strategy as he tried to trick the pig? (Each time he stated an earlier time to meet and HE turned up earlier, as well—all information that is IN the text, but in different places). Using color coded highlighters or arrows can help children with this process. Use all red arrows for information relevant to one question, green for another, etc.

Children can be taught that other information may depend on what is already in THEIR heads, what they know about similar situations (inferences). For example, they might speculate on how the town would now treat the third pig after the wolf was destroyed. They can be led through suggestive questions such as:

- What do you already know about wolves and pigs? (Wolves eat pigs), SO
- What can you guess about how the other pigs in town felt about the wolf? (Afraid of him), AND
- How do people often react when someone saves them from something scary or dangerous? (They reward them, treat them like heroes.), SO
- How might the town treat the third pig? (Like a hero, give him a parade, key to the town, elect him mayor, etc).

Even for inferences, some modifications can be made for students with disabilities. For example, though inferential questions usually involve recall responses, they can be provided as multiple choice recognition questions for students for whom recall is a problem.

Evaluative Comprehension

Evaluative comprehension is the ability to understand and sort facts, opinions, assumptions, persuasive elements, and the validity of a passage. Students with excellent evaluative comprehension skills can not only infer meaning from the text, but also compare, contrast, and apply what is read.

Evaluation requires the student to make a judgment by comparing ideas presented in the selection with external criteria provided by the teacher, or by some other external source, or with internal criteria provided by the student himself. Using *The Three Bears* again, evaluative questions might include:

- Judgment of reality or fantasy: Do you suppose that the story of *The Three Bears* really happened? Why or why not?
- Judgment of fact or opinion: Judge whether Baby Bear's furniture really was just right for Goldilocks. Why or Why not?
- Judgment of adequacy and validity: Give your opinion as to whether it was a good idea for the bears to take a walk while their porridge cooled.

- Judgment of appropriateness: Do you think it was safe for Goldilocks to enter an empty house?
- Judgment of worth, desirability, and acceptability: Was Goldilocks a guest or an intruder in the bears' home?

Appreciation

Appreciation deals with the psychological and aesthetic impact of the selection on the reader. True appreciation, goes beyond simply whether the reader likes the story or not, and requires a certain amount of self knowledge and self monitoring, as well as a certain amount of perspective. These can be abstract skills and can involve questions such as:

- Emotional response to the content: How did you feel when the three bears found Goldilocks asleep in Baby Bear's bed?
- Identification with characters or incidents: How do you suppose Goldilocks felt when she awakened and saw the three bears?
- Reaction to the author's use of language: Why do you think the author called the bears Papa, Mama, and Baby instead of Mr. Bear, Mrs. Bear and Jimmy Bear?

SKILL 3.4   Demonstrating knowledge of characteristics and functions of literary elements and devices (e.g., plot, point of view, setting); genres, themes, authors, and works of literature written for children; and strategies for developing students' literary response skills (e.g., making connections between texts and personal experiences)

LITERARY ELEMENTS

(See also Skill 3.03 for information on literary devices in various genre)
Most works of fiction contain a common set of elements that make them come alive to readers. In a way, even though writers do not consciously think about each of these elements when they sit down to write, all stories essentially contain these "markers" that make them the stories that they are. However, even though all stories share these elements, they are a lot like fingerprints: Each story's elements are different.

Let's look at a few of the most commonly discussed elements. The most commonly discussed story element in fiction is plot. Plot is the series of events in a story. Typically, but not always, plot moves in a predictable fashion:

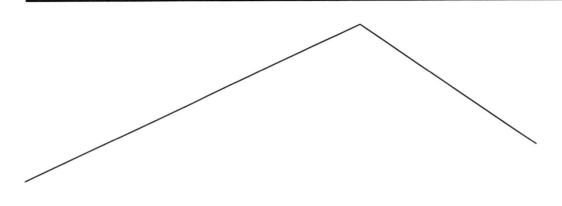

"Exposition"   "Rising Action"   "Climax" "Falling Action"   "Denouement"

Exposition is when characters and their situations are introduced. **Rising action** is the point at which conflict starts to occur. **Climax** is the highest point of conflict, often a turning point. **Falling action** is the result of the climax. **Denouement** is the final resolution of the plot.

In elementary school this sequence is often simplified into an initiating action or problem/goal, followed by events moving toward a resolution, and a final solution to the problem. Story maps and story grammar markers use this approach.

Character is another commonly studied story element. In stories, we often find heroes, villains, comedic characters, dark characters, etc. When we examine the characters of a story, we look to see who they are and how their traits contribute to the story. Often, because of their characteristics, plot elements become more interesting. For example, authors may pair unlikely characters together in a way that creates specific conflict.

The setting of a story includes both, the place or location where it occurs and the time period in which it occurs. Oftentimes, the specific place is not as important as some of the specifics about the setting. For example, the setting of *The Great Gatsby*, New York, is not as significant as the fact that it takes place amongst incredible wealth. Conversely, *The Grapes of Wrath*, although taking place in Oklahoma and California, has a more significant setting of poverty. In fact, as the story takes place *around* other migrant workers, the setting is even more significant. In a way, the setting serves as a reason for various conflicts to occur.

Themes of stories are the underlying messages, above and beyond all plot elements, that writers want to convey. Very rarely will one find that good literature is without a theme—or a lesson, message, point of view, or ideal. The best writers in the English language all seem to want to convey something about human nature or the world, and they turn to literature in order to do that.

Common themes in literature are jealousy, money, love, and human against corporation or government. These themes are never explicitly stated; rather, they are the result of the portrayal of characters, settings, and plots. Readers get the message even if the theme is not directly mentioned.

Finally, the mood of a story is the atmosphere or attitude the writer conveys through descriptive language. Often, mood fits nicely with theme and setting. For example, in Edgar Allen Poe's stories, we often find a mood of horror and darkness. We get that from the descriptions of characters and the setting, as well as from specific plot elements. Mood simply helps us better understand the writer's theme and intentions through descriptive, stylistic language.

Strategies for Developing Students' Literary Response Skills

While literature is a vehicle for teaching reading comprehension and writing, it is often overlooked that a very important reason for teaching literature is to help students understand how to appreciate written text, complex ideas, poetic language and ideas, and unique perspectives. However, just presenting good literature to students is not enough. They need active involvement with the literature. They also need to have a chance to respond to the literature in a variety of ways. Response helps students to personalize the literature (in other words, it helps students to understand that the literature comes from human instincts and issues); it helps them as they make sense of meaning; and it helps them to appreciate it more.

Appropriate responses to literature come in many forms. There are really too many forms to mention here, but we will provide a good overview of possible responses. Many students learn quite a bit by responding with additional works of art—whether it is further literature (poetry, fiction, etc.), visual art, or music. For example, students can write a poem expressing the mood of a character. They can also draw a picture that portrays a scene in a novel. They can even be asked to re-write the ending of a story. Giving students the opportunity to be creative in these ways help them to "enter" into the literature more fully. It gives them a real opportunity to interact with the ideas, characters, setting, and author.

Analytic writing is another good way to respond to literature. Of course, this may not seem as much fun from the student perspective, but analytic writing allows students to see that there is not just one way to view literature. They often learn best when they understand that their possibly unconventional ways of understanding literature must be defended with clear examples from the text. Drama is another very effective tool for responding to literature. When students act out scenes from a novel, for example, they begin to understand character motives more clearly.

In order to draw connections between personal experience and what they are reading, students can be asked to find something in the passage that reminds them of something that happened to them, or to someone they know. They can be asked to imagine how *they* would feel in a certain character's place. Would they have responded in the same way? What would they have done? Finding similarities or difference between themselves or someone they know and a character or their own environment and the setting of the story are other ways to respond to the literature on a personal level.

As you can see, the list of appropriate responses to literature could go on and on. It is important for teachers to match up appropriate responses with the literature and their students. Not every type of response will work well for all students and for all pieces of literature, so careful selection is important.

CHILDREN'S LITERATURE

Children's literature is a genre of its own and emerged as a distinct and independent form in the second half of the 18th century. *The Visible World in Pictures*, by John Amos Comenius, a Czech educator, was one of the first printed works and the first picture book. For the first time, educators acknowledged that children are different from adults in many respects. Literature designed for children must take into account the child's level of cognitive development as well as the child's interests. Since children of any age or grade will differ significantly on both these variables, modern educators acknowledge that introducing elementary students to a wide range of reading experiences plays an important role in their mental, social, and psychological development.

Children's literature can be found in virtually all of the genres described in Skill 3.03, both fiction and nonfiction. Examples of how various genres relate to children's literature include:

Traditional Literature of all sorts opens up a world where right wins out over wrong, where hard work and perseverance are rewarded, and where helpless victims find vindication—all worthwhile values that children identify with even as early as kindergarten. In traditional literature, children will be introduced to fanciful beings, humans with exaggerated powers, talking animals and heroes that will inspire them. For younger elementary children, these stories in Big Book format are ideal for providing predictable and repetitive elements that can be grasped by these children.

Folktales and Fairy tales are very popular with children and the themes of good and evil and the magical animals make them very interesting to young readers. . Some examples of these tales are: *The Three Bears, Little Red Riding Hood, Snow White, Sleeping Beauty, Puss-in-Boots, Rapunzel* and *Rumpelstiltskin.*

Fables such as *Aesop's Fables* provide short selections with easily comprehended, and usually clearly stated, lessons that can be used to help develop children's inferential comprehension skills.

Tall Tales and *legends* such as *Johnny Appleseed, Paul Bunyan, John Henry,* or *Pecos Bill* can help children develop an appreciation of various genre.

Fantasy is also very popular among young readers and many of the themes found in these stories are similar to those in traditional literature. Little people live in the walls in *The Borrowers*, and time travel is possible in *The Trolley to Yesterday*. Including some fantasy tales in the curriculum helps elementary-grade children develop their senses of imagination. These often appeal to ideals of justice and issues having to do with good and evil; and because children tend to identify with the characters, the message is more likely to be retained.

Science Fiction is another genre children like. Most children like these stories because of their interest in space and the "what if" aspect of the stories. Examples: *Outer Space and All That Junk* and *A Wrinkle in Time*.

Modern Realistic Fiction for children includes stories about real problems that real children face. By finding that others share their hopes and fears, young children can find insight into their own problems. Young readers also tend to experience a broadening of interests as the result of this kind of reading. It's good for them to know that a child can be brave and intelligent and can solve difficult problems

Historical Fiction can be an excellent way to introduce content area study for young readers. *Rifles for Watie*, for example, is presented in a historically accurate setting. It's about a young boy (16 years) who serves in the Union army. He experiences great hardship but discovers that his enemy is an admirable human being. It provides a good opportunity to introduce younger children to history in a beneficial way. It can also serve as a springboard to many responses to literature activities.

Biographies suitable to children would include anything written at their level, particularly modern or historical figures popular with children. Not only do they excite the imagination, they also open new vistas for children to think about when they choose an occupation to fantasize about.

Informational literature for children is becoming more available at more levels. When presenting informational text to children, it can help to emphasize that these are ways to learn more about something the child is interested in or something that the child knows nothing about. Encyclopedias are good resources, of course, but a book like *Polar Wildlife* by Kamini Khanduri shows pictures and facts that capture the imaginations of young children. (See Skill 3.5 for more on informational text)

In the classroom it is also important that the literature made available to children will contribute to their emerging and developing literacy. Fortunately, many of the available picture books and storybooks written for elementary children employ text structures and concepts found in literature for all ages, structures that will be found in books written for adolescents and adults, as well as for elementary students. With this in mind, an elementary teacher can select books with a variety of common text structures that are appropriate for very young readers. A brief representative list of such titles, arranged by text structure, is presented below.

Circular text

- Beard, Darleen Bailey (1999). *Twister.* New York: Farrar Straus Giroux.
- Fox, Mem (1997). *Whoever You Are.* San Diego: Harcourt Brace & Company.
- Turner, Ann (1993). *Apple Valley Year.* New York: Macmillan Publishing Company.
- Yolen, Jane (1991). *All Those Secrets of the World.* Boston: Little, Brown and Company.

Embedded facts text

- Manning, Mick (1994). *A Ruined House.* Cambridge, Massachusetts: Candlewick Press.
- Manning, Mick (2001). *Wash, Scrub, Brush!* Morton Grove, Illinois: Albert Whitman & Company.

Framing Question text

- Allington, Richard L. (1981). *Beginning to Learn About Summer.* Milwaukee: Raintree Childrens Books.
- Baylor, Byrd, and Peter Parnell. (1978). *The Other Way to Listen.* New York: Scribner.
- Cabrera, Jane (1997). *Cat's Colors.* New York: Dial Books for Young jReaders.
- Carlstrom, Nancy White (1992). *How Do You Say It Today, Jesse Bear?* New York: Macmillan Publishing Company.

- Carlstrom, Nancy White (1993). *How Does the Wind Walk?* New York: Macmillan Publishing Company.
- Carlstrom, Nancy White (1986). *Jesse Bear, What Will You Wear?* New York: Macmillan Publishing Company.
- Johnston, Tony (2001). *Cat, What Is that?* USA: HarperCollins Publishers.
- Moss, Thylias. (1993). *I Want To Be.* New York: Dial.
- Zolotow, Charlotte (1998). *The Bunny Who Found Easter.* Boston: Houghton Mifflin Company.
- Zolotow, Charlotte (2000). *Do You Know What I'll Do?* USA: HarperCollins Publishers
- Zolotow, Charlotte (1980). *If You Listen.* New York: Harper & Row Publishers.
- Zolotow, Charlotte (1993). *The Moon Was the Best.* . New York: Greenwillow Books
- Zolotow, Charlotte (1992) *The Seashore Book* New York: HarperCollins.

Lyrical fact text

- Bunting, Eve ( ) *Butterfly House.*
- Burleigh, Robert (1998) *Home Run.* San Diego: Harcourt Brace & Company.
- Winer, Yvonne (1999). *Spiders Spin Webs.* New York: Scholastic.
- Yolen, Jane (1993). *Welcome to the Green House.* New York: G. P. Putnam's Sons.

Memoir

- Kroll, Virginia (1995). *Fireflies, Peach Pies & Lullibies.* New York: Simon & Schuster Books for Young Readers.

Narrative sequenced by a series of objects, people, or animals

- Carlstrom, Nancy White (1997). *Raven and River.* Boston: Little, Brown and Company.
- Turner, Ann (1998). *Angel Hide and Seek.* USA: Harper Children

Participation text

- Allington, Richard L. (1981). *Beginning to Learn About Summer.* Milwaukee: Raintree Childrens Books.
- Manning, Mick (1994). *A Ruined House.* Cambridge, Massachusetts: Candlewick Press.

Pattern from nature text

- Fox, Mem ( ) *Possum.*
- Fox-Davies *Caribou*
- George, Jean Craighead (1993). *Look To the North: A Wolf Pup's Diary.* San Fransisco: HarperCollins.
- Gray, Libba Moore (1995). *My Mama Had a Dancing Heart.* New York: Orchard.
- Kroll, Steven *Girl, You're Amazing.*
- Lasky, Kathryn (1995). *Pond Year.* Cambridge, MA: Candlewick.
- Locker, Thomas (1997). *Water Dance.* New York: Harcourt Brace.
- Turner, Ann (1993). *Apple Valley Year.* New York: Macmillan Publishing Company.
- Zamorano, Ana (1996). *Let's Eat.* New York: Scholastic.

Repeated wrap around structure

- Carlstrom, Nancy White (1997). *Raven and River.* Boston: Little, Brown and Company.
- Rylant, Cynthia and Lisa Desmini ( ). *Tulip Sees America.* New York: Blue Sky Press, An Imprint of Scholastic, Inc.

Seesaw text

- Allington, Richard L. (1981). *Beginning to Learn About Summer.* Milwaukee: Raintree Childrens Books.
- Carlson, Nancy (2001). *My Best Friend Moved Away.* New York: Viking/Penguin Putnam Books for Young Readers.
- Carlstrom, Nancy White (2002). *Before You Were Born.* Grand Rapids, Michigan: Eardmans Books for Young Readers.
- Carlstrom, Nancy White (1991). *Goodbye Geese.* New York: Scholastic Inc.
- Carlstrom, Nancy White (1993). *How Does the Wind Walk?* New York: Macmillan Publishing Company.
- Carlstrom, Nancy White ( ) *Jesse Bear, What Will You Wear?*
- Crimi, Carolyn (1995). *Outside, Inside.* New York: Simon & Schuster Books for Young Readers.
- Fox, Mem (1994). *Tough Boris.* San Diego: Harcourt Brace & Company.
- Johnson, Paul Brett (1996). *Lost.* New York: Orchard Books.
- Kroll, Steven (1984). *The Biggest Pumpkin Ever.* New York: Scholastic Inc.
- Kroll, Virginia (1994). *The Seasons and Someone.* San Diego: Harcourt Brace & Company.
- Schaefer, Carole Lexa (2000). *Down In the Woods at Sleepytime.* Cambridge, Massachusetts: Candlewick Press.

- Walsh, Jill Paton (1995). *Connie Came to Play.* New York: Viking, Penguin Group.
- Yolen, Jane (1993). *Welcome to the Green House.* New York: G. P. Putnam's Sons.
- Zolotow, Charlotte *Big Brother.*

Threadback text

- Carlstrom, Nancy White (1992). *Baby-O.* Boston: Little, Brown and Company.
- Carlstrom, Nancy White (1998). *Better Not get Wet, Jesse Bear.* New York: Macmillan Publishing Company.
- Carlstrom, Nancy White (2001). *Glory.* Grand Rapids, Michigan: Eerdmans Books For Young Readers.
- Carlstrom, Nancy White (1997). *Raven and River.* Boston: Little, Brown and Company.
- Manning, Mick (2001). *Wash, Scrub, Brush!* Morton Grove, Illinois: Albert Whitman & Company.
- Schaefer, Carole Lexa (1996). *The Squiggle.* New York: Crown Publishers, Inc.
- Schaefer, Carole Lexa (1999). *Sometimes Moon.* New York: Crown Publishers, Inc.
- Sorensen, Henry (1996). *Your First Step.* New York: Lothrop, Lee and Shepard.

Time constant-Setting changes text

- Bunting, Eve (1996). *The Blue and the Gray.* New York: Scholastic.
- Frasier, Debra (1991). *On the Day You Were Born.* San Diego: Harcourt Brace Jovanovich, Publishers.
- Kurijan, Judy (1993). *In My Own Backyard.* Watertown, MA: Charlesbridge.
- Paulson, Gary (1995). *The Rifle.* New York: Harcourt Brace.
- Schaefer, Carole Lexa (2000). *Down In the Woods at Sleepytime.* Cambridge, Massachusetts: Candlewick Press.
- Shannon, George (1997). *This is the Bird.* New York: Houghton Mifflin.
- Shelby, Ann (1995). *Homeplace.* New York: Orchard.

Two part changing situation text

- Carlstrom, Nancy White (1997). *Raven and River.* Boston: Litttle Brown and Company.
- Fleming, Denise (1996). *Where Once There Was a Wood.* New York: Henry Holt and Company.
- Fox, Mem (1997). *Whoever You Are.* San Diego: Harcourt Brace & Company.

- Fox, Mem (1994). *Sophie.* New York: Harcourt Brace.
- Koll, Steven (1984). *The Biggest Pumpkin Ever.* New York: Scholastic, Inc.
- Quattlebaum, Mary (1997). *Underground Train.* New York: Doubleday Books for Young Readers.
- Rylant, Cynthia (1986). *Night in the Country.* Scarsdale, New York: Bradbury.
- Schaefer, Carole Lexa (2002). *The Little French Whistle.* New York: Alfred A. Knopf.
- Turner, Ann (1992). *Rainflowers.* USA: A Charlotte Zolotow Book, An Imprint of HarperCollins Publishers.
- Yolen, Jane (1995). *Before The Storm.* Honesdale, Pennsylvania: Boyds Mill Press.
- Zolotow, Charlotte (1960). *Big Brother.* New York: Harper & Row Publishers.

Umbrella/topic sentence—supporting details

- Maas, Robert (1998). *Garden.* New York: Henry Holt and Company.
- Houghton Mifflin Leveled Readers *Earthworms*

Vignettes with repeating lines

- Carlstrom, Nancy White (1998). *Better Not get Wet, Jesse Bear.* New York: Macmillan Publishing Company.
- Carlstrom, Nancy White (1990). *Grandpappy.* Boston: Little, Brown and Company.

Using children's books such as these and discussing text structures and ways to use the structure and vocabulary to understand what you are reading can contribute to students' growing literacy and comprehension of a variety of literary styles.

SKILL 3.5 **Applying knowledge of common patterns of organization in informational texts (e.g., chronological, cause-and-effect) and strategies for promoting comprehension of information texts (e.g., chronological, cause-and-effect) and strategies for promoting comprehension of informational texts (e.g., identifying explicit and implicit supporting details, using a glossary, using a graphic organizer)**

ORGANIZATION OF INFORMATIONAL TEXT

Common Text Features

Regardless of the specific subject matter, there are certain common text features children will encounter when reading and understanding the significance of these features significantly enhances comprehension of the text. This is particularly true of nonfiction informational text, which is often very *dense* in terms of amount of information conveyed.

Understanding the arrangement of nonfiction text with section and chapter titles, heads and subheads, (set in bold type) and other unique organizational devices can provide students with powerful tools to be successful. Students who use such headings as the main points can than fill in additional learning by reading the information below that heading. Also, if looking for a specific piece of information students can utilize Table of Contents and Indexes, which are generally a part of expository writing. By understanding the structure of the text, students save valuable time and decrease the amount of rereading required.

Generally, there is so much known and valuable information about topics that authors try to share all of that information with the reader. Since there is a large amount of information to be conveyed, authors use specific organizational tools to break the text into smaller, more manageable, chunks. These different structures require the reader to make adjustments to their own personal reading style in order to successfully manage the intake of the new learning.

Most texts provide brief **introductions.** These introductions can be used by the readers to determine if the information they are seeking is located within the passage to be read. By reading a short passage, the student can quickly ascertain whether he/she needs to do a complete reading or a quick skim will suffice.

When searching for information, students can become much more efficient if they learn to use a **glossary and index**. Students can find the necessary facts in a more rapid manner and also clarify information that was difficult to understand the first time. Additionally, charts, graphs, maps, diagrams, captions, and photos in text can work in the same way as looking up unknown words in the glossary. They can provide more insight and clarify the concepts and ideas the author is conveying.

When instructing young readers in the use of these and other text features to enhance comprehension, it helps to use material written at the students' reading level. As more and more research (see below) points to the need for earlier elementary instruction in nonfiction reading, more publishers are providing nonfiction texts that both follow national learning standards and are written at varying reading levels. Such texts can be invaluable in helping students learn how to read nonfiction and use its common text features.

Student writing can also help students expand their understanding of how to use these text features when they read. As mentioned earlier, reading and writing are complementary skills and one can be used to help the other. When students engage in expository writing of their own (See Objective 4), they can be taught to include many of these text features and this will help them understand how to use them when they read, as well.

Research has shown that students' ability to comprehend nonfiction or expository text--text that explains facts and concepts--is critical to their success on standardized tests, in their future education, and in adult life. Duke and Bennett-Armistead (2003) describe studies showing that nonfiction periodicals represent the single most common form of adult reading. They further explain that understanding informational text is key to future educational success.

In spite of this, surveys have shown that the vast majority of reading in primary grades is in the fiction genre. Far less attention is paid to nonfiction. This is a critical omission, because nonfiction text structures are more varied and difficult than those of fiction. Most fiction follows a fairly standard structure that is chronological in nature and can be outlined in terms of story grammar markers that list setting, characters, problem or initiating event, a sequence of events, and a resolution. Nonfiction text structures can be found in many different forms and it is important to teach strategies for comprehending them all.

In addition, expository texts are full of information that may or may not be factual and which may reflect the bias of the editor or author. Children need to learn that expository texts are organized around main ideas. They are usually found in newspapers, magazines, content textbooks, and informational reference books (i.e., an atlas, almanac, yearbook, or encyclopedia).

Common Expository Text Structures

The basic types of expository texts to which the children should be introduced to through modeled reading and a teacher-facilitated walk through are:

Description process—this usually describes a particular topic or provides the identifying characteristics of a topic. It can be depended upon to be factual. Within this type of text, the child reader has to use all of his or her basic reading strategies because these types of expository texts do not have explicit clue words. Graphic organizers that let the student state the topic or main idea then briefly list descriptive details are very useful aids. See below for more on graphic organizers.

Causation or Cause-Effect text—this is one where faulty reasoning may come into play, and the child reader has to use the inferential and self-questioning skills already mentioned to help assess whether the stated cause-effect relationship is a valid and correct one. This text appears in content area textbooks, newspapers, magazines, advertisements, and on some content area and general information web sites. Students should be taught to take note of certain clue words, such as: *therefore, the reasons for, as a result of, because, in consequence of,* and *since.* These clues point to a statement of cause and effect relationships. Again, students can differentially highlight cause and effect in the text and use graphic organizers to help with comprehension. Cause and effect organizers often resemble flow charts with arrows pointing to the results of various causes.

Chronological Text—like fiction, *some* nonfiction text will be organized chronologically or sequentially. This text structure puts events in an order from beginning to end or from the beginning of some segment to the end of that segment. This text structure is often an overall structure for historical and biographical text. It often contains an important text feature: a timeline. Timelines can be found in a number of formats (e.g., vertical, horizontal, by year, by decade, grouped by era, etc), and it is important for children to learn how to use them. In essence, a timeline presents a chronological arrangement of main ideas/events and is, itself, a good graphic organizer.

Comparison Text—this is an expository text that is centered on the reader's noting the contrasts and similarities between two or more objects and ideas. Many social studies, art, and science textbooks, as well as other non-fiction books include this structure. Sometimes newspaper columnists use it as well in their editorial commentary.

Again, strategies for helping children comprehend the comparison and contrast intended by the author include the use of key clue words and phrases. Among these are: *like, unlike, resemble, different, different from, similar to, in contrast with, in comparison to,* and *in a different vein.* It is important that as children examine texts that are talking about illustrated or photographed entities, they can also review the graphic representations for clues to support or contradict the text. Graphic organizers such as Venn diagrams can be very useful for recording and summarizing details.

Collection Text—this is an expository text that presents ideas in a group. The writer's goal is to present a set of related points or ideas. Another name for this structure of expository writing is a listing or a sequence. The author frequently uses clue words, such *as first, second, third, finally, and next* to alert the reader to the sequence. Based on how well the writer structures the sequence of points or ideas, the reader should be able to make connections.

Simple collection texts that can be literally modeled for young children include recipe making. A class of first graders, beginning readers and writers, were literally spellbound by the author's presentation of a widely-known copyrighted collection text. The children were thrilled as the author followed the sequences of this collection text and finally took turns stirring it until it was creamy and smooth. After it had cooled, they each had a taste using their plastic spoons. Can you guess what it was? No? What gourmet children's delight would have first graders begging for a taste? Can't guess? Cream Farina from a commercial cereal box that had cooking directions on it (i.e., known as a collection text).

You can bet that the children had constructed meaning from this five-minute class demonstration and that they would pay close attention to collection texts on other food and product instruction boxes now because this text had come to be an authentic part of their lives.

Response structure—this is an expository text that presents a question or problem followed by an answer or a solution. Of course, entire mathematics textbooks, and some science and social studies textbooks, are organized around this type of structure. Again, it is important here to walk the child reader through the excerpt and to sensitize the child to the clue words that signal this type of structure. These words include, but are not limited to: *the problem is, the questions is, you need to solve for, one probable solution would be, an intervention could be, the concerns is, and another way to solve this would be.* It can be helpful for the child to highlight the question or questions in some way and them mark or highlight sentences that provide answers to each question. Graphic organizers to record information can also be useful her.

Newspapers and Periodicals

Newspapers and magazines present excellent opportunities to bring "real" reading into the classroom. Children see their parents and other adults reading newspapers and magazines all the time. Students who understand the applications of the newspaper, technology and other real-life situations are able to make the final connection to life-long learning. Newspapers and magazines contain specialized text features that can aid comprehension if the student knows how to use them: headings, diagrams, captions, updates, side bars and newsy inserts, etc. A number of news magazines, such as Time For Kids, bring current events into the classroom written at various grade levels. Such tools can be very helpful in familiarizing students with these non-fiction text features.

What is really intriguing about the use of newspapers as a model and an authentic platform for introducing and teaching children to recognize and use expository text structures, features, and references, is that the children can demonstrate their mastery of these structures by using them to put out their own newspapers detailing their school. They can also create their own timelines for projects or research papers that they have done in class by using newspaper models.

STRATEGIES FOR PROMOTING COMPREHENSION OF INFORMATIONAL TEXT

There are several key strategies that can be used to increase children's abilities to read informational/expository texts.

- **Inferencing** (described in more detail in Skill 3.3) is a process that involves the reader in making a reasonable judgment based on the information given and engages children in literally constructing meaning. In order to develop and enhance inferencing in children, a teacher may consider having a mini-lesson in which this key skill is demonstrated by reading an expository book aloud (e.g., one on skyscrapers for young children) and then demonstrating for them the following reading habits: looking for clues, reflecting on what the reader already knows about the topic ("activating" prior knowledge), and using the clues, such as headings, diagrams and captions, in the expository text to figure out what the author means.
- Identifying **main ideas** in an expository text can be improved when children have an explicit strategy for identifying important information. They can be included in making this strategy part of their everyday reading style by being focused and "walked" through exercises as a part of a series of guided reading sessions. The child should read a passage so that the topic is readily identifiable to him or her.

- The child should be asked to be on the lookout for a sentence within the expository passage that summarizes the key information in the paragraph or in the lengthier excerpt. The child should then read the rest of the passage or excerpt in light of this information and also note which information in the paragraph is not important. The important information the child has identified in the paragraph can be used by the child reader to formulate the author's main idea. The child reader may even want to use some of the author's own language in formulating that idea.

- **Monitoring** means self-clarifying: As students read, they often realize that what are reading is not making sense. The reader then has to have a plan for making sensible meaning out of the excerpt. As discussed earlier, Cooper and other balanced literacy advocates have a "stop and think" strategy that they use with children. The child is asked to reflect, "Does this make sense to me?" When the child concludes that it does not, he or she then either: re-reads, reads ahead in the text, looks up unknown words, or asks for help from the teacher. This strategy can be modeled by the teacher and careful "leading" questions can be used to help the children learn to do this on their own.

- **Summarizing** engages the reader in pulling the essential bits of information within a longer passage or excerpt of text into a cohesive whole. Children can be taught to summarize informational or expository text by following these guidelines. First, they should look at the **topic sentence** of the paragraph or the text and delete the trivia. They should then search for information that has been mentioned more than once and make sure it is included only once in their summary. Students should find related ideas or items and group them under a unifying heading; they can then search for and identify a main idea sentence. Finally, they can put the summary together using all of these guidelines.

Generating questions can motivate and enhance children's comprehension of reading, in that they become actively involved in generating their own questions and then answer these questions based on their reading. In order to generate meaningful questions that trigger constructive reading in expository texts, children should preview the text by reading the titles and subheads (they should also look at the illustrations and the pictures). Students may then begin to read the first paragraph. These first previews should yield an impressive batch of specific questions.

Next, children should get into their "Dr. Seuss mode" by asking themselves a "think" question. For younger children, having a "think" silly hat in the classroom might be effective as well, as the children could actually go over and put it on. Teachers should make certain that the children write down the "think" question and encourage them to read to find important information to answer it. The children should be asked to write down the answer they found and to copy the sentence or sentences where they found the answer.

Also, children should be encouraged to consider whether, in light of their further reading through the text, their original question was a good one or not. The teacher should ask the students to be prepared to explain why their original question was a good one or not. Once the children have answered their original "think" question, they can generate additional ones.

Identifying Main Ideas and Topic Sentences

The **topic** of a paragraph or story is what the paragraph or story is about. The **main idea** of a paragraph or story states the important idea(s) that the author wants the reader to know about the topic. The topic and main idea of a paragraph or story are sometimes directly stated. There are times, however, when the topic and main idea are not directly stated, but simply implied. For example, look at this paragraph below:

> Henry Ford was an inventor who developed the first affordable automobile. The cars that were being built before Mr. Ford created his Model-T were very expensive. Only rich people could afford to have cars.

The topic of this paragraph is Henry Ford. The main idea is that Henry Ford built the first affordable automobile.

The **topic sentence** indicates what the passage is about; it is a statement about the main idea. It is the subject of that portion of the narrative. The ability to identify the topic sentence in a passage enables the student to focus on the concept being discussed and to better comprehend the information provided. In the paragraph above, the topic sentence is: "Henry Ford was an inventor who developed the first affordable automobile."

Students can be taught to find the main ideas by looking at the way in which paragraphs are written. A paragraph is a group of sentences about one main idea. Paragraphs usually have two types of sentences: a topic sentence, which contains the main idea, and two or more detail sentences that support, prove, provide more information, explain, or give examples.

Supporting Details

The supporting details are sentences that give more information about the topic and the main idea. The supporting details in the aforementioned paragraph about Henry Ford include:

A. that he was an inventor, and
B. that before he created his Model-T, only rich people could afford cars because they were too expensive.

You can only tell if you have a detail or topic sentence by comparing the sentences with each other. Look at this sample paragraph:

Fall is the best of the four seasons. The leaves change colors to create a beautiful display of golds, reds, and oranges. The air turns crisp and windy. The scent of pumpkin muffins and apple pies fill the air. Finally, Halloween marks the start of the holiday season. Fall is my favorite time of year!

Breakdown of these sentences:

- Fall is the best of the four seasons. (TOPIC SENTENCE)
- The leaves change colors to create a beautiful display of golds, reds, and oranges. (DETAIL)
- The air turns crisp and windy. (DETAIL)
- The scent of pumpkin muffins and apple pies fill the air. (DETAIL)
- Finally, Halloween marks the start of the holiday season. (DETAIL)
- Fall is my favorite time of year! (CLOSING SENTENCE – Often a restatement of the topic sentence)

Tips for Finding the Topic Sentence

Children can be taught to use both organizational and semantic clues to differentiate topic sentences and details.

- The topic sentence is often first, although it could be in any position in the paragraph.
- A topic is usually more "general" than the other sentences, that is, it addresses many things and looks at the big picture. Sometimes it refers to more than one thing. Plurals and the words "many," "numerous," or "several" often signal a topic sentence.
- Detail sentences are usually more "specific" than the topic, that is, they usually address one single aspect or side of an idea. Also, the words "for example," "i.e.," "that is," "first," "second," "third," and "finally" often signal a detail.
- Most of the detail sentences support, give examples, prove, talk about, or point toward the topic in some way.

Children can be taught that to be sure they have a topic sentence, they can try this trick: switch the sentence you think is the topic sentence into a question. If the other sentences seem to "answer" the question, then you've got it. For example:

Reword the topic sentence "Fall is the best of the four seasons" in one of the following ways:

> "Why is fall the best of the four seasons?"
> "Which season is the best season?"
> "Is fall the best season of the year?"

Then, as you read the remaining sentences (the ones you didn't pick), you will find that they answer (support) your question.

If you attempt this with a sentence other than the topic sentence, it won't work. For example:

> Suppose you select "Halloween marks the start of the holiday season," and you reword it in the following way:"Which holiday is the start of the holiday season?"

> You will find that the other sentences fail to help you answer (support) your question.

Restating the Main Idea

An accurate restatement of the main idea from a passage will usually summarize the concept in a concise manner; it will often present the same idea from a different perspective. A restatement should always demonstrate complete comprehension of the main idea.

To select an accurate restatement, identifying the main idea of the passage is essential. Once a reader comprehends the main idea of a passage, it is important to evaluate the choices to see which statement restates the main idea while eliminating statements that only restate a supporting detail.

Walk through the steps in the "Fall" paragraph above to see how to select the accurate restatement.

Steps:

- Identify the main idea (answer: "Fall is the best of the four seasons.")
- Decide which statement below restates the topic sentence:

   A. The changing leaves turn gold, red and orange.
   B. The holidays start with Halloween.
   C. Of the four seasons, Fall is the greatest of them all.
   D. Crisp wind is a fun aspect of Fall.

   The answer is C because it rewords the main idea of the first sentence (the topic sentence).

Additional **Strategies**

The point of comprehension instruction is not necessarily to focus just on the text(s) students are using at the very moment of instruction, but rather to help them to learn the strategies that they can use independently with any other text. Some common methods for doing this are as follows:

- **Graphic organizers**: Graphic organizers are graphical representations of content within a text. They provide more concrete, easily remembered formats for information. For example, graphic organizers can provide concrete pictorial representations of main ideas and details. An umbrella with the main idea and topic sentence in the top umbrella arc and the details on the handle (holding it up) can be useful, as can a building with the main idea/topic sentence in the roof portion and the details "supporting" it in the columns supporting the building. Venn Diagrams can be used to highlight the difference between two two similar political concepts in a Social Studies textbook, or the similarities in animal adaptations in science. A teacher can also use flow-charts with students to talk about the steps in a process (for example, the steps of setting up a science experiment). Semantic organizers are similar in that they graphically display information. The difference, however, is that semantic organizers focus on words or concepts. For example, a word web can help students to make sense of a word by mapping from the central word all the similar and related concepts to that word. (See Objective 2 on vocabulary).

- **Summarization:** This is where, either in writing or verbally, students go over the main point of the text, along with strategically chosen details that highlight the main point. The use of graphic organizers, above, can make this a much easier task. This is not the same as paraphrasing, which is saying the same thing in different words. Teaching students how to summarize is very important, as it will help them to look for the most critical areas in a text. For example, it will help them distinguish between main arguments and examples.

- **Question answering:** While this tends to be over-used in many classrooms, it is still a valid method of teaching students to comprehend. As the name implies, students answer questions regarding a text, either out loud, in small groups, or individually on paper. See Skill 3.03 for more on different types of questions for levels of comprehension. The best questions are those that cause students to have to think about the text (rather than just find an answer within the text). Note that a summary does not need to be written. Oral summaries are also useful. Highlighters and post-it arrows can be used to locate information that should be summarized in the text and then used for either oral or written summaries.

- **Question generating:** This is the opposite of question answering, although students can then be asked to answer their own questions or the questions of peer students. In general, students should constantly question texts as they read. This is important because it causes students to become more critical readers. Teaching students to generate questions helps them learn the types of questions they can ask, and it gets them thinking about how best to be critical of texts.

- **Monitoring comprehension:** Students need to be aware of their comprehension, or lack of it, in particular texts. As such, it is important to teach students what to do when text suddenly stops making sense. For example, students can go back and re-read the description of a life cycle process, or they can go back to the table of contents or the first paragraph of a chapter to see where they are headed.

- **Textual marking:** This is where students interact with the text as they read. For example, armed with sticky notes, students can insert questions or comments regarding specific sentences or paragraphs within the text. This helps students to focus on the importance of the small things, particularly when they are reading larger works (such as content area texts in high school). It also gives students a reference point on which to go back into the text when they need to review something.

- **Discussion**: Small group or whole-class discussion stimulates thoughts about texts and gives students a larger picture of the impact of those texts. For example, teachers can strategically encourage students to discuss related concepts to the text. This helps students to learn to consider texts within larger societal and social concepts. Teachers can also encourage students to provide personal opinions during discussions. By listening to various students' opinions, all students in a class are encouraged to see the wide range of possible interpretations and thoughts regarding one text.

One note to keep in mind: Many people mistakenly believe that the terms "research-based," "research-validated," or "evidence-based" relate mainly to specific programs, such as early reading textbook programs. While research does validate that some of these programs are effective, much research has been conducted regarding the effectiveness of particular instructional strategies. In reading, many of these strategies have been documented in the report from the National Reading Panel (2000). However, just because a strategy has not been validated as effective by research does not necessarily mean that it is not effective with certain students in certain situations. The numbers of strategies out there are much greater than researchers' ability to test their effectiveness. Some of the strategies listed above have been validated by rigorous research, while others have been shown consistently to help improve students' reading abilities in localized situations. There simply is not enough space to list all the strategies that have been proven effective; it is important to just know that the above strategies are very commonly cited ones that work in a variety of situations.

OBJECTIVE 4   UNDERSTAND SKILLS AND STRATEGIES INVOLVED IN WRITING FOR VARIOUS PURPOSES ACROSS THE CURRICULUM AND THE CONVENTIONS OF STANDARD ENGLISH GRAMMAR, USAGE, AND MECHANICS.

SKILL 4.1   Recognizing developmental stages of writing, including the use of pictures and developmental spelling; the writing process (e.g., prewriting, drafting, revising, editing) and strategies for promoting students' writing skills

DEVELOPMENTAL STAGES OF WRITING

Like reading, writing is a very complex skill that develops gradually as a child grows and learns. Just as reading skills can be divided into categories of decoding (understanding letter-sound code) and comprehension (understanding what a passage means), writing skills can be divided into categories of expression (composition of a coherent message to be communicated to the reader) and mechanics or conventions (the act of encoding the message into letters and words). Just as children vary in their ability to *decode* or *comprehend* a message when reading, they may also very in their abilities to *compose* or to *encode* a message when writing.

Like reading development, writing follows certain general stages of development. Although children vary in the age and speed at which they progress through these stages, most children move through them in a similar order. Though the stages may have varying titles in different writing systems, most include the following major stages:

Preliterate or Exploration: Initially, a child confuses **drawing** and writing, and often treats a drawing as if it is writing. A child may even "read" a drawing aloud. The child at this stage does understand that a drawing or writing contains a message, and this is key to progress in writing skills. Following this, the child begins to develop print concepts and begins **scribbling** in imitation of writing. The child understands that writing is different from drawing and that IT contains a message. The scribbling will often follow a line and look like nonsense symbols and the child will also "read" them aloud, expecting others to understand.

Children at this stage of development benefit from lots of drawing and writing opportunities in which the adult treats the child's "writing" seriously and listens to the message. Although most children have progressed beyond this stage by school age, children with disabilities may not have done so. In a classroom context, appropriate techniques at this stage include group or morning messages written together word by word as the children talk. Writing down what a child dictates word by word and reading it back can also be helpful. For children who already show problems with coherent expression, asking leading questions and offering choices for missing words helps.

Emergent or Experimental: In early Emergent writing the child begins to understand directionality in writing and to "write" symbols that look a bit like real letters, with straight lines and curves, though they are not yet real letters. Later in this stage, the child begins to use many real letters, but puts them in random order, often including fake letters, with no relationship to sounds. Although the children at this stage may be able to name some letters, they may write in different ways each time they use them. However, the child is developing the concept that the *message* carried by these letters should stay constant, and when "reading" back the message they have "written" it will tend to stay the same.

Instructional techniques that are helpful at this stage include reading Big Books as a group and remarking upon letters and words; making books with the students based upon their own words and drawings; writing captions and labels for drawings; and constructing simple story maps based on student compositions.

Transitional: At this stage the child begins to use more real letters, though rarely is the entire word spelled correctly. Often the child will write only initial or noticeable consonants. There is usually still some usage of mock letters. As children progress through this stage, they will begin to use invented spelling when they do not know the letter-sound code, and vowels will begin to be added to the words. Though there is little usage of spacing at the beginning of this stage, by the end, some word spacing will emerge, and some highly recognizable words may even be spelled correctly. A child at this stage can often compose a reasonably coherent story about something that has happened to them, though they will ramble, as well. Children often reach the end of this stage by the end of first grade, but children with disabilities may not do so.

Instructional techniques appropriate to this stage include anything that lets the child write for "real" reasons, letters to grandparents, daily journals, wish lists, "secret" messages passed around the class, etc. At this stage it is appropriate to begin word lists and cards with words important to the child, words he/she may like to use when writing. More formal writing process instruction often starts here, as does formal spelling instruction (see below). Having children dictate their ideas to a teacher, recorder, or computer before writing them down will help children who can compose coherent messages but struggle to write them down.

Fluent or Proficient: At this stage the child's writing looks like immature adult writing. Real letters are used. Spelling is age appropriate or at least phonetic. Capitalization and punctuation are reasonable. Children can write in paragraphs, organizing ideas so main ideas and details stay together and events stay in order. Children develop their own writing style and "voice." Writing workshops that focus on various aspects of the writing process and include mini-lessons on a variety of writing skills are appropriate at this point.

Developmental Spelling

Spelling is the major portion of the part of writing known as *encoding*. It is in large part dependent upon the child's developing phonics skills and is a more mechanical process than the expression of idea. Basically, the child is translating or encoding the words they use to express their ideas into the letter code of English. Spelling skills, themselves, tend to follow a pattern of development similar to that of writing overall. Spelling instruction should include learning words misspelled in daily writing, generalizing spelling knowledge, and mastering objectives in progressive phases of development. The developmental stages of spelling include:

- **Pre-phonemic spelling**—Children know that letters stand for a message, but they do not know the relationship between spelling and pronunciation.
- **Early phonemic spelling**—Children are beginning to understand spelling. They usually write the beginning letter correctly, while the rest of the word is composed of consonants or long vowels.
- **Letter-name spelling**—Some words are consistently spelled correctly. The student is developing a sight vocabulary and a stable understanding of letters as representing sounds. Long vowels are usually used accurately, but silent vowels are omitted. Unknown words are spelled by the child attempting to match the name of the letter to the sound.
- **Transitional spelling**—This phase is typically entered in late elementary school. Short vowel sounds are mastered and some spelling rules are known. Students are developing a sense of which spellings are correct and which are not.

- **Derivational spelling**—This is usually reached from high school to adulthood. This is the stage where spelling rules are mastered.

THE WRITING PROCESS

Writing is a recursive process. As students engage in the various stages of writing, they develop and improve not only their writing skills, but their thinking skills as well. The stages of the writing process are as follows:

- **Prewriting**--Students gather ideas before writing. Prewriting may include clustering, listing, brainstorming, mapping, free writing, and charting. Providing many ways for a student to develop ideas on a topic will increase his or her chances for success.
- **Writing**--Students compose the first draft.
- **Revising**--Students examine their work and make changes in sentences, wording, details, and ideas. Revise comes from the Latin word *revidere,* meaning "to see again."
- **Editing**--Students proofread the draft for punctuation and mechanical errors.
- **Publishing**--Students may have their work displayed on a bulletin board, read aloud in class, or printed in a literary magazine or school anthology. It is important to realize that these steps are recursive; as a student engages in each aspect of the writing process, he or she may begin with prewriting, writing, revising, writing, revising, editing, and publishing. They do not engage in this process in a lockstep manner; it is more circular.

TEACHING THE COMPOSING PROCESS

Prewriting Activities
- Have a class discussion of the topic.
- Map out ideas, questions, and graphic organizers on the chalkboard.
- Break into small groups to discuss different ways of approaching the topic, develop an organizational plan, and create a thesis statement.
- Research the topic, if necessary.
- Teacher models the activity by "prewriting" a topic of her own, recording ideas on chart paper.

Drafting/Revising
- Students write a first draft in class or at home.
- Students engage in peer response and class discussion.
- Using checklists or a rubric, students critique each other's writing and make suggestions for revising the writing. At this stage, you may stress organization and adequate details.

- Students revise the writing. They may alter the order of concepts presented, add details, choose more colorful words or try to add voice to the piece.
- Again, the teacher can first demonstrate this by referring to her prewriting chart and writing (perhaps with the students' help) her first draft.

Editing and Proofreading

- Students, working in pairs, analyze sentences for variety in structure, completeness and clarity.
- Students work in groups to read papers for punctuation and mechanics.
- Students perform final edit.

Teaching Special populations

As noted above, writing has two major parts: expression or composition and mechanics or encoding. Children with disabilities may have trouble with one or both of these classes of skills. Disabilities such as those that impact primarily the decoding or phonic portion of reading will impact primarily the encoding or conventions portion of writing. The child who struggles to master the letter-sound code in reading may also struggle to use the correct letters and spelling patterns to encode the written message. Just as such children may have relatively little difficulty comprehending a story read to them, they may have relatively little difficulty *composing or dictating* their ideas for a written composition.

Alternatively, some children can decode or read aloud individual words rapidly and correctly, but do not understand what they are reading. These children often spell and write words correctly, but have difficulty expressing their ideas. Sometimes this reflects itself in word finding and recalling difficulties or in difficulties organizing ideas and completing ideas or even sentences in composition. Some children with disabilities, of course, will have problems in both areas.

When teaching written communication to children with disabilities, it is often helpful to separate these two sets of skills and work on them separately until the child has mastered them. Doing this prevents a child's disability in one area from slowing down or restricting his/her progress in another area not impacted directly by the disability. In addition, the techniques used to help a child with composition and expression are different from those used to help with encoding and conventions, so separating the tasks makes it easier to provide training that is specific to the child's deficit.

For example, a child who is able to compose coherent, well organized ideas but who cannot encode or spell the words needed to write them down might be allowed to dictate the composition to a teacher, peer, or computer. The student can then work on revising ideas for word choice, language, etc. In order to work on the encoding and conventions, the composition can be read back to the student, who can practice the encoding skills separately in writing down the composition. The teacher can provide whatever assistance is necessary to help the student learn the conventions, and gradually reduce scaffolding over time. This allows the student to move ahead with expressive composition skills while working at a lower level on the more difficult (to him) conventions.

Similarly, ELL students may struggle more with the encoding portion of writing than the composition if heir conversational English is good. If they still struggle with English conversation, they may need to be allowed to *compose* their writing in their native language, then translate it into English and work on their encoding skills.

Alternatively, the student who can encode and use writing conventions well, but who cannot express coherent ideas would need other kinds of help. If word finding is a problem for the student, the student and teacher might brain storm a list of words relevant to the topic and record them in lists for the student to use in his composition. Graphic organizers of various sorts can help with organizational issues. Cloze procedures that allow the student to fill in key words (e.g., from the above mentioned word bank) might help the student produce a coherent piece of writing. Less help would be needed for the student to actually write the composition down, once the ideas are clear.

> **SKILL 4.2** **Analyzing factors to consider in writing for various audiences and purposes, and in writing in various genres, formats (e.g., essay, poem), and modes (e.g., descriptive, persuasive, evaluative)**

Developing the writing skills of students is a complex process. As with any other aspect of teaching, it's important to provide as many realistic opportunities as possible. When students read for an authentic purpose, the reading becomes more important and there is an increased interest in completing the task. The same is true of writing.

In writing, teachers often spend time having the students complete journals, write stories, or complete other assignments. While all of these types of writing provide skill development and can be important, it is when the teacher implements ways to incorporate authentic and relevant writing that students can find the same increased interest and understand the importance of writing.

Sometimes in schools these realistic reasons to write automatically present themselves. There will be times when the students are dissatisfied with a rule or decision that has been made within the school. During such a situation, the students could expand upon their persuasive writing skills to attempt to change the rule with which they disagree.

In other cases, students may keep pen pal letters with children in another state or country. This type of correspondence, even if accomplished via email, develops letter-writing skills in a more realistic setting than asking the students to write a fictitious letter for the teacher. It can also include descriptive writing or chronological writing as students describe their homes and lives or events in which they participated.

Similarly, students could write and add their own books to the library or even write books to share with younger students. Writing contests would provide another more realistic reason for students to write.

In the end, it is not the type of writing to be completed or the reason for which it is completed that is important. It is the understanding that children take away from the process that writing has a purpose in society, that writing is a relevant skill that needs to be developed.

Using these authentic methods, children will begin to see the relevance in their own lives. They will then be able to come up with their own ideas and reasons to write. This takes the skill to the next level, that of application. Bringing students to the application level is the goal of education.

Reading for Writing

Whatever purpose or style of writing is being studied, the *first step* the teacher should take is to **read quality examples of that form of writing to the students**, or have students read samples themselves. As mentioned earlier, research shows reading and writing skills to be closely intertwined. Human beings learn from watching models and imitating them. The more exposure students have to good, age appropriate examples of a style of writing, the better able they will be to incorporate relevant techniques into their own writing. In Skill 3.04 examples of children's literature in many structures and for many purposes were provided. The skillful teacher can introduce writing assignments by reading relevant works and helping the children identify text structures and writing techniques that made the books successful.

Writing Purposes

When we attempt to communicate, we are usually prompted by a purpose for our communication. We may want to:

- Express feelings
- Explore an idea
- Entertain
- Inform
- Persuade
- Argue
- Explain

For most narrative writing, the purpose is to explain or entertain. When beginning a narrative piece or brainstorming session, a writer should always ask herself, "Why am I writing?" For many students, the answer to this appears to be "I have an assignment due," or "To get a good grade." An effective teacher, however, will help students move past this response in order to realize that being cognizant of the purpose helps to focus the writing so that the main theme, point, idea or reason for the piece is clearly communicated to the reader.

Discourse, whether in speaking or writing, falls naturally into four different forms: narrative, descriptive, expository, and persuasive. The first question to be asked when reading a written piece, listening to a presentation, or writing is "What's the point?" This is usually called the thesis. When finished reading an essay, the reader should be able to say something along the lines of, "The point of this piece is that the foster-care system in America is a disaster." If it's a play, readers should also be able to say, "The point of that play is that good overcomes evil."

The same is true of any written document or performance. If it doesn't make a point, the reader/listener/viewer may become confused and feel that it's not worth the effort. Knowing this is very helpful when sitting down to write a document, be it essay, poem, or speech, as these forms have been the structure of Western thinking since the Greek Rhetoricians.

Exposition is discourse whose only purpose is to inform. Expository writing is not interested in changing anyone's mind or getting anyone to take a certain action. It exists to give information. Some examples include driving directions to a particular place, or the directions for putting together a toy. The writer doesn't care whether the readers do or do not follow the directions. The writer only wants to be sure that the information is available in case they do decide to use it.

Narration is discourse that is arranged chronologically—something happened, and then something else happened, and then something else happened. It is also called a story. News reports are often narrative in nature, as are records of trips.

Description is discourse whose purpose is to make an experience available through one of the five senses—seeing, smelling, hearing, feeling (as with the fingers), and tasting. Descriptive words are used to make it possible for the reader to "see" with his or her own mind's eye, hear through his or her own mind's ear, smell through his or her own mind's nose, taste with his or her own mind's tongue, and feel with his or her own mind's fingers. Description may also involve feelings and emotions. This is how language moves people. Only by experiencing an event can the emotions become involved. Poets are experts in descriptive language.

Persuasive writing often uses all forms of discourse. The introduction may be a history or a background of the idea being presented—exposition. Details supporting some of the points may be stories—narrations. Descriptive writing is used to make sure that the point is emotionally established. It is a piece of writing, a poem, a play, or a speech whose purpose is to change the minds of the audience members or to get them to do something. This is achieved in many ways:

- The credibility of the writer/speaker might lead the listeners/readers to a change of mind or a recommended action
- Reasoning is important in persuasive discourse. No one wants to believe that he or she accepts a new viewpoint or goes out and takes action just because he or she likes and trusts the person who recommended it. Logic comes into play in reasoning that is persuasive.
- The third and most powerful force that leads to acceptance or action is emotional appeal. Even if a person has been persuaded logically and reasonably that he or she should believe in a different way, the person is unlikely to act on it unless he or she is moved emotionally. A person with resources might be convinced that people suffered in New Orleans after Katrina, but he or she is not likely to do anything about it until he or she is emotionally moved. Sermons are good examples of persuasive discourse.

Paraphrase is the rewording of a piece of writing. The result is not necessarily shorter than the original, as it uses different vocabulary and possibly a different arrangement of details. Paraphrases are sometimes written to clarify a complex piece of writing. Sometimes, material is paraphrased because it cannot be copied for purposes of copyright restraints. In school settings, paraphrasing is often used to be sure material was fully understood by the reader or to help another reader understand the material.

Summary is a distilling of the elements of a piece of writing or speech. It is much shorter than the original. To write a good summary, the writer must determine what the "bones" of the original piece are. What is its structure? What are the main ideas and the critical details which support them? A summary does not make judgments about the original; it simply reports the original in condensed form.

Letters are often expository in nature—their purpose is to give information. However, letters are also often persuasive—the writer wants to persuade or get the recipient to do something. They are also sometimes descriptive or narrative—the writer may share an experience or tell about an event.

Research reports are a special kind of expository writing. A topic is researched—explored by some appropriate means such as searching literature, interviewing experts, or even conducting experiments—and the findings are written up in such a way that the audience may know what was discovered. They can be very simple, such as delving into the history of an event, or very complex, such as a report on a scientific phenomenon that requires complicated testing and reasoning to explain. A research reports often reports possible conclusions but puts forth one as the best answer to the question that inspired the research in the first place, which is what becomes the thesis of the report. These are common components of content area studies throughout educational settings.

Audience Considerations

The audience has a lot to do with how the author writes. It is important for a writer to be aware of the intended audience of a narrative piece before beginning since knowledge of one's audience will affect the tone, vocabulary and other choice of words, level of formality, subject, and sentence structure. For example, a story written to entertain sixth-graders will be quite different than a historical fiction piece for high school seniors. Young writers may need concrete examples of how to consider audience. They might be asked how they talk when chatting with friends about last night's Little League free for all and compare that to how they might describe the evening to their grandparent, the principal, or their minister during Sunday school. You might ask how they talk to a baby sibling or a puppy. Point out how they would use different words talking to "the guys" versus talking to Gramma; how they would adjust their language so the two year old can understand, etc. Discussion of how we talk to different audiences can lead into considerations of audience in writing.

Since a writer must anticipate a reader's questions or needs, the author must be knowledgeable about this audience in order to accurately anticipate these needs and to see the story through the readers' eyes. This is a challenging task as the author has to balance what the reader expects and needs, while also fulfilling the purpose of the writing. Sometimes it helps to literally make a list of the characteristics of the expected reader. Ask who is going to read it? How old are they? Why are they reading it? Make a web of descriptive terms for the expected members of the audience. It can even help to have children role play different audiences when reading a draft (see writing process above). For example, the students listening can be told to pretend they are teachers or small children, whatever, and respond to the author in that mode.

In upper elementary school it can be possible to have children write the same piece for different audiences. This can be made more authentic if groups of students are given the task of writing about some topic and each student group has a different audience. For example, the students might be writing a persuasive piece enlisting support for building a new playground. One student group will write letters to the PTO, another to the Principal or superintendent of schools, another to area businesses, and another to neighborhood children, etc. Discussions would cover how each group's writing would differ, and so forth.

SKILL 4.3 **Demonstrating knowledge of the use of writing strategies and language to achieve various effects (e.g., creating a point of view, showing author's voice, persuading, and establishing setting, describing sensory details[SAW10])**

Author's Voice and Point of View

The author's voice is his or her attitude as reflected in the statement or passage, his or her individual personality coming through in the written message. The choice of words and sentence structure can help the reader to determine the overall voice or point of view of a statement or passage. These are fairly abstract concepts and can be difficult for young writers to understand. They often feel that if they have simply recounted all the events or listed all the facts they have done their job as writers.

In order to make these concepts more concrete, the teacher might start with auditory voice. Have all the children close their eyes or turn their backs, or have several students stand behind a screen. The teacher points to one, who says something. Children then guess who is talking. Discuss how they knew who was talking. This can be taken a bit further once children have become sufficiently familiar with one another. The teacher can collect various children's comments about something familiar to them all (e.g., school lunch, the local sports team, whatever). It should be something of significance to the children. Then the teacher can read the comments to the class and students will guess who said what. Discussion of how they knew who said what can lead to a clearer idea of voice and point of view in writing.

As mentioned in the previous section, reading short selections where the author's voice or point of view is very clear can also be helpful.

Showing, not Telling

One strategy for helping students improve their expression of such characteristics as voice and point of view in their writing is to guide them to using words and sentences that *show* point of view or *demonstrate* voice rather than simply stating facts or listing events. Tell the students that they want the reader to understand, but don't make it TOO easy; make the reader do a little work. This is the flip side of understanding inferences when reading. Instead of just stating something literally (e.g., "Karen was a huge Atlanta Braves fan."), write a statement that illustrates it and let the reader figure it out (e.g., "Karen cried herself to sleep the night the Braves lost the World Series."). Talk about how the second sentence is more interesting than the first.

It can also help to have students dictate their compositions as if they were talking to someone. Of course, they may need to make revisions to take into account the expected audience, but more of their voice may come through anyway.

Figurative Language

Figurative language is present in both fiction and non-fiction. Figurative language is language that utilizes creative or poetic methods to convey points. Figurative language is used for effect and to make a point stand out. It can also be very effective in expressing the author's point of view and the selection of specific figurative language can also affect voice. The most common examples of figurative language include hyperbole, metaphor, personification, simile, and idiom. Each is explained below:

Hyperbole: The term, hyperbole, is the literary version of exaggeration. When authors exaggerate in their text, they are using hyperbole. Hyperbole is often used as irony, many times to over-emphasize a point. For example, the writer could simply write: "It's been a long time since they won the World Series." Or, using hyperbole: "The last time they won the world series the news had to be delivered by Pony Express."

Metaphor: A metaphor is a technique for comparing one thing to something very different that shares a particular quality. It simply states that one thing IS another. For example, one might say, of a very fast runner, that "He is lightning on the base paths." Obviously a person is not lightning, but we compare him to lightning, and *call* him lightning because, like lightning, he is fast. Authors use metaphor for emphasis, creativity, and often clarity. Sometimes, metaphors provide a better picture than accurate language.

Personification: Whenever an author gives human life to an inanimate item, personification is used. For example, we might say that the wind is whistling. Authors use personification to provide a more poetic look at common events. Personification often reveals a lot about an author's voice, as well. The manner in which a particular author talks about his antique Mustang as if it were his girlfriend may tell you a lot about the author.

Simile: Similes are comparisons between two things, that share a common characteristic using the words "like," or "as." The things compared can be objects, people, animals or events. Similes are like metaphors; however, they typically use "like" or "as" to identify the similarities. A simile is found in the phrase "love is like a rose," or "fast as lightning."

Idiom: Idioms are phrases or words used only in specific locations or cultures. For example, a common American idiom, found anywhere in the country, is "break a leg," which is a wish for good luck. However, each region of the country has its own distinctive idioms as well. Idioms are generally used in writing to spice the language with local flavor. Often, idioms are used to make characters seem more real, or even to indicate where in the country the action is taking place. Since the writer will have a repertoire of idioms common to his/her upbringing, the use of idioms can also enhance voice.

SKILL 4.4   Applying revision strategies to improve the unity, organization, clarity, precision, and effectiveness of written materials

Revision is an important step for the writer in the writing process. Here, students examine their work and make changes in wording, details, and ideas. So many times, students write a draft and then feel they're finished. On the contrary— students must be encouraged to develop, change, and enhance their writing once they've completed the draft as well as during initial composition. Refer to Skill 4.1 for an overview of the writing process and the place of revision in that process.

Sometimes teachers can begin instruction on revision by demonstrating how other writers revise. Find material from a famous writer and show how it went through various revisions before the final copy. For example, George Orwell's famous book, *1984,* is available in a large coffee table book that has a facsimile of the first draft, containing all the cross-outs, rewording, rearranging of sentences and paragraphs, etc, followed by second draft, and so forth to the final copy. Museums have copies for FDR's famous speeches ("A Day that will live in infamy" etc) in his handwriting with deletions, substitutions, etc. Students can be shown that if these famous writers had to revise and edit, surely the student can do so, too.

Effective teachers realize that revision and editing go hand-in-hand. They also know that students often move back and forth between these two stages during the course of one written work. These stages are often best practiced in small groups or pairs in addition to on an individual basis. Students must learn to analyze and improve their own work as well as the works of their peers. Some methods to use include:

- Students working in pairs to analyze sentences for variety.
- Students working in pairs or groups to ask questions about unclear areas or to help in adding details, information, etc.
- Students performing their final edit.

Many teachers introduce a Writer's Workshop to their students to maximize learning about the writing process. Writer's Workshops vary across classrooms, but the main idea is for students to become comfortable with the writing process. A basic Writer's Workshop includes a block of classroom time committed to writing various projects (e.g., narratives, memoirs, book summaries, fiction, book reports, etc). Students use this time to write, meet with others to review/edit writing, make comments on writing, revise their own work, proofread, meet with the teacher, and publish their work. (See Skill 4.01 for more on this writing process)

Teachers who facilitate effective Writer's Workshops are able to meet with students one at a time and can guide each student in his or her individual writing needs. This approach allows the teacher to differentiate instruction for each student's writing level.

REVISING AND CLARIFYING WRITING

Just as individual paragraphs have main ideas expressed as a topic sentence, details to support that topic sentence, and a concluding statement that restates the main idea, longer passages may have introductions that give an overview of the main idea or thesis, followed by paragraphs that provide details and support, and a conclusion or summary at the end. The introductory statement is at the beginning of the passage, and provides a bridge between any previous, relevant text and the content to follow. It provides information about the text and also sets the tone and parameters. The old axiom regarding presenting a body of information suggests that you should always "tell them what you are going to tell them; tell it to them; tell them what you just told them." In accordance with this, the introductory statement is where the writer "tell[s] them what [he or she is] going to tell them," the content portion (the main body of the narrative) is where the writer "tell[s] it to them," and the summary or concluding statement is where the writer "tell[s] them what [he or she] just told them." In short, the summary statement should be at or near the end of the passage; it is a concise presentation of the essential data from that passage.

Writing Introductions--It is important to remember that in the writing process, the introduction may be written first or last. Until the body of the paper has been determined, including the thesis and its development, it is sometimes difficult to make strategic decisions regarding the introduction. The Greek rhetoricians called this part of a discourse *exordium*, or "leading into." The basic purpose of the introduction, then, is to lead the audience into the discourse. It can let the reader know what the purpose of the discourse is, and it can condition the audience to be receptive to what the writer wants to say.

An introduction can be very brief or it can take up a large percentage of the total word count. Aristotle said that the introduction can be compared to the flourishes that flute players make before their performance—an overture in which the musicians display what they can play best in an attempt to gain the favor and attention of the audience for the main performance.

In order to do this, the writer must first know what to say; who the readership is likely to be; what the social, political, and economic climate is; what preconceived notions the audience is likely to have regarding the subject; and how long the discourse is going to be. There are many ways to do this:

- Show that the subject is important.
- Show that although the points being presented may seem improbable, they are true.
- Show that the subject has been neglected, misunderstood, or misrepresented in the past.
- Explain an unusual mode of development.
- Forestall any misconception of the purpose.
- Apologize for a deficiency.
- Arouse interest in the subject with an anecdotal lead-in.
- Ingratiate oneself with the readership.
- Establish one's own credibility.

The introduction often ends with the **thesis**—the point or purpose of the paper, somewhat analogous to the topic sentence in a single paragraph. However, this is not set in stone. The thesis may open the body of the discussion, or it may conclude the discourse. The most important thing to remember is that the purpose and structure of the introduction should be deliberate if it is to serve the purpose of "leading the reader into the discussion."

Writing Conclusions--It is easier to write a conclusion after the decisions regarding the introduction have been made. Aristotle taught that the conclusion should strive to do five things:

- Inspire the reader with a favorable opinion of the writer.
- Amplify the force of the points made in the body of the paper.
- Reinforce the points made in the body.
- Rouse appropriate emotions in the reader.
- Restate in a summary way what has been said.

The conclusion may be short or it may be long, depending on its purpose in the paper. Recapitulation, a brief summary or restatement of the main points (or of the thesis) is the most common form of effective conclusion writing. A good example is the closing argument in a court trial.

Text Organization--In studies of professional writers and how they produce their successful works, it has been revealed that writing is a process that can be clearly defined (although, in practice, it must have enough flexibility to allow for creativity). The teacher must be able to define the various stages that a successful writer goes through in order to make a statement that has value.

There must be a discovery stage when ideas, materials, and supporting details are deliberately collected. These may come from many possible sources: the writer's own experience and observations, deliberate research of written sources, interviews of live persons, television presentations, or the internet.

The next stage is organizing where the purpose, thesis, and supporting points will be. Most writers will put forth more than one possible thesis; in the next stage, the writing of the paper, they will then settle on one as the result of trial and error. Once the paper is written, the editing stage is probably the most important stage. This is not just the polishing stage. At this point, decisions must be made regarding whether the reasoning is cohesive—does it hold together? Is the arrangement the best possible one, or should the points be rearranged? Are there holes that need to be filled in? What form will the introduction take? Does the conclusion lead the reader out of the discourse, or is it inadequate or too abrupt?

It is important to remember that the best writers engage in all of these stages recursively. They may go back to discovery at any point in the process. They may go back and rethink the organization even once they have almost finished. To help students become effective writers, teachers need to give them adequate practice in the various stages. Students must be encouraged to engage deliberately in the creative thinking that makes writers successful.

Graphic Organizers

In the same way that graphic organizers can help readers make sense of what they read, such organizers can help the writer compose readable writing that will convey the message the writer wants to send. Young children, especially, have difficulty focusing on the topic, get sidetracked, and wander and ramble about the topic. Graphic organizers can help keep the focus and keep related ideas together in an organized fashion.

Graphic organizers are usually used during the prewriting stage of the writing process when the writer is collecting ideas or, in some cases, as the first step in the drafting process. If students are familiar with the use of graphic organizers in reading, it is a simple matter to turn them around to use for writing. Use a simple graphic organizer to illustrate how the writer of a familiar story book or nonfiction book organized ideas for the book. It can be effective to show how different types of organizers can be used for different types of writing (e.g., Venn diagrams for compare and contrast, buildings with pillars for main ideas and details, etc.). Children can be guided to select graphic organizers suitable to their topic and level of writing skill.

This is a good place for a teacher to differentiate writing instruction. More proficient students can use more complex organizers or multiple level organizers, whereas students who need more scaffolding can use simpler organizers, even Cloze forms that let the neediest students simply fill in the blanks with facts.

Managing Transitions

Even if the sentences that make up a given paragraph or passage are arranged in logical order, the document as a whole can still seem choppy, the various ideas disconnected. **Transitions**, words that signal relationships between ideas, can help improve the flow of a document. Transitions can help achieve clear and effective presentation of information by establishing connections between sentences, paragraphs, and sections of a document. With transitions, each sentence builds on the ideas in the last, and each paragraph has clear links to the preceding one. As a result, the reader receives clear directions on how to piece together the writer's ideas in a logically coherent argument. By signaling how to organize, interpret and react to information, transitions allow a writer to effectively and elegantly explain his ideas.

Logical Relationship	Transitional Expression
Exception/Contrast	but, however, in spite of, on the one hand ... on the other hand, nevertheless, nonetheless, notwithstanding, in contrast, on the contrary, still, yet
Sequence/Order	first, second, third, ... next, then, finally
Time	after, afterward, at last, before, currently, during, earlier, immediately, later, meanwhile, now, recently, simultaneously, subsequently, then
Example	for example, for instance, namely, specifically, to illustrate
Emphasis	even, indeed, in fact, of course, truly
Place/Position	above, adjacent, below, beyond, here, in front, in back, nearby, there
Cause and Effect	accordingly, consequently, hence, so, therefore, thus
Additional Support or Evidence	additionally, again, also, and, as well, besides, equally important, further, furthermore, in addition, moreover, then, in the same way, just as, to, likewise
Conclusion/Summary	finally, in a word, in brief, in conclusion, in the end, in the final analysis, on the whole, thus, to conclude, to summarize, in sum, in summary

Helping young writers to use such transitions is important. Depending upon the students' level of development, a simple chart such as the one above can be supplied to students for use during the revisions stage. Younger or less able writers may need simpler scaffolding or even modeled "think aloud" guidance on the use of various transitions. Such transitions would make a good topic for a mini-lesson in which the teacher and students rewrite a choppy piece of work together.

Word Choice

Activities such as word wallets and the use of thesauruses described in Objective 2 can be modified to help students revise their work to include more interesting word choices. When reading their work to peers or the teacher, a selection of overused or "boring" words can be highlighted and the vocabulary techniques outlined earlier can be used to replace them with more interesting words.

Help for Struggling Writers

Some writers will struggle more than others with revision. For some, they simply can't imagine saying it any other way, can't go beyond their original work to modify it. They may also find it difficult to edit for spelling, punctuation, and other mechanics. One way to differentiate the revision process and make it simpler for these students is to separate the revision and editing processes from *their* writing process. Start by providing samples of developmentally appropriate writing that contain errors or inadequacies the student CAN see. After practice and mastery of these tasks, move to material designed with errors and inadequacies *similar to those the student's writing shows*. This means much of the work will be individualized and this can be done by imitating a sample of the student's writing. Once the student can see and revise or correct someone else's errors, the student may be able to move on to correcting his or her own work.

Assessing Writing--Students need to be trained to become effective at proofreading, revising, and editing strategies. Begin by training them using both desk-side and scheduled conferences. Listed below are some strategies to use to guide students through the final stages of the writing process (and these can easily be incorporated into the Writer's Workshop).

Provide some guide sheets or forms for students to use during peer responses

- Allow students to work in pairs and limit the agenda
- Model the use of the guide sheet or form for the entire class
- Give students a time limit or number of written pieces to be completed in a specific amount of time
- Have the students read their partners' papers, and ask at least three who, what, when, why, how questions (the students should answer the questions and use them as a place to begin discussing the piece)

- At this point in the writing process, a mini-lesson that focuses on some of the problems students are having is appropriate

To help students revise, provide them with a series of questions that will assist them in revising their writing. For example:

- Do the details give a clear picture? Add details that appeal to more than just the sense of sight.
- How effectively are the details organized? Reorder the details if necessary.
- Are the thoughts and feelings of the writer included? Add personal thoughts and feelings about the subject.

These checklists and guides can be individualized or differentiated to match student level of functioning and writing.

SKILL 4.5   Demonstrating knowledge of the use of research skills and computer technology to support writing

Students must be able to research effectively in order to write about a specific assignment. Students need the skills to collect information, sort data, and make a decision as to what facts they will incorporate into their assignment or project.

Student Research Skills

- Learn to generate questions about a topic
- Form a research plan using a variety of strategies
- Restate factual information in the student's own words
- Collect and organize information on various topics
- Write grade-level-appropriate research drafts

Computer Technology

Computer technology, in the form of word processing programs, with the capability to add, delete, and rearrange text, are supportive of writing programs. The use of computer technology can lead to better writing outcomes.

Positive Outcomes Associated with the Use of Word Processors in Writing

- Longer written samples
- Greater variety of word usage
- More variety of sentence structure
- More accurate mechanics and spelling
- Better understanding of the writing process
- Better attitudes toward writing (Bialo and Sivin 1990)

Teachers should evaluate and select educational software based on problem solving, critical thinking, and curriculum standards. In so doing, they can create an environment where students are encouraged to research and write effectively while applying a variety of technology processes. Many software programs are designed to provide a template for the steps in research gathering, recording and drafting.

Locating information for research projects and compiling research sources using both print and electronic resources are vital steps in constructing written documents. The resources that are available in today's school communities include a large database of Internet resources and World Wide Web access, both of which provide individual navigation for print and electronic information. Research sources include looking at traditional commercial databases and using the Electronic Library to print and cite a diversity of informational resources.

One vital aspect of the research process includes learning to analyze the applicability and validity of the massive amounts of accessible information in cyberspace. Verifying and evaluating electronic resources should be a part of the writing process, as should sorting through the downloaded hardcopies or scrolling through the electronic databases. In using a diversity of research sources, the user must be able to discern authentic sources of information from the mass collections of websites and information databases with less-than-reputable sources.

In primary research, selecting a topic and setting up an outline for research information precedes using the secondary research of both print and electronic resources. Using conceptual graphic organizers to center the topic and brainstorm the peripheral information pertaining to the topic clarifies the purpose of the research. In addition, carefully constructed graphic organizers can provide the key words needed for locating both print and electronic information relevant to the topic. There are two aspects of the secondary research:

1. Using print sources
2. Using electronic research tools

Print sources provide guides on locations for specific or general information resources. Libraries have floors or designated areas dedicated to the collection of encyclopedias, specific resource manuals, card catalogs, and periodical indexes that provide information on the projected topic. Electronic research tools includes a listing of the latest and most effective search engines like Goggle, Microsoft, AOL, Infotrac, and Yahoo to find the topic of research, along with peripheral support information. Electronic databases that contain extensive resources help the user with selecting resources, choosing effective keywords, and constructing search strategies. The world of electronic research opens up a global library of resources for both print and electronic information.

Major online services such as Microsoft, Prodigy, and CompuServe provide users with specialized information that is either free or has a minimal charge assessed for that specific service or website. Online resources teach effective ways to bookmark sites of interest and provide information on how to cut and paste relevant information onto word documents for citation and reference.

Bookmarking favorite Internet searches that contain correct sources for reference can save a lot of research time. On AOL, bookmarking is known as "favorites"; with one click of the mouse, a user can type in the email address on the browser's location bar and create instant access to that location. Netscape uses the terminology of "bookmarks" to save browser locations for future research.

Online search engines and web portals create avenues of navigating the World Wide Web. Web portals provide linkages to other websites and are typically subdivided into other categories for searching. Portals are also specific to certain audience interests that index parts of the web. Search engines can provide additional strategic site searches.

Internet safety and security are important considerations when working with young writers. The skillful teacher may wish to provide a list of appropriate sites, already checked out for relevance and safety. These sites can be provided in print list or in a list on the computer with links or simply bookmarked, as above, for the student. The teacher will need to check this site list periodically to keep it up to date.

SKILL 4.6   Demonstrating knowledge of the parts of speech, elements of appropriate grammar and usage (e.g., subject verb agreement, antecedent-pronoun agreement, verb tense), and appropriate mechanics in writing (e.g., capitalization, punctuation)

English grammar, in conventional use, classifies words based on the following eight parts of speech:

- **Verb**: Essential to a sentence, a verb asserts something about the subject of the sentence and expresses an action, event, or state of being. The verb is the critical element of the predicate of a sentence. It is the only part of speech required for a sentence to be a sentence.
- **Noun**: A word used to name/identify a person, animal, place, thing, or abstract idea. Within the structure of a sentence, a noun can function as a subject, a direct or indirect object, a subject or object complement, or an appositive. Words that usually function as nouns can also be modified in spelling or use to function as adjectives or adverbs.

- **Pronoun**: This can be substituted for a noun or another pronoun. Pronoun classifications include the personal pronoun, the demonstrative pronoun, the interrogative pronoun, the indefinite pronoun, the relative pronoun, the reflexive pronoun, and the intensive pronoun. The appropriate use of pronouns (e.g., he, which, none, you) can make sentences less cumbersome and less repetitive (and, therefore, more readable).
- **Adjective**: A word that modifies a noun or a pronoun by describing, identifying, or quantifying other words. It answers the questions: What kind? How many? Which one? An adjective usually precedes the noun or the pronoun that it modifies. For example, "The sick child stayed in the bed." However, adjectives can also appear later in a sentence separated from the noun by the verb. For example, "The child is sick."
- **Adverb**: A part of a sentence that can modify a verb, an adjective, another adverb, a phrase, or a clause. An adverb indicates manner, time, place, cause, or degree; it answers questions such as "how," "when," "where," or "how much." For example, "Mary barely gets to work on time each day." While some adverbs can be identified by the characteristic "ly" suffix, most adverbs must be identified by analyzing the grammatical relationships within the sentence or clause as a whole. The adverb can be found in various places within the sentence.
- **Preposition**: This word links nouns, pronouns, and phrases to other words in a sentence, and shows the relationship between those elements. The word or phrase that the preposition introduces is the *object* of the preposition. A preposition usually indicates the temporal, spatial, or logical relationship of its object to the rest of the sentence (e.g., on, beneath, against, beside, over, during).
- **Conjunction**: This is used to link words, phrases, or clauses. For independent clauses, phrases, and individual words, **coordinating conjunctions** (e.g., and, but, or, nor, for, so, yet) are used. To introduce a dependent clause and indicate the nature of a relationship between the independent clause and dependent clause, a **subordinating conjunction** (e.g., after, although, as, because, before, how, if, once, since, than, that, though, until, when, where, whether, while) is used. Equivalent sentence elements are linked with **correlative conjunctions**, which always appear in pairs (e.g., both...and, either...or, neither...nor, not...only, but...also, so...as, whether...or). Strictly speaking, correlative conjunctions consist simply of a coordinating conjunction linked to an adjective or adverb.
- **Interjection**: A word added to a sentence to convey emotion, it usually compels the sentence to be closed with an exclamation mark. It is not grammatically related to any other part of the sentence. Some examples include "ouch," "hey," "wow," and "oh no!"

It is important to remember that each part of speech explains not what the word is, but how the word is used. For example, in some instances, the same word can be used as a noun in one sentence and as a verb or adjective in the next.

Subject-Verb Agreement

A verb agrees in number with its subject. Making the two agree relies on the ability to properly identify the subject.

- <u>One</u> of the boys <u>was playing</u> too rough.
- <u>No one</u> in the class, not the teacher nor the students, <u>was listening</u> to the message from the intercom.
- The <u>candidates,</u> including a grandmother and a teenager, <u>are debating</u> some controversial issues.

Note that intervening phrases containing plural nouns that are NOT the subject do not affect the verb. In the sentence above 'one' is the subject, so 'was' is used in the verb even though 'boys' occurs right before the verb. 'Boys' is not the subject; it is a prepositional phrase modifying 'one.'

If two singular subjects are connected by *and*, the verb must be plural.

A man *and* his dog <u>were jogging</u> on the beach.

If two singular subjects are connected by *or* or *nor,* a singular verb is required.

- Neither Dot *nor* Joyce <u>has missed</u> a day of school this year.
- Either Fran *or* Paul <u>is</u> missing.

If one singular subject and one plural subject are connected by *or nor,* the verb agrees with the subject nearest to the verb.

- Neither the coach *nor* the <u>players</u> <u>were</u> able to sleep on the bus.

If the subject is a collective noun, its sense of number in the sentence determines the verb: singular if the noun represents a group or unit, and plural if the noun represents individuals.

- The House of Representatives has adjourned for the holidays.
- The House of Representatives have failed to reach an agreement on the subject of adjournment.

Pronoun-Antecedent Agreement

A noun is any word that names a person, place, thing, idea, animal, quality, or activity. A pronoun is a word that is used in place of a noun or more pronouns. The word or word group that a pronoun stands for (or refers to) is called its antecedent.

We use pronouns in many of the sentences that we write. Pronouns add variety to writing by enabling the writer to avoid a monotonous repetition of nouns. Pronouns also help to maintain coherence within and among sentences. Pronouns must agree with their antecedents in number and person. Therefore, if the antecedent is plural, a plural pronoun must be used; if the antecedent is feminine, a feminine pronoun must be used. The pronouns must show a clear reference to their antecedents as well.

The following are the nine different types of pronouns: *personal, possessive, indefinite, reflexive, reciprocal, intensive, interrogative, relative, and demonstrative.*

In order to aid students in revising their texts to correct errors, teachers should have them complete the following steps:

- Read with a focus only on pronouns.
- Circle each pronoun and draw an arrow to its antecedent.
- Replace the pronoun with a noun to eliminate a vague pronoun reference.
- Supply missing antecedents where needed.
- Place the pronoun so that the nearest noun is its antecedent.

Once the students focus on pronoun antecedent agreement a few times, they will progress from correcting errors to avoiding errors. The only way to develop a student's skill with pronoun reference is to focus clear attention on pronouns until it becomes a habit of his or her writing.

Other Agreement

Possessive nouns are used in context to show that something is owned and belongs within a contextual framework of the sentence or the passage. Nouns have common usages in describing people, places, or things; they also provide the collective thought and meaning of the sentence. Nouns provide singular or plural contextual identity to the subject matter being addressed in sentences. The specificity of nouns can describe a diversity of familiar names, places, and things: New York, Statue of Liberty, Coca-Cola, Pacific Ocean, Mom, Dad, student, teacher, life, and America. Nouns provide a common language for the reader in understanding the context of information.

In contrast, pronouns are supportive descriptors that take the place of nouns in a sentence. Pronouns, like nouns, can either be singular or plural in usage. The first person pronoun in a sentence that can take the place of a name in the singular sense include "I," "me," or "my"; in the plural sense, the pronoun descriptor becomes "we," "us," or "our." In second person, pronoun terms include "you" or "yours" (singular and plural, respectively), whereas in the third-person usage, the singular words, "he/she," "him/her," or "his/hers," become "they," "them," or "their." Pronouns can become subjects in sentences and direct or indirect objects in sentences. For example, "I work with a great Professor, and I like her."

Adjectives and adverbs can be either comparative forms or superlative forms when comparisons occur in sentences "This book is lighter than the last book" or "She is the funniest sister in the family."

There are various forms of verbs that show action and the state of being in sentences. Verb forms can be present, present participle, past, or past participle. For example, in the sentence "She eats," the verbs become (respectively) "She is eating," "She ate," and "She has eaten." There are also irregular verbs used in sentences commonly containing "is," "were," and "been."

The importance of using the correct usage of possessive nouns, pronouns, verbs, adjectives, and adverbs is crucial in conveying meaning in written text. In connecting the reader with the written information, understanding how the information is presented creates an access to understanding the contextual aspect of the words. Using correct forms of support words is crucial in creating informative and accessible text.

USE OF VERBS (TENSE)

Present tense is used to express an action that is currently happening or is always true.

> Randy is playing the piano.
> Randy plays the piano like a pro.

Past tense is used to express an action that occurred in a past time.

> Randy learned to play the piano when he was six years old.

Future tense is used to express an action or a condition of future time.

> Randy will probably earn a music scholarship.

Present perfect tense is used to express an action or a condition that started in the past and is continued to or completed in the present, or one that has an unspecified time frame.

Randy has practiced piano every day for the last ten years.
Randy has never been bored with practice.

Past perfect tense expresses an action or a condition that occurred as a precedent to some other action or condition.

Randy had considered playing clarinet before he discovered the piano.

Future perfect tense expresses action that started in the past or the present and will conclude at some time in the future.

By the time he goes to college, Randy will have been an accomplished pianist for more than half of his life.

A note about participles: Participles are the forms of a verb that must be combined with a helping verb in various present or past tenses.

- The **present participle** is the –ing form of the verb. it always ends in –ing and is used to form either the present or the past tense (depending upon the helping verb) and indicates that the action is taking place at this moment or is/was taking place simultaneously with something else in the sentence. For example: "Randy is playing," means he is playing at this moment. "Randy was playing when I came in the room," indicates both actions, my entry into the room and his playing were occurring at the same time.
- The **past participle** can have –ed added for regular verbs, but may have various forms for irregular verbs. (e.g., talked is the past participle of talk, but done is the past participle of do) The past participle is used with a helping verb to form both perfect cases described above.

USE OF VERBS (MOOD)

Indicative mood is used to make unconditional statements.

I am wealthy.
I cannot fly.

Subjunctive mood is used for conditional clauses or wish statements that pose untrue conditions. Verbs in subjunctive mood are plural for both singular and plural subjects.

> If I were a bird, I would fly.
> I wish I were as rich as Donald Trump.

VERB CONJUGATION

The conjugation of verbs follows the patterns used in the discussion of tense above. However, the most frequent problems in verb use stem from the improper formation of past and past participial forms.

> Regular verb: believe, believed, (have) believed
> Irregular verbs: run, ran, run; sit, sat, sat; teach, taught, taught

Other problems arise from the use of verbs that are essentially homonyms and[SAW11] look the same in one tense but have forms of different words with different meanings in other tenses.

- I lie on the ground. I lay on the ground yesterday. I have lain down.
- I lay the blanket on the bed. I laid the blanket there yesterday. I have laid the blanket every night.

In the first set of sentences, "lay" is the past tense of "lie," an intransitive verb meaning 'recline' that does not take an object. In the second set of sentences, "lay" is a transitive verb meaning 'to put something down' and it does need an object (the blanket).

> Other examples:

- The sun rises. The sun rose. The sun has risen. (Rise is intransitive verb, no object, sun is going up)
- He raises the flag. He raised the flag. He had raised the flag. (Raise is a transitive verb for lifting something, requires an object: flag).
- I sit on the porch. I sat on the porch. I have sat in the porch swing. (Sit is an intransitive verb not requiring an object).
- I set the plate on the table. I set the plate there yesterday. I had set the table before dinner. (Set is a transitive verb, requiring an object-the plate).

It should be remembered that some verbs can be transitive in some sentences and intransitive in others.

Two other verb problems often stem from misusing the preposition *of* for the verb auxiliary *have* and misusing the verb *ought* (now rare).

> Incorrect: I should of gone to bed.
> Correct: I should have gone to bed.

> Incorrect: He hadn't ought to get so angry.
> Correct: He ought not to get so angry.

Use of Pronouns

The **case** of a pronoun depends upon how it is used in a sentence. A pronoun used as a subject or predicate nominative occurs in the nominative case.

> **She** was the drum majorette. The lead trombonists were **Joe** and **he**. The band director accepted **whoever** could march in step.

A pronoun used as a direct object, an indirect object, or as the object of a preposition occurs in the objective case.

> The teacher praised **him**. She gave **him** an "A" on the test. Her praise of **him** was appreciated. The students **whom** she did not praise will work harder next time.

Common pronoun errors typically occur from the misuse of reflexive pronouns:

> Singular: myself, yourself, herself, himself, itself
> Plural: ourselves, yourselves, themselves

> Incorrect: Jack cut hisself shaving.
> Correct: Jack cut himself shaving.

> Incorrect: They backed theirselves into a corner.
> Correct: They backed themselves into a corner.

Use of Adjectives

Comparative adjectives end in -er and superlatives in -est, with some exceptions like *worse* and *worst*. Some adjectives that cannot easily make comparative inflections are preceded by *more* and *most*.

> Mrs. Carmichael is the <u>better</u> of the two basketball coaches.
> That is the <u>hastiest</u> excuse you have ever contrived.

Avoid Double Comparisons

Incorrect: This is the worstest headache I ever had.
Correct: This is the worst headache I ever had.

When comparing one thing to others in a group, exclude the thing under comparison from the rest of the group.

Incorrect: Joey is larger than any baby I have ever seen.
(Since you have seen him, he cannot be larger than himself.)
Correct: Joey is larger than <u>any other</u> baby I have ever seen.

Include all necessary words to make a comparison clear in meaning.

I am as tall as my mother. I am as tall as she (is).
My cats are better behaved than those of my neighbor.

Plurals

The multiplicity and complexity of spelling rules based on phonics, letter doubling, and exceptions to rules—not mastered by adulthood—should be replaced by a good dictionary. As spelling mastery is also difficult for adolescents, the recommendation is the same. Learning the use of a dictionary and thesaurus is, overall, a rewarding use of time.
Most plurals of nouns that end in hard consonants or hard consonant sounds followed by a silent *e* are made by adding *s*. Some words ending in vowels only add *s*. For example:

fingers, numerals, banks, bugs, riots, homes, gates, radios, bananas

For nouns that end in soft consonant sounds *s, j, x, z, ch,* and *sh,* add *es*. Some nouns ending in *o* also add *es*.

dresses, waxes, churches, brushes, tomatoes

For nouns ending in *y* and preceded by a vowel, just add *s*.

boys, alleys

For nouns ending in *y* and preceded by a consonant, change the *y* to *i* and add *es*.

babies, corollaries, frugalities, poppies

Some nouns' plurals are formed irregularly or remain the same.

>   sheep, deer, children, leaves, oxen

Some nouns derived from foreign words, especially Latin, may make their plurals in two different ways—one of them Anglicized. Sometimes, the meanings are the same; other times, the two plurals are used in slightly different contexts. It is always wise to consult the dictionary.

>   appendices, appendixes   criterion, criteria
>   indexes, indices   crisis, crises

Make the plurals of closed (solid) compound words in the usual way.

>   timelines, hairpins

Some nouns with suffixes such as *ful*, can make their plurals on the root word OR the total word:

>   cupsful or cupfuls (Check the dictionary if you are unsure)

Make the plurals of open or hyphenated compounds by adding the change in inflection to the word that changed in number.

>   fathers-in-law, courts-martial, masters of art, doctors of medicine

Make the plurals of letters, numbers, and abbreviations by adding *s*.

>   fives and tens, IBMs, 1990s, *p*s and *q*s (Note that letters are italicized.)

Possessives

Make the possessives of singular nouns by adding an apostrophe followed by the letter *s* ('s).

>   baby's bottle, father's job, elephant's eye, teacher's desk, sympathizer's protests, week's postponement

Make the possessive of singular nouns ending in *s* by adding either an apostrophe or an ('s) depending upon common usage or sound. When making the possessive causes difficulty, use a prepositional phrase instead. Even with the sibilant ending, it is advisable to use the ('s) construction (with a few exceptions).

>   dress's color, species' characteristics or characteristics of the species, James' hat or James's hat, Delores's shirt.

Make the possessive of plural nouns ending in *s* by adding the apostrophe after the *s.*

> horses' coats, jockeys' times, four days' time

Make possessives of plural nouns that do not end in *s* the same as singular nouns by adding 's.

> children's shoes, deer's antlers, cattle's horns

Make possessives of compound nouns by adding the inflection at the end of the word or phrase.

> the mayor of Los Angeles' campaign, the mailman's new truck, the mailmen's new trucks, my father-in-law's first wife, the keepsakes' values, several daughters-in-law's husbands

Note: Because a gerund functions as a noun, any noun preceding it and operating as a possessive adjective must reflect the necessary inflection. However, if the gerundive following the noun is a participle, no inflection is added.

The general was perturbed by the private's sleeping on duty. (The word *sleeping* is a gerund, the object of the preposition *by).*

> but

The general was perturbed to see the private sleeping on duty. (The word *sleeping* is a participle modifying private.)

Mechanics in Writing

The candidate should be cognizant of proper rules and conventions of punctuation, capitalization, and spelling. Competency exams will generally test the ability to apply more advanced skills; thus, a limited number of more frustrating rules are presented here. Rules should be applied according to the American style of English, i.e. spelling *theater* instead of *theatre* and placing terminal marks of punctuation almost exclusively within other marks of punctuation.

CAPITALIZATION

Capitalize all proper names of persons (including specific organizations or agencies of government); places (countries, states, cities, parks, and specific geographical areas); things (political parties, structures, historical and cultural terms, and calendar and time designations); and religious terms (any deity, revered person or group, sacred writings).

> Percy Bysshe Shelley, Argentina, Mount Rainier National Park, Grand Canyon, League of Nations, the Sears Tower, Birmingham, Lyric Theater, Americans, Midwesterners, Democrats, Renaissance, Boy Scouts of America, Easter, God, Bible, Dead Sea Scrolls, Koran
> Capitalize proper adjectives and titles used with proper names.
> California gold rush, President John Adams, Homeric epic, Romanesque architecture, Senator John Glenn

Note: Some words that represent titles and offices are not capitalized unless used with a proper name.

Capitalized	**Not Capitalized**
Congressman McKay	the congressman from Florida
Commander Alger	commander of the Pacific Fleet
Queen Elizabeth	the queen of England

Capitalize all main words in titles of works of literature, art, and music. (See "Using Italics" in the Punctuation section.)

PUNCTUATION

Using Terminal Punctuation in Relation to Quotation Marks

In a quoted statement that is either declarative or imperative, place the period inside the closing quotation marks.

> "The airplane crashed on the runway during takeoff."

If the quotation is followed by other words in the sentence, place a comma inside the closing quotation marks and a period at the end of the sentence.

> "The airplane crashed on the runway during takeoff," said the announcer.

In most instances in which a quoted title or expression occurs at the end of a sentence, the period is placed before either the single or double quotation marks.

> "The middle school readers were unprepared to understand Bryant's poem 'Thanatopsis.'"

Early book-length adventure stories like *Don Quixote* and *The Three Musketeers* were known as "picaresque novels."

There are instances in which the final quotation mark does precede the period—for example, if the content of the sentence is about a speech or quote in which the meaning could be confused by the placement of the period.

The first thing out of his mouth was "Hi, I'm home." *but*
The first line of his speech began "I arrived home to an empty house".

In sentences that are interrogatory or exclamatory, the question mark or exclamation point should be positioned outside the closing quotation marks if the quote itself is a statement, command, or cited title.

- Who decided to lead us in the recitation of the "Pledge of Allegiance"?
- Why was Tillie shaking as she began her recitation, "Once upon a midnight dreary..."?
- I was embarrassed when Mrs. White said, "Your slip is showing"!

In sentences that are declarative but the quotation is a question or an exclamation, place the question mark or exclamation point inside the quotation marks.

- The hall monitor yelled, "Fire! Fire!"
- "Fire! Fire!" yelled the hall monitor.
- Cory shrieked, "Is there a mouse in the room?" (In this instance, the question supersedes the exclamation.)

Using Double Quotation Marks with Other Punctuation

Quotations—whether words, phrases, or clauses—should be punctuated according to the rules of the grammatical function they serve in the sentence.

The works of Shakespeare, "the bard of Avon," have been contested as originating with other authors.
"You'll get my money," the old man warned, "when 'Hell freezes over'."
Sheila cited the passage that began "Four score and seven years ago...."
(Note the ellipsis followed by an enclosed period.)
"Old Ironsides" inspired the preservation of the U.S.S. Constitution.

Use quotation marks to enclose the titles of shorter works: songs, short poems, short stories, essays, and chapters of books. (See "Using Italics" for punctuating longer titles.)

"The Tell-Tale Heart"   "Casey at the Bat"   "America the Beautiful"

Using Periods with Parentheses or Brackets

Place the period inside the parentheses or brackets if they enclose a complete sentence, independent of the other sentences around it.

Stephen Crane was a confirmed alcohol and drug addict. (He admitted as much to other journalists in Cuba.)

If the parenthetical expression is a statement inserted within another statement, the period in the enclosure is omitted.

Mark Twain used the character Indian Joe (who also appeared in *The Adventures of Tom Sawyer*) as a foil for Jim in *The Adventures of Huckleberry Finn*.

When enclosed matter comes at the end of a sentence requiring quotation marks, place the period outside the parentheses or brackets.

"The secretary of state consulted with the ambassador [Albright]."

Using Commas

Separate two or more coordinate adjectives modifying the same word and three or more nouns, phrases, or clauses in a list.

Maggie's hair was dull, dirty, and lice-ridden.

Dickens portrayed the Artful Dodger as skillful pickpocket, loyal follower of Fagin, and defendant of Oliver Twist.

Ellen daydreamed about getting out of the rain, taking a shower, and eating a hot dinner.

In Elizabethan England, Ben Johnson wrote comedy, Christopher Marlowe wrote tragedies, and William Shakespeare composed both.

Use commas to separate antithetical or complimentary expressions from the rest of the sentence.

The veterinarian, not his assistant, would perform the delicate surgery.
The more he knew about her, the less he wished he had known.
Randy hopes to, and probably will, get an appointment to the Naval Academy.
His thorough, though esoteric, scientific research could not easily be understood by high school students.

Using Semicolons

Use semicolons to separate independent clauses when the second clause is introduced by a transitional adverb. (These clauses may also be written as separate sentences, preferably by placing the adverb within the second sentence.)

The Elizabethans modified the rhyme scheme of the sonnet; thus, it was called the English sonnet.

Or

The Elizabethans modified the rhyme scheme of the sonnet. It was thus called the English sonnet.

Use semicolons to separate items in a series that are long and complex or have internal punctuation.

The Italian Renaissance produced masters in the fine arts: Dante Alighieri, author of the *Divine Comedy;* Leonardo da Vinci, painter of *The Last Supper;* and Donatello, sculptor of the *Quattro Coronati*, the four saints.

The leading scorers in the WNBA were: Zheng Haixia, averaging 23.9 points per game; Lisa Leslie, 22; and Cynthia Cooper, 19.5.

When using a semicolon in conjunction with quotation marks, the semicolon falls outside the final quotation mark (even when a period applied in the same situation falls inside the final quotation mark).

Jane Austen's final novel was "Persuasion."

But

Jane Austen's final novel was "Persuasion"; some critics consider it her best work.

Using Colons

Place a colon at the beginning of a list of items. (Note its use in the sentence about Renaissance Italians in the previous section.)

The teacher directed us to compare Faulkner's three symbolic novels: *Absalom, Absalom; As I Lay Dying;* and *Light in August*.

Do **not** use a colon if the list is preceded by a verb in an independent clause, as it separates the verb from its object.

> Three of Faulkner's symbolic novels are Absalom, Absalom; As I Lay Dying, and Light in August. (no colon after "are')

Using Dashes

Place dashes to denote sudden breaks in thought.

> Some periods in literature—the Romantic Age, for example—spanned different time periods in different countries.

Use dashes instead of commas if commas are already used elsewhere in the sentence for amplification or explanation.

> The Fireside Poets included three Brahmans—James Russell Lowell, Henry David Wadsworth, Oliver Wendell Holmes— and John Greenleaf Whittier.

Use italics to punctuate the titles of long works of literature, names of periodical publications, musical scores, works of art and motion picture television, and radio programs. (When unable to write in italics, students should be instructed to underline in their own writing where italics would be appropriate.)

The Idylls of the King	*Hiawatha*	*The Sound and the Fury*
Mary Poppins	*Newsweek*	*The Nutcracker Suite*

SKILL 4.7 **Demonstrating knowledge of various types of sentence structures (e.g., declarative, interrogative) and identifying appropriate corrections of errors in sentence structure (e.g., run-on sentences, misplaced modifiers, sentence fragments**

Teachers can instruct students to classify a sentence structure according to its purpose. Have the students ask themselves, "Why did the writer write this sentence this way?" The answer is then likely to lead them to the function of the sentence classification. Students can then classify sentences based on their purpose.

There are four types of sentences: declarative, interrogative, imperative, and exclamatory.

- A **declarative sentence** makes a statement and ends with a period. Declarative sentences consist of a subject and a predicate.
- An **interrogative sentence** asks a question and ends with a question mark, in addition to having a different tonal pattern (often a raised tone near the end of the sentence).
- An **imperative sentence** gives a command or makes a request. Sometimes the subject of an imperative sentence (you) is understood without being written. It usually ends with a period, but can use an explanation mark if it is also an exclamatory sentence (below).
- An **exclamatory sentence** emphasizes a statement (either declarative or imperative), shows strong feeling, and ends with an exclamation mark.

Declarative, imperative, or interrogative sentences can be made into exclamatory sentences by punctuating them with an exclamation point.

Students should be taught to utilize the various sentence types in their writing in order to create and combine diverse sentences for writing effective paragraphs.

Sentence Completeness

Fragments: A sentence fragment is a string of words that is not a complete sentence. In student writing, fragments usually occur 1) if word groups standing alone are missing either a subject or a verb, and 2) if word groups containing a subject and a verb, and standing alone are actually made dependent because of the use of subordinating conjunctions or relative pronouns.

> **Error**: The teacher waiting for the class to complete the assignment.
> **Problem**: This sentence is not complete because an -ing word alone does not function as a verb. When a helping verb is added (for example, was waiting), it will become a sentence.
> **Correction**: The teacher was waiting for the class to complete the assignment.

Run-on sentences: A run-on sentence is a "sentence" made up of independent clauses that should be separated into distinct sentences or joined by a conjunction.

> **Incorrect**: The dog ran into the house he grabbed the toy he jumped up and down.
> **Correct**: The dog ran into the house. He grabbed the toy and jumped up and down.

> Note that this problem can be corrected in more than one way. Avoid fragments and run-on sentences. Recognizing sentence elements necessary to make a complete thought, properly using independent and dependent clauses (see *Independent and dependent clauses*, below), and using correct punctuation will amend such errors.

Clauses-Independent and Dependent (Subordinate)

A clause is simply any group of words containing a subject and a predicate. An **independent clause** can stand alone as a complete sentence.

> Karen has a new puppy. (This has a subject—Karen-- and a predicate--has a new puppy.)

> In order to combine two independent clauses into one sentence, a conjunction is necessary: Karen has a new puppy and bobby has a new kitten. (Without the conjunction, and, this would be a run-on sentence: Karen has a new puppy Bobby has a new kitten.)

A **dependent, or subordinate, clause** has a subject and a predicate, but it cannot stand alone as a sentence. It depends upon an independent clause to express a complete thought.

We watched the movie that Pat had rented. (*that Pat had rented* is a dependent or subordinate clause. it has a subject—Pat—and a predicate—had rented—but it cannot stand alone. "That Pat had rented" is not a sentence. It would be a fragment standing alone. It modifies the object of the independent clause: *We watched the **movie**.*)

There are three kinds of dependent clauses:

- A **Noun clause** is a clause (with a subject and a predicate) that serves as a noun. it can function as a noun in any position where a noun can be found in a sentence. Examples with noun clauses in bold:

    o **The sport I like best** is baseball. ("The sport I like best" is the noun subject)

    o I saw **the man catch the ball**. ("the man catch the ball" is the noun object of 'saw')

- An **Adjective clause** is a clause (with subject and predicate) that acts like an adjective and modifies a noun or pronoun. Examples of adjective clauses in bold:

    o We watched the movie **that Pat had rented.** ("that Pat had rented" is an adjective clause modifying the noun, 'movie'.)

    o Mrs. Green, **the woman who babysits for me**, says I was a very good boy. ("the woman who babysits for me" is an adjective clause modifying the noun, 'Mrs. Green'.)

- An **adverb clause** has a subject and predicate and functions as an adverb, modifying a verb, adjective, or another adverb. Examples with adverb clause in bold:

    o **While you are at school**, work hard. ("when you are at school" is an adverb phrase modifying the verb, 'work', telling you when to do it.)

    o You may have a snack **as soon as you finish your homework**. ("as soon as you finish your homework" is an adverb phrase modifying the verb 'have' and telling you when you may have it).

Sentence Structure

Recognize simple, compound, complex, and compound-complex sentences. Use dependent (subordinate) and independent clauses correctly to create these sentence structures.

> **Simple:** Joyce wrote a letter.
> **Compound:** Joyce wrote a letter, and Dot drew a picture. (two independent clauses)
> **Complex:** While Joyce wrote a letter, Dot drew a picture. (use of a subordinate clause)
> **Compound/Complex:** When Mother asked the girls to demonstrate their new-found skills, Joyce wrote a letter, and Dot drew a picture.

Note: *Do not* confuse compound sentence *elements* with compound sentences. Simple sentences with compound subject:

> <u>Joyce</u> and <u>Dot</u> wrote letters.

> The <u>girl</u> in row three and the <u>boy</u> next to her were passing notes across the aisle.

Simple sentence with compound predicate:

> Joyce <u>wrote letters</u> and <u>drew pictures</u>.

> The captain of the high school debate team <u>graduated with honors</u> and <u>studied broadcast journalism in college</u>.

Simple sentence with compound object of preposition:

> Colleen graded the students' essays for <u>style</u> and <u>mechanical accuracy</u>.

Parallelism

Recognize parallel structures using phrases (prepositional, gerund, participial, and infinitive) and omissions from sentences that create the lack of parallelism.

Prepositional Phrase/Single Modifier

> **Incorrect:** Colleen ate the ice cream with enthusiasm and hurriedly. (mixing prepositional phrase and adverb)
> **Correct:** Colleen ate the ice cream with enthusiasm and in a hurry. (two prepositional phrases)
> **Correct:** Colleen ate the ice cream enthusiastically and hurriedly. (two adverbs)

Participial Phrase/Infinitive Phrase

Incorrect: After hiking for hours and to sweat profusely, Joe sat down to rest and drinking water.
Correct: After hiking for hours and sweating profusely, Joe sat down to rest and drink water.

Recognition of Dangling Modifiers

Dangling phrases are attached to sentence parts in a way that create ambiguity and incorrectness of meaning.

Participial Phrase

Incorrect: Hanging from her skirt, Dot tugged at a loose thread. (Is Dot hanging from her skirt?)
Correct: Dot tugged at a loose thread hanging from her skirt. (Ah, it's the thread that is hanging.)

Incorrect: Relaxing in the bathtub, the telephone rang.
Correct: While I was relaxing in the bathtub, the telephone rang.

Infinitive Phrase

Incorrect: To improve his behavior, the dean warned Fred. (*Whose* behavior needed improvement?)
Correct: The dean warned Fred to improve his behavior. (Ah, Fred's behavior needs improvement.)

Prepositional Phrase

Incorrect: On the floor, Father saw the dog eating table scraps. (*Who's* on the floor?)
Correct: Father saw the dog eating table scraps on the floor. (Ah, the dog is on the floor, as are the scraps.)

Recognition of Syntactical Redundancy or Omission

These errors occur when superfluous words have been added to a sentence or key words have been omitted from a sentence.

Redundancy

Incorrect: Joyce made sure that when her plane arrived **that** she retrieved all of her luggage.
Correct: Joyce made sure that when her plane arrived she retrieved all of her luggage.

Incorrect: He was a **mere** skeleton of his former self.
Correct: He was a skeleton of his former self.

Omission

Incorrect: Dot opened her book, recited her textbook, and answered the teacher's subsequent question.
Correct: Dot opened her book, recited **from** the textbook, and answered the teacher's subsequent question.

Avoidance of Double Negatives

This error occurs from positioning two negatives that, in fact, cancel each other's meaning.

Incorrect: Dot did**n't** have **no** double negatives in her paper.
Correct: Dot didn't have any double negatives in her paper.

OBJECTIVE 5   UNDERSTAND SKILLS AND STRATEGIES INVOLVED IN SPEAKING, LISTENING, AND VIEWING ACROSS THE CURRICULUM

SKILL 5.1   Applying knowledge of conventions (e.g., turn taking, responding to questions with appropriate information) of one-on-one and group verbal interactions[s14]

Communication occurs when one person sends a message and gets a response from another person. In fact, whenever two people can see or hear each other, they are communicating. The sender is the person who communicates the message; the receiver is the person who ultimately responds to the message. Once the response is given, the receiver changes roles and becomes the sender. The communication process may break down if the receiver's interpretation differs from that of the sender. It can also break down if sender and receiver are simply not following the same pragmatic social rules about communication.

Pragmatics refers to the set of rules and social skills that govern communication and social interaction. Pragmatics includes the rules of language as well as the accepted interpersonal behavior code such as taking turns, looking at the speaker, etc. These pragmatic rules can differ from culture to culture and even from one social setting to another. Most children learn their pragmatics at home as they interact with family and friends and as their language and cognitive ability develop. However, Gresham (1995) states that one of the most important venues for the development of these communication skills is the modern school. Children will arrive at school with varying amounts of background experience with communication and interpersonal interaction. Some will come from families who spend a lot of time talking to and with the children, or they will have spent time in play groups, or day care interacting verbally with adults and other children. Others will have had little opportunity to interact with other children, and may have socially impoverished backgrounds with little adult interaction and verbal stimulation. In addition, students with some disabilities (e.g., Autism spectrum disorders) may have extreme difficulty with such pragmatics.

Once in school, however, a more structured code of pragmatics is in place. Students raise their hands to ask or answer questions. They are expected to take turns in conversation and to make comments or replies that are relevant to the topic being discussed. They are expected to use appropriate oral cadence and prosody when they speak (e.g., down tone when ending a declarative sentence, or a lilt at the end for a question). They are expected to attend to each member of the conversational group as each speaks and to keep track of the flow and context of communication as it moves from person to person. They are expected to display certain elements of body language, such as looking at the speaker (in mainstream American culture), and nodding, etc.

Depending upon the developmental level of the students, teachers will need to make social communication and pragmatics skills a part of the regular curriculum. Skills to be covered might include

- Initiating conversations appropriately
- Participating in conversations appropriately (staying on topic)
- Taking turns in conversations
- Attending to others in conversations, both one on one and in groups
- Answering questions appropriately
- Understanding and displaying appropriate body language
- Manners and politeness
- Appreciating another's perspective (as appropriate developmentally)

Some of the methods the teacher can use to teach and reinforce these skills:

- Modeling
- Role play
- Guided practice
- Show and Tell or Book reviews where students relay straightforward information to the class
- Social stories and scripts
- Short plays and drama
- Video instruction
- Games and activities
- Reinforcement schedules and prizes to be used throughout the school year when the teacher sees a target behavior

SKILL 5.2   Analyzing ways in which oral language (e.g., grammar, usage), verbal cues (e.g., word choice, tone, volume) and nonverbal cues (e.g., body language, eye contact) affect communication in various situations

Verbal and nonverbal communication

It is the teacher's responsibility not only to provide instruction in communication skills, but to serve as a model for good communication skills, as well. Unclear communication between the teacher and students sometimes contributes to problems in academic and behavioral situations. In the learning environment, unclear communication can add to the students' confusion about certain processes or skills they are attempting to master.

There are many ways in which the teacher can improve the clarity of her communication. Giving clear, precise directions is one. Verbal directions can be simplified by using shorter sentences, familiar words, and relevant explanations.

Asking a student to repeat directions or to demonstrate understanding of them by carrying out the instructions is an effective way of monitoring the clarity of expression. In addition, clarification can be achieved by the use of concrete objects, multidimensional teaching aids, and by modeling or demonstrating what should be done in a practice situation.

Finally, a teacher can clarify her communication by using a variety of vocal inflections. The use of intonation can help make the message clearer, as can pauses at significant points in the communication. For example, verbal praise should be spoken with inflection that communicates sincerity. Pausing before starting key words, or stressing those that convey meanings, helps students learn concepts being taught.

Teachers can not only demonstrate these techniques, they might also use them in mini-lessons at appropriate times. When the teacher notices a communication issue in the class, an appropriate mini-lesson can be conducted, either with the class as a whole or with a small group of students who need the practice.

Paraphrasing

Paraphrasing, that is, restating what the speaker says using one's own words, can improve communication in many situations and learning to use this skill in the classroom can be helpful to students and teachers alike. First, when the teacher demonstrates paraphrasing by restating what the student has communicated, the teacher is not judging the content; she is simply relating what she understands the message to be. If the message has been interpreted differently from the way intended, the student is asked to clarify. Clarification should continue until both parties are satisfied that the message has been understood.

The act of paraphrasing sends the message that the teacher is trying to better understand the student. Restating the student's message as fairly and accurately as possible assists the teacher in seeing things from the student's perspective. It also reassures the student that the teacher is actually paying attention to the student's message and cares about what the student has to say.

Paraphrasing if often a simple restatement of what has been said. Lead-ins such as, "Your position is…" or "It seems to you that…" are helpful in paraphrasing a student's messages. A student's statement of, "I am not going to do my math today," might be paraphrased by the teacher as, "Did I understand you to say that you are not going to do your math today?" By mirroring what the student has just said, the teacher has telegraphed a caring attitude for that student and a desire to respond accurately to his message.

To paraphrase a student's message effectively, the teacher should

- restate the student's message in her own words;

preface her paraphrasing with such remarks as, "You feel..." or "I hear you say that..."; and avoid indicating any approval or disapproval of the student's statements.

Johnson (1978) states the following as a rule to remember when paraphrasing: "Before you can reply to a statement, restate what the sender says, feels, and means correctly and to the sender's satisfaction." (p.139)

Descriptive feedback is a factual, objective (i.e., unemotional) recounting of a behavioral situation or message sent by a student. Descriptive feedback has the same effect as paraphrasing in that: (1) when responding to a student's statement, the teacher restates (i.e., paraphrases) what the student has said, or factually describes what she has seen, and (2) it allows the teacher to check her perceptions of the student and his message. A student may do or say something, but because of the teacher's feelings or state of mind, the student's message or behavior might be totally misunderstood. The teacher's descriptive feedback, which Johnson (1972) refers to as "understanding," indicates that the teacher's intent is to respond only to ask the student whether his statement or behavior has been understood, how he feels about the problem, and how he perceives the problem. The intent of the teacher is to more clearly "understand" what the student is saying, feeling, or perceiving in relation to a stated message or a behavioral event.

Evaluative feedback is verbalized perception by the teacher that judges, evaluates, approves, or disapproves of the statements made by the student. Evaluative feedback occurs when the student makes a statement and the teacher responds openly with, "I think you're wrong," "That was a dumb thing to do," or "I agree with you entirely." The tendency to give evaluative responses is heightened in situations where feelings and emotions are deeply involved. The stronger the feelings, the more likely it is that two persons will each evaluate the other's statements or behaviors solely from his or her own point of view.

Since evaluative feedback intones a judgmental approval or disapproval of the student's remark or behavior; in most instances, it can be a major barrier to mutual understanding and effective communication. However, evaluative feedback typically has a different purpose than descriptive feedback. It is, of course, a necessary mechanism for providing feedback of a quantitative (and sometimes qualitative) instructional nature (e.g., test scores, homework results, classroom performance). It is also necessary to provide reinforcement and praise for student progress and effort. In order to be effective, evaluative feedback must be offered in a factual, constructive manner. Evaluative feedback is not, however, particularly effective in *simply determining whether communication has been effective.* Descriptive feedback tends to reduce defensiveness and feelings of being threatened because it will most likely communicate that the teacher is interested in the student as a person, has an accurate understanding of the student and what he is saying, and encourages the student to elaborate and further discuss his problems.

Nonverbal Communication and Responding to Feelings

Not all communication is delivered in a verbal manner. Indeed, words spoken are not always true indicators of what a person means and feels. Non-verbal communication, such as body language, facial expression, tone of voice, and speaking patterns, are all clues to the underlying message the student is attempting to deliver. The teacher demonstrates her willingness to listen by sitting close, leaning forward, making eye-to-eye contact, and showing understanding by nodding or smiling. By so doing, she is sending the message that she cares, is concerned about the student's feelings, and will take the time necessary to understand what is really being communicated.

To facilitate further communication, the teacher must become an active listener. This involves much more than just restating what the person has said. Her responses must reflect the student's feelings rather than merely the spoken language. It is essential that the teacher say back what she understands the student's message to mean, as well as the feelings she perceives, and asks for correctness of interpretation. Often, teachers enter into active listening, with body language conveying a willingness to listen, but respond in such a way that judgment or disapproval of the underlying message is conveyed. As noted above, evaluative responses from the listener will decrease attempts to communicate. Encouragement toward communicative efforts is enhanced by use of statements rather than questions, when spoken in the present tense and with use of personal pronouns, when reflective of current feelings about the situation, and when offering self-disclosure of similar experiences or feelings if the teacher feels inclined to do so.

Response to the child's feelings is particularly important since his message may not convey what he really feels. For example, a student who has failed a test may feel inadequate and have the need to blame someone else, such as his teacher, for his failure. The student might say to his teacher, "You didn't tell me that you were including all the words from the last six weeks on the spelling test." The teacher, if she were to respond solely to the spoken message, might say, "I know I told you that you would be tested over the entire unit. You just weren't listening!" The intuitive, sensitive teacher would look beyond the spoken words by saying, "You're telling me that it feels bad to fail a test." By responding to the child's feelings, the teacher lets him know her understanding of his personal crisis, and the student is encouraged to communicate further

Teachers can also construct short lessons and practice activities where students can practice these skills themselves. The teacher can ask students to paraphrase something she has told them to be sure they understand. She might have an oral activity where each student makes a brief statement about some issue and the next student needs to paraphrase it, etc. Similar activities can be designed for other elements of communication.

To summarize, in the learning environment, as in all situations, effective communication depends upon good sending and receiving skills. Teaching and managing students involves good communication. By using clear, non-threatening feedback, the teacher can provide students with information that helps them to understand themselves better, while at the same time providing a clearer understanding of each student on the teacher's part.

Public Speaking

In addition to everyday classroom and interpersonal communication situations, students will often be required to make oral reports or presentation in various content areas. Analyzing the speech of others is a very good technique for helping students to improve their own public speaking abilities. In most circumstances, because students cannot view themselves as they give speeches and presentations, they begin to learn what works and what doesn't work in effective public speaking when they get the opportunity to critique, question, and analyze others' speeches. However, a very important word of warning: DO NOT have students critique each others' public speaking skills. It could be very damaging to a student to have his or her peers point out what did not work in a speech. Instead, video is a great tool teachers can use. Any appropriate source of public speaking can be used in the classroom for students to analyze and critique.

Some of the things students can pay attention to include the following:

- **Volume:** A speaker should use an appropriate volume—not too loud to be annoying, but not too soft to be inaudible.
- **Pace:** The rate at which words are spoken should be appropriate—not too fast to make the speech incomprehensible, but not too slow so as to put listeners to sleep.
- **Pronunciation**: A speaker should make sure words are spoken clearly. Listeners do not have a text to go back to, and they cannot re-read things they didn't catch.
- **Body language:** While animated body language can help a speech, too much of it can be distracting. Body language should help to convey the message, not detract from it.
- **Word choice:** The words speakers choose should be consistent with their intended purpose as well as the audience.
- **Visual aids:** Visual aids, like body language, should enhance a message. Many visual aids can be distracting, which can detract from the message.

Overall, instead of telling students to keep these above factors in mind when presenting information orally, it may be beneficial to have them view speakers who do these things both well and poorly. Witnessing other speakers first-hand will help students to remember the "rules" the next time they give a speech.

Mini-lessons and guided practice of specific oral speaking techniques can also be helpful. Keeping all these things in mind can be difficult for young students. Instead, choose one of these factors at a time and provide brief, but repeated practice on it. For example, have a day when short readings or very brief presentation already made for the student are practiced at different volume or with different gestures, etc. After each individual skill has been practiced, begin to put them together and practice two or three at a time, depending upon the skill level of the students. This is a good place to differentiate your lessons. More advanced students can practice more complex presentations or more skills at a time, while struggling students can practice simpler, one dimensional presentations.

SKILL 5.3 Demonstrating knowledge of strategies for promoting effective listening skills

Listening is not a skill that is talked about much, except when someone clearly does not listen. The truth is, however, listening is a very specific skill for very specific circumstances. There are two aspects to listening that warrant attention. The first is comprehension. This is simply understanding what someone says, the reasons behind the message, and the context in which it is said. The second is purpose. Once you understand the message, what are you supposed to do with it? Just nod and smile? Go out and take action? Often, when we understand the purpose of listening in various contexts, comprehension will be much easier. Furthermore, when we know the purpose of listening, we can better adjust our comprehension strategies.

Oral speech can be very difficult to follow, as listeners typically have no written record in which to "re-read" things they didn't hear or understand and the auditory message must be kept in working memory while trying to understand it. In addition, oral speech can be much less structured than written language. At the same time, many of the skills and strategies that help students in reading comprehension can help them in listening comprehension. For example, as soon as we start listening to something new, we should tap into our prior knowledge in order to attach new information to what we already know. This will not only help in understanding, but it will also assist in remembering the material.

We can also look for transitions between ideas. Sometimes, in oral speech, this is fairly simple to find (such as when voice tone or body language change). Although we don't have the luxury of looking at paragraphs in oral language, we do have the animation that comes along with live speech. Human beings have to try very hard to be completely non-expressive in their speech. Listeners should take advantage of this and notice how the speaker changes character and voice to signal a transition of ideas.

Listeners can also better comprehend the underlying intent of a speaker when they notice nonverbal cues. For example, looking to see an expression on the face of a speaker that signals irony is often simpler than trying to extract irony from written words.

One good way to follow oral speech is to take notes and outline major points. Because oral speech can be more circular (as opposed to linear) than written text, it can be of great assistance to keep track of an author's message. Students can practice this strategy in many ways in the classroom, including taking notes during the teacher's oral messages as well as other students' presentations and speeches.

In many cultures and individual family homes, listening is often done for the purpose of enjoyment. We like to listen to stories; we enjoy poetry; we like radio dramas and theater. Listening to literature can also be a great pleasure. The problem today is that many students have not learned to extract great pleasure on a wide-spread scale from listening to literature, poetry, or language read aloud. Perhaps that is because we have not done a good job of showing students how listening to literature (or other oral communications) can indeed be more interesting than television or video games. In the classrooms of exceptional teachers, we will often find that students are captivated by the reading aloud of good literature. It is refreshing and enjoyable to just sit and soak in the language, story, and poetry of literature when it is read to us. Therefore, we must teach students *how* to listen and enjoy such work. We do this by making it fun and giving many possibilities and alternatives to capture the wide array of interests in each classroom.

Strategies to Enhance Listening Comprehension

Within the classroom setting, many opportunities will present themselves for students to speak and listen for various purposes and often these may be spontaneous. Activities for speaking and listening should be integrated throughout the language arts program, but there should also be times when speaking and listening are the focus of the instruction. By incorporating speaking and listening across the curriculum, students will begin to see the connection between the two and many ways these skills can be applied to all aspects of learning. In addition to reading aloud to children, several other classroom strategies can improve listening comprehension in various contexts:

Wordless picture books can be used to allow children to practice oral story telling skills, as well as to provide oral descriptions of pictures. This can be done by individual students, or the class as a group can make a sequential story in which each child's contribution is in part determined by the previous child's addition. This enhances both oral and listening skills, as well as cognitive concepts of making events match and follow a logical sequence.

Visualizing and describing what you see or visualize to other students so they can draw or describe it also promotes both oral language and listening skills. A variety of games and activities can use this format. These skills will contribute to eventual comprehension and writing tasks.

Oral Sharing and Questioning of all sorts can be helpful in developing language and listening skills. Whether it is "show and tell" time, book report time, or "news of the day" time, follow each child's sharing with several questions or comments from the audience and be sure everyone gets a chance to ask questions. This is an opportunity to help students learn to listen and make responses based on what they heard.

Listening for specific information in stories or articles read aloud to students is also helpful. If students are told to raise a hand when they hear a certain word or piece of information (or, for more inferential tasks, a *clue* of some sort), they will listen with more purpose. In addition, the resulting experience is very close to what they will need to do later when they must refer to something they have read to find specific information.

Listening to classmates is another skill that can improve language development. In any classroom discussion, the teacher can periodically ask a student what a classmate just said. This forces them to listen to one another and not only to attend, but to process the meaning of one another's comments.

Good listeners will respond emotionally, imaginatively, and intellectually to what they hear. Students need to be taught how to respond to presentations or comments by their classmates in ways that are not harmful or derogatory in any way. There are also different types of listening that the teacher can develop in the students:

Additional ways that speaking and listening can be integrated include:

- Conversations
- Small group discussions
- Brainstorming
- Interviewing
- Oral reading
- Readers' theater
- Choral speaking
- Storytelling
- Role playing
- Class debates
- Listening to guest speakers

For older or more advanced students, teachers can do mini-lessons on different purposes for listening:

- Appreciative listening to enjoy an experience
- Attentive listening to gain knowledge
- Critical listening to evaluate arguments and ideas

Setting a purpose: Many times it is obvious that students are hearing what the speaker is saying, but are not actively listening. Setting the purpose for an oral presentation and providing graphic organizers are two strategies that help structure listening activities. Having to develop graphic organizer gives students a purpose for listening and makes them focus on distinguishing between relevant and irrelevant information.

SKILL 5.4 Recognizing types, characteristics, and roles of visual and oral media (e.g., television, radio, film, electronic media)

The use of the media, television, radio, film, internet resources, and other electronic sources has become an asset in teaching, as they encourage students to practice critical thinking. The use of media offers new ways of engaging students in learning and in making connections among themselves, between school and life, and between educators and the outside world. Teachers should utilize a variety of media, as it is through the media that our culture largely expresses itself.

Media literacy is an informed, critical understanding gleaned from verbal and visual symbols that are experienced every day through television, radio, computers, and other electronic sources. Teachers should be aware of the need for students to develop critical *viewing* abilities along with critical *thinking* abilities when viewing various types of media. Critical viewing involves examining the techniques and characteristics that are involved in media production, critically analyzing media messages, and recognizing the roles that audiences play in deriving meaning from those messages.

When listening to a radio program, viewing a film, or watching a television program, students should ask themselves some key questions:

- What is this program's point of view?
- What persuasive techniques are used?
- What evidence is used to support the program's argument?
- Is there a media stereotyping, or are there correct representations of gender, race, and ethnicity?

Teachers should have an understanding of how to select, evaluate, and use information from television, radio, film, and electronic media sources. The key component of media literacy is understanding the symbols, information, ideas, values, and messages that emanate from the media. Teachers should make appropriate media selections by analyzing the various instructional media programs available. This will help them to achieve learning goals, which, after all, is the reason for the use of technology. See also Skill 4.05 for additional comments on internet and computer media use.

SKILL 5.5 **Demonstrating knowledge of the structures and elements of oral, visual, and multimedia presentations for diverse audiences and for various purposes**

The media's impact on today's society is immense and ever-increasing. As children, we watch programs on television that are amazingly fast-paced and visually rich. Parents' roles as verbal and moral teachers are diminishing in response to the much more stimulating guidance of the television set. Adolescence, which used to be the time for going out and exploring the world first-hand, is now consumed by the allure of MTV, popular music, and video games.

At the same time, the media's effect on society is also beneficial and progressive. In particular, its effect on education provides special challenges and opportunities for teachers and students.

Thanks to satellite technology, instructional radio and television programs can be received by urban classrooms and rural villages. CD-ROMs allow students to learn information through a virtual reality experience. The Internet allows instant access to unlimited data and connects people across cultures. Educational media, when used in a productive way, enrich instruction and make it more individualized, accessible, and economical.

Multimedia Teaching Model

Step 1. Diagnose
- Figure out what students need to know.
- Assess what students already know.

Step 2. Design
- Design tests of learning achievement.
- Identify effective instructional strategies.
- Select suitable media.
- Sequence learning activities within the program.
- Plan introductory activities.
- Plan follow-up activities.

Step 3. Procure
- Secure materials at hand.
- Obtain new materials.

Step 4. Produce
- Modify existing materials.
- Craft new materials.

Step 5. Refine
- Conduct a small-scale test of the program.
- Evaluate procedures and achievements.
- Revise the program accordingly.
- Conduct a classroom test of the program.
- Evaluate procedures and achievements.
- Revise the program in anticipation of the next school term.

Tips for Using Print Media and Visual Aids

- Use pictures over words whenever possible.
- Present one key point per visual.
- Use no more than three to four colors per visual to avoid clutter and confusion.
- Use contrasting colors such as dark blue and bright yellow.
- Use a maximum of twenty-five to thirty-five numbers per visual aid.
- Use bullets instead of paragraphs whenever possible.
- Make sure it is student-centered, not media-centered. The delivery is just as important as the media presented.

Tips for Using Film and Television

- Study the programs in advance.
- Obtain supplementary materials such as printed transcripts of the narrative or study guides.
- Provide students with background information, explain unfamiliar concepts, and anticipate outcomes.
- Assign outside readings based on the students' viewing.
- Ask cuing questions.
- Watch along with the students.
- Observe the students' reactions.
- Construct lessons and worksheets based on the video or presentation
- Follow up the viewing with discussions and related activities.

SUBAREA 2   MATHEMATICS

OBJECTIVE 6   UNDERSTAND APPROACHES FOR EXPLORING
                MATHEMATICS AND SOLVING PROBLEMS AND
                CONCEPTS AND SKILLS RELATED TO NUMBERS AND
                MATHEMATICAL OPERATIONS AND PROCESSES

SKILL 6.1   Applying concepts of quantities, numbers, and numeration to
              compare, order, estimate, and round

Rational numbers can be expressed as the ratio of two integers, $\frac{a}{b}$ where b ≠ 0,
for example $\frac{2}{3}$, $-\frac{4}{5}$, $5 = \frac{5}{1}$.

Rational numbers include integers, fractions, mixed numbers, and terminating
and repeating decimals. Every rational number can be expressed as a repeating
or terminating decimal and can be shown on a number line.

Integers are positive and negative whole numbers, and zero.
...-6, -5, -4, -3, -2, -1, 0, 1, 2, 3, 4, 5, 6...

Whole numbers are natural numbers and zero.
0, 1, 2, 3, 4, 5, 6...

Natural numbers are the counting numbers.
1, 2, 3, 4, 5, 6...

Irrational numbers are real numbers that cannot be written as the ratio of two
integers. These are infinite non-repeating decimals.

Examples:
$\sqrt{5}$ = 2.2360.., pi =π = 3.1415927...

A **fraction** is an expression of numbers in the form of x/y, where x is the
numerator and y is the denominator, which cannot be zero.

Example:
$\frac{3}{7}$ 3 is the numerator; 7 is the denominator

If the fraction has common factors for the numerator and denominator, divide
both by the common factor to reduce the fraction to its lowest form.

Example:
$$\frac{13}{39} = \frac{1 \times 13}{3 \times 13} = \frac{1}{3}$$ Divide by the common factor 13

A **mixed** number has an integer part and a fractional part.

Example:

$$2\frac{1}{4}, \ ^-5\frac{1}{6}, \ 7\frac{1}{3}$$

Percent = per 100 (written with the symbol %)

Example:

$$10\% = \frac{10}{100} = \frac{1}{10}$$

Decimals = deci = part of ten

To find the decimal equivalent of a fraction, use the denominator to divide the numerator, as shown in the following example.

Example:

Find the decimal equivalent of $\frac{7}{10}$.

Since 10 cannot divide into 7 evenly

$$\frac{7}{10} = 0.7$$

The **exponent form** is a shortcut method to write repeated multiplication. Basic form: b^n, where b is called the base and n is the exponent. Both b and n are real numbers. The b^n implies that the base b is multiplied by itself n times.

Examples:

$$3^4 = 3 \times 3 \times 3 \times 3 = 81$$

$$2^3 = 2 \times 2 \times 2 = 8$$

$$(^-2)^4 = (^-2) \times (^-2) \times (^-2) \times (^-2) = 16$$

$$^-2^4 = ^-(2 \times 2 \times 2 \times 2) = ^-16$$

Key exponent rules:

For 'a' nonzero, and 'm' and 'n' real numbers:

1) $a^m \cdot a^n = a^{(m+n)}$ Product rule[SAW18]

2) $\dfrac{a^m}{a^n} = a^{(m-n)}$ Quotient rule

3) $\dfrac{a^{-m}}{a^{-n}} = \dfrac{a^n}{a^m}$ Negative rule

When 10 is raised to any power, the exponent tells the numbers of zeroes in the product.

<u>Example</u>:

$10^7 = 10,000,000$

Caution: Unless the negative sign is inside the parentheses and the exponent is outside the parentheses, the sign is not affected by the exponent.

$(^-2)^4$ implies that -2 is multiplied by itself 4 times.

$^-2^4$ implies that 2 is multiplied by itself 4 times, then the answer is negated.

Scientific notation is a more convenient method for writing very large and very small numbers. It employs two factors. The first factor is a number between 1 and 10. The second factor is a power of 10. This notation is a "shorthand" for expressing large numbers (like the weight of 100 elephants) or small numbers (like the weight of an atom in pounds).

Recall that:

$10^n = (10)^n$ Ten multiplied by itself n times.
$10^0 = 1$ A nonzero number raised to power of zero is 1.
$10^1 = 10$
$10^2 = 10 \times 10 = 100$
$10^3 = 10 \times 10 \times 10 = 1000$ (kilo)
$10^{-1} = 1/10$ (deci)
$10^{-2} = 1/100$ (centi)
$10^{-3} = 1/1000$ (milli)
$10^{-6} = 1/1,000,000$ (micro)

Example:

Write 46,368,000 in scientific notation.

1)   Introduce a decimal point and decimal places.
46,368,000 = 46,368,000.0000

2)   Make a mark between the two digits that give a number
between[SAW19]
-9.9 and 9.9.
4 ∧ 6,368,000 .0000

3)   Count the number of digit places between the decimal point and the
∧ mark. This number is the '*n*'-the power of ten.

So, $46,368,000 = 4.6368 \times 10^7$

Example:

Write 0.00397 in scientific notation.

1)   Decimal is already in place.

2)   Make a mark between 3 and 9 to get a one number between
-9.9 and 9.9.

3)   Move decimal place to the mark (3 hops).

0.003 ∧ 97

Motion is to the right, so *n* of 10^n is negative.

Therefore, $0.00397 = 3.97 \times 10^{-3}$

Rounding numbers is a form of estimation that is very useful in many mathematical operations. For example, when estimating the sum of two three-digit numbers, it is helpful to round the two numbers to the nearest hundred prior to addition. Numbers can be rounded to any place value.

To **round whole numbers**, you first find the place value you want to round to (the rounding digit) and look at the digit directly to the right. If the digit is less than five, do not change the rounding digit and replace all numbers after the rounding digit with zeroes. If the digit is greater than or equal to five, increase the rounding digit by one and replace all numbers after the rounding digit with zeroes.

Example:

Round 517 to the nearest ten.

1 is the rounding digit because it occupies the ten's place.

517 rounded to the nearest ten = 520; because 7 > 5, we add 1 to the rounding digit.

Example:

Round 15,449 to the nearest hundred.

The first 4 is the rounding digit because it occupies the hundred's place.

15,449 rounded to the nearest hundred = 15,400; because 4 < 5 we do not add to the rounding digit.

Rounding decimals is identical to rounding whole numbers except that you simply drop all the digits to the right of the rounding digit.

Example:

Round 417.3621 to the nearest tenth.

3 is the rounding digit because it occupies the tenth place.

417.3621 rounded to the nearest tenth = 417.4; because 6 > 5, we add 1 to the rounding digit.

Teaching Strategies Appropriate to the Development of Number Concepts
Numbers appear in many daily situations. Children see numbers on clock faces, on telephone dials or buttons, on mailboxes, on car license plates, on price tags of toys, and on food items. How do children grow in their understanding and use of numbers? Early readiness skills involve classifying, comparing, and ordering numbers, activities that in essence provide some primitive practice in quantification. Stages of concept formation progress as children mature, develop,÷ and experience situations involving numbers.

- **One-to-one Matching**—children may be asked to match the items in two groups, one-by-one and to describe what they find. One group may be identified as having more or less than another.

- **Rote Counting**—many young children can count from one to ten or higher using rote memory. They can name the numbers in correct sequence, but may not really understand what the numbers mean. For example, they may be able to sing number songs, but cannot pick up five blocks upon request.

- **Selection of Correct Number of Objects**—Jean Piaget describes three phases through which children pass in mastering this concept. In the first, a child believes the number changes when the design or number of objects is rearranged. A child in the second phase understands conservation, in the sense that the number is the same no matter how different the set may appear. Children in the final stage can reverse their thinking and understand that the number does not change when objects are returned to their original positions. They can show one-to-one matching of rows of objects. Counting has become meaningful.

- **Ordinality and Cardinality**—*ordinality* refers to the relative position or order of an object within a set in relation to the other objects, like first, second and etc. *Cardinality* answers the question of "How many?" in reference to the total number of objects is a group. When counting, children use numbers cardinally as they say "one" for the first object, "two" for the second, and so on. It helps them to move the objects as they are counted. Thus, when the counting is complete, and children can tell that there are four balls in all, they can use the ordinal for any number of the group. The number "4"—a cardinal—is associated with all four objects; the last is the 4th—an ordinal.

- **Sequencing Numbers to Ten**—prior work in comparing and ordering quantities is gradually extended. Children learn that five, which is more than three, comes after three in counting sequence.

- **Zero**—developmental work with zero occurs within the 1 to 10 sequence rather than first. The meaning of zero as "none at all" is easier for children to understand when they can use it in relations to known quantities. For example, "There were two cookies on the plate. My dad and I each had one. Now they are all gone."

- **Symbols**—children learn to recognize and write numerals in a cognitive manner. The concepts of greater than and less than are also understood. Finally, children learn to name and use numerals of symbols for comparison, even when the objects are no longer present.

- **Sight Groups**—children learn to recognize, without counting, the number of objects in groups having four or less items. Eventually, children will learn to sight sub-groups with larger numbers of objects.

- **Writing numerals**—after children have learned to recognize a numeral and associate it with the correct number of objects, writing is begun. However, even when the focus is on writing, continued reference to quantities named should be made.

- **Sequencing Tasks**—earlier work, in which children used one-to-one matching to tell whether a group has more, less, or as many objects as another, is extended. Children come to recognize that when a number means more, it comes after another in the process of counting. Conversely, when a number means less, it comes before another in counting.

The stages just described serve as precursors in the development of number concepts. The conceptual understanding of number concepts further extends into mathematical operations, place value, re-groupings, and decimals later.

SKILL 6.2 **Demonstrating knowledge of the concepts of place value, prime numbers, multiples, and factors; equivalent forms of common fractions, decimal fractions, percentages, and ratios; and the properties of numbers and the number system (e.g., commutative, associative, distributive, identity, and property of zero)**

Whole Number Place Value
Our math system is a base ten math system. The value of each digit in a number depends on its *place* in the number, hence the term place value.

Consider the number 792. We can assign a place value to each digit.

Reading from left to right, the first digit (7) represents the hundred's place. The hundred's place tells us how many sets of 100 the number contains. Thus, there are 7 sets of 100 in the number 792.

The second digit (9) represents the ten's place. The ten's place tells us how many sets of 10 the number contains. Thus, there are 9 sets of 10 in the number 792.

The last digit (2) represents the one's place. The one's place tells us how many sets of 1 the number contains. Thus, there are 2 sets of 1 in the number 792.

Therefore, there are 7 sets of 100, plus 9 sets of 10, plus 2 sets of 1 in the number 792.

Moving to the left of the decimal point (whole numbers), place value moves through *periods*, each of which has three places (ones, tens, hundreds) within that larger value like this:

ones, tens, hundreds(ones period), thousands, ten thousands, hundred thousand(thousands period), millions, ten millions, hundred millions (millions period), billions (American system), etc.

Decimal Place Value

More complex numbers have additional place values to both the left and right of the decimal point. Consider the number 374.8.

Reading from left to right, the first digit (3) is in the hundred's place; it tells us that the number contains 3 sets of 100.

The second digit (7) is in the ten's place and tells us the number contains 7 sets of 10.

The third digit (4) is in the one's place and tells us the number contains 4 sets of 1.

Finally, the number after the decimal (8) is in the tenth's place; it tells us that the number contains 8 tenths.

Place Value for Older Students

Each digit to the left of the decimal point increases progressively in powers of 10. Each digit to the right of the decimal point decreases progressively in powers of 10.

Example:

12345.6789 occupies the following powers of 10 positions:

10^4	10^3	10^2	10^1	10^0	0	10^{-1}	10^{-2}	10^{-3}	10^{-4}
1	2	3	4	5	.	6	7	8	9

Names of power-of-10 positions:

10^0 = ones   (note that any non-zero base raised to power zero is 1)

10^1 = tens $\qquad\qquad\qquad\qquad$ (number 1 and 1 zero or 10)

10^2 = hundred $\qquad\qquad\qquad\qquad$ (number 1 and 2 zeros or 100)

10^3 = thousand $\qquad\qquad\qquad\qquad$ (number 1 and 3 zeros or 1000)

10^4 = ten thousand $\qquad\qquad\qquad$ (number 1 and 4 zeros or 10000)

$10^{-1} = \dfrac{1}{10^1} = \dfrac{1}{10}$ = tenths $\qquad\qquad$ (1st digit after decimal point or 0.1)

$10^{-2} = \dfrac{1}{10^2} = \dfrac{1}{100}$ = hundredth $\qquad$ (2nd digit after decimal point or 0.01)

$10^{-3} = \dfrac{1}{10^3} = \dfrac{1}{1000}$ = thousandth $\qquad$ (3rd digit after decimal point or 0.001)

$10^{-4} = \dfrac{1}{10^4} = \dfrac{1}{10000}$ = ten thousandth (4th digit after decimal point or 0.0001)

Example:

Write 73169.00537 in expanded form.

We start by listing all the powers of 10 positions.

$$10^4 \qquad 10^3 \quad 10^2 \quad 10^1 \quad 10^0 \quad . \quad 10^{-1} \quad 10^{-2} \quad 10^{-3} \quad 10^{-4} \quad 10^{-5}$$

Multiply each digit by its power of ten. Add all the results.

Thus $73169.00537 = (7\times10^4)+(3\times10^3)+(1\times10^2)+(6\times10^1)$
$\qquad\qquad\qquad\qquad +(9\times10^0)+(0\times10^{-1})+(0\times10^{-2})+(5\times10^{-3})$
$\qquad\qquad\qquad\qquad +(3\times10^{-4})+(7\times10^{-5})$

NOTE: In early elementary school, the term "expanded form" will be introduced by using full numbers rather than exponents. For example, the "expanded form of 4,523 would be written as: 4000+500+20+3

Example:

Determine the place value associated with the underlined digit in 3.16<u>9</u>5.

10^0	.	10^{-1}	10^{-2}	10^{-3}	10^{-4}
3	.	1	6	9	5

The place value for the digit 9 is 10^{-3} or $\dfrac{1}{1000}$.

NOTE: Again, in early elementary school, students would be told to simply move through the places to the right: tenths, hundredths, thousandths and label the place as thousandth.

Example:

Find the number that is represented by $(7 \times 10^3) + (5 \times 10^0) + (3 \times 10^{-3})$.
$= 7000 + 5 + 0.003$
$= 7005.003$

Example:

Write 21×10^3 in standard form.

$= 21 \times 1000 = 21,000$

Example:

Write 739×10^{-4} in standard form.

$= 739 \times \dfrac{1}{10000} = \dfrac{739}{10000} = 0.0739$

Common Factors

GCF is the abbreviation for the **greatest common factor.** The GCF is the largest number that is a factor of all the numbers given in a problem. The GCF can be no larger than the smallest number given in the problem. If no other number is a common factor, then the GCF is the number 1. To find the GCF, list all possible factors of the smallest number given (include the number itself). Starting with the largest factor (which is the number itself), determine if it is also a factor of all the other given numbers. If so, that is the GCF. If that factor doesn't work, try the same method on the next smaller factor. Continue until a common factor is found. That is the GCF.

Note: There can be other common factors besides the GCF.

Example:

Find the GCF of 12, 20, and 36.

The smallest number in the problem is 12. The factors of 12 are 1,2,3,4,6 and 12. 12 is the largest factor, but it does not divide evenly into 20. Neither does 6, but 4 will divide into both 20 and 36 evenly.

Therefore, 4 is the GCF.

Example:

Find the GCF of 14 and 15.

Factors of 14 are 1,2,7 and 14. 14 is the largest factor, but it does not divide evenly into 15. Neither does 7 or 2. Therefore, the only factor common to both 14 and 15 is the number 1.

The GCF is 1.

LCM is the abbreviation for **least common multiple.** The least common multiple of a group of numbers is the smallest number that all of the given numbers will divide into. The least common multiple will always be the largest of the given numbers or a multiple of the largest number.

Example:

Find the LCM of 20, 30, and 40.

The largest number given is 40, but 30 will not divide evenly into 40. The next multiple of 40 is 80 (2 x 40), but 30 will not divide evenly into 80 either. The next multiple of 40 is 120. 120 is divisible by both 20 and 30, so 120 is the LCM (least common multiple).

Example:

Find the LCM of 96, 16, and 24.

The largest number is 96. 96 is divisible by both 16 and 24, so 96 is the LCM.

Example:

Elly Mae can feed the animals in 15 minutes. Jethro can feed them in 10 minutes. How long will it take them if they work together?

If Elly Mae can feed the animals in 15 minutes, then she could feed 1/15 of them in 1 minute, 2/15 of them in 2 minutes, $x/15$ of them in x minutes. In the same fashion, Jethro could feed $x/10$ of them in x minutes. Together they complete 1 job. The equation is:

$$\frac{x}{15} + \frac{x}{10} = 1$$

Multiply each term by the LCD (least common denominator) of 30:

$$2x + 3x = 30$$
$$x = 6 \text{ minutes}$$ [SAW20]

Factors
A factor is any number that can be multiplied by another to get a certain product. All numbers have at least two factors, 1 and the number itself.

Composite numbers are whole numbers that have more than 2 different factors. For example, 9 is composite because besides factors of 1 and 9, 3 is also a factor. 70 is composite because besides the factors of 1 and 70, the numbers 2,5,7,10,14, and 35 are also all factors.

Prime numbers are whole numbers greater than 1 that have only 2 factors: 1 and the number itself. Examples of prime numbers are 2,3,5,7,11,13,17, and 19. Note that 2 is the only even prime number. When factoring into prime factors, all the factors must be numbers that cannot be factored again (without using 1). Initially, numbers can be factored into any 2 factors. Check each resulting factor to see if it can be factored again. Continue factoring until all remaining factors are prime. This is the list of prime factors. Regardless of which way the original number was factored, the final list of prime factors will always be the same.

Remember that the number 1 is neither prime nor composite.

Example:

Factor 30 into prime factors.

Factor 30 into any 2 factors.

$5 \cdot 6$	Now factor the 6.
$5 \cdot 2 \cdot 3$	These are all prime factors.

Factor 30 into any 2 factors.

$3 \cdot 10$	Now factor the 10.
$3 \cdot 2 \cdot 5$	These are the same prime factors even though the original factors were obtained differently.

Example:

Factor 240 into prime factors.

Factor 240 into any 2 factors.

$24 \cdot 10$	Now factor both 24 and 10.
$4 \cdot 6 \cdot 2 \cdot 5$	Now factor both 4 and 6.
$2 \cdot 2 \cdot 2 \cdot 3 \cdot 2 \cdot 5$	These are prime factors.

This can also be written as $2^4 \cdot 3 \cdot 5$.

Equivalent Forms of Common Fractions, Decimal Fractions, and Percentages

If we compare numbers in various forms, we see that:

The integer 400 = $\dfrac{800}{2}$ (fraction) = 400.0 (decimal) = 400% (percent).

From this, you should be able to determine that fractions, decimals, and percents can be used interchangeably within problems.

- To change a percent into a decimal, move the decimal point two places to the left and drop off the percent sign.
- To change a decimal into a percent, move the decimal two places to the right and add on a percent sign[SAW21].
- To change a fraction into a decimal, divide the numerator by the denominator.
- To change a decimal number into an equivalent fraction, write the decimal part of the number as the fraction's numerator. As the fraction's denominator, use the place value of the last column of the decimal. Reduce the resulting fraction as far as possible.

Example:

> J.C. Nickels has Hunch jeans for sale at 1/4 off the usual price of $36.00. Shears and Roadster have the same jeans for sale at 30% off their regular price of $40. Find the cheaper price.
>
> 1/4 = .25 so .25(36) = $9.00 off $36 - 9 = $27 sale price
>
> 30% = .30 so .30(40) = $12 off $40 - 12 = $28 sale price
>
> The price at J.C. Nickels is actually lower.

To convert a fraction to a decimal, as we did in the example above, simply divide the numerator (top) by the denominator (bottom). Use long division if necessary.

If a decimal has a fixed number of digits, the decimal is said to be **terminating**. To write such a decimal as a fraction, first determine what place value the farthest right digit is in (for example: tenths, hundredths, thousandths, ten thousandths, hundred thousands, etc). Then drop the decimal and place the string of digits over the number given by the place value.

If a decimal continues forever by repeating a string of digits, the decimal is said to be **repeating**. To write a repeating decimal as a fraction, follow these steps.

a. Let $x =$ the repeating decimal (ex. $x = .716716716...$)
b. Multiply x by the multiple of ten that will move the decimal just to the right of the repeating block of digits. (ex. $1000x = 716.716716...$)
c. Subtract the first equation from the second (ex. $1000x - x = 716.716.716... - .716716...$)
d. Simplify and solve this equation. The repeating block of digits will subtract out (ex. $999x = 716$ so $x = {}^{716}\!/_{999}$)
e. The solution will be the fraction for the repeating decimal

Properties of Numbers and the Number System
The real number properties are best explained in terms of a small set of numbers. For each property, a given set will be provided.

Axioms of Addition
Closure—For all real numbers a and b, $a + b$ is a unique real number.

Associative—For all real numbers $a, b,$ and c, $(a + b) + c = a + (b + c)$.

Additive Identity—There exists a unique real number 0 (zero) such that $a + 0 = 0 + a = a$ for every real number a.

Additive Inverses—For each real number a, there exists a real number $-a$ (the opposite of a) such that $a + (-a) = (-a) + a = 0$.

Commutative—For all real numbers a and b, $a + b = b + a$.

Axioms of Multiplication

Closure—For all real numbers a and b, ab is a unique real number.

Associative—For all real numbers a, b, and c, $(ab)c = a(bc)$.

Multiplicative Identity—There exists a unique nonzero real number 1 (one) such that $1 \cdot a = a \cdot 1 = a$ [SAW22].

Multiplicative Inverses—For each nonzero real number, there exists a real number $1/a$ (the reciprocal of a) such that $a(1/a) = (1/a)a = 1$.

Commutative—For all real numbers a and b, $ab = ba$.

The Distributive Axiom of Multiplication over Addition
For all real numbers a, b, and c, $a(b + c) = ab + ac$.

Recognizing the Property of Denseness
The **Denseness Property** of real numbers states that if all real numbers are ordered from least to greatest on a number line, there is an infinite set of real numbers between any two given numbers on the line.

Example:

>   Between 7.6 and 7.7, there is the rational number 7.65 in the set of real numbers.
>   Between 3 and 4 there exists no other natural number.

Applying Inverse Operations

>   Subtraction is the inverse of Addition, and vice-versa.
>   Division is the inverse of Multiplication, and vice-versa.
>   Taking a square root is the inverse of squaring, and vice-versa.

These inverse operations are used when solving equations.

SKILL 6.3   Applying knowledge of the relationships among mathematical operations and strategies for using the basic four operations with variables and numbers[SAW23]

For standardization purposes, there is an accepted order in which operations are performed in any given algebraic expression. The following pneumonic is often used for the order in which operations are performed.

Please	Parentheses	
Excuse	Exponents	
My	Multiply	(Multiply or Divide depending on which
Dear	Divide	operation is encountered first from left to right.)
Aunt	Add	(Add or Subtract depending on which
Sally	Subtract	operation is encountered first from left to right.)

This **Order of Operations** should be followed when evaluating algebraic expressions:

1. Simplify inside grouping characters such as parentheses, brackets, square root, fraction bar, etc.

2. Multiply out expressions with exponents.

3. Do multiplication or division, from left to right.

4. Do addition or subtraction, from left to right.
   Samples of simplifying expressions with exponents:

$$(^-2)^3 = -8 \qquad ^-2^3 = ^-8$$
$$(^-2)^4 = 16 \qquad ^-2^4 = 16 \qquad \text{Note change of sign.}$$
$$(\tfrac{2}{3})^3 = \tfrac{8}{27}$$
$$5^0 = 1$$
$$4^{-1} = \tfrac{1}{4}$$

Instruction for Whole Numbers: Addition, Subtraction, Multiplication and Division

- Phase 1—Conceptualization

   a. Relate arithmetic operations to physical operations.

   b. Develop a process for finding answers using concrete objects or pictures of objects.

- Phase 2—Fact Mastery

    a. Easy facts

        i. Figure them out using already developed processes.

        ii. Organize them in different ways to see relationships.

        iii. Memorize them.

    b. Develop more efficient techniques for remembering facts that:

        i. Are mental processes.

        ii. Use easier facts already memorized.

    c. Harder facts

        i. Figure them out using new efficient processes.

        ii. Organize them.

- Phase 3—Algorithm Learning

    a. De-emphasize superficial rules.

    b. Stress big ideas, and relate them to concrete models.

    c. Develop computational expertise apart from models.

The conceptualization phase should include

(1) interaction with concrete, tangible materials;

(2) use of pictures or dots, number lines, representation manipulatives, such as semi concrete representations; and last,

(3) work on a symbolic or abstract level (Henley, Ramsey, & Algozzine, 1993: Morsink, 1984).

Too often, teachers use the pictures in math texts as their sole means of offering a meaningful foundation to a newly-introduced concept, rather than providing concrete, manipulative aids. Understanding is better assured whenever a relationship between manipulatives, pictures, and the abstract concept is fostered. Many things that children do are naturally related to numbers.

Activities considered pre-addition or pre-subtraction in math include:

    (1) basic number meanings,

    (2) visual and meaningful recognition of numerals, and

    (3) counting skills.

Children learn that = + = means put together and that * - * means take away as they manipulate objects within groups. When children are making final steps toward fact mastery, instruction usually moves into writing addition and subtraction algorithms. They are taught to use a written computational procedure in order to obtain an answer. Clustering facts that use the same strategy or relationships aids efforts toward understanding cognitive processes. There are basically two things to remember when teaching addition to facilitate learning:

    (1) add like or similar units,

    (2) make a trade whenever there are 10 or more of a kind.

Similarly, two Ideas prevail when teaching subtraction:

    (1) subtract like units, and

    (2) if the value is insufficient within a given place unit, make a trade (regroup or borrow).

The concept of multiplication is closely related to the concept of addition. In fact, multiplication is initially taught as repeated addition. Two or more sets are combined to form a new set; thus, multiplication can be conceptualized as the union of sets, as in addition. However, in multiplication, each of the groups joined must have the same number of objects. The symbol "x" (or the multiplication dot, or parentheses, whichever symbol you use) needs to connote an understanding of equal units. For example, 2 x 3 should be conceptualized as two groups of three objects, or three objects combined two times.

Like multiplication, division is a process that involves groups of equal size. In multiplication, the equal-sized groups are joined. Since division is the inverse operation of multiplication, division can be related to the act of separating a group into parts of equal size.

SKILL 6.4   Performing calculations with whole numbers, decimals, and fractions and applying methods for making estimations and evaluating the accuracy of estimate solutions

Addition of Whole Numbers

Example:

At the end of a day of shopping, a shopper had $24 remaining in his wallet. He spent $45 on various goods. How much money did the shopper have at the beginning of the day?

The total amount of money the shopper started with is the sum of the amount spent and the amount remaining at the end of the day.

```
   24
+  45
  ───
   69 ──────▶    The original total was $69.
```

Example:

A race took the winner 1 hr. 58 min. 12 sec. on the first half of the race and 2 hr. 9 min. 57 sec. on the second half of the race. How much time did the entire race take?

```
   1 hr. 58 min. 12 sec.
+  2 hr.  9 min. 57 sec.     Add these numbers
   3 hr. 67 min. 69 sec.
+  1 min           -60 sec.  Change 60 seconds to 1 min.
   3 hr. 68 min. 9 sec.
+  1 hr.-60 min.             Change 60 minutes to 1 hr.
   4 hr. 8 min.   9 sec.  ←  final answer
```

Subtraction of Whole Numbers

Example:

At the end of his shift, a cashier has $96 in the cash register. At the beginning of his shift, he had $15. How much money did the cashier collect during his shift?

The total collected is the difference of the ending amount and the starting amount.

$$
\begin{array}{r}
96 \\
-\ \ 15 \\
\hline
81
\end{array}
$$
→ The total collected was $81.

Multiplication of Whole Numbers

Multiplication is one of the four basic number operations. In simple terms, multiplication is the addition of a number to itself a certain number of times. For example, 4 multiplied by 3 is the equal to 4 + 4 + 4 or 3 + 3 + 3 +3. Another way of conceptualizing multiplication is to think in terms of groups. For example, if we have 4 groups of 3 students, the total number of students is 4 multiplied by 3. We call the solution to a multiplication problem the **product**.

One common algorithm for whole number multiplication begins with aligning the numbers by place value with the number containing more places on top.

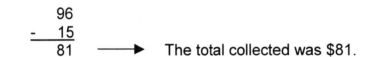

$$
\begin{array}{r}
172 \\
\times\ 43
\end{array}
$$
→ Note that we placed 172 on top because it has more places than 43 does.

Next, we multiply the one's place of the second number by each place value of the top number sequentially.

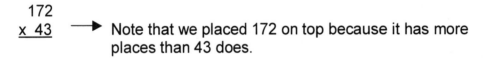

$$
\begin{array}{r}
(2) \\
172 \\
\times\ 43 \\
\hline
516
\end{array}
$$
→ {3 x 2 = 6, 3 x 7 = 21, 3 x 1 = 3}
Note that we had to carry (regroup) a 2 to the hundred's column because 3 x 7 = 21. Note also that we add, not multiply, carried numbers to the product.

Next, we multiply the number in the ten's place of the second number by each place value of the top number sequentially. Because we are multiplying by a number in the ten's place, we place a zero at the end of this product.

(2)
172
x 43 ⟶ {4 x 2 = 8, 4 x 7 = 28, 4 x 1 = 4}
516
6880

Finally, to determine the final product, we add the two partial products.

172
x 43
516
+ 6880
7396 ⟶ The product of 172 and 43 is 7396.

NOTE: There are other algorithms for this operation, including those often taught first in elementary school, where the number is multiplied first in its expanded form, then added together:

45 x 23 = (45x20) + (45x3), so
45x 20=900 and 45x3=135, and 900+135=1035

Example:

A student buys 4 boxes of crayons. Each box contains 16 crayons. How many total crayons does the student have?
The total number of crayons is 16 x 4.

16
x 4
64 ⟶ The total number of crayons equals 64.

Division of Whole Numbers
Division, the inverse of multiplication, is another of the four basic number operations. When we divide one number by another, we determine how many times we can multiply the divisor (number divided by) before we exceed the number we are dividing (dividend). For example, 8 divided by 2 equals 4 because we can multiply 2 four times to reach 8 (2 x 4 = 8 or 2 + 2 + 2 + 2 = 8). Using the grouping conceptualization we used with multiplication, we can divide 8 into 4 groups of 2, or 2 groups of 4. We call the answer to a division problem the **quotient**.

If the divisor does not divide evenly into the dividend, we express the leftover amount either as a remainder or as a fraction with the divisor as the denominator. For example, 9 divided by 2 equals 4 with a remainder of 1 or 4 ½.

The basic algorithm for division is long division. We start by representing the quotient as follows.

$14\overline{)293}$ ⟶ 14 is the divisor and 293 is the dividend.

This represents 293 ÷ 14.

Next, we divide the divisor into the dividend, starting from the left.

$\begin{array}{r} 2 \\ 14\overline{)293} \end{array}$ ⟶ 14 divides into 29 two times with a remainder.

Next, we multiply the partial quotient by the divisor, subtract this value from the first digits of the dividend, and bring down the remaining dividend digits to complete the number.

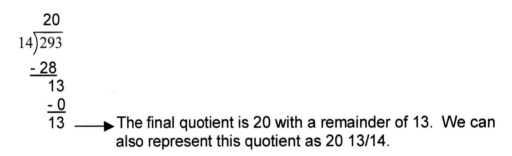

⟶ 2 x 14 = 28, 29 – 28 = 1, and bringing down the 3 yields 13.

Finally, we divide again (the divisor into the remaining value) and repeat the preceding process. The number left after the subtraction represents the remainder.

$$\begin{array}{r} 20 \\ 14\overline{)293} \\ \underline{-28} \\ 13 \\ \underline{-0} \\ 13 \end{array}$$

⟶ The final quotient is 20 with a remainder of 13. We can also represent this quotient as 20 13/14.

Example:

Each box of apples contains 24 apples. How many boxes must a grocer purchase to supply a group of 252 people with one apple each?

The grocer needs 252 apples. Because he must buy apples in groups of 24, we divide 252 by 24 to determine how many boxes he needs to buy.

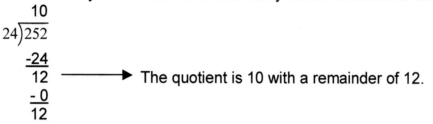

The quotient is 10 with a remainder of 12.

Thus, the grocer needs 10 boxes plus 12 more apples. Therefore, the minimum number of boxes the grocer can purchase is 11.

Example:

At his job, John gets paid $20 for every hour he works. If John made $940 in a week, how many hours did he work?

This is a division problem. To determine the number of hours John worked, we divide the total amount made ($940) by the hourly rate of pay ($20). Thus, the number of hours worked equals 940 divided by 20.

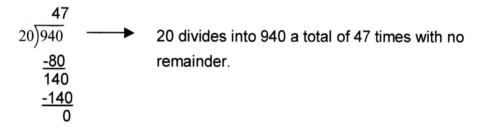

20 divides into 940 a total of 47 times with no remainder.

John worked 47 hours.

Addition and Subtraction of Decimals
When adding and subtracting decimals, we align the numbers by place value as we do with whole numbers. After adding or subtracting each column, we bring the decimal down, placing it in the same location as in the numbers added or subtracted.

Example:

Find the sum of 152.3 and 36.342.

$$
\begin{array}{r}
152.300 \\
+36.342 \\
\hline
188.642
\end{array}
$$

Note that we placed two zeroes after the final place value in 152.3 to clarify the column addition.

Example:

Find the difference of 152.3 and 36.342.

$$
\begin{array}{cc}
2\ 9\ 10 & (4)11(12) \\
152.\cancel{300} & 1\cancel{52}.\cancel{300} \\
-36.342 & -36.342 \\
\hline
58 & 115.958
\end{array}
$$

Note how we borrowed (or regrouped) to subtract from the zeroes in the hundredth's and thousandth's place of 152.300.

Multiplication of Decimals

When multiplying decimal numbers, we multiply exactly as with whole numbers, with the product having the same number of places to the right of the decimal as the factors have combined.[SAW24] For example, when multiplying 1.5 and 2.35, we place the decimal point in the product so there are three places to its right, since that is the total number of places found to the right of the two factors used. (3.525).

<u>Example</u>:

Find the product of 3.52 and 4.1.

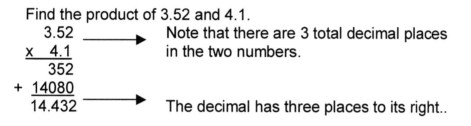

Note that there are 3 total decimal places in the two numbers.

The decimal has three places to its right..

Thus, the final product is 14.432.

<u>Example</u>[SAW25]:

A shopper has 5 one-dollar bills, 6 quarters, 3 nickels, and 4 pennies in his pocket. How much money does he have?

$$
\begin{array}{cccc}
 & 3 & 1 & \\
5 \times \$1.00 = \$5.00 & \$0.25 & \$0.05 & \$0.01 \\
 & \underline{\times \quad 6} & \underline{\times \quad 3} & \underline{\times \quad 4} \\
 & \$1.50 & \$0.15 & \$0.04 \\
\end{array}
$$

Note the placement of the decimals in the multiplication products. Thus, the total amount of money in the shopper's pocket is:

$$
\begin{array}{r}
\$5.00 \\
1.50 \\
0.15 \\
\underline{+ \ 0.04} \\
\$6.69 \\
\end{array}
$$

When adding, the decimal stays in the same place.

Division of Decimals

When dividing decimal numbers, we first remove the decimal in the divisor by moving the decimal in the dividend the same number of spaces to the right. For example, when dividing 1.45 into 5.3 we convert the numbers to 145 and 530 and perform normal whole number division.

Example:

Find the quotient of 5.3 divided by 1.45.

Convert to 145 and 530.

Divide.

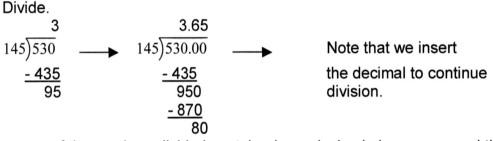

Note that we insert the decimal to continue division.

Because one of the numbers divided contained one decimal place, we round the quotient to one decimal place. Thus, the final quotient is 3.7.

Operating with Percents

Example:

5 is what percent of 20?

This is the same as converting $\frac{5}{20}$ to % form.

$$\frac{5}{20} \times \frac{100}{1} = \frac{5}{1} \times \frac{5}{1} = 25\%$$

Example:

There are 64 dogs in the kennel. 48 are collies. What percent are collies?

Restate the problem.   48 is what percent of 64?
Write an equation. $48 = n \times 64$
Solve. $\frac{48}{64} = n$

$n = \frac{3}{4} = 75\%$

75% of the dogs are collies.

Example:

The auditorium was filled to 90% capacity. There were 558 seats occupied. What is the capacity of the auditorium?

Restate the problem.	90% of what number is 558?
Write an equation.	$0.9n = 558$
Solve.	$n = \frac{558}{.9}$
	$n = 620$

The capacity of the auditorium is 620 people.

Example:

A pair of shoes costs $42.00. Sales tax is 6%. What is the total cost of the shoes?

Restate the problem.	What is 6% of 42?
Write an equation.	$n = 0.06 \times 42$
Solve.	$n = 2.52$

Add the sales tax to the cost. $42.00 + $2.52 = $44.52
The total cost of the shoes, including sales tax, is $44.52.

Addition and Subtraction of Fractions
Key Points

1. You need a common denominator in order to add and subtract reduced and improper fractions.

Example:

$$\frac{1}{3}+\frac{7}{3}=\frac{1+7}{3}=\frac{8}{3}=2\frac{2}{3}$$

Example:

$$\frac{4}{12}+\frac{6}{12}-\frac{3}{12}=\frac{4+6-3}{12}=\frac{7}{12}$$

2. Adding an integer and a fraction of the same sign results directly in a mixed fraction.

Example: $2+\frac{2}{3}=2\frac{2}{3}$

Example: $^{-}2-\frac{3}{4}={}^{-}2\frac{3}{4}$

3. Adding an integer and a fraction with different signs involves the following steps:

- Get a common denominator
- Add or subtract as needed
- Change to a mixed fraction if possible

Example:

$$2 - \frac{1}{3} = \frac{2 \times 3 - 1}{3} = \frac{6-1}{3} = \frac{5}{3} = 1\frac{2}{3}$$

Example:

Add $7\frac{3}{8} + 5\frac{2}{7}$

Add the whole numbers, add the fractions, and combine the two results:

$$7\frac{3}{8} + 5\frac{2}{7} = (7+5) + (\frac{3}{8} + \frac{2}{7})$$
$$= 12 + \frac{(7 \times 3) + (8 \times 2)}{56} \quad \text{(LCM of 8 and 7)}$$
$$= 12 + \frac{21+16}{56} = 12 + \frac{37}{56} = 12\frac{37}{56}$$

Example:

Perform the operation.

$$\frac{2}{3} - \frac{5}{6}$$

We first find the LCM of 3 and 6, which is 6.

$$\frac{2 \times 2}{3 \times 2} - \frac{5}{6} \rightarrow \frac{4-5}{6} = \frac{^-1}{6} \quad \text{(Using method A)}$$

Example:

$$^-7\frac{1}{4}+2\frac{7}{8}$$

$$^-7\frac{1}{4}+2\frac{7}{8}=(^-7+2)+(\frac{^-1}{4}+\frac{7}{8})$$

$$=(^-5)+\frac{(^-2+7)}{8}=(^-5)+(\frac{5}{8})$$

$$=(^-5)+\frac{5}{8}=\frac{^-5\times8}{1\times8}+\frac{5}{8}=\frac{^-40+5}{8}$$

$$=\frac{^-35}{8}=^-4\frac{3}{8}$$

Divide 35 by 8 to get 4, remainder 3.

Caution: A common error would be:

$$^-7\frac{1}{4}+2\frac{7}{8}=^-7\frac{2}{8}+2\frac{7}{8}=^-5\frac{9}{8}$$ Wrong.

It is correct to add -7 and 2 to get -5, but adding $\frac{2}{8}+\frac{7}{8}=\frac{9}{8}$ is wrong. It should

have been $\frac{^-2}{8}+\frac{7}{8}=\frac{5}{8}$. Then, $^-5+\frac{5}{8}=^-4\frac{3}{8}$ as before.

Multiplication of Fractions

Using the following example: $3\frac{1}{4}\times\frac{5}{6}$

1. Convert each number to an improper fraction.

$$3\frac{1}{4}=\frac{(12+1)}{4}=\frac{13}{4}\qquad\qquad\frac{5}{6}\text{ is already in reduced form.}$$

2. Reduce (cancel) common factors of the numerator and denominator if they exist.

$$\frac{13}{4}\times\frac{5}{6}\quad\text{No common factors exist.}$$

3. Multiply the numerators by each other and the denominators by each other.

$$\frac{13}{4} \times \frac{5}{6} = \frac{65}{24}$$

4. If possible, reduce the fraction back to its lowest term.

$$\frac{65}{24}$$ Cannot be reduced further

5. Convert the improper fraction back to a mixed fraction by using long division.

$$\frac{65}{24} = 24\overline{)65} \qquad = 2\frac{17}{24}$$
$$\frac{48}{17}$$

Summary of Sign Changes for Multiplication

a. $(+) \times (+) = (+)$

b. $(-) \times (+) = (-)$

c. $(+) \times (-) = (-)$

d. $(-) \times (-) = (+)$

Example:

$$7\frac{1}{3} \times \frac{5}{11} = \frac{22}{3} \times \frac{5}{11}$$

Reduce like terms (22 and 11)

$$= \frac{2}{3} \times \frac{5}{1} = \frac{10}{3} = 3\frac{1}{3}$$

Example:

$$^-6\frac{1}{4} \times \frac{5}{9} = \frac{^-25}{4} \times \frac{5}{9}$$

$$= \frac{^-125}{36} = ^-3\frac{17}{36}$$

Example:

$$\frac{^-1}{4} \times \frac{^-3}{7}$$

Negative times a negative equals positive.

$$= \frac{1}{4} \times \frac{3}{7} = \frac{3}{28}$$

Division of Fractions
Change mixed fractions to improper fractions.

Change the division problem to a multiplication problem by using the reciprocal of the number after the division sign.

Find the sign of the final product.

Cancel if common factors exist between the numerator and the denominator.

Multiply the numerators together and the denominators together.

Change the improper fraction to a mixed number.

Example:

$$3\frac{1}{5} \div 2\frac{1}{4} = \frac{16}{5} \div \frac{9}{4}$$

$$= \frac{16}{5} \times \frac{4}{9} \qquad \text{Reciprocal of } \frac{9}{4} \text{ is } \frac{4}{9}.$$

$$= \frac{64}{45} = 1\frac{19}{45}$$

Example:

$$7\frac{3}{4} \div 11\frac{5}{8} = \frac{31}{4} \div \frac{93}{8}$$

$$= \frac{31}{4} \times \frac{8}{93} \qquad \text{Reduce like terms.}$$

$$= \frac{1}{1} \times \frac{2}{3} = \frac{2}{3}$$

Example:

$$\left({}^{-}2\frac{1}{2} \right) \div 4\frac{1}{6} = \frac{{}^{-}5}{2} \div \frac{25}{6}$$

$$= \frac{{}^{-}5}{2} \times \frac{6}{25} \qquad \text{Reduce like terms.}$$

$$= \frac{{}^{-}1}{1} \times \frac{3}{5} = \frac{{}^{-}3}{5}$$

Example:

$$\left(-5\frac{3}{8}\right) \div \left(\frac{^-7}{16}\right) = \frac{^-43}{8} \div \frac{^-7}{16}$$

$$= \frac{^-43}{8} \times \frac{^-16}{7} \quad \text{Reduce like terms.}$$

$$= \frac{43}{1} \times \frac{2}{7} \quad \text{Negative times a negative equals a positive.}$$

$$= \frac{86}{7} = 12\frac{2}{7}$$

Making Estimations and Evaluating the Accuracy of Estimated Solutions
Estimation and approximation may be used to check the reasonableness of answers.

Example:

Estimate the answer.

$$\frac{58 \times 810}{1989}$$

58 becomes 60, 810 becomes 800 and 1989 becomes 2000.

$$\frac{60 \times 800}{2000} = 24$$

For word problems, an estimate may sometimes be all that is needed to find the solution.

Example:

Janet goes into a store to purchase a CD on sale for $13.95. While shopping, she sees two pairs of shoes priced at $19.95 and $14.50. She only has $50. Can she purchase everything?

Solve by rounding:

$19.95→$20.00
$14.50→$15.00
$13.95→$14.00
$49.00   Yes, she can purchase the CD and the shoes.

SKILL 6.5 **Demonstrating knowledge of strategies for investigating, developing, and evaluating mathematical arguments and strategies (e.g., determining relevant information, estimating, simplifying) for solving single-step and multi-step problems**[s26]

A valid argument is a statement made about a pattern or relationship between elements, thought to be true, which is subsequently justified through repeated examples and/or logical reasoning. Another term for a valid argument is a proof.

For example, the statement that the sum of two odd numbers is always even could be tested through actual examples:

Two Odd Numbers	Sum	Validity of Statement
1+1	2 (even)	Valid
1+3	4 (even)	Valid
61+29	90 (even)	Valid
135+47	182 (even)	Valid
253+17	270 (even)	Valid
1,945+2,007	3,952 (even)	Valid
6,321+7,851	14,172 (even)	Valid

Adding two odd numbers always results in a sum that is even. It is a valid argument based on the justifications in the table above.

Here is another example. The statement that a fraction of a fraction can be determined by multiplying the numerator by the numerator and the denominator by the denominator can be proven through logical reasoning. For example, one-half of one-quarter of a candy bar can be found by multiplying ½ * ¼. The answer would be one-eighth. The validity of this argument can be demonstrated as valid with a model:

The entire rectangle represents one whole candy bar. The top half section of the model is shaded in one direction to demonstrate how much of the candy bar remains from the whole candy bar. The left quarter, shaded in a different direction, demonstrates that one-quarter of the candy bar has been given to a friend. Since the whole candy bar is not available to give out, the area that is double-shaded is the fractional part of the ½ candy bar that has been actually given away. That fractional part is one-eighth of the whole candy bar, as shown in both the sketch and the algorithm.

Write Simple Proofs in Two-Column Form

In a two-column proof, the left side should be the given information, or statements that could be proven by deductive reasoning. The right column should consist of the methods used to determine that each statement to the left is verifiably true. The right side can identify given information or state theorems, postulates, definitions, or algebraic properties used to prove that each particular line of the proof is true.

Write Indirect Proofs

Assume the opposite of the conclusion. Keep the hypothesis and the given information the same. Proceed to develop the steps of the proof, looking for a statement that contradicts the original assumption or some other known fact. This contradiction indicates that the assumption made at the beginning of the proof was incorrect; therefore, the original conclusion has to be true.

Classify Conclusions as Examples of Inductive or Deductive Thinking

Inductive thinking is the process of finding a pattern from a group of examples. That pattern is the conclusion that this set of examples *seemed* to indicate. It may be a correct conclusion, or it may be an incorrect conclusion because other examples may not follow the predicted pattern. Inductive reasoning is good for developing a hypothesis, but it is not definitive. It gives a *probable* conclusion based on past events or examples.

Deductive thinking is the process of arriving at a conclusion based on other statements that are all known to be true, known to be facts, such as theorems, axioms postulates, or postulates. Conclusions found by deductive thinking based on true statements will <u>always</u> be true.

<u>Examples:</u>

1) Suppose:
On Monday, Mr. Peterson eats breakfast at McDonald's.
On Tuesday, Mr. Peterson eats breakfast at McDonald's.
On Wednesday, Mr. Peterson eats breakfast at McDonald's.
On Thursday, Mr. Peterson eats breakfast at McDonald's.

Conclusion:
On Friday, Mr. Peterson will eat breakfast at McDonald's again.

This is a conclusion based on inductive reasoning. Based on several days[SAW27] of observations, it can be concluded that Mr. Peterson will eat at McDonald's. This may or may not be true, but it is a conclusion developed by inductive thinking. We would say it is the best guess, the most probable result. The fact that he ate there the first four days of the week, however, does not **prove** he will eat there on Friday.

2) Suppose you know the following to be facts:
Mr. Peterson is the dinner manager at McDonalds.
Mr. Peterson works Friday evenings.
Evening managers at this McDonalds are required to eat their dinners at McDonalds.

Conclusion: Mr. Peterson will eat dinner at McDonalds Friday night.

This conclusion is based on deductive reasoning. It is based on the three facts listed above. Since he is the evening manager and evening managers must eat dinner there, it can be concluded that he eats dinner there on Friday night. This is a valid conclusion or proof, *provided* the earlier facts are indeed correct.

Make Conditional Statements[s28]

Conditional statements are frequently written in "if-then" form. The "if" clause of the conditional is known as the **hypothesis**, and the "then" clause is called the **conclusion**. In a proof, the hypothesis is the information that is proposed to be true, while the conclusion is what is to be proven true. A conditional statement often follows a basic form:

If p, then q.
p is the hypothesis and q is the conclusion

Conditional statements can be diagrammed using a **Venn diagram**. This diagram can be drawn with one circle inside another circle. The inner circle represents the hypothesis. The outer circle represents the conclusion. If the hypothesis is taken to be true, then you are located inside the inner circle. If you are located in the inner circle then you are also inside the outer circle, so that proves the conclusion is true.

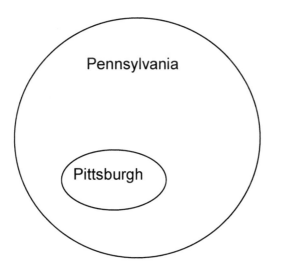

Example:

> If you are in Pittsburgh, then you are in Pennsylvania.
> In this statement, "you are in Pittsburgh" is the hypothesis.
> In this statement, "you are in Pennsylvania" is the conclusion.

Example:

> If an angle has a measure of 90 degrees, then it is a right angle.
> In this statement, "an angle has a measure of 90 degrees" is the hypothesis.
> In this statement, "it is a right angle" is the conclusion.

Conditional: If p, then q.
p is the hypothesis and q is the conclusion

Inverse: If not p, then not q.
Negate both the hypothesis (If p) and the conclusion (then q) from the original conditional.

Converse: If q, then p.
Reverse the two clauses. The original hypothesis becomes the conclusion. The original conclusion then becomes the new hypothesis.

Contrapositive: If not q, then not p.
Reverse the two clauses. The original hypothesis becomes the conclusion and the original conclusion becomes the hypothesis. Then negate both the new hypothesis and the new conclusion.

Example:

Given the *conditional*:
If an angle has 60°, then it is an acute angle.

Its *inverse* form would be:
If an angle doesn't have 60°, then it is not an acute angle.

NOTICE that the inverse is not true, even though the conditional statement was true.

Its *converse* form would be:
If an angle is an acute angle, then it has 60°.

NOTICE that the converse is not necessarily true, even though the conditional statement was true.

Its *contrapositive* form would be:
If an angle isn't an acute angle, then it doesn't have 60°.

NOTICE that the contrapositive is true, assuming the original conditional statement was true.

TIP: If you are asked to pick a statement that is logically equivalent to a given conditional, look for the contrapositive. The inverse and converse are not always logically equivalent to every conditional. The contrapositive is ALWAYS logically equivalent.

Find the inverse, converse, and contrapositive of the following conditional statements. Also, determine if each of the statements is true or false.

Conditional: If $x = 5$, then $x^2 - 25 = 0$.   TRUE
Inverse: If $x \neq 5$, then $x^2 - 25 \neq 0$.   FALSE, x could be $^-5$
Converse: If $x^2 - 25 = 0$, then $x = 5$.   FALSE, x could be $^-5$
Contrapositive: If $x^2 - 25 \neq 0$, then $x \neq 5$.   TRUE

Conditional: If $x = 5$, then $6x = 30$.   TRUE
Inverse: If $x \neq 5$, then $6x \neq 30$.   TRUE
Converse: If $6x = 30$, then $x = 5$.   TRUE
Contrapositive: If $6x \neq 30$, then $x \neq 5$.   TRUE

Sometimes, as in the latter example, all four statements can be logically equivalent; however, the only statement that will always be logically equivalent to the original conditional is the contrapositive.

The use of Venn diagrams (explained above) can help to visualize this process. Suppose that the following statements were given to you, and you were asked to try to reach a conclusion.

1)   All swimmers are athletes.
        All athletes are scholars.

In "if-then" form, these would be:

If you are a swimmer, then you are an athlete.
If you are an athlete, then you are a scholar.

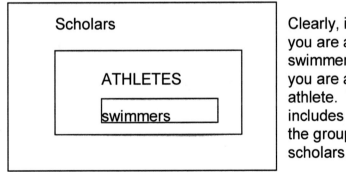

Clearly, if you are a swimmer, then you are also an athlete. This includes you in the group of scholars.

2)   All swimmers are athletes.
        All wrestlers are athletes.
In "if-then" form, these would be:

If you are a swimmer, then you are an athlete.

If you are a wrestler, then you are an athlete.

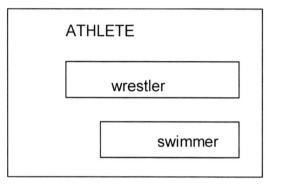

Clearly, if you are a swimmer or a wrestler, then you are also an athlete. This does NOT allow you to come to any other conclusions.

A swimmer may or may NOT also be a wrestler. Therefore, NO CONCLUSION IS POSSIBLE.

3)   All rectangles are parallelograms.
        Quadrilateral ABCD is not a parallelogram.

In "if-then" form, the first statement would be:

If a figure is a rectangle, then it is also a parallelogram.

Note that this second statement is the negation of the conclusion of statement one. Remember also that the contrapositive is logically equivalent to a given conditional. That is, "If not q, then not p." Since "ABCD is NOT a parallelogram" is like saying "if not q," then you can come to the conclusion "then not p." Therefore, the conclusion is "ABCD is not a rectangle." Looking at the Venn diagram below, if all rectangles are parallelograms, then rectangles are included as part of the parallelograms. Since quadrilateral ABCD is not a parallelogram, it is excluded from anywhere inside the parallelogram box. This allows you to conclude that ABCD cannot be a rectangle either.

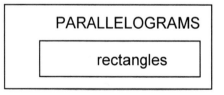

quadrilateral CD

A **counterexample** is an exception to a proposed rule or conjecture that disproves the conjecture. For example, the existence of a single non-brown dog disproves the conjecture "all dogs are brown." Thus, any non-brown dog is a counterexample.

In searching for mathematic counterexamples, one should consider extreme cases near the ends of the domain of an experiment as well as special cases where an additional property is introduced. Examples of extreme cases are numbers near zero and obtuse triangles that are nearly flat. An example of a special case for a problem involving rectangles is a square because a square is a rectangle with the additional property of symmetry.

Example:

Identify a counterexample for the following conjectures.

If n is an even number, then $n +1$ is divisible by 3.

$n = 4$
$n + 1 = 4 + 1 = 5$
5 is not divisible by 3.

If n is divisible by 3, then $n^2 - 1$ is divisible by 4.

$n = 6$
$n^2 - 1 = 6^2 - 1 = 35$
35 is not divisible by 4.

PROBLEM SOLVING STRATEGIES

The primary reason for studying mathematics is to acquire the ability to perform problem-solving skills. Problem solving is the process of applying previously acquired knowledge to new and novel situations. Mathematical problem solving is generally thought of as solving word problems; however, there are more skills involved in problem solving than merely reading word problems, deciding on correct conceptual procedures, and performing the computations. Problem-solving skills involve posing questions; analyzing situations; hypothesizing, translating and illustrating results; drawing diagrams; and using trial and error. When solving mathematical problems, students need to be able to apply logic, and thus, determine which facts are relevant.

Problem solving has proven to be the primary area of mathematical difficulty for students. The following methods for developing problem-solving skills have been recommended.

- Allot time for the development of successful problem-solving skills. It is complex process and needs to be taught in a systematic way.

Be sure prerequisite skills have been adequately developed. The ability to perform the operations of addition, subtraction, multiplication and division are necessary sub-skills.

Use error analysis to diagnose areas of difficulty. One error in procedure or choice of mathematical operation, once corrected, will eliminate subsequent mistakes, following the initial error, like the domino effect. Look for patterns of similar mistakes to prevent a series of identical errors. Instruct children on the usage of error analysis to perform self-appraisal of their own work.

Teach students appropriate terminology. Many words have a different meaning when used in a mathematical context than in everyday life. For example, "set" in mathematics refers to a grouping of objects, but it may also be used as a verb, such as in "set the table." Other words that should be defined include "order," "base," "power" and "root."

Have students estimate answers. Teach them how to check their computed answer to determine how reasonable it is. For example, Teddy is asked how many hours he spent doing his homework. If he worked on it two hours before dinner and one hour after dinner, and his answer came out to be 21, Teddy should be able to conclude that 21 hours is the greater part of a day, and is far too large to be reasonable.

Remember that development of math readiness skills enables students to acquire prerequisite concepts and to build cognitive structures. These prerequisite skills appear to be related to problem-solving performance.

There are a variety of specific problem solving strategies that can be taught to help students learn to solve mathematic problems on many levels.

The **questioning technique** is a mathematic process in which students devise questions to clarify the problem, eliminate possible solutions, and simplify the problem-solving process. By developing and attempting to answer simple questions, students can tackle difficult and complex problems.

Sometimes, the discourse may be teacher-guided though a process in which the teacher asks questions to generate dialogue and lead discussions. Other times, the students might be encouraged to generate their own inquiry discussions by sharing their questions and thoughts among themselves. A third type of discourse can take place in small groups where the students work both independently and collaboratively.

Teachers might ask the following types of questions to encourage higher order thinking:

- Questions that require manipulation of prior knowledge
- Asking students to state ideas or definitions in their own words
- Questions that require students to solve a problem
- Questions that require observations and/or descriptions of an object or event
- Questions that call for comparison and contrast

It is also recommended that teachers give students enough time to attempt to answer the question before calling on another student. When a student is having trouble responding to a question, a teacher should ask probing questions such as:

- Asking for clarification
- Rephrasing the question
- Asking related questions
- Restating the student's ideas

Strategies for Solving Single-Step and Multi-Step Problems
Successful math teachers introduce their students to multiple problem-solving strategies. They create classroom environments where free thought and experimentation are encouraged. Teachers can promote problem-solving among their students by allowing them to make multiple attempts at problems, giving credit for reworking test or homework problems, and encouraging students to share their ideas through class discussion. To maximize efficacy, there are several specific problem-solving skills with which teachers should be familiar.

The **guess-and-check** strategy calls for students to make an initial guess at the solution, check the answer, and use that outcome to guide the next guess. With each successive guess, the student should get closer to the correct answer. **Constructing a table** from the guesses can help to organize the data.

Example:

There are 100 coins in a jar. 10 are dimes. The rest are pennies and nickels. There are twice as many pennies as nickels. How many pennies and nickels are in the jar?

This is a multi-step problem. There are 90 total nickels and pennies in the jar (100 coins – 10 dimes).

There are twice as many pennies as nickels. Students can take guesses that fulfill the criteria and adjust these guesses based on the answer found. They can continue until they find the correct answer: 60 pennies and 30 nickels.

Number of Pennies	Number of Nickels	Total Number of Pennies and Nickels
40	20	60
80	40	120
70	35	105
60	30	90

The **working backwards** strategy requires students to determine a starting point when solving a problem where the final result and the steps to reach the result are given.

Example:

John subtracted 7 from his age, and divided the result by 3. The final result was 4. What is John's age?

Work backward by reversing the operations.

4 x 3 = 12;

12 + 7 = 19

John is 19 years old.

The strategies of **estimation** and testing for **reasonableness** are related skills that students should employ prior to and after solving a problem. These skills are particularly important when students use calculators to find answers.

Example:

Find the sum of 4387 + 7226 + 5893.

4300 + 7200 + 5800 = 17300   Estimation
4387 + 7226 + 5893 = 17506   Actual sum

By comparing the estimate to the actual sum, students can determine whether their answer is reasonable.

Distinguishing relevant from irrelevant information is an important skill for use in math problems solving. Many times, the description of a problem may contain more information than is needed to solve the problem. Some of the information may actually be irrelevant. It is important to focus on what information is relevant to the problem.

Example:

> Jonathan went to the mall and bought a baseball cap for $14, gloves for $10, a stocking cap for $8, a headband for $7, and an umbrella for $15. What was the average price of the headwear that Jonathan bought?

> In this problem, we are interested only in the items Jonathan bought that could be worn on the head: a baseball cap, a stocking cap, and a headband. We would not be interested in the gloves or the umbrella. Therefore, we average $14, $8, and $7 to get $9.67.

The strategy of **simplifying** is used when the best way to solve a problem is to break it into a series of simpler problems. This may be most appropriate when:

> A direct solution to the problem is too complicated
> The problem involves numbers that are either too small or too large
> The student needs to better understand the problem
> The computations are too complex
> The problem involves a diagram or a large array

Example:

> There are 20 people at a party. If each person shakes hands with every other person, how many handshakes will there be?

We could take the long approach by determining that the first person shakes hands with 19 other people, the second person has 18 other people with whom to shake hands, the third person has 17 other people with whom to shake hands, etc., and then adding each of these numbers together.

A simpler approach would be to break the problem down into a smaller problem—such as 4 people at a party. We determine that the first person would shake hands with 3 other people, the second would shake hands with 2 other people, and the third person would shake hands with 1 other person. We can represent this as

$$(4-1)+(4-2)+(4-3) = 3+2+1 = 6$$

or

$$(n-1)+(n-2)+(n-3) = 3n-6 = 6$$

where n = the total number of people at the party. If we set the answer equal to x, we can solve for x as follows:

$$(n-1)n - x = x$$
$$(20-1)(20) = 2x$$
$$(19)(20) = 2x$$
$$380 = 2x$$
$$190 = x$$

Other effective problem solving strategies appropriate for elementary students include:

- Acting out the problem. This might be particularly helpful if the problem involved money And change, for example.

- Using manipulatives to illustrate problem. This is similar to acting the problem out and can be effective when place value or money is involved.

- Looking for patterns that are clues to predict information not provided. This can be facilitated by using tables or diagrams for recording the information.

- Drawing pictures or symbols to represent the information and follow through the processes used to solve. Simple symbols such as x's, O's, or tally marks can help students visualize a problem.

- Flowcharts and templates for setting up and following the steps in a multi-step problem. Such a strategy can help keep the student focused and avoid leaving out steps.

SKILL 6.6   Demonstrating knowledge of the ways in which the language and vocabulary of mathematics are used to communicate ideas precisely and the variety of materials, models, and methods used to explore mathematical concepts and solve problems

Mathematical concepts and procedures can take many different forms. Students of mathematics must be able to recognize different forms of equivalent concepts.

For example, the slope of a line can be represented graphically, algebraically, verbally, and numerically. A line drawn on a coordinate plane will show the slope. In the equation of a line, $y = mx + b$, the term m represents the slope. The slope of a line can be defined in several different ways; it is the change in the value of the y divided by the change in the value of x over a given interval. Alternatively, the slope of a line is the ratio of "rise" to "run" between two points. The numeric value of the slope can be calculated by using the verbal definitions and the algebraic representation of the line.

In order to understand mathematics and to solve problems, it is important to know the definitions of basic mathematic terms and concepts. Many of the terms used in math have definitions and uses that differ from those of everyday language. A line in math is straight, two dimensional, and without a beginning or end. This is at sharp variance from the meaning of a line that is used outside of school (e.g. curves can be lines in art, people can be in lines in the cafeteria, etc.). For a list of definitions and explanations of basic math terms, visit the following website: http://home.blarg.net/~math/deflist.html.

Additionally, one must use the language of mathematics correctly and precisely to communicate concepts and ideas. For example, the statement "minus 10 times minus 5 equals plus 50" is incorrect because "minus" and "plus" are arithmetic operations, not numerical modifiers. The statement should read "negative 10 times negative 5 equals positive 50."

Instruction in the understanding and use of the language of math is particularly critical, as many students who can handle the basic math concepts and calculations will still struggle with the language of math. This is particularly true of ELL populations and students with language learning disabilities.

The development of math concepts in elementary students
In order to identify and select appropriate instructional and support materials for teaching math, it is first necessary to understand something about the developmental processes that influence the child's acquisition of mathematic concepts. Hatfield, et al (2005) describes the child's developing sense of number and math concepts in terms of Piaget's observations on child development.

Preoperational stage: Although movement through developmental stages is highly individual in terms of exact age, most preschool and first grade children are still in what Piaget calls the *Preoperational Stage.* They are aware that objects have a reality outside that of the child itself, and that objects have properties, which they can describe in a limited way. However, they do not yet understand many of the concepts that are critical to basic, underlying math concepts, and they need a great deal of interaction with objects and manipulatives, as well as guiding questions and time, to develop these concepts.

Concrete Operational Stage: By second grade, many children are beginning to enter the *Concrete operational stage* during which a number of concepts critical to the development of math sense can be learned. Children at this stage can act on operations, can understand an *operation* on an object. They can begin to understand relationships between objects (e.g., size, order) and can carry out operations on objects and *reverse* operations on objects. At this stage, children can learn to sort and classify objects according to a variety of criteria. They can understand that an entire group can be a *part or subset* of another group. They can *reverse actions and operations.* They can successively compare objects and *put them in order.* Most important of all for developing math concepts, they can begin to *conserve number* or to understand that the number of objects remains the same even when their arrangement or appearance changes. These concepts are critical to the ability to understand the nature of addition and subtraction, as well as other operations in math.

Formal Operational Stage: By the time children enter middle or high school, many of them will be at the *Formal Operational stage* and they will be capable of learning to conduct operations on other operations independent of any objects or concrete stimuli.

Based on the child's development, Baratta-Lorton described three levels of instruction necessary to help a child move through any mathematics curriculum.

- **Concept Level:** At this level, the child needs *repeated and varied* interaction with manipulatives. The child needs to interact intensively with a variety of objects, to see patterns, combinations, and relationships among the objects before the child can internalize concepts. When introducing new concepts, this is the level at which the child will spend the most time. It is important to remember that the objects are not being used by the teacher to demonstrate concepts, but by the child to *discover* concepts and relationships. The teacher's role is to ask questions that trigger higher order thinking and learning from the child.

- **Connecting Level:** At this level the child learns to assign symbols or representations to the objects and the operations carried out on the objects. However, the objects or manipulatives are still very present and part of the process. Labeling the objects and operations with symbols in the presence of the objects or manipulatives serves as a connection from the concrete level to the next level. The child can move on from this level more quickly and whenever ready to do so.

- **Symbolic Level:** At this level, the child can use symbols without manipulatives. The child understands the abstract concepts behind the symbols and can operate on and with symbols alone.

The National Council of Teachers of Mathematics (NCTM)'s 2000 outline of principles upon which mathematics instruction should be based outlined a similar process by which math concepts should be taught. This document states that instruction and exploration should go through three stages of *representation* (the procedure for modeling and interpreting organization of objects and mathematical operations.

- Concrete Representations: the extensive exploration and use of objects and manipulatives to discover and then demonstrate operations and relationships.

- Pictorial Representations: The use of concrete pictures of objects and actions often in the presence of the objects as discoveries and demonstrations are made.

- Symbolic Representations: The use of symbols exclusively to conduct operations, explorations and discoveries about math concepts.

The Language of Math
For many students, it is the language of math that is most difficult. Although the specific language issues will depend upon the precise math concepts and operations being taught, there are some strategies for helping students master the specialized language of math:

- Model and talk aloud as you work problems and encourage students to do so under your supervision. Stop periodically and ask other students to describe (using good math language!) what another student or you yourself are doing and why. Such practice helps the students learn the reasoning process, the correct words to use, and problem solving strategies.

- DO the math operation manually or have the student do it and talk about it AS you are doing it, not just before or after.

- Explicitly teach math vocabulary using visuals and objects.

- Rephrase a student's words to use math terminology and reward the student's use of correct math language.

Materials, Models, and Methods Used to Explore Mathematical Concepts and Solve Problems

Manipulatives can foster learning for all students. The subject of Mathematics needs to be derived from something that is real to the learner (see above). If the learner can "touch" it, he or she will better understand and remember it. Students can use fingers, ice cream sticks, tiles, and paper folding (as well as commercially available manipulatives) to visualize operations and concepts. The teacher needs to solidify concrete examples into abstract mathematics.

<u>Example</u>:

Use tiles to demonstrate both geometric ideas and number theory.

Give each group of students 12 tiles and instruct them to build rectangles. Students draw their rectangles on paper.

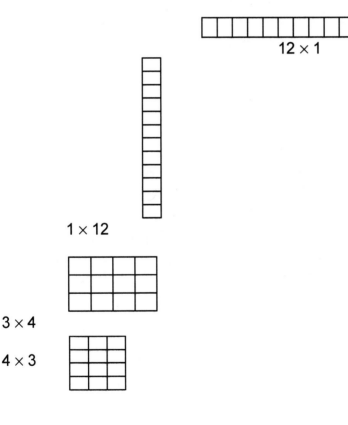

12×1

1×12

3×4

4×3

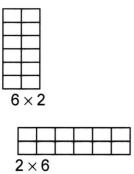

6×2

2×6

Encourage students to describe their reactions. Extend to 16 tiles. Ask students to form additional problems.

Models are another means of representing mathematical concepts by relating them to real-world situations. Teachers must choose wisely when devising and selecting models because, to be effective, models must be properly applied. For example, a building with floors above and below ground is a good model for introducing the concept of negative numbers. It would be difficult, however, to use the building model in teaching subtraction of negative numbers.

When introducing a new mathematical concept to students, teachers should utilize the concrete-to-representational-to-abstract sequence of instruction. The first step of this instructional progression is the introduction of a concept modeled with concrete materials. The second step is the translation of concrete models into representational diagrams or pictures. The third and final step is the translation of representational models into abstract models using only numbers and symbols.

Teachers should first use concrete models to introduce a mathematical concept because they are easiest to understand. For example, teachers can allow students to use counting blocks to learn basic arithmetic. Teachers should give students ample time and many opportunities to experiment, practice, and demonstrate mastery with the concrete materials.

The second step in the learning process allows for a deeper understanding of the first step. For example, students may use tally marks or pictures to represent the counting blocks they used in the previous stage. Once again, teachers should give students ample time to master the concept on the representational level.

The final step in the learning process is necessary for more abstract levels of thought. For example, students represent the processes carried out in the previous stages using only numbers and arithmetic symbols. To ease the transition, teachers should associate numbers and symbols with the concrete and representational models throughout the learning progression.

Sometimes, using a model is the best way to see the solution to a problem, as in the case of fraction multiplication.

Example:

Model $\dfrac{5}{6} \times \dfrac{2}{3}$.

Draw a rectangle. Divide it vertically into 6 equal sections (the denominator of the first number.)

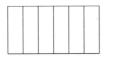

Divide the rectangle horizontally into 3 equal sections (the denominator of the second number).

Color in a number of vertical strips equal to the numerator of the first number.

Use a different color to shade a number of horizontal strips equal to the numerator of the second number.

By describing the area where both colors overlap, we have the product of the two fractions. The answer is $\dfrac{10}{18}$.

Diagrams
Drawing pictures or diagrams can also help to make relationships in a problem clearer.

For example: In a women's marathon, the first five finishers (in no particular order) were Frieda, Polly, Christa, Betty, and Dora. Frieda finished 7 seconds before Christa. Polly finished 6 seconds after Betty. Dora finished 8 seconds after Betty. Christa finished 2 seconds before Polly. In what order did the women finish the race?

Drawing a picture or diagram will help to demonstrate the answer more easily.

From the diagram, we can see that the women finished in the following order: 1st – Frieda, 2nd – Betty, 3rd – Christa, 4th – Polly, and 5th – Dora.

Technology

Finally, there are many forms of **technology** available to math teachers. For example, students can test their understanding of math concepts by working on skill-specific computer programs and websites. Graphing calculators can help students to visualize the graphs of functions. Teachers can also enhance their lectures and classroom presentations by creating multimedia presentations.

A mathematics program based on NCTM standards and current research will have certain characteristics.

- Children will be actively engaged in exploring math concepts and *doing* math. There will be hands-on, concrete exploration, as well talking about, reading about, and writing about math.

- Students will be encouraged to "stretch" their math sense and "think like mathematicians." High standards will be expected, but the learning setting will be safe enough for children to take risks and make mistakes in order to learn, and enjoy learning.

- Teachers will be asking questions that stimulate children to make new discoveries and to reveal concepts they already know. Questioning will lead students to make connections between what they know and what they learn.

- Cooperative learning will take place. Children will learn from talking to one another about math and working together.

- Math will be part of the "real world" and connections to that real world will be made for all activities and concepts.

- Content taught will cover a wide range of topics and applications. Children will learn not only computation, but the concepts behind computation and use, and the math language to discuss these connections.

SKILL 6.7 **Demonstrating knowledge of the interconnections among mathematical concepts; the applications of mathematics in other content areas; and the applications of measurement, geometry, algebra, and data analysis in everyday life**

Recognition and understanding of the relationships between concepts and topics is of great value in mathematical problem-solving as well as in the explanation of more complex processes.

For instance, multiplication can be seen simply as repeated addition. This relationship explains the concept of **variable addition**. We can show that the expression $4x + 3x = 7x$ is true by rewriting 4 times x and 3 times x as repeated addition, yielding the expression $(x + x + x + x) + (x + x + x)$. Thus, because of the relationship between multiplication and addition, variable addition is accomplished by **coefficient addition**.

In this same way, division and multiplication are also linked. Many students find multiplication to be much easier to understand than division. Teaching them that they are two sides of the same concept may make all the difference.

For example, knowing that $6 \times 8 = 48$ off the top one's head makes understanding $48 \div 6 = 8$ even easier. This is why multiplication charts have always held a place in many elementary education classrooms.

Students will react differently to this type of mathematical breakdown. Some may find that explaining multiplication (or any other complex mathematical concept) in terms of an already mastered concept—in this case, addition—will help to strengthen their ability to understand and even enjoy mathematics. However, others may find difficulty in understanding the underlying concepts behind the correlation—either because they don't grasp the connection or because they have moved beyond it.

Although this may make teaching mathematical relationships more difficult for the teacher, it is important to recognize that mathematical concepts and procedures can take many different forms, and instruction will need to be differentiated in order to reach all students. Students of mathematics must be able to recognize different forms of equivalent concepts. These basic skill sets will lead to a higher level of understanding as the level of difficulty in mathematical concepts increases.

Applications of Mathematics in Other Content Areas and in Everyday Life
Real-world applications of mathematics abound and offer highly-motivating opportunities for computational practice and the development of number sense and mathematical reasoning that can give students confidence in their mathematical abilities. Finding the mathematical connections in outdoor games, planning for the purchase of lunch, comparing heights among classmates, calculating the time until recess, and figuring out which sports team is headed for the playoffs are just a few examples.

Teachers can increase interest in math and promote learning and understanding by relating mathematical concepts to the lives of students. Instead of using only abstract presentations and examples, teachers should relate concepts to real-world situations that then shift the emphasis from memorization and abstract application to understanding and applied problem-solving. The skillful teacher will make an effort to understand students as individuals and learn what interests them. Young baseball fans, for example, will probably work harder on math problems related to batting average and winning percentages than to contrived problems with Susie and Becky and their vegetable garden, or whatever generic problem is found in the textbook. In addition, relating math to careers and professions helps to illustrate the relevance of math; it may even aid in the career exploration process.

For example, when teaching a unit on the geometry of certain shapes, teachers can ask students to design a structure of interest using the shapes in question.

This exercise serves the dual purpose of teaching students to learn and apply the properties (e.g., area, volume) of shapes while demonstrating the relevance of geometry to architectural and engineering professions.

Artists, musicians, scientists, social scientists, and business people use mathematical modeling to solve problems in their disciplines. These disciplines rely on the tools and symbols of mathematics to model natural events and manipulate data.

Mathematics is a key aspect of visual art. Artists use the geometric properties of shapes, ratios, and proportions in creating paintings and sculptures. For example, mathematics is essential to the concept of perspective. Artists must determine the appropriate lengths and heights of objects to portray three-dimensional distance in two dimensions. The "Golden Mean" used historically in all great art is basically a mathematic concept.

Mathematics is also an important part of music. Many musical terms have mathematical connections. For example, the musical octave contains twelve notes and spans a factor of two in frequency. In other words, the frequency, the speed of vibration that determines tone and sound quality, doubles from the first note in an octave to the last. Thus, starting from any note, we can determine the frequency of any other note with the following formula.

Freq = note x $2^{N/12}$

In this equation, N is the number of notes from the starting point, and *note* is the frequency of the starting note. Mathematical understanding of frequency plays an important role in tuning musical instruments.

In addition to the visual and auditory arts, mathematics is an integral part of most scientific disciplines. The uses of mathematics in science are almost endless.

The following are but a few examples of how scientists use mathematics, but it is certainly not a comprehensive list. Physical scientists use vectors, functions, derivatives, and integrals to describe and model the movement of objects.

Biologists and ecologists use mathematics to model ecosystems and study DNA. Chemists use mathematics to study the interaction of molecules and to determine proper amounts and proportions of reactants.

Many social science disciplines use mathematics to model and solve problems as well. Economists, for example, use functions, graphs, and matrices to model the activities of producers, consumers, and firms.

Scales
Students need to understand that ratios and proportions are used to create scale models of real-life objects. They also must understand the principles of ratio and proportion, and how to calculate scale using ratio and proportion.

Scaled drawings (maps, blueprints, and models) are used in many real-world situations. Architects make blueprints and models of buildings. These drawings and models are then used by the contractors to build the buildings. Engineers make scaled drawings of bridges, machine parts, roads, airplanes, and many other things. Maps of the world, countries, states, and roads are scaled drawings too. Landscape designers use scale drawings and models of plants, decks, and other structures to show how they should be placed around a building. Models of cars, boats, and planes made from kits are scaled. Automobile engineers construct models of cars before the actual assembly is done. Many museum exhibits are actually scaled models because the real size of the items displayed would be too large.

Examples of real-world problems that students might solve using scaled drawings include:

- Reading road maps and determining the distance between locations by using the map scale
- Creating a scaled drawing (floor plan) of the classroom to determine the best use of space
- Creating an 8 ½" x 11" representation of a quilt to be pieced together
- Drawing blueprints of their rooms and creating models from them

It is not enough to simply tell students that math is a part of many disciplines as well as their everyday life. In designing daily lessons in all subjects, the role of math should be noted and practiced. Instead of limiting math work to one class period per day, the teacher should be searching the lessons and standards of other subjects for the math concepts that are relevant to those standards. Then math practice or lessons should be coordinated with those subjects. If, for example, the math class is studying the ordering of large numbers, the teacher might consider having students in geography class order the height of the mountains they are studying or the depths of the various oceans, and so forth.

OBJECTIVE 7   **UNDERSTAND PRINCIPLES AND SKILLS OF MEASUREMENT AND THE CONCEPTS AND PROPERTIES OF GEOMETRY**

SKILL 7.1   **Identifying appropriate measurement procedures, tools, and units (e.g., customary and metric) for problems involving length, perimeter, area, capacity, weight, time, money, and temperature**

Measurements of length (English system)

12 inches (in)	=	1 foot (ft)
3 feet (ft)	=	1 yard (yd)
1760 yards (yd)	=	1 mile (mi)

Measurements of length (Metric system)

kilometer (km)	=	1000 meters (m)
hectometer (hm)	=	100 meters (m)
decameter (dam)	=	10 meters (m)
meter (m)	=	1 meter (m)
decimeter (dm)	=	1/10 meter (m)
centimeter (cm)	=	1/100 meter (m)
millimeter (mm)	=	1/1000 meter (m)

Conversion of length from English to Metric

1 inch	=	2.54 centimeters
1 foot	$\approx$	30 centimeters
1 yard	$\approx$	0.9 meters
1 mile	$\approx$	1.6 kilometers

Measurements of weight (English system)

28 grams (g)	=	1 ounce (oz)
16 ounces (oz)	=	1 pound (lb)
2000 pounds (lb)	=	1 ton (t) (short ton)
1.1 ton (t)	=	1 ton (t)

Measurements of weight (Metric system)

kilogram (kg)	=	1000 grams (g)
gram (g)	=	1 gram (g)
milligram (mg)	=	1/1000 gram (g)

Conversion of weight from English to metric

1 ounce	$\approx$	28 grams
1 pound	$\approx$	0.45 kilogram (454 grams)

Measurement of volume (English system)

8 fluid ounces (oz)	=	1 cup (c)
2 cups (c)	=	1 pint (pt)
2 pints (pt)	=	1 quart (qt)
4 quarts (qt)	=	1 gallon (gal)

Measurement of volume (Metric system)

kiloliter (kl)	=	1000 liters (l)
liter (l)	=	1 liter (l)
milliliter (ml)	=	1/1000 liters (ml)

Conversion of volume from English to metric

1 teaspoon (tsp)	≈	5 milliliters
1 fluid ounce	≈	15 milliliters
1 cup	≈	0.24 liters
1 pint	≈	0.47 liters
1 quart	≈	0.95 liters
1 gallon	≈	3.8 liters

Measurement of time

1 minute	=	60 seconds
1 hour	=	60 minutes
1 day	=	24 hours
1 week	=	7 days
1 year	=	365 days
1 century	=	100 years

Note: (') represents feet and (") represents inches.

Square Units
Square units can be derived from the knowledge of basic units of length by squaring the equivalent measurements.

> 1 square foot (sq. ft.) = 144 sq. in.
> 1 sq. yd. = 9 sq. ft.
> 1 sq. yd. = 1296 sq. in.

Example:

14 sq. yd. = _____ sq. ft.
14 × 9 = 126 sq. ft.

Weight

Example:

Kathy has a bag of potatoes that weighs 5 lbs., 10 oz. She uses one-third of the bag to make mashed potatoes. How much does the bag weigh now?

1 lb. = 16 oz.
5(16 oz.) + 10 oz. = 80 oz. + 10 oz. = 90 oz.
$90 - (\frac{1}{3})$ 90 oz.   = 90 oz. − 30 oz. = 60 oz.
60 ÷ 16 = 3.75 lbs.
.75 = 75%
75% = $\frac{75}{100}$ = $\frac{3}{4}$
$\frac{3}{4}$ x 16 oz. = 12 oz.

The bag weighs 3 lbs., 12 oz.

Example:

The weight limit of a playground merry-go-round is 1000 pounds. There are 11 children on the merry-go-round. 3 children weigh 100 pounds. 6 children weigh 75 pounds. 2 children weigh 60 pounds. George weighs 80 pounds. Can he get on the merry-go-round?

3(100) + 6(75) + 2(60)
= 300 + 450 + 120
= 870
1000 − 870
= 130

Since 80 is less than 130, George can get on the merry-go-round.

Perimeter and Area

The **perimeter** of any polygon is the sum of the lengths of the sides.

The **area** of a polygon is the number of square units covered by the figure.

FIGURE	AREA FORMULA	PERIMETER FORMULA
Rectangle	LW	$2(L+W)$
Triangle	$\frac{1}{2}bh$	$a+b+c$
Parallelogram	bh	sum of lengths of sides
Trapezoid	$\frac{1}{2}h(a+b)$	sum of lengths of sides

Example:

A farmer has a piece of land shaped as shown below. He wishes to fence this land at an estimated cost of $25 per linear foot. What is the total cost of fencing this property to the nearest foot?

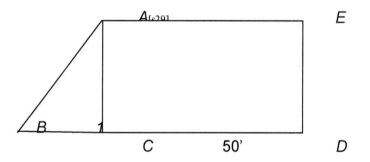

From the right triangle ABC, AC = 30 and BC = 15.

Since $(AB) = (AC)^2 + (BC)^2$
$(AB) = (30)^2 + (15)^2$

So $\sqrt{(AB)^2} = AB = \sqrt{1125} = 33.5410$ feet

To the nearest foot AB = 34 feet.

Perimeter of the piece of land is $= AB + BC + CD + DE + EA$

= 34 + 15 + 50 + 30 + 50 = 179 feet

cost of fencing = $25 x 179 = $4, 475.00

Example:

What will be the cost of carpeting a rectangular office that measures 12 feet by 15 feet if the carpet costs $12.50 per square yard?

12 ft

15 ft

The problem is asking you to determine the area of the office. The area of a rectangle is *length x width = A*

Substitute the given values in the equation *A = lw*

A = (12 ft.)(15 ft.)

A = 180 ft. ^{2}

The problem asked you to determine the cost of carpet at $12.50 per square yard.

First, you need to convert 180 ft.^{2} into yards^2.

1 yd. = 3 ft.
(1 yard)(1 yard) = (3 feet)(3 feet)
$1 \text{ yd}^2 = 9 \text{ ft}^2$

Hence, $\dfrac{180 \text{ ft}^2}{1} \quad \dfrac{1 \text{ yd}^2}{9 \text{ ft}^2} = \dfrac{20}{1} = 20 \text{ yd}^2$

The carpet cost $12.50 per square yard; thus the cost of carpeting the office described is $12.50 x 20 = $250.00.

Example:

Find the area of a parallelogram whose base is 6.5 cm and the height of the altitude to that base is 3.7 cm.

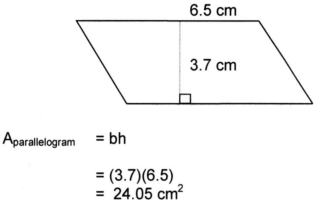

$A_{parallelogram}$ = bh

= (3.7)(6.5)
= 24.05 cm^2

Example:

Find the area of this triangle.

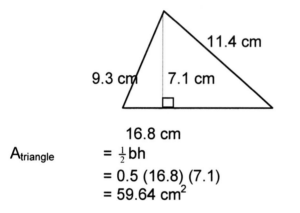

$A_{triangle}$ = $\frac{1}{2}$bh
= 0.5 (16.8) (7.1)
= 59.64 cm^2

<u>Example</u>:

Find the area of this trapezoid.

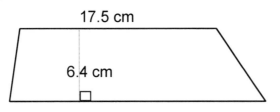

17.5 cm

6.4 cm

23.7 cm

The area of a trapezoid equals one-half the sum of the bases times the altitude.

$$A_{trapezoid} = \tfrac{1}{2}h(b_1 + b_2)$$
$$= 0.5\,(6.4)\,(17.5 + 23.7)$$
$$= 131.84 \text{ cm}^2$$

Circles

The distance around a circle is the **circumference**. The ratio of the circumference to the diameter is represented by the Greek letter pi, $\pi \sim 3.14 \sim \dfrac{22}{7}$.

The circumference of a circle is found by the formula $C = 2\pi r$ or $C = \pi d$, where r is the radius of the circle and d is the diameter.

The area of a circle is found by the formula $A = \pi r^2$.

<u>Example</u>:

Find the circumference and area of a circle whose radius is 7 meters.

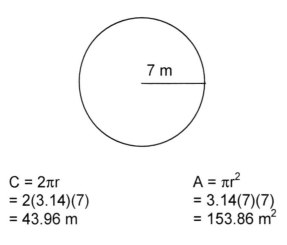

7 m

$C = 2\pi r$

$= 2(3.14)(7)$

$= 43.96$ m

$A = \pi r^2$

$= 3.14(7)(7)$

$= 153.86 \text{ m}^2$

Reading Instruments

When reading an instrument, students should first determine the interval of scale on that particular instrument. To achieve the greatest accuracy, they should read the scale to the nearest measurement mark.

If they are using a scale with a needle that has a mirrored plate behind it, the scale should be viewed so that the needle's reflection is hidden behind the needle itself. Students should not look at it from an angle. In order to read a balance scale accurately, it is necessary to place the scale on a level surface and make sure that the hand points precisely at 0. Objects should be placed on the plate gently and taken away gently. The dial should be faced straight on to read the graduation accurately. Students should read from the large graduation to smaller graduation. If the dial hand points between two graduations, they should choose the number that is closest to the hand.

When reading inches on a ruler, the student needs to understand that each inch is divided into halves by the longest mark in the middle; into fourths by the next longest marks; into eighths by the next; and into sixteenths by the shortest. When the measurement falls between two inch marks, they can give the whole number of inches, count the additional fractional marks, and give the answer as the number and fraction of inches. Remind students that the convention is always to express a fraction by its lowest possible denominator.

If students are using the metric system on a ruler, have them focus on the marks between the whole numbers (centimeters). Point out that each centimeter is broken into tenths, with the mark in the middle being longer to indicate a halfway mark. Students should learn to measure things accurately to the nearest tenth of a centimeter, then the nearest hundredth, and finally the nearest thousandth. Measurements using the metric system should always be written using the decimal system, for example, 3.756 centimeters.

Whether using standard or metric rulers, it is critically important that students understand the nature of the units on the ruler and the fact that the lengths of the spaces between marks are standard and uniform. When measuring, they need to place the ruler so the end mark before the first unit, *not the edge of the ruler* is at the beginning of whatever they are measuring. In addition, they need to understand that they can start measuring at any point of the ruler and get a correct measurement. For example, if they need to place the ruler at the two-inch point and the item ends at the six-inch point, the item is four, not six inches long.

When reading a thermometer, it should be held vertically at eye level. Students should check the scale of the thermometer to make certain they read as many significant digits as possible. Thermometers with heavy or extended lines that are marked 10, 20, 30 … should be read to the nearest 0.1 degree. Thermometers with fine lines every two degrees may be read to the nearest 0.5 degree.

In order to get an accurate reading in a liquid measuring cup, students should set the cup on a level surface and[SAW30] read it at eye level. The measurement should be read at the bottom of the concave arc at the liquid's surface (the **meniscus** line). When measuring dry ingredients, dip the appropriately sized measuring cup into the ingredient and sweep away the excess across the top with a straight-edged object.

Protractors measure angles in degrees. To measure accurately, students must find the center hole on the straight edge of the protractor and place it over the vertex of the angle they wish to measure. They should line up the zero on the straight edge with one of the sides of the angle, and find the point where the second side of the angle intersects the curved edge of the protractor. They can then read the number that is written at the point of intersection.

When reading an instrument such as a rain gauge, it is again important to read at eye level and at the base of the meniscus. The measuring tube is divided, marked, and labeled in tenths and hundredths. The greatest number of decimal places there will be is two.

Most numbers in mathematics are "exact" or "counted." Measurements are "approximate." They usually involve interpolation, or figuring out which mark on the ruler is closest. Any measurement acquired with a measuring device is approximate. These variations in measurement are called precision and accuracy.

Precision is a measurement of how exactly a measurement is made, without reference to a true or real value. If a measurement is precise, it can be made again and again with little variation in the result. The precision of a measuring device is the smallest fractional or decimal division on the instrument. The smaller the unit or fraction of a unit on the measuring device, the more precisely it can measure.

The greatest possible error of measurement is always equal to one-half the smallest fraction of a unit on the measuring device.

Accuracy is a measure of how close the result of measurement comes to the "true" value.

If throwing darts, the true value is the bull's eye. If the three darts land on the bull's eye, the dart thrower is both precise (all land near the same spot) and accurate (the darts all land on the "true" value).

The greatest measure of error allowed is called the **tolerance**. The least acceptable limit is called the **lower limit,** and the greatest acceptable limit is called the **upper limit**. The difference between the upper and lower limits is called the **tolerance interval**. For example, a specification for an automobile part might be 14.625 ± 0.005 mm. This means that the smallest acceptable length of the part is 14.620 mm and the largest length acceptable is 14.630 mm. The tolerance interval is 0.010 mm. One can see how it would be important for automobile parts to be within a set of limits in terms of length. If the part is too long or too short it will not fit properly, and vibrations will occur that weaken the part and may eventually cause damage to other parts.

SKILL 7.2   Applying knowledge of approaches to direct measurement through the use of standard and nonstandard units and indirect measurement through the use of algebra or geometry

There are two types of measurement: **direct measurement** and **indirect measurement**. As the name implies, direct measurement is the action of directly measuring something. For example, the length of a boat can be measured with a measuring tape, or elapsed time can be measured with a stop watch.

Indirect measurement is measurement that is not done with a tool such as a ruler or watch. Instead, other mathematical approaches are used to *derive* the desired measurement. Using similar triangles is an example of indirect measurement. Similar triangles have the same angles and proportionate sides, but they are different sizes. They can be used to determine the distance from one point to another without measuring it directly. In the diagram below, *X* represents the distance between two points with an unknown length.

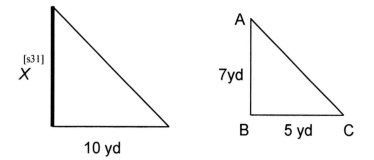

The problem can be determined by setting up the proportion below and solving for *X*.

$$\frac{X}{10 \text{ yd}} = \frac{7\text{yd}}{5\text{yd}}$$

After cross-multiplying, the equation can be written as 5X = 70; X equals 14 yards. Without actually measuring the distance with a measuring tape or other tools, the distance between the points is determined.

Indirect measurement also occurs in instances other than simply measuring length. The area of a room can be measured using a scale drawing. Measuring the weight of the moon is possible using the measurable effects the moon exerts on the earth, such as the changes in tides. Another familiar indirect measurement is the Body Mass Index (BMI), which indicates body composition. The body composition uses height and weight measurements to measure health risks.

SKILL 7.3 Classifying plane and solid geometric figures (e.g., triangle, quadrilateral, sphere, cone)

A **triangle** is a polygon with three sides.

Triangles can be classified by the types of angles or the lengths of their sides.

Classifying By Angles

An **acute** triangle has exactly three acute angles.
A **right** triangle has one right angle.
An **obtuse** triangle has one obtuse angle.

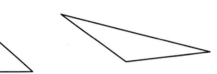

acute   right   obtuse

Classifying By Sides

All three sides of an **equilateral** triangle are the same length.
Two sides of an **isosceles** triangle are the same length.
None of the sides of a **scalene** triangle are the same length.

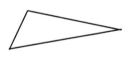

equilateral   isosceles   scalene

A **quadrilateral** is a polygon with four sides.
The sum of the measures of the angles of a convex quadrilateral is 360°.

A **trapezoid** is a quadrilateral with exactly <u>one</u> pair of parallel sides.

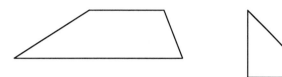

In an **isosceles trapezoid**, the non-parallel sides are congruent.

A **parallelogram** is a quadrilateral with <u>two</u> pairs of parallel sides.

A **rectangle** is a four sided polygon, a parallelogram with four right angles (all four interior angles are right angles).

A **rhombus** is a parallelogram with all sides of equal length.

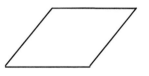

A **square** is a rectangle with all sides of equal length.

The union of all points on a simple closed surface and all points in its interior form a space figure called a **solid**. The five regular solids, or **polyhedra**, are the cube, tetrahedron, octahedron, icosahedron, and dodecahedron. A **net** is a two-dimensional figure that can be cut out and folded up to make a three-dimensional solid. Below are models of the five regular solids with their corresponding face polygons and nets.

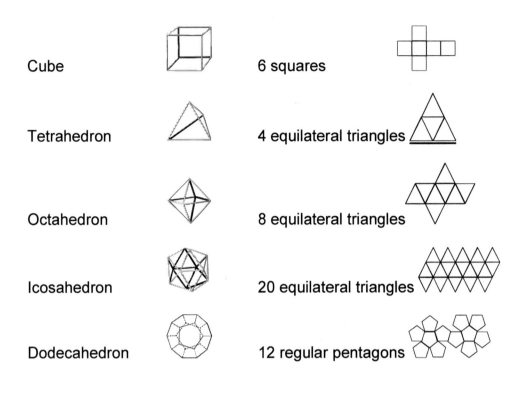

Cube		6 squares
Tetrahedron		4 equilateral triangles
Octahedron		8 equilateral triangles
Icosahedron		20 equilateral triangles
Dodecahedron		12 regular pentagons

Other examples of solids:

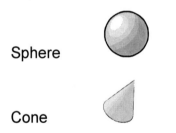

Sphere

Cone

A **sphere** is a space figure having all its points the same distance from the center.

A **cone** is a space figure having a circular base and a single vertex.

SKILL 7.4   Applying knowledge of basic geometric concepts (e.g., similarity, congruence, parallelism) and knowledge of strategies for measuring the component parts (e.g., angles, segments) of geometric figures and computing the volume of simple geometric solids

Congruent figures have the same size and shape. If one is placed above the other, they will fit exactly. Congruent lines have the same length. Congruent angles have equal measures.

The symbol for congruent is $\cong$.

Polygons (pentagons) *ABCDE* and *VWXYZ* are congruent. They are exactly the same size and shape.

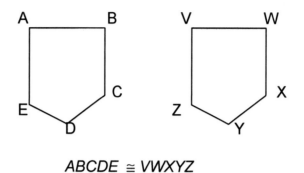

$$ABCDE \cong VWXYZ$$

Corresponding parts are the congruent angles and congruent sides. They are:

corresponding angles	corresponding sides
$\angle A \leftrightarrow \angle V$	$AB \leftrightarrow VW$
$\angle B \leftrightarrow \angle W$	$BC \leftrightarrow WX$
$\angle C \leftrightarrow \angle X$	$CD \leftrightarrow XY$
$\angle D \leftrightarrow \angle Y$	$DE \leftrightarrow YZ$
$\angle E \leftrightarrow \angle Z$	$AE \leftrightarrow VZ$

Example:

Given two similar quadrilaterals, find the lengths of sides *x, y,* and *z.*

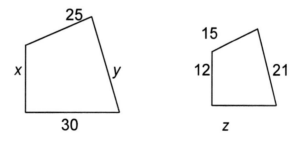

Since corresponding sides are proportional, the scale is:

$$\frac{12}{x} = \frac{3}{5} \qquad \frac{21}{y} = \frac{3}{5} \qquad \frac{z}{30} = \frac{3}{5}$$

$3x = 60$ $3y = 105$ $5z = 90$
$x = 20$ $y = 35$ $z = 18$

Similarity

Two figures that have the same shape are **similar**. Polygons are similar if and only if corresponding angles are congruent and corresponding sides are in proportion. Corresponding parts of similar polygons are proportional.

<u>Example:</u>

Given the rectangles below, compare the area and perimeter.

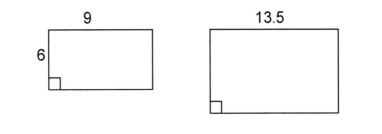

$A = LW$ $A = LW$ 1. Write formula
$A = (6)(9)$ $A = (9)(13.5)$ 2. Substitute known
                                    values
$A = 54$ sq. units $A = 121.5$ sq. units   3. Compute

$P = 2(L + W)$ $P = 2(L + W)$ 1. Write formula
$P = 2(6 + 9)$ $P = 2(9 + 13.5)$ 2. Substitute known
                                    values
$P = 30$ units $P = 45$ units   3. Compute

Notice that the areas relate to each other in the following manner:
Ratio of sides $9/13.5 = 2/3$

Multiply the first area by the square of the reciprocal $(3/2)^2$ to get the second area.
$54 \times (3/2)^2 = 121.5$

The perimeters relate to each other in the following manner:
Ratio of sides $9/13.5 = 2/3$

Multiply the perimeter of the first by the reciprocal of the ratio to get the perimeter of the second.
$30 \times 3/2 = 45$

Measuring the Component Parts of Geometric Figures and Computing the Volume of Simple Geometric Solids

In geometry, the point, line, and plane are key concepts that can be discussed in relation to each other.

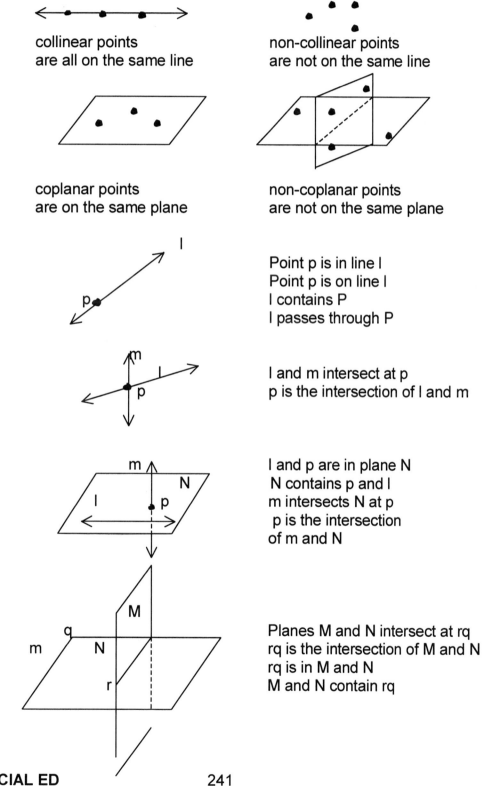

collinear points
are all on the same line

non-collinear points
are not on the same line

coplanar points
are on the same plane

non-coplanar points
are not on the same plane

Point p is in line l
Point p is on line l
l contains P
l passes through P

l and m intersect at p
p is the intersection of l and m

l and p are in plane N
N contains p and l
m intersects N at p
p is the intersection
of m and N

Planes M and N intersect at rq
rq is the intersection of M and N
rq is in M and N
M and N contain rq

The classifying of angles refers to the angle measure. The naming of angles refers to the letters or numbers used to label the angle.

Example:

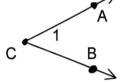

$\overrightarrow{CA}$ (read ray CA) and $\overrightarrow{CB}$ are the sides of the angle.
The angle can be called $\angle ACB$, $\angle BCA$, $\angle C$ or $\angle 1$.

Angles are classified according to their size as follows:

Acute: greater than 0 and less than 90 degrees.
Right: exactly 90 degrees.
Obtuse: greater than 90 and less than 180 degrees.
Straight: exactly 180 degrees

Angles can be classified in a number of other ways. Some of those classifications are outlined here.

Adjacent angles have a common vertex and one common side but no interior points in common.

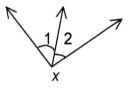

Complementary angles add up to 90 degrees.

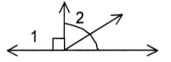

Supplementary angles add up to 180 degrees.

Vertical angles have sides that form two pairs of opposite rays.

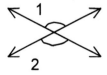

Corresponding angles are in the same corresponding position on two parallel lines cut by a transversal.

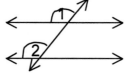

Alternate interior angles are diagonal angles on the inside of two parallel lines cut by a transversal.

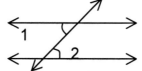

Alternate exterior angles are diagonal on the outside of two parallel lines cut by a transversal.

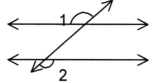

Parallel lines or planes do not intersect.

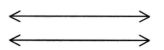

Perpendicular lines or planes form a 90 degree angle to each other.

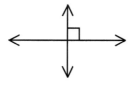

Intersecting lines share a common point, and intersecting planes share a common set of points or line.

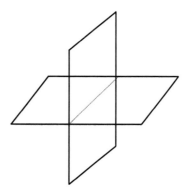

Skew lines do not intersect and do not lie on the same plane.

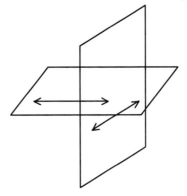

The three undefined terms of geometry are point, line, and plane.

A **plane** is a flat surface that extends forever in two dimensions. It has no ends or edges. It has no thickness to it. It is usually drawn as a parallelogram that can be named either by three non-collinear points (three points that are not on the same line) on the plane, or by placing a letter in the corner of the plane that is not used elsewhere in the diagram.

A **line** extends forever in one dimension. It is determined and named by two points that are on the line. The line consists of every point that is between those two points as well as the points that are on the "straight" extension each way. A line is drawn as a line segment with arrows facing opposite directions on each end to indicate that the line continues in both directions forever.

A **point** is a position in space, on a line, or on a plane. It has no thickness and no width. Only one line can go through any two points. A point is represented by a dot named by a single letter.

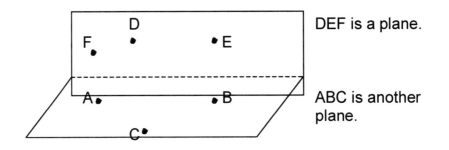

DEF is a plane.

ABC is another plane.

<--•-----•-------------•-------->

G   H   I

This line can be named by any two points on the line.

For example, the line could be named $\overline{GH}$, $\overline{HI}$, $\overline{GI}$, $\overline{IG}$, $\overline{IH}$, or $\overline{HG}$. Any two points (letters) on the line can be used, and their order is not important in naming a line. In the above diagrams, A, B, C, D, E, F, G, H, and I are all locations of individual points.

A **ray** is not an undefined term. A ray consists of all the points on a line starting at one given point and extending in only one of the two opposite directions along the line. The ray is named by naming two points on the ray. The first point must be the endpoint of the ray, while the second point can be any other point along the ray. The symbol for a ray is a ray above the two letters used to name it. The endpoint of the ray MUST be the first letter.

J •----•-------------•------>
     K   L

This ray could be named $\overrightarrow{JK}$ or $\overrightarrow{JL}$. It cannot be called $\overrightarrow{KJ}$ or $\overrightarrow{LJ}$ or $\overrightarrow{LK}$ or $\overrightarrow{KL}$, because none of these names starts with the endpoint, J.

The **distance** between two points on a number line is equal to the absolute value of the difference of the two numbers associated with the points.

If one point is located at "a" and the other point is at "b," then the distance between them is found by this formula:

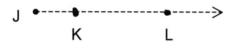

$$\text{distance} = |a - b| \text{ or } |b - a|$$

If one point is located at $^-3$ and another point is located at 5, the distance between them is found by:

$$\text{distance} = |a - b| = |(^-3) - 5| = |^-8| = 8$$

Volume and **surface area** are computed using the following formulas:

FIGURE	VOLUME	TOTAL SURFACE AREA
Right Cylinder	$\pi r^2 h$	$2\pi rh + 2\pi r^2$
Right Cone	$\dfrac{\pi r^2 h}{3}$	$\pi r\sqrt{r^2 + h^2} + \pi r^2$
Sphere	$\dfrac{4}{3}\pi r^3$	$4\pi r^2$
Rectangular Solid	LWH	$2LW + 2WH + 2LH$

FIGURE	LATERAL AREA	TOTAL AREA	VOLUME
Regular Pyramid	1/2Pl	1/2Pl+B	1/3Bh

P = Perimeter
h = height
B = Area of Base
l = slant height

Example:

What is the volume of a shoe box with a length of 35 cm, a width of 20 cm, and a height of 15 cm?

Volume of a rectangular solid= Length x Width x Height

= 35 x 20 x 15
= 10500 cm^3

Example:

A water company is trying to decide whether to use traditional cylindrical paper cups or to offer conical paper cups, since both cost the same. The traditional cups are 8 cm wide and 14 cm high. The conical cups are 12 cm wide and 19 cm high. The company will use the cup that holds the most water.

Draw and label a sketch of each.

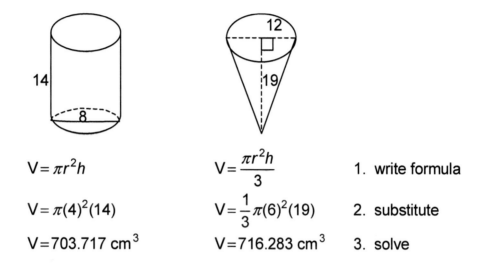

$V = \pi r^2 h$ $V = \dfrac{\pi r^2 h}{3}$ 1. write formula

$V = \pi(4)^2(14)$ $V = \dfrac{1}{3}\pi(6)^2(19)$ 2. substitute

$V = 703.717 \text{ cm}^3$ $V = 716.283 \text{ cm}^3$ 3. solve

The choice should be the conical cup since its volume is more.

Example:

How much material is needed to make a basketball that has a diameter of 15 inches? How much air is needed to fill the basketball?

Draw and label a sketch:

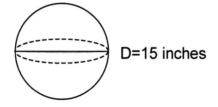
D=15 inches

Total surface area   Volume

$TSA = 4\pi r^2$ $V = \dfrac{4}{3}\pi r^3$ 1. Write formula

$= 4\pi(7.5)^2$ $= \dfrac{4}{3}\pi(7.5)^3$ 2. Substitute

$= 706.858 \text{ in}^2$ $= 1767.1459 \text{ in}^3$ 3. Solve

SKILL 7.5   Applying knowledge of coordinate systems to identify representations of basic geometric figures and concepts

We can represent any two-dimensional geometric figure in the **Cartesian** or **rectangular coordinate system**. The Cartesian or rectangular coordinate system is formed by two perpendicular axes (coordinate axes): the X-axis and the Y-axis. If we know the dimensions of a two-dimensional (planar) figure, we can use this coordinate system to visualize the shape of the figure.

<u>Example</u>:

Represent an isosceles triangle with two sides of length 4.

Draw the two sides along the x- and y- axes and connect the points (vertices).

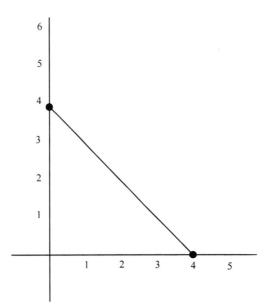

In order to represent three-dimensional figures, we need three coordinate axes (X, Y, and Z) that are all mutually perpendicular to each other. Since we cannot draw three mutually perpendicular axes on a two-dimensional surface, we use oblique representations.

Example:

Represent a cube with sides of 2.

Once again, we draw three sides along the three axes to make things easier.

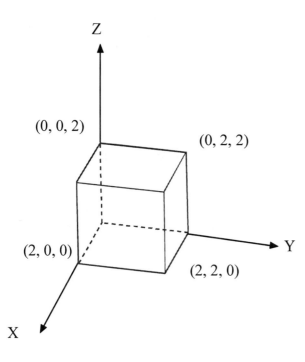

Each point has three coordinates (x, y, z).

OBJECTIVE 8   UNDERSTAND CONCEPTS AND SKILLS RELATED TO ALGEBRA

SKILL 8.1   Recognizing the characteristics of patterns, identifying correct extensions of patterns, and recognizing relationships (e.g., color, shape, texture, number) among patterns

The following table represents the number of problems Mr. Rodgers is assigning his math students for homework each day, starting with the first day of class.

Day	1	2	3	4	5	6	7	8	9	10	11
Number of Problems	1	1	2	3	5	8	13				

If Mr. Rodgers continues this pattern, how many problems will he assign on the eleventh day?

If we look for a pattern, it appears that the number of problems assigned each day is equal to the sum of the problems assigned for the previous two days. We test this as follows:

Day 2 = 1 + 0 = 1
Day 3 = 1 + 1 = 2
Day 4 = 2 + 1 = 3
Day 5 = 3 + 2 = 5
Day 6 = 5 + 3 = 8
Day 7 = 8 + 5 = 13

Therefore, Day 8 would have 21 problems; Day 9, 34 problems; Day 10, 55 problems; and Day 11, 89 problems.

A sequence is a pattern of numbers arranged in a particular order. When a list of numbers is in a sequence, a pattern may be expressed in terms of variables. Suppose we have the sequence 8, 12, 16…. If we assign the variable a to the initial term, 8, and assign the variable d to the difference between the first two terms, we can formulate a pattern of $a, a + d, a + 2d … a + (n-1)d$. With this formula, we can determine any number in the sequence. For example, let's say we want to know what the 400th term would be. Using the formula,

$$a + (n-1)d =$$
$$8 + (400-1)4 =$$
$$8 + 399(4) =$$
$$8 + 1596 = 1604$$

We determine that the 400th term would be 1604.

Suppose we have an equation, $y = 2x + 1$. We construct a table of values in order to graph the equation to see if we can find a pattern.

x	y
-2	-3
-1	-1
0	1
1	3
2	5

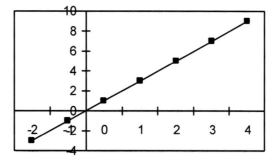

The pattern formed by the points is that they all lie on a line. Therefore, we can determine any solution of *y* by picking an *x*-coordinate and finding the corresponding point on the line. For example, if we want to know the solution of *y* when *x* is equal to 4, we find the corresponding point and see that *y* is equal to 9.

Teaching Recognition of Patterns and Relationships

When teaching any math concept, it is important to remember that there will be a hierarchy of concepts that act as steps leading to the concept being taught. In order to fully master any concept in math, it is necessary to first master the mathematical "stepping stones" to that concept. According to Hatfield, et al (2005), an understanding of patterns, their combinations, and functions is critical to understanding algebraic reasoning as something that goes beyond symbols on the page. It is important that instruction in the most basic elements of these concepts begin in the earliest school years.

Patterns

When students are asked to recognize a pattern, they are being asked to identify the repetitive nature of something. This requires at least two prerequisite skills:

- Identifying similarities
- Detecting differences

Prior to beginning any lessons on pattern recognition, the teacher needs to assure that students have these two prerequisite skills.

The National Council of Teachers of Mathematics (NCTM) states that elementary students should engage in many repeated activities involving the recognition, extension, transfer, translation, creation, and description of patterns on a concrete, meaningful level. These experiences should include visual, auditory, and kinesthetic activities.

As noted in Skill 6.6, children should spend the most time at this concrete conceptual level when learning any new concept. This is particularly true of students with learning disabilities, as many will need more time at the concrete concept level. Care must be taken to be sure that students with perceptual difficulties have adequate practice using whatever sensory modality is best for them.

In early elementary school, this means sorting and classifying a wide variety of simple, concrete objects and pictures, creating and duplicating patterns with them, and discussing and *describing the patterns.* It should also involve beginning to describe changes in quality (bigger, louder) and quantity (more or less).

In later elementary school, activities can involve more pictures and representations and include geometric and number patterns; use of words, tables, and graphs; properties of numbers; modeling problems with objects; and discussing rates of change. At this stage students begin to move to more pictorial and symbolic materials. Equivalent patterns with different materials can also be introduced for some students.

In middle and high school, students can typically begin to handle patterns with multiple attributes and operate on a more symbolic level.

SKILL 8.2   Applying knowledge of the concepts of variable, function, and equation to the expression of algebraic relationships

A **variable** is a letter that is used to represent one or more numbers. An algebraic expression is a collection of numbers, variables, operations, and grouping symbols.

Example:

16 times a, divided by b may be expressed algebraically as $\dfrac{16a}{b}$

An **equation** is formed when an equal sign is placed between two expressions.

Example:

$3x + y = 24$.

A **function** is a special type of relationship between two values, in which each input value corresponds to exactly one output value. Another way of defining a function is as a relation in which no two ordered pairs have the same x value.

Example:

$$\{(a,1),(b,4),(c,4)\}$$

Teaching Functions and Basic Algebraic Relationships

Functions

From an instructional standpoint, functions can be seen in one of two ways: as relationships between sets or as input/output changes. Use of the Input/output changes model can be used even with very young children.

Again, as with all math concepts, instruction should begin at the most concrete level. Hatfield, et al (2005), suggest actually "building" an input/output box from a shoe box or any handy box. Label one end with "In" or even an arrow in, and the other end with "out" or an out arrow, etc. The teacher should have two sets of objects that vary on only one consistent dimension (e.g., size, color, number).

The student can put an object in one end and the teacher pulls the corresponding object out of the other end. It might be a big, then little ball, cube, pyramid, etc or a red then blue version of the same object, and so forth. Students discuss and discover the "rule" for in and out as they go. There are many variations in such procedures, but all should start at the most concrete level. In the discussion, the teacher can begin using math language to discuss the operation.

As students progress, instruction can include drawings of the objects that go in and out, and move to more pictorial, then more symbolic levels. Always include the connecting step of having pictures and objects together at first, then of having pictures and symbols together before moving to symbols alone.

Students with disabilities may need much more time at the concrete level. Some may continue to need sample pictures to help them remember various functions. If these early foundation exercises are mastered, students will have a sound basis on which to build later more symbolic concepts.

Algebraic Reasoning

Although algebra was once thought of as a secondary school topic, modern research shows its foundations, again, lie in concepts learned at an early age. Usiskin (1992) outlined three basic facts about learning algebraic concepts to the NCTM:

1. Algebraic concepts are best learned in context.
2. Almost any human being can learn algebra
3. Algebraic concepts are best learned at a very young age.

In teaching algebraic reasoning at any age, it is important to remember that algebra has two parts:

- Language describing patterns, functions, and relationships, and
- An abstract system with its own rules and definitions

The first of these, patterns, functions and relationships, can be taught in elementary school to almost any student at *some* level. The foundations of patterns and functions described above can lead into very concrete activities that mirror algebraic concepts. Students need to be able to identify equality (equal numbers or equal sizes, etc) when they see it, and, as noted in patterns in the earlier section, detect similarities and differences. Once basic work with patterns and functions is accomplished, activities that explore balance and equality become central to instruction. This can involve actual scales so students can explore how many blocks are necessary to balance something on the other side of the scale, figure out how many more or less of something is necessary to make it equal, etc. Similar activities with snap together cubes (to get the same length with different size cubes, etc) can be used. Dominoes can help move to a connecting level (different combinations of dots equal the same number, etc).

As in all math activities, move from the concrete to the pictorial to the symbolic. It is crucial to be **talking about** what you are doing and using math language as you do. Frequently asking for the missing variable (e.g., "how many more small paper clips do we need to balance the large one?") is crucial.

Again, students with some disabilities will need more time at the concrete level. Even students who have very rudimentary skills, however, can do at least some work in these algebraic concepts. The key is to take *whatever materials at whatever their level* and design such balance activities for them. For later use, there are math programs that use scales and objects that represent different numbers to help upper level students with these concepts. Such manipulatives are intended for middle and high school level, as well.

There are a variety of computer programs that can be used to enhance math learning once the most concrete concept stage is mastered. However, it is important that such programs have a solid connecting level that is used to *show* objects first, then connect to words and symbols, etc. before moving to symbols, alone.

Given a strong introduction to algebraic concepts, middle school and high school students will be more ready to deal with the abstract system of rules and definitions, and handle complex reasoning exercises, such as if-then propositions.

SKILL 8.3   Identifying relationships among variables based on mathematical expressions, tables, graphs, and rules

A relationship between two quantities can be shown using a table, graph, or rule. In this example, the rule y= 9x describes the relationship between the total amount earned, *y*, and the total amount of $9 sunglasses sold, *x*.

A table using this data would appear as:

number of sunglasses sold	1	5	10	15
total dollars earned	9	45	90	135

Each *(x,y)* relationship between a pair of values is called the **coordinate pair** that can be plotted on a graph. The coordinate pairs (1,9), (5,45), (10,90), and (15,135) are plotted on the graph below.

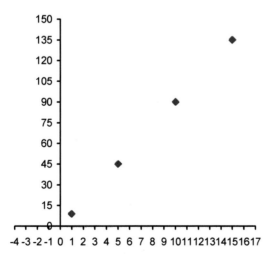

The graph to the left shows a **linear relationship**. A linear relationship is one in which two quantities are proportional to each other. Doubling *x* also doubles *y*. On a graph, a straight line depicts a linear relationship.

The function or relationship between two quantities may be analyzed to determine how one quantity depends on the other.

The relationship between two or more variables can be analyzed using a table, graph, written description, or symbolic rule. The function, $y=2x+1$, is written as a symbolic rule. The same relationship is also shown in the table below:

x	0	2	3	6	9
y	1	5	7	13	19

This relationship could be written in words by saying that the value of *y* is equal to two times the value of *x*, plus one. This relationship could be shown on a graph by plotting given points such as the ones shown in the table above.

Another way to describe a function is as a process in which one or more numbers are input into an imaginary machine that produces another number as the output. If 5 is input, (x), into a machine with a process of $x+1$, the output, (y), will equal 6. (See Skill 8.02 for guidance on teaching this concept to elementary children.)

In real situations, relationships can be described mathematically. The function, $y=x+1$, can be used to describe the idea that people age one year on their birthday. To describe the relationship in which a person's monthly medical costs are 6 times a person's age, we could write $y=6x$. The monthly cost of medical care could be predicted using this function. A 20 year-old person would spend $120 per month (120=20*6). An 80 year-old person would spend $480 per month (480=80*6). Therefore, one could analyze the relationship to say: as you get older, medical costs increase by a factor of $6.00 each year.

SKILL 8.4   Applying the methods of algebra to solve equations and inequalities

Procedure for Solving Algebraic Equations

<u>Example</u>:

$$3(x+3) = {}^-2x+4 \quad \text{Solve for } x.$$

1. Expand to eliminate all parentheses. $3x+9 = {}^-2x+4$

2. Multiply each term by the LCD to eliminate all denominators.

3. Combine like terms on each side when possible.

4. Use the properties to put all variables on one side and all constants on the other side.

$$\rightarrow 3x+9-9 = {}^-2x+4-9 \quad \text{(subtract nine from both sides)}$$

$$\rightarrow 3x = {}^-2x-5$$

$$\rightarrow 3x+2x = {}^-2x+2x-5 \quad \text{(add } 2x \text{ to both sides)}$$

$$\rightarrow 5x = {}^-5$$

$$\rightarrow \frac{5x}{5} = \frac{{}^-5}{5} \qquad\qquad \text{(divide both sides by 5)}$$

$$\rightarrow x = {}^-1$$

<u>Example</u>:

Solve: $3(2x+5)-4x = 5(x+9)$

$$6x+15-4x = 5x+45$$

$$2x+15 = 5x+45$$

$${}^-3x+15 = 45$$

$${}^-3x = 30$$

$$x = {}^-10$$

Example:

Mark and Mike are twins. 3 times Mark's age, plus 4, equals 4 times Mike's age minus 14. How old are the boys?

Since the boys are twins, their ages are the same. "Translate" the English into Algebra. Let x = their age.

$3x + 4 = 4x - 14$

$18 = x$

The boys are each 18 years old.

Procedure for Solving Algebraic Inequalities

We use the same procedure used above for solving linear equations, but the answer is either represented in graphical form on the number line or in interval form.

Example:

Solve the inequality, show its solution using interval form, and graph the solution on the number line.

$$\frac{5x}{8} + 3 \geq 2x - 5$$

$$8\left(\frac{5x}{8}\right) + 8(3) \geq 8(2x) - 5(8) \quad \text{Multiply by LCD = 8.}$$

$$5x + 24 \geq 16x - 40$$

$$5x + 24 - 24 - 16x \geq 16x - 16x - 40 - 24$$

Subtract 16x and 24 from both sides of the equation.

$$^-11x \geq\, ^- 64$$

$$\frac{^-11x}{^-11} \leq \frac{^-64}{^-11}$$

$$x \leq \frac{64}{11} \;;\; x \leq 5\frac{9}{11}$$

Solution in interval form: $\left(^{-}\infty, 5\frac{9}{11}\right]$

Note: "] " means $5\frac{9}{11}$ is included in the solution.

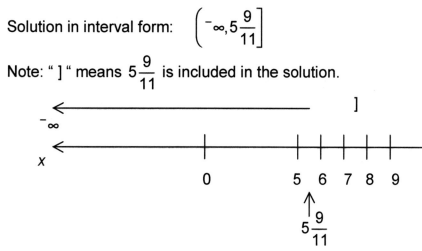

Example:

Solve the following inequality and express your answer in both interval and graphical form.

$3x - 8 < 2(3x - 1)$

$3x - 8 < 6x - 2$ Distributive property.

$3x - 6x - 8 + 8 < 6x - 6x - 2 + 8$

Add 8 and subtract 6x from both sides of the equation.

$^{-}3x < 6$

$\dfrac{^{-}3x}{^{-}3} > \dfrac{6}{^{-}3}$ Note the change in direction of the equality.

$x >^{-} 2$

Graphical form:

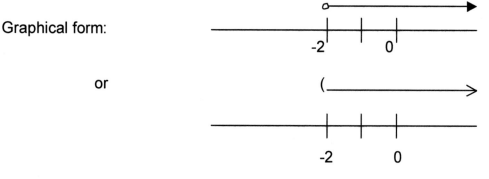

        or

Interval form: $(^{-}2, \infty)$

Recall:

a) Using a parentheses or an open circle implies the point is not included in the answer.

b) Using a bracket or a closed circle implies the point is included in the answer.

Example:

Solve: $6x + 21 < 8x + 31$

$^-2x + 21 < 31$

$^-2x < 10$

$x > ^-5$

Note that the inequality sign has changed.

The solution set of linear equations is all the ordered pairs of real numbers that satisfy both equations, thus the intersection of the lines. There are two methods for solving linear equations: *linear combinations* and *substitution*.

In the **substitution** method, an equation is solved for either variable. That solution is then substituted in the other equation to find the remaining variable.

Example:

(1) $2x + 8y = 4$
(2) $x - 3y = 5$

(2a) $x = 3y + 5$ Solve equation (2) for x.
(1a) $2(3y + 5) + 8y = 4$ Substitute x in equation (1)
        $6y + 10 + 8y = 4$ Solve.
                $14y = -6$
                 $y = \frac{-3}{7}$ Solution

(2) $x - 3y = 5$
        $x - 3(\frac{-3}{7}) = 5$ Substitute the value of y.
        $x = \frac{26}{7} = 3\frac{5}{7}$ Solution

Thus, the solution set of the system of equations is $(3\frac{5}{7}, \frac{-3}{7})$.

In the **linear combinations** method, one or both of the equations are replaced with an equivalent equation so that the two equations can be combined (added or subtracted) to eliminate one variable.

Example:

(1) $4x + 3y = -2$
(2) $5x - y = 7$

(1) $4x + 3y = -2$
(2a) $15x - 3y = 21$ Multiply equation (2) by 3

       $19x = 19$ Combining (1) and (2a)
        $x = 1$ Solve.

To find y, substitute the value of x in equation 1 (or 2).

(1) $4x + 3y = -2$
      $4(1) + 3y = -2$
      $4 + 3y = -2$
      $3y = -2$
      $y = -2$

Thus the solution is $x = 1$ and $y = -2$ or the order pair (1, -2).

Some word problems can be solved using a system (group) of equations or inequalities. Watch for words like *greater than, less than, at least, or no more than*, which indicate the need for inequalities.

Example:

Farmer Greenjeans bought 4 cows and 6 sheep for $1700. Mr. Ziffel bought 3 cows and 12 sheep for $2400. If all the cows were the same price and all the sheep were another fixed price, find the price charged for a cow or for a sheep.

Let x = price of a cow
Let y = price of a sheep

Then Farmer Greenjeans' equation would be: $4x + 6y = 1700$
Mr. Ziffel's equation would be: $3x + 12y = 2400$

To solve by **addition-subtraction**:

Multiply the first equation by $^-2$: $^-2(4x + 6y = 1700)$
Keep the other equation the same: $(3x + 12y = 2400)$

By doing this, the equations can be added to each other to eliminate one variable and solve for the other variable.

$$^-8x - 12y = {}^-3400$$
$$\underline{3x + 12y = 2400} \qquad \text{Add these equations.}$$
$$^-5x \qquad = {}^-1000$$

$x = 200 \leftarrow$ the price of a cow was \$200.

Solving for y, $y = 150 \leftarrow$ the price of a sheep was \$150.

To solve this same equation by **substitution**:

Solve one of the equations for a variable. (Try to make an equation without fractions if possible.) Substitute this expression into the equation that you have not yet used. Solve the resulting equation for the value of the remaining variable.

$$4x + 6y = 1700$$
$$3x + 12y = 2400 \leftarrow \text{Solve this equation for } x.$$

It becomes $x = 800 - 4y$. Now substitute $800 - 4y$ in place of x in the OTHER equation. $4x + 6y = 1700$ now becomes:
$$4(800 - 4y) + 6y = 1700$$
$$3200 - 16y + 6y = 1700$$
$$3200 - 10y = 1700$$

$$^-10y = {}^-1500$$
$y = 150$, or \$150 for a sheep.

Substituting 150 back into an equation for y, find x.
$$4x + 6(150) = 1700$$
$$4x + 900 = 1700$$
$4x = 800$ so $x = 200$, or \$200 for a cow.

Example:

Sharon's Bike Shoppe can assemble a 3 speed bike in 30 minutes or a 10 speed bike in 60 minutes. The profit on each bike sold is $60 for a 3 speed or $75 for a 10 speed bike. How many of each type of bike should they assemble during an 8 hour day (480 minutes) to make the maximum profit? Total daily profit must be at least $300.

Let x = number of 3 speed bikes.
y = number of 10 speed bikes.

Since there are only 480 minutes to use each day,
$30x + 60y \leq 480$ is the first inequality.

Since the total daily profit must be at least $300,
$60x + 75y \geq 300$ is the second inequality.

$32x + 65y \leq 480$ solves to $y \leq 8 - 1/2\,x$
$60x + 75y \geq 300$ solves to $y \geq 4 - 4/5\,x$

Graph these 2 inequalities:

$y \leq 8 - 1/2\,x$
$y \geq 4 - 4/5\,x$

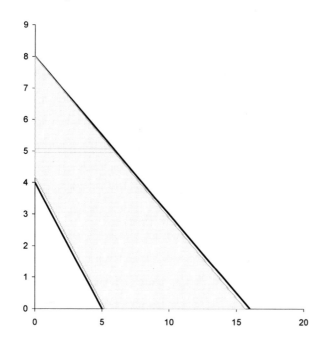

Realize that $x \geq 0$ and $y \geq 0$, since the number of bikes assembled cannot be a negative number. Graph these as additional constraints on the problem. The number of bikes assembled must always be an integer value, so points within the shaded area of the graph must have integer values. The maximum profit will occur at or near a corner of the shaded portion of this graph. Those points occur at (0,4), (0,8), (16,0), or (5,0).

Since profits are $60/3$-speed or $75/10$-speed, the profit would be:

(0,4) $60(0)+75(4) = 300$
(0,8) $60(0)+75(8) = 600$
(16,0) $60(16)+75(0) = 960 \leftarrow$ Maximum profit
(5,0) $60(5)+75(0) = 300$

The maximum profit would occur if 16 3-speed bikes are made daily.

Example:

The YMCA wants to sell raffle tickets to raise at least $32,000. If they must pay $7,250 in expenses and prizes out of the money collected from the tickets, how many tickets worth $25 each must they sell?

Since they want to raise at least $32,000, that means they would be happy to get 32,000 or more. This requires an inequality.

Let $x =$ number of tickets sold
Then $25x =$ total money collected for x tickets

Total money minus expenses is greater than $32,000.

If they sell 1,570 tickets or more, they will raise at least $32,000.

Example:

The Simpsons went out for dinner. All 4 of them ordered the aardvark steak dinner. Bert paid for the 4 meals and included a tip of $12 for a total of $84.60. How much was one aardvark steak dinner?

Let $x =$ the price of one aardvark dinner.
So $4x =$ the price of 4 aardvark dinners.

$4x +12 = 84.60$
$4x = 72.60$
$x = \$18.50$ for each dinner.

SKILL 8.5   Analyzing how algebraic functions are used to plot points, describe graphs, and determine slope

Graphically

A first degree equation has an equation of the form $ax + by = c$. To find the slope of a line, solve the equation for y. This gets the equation into **slope intercept form**, $y = mx + b$. In this equation, m is the line's slope.

The y intercept is the coordinate of the point where a line crosses the y axis. To find the y intercept, substitute 0 for x and solve for y. This is the y intercept. In slope intercept form, $y = mx + b$, b is the y intercept.

To find the x intercept, substitute 0 for y and solve for x. This is the x intercept.

If the equation solves to $x =$ **any number**, then the graph is a vertical line, because it only has an x intercept. Its slope is **undefined**.

If the equation solves to $y =$ **any number**, then the graph is a horizontal line, because it only has a y intercept. Its slope is 0 (zero).

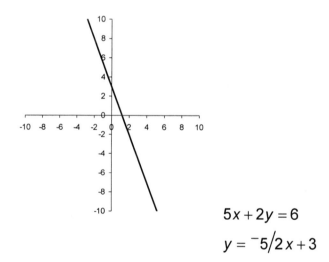

$$5x + 2y = 6$$
$$y = {}^-5/2\, x + 3$$

The equation of a line from its graph can be found by finding its slope and its y intercept. The slope formula looks like this:

$$m = \frac{y_2 - y_1}{x_2 - x_1}$$

The y intercept can be found using this equation:

$$Y - y_a = m(X - x_a)$$

(x_a, y_a) can be (x_1, y_1) or (x_2, y_2) If **m**, the value of the slope, is distributed through the parentheses, the equation can be rewritten into other forms of the equation of a line.

Example:
Find the equation of a line through $(9, {}^-6)$ and $({}^-1, 2)$.

$$\text{slope} = \frac{y_2 - y_1}{x_2 - x_1} = \frac{2 - {}^-6}{{}^-1 - 9} = \frac{8}{{}^-10} = \frac{{}^-4}{5}$$

$$Y - y_a = m(X - x_a) \rightarrow Y - 2 = {}^-4/5(X - {}^-1) \rightarrow$$
$$Y - 2 = {}^-4/5(X + 1) \rightarrow Y - 2 = {}^-4/5 X - 4/5 \rightarrow$$
$$Y = {}^-4/5 X + 6/5 \quad \text{This is the slope-intercept form.}$$

Multiplying by 5 to eliminate fractions, it is:

$$5Y = {}^-4X + 6 \rightarrow 4X + 5Y = 6 \quad \text{Standard form.}$$

Example:
Find the slope and intercepts of $3x + 2y = 14$.
$$3x + 2y = 14$$
$$2y = {}^-3x + 14$$
$$y = {}^-3/2\, x + 7$$

The slope of the line is ${}^-3/2$. The y intercept of the line is 7.

The intercepts can also be found by substituting 0 in place of the other variables in the equation.

To find the y intercept:
let $x = 0$; 3(0) + 2y = 14
0 + 2y = 14
2y = 14
y = 7
(0,7) is the y intercept.

To find the x intercept:
let $y = 0$; 3x + 2(0) = 14
3x + 0 = 14
3x = 14
x = 14/3
(14/3 ,0) is the x intercept.

<u>Example</u>:

Sketch the graph of the line represented by $2x + 3y = 6$.

Let $x = 0 \rightarrow 2(0) + 3y = 6$

$\rightarrow 3y = 6$
$\rightarrow y = 2$
$\rightarrow (0,2)$ is the y intercept.

Let $y = 0 \rightarrow 2x + 3(0) = 6$
$\qquad \rightarrow 2x = 6$
$\qquad \rightarrow x = 3$
$\qquad \rightarrow (3,0)$ is the x intercept.

Let $x = 1 \rightarrow 2(1) + 3y = 6$
$\qquad \rightarrow 2 + 3y = 6$
$\qquad \rightarrow 3y = 4$
$\qquad \rightarrow y = \dfrac{4}{3}$
$\qquad \rightarrow \left(1, \dfrac{4}{3}\right)$ is the third point.

Plotting the three points on the coordinate system, we get the following:

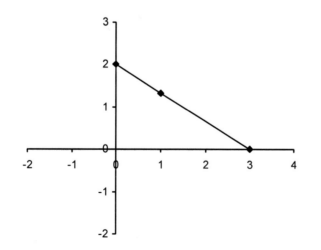

To graph an inequality, solve the inequality for *y*. This gets the inequality in slope intercept form, (for example: $y < mx + b$). The point (0,b) is the *y* intercept, and *m* is the line's slope.

If the inequality solves to $x \geq$ **any number**, then the graph includes a vertical line.

If the inequality solves to $y \leq$ **any number**, then the graph includes a horizontal line.

When graphing a linear inequality, the line will be dotted if the inequality sign is $<$ or $>$. If the inequality signs are either $\geq$ or $\leq$, the line on the graph will be a solid line. Shade above the line when the inequality sign is $\geq$ or $>$. Shade below the line when the inequality sign is $<$ or $\leq$. For inequalities of the forms $x >$ number, $x \leq$ number, $x <$ number, or $x \geq$ number, draw a vertical line (solid or dotted). Shade to the right for $>$ or $\geq$. Shade to the left for $<$ or $\leq$.

Remember: **Dividing or multiplying by a negative number will reverse the direction of the inequality sign.**

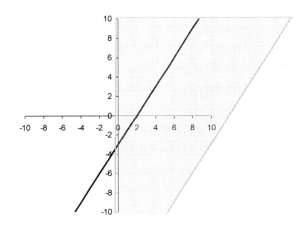

$3x - 2y \geq 6$

$y \leq 3/2\,x - 3$

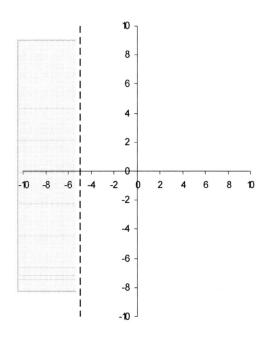

$$3x + 12 < -3$$
$$x < {}^-5$$

Example:

Solve by graphing:

$$x + y \le 6$$
$$x - 2y \le 6$$

Solving the inequalities for y, they become:

$y \le {}^-x + 6$ (y intercept of 6 and slope = $^-1$)

$y \ge 1/2\,x - 3$ (y intercept of $^-3$ and slope = $1/2$)

A graph with shading is shown below:

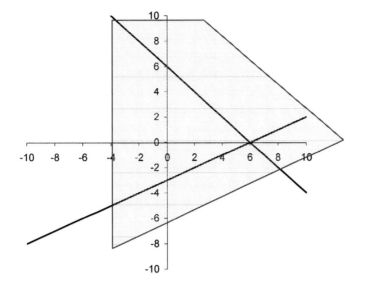

OBJECTIVE 9   **UNDERSTAND CONCEPTS AND SKILLS RELATED TO DATA ANALYSIS**

SKILL 9.1   **Applying knowledge of methods for organizing and interpreting data in a variety of formats (e.g., tables, frequency distributions, line graphs, circle graphs)**

To make a **bar graph** or a **pictograph**, determine the scale to be used for the graph. Then determine the length of each bar on the graph, or determine the number of pictures needed to represent each item of information. Be sure to include an explanation of the scale in the legend of a pictograph.

Example:

A class had the following grades: 4 As, 9 Bs, 8 Cs, 1 D, and 3 Fs. Graph these on a bar graph and a pictograph.

Pictograph

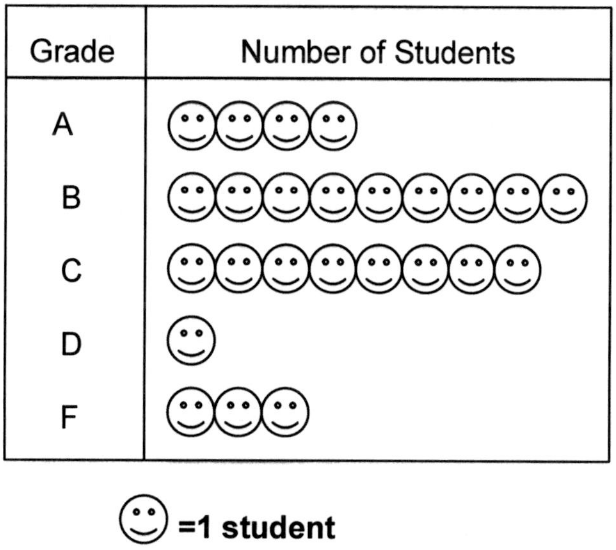

☺ =1 student

Bar graph

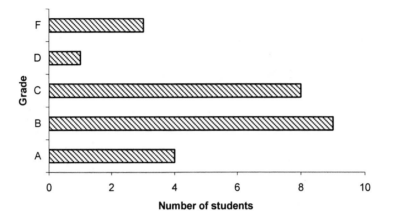

To make a **line graph**, determine appropriate labels for both the vertical and horizontal axes (based on the information to be graphed). It is important to use a scale that is appropriate to the measurement and resulting data. Describe what each axis represents and mark the scale periodically on each axis. Graph the individual points of the graph and connect the points on the graph from left to right.

Example:

Graph the following information using a line graph.

The number of National Merit finalists/school year

	90-91	91-92	92-93	93-94	94-95	95-96
Central	3	5	1	4	6	8
Wilson	4	2	3	2	3	2

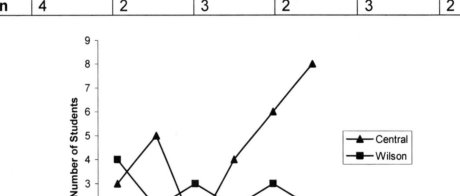

To make a **circle graph**, total all the information that is to be included on the graph. Determine the central angle to be used for each sector of the graph using the following formula:

$$\frac{\text{information}}{\text{total information}} \times 360° = \text{degrees in central} \square$$

Lay out the central angles to these sizes, label each section, and include each section's percent.

Example:
   Graph this information on a circle graph: Monthly expenses:

   Rent, $400
   Food, $150
   Utilities, $75
   Clothes, $75
   Church, $100
   Misc., $200

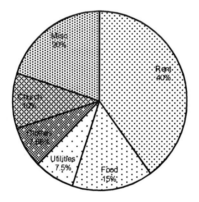

To read a bar graph or a pictograph, read the explanation of the scale that was used in the legend. Compare the length of each bar with the dimensions on the axes and calculate the value each bar represents. On a pictograph, check the legend to see what the value of each symbol or picture is, count the number of pictures used in the chart, and calculate the value of all the pictures.

To read a circle graph, find the total of the amounts represented on the entire circle graph. To determine the actual amount that each sector of the graph represents, multiply the percent in a sector times the total amount number.

To read a chart, be sure to look at the row and column headings on the table. Use this information to evaluate the given information in the chart.

Scatter plots compare two characteristics of the same group of things or people and usually consist of a large body of data. They show how much one variable is affected by another. The relationship between the two variables is their **correlation**. The closer the data points come to making a straight line when plotted, the closer the correlation.

Stem and leaf plots are visually similar to line plots. The **stems** are the digits in the greatest place value of the data values, and the **leaves** are the digits in the next greatest place values. Stem and leaf plots are best suited for small sets of data and are especially useful for comparing two sets of data. The following is an example using test scores:

4	9
5	4 9
6	1 2 3 4 6 7 8 8
7	0 3 4 6 6 6 7 7 7 7 8 8 8 8
8	3 5 5 7 8
9	0 0 3 4 5
10	0 0

Histograms are used to summarize information from large sets of data that can be naturally grouped into intervals. The vertical axis indicates **frequency** (the number of times any particular data value occurs), and the horizontal axis indicates data values or ranges of data values. The number of data values in any interval is the **frequency of the interval**.

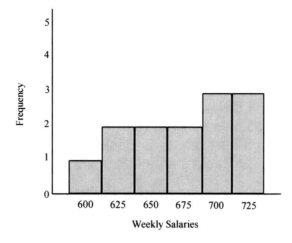

Teaching Concepts of Data Collection and Statistics

Instructional strategies for teaching concepts and operations in data collection and statistics should begin at an early age and follow the same sequence from concrete conceptual development activities, through connecting activities with pictures and symbols in the presence of objects, to the purely symbolic level. There are several underlying concepts or skills important to data collection and statistics, and probability that can be practiced in many contexts besides math.

- Recording data: At the earliest age simply have students record information based upon observation. Whether they use language, stickers, pictures or numbers, just give them lots of experience recording information.

- Make decisions: Choosing from among various options and discussing the reasons for the choice are basic skills they will need for later interpretation of data, and these skills can be practiced all day in many contexts.

- Concepts of fairness and equality. Even Kindergarten and first grade students have a rudimentary concept of fairness, and regardless of their level of development, they will need to be able to identify equality in *some* context. Even if they do not yet have conservation of number or size, they can see that it is unfair for one child to get a bigger cookie than another.

- Making predictions and checking their accuracy: Students can make predictions in many contexts, from daily weather predictions, to story and reading predictions, to more standard "What's in the bag?" predictions. Teachers can also model predicting and checking each prediction's accuracy (e.g., "Well, I thought it might rain today, but that prediction did not come true—it's sunny out!"). Children need lots of practice making predictions and then stating whether the prediction was correct or not.

Such activities should continue at increasingly abstract levels throughout a student's learning career. Once some proficiency is accomplished, however, move to activities more directly related to data collection and analysis. At the earliest level, several foundation skills must be practiced extensively:

- Collecting data and recording it: This should be as concrete and relevant to the child's daily life as possible (e.g., counting and recording the number of books on the shelves, or desks in the room, or lunch choices, or canned food in the cabinet at home, or Halloween candy, etc.)

- Making "real" graphs: Most text books begin with pictographs, but prior to this connecting level activity, students need repeated experience with concrete graphs made of real things. Legos make great graphs and allow for exploration of different scales (it takes more small Legos to make the same tower and large Legos), charts made of candy are a staple in many Kindergarten and first grade classes, as well.

- Move from real to pictures of real, then to pictograph symbols and only gradually to symbolic graphs and analysis. Students with disabilities may have considerable difficulty with variable scales and keys, and need even more practice at the concrete level.

- Again, model thinking aloud and making decisions based on the data collected, the graphs, and the analysis.

Probability can be particularly difficult for some students. Like other math skills, instruction begins at the most concrete level. Traditional coin tosses, rolls of the dice, or two colored chips can be good introductions, but it is critical to remember that the students need to record the data and talk about it. The concept of "more likely" must be tied to "more often happens" during the earliest stages of development. Instead of recording the number of heads or tails tossed, earliest activities could involve two jars, with a heads up and a tails up coin taped onto them, and children put a chip in each one for each toss. Chips can be stacked later for analysis. The same procedure can be used when moving to choosing colored marbles from a closed bag (e.g., there are 10 red marbles and 3 blue ones, which are we most likely to pull out? etc.).

Students can move on to the connecting, pictorial level and then to the symbolic as they move through the school curriculum. However, since some students will struggle to move to higher cognitive levels or move through the levels more slowly than peers, it will often be necessary to differentiate instruction (see test 004, next for more on differentiating instruction.). When addressing a particular standard on statistics or probability in the curriculum, remember that one good way to differentiate your lessons so all students can participate is to present the task or lesson on a more concrete level of instruction. If most of your class is operating at the connecting level, using pictures alone, some students might be given the same task with pictures and objects, others given just objects, and some gifted students might already be using symbols alone.

SKILL 9.2   Identifying trends and patterns in data

Random sampling supplies every combination of items from a frame, or stratum, with a known probability of occurring. However, the term "random" is somewhat misleading, as sampling is typically a very structured and scientific process. A large body of statistical theory quantifies the risk, thus enabling statisticians to determine the appropriate sample size to make it valid.

Systematic sampling selects items in a frame according to the kth sample. The first item is chosen to be the rth, where r is a random integer in the range $1,...,k-1$.

There are three stages to **cluster** or **area sampling**: the target population is divided into many regional clusters (groups), a few clusters are randomly selected for study, and a few subjects are randomly chosen from within a cluster.

Convenience sampling is the method of choosing items arbitrarily and in an unstructured manner from the frame.

Correlation is a measure of association between two variables. It varies from -1 to 1, with 0 being a random relationship, 1 being a perfect positive linear relationship, and -1 being a perfect negative linear relationship.

The **correlation coefficient** (r) is used to describe the strength of the association between the variables as well as the direction of the association.

<u>Example</u>:

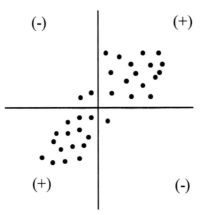

Horizontal and vertical lines are drawn through the **point of averages**, which is the point on the respective averages of the *x* and *y* values. Doing this divides the scatter plot into four quadrants. If a point is in the lower left quadrant, the product of two negatives is positive; in the upper right, the product of two positives is positive. The positive quadrants are depicted with the positive sign (+). In the two remaining quadrants (upper left and lower right), the product of a negative and a positive is negative. The negative quadrants are depicted with the negative sign (-). If *r* is positive, then there are more points in the positive quadrants; if *r* is negative, then there are more points in the two negative quadrants.

Regression is a form of statistical analysis used to predict a dependent variable (*y*) from values of an independent variable (*x*). A **regression equation** is derived from a known set of data.

The simplest regression analysis models the relationship between two variables using the following equation: $y = a + bx$, where *y* is the dependent variable and *x* is the independent variable. This simple equation denotes a linear relationship between *x* and *y*. This form would be appropriate if, when you plotted a graph of *x* and *y*, you saw the points roughly form along a straight line.

Example:

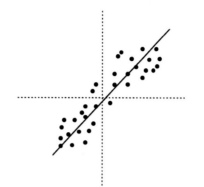

The line can then be used to make predictions.

If all of the data points fell on the line, there would be a perfect correlation ($r = 1.0$) between the x and y data points. These cases represent the best scenarios for prediction. A positive or negative r value represents how y varies with x. When r is positive, y increases as x increases. When r is negative, y decreases as x increases.

A **linear regression** equation is of the form: $Y = a + bX$.

Example:

A teacher wanted to determine how a practice test influenced a student's performance on the actual test. The practice test grade and the subsequent actual test grade for each student are given in the table below:

Practice Test (x)	Actual Test (y)
94	98
95	94
92	95
87	89
82	85
80	78
75	73
65	67
50	45
20	40

We determine the equation for the linear regression line to be $y = 14.650 + 0.834x$.

A new student comes into the class and scores 78 on the practice test. Based on the equation obtained above, what would the teacher predict this student would get on the actual test?

y = 14.650 + 0.834 (78)
y = 14.650 + 65.052
y = 79.7

It is predicted that the student will get an 80.

SKILL 9.3   Demonstrating knowledge of standard measures (e.g., mean, median, mode, and range) used to describe data

Mean, median, and mode are three measures of central tendency. The **mean** is the average of the data items. The **median** is found by putting the data items in order from smallest to largest and selecting the item in the middle (or the average of the two items in the middle). The **mode** is the most frequently occurring item.

Range is a measure of variability. It is found by subtracting the smallest value from the largest value.

Example:

Find the mean, median, mode, and range of the test scores listed below:

85	77	65
92	90	54
88	85	70
75	80	69
85	88	60
72	74	95

Mean (X) = sum of all scores ÷ number of scores
= 78

Median = put numbers in order from smallest to largest. Pick middle number.
54, 60, 65, 69, 70, 72, 74, 75, 77, 80, 85, 85, 85, 88, 88, 90, 92, 95
-- --
both in middle

Therefore, the median is the average of two numbers in the middle, 78.5.

Mode = most frequent number
= 85

Range = largest number minus the smallest number
= 95 – 54
= 41

Different situations require different information. For example, examine the circumstances under which each of the following three scenarios use the numbers provided.

   1) Over a 7-day period, the store owner collected data on the ice cream flavors sold. He found the mean number of scoops sold was 174 per day. The most frequently sold flavor was vanilla. This information was useful in determining how much ice cream to order overall as well as the amounts of each flavor. In the case of the ice cream store, the median and range had little business value for the owner.

   2) Consider the set of test scores from a math class: 0, 16, 19, 65, 65, 65, 68, 69, 70, 72, 73, 73, 75, 78, 80, 85, 88, and 92. The mean is 64.06 and the median is 71. Since there are only three scores less than the mean out of the entire class, the median (71) would be a more descriptive score.

   3) Retail storeowners may be most concerned with the most common dress size so they may order more of that size than any other.

An understanding of the definitions is important in determining the validity and uses of statistical data. All definitions and applications in this section apply to ungrouped data.
Data item: each piece of data is represented by the letter X.

Mean: the average of all data, with is represented by the symbol $\overline{X}$.

Range: the difference between the highest and lowest value of data items.

Sum of the squares: the sum of the squares of the differences between each item and the mean.

$$Sx^2 = (X - \overline{X})^2$$

Variance: the sum of the squares quantity divided by the number of items. The lower case Greek letter sigma squared (σ^2) represents variance.

$$\frac{Sx^2}{N} = \sigma^2$$

The larger the value of the variance, the larger the spread.

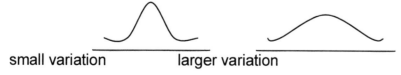

    small variation   larger variation

Standard deviation: the square root of the variance. The lower case Greek letter sigma (σ) is used to represent standard deviation.

$$\sigma = \sqrt{\sigma^2}$$

Most statistical calculators have standard deviation keys on them; they should be used when asked to calculate statistical functions. It is important to become familiar with the calculator and the location of the keys needed.

Example:
>Given the ungrouped data below, calculate the mean, range, standard deviation, and the variance.
>
>15   22   28   25   34   38
>18   25   30   33   19   23
>
>Mean ($\overline{X}$) = 25.8333333
>Range: $38 - 15 = 23$
>Standard deviation (σ) = 6.6936952
>Variance (σ^2) = 44.805556

Using graphing calculators or computer software has many advantages. The technology is better able to handle large data sets (such as the results of a science experiment), and it is much easier to edit and sort the data and to change the style of the graph to find its best representation. Furthermore, graphing calculators also provide a tool to plot statistics.

0009.04   Drawing valid conclusions based on data

Both averages and graphs can be misleading if the data are not presented appropriately. The three types of averages used in statistics are mean, median, and mode.

If a data set contains one very high or very low value, the mean will not be representative: for example, including the teacher's height in the mean height of a classroom.

If the data are clustered around two numbers with a large gap between them, the median will not be representative: for example, expressing the median height in a family of two parents and two small children.

Modes are best used with categorical data. In other words, do not mix apples with oranges; a mode of the sale of men's shoe sizes would be helpful to a store for reordering stock of men's shoes. However, finding the mode of men and women's shoe sizes combined would not be a good indicator of the stock that needed to be reordered.

Pictographs can also be misleading, especially if they are drawn to represent three-dimensional objects. If two or more dimensions are changed in reflecting ratio, the overall visual effect can be misinterpreted.

Bar and line graphs can be misleading if the scales are changed; for example, using relatively small scale increments for large numbers will make the comparison differences seem much greater than if larger scale increments are used.

Circle graphs, or pie charts, are excellent for comparing relative amounts. However, they cannot be used to represent absolute amounts, and if interpreted as such, they are misleading.

Line graphs are most appropriate for analyzing trend or changes over time.

TEST 1 SUBAREA 3.   SCIENCE, SOCIAL STUDIES, HEALTH, PHYSICAL EDUCATION, AND THE ARTS

OBJECTIVE 0010 UNDERSTAND THE CHARACTERISTICS AND PROCESSES OF SCIENCE AND THE CONCEPTS AND PRINCIPLES OF LIFE SCIENCE

0010.01   Recognizing the nature of scientific knowledge; the values of science (e.g., importance of curiosity, honesty, openness, and skepticism; reliance on verifiable evidence); the unifying concepts of science (e.g., systems, models, scale); the principles of scientific inquiry; and the design of scientific investigations

Learning can be broadly divided into two kinds: active and passive. Active learning, as the name indicates, involves a learning atmosphere full of action. In passive learning, students are taught in a non-stimulating and inactive atmosphere. Active learning draws students into it, thereby interesting them to the point of participating and purposely engaging in learning.

It is crucial that students are actively engaged, not entertained. They should be taught the answers for "How" and "Why" questions and encouraged to be inquisitive and interested.

Active learning is conceptualized as follows:

A Model of Active Learning

Experience of	Dialogue with
Doing	Self
Observing	Others

This model suggests that all learning activities involve some kind of experience or some kind of dialogue. The two main kinds of dialogue are "Dialogue with self" and "Dialogue with others." The two main kinds of experience are "Observing" and "Doing."

Dialogue with self: This is what happens when learners think reflectively about a topic. They ask themselves a number of things about the topic.

Dialogue with others: When the students are listening to a book being read by another student or when the teacher is teaching, a partial dialogue takes place because the dialogue is only one-sided. When they are listening to another and when there is an exchange of ideas back and forth, it is said to be a dialogue with others.

Observing: This is a very important skill in science. This occurs when a learner carefully watches or observes someone else doing an activity or experiment. This is a good experience, although it is not quite like doing something for oneself.

Doing: This refers to any activity where a learner actually does something, giving the learner a firsthand experience that is very valuable. Of course, what the learner might be *doing* is *observing and recording events.*

The scientific attitude is to be curious, open to new ideas, and skeptical. In science, there are always new discoveries, new research, and new theories proposed. Sometimes, old theories are disproved; sometimes parts of them are modified. As a rule research, observation, and experimentation result not only in new knowledge, but in new questions, as well. To view these changes rationally, one must have openness, curiosity, and skepticism. (Skepticism is a Greek word, meaning a method of obtaining knowledge through systematic doubt and continual testing. A scientific skeptic is one who refuses to accept certain types of claims without subjecting them to a systematic investigation.)

Many students will be naturally curious about the world. In fact most students will be curious about *something*, though what excites each child's individual curiosity may vary considerably. Even given natural curiosity, however, they may not naturally think of investigating and gathering information in a systematic way. It is the responsibility of the teacher to encourage, nurture, and practice these attitudes so that students will have a good role model.

Unifying Concepts and Processes among the Sciences

The following are the concepts and processes generally recognized as those common to all scientific disciplines:

1. Systems, order, and organization
2. Constancy, change, and measurement
3. Evolution and equilibrium
4. Form and function
5. Evidence, models, and explanation

Systems, order, and organization

Because the natural world is so complex, the study of science involves the **organization** of items into smaller groups based on interaction or interdependence. These groups are called **systems**. Examples of organization include the periodic table of elements and the five-kingdom classification scheme for living organisms. Examples of systems include the solar system, the cardiovascular system, Newton's laws of force and motion, and the laws of conservation.

Order refers to the behavior and measurability of organisms and events in nature. The arrangement of planets in the solar system and the life cycle of bacterial cells are examples of order.

Constancy, Change, and Measurement

Constancy and **change** describe the observable properties of natural organisms and events, whether and in what part they remain the same (constancy), and whether and in what part they change (change)/. The freezing and melting points of given substances and the speed of sound are examples of variables that are constant under constant conditions. Growth, decay, and erosion are all examples of natural change. Scientists use different systems of **measurement** to observe change and constancy. The choice of measurement must be appropriate to the phenomenon being measured.

Evolution and Equilibrium

Evolution is the process of change over a long period of time. While biological evolution is the most common example, one can also classify technological advancements, changes in the universe, and changes in the environment as evolution.

Equilibrium is the state of balance between opposing forces of change. Homeostasis and ecological balance are examples of equilibrium.

Form and Function

Form and **function** are properties of organisms and systems that are closely related. The function of an object usually dictates its form, and the form of an object usually facilitates its function. For example, the form of the heart (e.g., muscle and valves) allows it to perform its function of circulating blood through the body.

Evidence, Models, and Explanations

Scientists use **evidence** and **models** to form **explanations** of natural events. Models are miniaturized representations of a larger event or system. Evidence is anything that furnishes proof.

Some things happen at too fast or too slow a rate, or are too small or too large for use to see. In these cases, we have to rely on indirect evidence to develop models of what is intangible. Once data has been collected and analyzed, it is useful to generalize the information by creating a model. A model is a conceptual representation of a phenomenon. Models are useful in that they clarify relationships, helping us to understand the phenomenon and make predictions about future outcomes. The natural sciences and social sciences employ modeling for this purpose.

Many scientific models are mathematical in nature and contain a set of variables linked by logical and quantitative relationships. These mathematical models may include functions, tables, formulas, and graphs. Typically, such mathematical models include assumptions that restrict them to very specific situations.

Oftentimes, this means they can only provide an *approximate* description of what occurs in the natural world. These assumptions, however, prevent the model from becoming overly complicated. For a mathematical model to fully explain a natural or social phenomenon, it has to contain many variables and may become too cumbersome to use. Accordingly, it is critical that assumptions be carefully chosen and thoroughly defined.

Certain models are abstract and contain sets of logical principles rather than relying on mathematics. These types of models are generally vaguer and are more useful for discovering and understanding new ideas. Abstract models can also include actual physical models built to make concepts more tangible. Abstract models, to an even greater extent than mathematical models, make assumptions and simplify actual phenomena.

Proper scientific models must be able to be tested and verified using experimental data. Often these experimental results are necessary to demonstrate the superiority of a model when two or more conflicting models seek to explain the same phenomenon. Computer simulations are increasingly used in both testing and developing mathematical and even abstract models. These types of simulations are especially useful in situations, such as ecology or manufacturing, where experiments are not feasible or variables are not fully under control.

PRINCIPLES OF SCIENTIFIC INQUIRY AND THE DESIGN OF SCIENTIFIC INVESTIGATIONS

Processes by which Hypotheses are Generated and Tested

Science can be defined as a body of knowledge that is systematically derived from study, observations, and experimentation. Its goal is to identify and establish principles and theories that may be applied to solve problems.

Pseudoscience, on the other hand, is a belief that is not warranted, but may imitate scientific terminology. There is no scientific methodology or application. Some of the classic examples of pseudoscience include witchcraft, astrology, alien encounters, or any topic that is explained by hearsay.

Scientific theory and experimentation must be repeatable, meaning that the findings of one experiment can be duplicated during any number of repetitions. They are also capable of change and can capable of being disproved. Science depends on communication, agreements, and disagreements among scientists. It is composed of theories, laws, and hypotheses.

Theory - the formation of principles or relationships that have been verified and accepted. (the term 'theory' can have several meanings within scientific literature, but when used with the upper case 'T' usually signifies the above.)

Law - an explanation of events that occur with uniformity under the same conditions (e.g., laws of nature, law of gravitation) and for which concrete evidence exists.

Hypothesis - an unproved theory or educated guess, designed to best explain a phenomena. A hypothesis should be consistent with facts already known and generally leads to research designed to test its validity.

Science is limited by the available technology. An example of this would be the relationship between the discovery of the cell and the invention of the microscope. As our technology improves, more hypotheses will become theories and possibly laws.

Science is also limited by the data that can be collected. Data may be interpreted differently on different occasions. Scientific limitations cause explanations to be changeable as new technologies emerge.

The first step in scientific inquiry is posing a question to be answered. Next, a hypothesis is formed to provide a plausible explanation. An experiment is then proposed and performed to test this hypothesis. A comparison between the predicted and observed results is the next step. Conclusions are then formed, and it is determined whether the hypothesis is correct or incorrect. If incorrect, the next step is to form a new hypothesis and the process is repeated.

One[s32] of the most important things to remember about scientific inquiry is that it is ongoing, and our "scientific" knowledge is always changing. Whether it is the number of elements on the periodic table, the number of moons of Jupiter, the number of kingdoms classifying life, or the definition of a planet, our knowledge of the world and ourselves changes constantly with scientific inquiry and what was considered a "fact" even last year may now be obsolete. It is important to constantly review and update one's knowledge of current scientific "facts" so as to provide the most up to date instruction possible to students. The science overview in this guide is current as of publication date, but teachers are responsible for keeping up with new scientific developments that might affect their content area instruction.

0010.02   **Applying knowledge of strategies for observing, collecting, analyzing, and communicating scientific data (e.g., using graphs, charts, and tables); appropriate tools, instruments, methods, process skills, and safety procedures associated with given scientific investigations; and the connections among science, mathematics, technology, society, and everyday life**

The scientific method is the basic process behind science. It involves several steps beginning with hypothesis formulation and working through to the conclusion.

Pose a question: Although many discoveries happen by chance, the standard thought process of a scientist begins with forming a question to research. The more limited the question, the easier it is to set up an experiment to answer it. *Form a hypothesis*: Once the question is formulated, scientists take an educated guess about the answer to the problem or question. This "best guess" is the hypothesis. It should be consistent with what is already known about the phenomenon in questions.

Conducting the test: Data collected for an experiment must have a variable or any condition that can be changed, such as temperature or mass. A good test will try to manipulate as few variables as possible so as to see which variable is responsible for the result. This requires a second example of a control. A control is an extra setup in which all the conditions are the same except for the variable being tested.

Observe and record the data: Reporting data should include specifics of how the measurements were calculated. For example, a graduated cylinder needs to be read with proper procedures. As beginning students, technique must be part of the instructional process so as to give validity to the data.

Drawing a conclusion: After recording data, compare it with that of other groups. A conclusion is the judgment derived from the data results.

Methods or Procedures for Collecting Data

The procedure used to obtain data is important to the outcome. Experiments consist of **controls** and **variables**. A control is the experiment run under normal conditions. The variable includes a factor that is changed. In biology, the variable may be light, temperature, pH, or time. The differences in tested variables may be used to make a prediction or to form a hypothesis. Usually only one variable should be tested at a time; for example, one would not alter both the temperature and pH of the experimental subject.

The **independent variable** is the one that is changed or manipulated by the researcher in order to determine its relationship to or effect upon an observed phenomenon. An independent variable might be the amount of light given to a plant or the temperature at which bacteria is grown, etc. The **dependent variable** is that which is influenced by the independent variable, the variable expected to change when the independent variable is changed (it is hypothesized to be *dependent* in part upon the independent variable).

Controls or control variables are variables or conditions that might be expected to affect the experiment if they vary or are changed. So these variables or conditions are purposely kept *exactly the same* from group to group in order to be sure any effects you see in the dependent variable are not due to changes in conditions other than the independent variable. For example, if you are studying the effect of amount of light (independent variable) on the growth of a plant (dependent variable), you would want to keeps things such as amount of water or fertilizer given exactly the same in each group. If you don't control these factors, then you won't know whether any differences in growth were due to the light or the water or the fertilizer. Any differences in water or fertilizer would be considered *confounding variables* or variables that *confound* the results and make it impossible to say for sure whether a relationship exists between the independent and dependent variables. Since one cannot always know in advance exactly *which* variables or conditions *might* have an effect on the dependent variable, scientific experiments are designed to keep all (or as many as can be controlled) conditions the same from group to group *except* the independent variable. If the independent variable is the ONLY difference between the groups, any change can be considered to indicate a relationship between the independent and dependent variables.

Graphing Data

Graphing is an important skill used to visually display collected data for analysis. It utilizes numbers to demonstrate patterns. The patterns offer a visual representation, making it easier to draw conclusions.

Two types of commonly used graphs are the **line graph** and the **bar graph**. The[SAW34] X axis is the horizontal axis. on which the Independent variable (the one manipulated) is usually placed. The Y axis is the vertical axis along which the dependent variable (the one you expect to change when you change the independent one) will be placed. For example, if you are studying the height of a plant (dependent variable) given differing amounts of light (independent variable), you would normally put the amount of light (say, high, medium or low) on the X axis and the height of the plant when you measure it on the Y axis. For a bar graph, you would draw a bar from the X axis to the end point of growth for each level of the variable on the Y axis.

Line graphs are usually used to show changes over time. Time, then, is the independent variable (*you* don't manipulate it, but it does change independently of anything else going on and you want to see what happens when it changes or passes). Therefore, time is usually on the X axis and the dependent variable (say, a child's height) is on the Y axis (you expect the child's height to change with the passage of time).

It is possible to have multiple independent variables, or multiple groups being compared on the one independent variable (say tomatoes and peppers in the light experiment above) and these would need to be shown differentially on a graph, say with symbols or colors.

Graphs should be calibrated at equal intervals. If one space represents one day, the next space may not represent ten days. A "best fit" line can be drawn to join the points, and it does not always include all the points in the data. Axes must always be labeled for the graph to be meaningful. A good title will describe both the dependent and the independent variables.

[SAW36] (See Skill 9.01 for more on constructing graphs.)

Apply Knowledge of Designing and Performing Investigations

Normally, knowledge is integrated in the form of a lab report. A report has many sections. It should include a specific **title** that tells exactly what is being studied. The **abstract** is a summary of the report; it is written at the beginning of the paper. The **purpose** should always be defined, as it will state the problem. The purpose should include the **hypothesis** (educated guess) of what is expected from the outcome of the experiment. The entire experiment should relate to this problem.

It is important to describe exactly what was done to prove or disprove a hypothesis (usually referred to as the 'procedure' section). A **control** is necessary to prove that the results were related to the changed conditions and would not have normally happened. Only one variable should be manipulated at a time. **Observations** and **results** of the experiment should be recorded, including all results from data. Drawings, graphs, and illustrations should be included to support information. Observations are objective, whereas analysis and interpretation is subjective. A **conclusion** should explain why the results of the experiment either proved or disproved the hypothesis. I might also include recommendations on any additional research that needs to be done to clarify the results.

A scientific theory is an explanation of a set of related observations based on a proven hypothesis. A scientific law usually lasts longer than a scientific theory and has more experimental data to support it.

Scientific inquiry often uses the metric system, as it is accepted worldwide and allows easier comparison among experiments done by scientists around the world. It is important to learn the following basic units and prefixes:

meter - measure of length
liter - measure of volume
gram - measure of mass

deca-(meter, liter, gram)= 10X the base unit   *deci*= 1/10 the base unit
hecto-(meter, liter, gram)= 100X the base unit   *centi*= 1/100 the base unit
kilo-(meter, liter, gram)= 1000X the base unit   *milli*= 1/1000 the base unit

Procedures and Tools--The Appropriate Use of Laboratory Materials

The specific tools and equipment used will depend upon the experiment being done and the grade level of the students. Not all scientific equipment is a form of high technology. Long before modern technology was available, Aristotle's students were crawling around the woods, recording observations on scrolls with quills and charcoal. We still use some of the information they collected.

The important thing in any investigation is to plan carefully and make a list of tools and supplies, whether they be pen and paper and a magnifying glass or an electron microscope, and design lessons to be sure students know how to use them safely. Examples of some common types of equipment are provided here.

Microscopes are commonly used in both elementary and high school experiments[s37]. Total magnification is determined by multiplying the ocular (usually 10X) and the objective (usually 10X on low, 40X on high) lenses. Several procedures should be followed to properly care for this equipment.

- Clean all lenses with lens paper only.
- Carry microscopes with two hands; one on the arm and one on the base.
- Always begin focusing on low power, then switch to high power.
- Store microscopes with the low power objective down.
- Always use a coverslip when viewing wet mount slides.
- Bring the objective down to its lowest position, then focus, moving up to avoid breaking the slide or scratching the lens.

Wet mount slides should be made by placing a drop of water on the specimen and then putting a glass coverslip on top of the drop of water. Dropping the coverslip at a forty-five degree angle will help to avoid air bubbles.

Chromatography uses the principles of capillarity to separate substances such as plant pigments. Molecules of a larger size will move slowly up the paper, whereas smaller molecules will move more quickly, producing lines of pigment. The paper slips should not be contaminated by other materials (school lunch, sticky fingers, etc), so careful washing or use of gloves is recommended.

An **indicator** is any substance used to assist in the classification of another substance. An example of an indicator is **litmus paper**. Litmus paper is a way to measure whether a substance is acidic or basic. Blue litmus turns pink when an acid is placed on it, and pink litmus turns blue when a base is placed on it. A more accurate measure of pH is pH paper; the paper turns different colors depending on the pH value.

Spectrophotometry measures the percent of light at different wavelengths absorbed and transmitted by a pigment solution. This is usually done via complex equipment.

Centrifugation involves spinning substances at a high speed. The more dense part of a solution will settle to the bottom of the test tube, whereas the lighter material will stay on top. Centrifugation is used to separate blood into blood cells and plasma, with the heavier blood cells settling to the bottom. A variety of simpler processes can illustrate this at the elementary level.

Electrophoresis[s38] uses electrical charges of molecules to separate them according to their size. The molecules, such as DNA or proteins, are pulled through a gel towards either the positive end of the gel box (if the material has a negative charge) or the negative end of the gel box (if the material has a positive charge). DNA is negatively charged and moves towards the positive charge.

Storing, Identifying, and Disposing of Chemicals and Biological Materials

All laboratory solutions should be prepared as directed in the lab manual. Care should be taken to avoid contamination. All glassware should be rinsed thoroughly with distilled water before using, and cleaned well after use. To prevent injury from accidents, safety goggles should be worn while working with glassware. All solutions should be made with distilled water, as tap water contains dissolved particles that may affect the results of an experiment. Chemical storage should be located in a secured, dry area. Chemicals should be stored in accordance with reactability. Acids are to be locked in a separate area. Used solutions should be disposed of according to local disposal procedures. Any questions regarding safe disposal or chemical safety may be directed to the local fire department.

The "Right to Know Law" covers science teachers who work with potentially hazardous chemicals. Briefly, the law states that employees must be informed of potentially toxic chemicals. An inventory must be made available if requested. The inventory must contain information about the hazards and properties of the chemicals. This inventory is to be checked against the "substance list." Training must be provided on the safe handling and interpretation of the Material Safety Data Sheet.

The following chemicals are potential carcinogens and are not allowed in school facilities: acrylonitrile, arsenic compounds, asbestos, benzidine, benzene, cadmium compounds, chloroform, chromium compounds, ethylene oxide, ortho-toluidine, nickel powder, and mercury.

Chemicals should not be stored on bench tops or heat sources. They should be stored in groups based on their reactivity with one another and in protective storage cabinets. All containers within the lab must be labeled.

[s39]
Chemical waste should be disposed of in properly labeled containers. Waste should be separated based on its reactivity with other chemicals.

Biological material should never be stored near food or water used for human consumption. All biological materials should be appropriately labeled. All blood and bodily fluids should be put into well-contained containers with secure lids to prevent leaking. All biological waste should be disposed of in biological hazardous waste bags.

Material Safety Data Sheets are available for every chemical and biological substance. These are available directly from the company of acquisition or the internet. The manuals for equipment used in the lab should be read and understood before using them.

Even in elementary schools, where less sophisticated and less obviously dangerous materials are in use, the teacher must take measures to keep students safe. Even a protractor can seriously injure a child if used incorrectly. Glass instruments can break and cause injury, dry ice can burn, etc. A part of the lesson plan should always center on proper use of the materials. This part of the lesson can also be used to reinforce the scientific principles regarding being responsible for the actions and results of the experiment.

Dissection and Alternatives to Dissection

Dissections - Animals that are not obtained from recognized sources should never be used. Decaying animals or those of unknown origin may harbor pathogens and/or parasites. Specimens should be rinsed before handling. Latex gloves are desirable. If gloves are not available, students with sores or scratches should be excused from the activity. Formaldehyde is a carcinogen and should be avoided or disposed of according to district regulations.

Students objecting to dissections for moral reasons should be given an alternative assignment. Interactive dissections are available online or from software companies for those students who object to performing dissections. There should be no penalty for those students who refuse to physically perform a dissection.

Live specimens - No dissections may be performed on living mammalian vertebrates or birds. Lower order life and invertebrates may be used. Biological experiments may be done with all animals except mammalian vertebrates or birds. No physiological harm may result to the animal. All animals housed and cared for in the school must be handled in a safe and humane manner. Animals are not to remain on school premises during extended vacations unless adequate care is provided. Many state laws stipulate that any instructor who intentionally refuses to comply with the laws may be suspended or dismissed.

Microbiology - Pathogenic organisms must never be used for experimentation. Students should adhere to the following rules at all times when working with microorganisms to avoid accidental contamination:

1. Treat all microorganisms as if they were pathogenic.
2. Maintain sterile conditions at all times

If taking a national level exam[s40], it is important to check with the Department of Education for specific state safety procedures. Teachers should know what their state expects not only for the test, but also for performance in the classroom and for the welfare of students. It is the responsibility of the teacher to provide a safe environment for the students. Proper supervision greatly reduces the risk of injury, and a teacher should never leave a class for any reason without providing alternate supervision.

After an accident, two factors are considered: *foreseeability* and *negligence*. **Foreseeability** is the anticipation that an event may occur under certain circumstances (and measures should, therefore, have been in place to prevent or treat it). **Negligence** is the failure to exercise ordinary or reasonable care. Safety procedures should be a part of the science curriculum, and a well-managed classroom is important to avoid student injury and potential lawsuits. All science labs should contain the following items of safety equipment. The following are requirements by law:

- Fire blanket that is visible and accessible
- Ground Fault Circuit Interrupters (GFCI) within two feet of water supplies
- Emergency shower capable of providing a continuous flow of water (where chemicals are in use)
- Signs designating room exits
- Emergency eye wash station that can be activated by the foot or forearm
- Eye protection for every student as well as a means of sanitizing equipment
- Emergency exhaust fans providing ventilation to the outside of the building
- Master cut-off switches for gas, electric, and compressed air. Switches must have permanently attached handles. Cut-off switches must be clearly labeled.
- An ABC fire extinguisher
- Storage cabinets for flammable materials

Also recommended, but not required by law:

- Chemical spill control kit
- Fume hood with a motor that is spark proof
- Protective laboratory aprons made of flame retardant material
- Signs that will alert people to potential hazardous conditions
- Containers for broken glassware, flammables, corrosives, and waste
- Containers should be labeled

While some of these requirements apply primarily to secondary school situations, the *principles* involved should be followed at all levels of scientific inquiry.

Connections among Science, Mathematics, Technology, Society, and Everyday Life

Biological science is closely connected to technology and the other sciences; it greatly impacts society and everyday life. Scientific discoveries often lead to technological advances and, conversely, technology is often necessary for scientific investigation. Biology and the other scientific disciplines share several concepts and processes that help to unify the study of science. Because biology is the science of living systems, biology directly impacts society and everyday life.

Science and technology, while distinct concepts, are closely related. Science attempts to investigate and explain the natural world, while technology attempts to solve human adaptation problems. Technology often results from the application of scientific discoveries, and advances in technology can increase the impact of scientific discoveries. For example, Watson and Crick used science to discover the structure of DNA; their discovery led to many biotechnological advances in the manipulation of DNA. These technological advances greatly influenced the medical and pharmaceutical fields. The success of Watson and Crick's experiments, however, was dependent on the technology available. Without the necessary technology, the experiments would have failed.

Biologists use a variety of tools and technologies to perform tests, to collect and display data, and to analyze relationships. Examples of commonly used tools include computer-linked probes, spreadsheets, and graphing calculators.

Biologists use **computer-linked probes** to measure various environmental factors including temperature, dissolved oxygen, pH, ionic concentration, and pressure. The advantage of computer-linked probes, as compared to more traditional observational tools, is that the probes automatically gather data and present it in an accessible format. This property of computer-linked probes eliminates the need for constant human observation and manipulation.

Biologists use **spreadsheets** to organize, analyze, and display data. For example, conservation ecologists use spreadsheets to model population growth and development, to apply sampling techniques, and to create statistical distributions to analyze relationships. Spreadsheet use simplifies data collection and manipulation, and it also allows the presentation of data to be done in a logical and understandable format.

Graphing calculators are another technology with many applications to biology. For example, biologists use algebraic functions to analyze growth, development, and other natural processes. Graphing calculators can manipulate algebraic data and create graphs for analysis and observation. In addition, biologists use the matrix function of graphing calculators to model problems in genetics. The use of graphing calculators simplifies the creation of graphical displays, including histograms; scatter plots, and line graphs. Biologists can transfer data and displays to computers for further analysis. Finally, biologists also connect computer-linked probes, used to collect data, to graphing calculators to ease the collection, transmission, and analysis of data.

The combination of biology and technology has improved the human standard of living in many ways. However, the negative impact of increasing human life expectancy and population on the environment is problematic. In addition, advances in biotechnology (e.g. genetic engineering, cloning) produce ethical dilemmas that society must consider.

0010.03   Demonstrating knowledge of the differences between living and nonliving things; different types of organisms and methods of classification; and the basic needs, characteristics, structures, and life processes of organisms

The organization of living systems builds by levels from small to increasingly larger and more complex. All aspects, whether they are cells or ecosystems, have similar requirements to sustain life. Life is organized from simple to complex in the following way:

Organelles make up **cells**, which make up **tissues**. Tissues make up **organs**, and groups of organs make up **organ systems**. Organ systems work together to provide life for the **organism**.

Several characteristics have been described to identify living versus non-living substances.

Living things are made of cells. They grow, are capable of reproduction, and respond to stimuli.

- Living things must adapt to environmental changes or perish.
- Living things carry on metabolic processes. They use and make energy.

All organic life on Earth has a common element: carbon. Carbon is recycled through the ecosystem through both biotic and abiotic means. It is the link between biological processes and the chemical make-up of life.

Different Types of Organisms and Methods of Classification

Carolus Linnaeus is termed the father of taxonomy. **Taxonomy** is the science of classification. **Classifying** is the grouping of items according to their similarities. It is important for students to realize relationships and similarity as well as differences to reach a reasonable conclusion in a lab experience. Linnaeus based his system on morphology (study of structure). Later on, evolutionary relationships (phylogeny) were also used to sort and group species. The modern classification system uses binomial nomenclature. This consists of a two-word name for every species. The genus is the first part of the name and the species is the second part. Notice in the levels explained below that Homo sapiens is the scientific name for humans.

Starting with the kingdom, the groups get smaller and more alike as one moves down the levels in human classification:

Kingdom: Animalia
Phylum: Chordata
Subphylum: Vertebrata
Class: Mammalia
Order: Primate
Family: Hominidae
Genus: Homo
Species: sapiens

Species are defined by the ability to successfully reproduce with members of their own kind.

Characteristics of the Five (or Six) Kingdoms

Linnaeus' original taxonomy of life contained five kingdoms, and that list is still widely used. Recently, however, many textbooks divide the bacterial kingdom into two kingdoms, resulting in six kingdoms (see below).Members of the various kingdoms of the classification system of living organisms often differ in their basic life functions. Here we compare and analyze how members of these kingdoms obtain nutrients, excrete waste, and reproduce.

Bacteria are prokaryotic, single-celled organisms that lack cell nuclei. The different types of bacteria obtain nutrients in a variety of ways. Most bacteria absorb nutrients from the environment through small channels in their cell walls and membranes (chemotrophs), while some perform photosynthesis (phototrophs). Chemoorganotrophs use organic compounds as energy sources while chemolithotrophs can use inorganic chemicals as energy sources. Depending on the type of metabolism and energy source, bacteria release a variety of waste products (e.g., alcohols, acids, carbon dioxide) to the environment through diffusion.

All bacteria reproduce through binary fission (asexual reproduction), producing two identical cells. Bacteria reproduce very rapidly, dividing or doubling every twenty minutes in optimal conditions. Asexual reproduction does not allow for genetic variation, but bacteria achieve genetic variety by absorbing DNA from ruptured cells and conjugating or swapping chromosomal or plasmid DNA with other cells.

In recent years many scientists have argued for splitting this kingdom into two kingdoms: Eubacteria ("True Bacteria", as described above) and Archaebacteria, bacteria-like organism that live in profoundly harsh environments in which Eubacteria (and other life forms) cannot survive (e.g., hot springs, oceanic volcanic vents, sewage systems).

Protists are eukaryotic, single-celled organisms. Most protists are heterotrophic, obtaining nutrients by ingesting small molecules and cells and digesting them in vacuoles. All protists reproduce asexually by either binary or multiple fission. Like bacteria, protists achieve genetic variation by exchange of DNA through conjugation.

Animals are multi-cellular, eukaryotic organisms. Animal cells have a cell membrane, but no cell wall. Their cells do not have chloroplasts. All animals obtain nutrients by eating food (ingestion). Different types of animals derive nutrients from eating plants, other animals, or both. Animal cells perform respiration, which converts food molecules—mainly carbohydrates and fats—into energy. The excretory systems of animals, like animals themselves, vary in complexity. Simple invertebrates eliminate waste through a single tube, while complex vertebrates have a specialized system of organs that process and excrete waste.

Most animals, unlike bacteria, exist in two distinct sexes. Members of the female sex give birth or lay eggs. Some less developed animals can reproduce asexually. For example, flatworms can divide into two, and some unfertilized insect eggs can develop into viable organisms. Most animals reproduce sexually through various mechanisms. For example, aquatic animals reproduce by external fertilization of eggs, while mammals reproduce by internal fertilization. More developed animals possess specialized reproductive systems and cycles that facilitate reproduction and promote genetic variation.

Plants, like animals, are multi-cellular, eukaryotic organisms. Plant cells have a cell membrane and a cell wall made of cellulose, which makes the cells stronger and capable of withstanding the pressure associated with water transfer. Plant cells also have chloroplasts which contain chlorophyll. Plants obtain nutrients from the soil through their root systems and convert sunlight into energy through photosynthesis. Many plants store waste products in vacuoles or organs (e.g., leaves, bark) that are discarded. Some plants also excrete waste through their roots.

More than half of the plant species reproduce by producing seeds from which new plants grow. Depending on the type of plant, flowers or cones produce seeds. Other plants reproduce by spores, tubers, bulbs, buds, and grafts. The flowers of flowering plants contain the reproductive organs. *Pollination* is the joining of male and female gametes; it is often facilitated through the movement of wind or animals.

Fungi are eukaryotic, mostly multi-cellular organisms. All fungi are heterotrophs, obtaining nutrients from other organisms. More specifically, most fungi obtain nutrients by digesting and absorbing nutrients from dead organisms. Fungi secrete enzymes outside of their body to digest organic material and then absorb the nutrients through their cell walls.

Most fungi can reproduce asexually and sexually. Different types of fungi reproduce asexually by mitosis, budding, sporification, or fragmentation. Sexual reproduction of fungi is different from sexual reproduction of animals. The two mating types of fungi are plus and minus, not male and female. The fusion of hyphae, the specialized reproductive structure in fungi, between plus and minus types produces and scatters diverse spores.

Behavioral Responses to External and Internal Stimuli

Response to stimuli is one of the key characteristics of any living thing. Any detectable change in the internal or external environment (the stimulus) may trigger a response in an organism. Just like physical characteristics, organisms' responses to stimuli are adaptations that allow them to better survive. While these responses may be more noticeable in animals that can move quickly, all living organisms are actually capable of responding to changes.

   Single-Celled Organisms: These organisms are able to respond to basic stimuli such as the presence of light, heat, or food. Changes in the environment are typically sensed via cell surface receptors. These organisms may respond to such stimuli by making changes in internal biochemical pathways or by initiating reproduction or phagocytosis. Those capable of simple motility, using flagella for instance, may respond by moving toward food or away from heat.

Plants: Plants typically do not possess sensory organs; thus, individual cells recognize stimuli through a variety of pathways. When many cells respond to stimuli together, a response becomes apparent. Logically then, the responses of plants occur on a rather longer timescale that those of animals. Plants are capable of responding to a few basic stimuli including light, water, and gravity. Some common examples include the way plants turn and grow toward the sun, the sprouting of seeds when exposed to warmth and moisture, and the growth of roots in the direction of gravity.

Animals: Lower members of the animal kingdom have responses similar to those seen in single-celled organisms. However, higher animals have developed complex systems to detect and respond to stimuli. The nervous system, sensory organs (eyes, ears, skin, etc), and muscle tissue all allow animals to sense and quickly respond to changes in their environment. As in other organisms, many responses to stimuli in animals are involuntary. For example, pupils dilate in response to the reduction of light. Such reactions are typically called reflexes. However, many animals are also capable of voluntary response. In many animal species, voluntary reactions are instinctual. For instance, a zebra's response to a lion is a voluntary one, but, instinctually, it will flee quickly as soon as the lion's presence is sensed. Complex responses, which may or may not be instinctual, are typically termed **behavior**. An example is the annual migration of birds when seasons change.

Basic Needs, Characteristics, Structures, and Life Processes of Organisms

Ecology is the study of organisms, where they live, and their interactions with the environment. A **population** is a group of the same species in a specific area. A **community** is a group of populations residing in the same area.

There are three critical levels of environmental understanding:

- An **ecosystem** is a community (of any size) consisting of a physical environment and the organisms that live within it.
- A **biome** is a large area of land with characteristic climate, soil, and mixtures of plants and animals. Biomes are made up of groups of ecosystems. The major biomes include: desert, chaparral, savanna, tropical rain forest, temperate grassland, temperate deciduous forest, taiga, and tundra.
- A **habitat** is the set of surroundings within which members of a species normally live. Elements of the habitat include soil, water, predators, and competitors.

Communities that are ecologically similar in regards to temperature, rainfall, and the species that live there are called **biomes**. Although classification of biomes can vary, specific biomes include:

- *Marine:* This is the saltwater that covers 75 percent of the earth. This biome is organized by the depth of water. The *intertidal* zone is located from the tide line to the edge of the water. The *littoral* zone is found from the water's edge to the open sea. It includes coral reef habitats and is the most densely populated area of the marine biome. The open sea zone is divided into the *epipelagic* zone and the *pelagic* zone. The epipelagic zone receives more sunlight and has a larger number of species. The ocean floor is called the *benthic* zone. It is populated with bottom feeders.
- *Tropical Rain Forest:* Here, temperature is fairly constant (25 degrees C) and rainfall exceeds 200 cm per year. Located around the equator, rain forests have abundant, diverse species of plants and animals.
- *Savanna:* The temperatures range from 0-25 degrees C depending on the location. Rainfall is from 90 to 150 cm per year. Plants include shrubs and grasses. The savanna is a transitional biome between the rain forest and the desert.
- *Desert*[SAW41]: A desert is defined by its dryness, and a lack of water. There is a lack of precipitation (less than 10 inches per year), or a a high ratio of evaporation to precipitation (low), or a lack of useable water because the water is continuously bound up in ice.. In hot deserts, temperatures range from 10-38 degrees C, and plant species include xerophytes and succulents. Lizards, snakes, and small mammals are common animals in hot deserts. In cold deserts e.g., Antarctica), temperatures stay below freezing and there is little if any plant life. (See Polar or Permafrost).
- *Temperate Deciduous Forest:* In this biome, temperatures range from -24 to 38 degrees C. Rainfall is 65 to 150 cm per year. Deciduous trees are common, as well as deer, bear, and squirrels.
- *Taiga:* Here, temperatures range from -24 to 22 degrees C. Rainfall is 35 to 40 cm per year. Taiga is located north and south of the equator, close to the poles. Plant life includes conifers and plants that can withstand harsh winters. Animals include weasels, mink, and moose.
- *Tundra:* Temperatures range from -28 to 15 degrees C in the tundra. Rainfall is limited, ranging from 10 to 15 cm per year. The tundra is located even further north and south of the taiga. Common plants include lichens and mosses. Animals include polar bears and musk ox.
- *Polar or Permafrost (also called cold deserts):* This is where temperatures range from -40 to 0 degrees C. It rarely gets above freezing. Rainfall is below 10 cm per year. Most water is bound up as ice. Life is limited.

- *Freshwater* biomes: Some systems of classification consider freshwater to be a biome of its own. However, fresh water habitats, such as rivers, ponds and lakes, usually reflect characteristics of the larger biome of which they are a part (e.g., Deciduous forest).

Succession is an orderly process of replacing a community that has been damaged or has begun where no life previously existed. Primary succession occurs after a community has been totally wiped out by a natural disaster or where life never existed before, as in a flooded area. Secondary succession takes place in communities that were once flourishing but disturbed by some force, either human or natural, but not totally stripped. A climax community is a community that is established and flourishing.

Biodiversity refers to the variety of species and organisms on the earth, as well as the variety of available habitats for them. Biodiversity provides the life-support system for all the earth's habitats and species. The greater the degree of biodiversity, the more species and habitats will continue to survive.

Definitions of Relationships

Interactions between members of the species occur within habitats. These interactions can vary considerably in terms of the relative benefits to each species:

Competition occurs between members of the same species or between members of different species for resources required to continue life, to grow, or to reproduce. For example, competition for acorns can occur between individual squirrels, or it can occur between squirrels and woodpeckers. One species can either push out or cause the demise of another species if it is better adapted to obtain the resource. When a new species is introduced into a habitat, the result can be a loss of the native species and/or significant changes to the habitat. For example, the introduction of the Asian plant Kudzu into the American South has resulted in the destruction of several species because Kudzu grows and spreads very quickly, often smothering everything in its path.

Predation occurs when predators, organisms that live by hunting and eating others, consume the organisms in an area. The species best suited for hunting other species in the habitat will be the species that survives. Larger species that have better hunting skills reduce the amount of prey available for smaller and/or weaker species. This affects both the amount of available prey and the diversity of species that are able to survive in the habitat.

Symbiosis is a condition in which two organisms of different species are able to live in the same environment over an extended period of time without harming one another. In some cases, one species may benefit without harming the other. In some cases only one benefits, but the other is not harmed. In other cases, both species benefit.

Parasitism is when two species occupy a similar place, but the parasite benefits from the relationship while the host is harmed.

Commensalism occurs when two species occupy a similar place, and neither species is harmed by or benefits from the relationship.

Mutualism is when two species occupy a similar place and both species benefit from the relationship.

Carrying Capacity is the total amount of life a habitat can support. Once the habitat runs out of food, water, shelter or space, the carrying capacity decreases, and then stabilizes.

Biotic factors are living things in an ecosystem: plants, animals, bacteria, fungi, etc.

Abiotic factors are non-living aspects of an ecosystem: soil quality, rainfall, temperature, etc.

Biogeochemical cycles

Essential elements are recycled through an ecosystem. At times, the element needs to be "fixed" in a useable form. Some cycles are dependent on plants, algae, and bacteria to fix nutrients for use by animals.

Water cycle: Two percent of all the available water is fixed and unavailable in ice or the bodies of organisms. Available water includes surface water (lakes, ocean, and rivers) and ground water (aquifers, wells). Ninety-six percent of all available water is from ground water. Water is recycled through the processes of evaporation, condensation, and precipitation. The water present on the earth now is the water that has been here since our atmosphere formed.

Carbon cycle: Ten percent of all available carbon in the air (from carbon dioxide gas) is fixed by photosynthesis. Plants fix carbon in the form of glucose, and animals then eat the plants and are able to obtain their source of carbon. When animals release carbon dioxide through respiration, the plants have a source of carbon to fix once more.

Nitrogen cycle: Eighty percent of the atmosphere is nitrogen gas. Nitrogen must be in non-gaseous form to be incorporated into an organism. Only a few genera of bacteria have the correct enzymes to break the triple bond between nitrogen atoms. These bacteria live within the roots of legumes (peas, beans, alfalfa) and add bacteria to the soil so that it may be taken up by plants. Nitrogen is necessary to make amino acids and the nitrogenous bases of DNA.

Phosphorus cycle: Phosphorus is a mineral not found in the atmosphere. Fungi and plant roots have a structure called mycorrhizae that are able to fix insoluble phosphates into useable phosphorus. Urine and decayed matter return phosphorus to the earth where it can be incorporated in the plant. Phosphorus is needed for the backbone of DNA and for ATP manufacture.

Ecological Problems

Non-renewable resources are fragile and must be conserved for use in the future. Man's impact on the environment and knowledge of conservation will determine the future.

Biological magnification: Chemicals and pesticides accumulate in the food chain (See Skill 10.04). Tertiary consumers have more accumulated toxins than animals at the bottom of the food chain.

Simplification of the food web: Three major crops feed the world (rice, corn, and wheat). Planting these crops wipes out other habitats and pushes animals into smaller areas, causing overpopulation or extinction.

Fuel sources: Strip mining and the overuse of oil reserves have depleted these resources. At the current rate of consumption, conservation or alternate fuel sources will be key to our future.

Pollution: Although technology gives us many advances, pollution is a side effect of production. Waste disposal and the burning of fossil fuels have polluted our land, water, and air. Global warming and acid rain are two results of the burning of hydrocarbons and sulfur.

Global warming: Rain forest depletion, fossil fuels, and aerosols have caused an increase in carbon dioxide production. This leads to a decrease in the amount of oxygen, which is directly proportional to the amount of ozone. As the ozone layer depletes, more heat enters our atmosphere and is trapped. This causes an overall warming effect that may eventually melt the polar ice caps, causing a rise in water levels and changes in climate. This will, in turn, affect weather systems.

Endangered species: Construction to house our overpopulated world has caused a destruction of habitats for other animals, often leading to their extinction.

Overpopulation: The human race is still growing at an exponential rate. Carrying capacity has not been met due to our ability to use technology to produce more food.

0010.04 **Demonstrating knowledge of the interactions of organisms with one another and their environment, the flow of energy and matter within an ecosystem, the basic principles of heredity and life cycles, factors that affect the survival or extinction of species, and the effects of humans on the environment**

FLOW OF ENERGY IN AN ECOSYSTEM

Trophic levels are based on the feeding relationships that determine energy flow and chemical cycling.

Autotrophs are the primary **producers** of the ecosystem. They consist mainly of plants. They produce food, usually from sunlight and chlorophyll.

Consumers are living things that eat or consume other living things for nourishment.

Primary consumers are the next trophic level. The primary consumers are the herbivores that eat plants or algae.

Secondary consumers are the carnivores that eat the primary consumers..

Tertiary consumers eat the secondary consumers. These trophic levels may go higher depending on the ecosystem.

Omnivores are consumers that eat either plants or other consumers.

Decomposers are consumers that feed off animal waste and dead organisms. In the process, they break down the dead organism or waste.

This pathway of food and energy transfer is known as a food chain. Most food chains are more elaborate, becoming food webs

.

Energy is lost as the trophic levels progress from producer to tertiary consumer. The amount of energy that is transferred between trophic levels is called the **ecological efficiency**. This accounts for the relative numbers of each type of organism in a habitat. Producers will be the most populous, and tertiary consumers, the fewest. The visual of this energy flow is represented in a **pyramid of productivity**, seen below:

Tertiary

Consumers

Secondary Consumers

P r i m a r y C o n s u m e r s

P   r   o   d   u   c   e   r   s

The **biomass pyramid** represents the total dry weight of organisms in each trophic level. A **pyramid of numbers** is a representation of the population size of each trophic level. The producers, being the most populous, are on the bottom of this pyramid with the tertiary consumers on the top with the fewest numbers.

PRINCIPLES OF GENETICS

Gregor Mendel is recognized as the father of genetics. His work in the late 1800s is the basis of our knowledge of genetics. Although unaware of the presence of DNA or genes, Mendel realized there were factors (now known as **genes**) that were transferred from parents to their offspring. Mendel worked with pea plants, fertilizing them himself and keeping track of subsequent generations. His findings led to the Mendelian laws of genetics. Mendel found that two "factors" governed each trait, one from each parent. Traits or characteristics came in several forms, known as **alleles**. For example, the trait for flower color had both white alleles and purple alleles.

Mendel formed three laws:

Law of dominance - In a pair of alleles, one trait may cover up the allele of the other trait. Example: brown eyes are dominant to blue eyes.

Law of segregation - Only one of the two possible alleles from each parent is passed on to the offspring from each parent. (During meiosis, the haploid number insures that half the sex cells get one allele, half get the other.)

Law of independent assortment - Alleles sort independently of each other. (Many combinations are possible depending on which sperm ends up with which egg. Compare this to the many combinations of hands possible when dealing a deck of cards).

Punnet squares are used to show the possible ways that genes combine and indicate the probability of the occurrence of a certain genotype or phenotype. One parent's genes are put at the top of the box and the other parent at the side of the box. Genes combine on the square just like numbers that are added in addition tables learned in elementary school. Below is an example of a **monohybrid cross**, which is a cross using only one trait—in this case, a trait labeled "g."

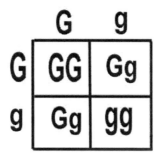

In a **dihybrid cross**, sixteen gene combinations are possible, as each cross has two traits.

DEFINITIONS TO KNOW:

Dominant - the stronger of the two traits. If a dominant gene is present, it is expressed as a capital letter.

Recessive - the weaker of the two traits. In order for the recessive gene to be expressed, there must be two recessive genes present. It is expressed as a lower case letter.

Homozygous - (purebred) having two of the same genes present. An organism may be homozygous dominant, with two dominant genes, or homozygous recessive, with two recessive genes.

Heterozygous - (hybrid) having one dominant gene and one recessive gene. The dominant gene is the one that is expressed (seen), but the recessive gene can be passed on to offspring.

Genotype - the genes the organism has. Genes are represented with letters. AA, Bb, and tt are examples of genotypes.

Phenotype - how the trait is expressed in an organism. Blue eyes, brown hair, and red flowers are examples of phenotypes.

Incomplete dominance - neither gene masks the other so that a new phenotype is formed. For example, red flowers (R) and white flowers (r) in a particular plant may have equal strength. A heterozygote (Rr) would have pink flowers. If a problem occurs with a third phenotype, incomplete dominance is occurring.

Co-dominance - genes may form new phenotypes. The ABO blood grouping is an example of co-dominance. A and B are of equal strength and O is recessive. Therefore, type A blood may have the genotypes of AA or AO, type B blood may have the genotypes of BB or BO, type AB blood has the genotype A and B, and type O blood has two recessive O genes.

Linkage - genes that are found on the same chromosome usually appear together unless crossing over has occurred in meiosis (for example, blue eyes and blonde hair often show up together).

Lethal alleles – maladaptive, and usually recessive due to the early death of the offspring. If a 2:1 ratio of alleles is found in offspring, a lethal gene combination is usually the reason. Some examples of lethal alleles include sickle cell anemia, Tay-Sachs disease, and cystic fibrosis. In these cases, the coding for an important protein is usually affected.

Inborn errors of metabolism – the affected protein is an enzyme. Examples include PKU (phenylketonuria) and albinism.

Polygenic characters - many alleles code for a phenotype. There may be as many as twenty genes that code for skin color. This is why there is such a variety of skin tones. Another example is height. A couple of medium height may have very tall offspring.

Sex linked traits - the Y chromosome found only in males (XY) carries very little genetic information, whereas the X chromosome found in females (XX) carries a great deal of information. Since men have no second X chromosome to cover up a recessive gene on the single X chromosome, the recessive trait is expressed more often in men. Women need the recessive gene on both X chromosomes to show the trait. Examples of sex-linked traits include hemophilia and color-blindness.

Sex influenced traits - traits that are influenced by the sex hormones. Male pattern baldness is an example of a sex-influenced trait. Testosterone influences the expression of the gene. Mostly men who lose their hair do so due to this trait.

COMMON LIFE CYCLES

Bacteria are commonly used in laboratories for research. Bacteria reproduce by binary fission. This **asexual** process is simply a division of the bacterium in half. All new organisms are exact copies of the parent. The obvious advantage of asexual reproduction is that it does not require a partner. This is a huge advantage for organisms that do not move around; not having to move around to reproduce allows organisms to conserve energy. Asexual reproduction also tends to be faster. However, as asexual reproduction produces only exact copies of the parent organism, it does not allow for genetic variation, which means that mutations, or weaker qualities, will always be passed on.

Plants typically start from a seed, which germinates (puts out roots and a stem), under the right conditions (usually involving water and warmth). Plants grow at widely varying rates and when grown produce flowers. Flowers, when pollinated, produce seeds. Seeds are dispersed into the environment in a variety of ways (wind, animals, water, etc.) and the process begins again.

Insects go through a process called **metamorphosis**, either complete or partial. Insects such as butterflies go through complete metamorphosis, involving four different stages of life, but they only look like butterflies in the final stage. In the first stage, the adult butterfly lays an egg. In the second stage, the egg hatches into a caterpillar or larva, the stage at which most feeding occurs. The third stage is when the caterpillar forms the chrysalis or pupa, when the organism is inactive but going through major changes. Finally, the chrysalis matures and the adult butterfly emerges. Adults repeat the reproductive process.

Some insects, such as grasshoppers, go through incomplete metamorphosis and only go through three stages: egg, larva, adult (no Pupa stages).

Amphibians spend a part of their life cycle in the water and another part on land. Frogs, for example, go through their own metamorphosis, and have multiple stages in their life cycle. Initially, an adult frog lays its eggs in the water (all amphibians require water for reproduction). In the second stage, tadpoles hatch from the eggs. The tadpoles have tails, but no legs, swim in the water, and use gills for breathing. Tadpoles have a tail that is used for locomotion, but the tail will eventually disappear and they will grow legs instead. Somewhere between two and four months old, the tadpole is known as a froglet. You can recognize a froglet because the rim around its tail, which appears fish-like, has disappeared, its tail is shorter, and its four legs have grown to the extent that its rear legs are bent underneath it. The final stage of a frog's life is spent as an adult on land. Its tail has been entirely reabsorbed, it uses lungs, not gills, to breathe air, it has a chubby frog-like appearance instead of the tadpole's fish-like appearance, and as a mature frog, it can lay eggs.

Most other animals, **reptiles, bird, and mammals**, start their life cycle when they are born (either from eggs or alive), look somewhat similar to the adult even when young, then simply grow larger until they are adults and can reproduce.

SURVIVAL OF SPECIES

Factors that Affect the Survival or Extinction of Organisms

There are many interactions that may occur between different species living together. Predation, parasitism, competition, commensalisms, and mutualism are the different types of relationships populations have with each other.

Predation and **parasitism** result in a benefit for one species and a detriment for the other. Predation occurs when a predator eats its prey. The common conception of predation is of a carnivore consuming other animals. This is one form of predation. Although not always resulting in the death of the plant, herbivory is a form of predation. Some animals eat enough of a plant to cause death. However, many plants and animals have defenses against predators. Some plants have poisonous chemicals that will harm the predator if ingested, and some animals are camouflaged so they are harder to detect.

Parasitism involves a predator that lives on or in its host, causing detrimental effects to the host but not the parasite. Insects and viruses living off and reproducing in their hosts are examples of parasitism.

Competition occurs when two or more species in a community use the same resources. Competition is usually detrimental to both populations. It is often difficult to find in nature, because competition between two populations is not continuous. Either the weaker population will no longer exist, or one population will evolve to utilize other available resources.

Symbiosis is when two species live close together. Parasitism, described above, is one example of symbiosis. Another example of symbiosis is commensalism. **Commensalism** occurs when one species benefits from the other without harmful effects. **Mutualism** is when both species benefit from the other. Species involved in mutualistic relationships must co-evolve to survive; as one species evolves, the other must as well. For example, grouper and a species of shrimp live in a mutualistic relationship. The shrimp feed off parasites living on the grouper; thus, the shrimp are fed and the grouper stays healthy and parasite-free. Many microorganisms are in mutualistic relationships.

Adaptations

Animals and plants have basic needs that must be met in their habitats. All living things have the same basic needs for

- Nourishment
- Protection (from the environment-shelter- and from predators)
- Growth
- Reproduction

Animals and plants will have *adaptations,* in body parts or behavior, that help them adapt to their environments and meet their needs in those environments. Many adaptations are found in the basic structures of the body. For example, cactus plants have thick, waxy stems to retard water loss so they can live in the desert. A turtle has a hard shell which provides both shelter and safety from predators. A camel had very broad foot pads that make walking on sand easier, and so forth.

Sometimes animals have developed (or have instinctive) behaviors that help them adapt to their environments. Some spiders spin elaborate rectangular nets out of spider silk and throw these nets over prey. Some birds and insects engage in elaborate "dances" and mating rituals prior to reproduction.

The Concepts of Niche and Carrying Capacity

The term **niche** describes the relational position of a species or population in an ecosystem. It includes how a population responds to the amount of its resources and its enemies (e.g., growing when resources are abundant and predators, parasites, and pathogens are scarce).

Niche also involves the life history of an organism, its habitat, and its place in the food chain. According to the competitive exclusion principle, no two species can occupy the same niche in the same environment for a long time. They would be considered *competitors* (see above) in that niche.

The full range of environmental conditions (biological and physical) under which an organism can exist describes its **fundamental niche**. Because of the pressure from superior competitors, organisms that survive over the long term are driven to occupy a niche that is narrower than their previous one. This is known as the **realized niche**.

Examples of niches include:

Oak trees

- live in forests
- absorb sunlight by photosynthesis
- provide shelter for many animals
- act as support for creeping plants
- serve as a source of food for animals
- cover their ground with dead leaves in the autumn

If the oak trees were cut down or destroyed by fire or storms, they would no longer be doing these jobs. In turn, this would have a disastrous effect on all the other organisms living in the same habitat.

Hedgehogs

- eat a variety of insects and other invertebrates that live underneath the dead leaves and twigs in the garden
- have spines that are a superb environment for fleas and ticks
- put the nitrogen back into the soil when they urinate
- eat slugs and protect plants from them

If the hedgehog population was drastically reduced, the number of slugs would explode and the nutrients in the dead leaves and twigs would not recycle.

A **population** is a group of individuals of one species that live in the same general area. Many factors can affect the population size and its growth rate. For example, population size depends on the total amount of life a habitat can support. This is called the **carrying capacity** of the environment.

Limiting factors can also affect population growth. As a population increases, the competition for resources is more intense, and the growth rate declines. This is a **density-dependent** growth factor. The carrying capacity can be determined by the density-dependent factor.

Density-independent factors affect individuals regardless of population size. The weather and climate are good examples. Temperatures that are too hot or too cold may kill many individuals from a population even if it has not reached the carrying capacity of the habitat.

HUMAN INFLUENCES

Human population increased slowly until 1650. Since 1650, the human population has grown almost exponentially, reaching its current population of over six billion. Factors that have led to this increased growth rate include improved nutrition, sanitation, and health care. In addition, advances in technology, agriculture, and scientific knowledge have made the use of resources more efficient and readily available.

While the earth's ultimate carrying capacity for humans is uncertain, some factors that may limit growth are the availability of food, water, space, and fossil fuels. There is a finite amount of land on Earth available for food production. In addition, providing clean, potable water for a growing human population is a real concern. Fossil fuels, important energy sources for human technology, are scarce. The inevitable shortage of energy in the earth's future will require the development of alternative energy sources to maintain or increase human population growth.

Effects of Humans on the Environment

For centuries, humans have been increasingly altering the environments in which they live. Everything from driving cars to logging has had a toll on the environment.

Pollutants are impurities in the air, water, and soil that may be harmful to life. Oil is a major pollutant that can cause severe destruction of the oceans, beaches, and animal life when there is a spill. Other pollutants, such as chemical and radioactive spills endanger all forms of life, including humans.

Global warming is an enormous environmental issue today; it is caused by the "greenhouse effect." Atmospheric greenhouse gases such as water vapor, carbon dioxide, and other gases trap some of the outgoing energy, retaining heat near the planet, somewhat like the glass panels of a greenhouse. This occurs naturally; without it, the temperature on the earth would be too low to sustain life. The problem occurs when these gases enter the atmosphere in large amounts; their heat-trapping ability results in global warming.

Over the past 100 years, the earth's surface temperature has risen one degree Fahrenheit, with accelerated warming occurring in the past two decades. The increase of gases in the atmosphere is caused by the burning of fossil fuels and emissions of carbon dioxide from cars and factories.

All acids contain hydrogen. Substances from factory and car exhaust dissolve in rainwater, forming **acid rain**. When this rain falls onto stone, the acids can react with metallic compounds and gradually wear the stone away. It can also be harmful to many forms of plant life—the base of the biodiversity pyramid—as well as aquatic life.

Since radioactive material has become readily available, it has been a major concern as a threat of **nuclear disaster**. Radioactivity ionizes the air through which it travels. It is strong enough to kill cancer cells or dangerous enough to cause illness or even death. Gamma rays can penetrate the body and damage cells. In a nuclear disaster, damage to the land and all living organisms is inevitable.

Logging also has a negative impact on the environment. Clear-cutting forests leaves the soil unprotected and can cause disasters such as mudslides. Also, the quality of soil in that area diminishes the chances of successful re-growth for living organisms. In addition, loss of forests, particularly rain forests, impacts air quality and the rate at which plants return oxygen to the air and clean carbon dioxide out of it.

There are some benefits of human activities in the environment. The populations of many animal species that were endangered have risen because of protection laws and the study of the animals and their habitats.

With the development of new technology, other benefits accrue to the environment. The recycling process has prevented the unnecessary waste of plastics, glass, and paper.

OBJECTIVE 0011   UNDERSTAND CONCEPTS AND PRINCIPLES OF PHYSICAL AND EARTH SCIENCE

0011.01   Demonstrating knowledge of the structure and properties of matter (e.g., atoms, elements, molecules, density, boiling and freezing points); the differences between physical and chemical changes; and the concepts of conservation of matter and conservation of energy as they are applied to physical systems

An **atom** is the smallest particle of an element that retains the properties of that element. All of the atoms of a particular element are the same. The atoms of each element are different from the atoms of other elements.

An **element**[s42] is a substance that cannot be broken down into other substances. As of July, 2009,, scientists have identified 117 elements (numbers 1-116 and # 118); 94 are found in nature and twenty-three are synthetic, often occurring only briefly in laboratories. It should be remembered that the numbers of both naturally occurring and synthetic elements are always changing. For example, as of July, 2009, there was one "undiscovered" element (#117) that has been given a "placeholder" number and name because laboratory work is on the verge of creating or discovering it. Elements are assigned an identifying symbol of one or two letters. For example, the symbol for oxygen is O, which stands for one atom of oxygen. However, because oxygen atoms in nature are joined together in pairs, the symbol O_2 represents oxygen as we know it.

This pair of oxygen atoms is a molecule. A **molecule** is the smallest particle of a substance that can exist independently and has all of the properties of that substance. A molecule of most elements is made up of one atom. However, oxygen, hydrogen, nitrogen, and chlorine molecules are made of two atoms each.

A **compound** is made of two or more elements that have been chemically combined. Each element's atoms join together when they bind chemically; the result is that the elements lose their individual identities. The compound that they become has different properties.

We use a formula to show the elements of a chemical compound. A **chemical formula** is a shorthand way of showing what is in a compound by using symbols and subscripts. The letter symbols let us know which elements are involved, and the number subscript tells how many atoms of each element are involved. No subscript is used if there is only one atom involved. For example, carbon dioxide is made up of one atom of carbon (C) and two atoms of oxygen (O_2), so the formula would be represented as CO_2.

Substances can combine without a chemical change. A **mixture** is any combination of two or more substances in which the substances keep their own properties. A fruit salad is a mixture. So is an ice cream sundae, although you might not recognize each part if it is stirred together. Colognes and perfumes are other examples. You may not readily recognize the individual elements; however, they can be separated.

Compounds and mixtures are similar in that they are made up of two or more substances. However, they have the following opposite characteristics:

Compounds:

1. Made up of one kind of particle
2. Formed during a chemical change
3. Broken down only by chemical changes
4. Properties are different from its parts
5. Has a specific amount of each ingredient.

Mixtures:

1. Made up of two or more particles
2. Not formed by a chemical change
3. Can be separated by physical changes
4. Properties are the same as its parts
5. Does not have a definite amount of each ingredient

Common compounds are acids, bases, salts, and oxides. They are classified according to their characteristics.

An **acid** contains one element of hydrogen (H). Although it is never wise to taste a substance to identify it, acids have a sour taste. Vinegar and lemon juice are both acids, and acids occur in many foods in a weak state. Strong acids can burn skin and destroy materials. Common acids include:

- Sulfuric acid (H_2SO_4) -Used in medicines, alcohol, dyes, and car batteries
- Nitric acid (HNO_3) -Used in fertilizers, explosives, and cleaning materials
- Carbonic acid (H_2CO_3)-Used in soft drinks
- Acetic acid ($HC_2H_3O_2$)-Used in making plastics, rubber, photographic film, and as a solvent.

Bases have a bitter taste, and the stronger ones feel slippery. Like acids, strong bases can be dangerous and should be handled carefully. All bases contain the elements oxygen and hydrogen (OH). Many household cleaning products contain bases. Common bases include:

- Sodium hydroxide (NaOH): Used in making soap, paper, vegetable oils, and refining petroleum.
- Ammonium hydroxide (NH_4OH): Used for making deodorants, bleaching compounds, and cleaning compounds
- Potassium hydroxide (KOH): Used for making soaps, drugs, dyes, alkaline batteries, and purifying industrial gases
- Calcium ($Ca(OH)_2$): Used in making cement and plaster hydroxide

An **indicator** is a substance that changes color when it comes in contact with an acid or a base. Litmus paper is an indicator. Blue litmus paper turns red in an acid. Red litmus paper turns blue in a base.

A substance that is neither acid nor base is **neutral**. Neutral substances do not change the color of litmus paper.

Salt is formed when an acid and a base combine chemically. Water is also formed. The process is called neutralization. Table salt (NaCl) is an example of this process. Salts are also used in toothpaste, epsom salts, and cream of tartar. Calcium chloride ($CaCl_2$) is used on frozen streets and walkways to melt the ice.

Oxides are compounds that are formed when oxygen combines with another element. Rust is an oxide formed when oxygen combines with iron.

Melting point refers to the temperature at which a solid becomes a liquid. Melting takes place when there is sufficient energy available to break the intermolecular forces that hold molecules together in a solid.

Boiling point refers to the temperature at which a liquid becomes a gas. Boiling occurs when there is enough energy available to break the intermolecular forces holding molecules together as a liquid.

Density is the mass of a substance contained per unit of volume. It is stated in grams per cubic centimeter (g/cm^3).

Physical and Chemical Changes

Everything in the world is made up of **matter**, whether it is a rock, a building, an animal, or a person. Matter is defined by its characteristics: <u>It takes up space and it has mass.</u>

Mass is a measure of the amount of matter in an object. Two objects of equal mass will balance each other on a simple balance scale no matter where the scale is located. For instance, two rocks with the same amount of mass that are in balance on the earth will also be in balance on the moon. They will feel **heavier** on earth than on the moon because of the gravitational pull of the earth. So, although the two rocks have the same mass, they will have different weight.

Weight is the measure of the earth's pull of gravity on an object. It can also be defined as the pull of gravity between other bodies. The units of weight measure commonly used are the pound in English measure and the **kilogram** in metric measure.

In addition to mass, matter also has the property of volume. **Volume** is the amount of cubic space that an object occupies. Volume and mass together give a more exact description of the object. Two objects may have the same volume, but different mass, the same mass but different volumes, etc. For instance, consider two cubes that are each one cubic centimeter, one made from plastic, one from lead. They have the same volume, but the lead cube has more mass. The measure that we use to describe the cubes takes into consideration both the mass and the volume. **Density** is the mass of a substance contained per unit of volume. If the density of an object is less than the density of a liquid, the object will float in the liquid. If the object is denser than the liquid, the object will sink.

Density is stated in grams per cubic centimeter (g/cm^3), where the gram is the standard unit of mass. To find an object's density, one must measure its mass and its volume, then divide the mass by the volume ($D = m / V$).

To find an object's density, first use a balance to find its mass. Then calculate its volume. If the object is a regular shape, one can find the volume by multiplying the length, width, and height together. However, if it is an irregular shape, one can find the volume by seeing how much water it displaces. Measure the water in the container before and after the object is submerged. The difference will be the volume of the object.

Specific gravity is the ratio of the density of a substance to the density of water. For instance, the specific density of one liter of turpentine is calculated by comparing its mass (0.81 kg) to the mass of one liter of water (1 kg):

$$\frac{\text{mass of 1 L alcohol}}{\text{mass of 1 L water}} = \frac{0.81 \text{ kg}}{1.00 \text{ kg}} = 0.81$$

Physical properties and chemical properties of matter describe the appearance or behavior of a substance. A **physical property** can be observed without changing the identity of a substance. For instance, one can describe the color, mass, shape, and volume of a book. **Chemical properties** describe the ability of a substance to be changed into new substances. Baking powder goes through a chemical change as it changes into carbon dioxide gas during the baking process.

Matter constantly changes. A **physical change** is a change that does not produce a new substance. The freezing and melting of water is an example of physical change. A **chemical change** (or **chemical reaction**) changes the inherent properties of a substance. This includes things such as burning materials that turn into smoke or a seltzer tablet that fizzes into gas bubbles when submerged in water.

The **phase of matter** (solid, liquid, or gas) is identified by its shape and volume. A **solid** has a definite shape, which it keeps when you move it around, and definite volume. A **liquid** has a definite volume, but no shape; its shape changes to fit that if its container. A **gas** has no shape or volume because it will spread out to occupy the entire space of whatever container it is in.

Energy is the ability to cause change in matter. Applying heat to a frozen liquid changes it from solid to liquid. Continue heating it, and it will boil and give off steam, a gas.

Evaporation is the change in phase from liquid to gas. **Condensation** is the change in phase from gas to liquid.

Conservation of Matter and Conservation of Energy

The **law of conservation of energy** states that energy is neither created nor destroyed. Thus, energy changes form whenever energy transactions occur in nature. Because the total energy in the universe is constant, energy continually transitions between forms. For example, an engine burns gasoline, converting the chemical energy of the gasoline into mechanical energy. A plant converts radiant energy of the sun into chemical energy found in glucose. A battery converts chemical energy into electrical energy.

Chemical reactions are the interactions of substances that result in chemical changes and changes in energy. Chemical reactions involve changes in electron motion as well as the breaking up and formation of chemical bonds. **Reactants** are the original substances that interact to form distinct products. **Endothermic** chemical reactions consume energy, while **exothermic** chemical reactions release energy with product formation. Chemical reactions occur continually in nature and are also induced by man for many purposes.

Nuclear reactions, or **atomic reactions**, are reactions that change the composition, energy, or structure of atomic nuclei. Nuclear reactions change the number of protons and neutrons in the nucleus. The two main types of nuclear reactions are **fission** (splitting of nuclei) and **fusion** (joining of nuclei). Fusion reactions are exothermic, releasing heat energy. Fission reactions are endothermic, absorbing heat energy. Fission of large nuclei (e.g. uranium) releases energy because the products of fission undergo further fusion reactions. Fission and fusion reactions can occur naturally, but are most recognized as man-made events. Particle acceleration and bombardment with neutrons are two methods of inducing nuclear reactions.

The law of conservation can also be applied to physical and biological processes that affect matter. For example, when a rock is weathered, it does not just lose pieces; instead, it is broken down into its composite minerals, many of which enter the soil. In nature decomposers recycle decaying material. Since energy is neither created nor destroyed, we know that it must change form. An animal may die, but its body will either be consumed by other animals or decay into the ecosystem. Either way, it enters another form and the matter still exists.

0011.02　　**Recognizing forms of energy (e.g., heat, light), processes of energy transfer, and the interactions of energy and matter; types of forces (e.g., gravity, friction) and their effects on the position, motion, and behavior of objects; the types and characteristics of simple machines (e.g., lever, pulley); and the characteristics of light, sound, electricity, and magnetism**

The relationships between heat, forms of energy, and work (mechanical, electrical, etc.) are described by the **laws of thermodynamics**. These laws deal strictly with systems in thermal equilibrium and not those within the process of rapid change or in a state of transition. Systems that are nearly always in a state of equilibrium are called **reversible systems**.

The **first law of thermodynamics** is a restatement of the conservation of energy. The change in heat energy supplied to a system (Q) is equal to the sum of the change in the internal energy (U) and the change in the work done by the system against internal forces.

$$\Delta Q = \Delta U + \Delta W$$

The **second law of thermodynamics** is stated in two parts:

1. No machine is 100 percent efficient. It is impossible to construct a machine that only absorbs heat from a heat source and performs an equal amount of work because some heat will always be lost to the environment.

2. Heat cannot spontaneously pass from a colder to a hotter object. An ice cube sitting on a hot sidewalk will melt into a little puddle, but it will never spontaneously cool and form the same ice cube. Certain events have a preferred direction called the **arrow of time**.

Entropy is the measure of how much energy or heat is left for work. Work occurs only when heat is transferred from hot to cooler objects. Once this is done, no more work can be extracted. The energy is still being conserved, but it is not available for work when the objects are the same temperature. Theory has it that, eventually, all things in the universe will reach the same temperature. If this happens, energy will no longer be usable.

Remember that the law of conservation of energy states that energy is neither created nor destroyed. Thus, energy changes form when energy transactions occur in nature. The following are the major forms energy can take:

Thermal energy is the total internal energy of objects created by the vibration and movement of atoms and molecules. Heat is the transfer of thermal energy.

Acoustical energy, or sound energy, is the movement of energy through an object in waves. Energy that forces an object to vibrate creates sound.

Radiant energy is the energy of electromagnetic waves. Light—visible and otherwise—is an example of radiant energy.

Electrical energy is the movement of electrical charges in an electromagnetic field. Examples of electrical energy are electricity and lightning.

Chemical energy is the energy stored in the chemical bonds of molecules. For example, the energy derived from gasoline is chemical energy.

Mechanical energy is the potential and kinetic energy of a mechanical system. Rolling balls, car engines, and body parts in motion exemplify mechanical energy.

Nuclear energy is the energy present in the nucleus of atoms. The division, combination, or collision of nuclei release nuclear energy.

Types of Forces and Their Effects on the Position, Motion, and Behavior of Objects

Dynamics is the study of the relationship between motion and the forces affecting motion. **Force** causes motion.

Mass and weight are not the same quantities. An object's **mass** gives it a reluctance to change its current state of motion. It is also the measure of an object's resistance to acceleration. The force that the earth's gravity exerts on an object with a specific mass is called the object's weight on earth. Weight is a force that is measured in newtons. Weight (W) = mass times acceleration due to gravity (W = mg).

Newton's Laws of Motion

Newton's first law of motion is also called the law of inertia. It states that an object at rest will remain at rest and an object in motion will remain in motion at a constant velocity unless acted upon by an external force.

Newton's second law of motion states that if a net force acts on an object, it will cause the acceleration of the object. The relationship between force and motion is: force equals mass times acceleration (F = ma).

Newton's third law states that for every action there is an equal and opposite reaction. Therefore, if an object exerts a force on another object, that second object exerts an equal and opposite force on the first.
Surfaces that touch each other have a certain resistance to motion. This resistance is **friction**. Friction has certain characteristics:

- The materials that make up the touching surfaces will determine the magnitude of the frictional force.
- The frictional force is independent of the area of contact between the two surfaces.
- The direction of the frictional force is opposite to the direction of motion.
- The frictional force is proportional to the normal force between the two surfaces in contact.

Static friction describes the force of friction of two surfaces that are in contact but do not have any motion relative to each other, such as a block sitting on an inclined plane. **Kinetic friction** describes the force of friction of two surfaces in contact with each other when there is relative motion between the surfaces. When an object moves in a circular path, a force must be directed toward the center of the circle in order to keep the motion going. This constraining force is called **centripetal force**. Gravity is the centripetal force that keeps a satellite circling the earth.

Push and pull - Pushing a volleyball or pulling a bowstring applies muscular force as the muscles expand and contract. Elastic force occurs when any object returns to its original shape (for example, when the bow is released).

Rubbing - Friction opposes the motion of one surface past another. Friction is common when slowing down a car or sledding down a hill.

Pull of gravity - The pull of gravity is a force of attraction between two objects. Gravity questions can be raised not only on Earth but also between planets and even black hole discussions.

Inertia and circular motion - The centripetal force is provided by the high banking of a curved road and by friction between the wheels and the road. This inward force that keeps an object moving in a circle is another example of a centripetal force.

Forces on objects at rest - The formula F= m/a is shorthand for force equals mass over acceleration. An object will not move unless the force is strong enough to move the mass. Also, there can be opposing forces holding the object in place. For instance, a boat may be influenced (forced) by the currents to drift away, but an equal and opposite force is a rope holding it to a dock.

Forces on a moving object - Inertia is the tendency of any object to oppose a change in motion. An object at rest tends to stay at rest. An object that is moving tends to keep moving.
Work is done on an object when an applied force moves through a distance.

Power is the work done divided by the amount of time that it took to do it. (Power = Work / time)

Simple machines include the following:

1. Inclined plane
2. Lever
3. Wheel and axle
4. Pulley

Compound machines are two or more simple machines working together. A wheelbarrow is an example of a complex machine. It uses a lever and a wheel and axle. Machines of all types ease workload by changing the size or direction of an applied force. The amount of effort saved when using simple or complex machines is called mechanical advantage, or MA.

Light, Sound, Electricity, and Magnetism

Shadows illustrate one of the basic properties of light. Light travels in a straight line. If you put your hand between a light source and a wall, you will interrupt the light and produce a shadow.

When light hits a surface, it is **reflected**. The angle of the incoming light (angle of incidence) is the same as the angle of the reflected light (angle of reflection). It is this reflected light that allows you to see objects. You see the objects when the reflected light reaches your eyes.

Different surfaces reflect light differently. Rough surfaces scatter light in many different directions. A smooth surface reflects the light in one direction. If it is smooth and shiny (like a mirror) you see your image in the surface.

When light enters a different medium (e.g., water), it bends. This bending, or change of speed, is called **refraction**.

Light can be **diffracted**, or bent around the edges of an object. Diffraction occurs when light goes through a narrow slit. As light passes through it, the light bends slightly around the edges. You can demonstrate this by pressing your thumb and forefinger together, making a very thin slit between them. Hold them about eight cm from your eye and look at a distant source of light. The pattern you observe is caused by the diffraction of light.

Wave **interference** occurs when two waves meet while traveling along the same medium. The medium takes on a shape that results from the net effect of the individual waves upon the particles of the medium. There are two types of interference: constructive and destructive.

Constructive interference occurs when two crests or two troughs of the same shape meet. The medium will take on the shape of a crest or a trough with twice the amplitude of the two interfering crests or troughs. If a trough and a crest of the different shapes meet, the two pulses will cancel each other out, and the medium will assume the equilibrium position. This is called **destructive** interference.

Destructive interference in sound waves will reduce the loudness of the sound. This is a disadvantage in rooms such as auditoriums, where sound needs to be at its optimum. However, it can be used as an advantage in noise reduction systems. When two sound waves differing slightly in frequency are superimposed, beats are created by the alternation of constructive and destructive interference. The frequency of the beats is equal to the difference between the frequencies of the interfering sound waves.

Wave interference occurs with light waves in much the same manner that it does with sound waves. If two light waves of the same color, frequency, and amplitude are combined, the interference shows up as fringes of alternating light and dark bands. In order for this to happen, the light waves must come from the same source.

Wave-particle duality is the exhibition of both wavelike and particle-like properties by a single entity. Wave-particle duality is usually a quantum phenomenon relating to photons, electrons, and protons. Quantum mechanics shows that such objects sometimes behave like particles, sometimes like waves, and sometimes both. All objects exhibit wave-particle duality to some extent, but the larger the object, the harder it is to observe. Individual molecules are often too large to show their quantum mechanical behavior.

An everyday example of wave-particle duality is sunlight. When standing in the sun, the shadow your body makes suggests that the light travels straight from the sun and is blocked by your body. Here the light is behaving like a collection of particles sent from the sun. However, if you take two pieces of glass with a little water between them and hold them in the sun, you will see fringes; these are formed by the interference of waves.

When a piano tuners tune a piano, they only use one tuning fork, even though there are many strings on the piano. They adjust the first string to be the same as that of the tuning fork. Then they listen to the beats that occur when both the tuned and un-tuned strings are struck. They adjust the un-tuned string until they can hear the correct number of beats per second. This process of striking the un-tuned and tuned strings together and timing the beats is repeated until all the piano strings are tuned.

Pleasant sounds have a regular wave pattern that is repeated over and over. Sounds that do not happen with regularity are typically unpleasant and are called *noise*. Change in experienced frequency due to relative motion of the source of the sound is called the **Doppler Effect**. When a siren approaches, the pitch is high. When it passes, the pitch drops. As a moving sound source approaches a listener, the sound waves are closer together, causing an increase in frequency in the sound that is heard. As the source passes the listener, the waves spread out and the sound experienced by the listener is lower.

A **converging lens** produces a real image whenever the object is far enough from the lens that the rays of light from the object can hit the lens and be focused into a real image on the other side of the lens.

Electrostatics is the study of stationary electric charges. A plastic rod that is rubbed with fur or a glass rod that is rubbed with silk will become electrically charged and will attract small pieces of paper. The charge on the plastic rod rubbed with fur is negative, and the charge on glass rod rubbed with silk is positive.

Electrically charged objects share these characteristics:

1. Like charges repel one another.
2. Opposite charges attract each other.
3. Charge is conserved. A neutral object has no net change.

Imagine if the plastic rod and fur are initially neutral. When the rod becomes charged by the fur, a negative charge is transferred from the fur to the rod. The net negative charge on the rod is equal to the net positive charge on the fur.

Materials through which electric charges can easily flow are called **conductors**. Conversely, an **insulator** is a material through which electric charges do not move easily, if at all. A simple device used to indicate the existence of a positive or negative charge is called an **electroscope**. An electroscope is made up of a conducting knob and attached very lightweight conducting leaves—usually made of gold foil or aluminum foil. When a charged object touches the knob, the leaves push away from each other because like charges repel. It is not possible to tell whether or not the charge is positive or negative.

If one touches the electroscope knob with a finger while a charged rod is nearby, the electrons will be repulsed and flow out of the electroscope through the hand. If the hand is removed while the charged rod remains close, the electroscope will retain the charge.

When an object is rubbed with a charged rod, the object will take on the same charge as the rod. However, *charging by induction* gives the object the opposite charge as that of the charged rod.

Charge can be removed from an object by connecting it to the earth through a conductor. The removal of static electricity by conduction is called **grounding**.

Magnets have a north pole and a south pole. Like poles repel and different poles attract. A **magnetic field** is the space around a magnet where its force will affect objects. The closer you are to a magnet, the stronger the force. As you move away, the force becomes weaker.

Some materials act as magnets and some do not. This is because magnetism is the result of electrons in motion. The most important motion in this case is the spinning of the individual electrons. Electrons spin in pairs in opposite directions in most atoms. Each spinning electron has the magnetic field that it creates canceled out by the electron that is spinning in the opposite direction.

In an atom of iron, there are four unpaired electrons. The magnetic fields of these are not canceled out. Their fields add up to make a tiny magnet. Their fields exert forces on each other, setting up small areas in the iron called **magnetic domains** where atomic magnetic fields line up in the same direction.

You can make a magnet out of an iron nail by stroking the nail in the same direction repeatedly with a magnet. This causes poles in the atomic magnets in the nail to be attracted to the magnet. The tiny magnetic fields in the nail line up in the direction of the magnet. The magnet causes the domains pointing in its direction in the nail to grow. Eventually, one large domain results and the nail becomes a magnet.

A bar magnet has a north pole and a south pole. If you break the magnet in half, each piece will have a north and south pole.

The earth has a magnetic field. In a compass, a tiny, lightweight magnet is suspended and will line its south pole up with the north pole magnet of the earth. A magnet can be made out of a coil of wire by connecting the ends of the coil to a battery. When the current goes through the wire, the wire acts in the same way that a magnet does; it is called an **electromagnet**.

The poles of the electromagnet will depend upon which way the electric current runs. An electromagnet can be made more powerful in three ways:

1. Make more coils.
2. Put iron core (nail) inside the coils.
3. Use more battery power.

0011.03   Comparing characteristics of objects in the solar system and universe (e.g., stars, planets) and analyzing the effects (e.g., seasons, phases of the moon) of the relative positions and motions of the earth, moon, and sun; and demonstrating knowledge of the composition, structure, and processes of the earth's lithosphere (e.g., rocks, minerals), hydrosphere, and atmosphere and the interactions among these systems (e.g., water cycle, weather patterns)

As mentioned in Skill 10.01, our scientific knowledge grows and changes every day. Certainly our knowledge of the Solar System has grown considerably as data from telescopes and space probes and exploration vessels become available. Information presented here was current as of publication.

THE SOLAR SYSTEM AND BEYOND

Planets

In order to be classified as a planet, a celestial body must meet three criteria:

- it must orbit the sun
- be big enough for its gravity to shape it into a basically roundish shape
- and have cleared everything else out of its orbital path

There are eight bodies defined as planets in our solar system: Mercury, Venus, Earth, Mars, Jupiter, Saturn, Uranus, and Neptune. Pluto was defined as a planet in our solar system until the summer of 2006. It has since been reclassified as a dwarf planet (see below). The planets are divided into two groups based on distance from the sun. The inner planets include Mercury, Venus, Earth, and Mars. The inner planets are made mostly of rock. The outer planets include Jupiter, Saturn, Uranus, and Neptune and are called gas giants because they are made primarily of hydrogen and helium and are massive compared to the inner planets.

Mercury is the closest planet to the sun. Its surface has craters and rocks. The atmosphere is composed of hydrogen, helium, and sodium. It has no known satellites (moons). Mercury was named after the Roman messenger god. *Venus* has a slow rotation when compared to Earth. Venus and Uranus rotate in opposite directions from the other planets (this opposite rotation is called **retrograde rotation**). The surface of Venus is not visible due to the extensive cloud cover. The atmosphere is composed mostly of carbon dioxide, and sulfuric acid droplets in the dense cloud cover give Venus a yellow appearance. It has a greater greenhouse effect than observed on Earth; the dense clouds combined with carbon dioxide trap heat. It has no known moons. Venus was named after the Roman goddess of love.

Earth is considered a water planet, with 70 percent of its surface covered by water. Gravity holds the masses of water in place. The different temperatures observed on Earth allow for the different states (solid, liquid, and gas) of water to exist. The atmosphere is composed mainly of oxygen and nitrogen. Earth is the only planet that is known to support life. It has one moon.

Mars has a surface that contains numerous craters, active and extinct volcanoes, ridges, and valleys with extremely deep fractures. Iron oxide found in the dusty soil makes the surface seem rust-colored and the skies seem pink in color. The atmosphere is composed of carbon dioxide, nitrogen, argon, oxygen, and water vapor. Mars has Polar Regions with icecaps composed of water. Mars has two satellites. Mars was named after the Roman war god.

Jupiter is the largest planet in the solar system. It has many, many moons and more are being discovered all the time. At last count it had between 49 and 62 moons. Twenty three new moons were discovered in 2003 alone. Four of its moons are the size of planets and one of them, Ganymede is big enough to generate its own magnetic field—the only known moon to do so. Another of its moons, Io, is the most volcanically active body in the Solar System. Jupiter also has a simple set of rings. Jupiter's atmosphere is composed of hydrogen, helium, methane, and ammonia. There are white-colored bands of clouds indicating rising gases, and dark-colored bands of clouds indicating descending gases. The gas movement is caused by heat resulting from the energy of Jupiter's core. Jupiter has a Great Red Spot that is thought to be a hurricane-like cloud. Jupiter has a strong magnetic field.

Saturn is the second largest planet in the solar system. Saturn has thousands of rings of ice, rock, and dust particles circling it, covering a distance about half that from Earth to the moon. It also has a great many moons, 50-60 at last count. Saturn's atmosphere is composed of hydrogen, helium, methane, and ammonia. Saturn was named after the Roman god of agriculture.

Uranus is the second largest planet in the solar system with retrograde revolution. Uranus is a gaseous planet. It has at least eleven dark rings and at least 27 satellites. One of its moons, Miranda, has canyons twelve times and deep as the Grand Canyon. Uranus has an atmosphere composed of hydrogen, helium, and methane. Uranus was named after the Greek god of the heavens.

Neptune is another gaseous planet with an atmosphere consisting of hydrogen, helium, and methane. Neptune has a number of rings and at least thirteen satellites. Due to Pluto's erratic orbit, for 20 out of every 248 Earth years, Neptune is further from the Sun than Pluto. Neptune was named after the Roman sea god because its atmosphere is the same color as the seas.

Dwarf Planets and Plutoids

Until 2006, Pluto was considered a planet. However, the new definition of a planet means Pluto does not qualify as a planet. Although it meets the first two criteria (it orbits the sun and has enough gravity to make it round), it does not meet the third criterion: It has not cleared its orbital path of other objects. In addition, other celestial bodies, at least one even bigger than Pluto, have been discovered, necessitating two new categories of celestial body.

A *dwarf planet* is a celestial body that orbits the sun, has enough gravity to make it round, is **not** a satellite of a planet, but has **not** cleared its path of other things.

Pluto is a dwarf planet. Pluto's atmosphere probably contains methane, ammonia, and frozen water. Pluto has one satellite. It revolves around the sun every 250 years. Pluto's orbit keeps it beyond Neptune and the Kuiper Belt most of the time, but for twenty years out of every 248, Pluto's orbit moves it slightly closer to the sun than Neptune. Pluto was named after the Roman god of the underworld.

A *Plutoid,* named after Pluto, is basically a dwarf planet that has an orbit that moves beyond Neptune and the Kuiper Belt. As of publication date, three such Plutoids have been named: Pluto, itself, Eris, and Makemake. Eris is the largest of the three, but astronomers expect to discover more Plutoids, as more data from space probes and telescopes is analyzed.

Extrasolar Planets

Extrasolar planets, also called *Exoplanets,* are planets found outside of our Solar System. Once discussed only in the realm of science fiction and speculation, as of August, 2009, 373 such planets have been discovered outside our Solar System. Most were discovered through radial velocity or spectral or infrared analysis of Hubble Telescope images or space probes. Most of those discovered so far are gas giants like our outer planets, but this is considered to be because they are larger and simply easier to find. Based on recent findings, astronomers expect that the number of lighter, rocky planets (similar to our inner planets) discovered will soon outnumber the gas giants. At least some of those discovered inhabit an area relative to their galaxy and solar system that is comparable to that of Earth and this is considered evidence to support the possibility that life similar to that on Earth could eventually be found.

Comets, Asteroids, and Meteors

Astronomers believe that many of these rocky, icy fragments may be the remains of the birth of the solar system, pieces of matter that never formed into a planet.

Asteroids are found in the region between Mars and Jupiter. The definition of an asteroid is somewhat fluid, but they are generally considered to be composed primarily of rocky particles and dust, to be smaller than planets, but bigger than meteoroids, and to originate in the inner part of the Solar System.

Comets are masses of frozen gases, cosmic dust, and small rocky particles. Astronomers think that most comets originate in a dense comet cloud beyond Pluto. Comets consist of a nucleus, a coma, and a tail. A comet's tail always points away from the sun. Comets[s43] orbit the sun, so many return to the vicinity of Earth on a predictable, regular basis, and are known as *periodic comets*. One of the most famous comets, and the earliest to be specifically identified as periodic and its return accurately predicted is **Halley's Comet.** Although Halley's Comet was discovered in 240 BC, it is named after Edmund Halley, who first recognized it as a returning comet and accurately predicted the date of its return. It returns to the skies near the earth every seventy-five to seventy-six years.

Meteoroids are composed of particles of rock and metal of various sizes, but are smaller than asteroids. When a meteoroid travels through the earth's atmosphere, friction causes its surface to heat up and it begins to burn. The burning meteoroid falling through the earth's atmosphere is called a **meteor** (also known as a "shooting star").

Meteorites are meteors that strike the earth's surface. A physical example of a meteorite's impact can be seen in Arizona; the *Barringer Crater* is a huge crater left by a meteorite strike. There are many other meteor craters throughout the world.

Stars

Stars are luminous celestial bodies made of plasma and held together by their own gravity. They shine because of the thermonuclear fusion at their cores. They give off light and heat, and are typically massive compared to planets.

Sun

The Sun is the star at the center of our Solar System, the one around which Earth and the other planets and celestial bodies orbit. It is a G2 (Yellow Dwarf) star and is bigger than 90% of the stars discovered so far. It is massive compared to the planets in our Solar System, and its mass makes up over 99.8% of the total mass of all objects in our Solar System. Energy from the Sun is responsible for the existence of all life on Earth.
Parts of the sun include:

- The **core,** the inner portion of the sun where fusion takes place.
- The **photosphere,** or the surface of the sun that produces **sunspots** (cooler, dark areas that can be seen on its surface).
- The **chromosphere**, which includes hydrogen gases that cause this portion to be red in color; **solar flares** (sudden brightness of the chromosphere); and **solar prominences** (gases that shoot outward from the chromosphere).

- The **corona**, which is the transparent area of the sun visible only during a total eclipse.

Solar radiation is energy traveling from the Sun into space. **Solar flares** produce excited protons and electrons that shoot outward from the chromosphere at great speeds, reaching Earth. These particles disturb radio reception and also affect the magnetic field on Earth.

Earth's orbit around the sun and the Earth's axis of rotation determine the seasons of the year. When a hemisphere (Northern or Southern) of Earth is pointed towards the sun, it is summer in that hemisphere, and when that hemisphere is pointed away from the sun, it is winter there. Because of the axis of rotation, both hemispheres cannot be in the same season simultaneously. The two hemispheres have opposite seasons at all times.

Moon

A *moon* is a natural satellite that orbits a planet. Many planets have moons (see above).

The Earth's *moon* is a rocky spheroid in a *synchronous* orbit of Earth. This means that the same half always faces the Earth. It "shines" because it reflects light from the Sun. The illuminated (or "day") side of the moon has a temperature of 107 degrees Celsius (225 degrees Fahrenheit) while the dark side has a temperature of -153 degrees Celsius (-243 degrees Fahrenheit). The moon is about one fourth the size of the Earth and has gravity about 17% of Earth's gravity. It has no measureable atmosphere and no water.

The moon phase we see is dependent of the position of the moon relative to the Earth and Sun. During each lunar orbit (a lunar month), we see the moon's appearance change from not visibly illuminated to partially illuminated to fully illuminated, then back through partially illuminated to not illuminated again. Although this cycle is a continuous process, there are eight distinct, traditionally recognized stages, called **phases**. The phases designate both the degree to which the moon is illuminated and the geometric appearance of the illuminated part.

New Moon: This occurs when the Sun and moon are on the same side of earth, so the moon's non-illuminated side is facing the earth. The moon is not visible or looks dark.

Waxing Crescent: This is when the moon appears to be less than one-half illuminated by direct sunlight. The fraction of the moon's disk that is illuminated is increasing.

First Quarter: One-half of the moon appears to be illuminated by direct sunlight during this time. The fraction of the moon's disk that is illuminated is increasing. *Waxing Gibbous:* In this phase, the moon appears to be more than one-half but not fully illuminated by direct sunlight. The fraction of the Moon's disk that is illuminated is increasing.

Full Moon: This occurs when the Sun and moon are on opposite sides of the Earth so the moon's illuminated side is facing the earth. The moon appears to be completely illuminated by direct sunlight.

Waning Gibbous: This is when the moon appears to be more than one-half but not fully illuminated by direct sunlight. The fraction of the moon's disk that is illuminated is decreasing.

Last Quarter: One-half of the moon is illuminated by direct sunlight in this phase. The fraction of the moon's disk that is illuminated is decreasing.

Waning Crescent: During this time, the moon is less than one-half illuminated by direct sunlight. The fraction of the moon's disk that is illuminated is decreasing. The moon takes approximately 27.3 days to orbit the Earth, but it takes about 29.5 days to move from full moon to full moon (or from any phase to the same phase next month) due to variations caused by the fact that while the moon orbits the Earth, the Earth and moon together are orbiting the sun. Our concept of a month comes from this regular orbit and phases of the moon.

The moon, the earth, and the sun affect ocean tides. Along the west coast of the United States, we experience four different tides per day: two highs and two lows. When the moon, the earth, and the sun are in a line, **spring tides** occur. During these tides, one may observe higher and lower than normal tides. In other words, there will be very high tides and very low tides. When the moon, the earth, and sun are at right angles to each other, **neap tides** are formed. During these tides, one is not able to observe a great deal of difference in the heights of the high and low tides.

Eclipses

Eclipses occur when the Earth, the moon, and the sun are in a line and the plane of the Earth's orbit of the Sun and that of the moon's orbit of Earth intersect more or less directly.

A **solar eclipse** occurs during a new moon, when the moon comes between the earth and the Sun, so it blocks all or part of the view of the Sun from parts of the earth's surface. Although the Sun is far larger than the moon, the moon is much closer to Earth, so from a location in line with the moon as it blocks the Sun, the Sun can be completely blocked (a total eclipse) with only a corona showing part time. Anywhere from two to five partial Solar eclipses happen per year, but total eclipses are rare.

A **Lunar Eclipse** occurs during a full moon, when the Earth is between the moon and the Sun and blocks light from the Sun, preventing it from illuminating the moon. There are at least two partial lunar eclipses per year, though total lunar eclipses are much rarer.

EARTH'S ATMOSPHERE

Earth's atmosphere is a layer of gases held around the Earth by Earth's gravity. It is composed primarily of Nitrogen (78%) and Oxygen (20.95%), as well as smaller amounts of Argon (.93%) and Carbon Dioxide (.038%) and a few trace gases. Most of the atmosphere lies within eleven kilometers (6.8 miles) of the surface of the planet. It is thickest at the surface and thins out as altitude increases, so that by about 120 kilometers (25 miles) above Earth, it is so thin as to be negligible[s44].

Air Pressure is simply the weight of the air pressing down upon the Earth. It is greatest at sea level and decreases as altitude increases.

Air masses[SAW45] in motion are referred to as **wind** or **air currents**, and they can move vertically or horizontally. Horizontal winds typically move at much greater speeds than vertical winds. Horizontal winds near the Earth's surface typically move from areas of high pressure to areas of low pressure, while vertical winds move from areas of low pressure to areas of high pressure. Weather conditions are generated by winds and air currents moving from one location to another and carrying large amounts of heat and moisture from one part of the atmosphere to another. Wind is usually described in terms of two dimensions: speed and direction.

Wind direction is labeled based on the source of the wind or the *direction from which it blows.* SO a *northerly* wind is blowing from the north to the south, and a *southeast* wind is blowing from the southeast to the northwest, etc. Direction is measured by wind vanes or wind socks, usually placed about 10 meters above ground. Wind direction, of course, like wind speed, can vary from one altitude level to another.

Wind speeds are measured by instruments called **anemometers**. An anemometer looks like four halved or open cups attached to a spindle that rotates. It can measure wind velocity in kilometers, miles, or knots per hour. Wind speed is determined by the steepness or *gradient* of the change in air pressure from one location to another. The steepness or gradient of change is determined by a combination of the magnitude of the difference in pressure from one location to the other and the distance between the two locations. So, a large change in pressure over a short distance would produce a steep gradient, whereas a small change in pressure spread out over a longer distance would produce a less steep gradient of the change The steeper the change (i.e., the greater the change in air pressure over a short distance), the higher the velocity of the wind. Since cold air is denser, it produces higher air pressure than warm air, which is lighter. For this reason, wind is also related to the movement of hot and cold air masses.

The sun heats the air all over the planet, but the heat is distributed unevenly. In addition, the Earth rotates constantly. Therefore, air is always in motion *somewhere*, and there are areas where certain bands or *belts.* The wind belts in each hemisphere consist of convection cells that encircle Earth like belts. There are three major wind belts on Earth: 1) trade winds, 2) prevailing westerlies, and 3) polar easterlies. Wind belt formation depends on the differences in air pressures that develop in the doldrums, the horse latitudes, and the polar regions. The **doldrums** surround the equator. Within this belt, heated air usually rises straight up into Earth's atmosphere. The **horse latitudes** are regions of high barometric pressure with calm and light winds, and the **polar regions** contain cold dense air that sinks to Earth's surface.

Winds caused by local temperature changes include sea breezes and land breezes. **Sea breezes** are caused by the unequal heating of the land and a large, adjacent body of water. Land heats up faster than water. The movement of cool ocean air toward the land is called a sea breeze. Sea breezes usually begin blowing about mid-morning; ending about sunset. A breeze that blows from the land to the ocean or a large lake is called a **land breeze**.

El Niño refers to a sequence of changes in the ocean and atmospheric circulation across the Pacific Ocean. It causes the water around the equator to be unusually hot every two to seven years. Trade winds normally blow east to west across the equatorial latitudes, piling warm water into the western Pacific. A huge mass of heavy thunderstorms usually forms in the area and produces vast currents of rising air that displace heat pole-ward. This helps to create the strong mid-latitude jet streams. When it occurs, the world's climate patterns are disrupted by a change in location of thunderstorm activity.

Both wind speed and its direction are critical factors in weather and climate, since wind and air currents bring moisture in terms of clouds and humidity with them, or take it away, and they change the prevailing ground temperature as they move into a new area.

Monsoons are huge wind systems that cover large geographic areas and that reverse direction seasonally. The monsoons of India and Asia are examples of these seasonal winds. They alternate wet and dry seasons. As denser, cooler air over the ocean moves inland, a steady seasonal wind called a summer or wet monsoon is produced.

Cloud types

- *Cirrus clouds* - white and feathery; high in the sky
- *Cumulus* - thick, white, and fluffy
- *Stratus* - layers of clouds that cover most of the sky
- *Nimbus* - heavy, dark clouds that represent thunderstorm clouds

Variations on the clouds mentioned above:

- *Cumulo-nimbus*
- *Strato-nimbus*

The air temperature at which water vapor begins to condense at a certain pressure level is called the **dew point**.

Relative humidity is the actual amount of water vapor in a certain volume of air compared to the maximum amount of water vapor this air could hold at a given temperature.

Types of Storms

A **thunderstorm** is a brief, local storm produced by the rapid upward movement of warm, moist air within a cumulo-nimbus cloud. Thunderstorms produce lightning and thunder, and are accompanied by strong wind gusts and heavy rain or hail.

A severe storm with swirling winds that may reach speeds of hundreds of km per hour is called a **tornado**. The winds in a tornado circle around an "eye' and are the strongest winds of any storm. Such a storm is also referred to as a "twister." Tornados typically form over land. When it occurs, the sky is covered by large cumulo-nimbus clouds and violent thunderstorms. A funnel-shaped swirling cloud may extend downward from a cumulo-nimbus cloud and reach the ground. Tornadoes are very destructive storms, but typically leave a narrow path of destruction on the ground. Tornados appear and depart very suddenly, with little warning. A swirling, funnel-shaped cloud that extends downward and touches a body of water is called a **waterspout**.

Hurricanes are storms that form over water and develop when warm, moist air carried by trade winds rotates around a low-pressure "eye." A large, rotating, low-pressure system accompanied by heavy precipitation and strong winds is called a tropical cyclone (better known as a hurricane). In the Pacific region, a hurricane is called a typhoon. These winds are not as strong as those in a tornado, but a hurricane is much larger, often hundreds of miles in diameter. This greater size, plus a hurricane's longer duration, makes it the most destructive of storms. Hurricanes build slowly, however, and there is usually ample time to predict their land fall and make preparations.

Storms that occur only in the winter are known as blizzards or ice storms. A **blizzard** is a storm with strong winds, blowing snow and frigid temperatures. An **ice storm** consists of falling rain that freezes when it strikes the ground, covering everything with a layer of ice.

Hydrologic (water) Cycle

Water that falls to Earth in the form of rain, snow, sleet, hail, etc., is called **precipitation**. Precipitation is part of a continuous process in which water at Earth's surface evaporates, condenses into clouds, and returns. This process is termed the **water cycle**. The water located below the land surface is called **groundwater**.

The impact of **altitude** upon climatic conditions is primarily related to temperature and precipitation. As altitude increases, climatic conditions become increasingly drier and colder; solar radiation becomes more severe, while the effects of convection forces are minimized.

Climatic changes as a function of latitude follow a similar pattern (as a reference, latitude moves either north or south from the equator). The climate becomes colder and drier as the distance from the equator increases. Proximity to land or water masses produces climatic conditions based upon the available moisture. Dry and arid climates prevail where moisture is scarce; lush tropical climates can prevail where moisture is abundant. Climate, as described above, depends upon the specific combination of conditions making up an area's environment. Man impacts all environments by producing pollutants in earth, air, and water. It follows then, that man is a major player in world climatic conditions.

PLANET EARTH

Lithosphere

The *lithosphere* is made up of the outer two layers of the Earth, **the crust and the mantle.** It is the hard outer covering of the planet. **Plates** are rigid blocks of the earth's crust and upper mantle. These rigid solid blocks make up the lithosphere. The earth's lithosphere is broken into nine large sections and several small ones. These moving slabs are called plates. The major plates are named after the continents they are "transporting."

The plates float on and move with a layer of hot, plastic-like rock in the upper mantle. Geologists believe that the heat currents circulating within the mantle cause this plastic zone of rock to slowly flow, carrying along the overlying crustal plates.

Earth/Water Interactions

Erosion is the removal and transportation of surface materials by another moveable material (usually water, wind, or ice). The most important cause of erosion is running water. Streams, rivers, and tides are constantly at work removing weathered fragments of bedrock and carrying them away from their original location.

A stream erodes bedrock through the grinding action of the sand, pebbles, and other rock fragments. This grinding is called **abrasion**. Streams also erode rocks by dissolving or absorbing their minerals. Limestone and marble are readily dissolved by streams.

The breaking down of rocks at or near to the earth's surface is known as **weathering**. Weathering breaks down these rocks into smaller and smaller pieces. There are two types of weathering: physical weathering and chemical weathering.

Physical weathering is the process by which rocks are broken down into smaller fragments without undergoing any change in chemical composition. Physical weathering is mainly caused by the freezing of water, the expansion of rock, and the activities of plants and animals.

Some examples of physical weathering include frost wedging and exfoliation.

Frost wedging is the cycle of daytime thawing and refreezing at night. This cycle causes large rock masses, especially the rocks exposed on mountaintops, to be broken into smaller pieces. The peeling away of the outer layers from a rock is called **exfoliation**. Rounded mountaintops are called exfoliation domes because they have been formed in this way.

Chemical weathering is the breakdown of rocks through changes in their chemical composition. An example would be the change of feldspar in granite to clay. Water, oxygen, and carbon dioxide are the main agents of chemical weathering. When water and carbon dioxide combine chemically, they produce a weak acid that breaks down rocks.

Soils are composed of particles of sand, clay, various minerals, tiny living organisms, and humus, plus the decayed remains of plants and animals. Soils are divided into three classes according to their texture. These classes are *sandy soils, clay soils*, and *loamy soils*. Sandy soils are gritty and their particles do not bind together firmly. Sandy soils are porous; water rapidly passes through them. Therefore, sandy soils do not hold much water and have poor **absorption**. Clay soils are smooth and greasy; their particles bind together firmly. Clay soils are moist and usually do not allow water to pass through easily. This type of soil has the lowest potential for **run off**. Loamy soils feel somewhat like velvet and their particles clump together. Loamy soils are made up of sand, clay, and silt. Loamy soils hold water but some water can pass through. **Percolation** is best in this type of soil.

Sinkholes

Large features formed by dissolved limestone (calcium carbonate), include sinkholes, caves, and caverns. **Sinkholes** are funnel-shaped depressions created by dissolved limestone. Many sinkholes started life as limestone caverns. Erosion weakens the cavern roof causing it to collapse, forming a sinkhole.

Groundwater usually contains large amounts of dissolved minerals, especially if the water flows through limestone. As groundwater drips through the roof of a cave, gases dissolved in the water can escape into the air. A deposit of calcium carbonate is left behind. **Stalactites** are icicle-like structures of calcium carbonate that hang from the roofs of caves. Water that falls on a constant spot on the cave floor and evaporates, leaving a deposit of calcium carbonate, builds a **stalagmite**.

0011.04   Demonstrating knowledge of strategies and tools for observing, measuring, predicting, and communicating weather data; the natural and human-caused constructive and destructive processes that shape the earth's surface; and how fossils are formed and provide evidence of organisms that lived long ago

Every day, each person on Earth is affected by weather. It may be in the form of a typical thunderstorm, bringing moist air and cumulo-nimbus clouds, or a severe storm with pounding winds that can cause either hurricanes or tornadoes. These are familiar terms.

The daily newscast relates terms such as dew point, barometric pressure, and relative humidity. Suddenly, all too common terms become clouded with those more frequently used by a meteorologist (someone who forecasts weather). Yet it is important to understand the terms in order to understand the weather.

The **dew point** is the air temperature at which water vapor begins to condense at a certain pressure level.

Weather instruments that forecast weather include the aneroid barometer and the mercury barometer, both of which measure air pressure (**barometric pressure**). The aneroid barometer works because air exerts varying pressures on a metal diaphragm that will then read air pressure. The mercury barometer operates when atmospheric pressure pushes on a pool of (mercury) in a glass tube. The higher the pressure, the higher up the tube mercury will rise.

Relative humidity is measured by two kinds of weather instruments, the **psychrometer** and the **hair hygrometer**. Relative humidity simply indicates the amount of moisture in the air. Relative humidity is defined as a ratio of existing amounts of water vapor and moisture in the air when compared to the maximum amount of moisture that the air can hold at the same given pressure and temperature. Relative humidity is stated as a percentage; for example, if you were to analyze relative humidity from data, a parcel of air may be saturated (meaning it now holds all the moisture it can hold at a given temperature), placing the relative humidity at 100 percent.

Lesson Plans for teachers to analyze data and predict weather can be found at: http://www.srh.weather.gov/srh/jetstream/synoptic/ll_analyze.htm.

Weather Maps

The following are a few sources of current weather maps. Sometimes a site may be down or experiencing data losses. In such a case, try another site listed. This is not meant to be an exhaustive list. These are provided for your convenience.

1. NCAR, pick your regional plot: http://www.rap.ucar.edu/weather/surface/
2. UNISYS: http://weather.unisys.com/surface/sfc_map.html
3. College of DuPage: http://weather.cod.edu/analysis/analysis.sfcplots.html
4. NOAA http://www.nws.noaa.gov/
5. Ohio State University: http://asp1.sbs.ohio-state.edu/ (Click on "Current Weather" and choose your map)

CONSTRUCTIVE AND DESTRUCTIVE PROCESSES THAT SHAPE THE EARTH'S SURFACE

Mountain Building

Orogeny is the term given to natural mountain building. A mountain is terrain that has been raised high above the surrounding landscape by volcanic action or some form of tectonic plate collision. Mountains are produced by different types of mountain-building processes. Most major mountain ranges are formed by the processes of folding and faulting. The plate collisions could be either intercontinental or an ocean floor collision with a continental crust (**subduction**). The physical composition of mountains includes igneous, metamorphic, and sedimentary rocks; some may have rock layers that are tilted or distorted by plate collision forces.

There are many different types of mountains. The physical attributes of a mountain range depend upon the angle at which plate movement thrust layers of rock to the surface. Many mountains (Adirondacks, Southern Rockies) were formed along high angle faults.

Faults are fractures in the earth's crust that have been created by either tension or compression forces transmitted through the crust. These forces are produced by the movement of separate blocks of crust.

Fault lines are categorized based on the relative movement between the blocks on both sides of the fault plane. The movement can be horizontal, vertical, or oblique.

A **dip-slip fault** occurs when the movement of the plates is vertical and opposite. The displacement is in the direction of the inclination, or dip, of the fault. Dip-slip faults are classified as normal faults wherein the rock above the fault plane moves down relative to the rock below.

Reverse faults are created when the rock above the fault plane moves up relative to the rock below. Reverse faults with a very low angle to the horizontal are also referred to as **thrust faults**.

Faults in which the dominant displacement is horizontal movement along the trend or strike (length) of the fault are called **strike-slip faults**. When a large strike-slip fault is associated with plate boundaries, it is called a **transform fault**. The San Andreas Fault in California is a well-known transform fault. Faults that have both vertical and horizontal movement are called **oblique-slip faults**.

Movement of Tectonic Plates

Data obtained from many sources led scientists to develop the theory of plate tectonics. This theory is the most current model to explain not only the movement of the continents, but also the changes in the earth's crust caused by internal forces.

Plates are rigid blocks of the earth's crust and upper mantle. Movement of these crustal plates creates areas where the plates diverge as well as areas where the plates converge. A major area of divergence is located in the Mid-Atlantic. Hot mantle rock rises and separates at the point of divergence, creating new oceanic crust at the rate of two to ten centimeters per year.

Convergence occurs when the oceanic crust collides with either another oceanic plate or a continental plate. The oceanic crust sinks, forming an enormous trench and generating volcanic activity. Convergence also includes continent-to-continent plate collisions. When two plates slide past one another, a transform fault is created.

These movements produce many major features of the earth's surface, including mountain ranges, volcanoes, and earthquake zones. Most of these features are located at plate boundaries, where the plates interact by spreading apart, pressing together, or sliding past each other. These movements are very slow, averaging only a few centimeters a year.

Boundaries form between spreading plates where the crust is forced apart in a process called **rifting**. Rifting generally occurs at mid-ocean ridges. Rifting can also take place within a continent, splitting the continent into smaller landmasses that drift away from each other, thereby forming an ocean basin between them. The Red Sea is a product of rifting. As the seafloor spreading takes place, new material is added to the inner edges of the separating plates. In this way, the plates grow larger and the ocean basin widens. This is the process that broke up the super continent Pangaea and created the Atlantic Ocean.

Boundaries between colliding plates are zones of intense crustal activity. When a plate of ocean crust collides with a plate of continental crust, the more dense oceanic plate slides under the lighter continental plate and plunges into the mantle. This process is called **subduction**, and the site where it takes place is called a **subduction zone**. A subduction zone is usually visible on the sea floor as a deep depression called a **trench**.

The crustal movement identified by plates sliding sideways past each other produces a plate boundary that is characterized by major faults. These faults are capable of unleashing powerful earthquakes. The San Andreas Fault forms such a boundary between the Pacific Plate and the North American Plate.

Types of Mountains

Folded mountains (Alps, Himalayas, Rocky Mountains) are produced by the folding of rock layers that occurs when tectonic plates push against each other. Crustal movements may press horizontal layers of sedimentary rock together from the sides, squeezing them into wavelike folds. Up-folded sections of rock are called **anticlines**; down-folded sections of rock are called **synclines**. The Appalachian Mountains are an example of folded mountains, with long ridges and valleys in a series of anticlines and synclines formed by folded rock layers. The Himalayas are the highest mountains in the world and contain Mount Everest, which rises almost nine km above sea level. The Himalayas were formed when India collided with Asia. The movement that created this collision is still in process at the rate of a few centimeters per year.

Fault-block mountains (Utah, Arizona, and New Mexico) are created when plate movement produces a combination of tension and uplifting forces instead of compression forces. The area under tension produces normal faults; rock along these faults is displaced upward. These mountains form, obviously along a fault (see below) and produce very steep, cliff-like rises on one side and gentler declines on the other. The Tetons of Wyoming are a good example.

Dome mountains are formed as magma tries to push up through the crust but fails to break the surface. Dome mountains resemble huge blisters on the earth's surface.

Upwarped mountains (Black Hills of South Dakota) are created in association with a broad arching of the crust. They can also be formed by rock thrust upward along high angle faults.

Volcanic mountains are built up by successive deposits of volcanic materials.

Volcanism is the term given to the movement of magma through the crust as well as its emergence as lava onto the earth's surface

An **active volcano** is one that is presently erupting or building to an eruption. A **dormant volcano** is one that is between eruptions but still shows signs of internal activity that might lead to an eruption in the future. An **extinct volcano** is said to be no longer capable of erupting. Most of the world's active volcanoes are found along the rim of the Pacific Ocean, which is also a major earthquake zone. This curving belt of active faults and volcanoes is often called the Ring of Fire. The world's best known volcanic mountains include Mount Etna in Italy and Mount Kilimanjaro in Africa. The Hawaiian Islands are actually the tops of a chain of volcanic mountains that rise from the ocean floor.

There are three types of volcanic mountains: shield volcanoes, cinder cones, and composite volcanoes.

Shield Volcanoes are associated with quiet eruptions. Lava emerges from the vent or opening in the crater and flows freely out over the earth's surface until it cools and hardens into a layer of igneous rock. A repeated lava flow builds this type of volcano into the largest volcanic mountain. Mauna Loa in Hawaii is the largest shield volcano on Earth.

Cinder Cone Volcanoes are associated with explosive eruptions as lava is hurled high into the air in a spray of droplets of various sizes. These droplets cool and harden into cinders and particles of ash before falling to the ground. The ash and cinder pile up around the vent to form a steep, cone-shaped hill called the cinder cone. Cinder cone volcanoes are relatively small but may form quite rapidly.

Composite Volcanoes are described as being built by both lava flows and layers of ash and cinders. Mount Fuji in Japan, Mount St. Helens in Washington, USA, and Mount Vesuvius in Italy are all famous composite volcanoes.

When lava cools, **igneous rock** is formed. This formation can occur either above ground or below ground.

> **Intrusive rock** includes any igneous rock that was formed below the earth's surface. **Batholiths** are the largest structures of intrusive type rock; they are composed of near-granite materials and are the core of the Sierra Nevada Mountains.

> **Extrusive rock** includes any igneous rock that was formed at the earth's surface.

Dikes are old lava tubes formed when magma entered a vertical fracture and hardened. Sometimes, magma squeezes between two rock layers and hardens into a thin horizontal sheet called a **sill**. A **laccolith** is formed in much the same way as a sill, but the magma that creates a laccolith is very thick and does not flow easily. It pools and forces the overlying strata into creating an obvious surface dome.

A **caldera** is normally formed by the collapse of the top of a volcano. This collapse can be caused by a massive explosion that destroys the cone and empties most if not all of the magma chamber below the volcano. The cone collapses into the empty magma chamber, forming a caldera.

An inactive volcano may have magma solidified in its pipe. This structure, called a volcanic neck, is resistant to erosion; today, it may be the only visible evidence of the past presence of an active volcano.

Glaciation

A **glacier** is a large mass of ice that moves or flows over the land in response to gravity. Glaciers form when temperatures stay cold enough that snow remains year round for an extended period of time. Since the snow does not melt, it becomes compressed into harder and harder ice. Eventually, glaciers form. About 12,000 years ago, a vast sheet of ice covered a large part of the northern United States. This huge, frozen mass had moved southward from the northern regions of Canada as several large bodies of slow-moving ice, or **glaciers.** A time period in which glaciers advance over a large portion of a continent is called an **ice age**. Glaciers form among high mountains and in other cold regions. As glaciers move over the surface of the Earth, they scrape, erode, and change the face of the earth.

There are two main types of glaciers: valley glaciers and continental glaciers. Erosion by **valley glaciers** is characteristic of U-shaped erosion. They produce sharp-peaked mountains such as the Matterhorn in Switzerland.

Continental glaciers ride over mountains in their paths, leaving smoothed, rounded mountains and ridges.

Evidence of the North American glacial coverage during the most recent ice age remains as large boulders from northern environments dropped in southerly locations; abrasive grooves; glacial troughs created by the rounding out of steep valleys through glacial scouring; and the remains of glacial sources, called cirques, that were created by frost wedging the rock at the bottom of the glacier. Remains of plants and animals typically found in warm climates that have been discovered in the moraines and outwash plains help to support the theory of periods of warmth during the past ice ages.

There have been four major **ice ages** on Earth. The oldest, for which we have evidence, was 800-600 million years ago, followed by one from 460-430 million years ago, another 350-250 million years ago, and the present ice age, which began in the Pleistocene age. This Ice Age began about 2 -3 million years ago. This age saw the advancement and retreat of glacial ice over millions of years. Earth is currently in an interglacial period of this ice age, when glaciers are not growing.

Theories relating to the origin and cause of the ice ages include **plate tectonics**, and the movement of continents which affects temperature; changes in the earth's orbit around the sun or changes in the angle of the earth's axis, and the wobbling of the earth's axis; and atmospheric composition, notably the amounts of carbon dioxide and methane.

Natural Disasters

An important topic in science is the effect of natural disasters and events on society, as well as the effect human activity has on inducing such events. Naturally occurring geological, climatic, and environmental events can greatly affect the lives of humans. At the same time, the activities of humans can induce such events that would not normally occur.

Nature-induced hazards include floods, landslides, avalanches, volcanic eruptions, wildfires, earthquakes, hurricanes, tornadoes, droughts, and disease. Such events often occur naturally due to changing weather patterns or geological conditions. Property damage, resource destruction, and the loss of human life are the possible outcomes of natural hazards. Thus, natural hazards are often extremely costly on both an economic and personal level.

While many nature-induced hazards occur naturally, human activity can often stimulate such events. For example, destructive land use practices such as mining can induce landslides or avalanches if not properly planned and monitored. In addition, human activities can cause other hazards, including global warming and waste contamination. Global warming is an increase in the earth's average temperature resulting, at least in part, from the burning of fuels by humans. Global warming is hazardous because it disrupts the earth's environmental balance and can negatively affect weather patterns. Ecological and weather pattern changes can promote some of the natural disasters listed above.

Improper hazardous waste disposal by humans can contaminate the environment, resulting in a variety of changes. One devastating effect of hazardous waste contamination is the stimulation of disease in human populations. Thus, hazardous waste contamination negatively affects both the environment and the people that live in it.

HOW FOSSILS ARE FORMED AND HOW THEY PROVIDE EVIDENCE OF ORGANISMS THAT LIVED LONG AGO

A **fossil** is the remains or trace of an ancient organism that has been preserved naturally in the earth's crust. Sedimentary rocks usually are rich sources of fossil remains. Those fossils found in layers of sediment were embedded in the slowly forming sedimentary rock strata. The oldest fossils known are the traces of 3.5 billion-year-old bacteria found in sedimentary rocks. Few fossils are found in metamorphic rock, and virtually none are found in igneous rocks. The magma is so hot that any organism trapped in the magma is destroyed.

Although the fairly well preserved remains of a woolly mammoth embedded in ice were found in Russia in May of 2007, the best-preserved animal remains are typically discovered in natural tar pits. When an animal accidentally falls into the tar, it becomes trapped, sinking to the bottom. Preserved bones of the saber-toothed cat have been found in tar pits.

Prehistoric insects have been found trapped in ancient amber or fossil resin that was excreted by some extinct species of pine trees. Fossil molds are the hollow spaces in a rock previously occupied by bones or shells. A fossil cast is a fossil mold that fills with sediments or minerals that later hardens to form a cast. Fossil tracks are the imprints in hardened mud left behind by birds or animals.

OBJECTIVE 0012   UNDERSTAND IMPORTANT EVENTS, CONCEPTS, AND METHODS OF INQUIRY RELATED TO GEORGIA, U.S., AND WORLD HISTORY

0012.01   Recognizing chronological relationships among historical events and analyzing various perspectives, interpretations, and implications of events, issues, and developments in Georgia and the United States, including early Native American cultures in North America and their interactions with early explorers

Chronology is the ordering of events through time. Chronologies are often listed along a timeline or in a list by date.

Chronologies allow for an easy visualization of a wide expanse of history. Information condensed this way allows a student to quickly get an overview of the major events and changes over time. By focusing on important related events, the causes and effects of major developments can be emphasized. In addition, in placing chronologies for different societies parallel to one another, comparisons in relative development can be quickly interpreted, providing material for further historical exploration.

Historic causation is the concept that events in history are linked to one another by and endless chain of cause and effect. The root causes of major historical events cannot always be seen immediately; they are often only apparent when looking back from many years later.

In some cases, individual events do have an immediate, clear effect. In 1941, Europe was embroiled in war. On the Pacific Rim, Japan was engaged in a military occupation of Korea and other Asian countries. The United States took a position of isolation, choosing not to become directly involved with the conflicts. This position changed rapidly, however, on the morning of December 7, 1941, when Japanese forces launched a surprise attack on a U.S. naval base at Pearl Harbor in Hawaii. The United States immediately declared war on Japan and became involved in Europe shortly afterward. The entry of the United States into the Second World War undoubtedly contributed to the eventual victory of the Allied forces in Europe and the defeat of Japan after two atomic bombs were dropped there by the United States. The surprise attack on Pearl Harbor affected the outcome of the war and the shape of the modern world. Interactions between cultures—either by exploration, migration, or war—often contribute directly to major historical events; however, other forces can influence the course of history as well. Religious movements, such as the rise of Catholicism in the Middle Ages, created social changes throughout Europe and culminated in the Crusades and the expulsion of Muslims from Spain.

Technological developments can also lead to major historical events, as in the case of the Industrial Revolution, which was driven by the replacement of water power with steam power.

Social movements can also cause major historical shifts. Between the Civil War and the early 1960s in the United States, racial segregation was practiced legally in many parts of the country through "Jim Crow" laws. Demonstrations and activism opposing segregation began to escalate during the late 1950s and early 1960s, eventually leading to the passage in the U.S. Congress of the Civil Rights Act of 1964, effectively ending legal segregation in the United States.

Even now, all of these examples of historical occurrences can be changed by the passage of time. Viewed in light of the entire scope of U.S. history, the events of fifty years ago are still incredibly pertinent to today's society. Viewed in light of the entire scope of world history, the events of 500 years ago may have less of an overall impact than those changes wrought 5,000 years ago. Chronology, like time, is relative. Students must have a grasp of how events relate to one another and to history as a whole in order to understand what the events mean in a greater context.

The practice of dividing time into a number of discrete periods or blocks of time is called "periodization." Because history is continuous, all systems of periodization are, to some extent, arbitrary. However, dividing time into segments helps to facilitate an understanding of the changes that occur over time as well as the ability to identify similarities between events, knowledge, and experiences within the defined period.

Divisions of time may be determined by date, by cultural advances or changes, by historical events, by the influence of particular individuals or groups, or by geography. For example, the World War II era is defined as a particular period of time in which key historical, political, social, and economic events occurred throughout the entire world. However, the Jacksonian Era only has meaning in terms of American history. In that same vein, defining the "Romantic period" is only applicable in England, Europe, and countries under their direct influence.

Many of the commonly used divisions of time are open to controversy and discussion. For example, the use of BC and AD dating has clear reference only in societies that account time according to the Christian calendar. Similarly, speaking of "the year of the pig" has the greatest meaning in China.

An example of the kind of questions that can be raised about designations of time periods can be understood in the context of "Victorian." For example, is it possible to speak of a Victorian era beyond England? Is literature written in the style of the English poets and writers "Victorian" if it is written beyond the borders of England? Time designations can also carry both positive and negative connotations. For example, the term "Victorian" is often used to refer to class conflict, sexual repression, and heavy industry. These can be construed with negative connotations or positive connotations depending on the issue at hand.

Sometimes, several designations can be applied to the same period. The period known as the "Elizabethan Period" in English history is also called "the English Renaissance." In some cases, the differences in designation refer primarily to the specific aspect of history that is being considered. For example, one designation may be applied to a specific period of time when analyzing cultural history, while a different designation can be applied to the same period of time when considering military history.

Early Native American Cultures in North America

Native American peoples lived throughout what we now call the United States in varying degrees of togetherness. They had established cultures long before Columbus or any other European explorer arrived on the scene. Each people adopted different customs, pursued different avenues of agriculture and food gathering, and made slightly different weapons. They also fought among themselves and with other groups.

Perhaps the most famous of the Native American people is the *Algonquians*. Historians know much about this group because it was one of the first to interact with the newly arrived English settlers in Plymouth (and elsewhere). The Algonquians lived in wigwams and wore clothing made from animal skins. They were proficient hunters, gatherers, and trappers who also knew quite a bit about farming.

Beginning with a brave man named Squanto, the Algonquians shared their agricultural knowledge with the English settlers, including how to plant and cultivate corn, pumpkins, and squash. Other famous Algonquians include Pocahontas and her father, Powhatan—both of whom are immortalized in English literature—and Tecumseh and Black Hawk—known foremost for their fierce fighting abilities. To the overall Native American culture, they were responsible for contributing wampum and dream catchers.

Another group of people who lived in the Northeast was the *Iroquois*, who were fierce fighters but also forward thinkers. They lived in long houses and wore clothes made of buckskin. They, too, were expert farmers, growing the "Three Sisters" (corn, squash, and beans). Five of the Iroquois groups formed a Confederacy, which functioned as a shared form of government. This Confederacy had a detailed constitution that left each member nation independent to rule its own affairs, while establishing a supreme council to rule the entire body. Members of the Council were chosen from among the leaders of each member nation and were equal in power. This council ruled on all "foreign" affairs with other nations, and made laws applicable to the Confederacy as a whole. Member nations policed internal affairs with autonomy so long as they obeyed the confederacy laws. Men and women were equal voters and contributors to laws, treaties and policies. The Confederacy had an internal council for civil affairs, a military council, a military council with a two member head, and a religious council.

The Iroquois Confederacy was established in 1142 (a date recently updated based on data from a total eclipse). It has significant similarities in structure and concept to the U.S. Constitution, and although the *degree* to which the Iroquois Confederacy influenced the U.S. Constitution is hotly debated, there is no doubt some influence was there. Published speeches and writings by both Ben Franklin and Thomas Jefferson refer to the importance of some of the provisions and characteristics of the Iroquois Confederacy's constitution and suggest using parts of it as a model for the embryonic U.S government.

The Iroquois also formed the False Face Society, a group of medicine men who shared their medical knowledge with others but kept their identities secret. The masks they wore are one of the enduring symbols of the Native American era.

Among those living in the Southeast were the *Seminoles* and *Creeks*, a huge collection of people who lived in chickees (open, bark-covered houses) and wore clothes made from plant fibers. They were expert planters and hunters; they were also proficient at making and paddling dugout canoes. The beaded necklaces they created were some of the most beautiful on the continent. They are best known, however, for their struggles against Spanish and English settlers, especially those struggles led by the great Osceola.

The *Cherokee* also lived in the Southeast. They were one of the most influential groups, living in domed houses and wearing deerskin and rabbit furs. Accomplished hunters, farmers, and fishermen, the Cherokee were known the continent over for their intricate and beautiful basketry and clay pottery. They also played a game called lacrosse, which survives to this day in countries around the world.

In the middle of the continent lived the Plains tribes such as the *Sioux, Cheyenne, Blackfeet, Comanche,* and *Pawnee.* These peoples lived in teepees and wore buffalo skins and feather headdresses. (It is this image of the Native American that has made its way into most movies depicting the period.) They hunted wild animals on the Plains, especially the buffalo. They were well-known for their many ceremonies, including the Sun Dance, and for the peace pipes that they smoked. Famous Plains people include Crazy Horse and Sitting Bull, authors of the Custer Disaster; Sacagawea, leader of the Lewis and Clark expedition; and Chief Joseph, the famous Nez Perce leader.

Dotting the deserts of the Southwest were a handful of peoples, including the famous *Pueblo* nations, who lived in houses from which the name comes. They built multi-level apartment buildings of adobe that contained both above and below ground floors, and were often built into cliff faces for security. They wore clothes made of wool and woven cotton, farmed crops in the middle of desert land, herded sheep, created exquisite pottery and Kachina dolls, and had complex and flourishing religious customs, many of which survive today. They are perhaps best known for the challenging vista-based villages that they constructed out of the sheer faces of cliffs and rocks as well as for their *adobes*, which were mud-brick buildings that housed their living and meeting quarters. Theirs was perhaps one of the oldest representative governments in the world; the Pueblos chose their own chiefs.

Another well-known Southwestern group included the *Apache*, with their famous leader Geronimo. The Apache lived in homes called wickiups, which were made of bark, grass, and branches. They wore cotton clothing and were excellent hunters and gatherers. Adept at basketry, the Apache believed that everything in nature had special powers and that they were honored just to be part of it all.

The *Navajo,* (Dine) also residents of the Southwest, lived in hogans (round homes built of adobe) and wore clothes of rabbit skin and other natural fibers. They herded sheep and followed herds from place to place over a wide area. Still famous today are their skills in sand painting, weapon making, silversmithing, and weaving. Some of the most beautiful woven rugs were crafted by Navajo hands.

Living in the Northwest were the *Inuit,* who lived in tents made from animal skins or, in some cases, igloos. They wore clothes also made from animal skins, usually seal or caribou. They were excellent fishermen and hunters; they crafted efficient kayaks and umiaks to take them through waterways as well as harpoons with which to hunt animals. The Inuit are perhaps best known for the great carvings that they built. Among these are ivory figures and tall totem poles.

Colonists from England, France, Holland, Sweden, and Spain all settled in North America on lands once inhabited by Native Americans. Spanish colonies were mainly in the south, French colonies were mainly in the extreme north and in the middle of the continent, and the rest of the European colonies were in the northeast and along the Atlantic coast. These colonists got along with their new neighbors with varying degrees of success.

Of all of them, the French colonists seemed the most willing to work with the Native Americans. Even though their pursuit of animals to fill the growing demand for the fur trade was overpowering, they managed to find a way to keep their new neighbors happy. The French and Native Americans even fought on the same side of the war against England.

The Dutch (mostly in what is now New York and New Jersey) and Swedish (mostly in what is now Delaware) colonists were mainly interested in surviving in their new homes. However, they were conquered by the English early in their tenure on this continent.

The English and Spanish colonists had the worst relations with the Native Americans, mainly because the Europeans made a habit of taking land, signing and then breaking treaties, massacring, and otherwise abusing their new neighbors. Early on, many Native Americans were only too happy to share their agriculture and jewel-making secrets with the Europeans. However, the European (and later American) concept of "Manifest Destiny," (a policy of imperialistic expansion defended as right or necessary, or even divinely ordained) created serious problems, and from the Native American point of view what they got in return for their initial help was grief and deceit. The term "Manifest Destiny" meant nothing to the Native Americans, who believed that they lived on land granted access to them by the gods above. The Europeans and early Americans believed it was their right or destiny to push across the continent and bring "civilization" to the New World. This inevitably created enormous conflict, since the "push" of Manifest Destiny" generally meant pushing Native American groups further and further out of the picture.

The conflicts between Europeans and the various Native American groups formed the basis for an incredibly large portion of early U.S. history; the repercussions of many of these conflicts are still evident in society today.

HISTORY OF GEORGIA

During the seventeenth century, the east coast of North America was rapidly being settled by European colonists in the north and by the Spanish in the south. In 1670, the British colony of South Carolina was founded directly north of Spanish-controlled Florida, creating a tense frontier in what is now *Georgia*. Military conflict followed until the Spanish missions were withdrawn in 1704 and the area occupied by Yamasee Native Americans became friendlier to the British.

However, relations grew sour between the Yamasee and the British in 1715 over the fur trade, and the Yamasee began attacking British colonists. The colonists responded with force and the Yamasee were driven out of the area toward Florida. This largely depopulated the coastal region between Charleston, the capital of British Carolina, and St. Augustine, the capital of Spanish Florida.

In the early 1730s, James Oglethorpe, a British Member of Parliament, was engaged in a campaign of prison reform in England. English citizens who fell into debt could be thrown into debtor's prisons under deplorable conditions, where they were usually mistreated and often died. Oglethorpe presented a plan to colonize the newly available land in North America with some of these debtors to give them an opportunity to escape the horrors of prison and start over in the New World.

King George II approved Oglethorpe's scheme, and on June 9, 1732, granted a royal charter to Oglethorpe and a group of twenty other philanthropists to found a colony in North America. These twenty-one trustees called the new colony "Georgia" in honor of the king.

In the end, the first people chosen to go to the new colony were not debtors, but individuals chosen by the trustees based on their skills, professions, and potential usefulness in the new colony. The first group of 114 people, including Oglethorpe, sailed from England on the *Anne* in November 1732 and arrived in Charleston two months later. Oglethorpe scouted ahead into the Georgia region and selected a bluff on the Savannah River to build the first settlement, which became called Savannah.

Oglethorpe and the trustees wished to avoid duplicating England's strict class system in the new colony, as they felt it had led to the practice of imprisoning debtors. They implemented a series of rules in the colony that prohibited slavery and required each man to work his own land. Identical houses were built on equal-sized lots to emphasize the equality of all.

The peaceful agrarian community that was envisioned by Oglethorpe grew happily for a time, but positioned as it was on the British frontier with the Spanish, the realities of potential warfare occupied the colony's attentions. Oglethorpe successfully petitioned the British government to grant him military authority in the area and to provide him with a regiment of British troops to defend the frontier. Oglethorpe unsuccessfully attempted to capture St. Augustine, spurring a series of battles between the Spanish and the British allied troops under Oglethorpe. The British emerged victorious after holding the line at the Battle of Bloody Marsh in 1742, after which the Spanish did not try to invade Georgia again.

As dissatisfaction with taxation increased in the northern colonies, similar rumblings began in Georgia, which joined the other colonies in 1765 in renouncing the Stamp Act. Georgia had prospered under its royal charter, however, and many Georgians believed that they needed British protection from neighboring Native Americans.

When news of the Battle of Lexington and Concord reached Georgia, patriotic resolve was strengthened; in May of 1775, a group of patriots raided the arsenal at Savannah and took a supply of British gunpowder. Georgian colonists set up their own government shortly thereafter and joined the association of colonies in enforcing a ban on trade with the British. While British Governor James Wright was still the official authority in Georgia, the provincial government founded in July 1775 gave executive authority to Council of Safety, which held the real power.

Wright was eventually expelled in 1776, after being held hostage by the colonists once British warships approached Savannah. Without a governor, provincial congress was convened at Augusta in April 1776, and a set of Rules and Regulations was adopted outlining a simple structure of government. Three delegates were sent to the Second Continental Congress in Philadelphia in time to sign the Declaration of Independence in July.

Three months later, a convention was called in Savannah to provide for a more permanent form of government in Georgia. The result of this convention was Georgia's first constitution, the Constitution of 1777. The new constitution created a single elected assembly that, in turn, chose a governor. Although only white men were allowed to vote, the constitution was remarkable for its time in granting voting rights to any man who paid taxes or had a trade. The Georgia Constitution also provided for future amendments by state convention. This provision, which was not included in all state constitutions at the time, eventually became common practice throughout the United States. This constitution also guaranteed freedom of religion and the press, as well as right to a trial by jury. However, the Constitution of 1777 lacked many of the internal balances of political power that would be included in the United States Constitution, and serious movements began in 1788 to redraft it.

Following the American victory in the Revolutionary War, Georgia engaged with the rest of the new states in the debate over a federal constitution. Along with its southern neighbors, Georgia opposed a strong central government advocated by the Federalists, fearing the concentration of political power in the northern states. The Bill of Rights, the first ten amendments to the U.S. Constitution that spell out limits on governmental authority, were included in the proposed Constitution to ensure the rights of the states. In this way, Georgia and the other southern states greatly influenced the shape of the Constitution. Georgia ratified the U.S. Constitution in January 1788.

Please refer to Skill 12.03 for details on the Civil War.

"New South" is a term sometimes used to describe the South after the Civil War; it refers to a South no longer dependent on slave labor and based on industry instead. In Georgia, Henry Grady is closely associated with the New South movement of the 1880s. This movement sought to bring northern investments and industry to the state, particularly in the Atlanta region.

The New South was more of an ideal than a reality for Georgia farmers, who found themselves stressed by falling cotton prices after the Civil War. The growing Populist movement in the 1890s blamed the entrenched Democratic Party for many of the farmer's woes and mounted a challenge to the party. Georgia populists sought to include Blacks in the movement and called for prison reform. By the turn of the century, Populism as a movement had largely faded from Georgia politics, although it did have lasting effects.

Jim Crow laws were laws enacted after the Civil War that resulted in the segregation of whites and blacks, with blacks being forced to use inferior facilities. During Reconstruction, southern states were forced to adopt protections for free black citizens. Once the Reconstruction governments were replaced with "Redeemer" governments, laws were enacted that required separate schools and public facilities for blacks and whites, thereby replacing the Black Codes that had been in effect prior to the Civil War.

Jim Crow laws had the effect of denying voting rights to many black citizens by requiring the payment of a poll tax. The Democratic Party also discouraged black participation in politics and elections. The fifteenth Amendment to the US Constitution (ratified in 1870) gave blacks the right to vote, though this right was often not enforced until the 1960's.

Despite these prejudices, many blacks prospered following the war, especially in the growing industrial center of Atlanta. As the white elite witnessed the emergence of a black economic elite in Atlanta, some argued that allowing blacks to vote had caused them to think of themselves as equal to whites, and that the vote should be taken away from them.

Tension grew between the races, eventually erupting in violence in Atlanta in 1906. Unsubstantiated reports circulated that black men had attacked four white women. A mob of white men and boys gathered and raided black neighborhoods, destroying businesses and killing several people. The state militia was called in to control the mob, which eventually subsided. As a result of the riot, even further restrictions were placed on black voting rights.

World War I greatly impacted Georgia, which became the location of several military training camps. Thousands of troops from all over the country passed through Georgia on their way to war. In 1918, the troop ship *Otranto* tragically sank, killing almost 400 men, 130 from Georgia.

When President Wilson instituted the draft, many white Georgians (especially landowners who employed black sharecroppers) tried to prevent black men from being called into service. Not wanting to lose their labor force, they would sometimes refuse to deliver draft notices and succeeded in preventing many blacks from registering. Many blacks were arrested and jailed for evading the draft as a result.

Agriculture during this time was threatened by more than just the potential loss of farm labor. The boll weevil is an insect that affects cotton. It began its spread northward from Mexico in the late nineteenth century and reached Georgia around 1915. Within ten years, the number of acres planted in cotton in Georgia halved because of the pest. The boll weevil forced farmers to diversify their crops. This need plus the work of George Washington Carver, led to the rise of peanut farming, which became an important agricultural product.

Eugene Talmadge began his career in state politics as the Commissioner of Agriculture in 1926. Outspoken and opinionated, Talmadge won popular support from the rural community and rapidly became a polarizing influence in the Democratic Party. He was elected governor in 1932 and re-elected in 1934. After unsuccessful bids for the U.S. Senate, Talmadge was again elected governor in 1940.

Talmadge was a forceful leader who bypassed legislative action and removed appointees who disagreed with his views. Talmadge undertook to remove faculty members from the state university system if he thought they wanted to integrate the schools or held the belief of racial equality. As a result of his raid on the system, the university lost its accreditation. The more moderate Ellis Arnall challenged Talmadge in the gubernatorial race of 1942, promising to restore accreditation, and won. Talmadge was re-elected governor in 1946, but died before taking office.

Talmadge was a major opponent of President Franklin Roosevelt's New Deal, a series of public programs beginning in 1933 designed to assist Depression-wracked Americans and to promote economic recovery. Talmadge and others saw the New Deal as federal interference with local affairs, but the program, which provided farm subsidies, built new infrastructure, and provided direct assistance to poor Georgians was popular among the people. President Roosevelt himself was popular in Georgia, having adopted Warm Springs as a second home during his time in office.

The New Deal did help many poor Southerners, although it failed to bring the dramatic turnaround that had been hoped for in the South. It was World War II and the related boom in the war industry that transformed Georgia's economy. Defense contractors found a large and willing labor force in Georgia, and shipbuilding and aircraft manufacturing became important industries that employed hundreds of thousands of people. With many men away in the military, women entered the workforce in large numbers for the first time.

Black workers also benefited from the labor shortage, entering positions that had formerly been reserved for white men. Segregation, however, was still enforced. New methods of agriculture made farming a viable endeavor once again, but Georgia was no longer entirely dependent on agriculture. The city of Atlanta made an early commitment to develop air travel when it establishment an airfield in 1925. The airfield grew throughout the twentieth century; under the administration of Mayor Maynard Jackson, it was transformed into the Hartsfield International Airport, a huge building project that opened in 1980. Later named the Hartsfield-Jackson International airport, the facility is currently the busiest airport in the world.

Ellis Arnall was elected governor of Georgia in 1942 at the age of thirty-five. Arnall made several significant reforms, including eliminating poll taxes and lowering the voting age. He also proposed checks to the power of the governor, feeling that Eugene Talmadge had previously abused his power. Arnall left office in 1947, although he ran again in 1966 against the segregationist Lester Maddox. Maddox emerged the victor in that race and served as governor until 1971.

Herman Talmadge was the only son of former Governor Eugene Talmadge. He ran his father's successful campaign for governor in 1946 and was briefly appointed to the position by the legislature when his father died before taking office. Herman Talmadge was himself elected governor in 1948. Talmadge supported segregation and worked to bring industry to Georgia. He served as Governor until 1954, when he ran for the U.S. Senate and was elected. Talmadge served in the Senate until 1981.

Between Reconstruction and the 1960s, the Democratic Party dominated Georgia politics. Republicans had been installed by the federal government during Reconstruction, but they were quickly replaced by Democrats after the federal troops that supported the Republican state governments were withdrawn. The civil rights era began drawing sharp lines between old-line Democrats and more moderate Democrats, sometimes splitting the vote and allowing Republicans to gain footholds.

Another change in Georgia politics in the 1960s was the end of the county unit system of conducting state primaries. Under this system, all of a county's unit votes were awarded to the candidate that received the most individual votes within that county. This system favored rural counties, and allowed for the election of candidates who had actually lost the popular vote, as was the case in 1946 when Eugene Talmadge won the primary for Governor. Primary politics were important in Georgia. Because of the dominance of the Democratic Party, winning the primary virtually ensured winning the general election. The U.S. Supreme Court declared the county unit system illegal in 1963.

In 1962, Jimmy Carter was elected to the Georgia legislature after challenging fraudulent returns in his election. He went on to serve as the governor of Georgia and was elected President of the United States in 1976, defeating President Gerald Ford.

0012.02   Recognizing chronological relationships among historical events and analyzing various perspectives, interpretations, and implications of events, issues, and developments in world history

History is the study of the past, especially aspects of human past: political incidents, economic events, and cultural and social conditions. Students study history through textbooks, research, field trips to museums and historical sights, and other hands-on methods. Most nations set requirements in history around the study of their own country's heritage, usually to develop an awareness and feeling of loyalty and patriotism.

For better comprehension, history can be divided into the three main classifications: a) *time periods*, b) *nations* (in terms of a group of peoples sharing political and social boundaries, not necessarily nations as we know them today), and c) *specialized topics*. In the following pages, all of the provided historical information for study falls into one or the other of these three divisions. Note that the three categories can and do overlap in some of their content; this is a natural outcome of the complex details that make up our world's history. For example, Imperial and Feudal Japan can fall under the categories of both time period and nation. It is a time period in that there were definite years when Imperialism and Feudalism were common forms of government. At the same time, the provided information deals only with those forms of government in Japan. In order to understand history in a greater context, the reader must grasp that with history, all things are relative to the time period and context in which they occur. Reasoning about relationships, causal and otherwise, between events, time periods, or nations, etc., can begin with any of these divisions and move around through them in any way the reader may wish.

EXAMPLES OF TIME PERIODS

The names of time periods and the manner in which history is divided into periods may vary with the source or the purpose of the discussion. However, many divisions stress major elements such as key governments or social or scientific developments that are seen as causal or characteristic of a particular period. Time periods are used to describe a period of years during which many of the events can be described in terms of a particular factor or development. Some common such divisions are presented here.

Prehistory is defined as the period of mankind's achievements before the development of writing. In the Stone Age cultures, there were three different periods. They include the *Lower Paleolithic Period*, which is characterized by the use of crude tools; the *Upper Paleolithic Period*, which exhibited a greater variety of more intricate tools and implements, the adoption of wearing clothing, a highly organized group life, and skills in art; and finally, the *Neolithic Period*, during which time the people domesticated animals; formalized food production; practiced the arts of knitting, spinning, and weaving cloth; started fires through friction; built domestic shelters; and developed the institutions of family, religion, and government.

The *Tang Dynasty* of China extended from 618 to 907 CE (Common Era). Its capital was the most heavily populated of any city in the world at the time. Buddhism was adopted by the imperial family (Li) and became an integral part of Chinese culture. The emperor, however, feared the monasteries and began to take action against them in the tenth century. Confucianism experienced a rebirth during the time of this dynasty as an instrument of state administration. Following a civil war, the central government lost control of local areas. Warlords arose in 907, and China was divided into North and South. These areas came to be ruled by short-lived minor dynasties. A major political accomplishment of this period was the creation of a class of career government officials who functioned between the populace and the government. This class of "scholar-officials" continued to fulfill this function in government and society until 1911.

The period of the Tang Dynasty is generally considered a pinnacle of Chinese civilization. Through contact with the Middle East and India, the period was marked by great creativity in many areas. Block printing was invented; it made much information and literature available to wide audiences. In science, astronomers calculated the paths of the sun and the moon as well as the movements of the constellations. This facilitated the development of the calendar. In agriculture, such technologies as land cultivation by setting it on fire, the curved-shaft plow, separate cultivation of seedlings, and sophisticated irrigation systems increased productivity. Hybrid breeds of horses and mules were created to strengthen the labor supply. In medicine, there were achievements like the understanding of the circulatory and digestive systems as well as great advances in pharmacology. Gunpowder was commonly used for a variety of purposes during this time, as well.

Ceramics was another area in which great advances were made. A new type of glazing was invented; it gave the dynasty's porcelain and earthenware its unique appearance through three-colored glazing.

In literature, the poetry of the period is generally considered the best in the entire history of Chinese literature. The rebirth of Confucianism led to the publication of many commentaries on his classical writings. Encyclopedias on several subjects were produced, as well as histories and philosophical works.

Middle Ages

The term *Middle Ages* is used in two time period classifications, Early Middle Ages (often called the Dark Ages, from the fall of Rome in 507CE to 1000CE), and High Middle Ages (from 1000-1300CE). When used alone, the term Middle Ages often refers to this latter definition, covering the 11th, 12th, and 13th centuries. It is important to note that the term refers to *European history.*

During the Middle Ages, the population of Europe was growing rapidly. Its system of *feudalism* was one of loyalty and protection. The strong and wealthy protected the weak, who in turn provided services in farm labor, military service, and lifelong allegiances. Life was typically lived on a vast estate, owned by a nobleman and his family, called a "manor." It was a complete village supporting a few hundred people, mostly peasants. Improved tools and farming methods made life more bearable, although most people never left the manor or traveled from their village during their entire lifetimes.

In feudal societies, a very small number of people actually owned land. Instead, they held it as a hereditary trust from some social or political superior in return for services. The superiors were a small percentage of the people; they were a fighting and ruling aristocracy. The vast majority of the people were simply workers. One of the largest landowners of the time was the Roman Catholic Church. It was estimated that during the twelfth and thirteenth centuries, the Church controlled one-third of the useable land in Western Europe.

In addition to the tremendous influence of the Church, the era of knighthood and its code of chivalry also came into importance at this time. Until the period of the Renaissance, the Church was the only place where people could be educated. The Bible and other books were hand-copied by monks in the monasteries. Cathedrals were built and decorated with art depicting religious subjects.

With the increase in trade and travel, cities sprang up and began to grow. Craft workers in the cities developed their skills to a high degree, eventually organizing guilds to protect the quality of the work and to regulate the buying and selling of their products. City government, centered on strong town councils, developed and flourished. The wealthy businessmen who made up the rising middle class were the most active in city government and town councils.

The end of the feudal manorial system was sealed by the outbreak and spread of the infamous *Black Death*, which killed over one-third of the total population of Europe. Those who survived and were skilled in any job or occupation were in demand; for the first time, many serfs and peasants found freedom and (for that time period) a decidedly improved standard of living. Strong *nation-states* became powerful, and people developed a renewed interest in life and learning.

Imperial and Feudal Japan

From its beginnings, Japan operated under an Imperial form of government. The divine emperor was believed to do no wrong and, therefore, served for his entire life. *Kyoto*, the capital, became one of the largest and most powerful cities in the world. As in Europe, however, the rich and powerful landowners—the nobles— grew powerful over time. Eventually, the nobles had more power than the emperor, which required a change in attitude in the minds of the Japanese people.

During the **Feudal Period** (from the 12th to the 19th century), the nobles of Japan were lords of great lands; they were called *Daimyos*. They were of the highest social class, and people of lower social classes worked for them. In return for their work and loyalty, the Daimyos (similar to the lards in feudal Europe) provided a home and protection. The workers included the lowly peasants, who had few privileges other than being allowed to work for the great men that the Daimyos told everyone they were. Serving them, the Daimyos had warriors known as Samurai, who were answerable only to the Daimyo. The most powerful of the Samurai became the Shogun, the military leader of the country and its de facto ruler. During this period, the Emperor became a ceremonial head of state. The Shogun code of honor was an exemplification of the overall Japanese belief that every man was a soldier and a gentleman. Women could also be Samurai and sometimes fought alongside the men. However, the status of Japanese women deteriorated during this period as it became more and more common for women to be seen as secondary to men and the ideal woman to be seen as subservient to men. Even so, women in the military could command men of a lower station, though men in their own station could command any woman.

The main economic difference between Imperial and Feudal Japan was that the money that continued to flow into the country from trade with China, Korea, and other Asian countries (and from good old-fashioned plundering on the high seas) made its way into the pockets of the Daimyos rather than the emperor's coffers. Feudalism developed in Japan later than it did in Europe, and it lasted longer as well. Japan dodged one historical bullet when a huge Mongol invasion was driven away by a huge typhoon, the famed *kamikaze*, or "divine wind," in the twelfth century. Japan was thus free to continue to develop itself as it saw fit and to refrain from interacting with the West. This isolation lasted until the nineteenth century.

Scientific Revolution

The *Scientific Revolution* was characterized by a shift in patterns of thought about reason and proof. Most scientists date the beginning of the scientific revolution to the publication, in 1543, of the works of Copernicus on planetary orbits and the works of Vesalius on the human body, but it is Galileo who has been called the father of Modern Science.. Near the end of the sixteenth century, *Galileo Galilei,*a vocal proponent of Copernicanism (the statement that the Earth and other planets orbit the Sun, rather than the then popular belief that the Earth was the center of the universe.), introduced a radical approach to the study of motion. He moved from the then current attempt to use thought and reason alone to explain the general reasons why objects move the way they do to the use of experiments to describe precisely how they do, in fact, move. He also used experimentation to describe how forces affect non-moving objects. Other scientists continued in the same approach. Once this approach became possible, philosophers, thinkers, and scientists began to question almost everything and subject long held ideas to scrutiny with scientific approaches and methods. This period has been marked by extensive use of experimentation and the Scientific Method of investigation, as well as technological advancement. The scientific fields of astronomy, physics, and biology began to make great advances.

Outstanding scientists of the period also included: *Johannes Kepler, Evangelista Torricelli, Blaise Pascal, Isaac Newton*, and *Gottfried Wilhelm Leibniz*. This was the period when experiments dominated scientific study. This method was particularly applied to the study of physics.

Agricultural Revolution

The term *Agricultural Revolution* has been used for a number of such "revolutions" during which great advances in agriculture have occurred. The Original Agricultural Revolution was the *Neolithic agricultural revolution,* during which time human beings moved from a hunter-gatherer society one based more firmly on agriculture. Coinciding with the shift from hunting wild game to the domestication of animals, this period was one of dramatic social and economic change.

Numerous changes in lifestyle and thinking accompanied the development of stable agricultural communities. Rather than gathering a wide variety of plants as hunter-gatherers, agricultural communities were dependent on a limited number of plants and crops. Subsistence was vulnerable to the weather and dependent upon planting and harvesting times. Agriculture also required a great deal of physical labor as well as a sense of discipline. Agricultural communities were also more sedentary and stable in terms of location. This made the construction of dwellings possible—especially dwellings relatively close together, creating villages and towns.

Stable communities also freed people from the need to carry everything with them in the move from hunting ground to hunting ground. In addition to pottery, this facilitated the invention of larger, more complex tools. As new tools were envisioned and developed, it began to make sense to have some specialization within the society.

In the beginning of the transition to agriculture, the tools that were used for hunting and gathering were adequate to the tasks of agriculture. The initial challenge was in adapting to a new way of life. Once that challenge was met, attention turned to the development of more advanced tools and sources of energy. Six thousand years ago, the first plow was invented in Mesopotamia. This plow was pulled by animals. With this invention, agriculture became possible on a much larger scale. Soon, tools were developed that make such basic tasks as gathering seeds, planting, and cutting grain faster and easier.

It also becomes necessary to maintain social and political stability to ensure that planting and harvesting times are not interrupted by internal discord or a war with a neighboring community. It was also necessary to develop ways to store the crop and to prevent its destruction by the elements and animal (not to mention protection from thieves).

Settled communities that produced the necessities of life were largely self-supporting. Advances in agricultural technology and the ability to produce a surplus of produce created two opportunities: first, the opportunity to trade the surplus goods for other desired goods, and second, vulnerability to others who might steal the goods. Protecting domesticated livestock and surplus crops become an issue for the early communities. This, in turn, led to the construction of walls and other fortifications around the community.

The ability to produce surplus crops also created the opportunity to trade or barter with other communities in exchange for desired goods. Traders and trade routes began to develop between villages and cities. With the expansion of trade and travel between communities came the exchange of ideas and knowledge. The *Muslim Agricultural Revolution* took place in the 8th-13th centuries when traders contributed to the *Globalization* of both crops and farming techniques, bringing such crops as sorghum from Africa, citrus from China, and rice and cotton from India to the Arabic Peninsula. Agricultural revolutions are characterized by a sharp increase in food production and often lead to other advances, as well as to population growth.

The modern *Agricultural Revolution* began in England in the early 18th century. It was marked by experimentation that resulted in the increased production of crops as well as a new and more technical approach to the management of agriculture. In the Americas, it was further advanced by improvements in farm equipment, particularly plows, seed drill, and reapers and harvesters. Important names associated with these advances include John Deere (first cast steel plows), Jethro Tull (seed drills), and Cyrus McCormick (reapers and harvesters). These advances created massive increases in agricultural production, particularly food production, which then fueled population increases.

This revolution both helped fuel (literally) and was hugely enhanced by the Industrial Revolution. The invention of the steam engine and the introduction of steam-powered tractors greatly increased crop production and significantly decreased labor costs. Developments in agriculture were also enhanced by the Scientific Revolution and the process of learning from experimentation (which ultimately led to philosophies of crop rotation and soil enrichment). Improved systems of irrigation and harvesting also contributed to the growth of agricultural production.

Industrial Revolution

The *Industrial Revolution* of the late 18th and the 19th centuries began in Great Britain and spread elsewhere. It was the based on the development of power-driven machinery (fueled by coal and steam). This revolution led to the accelerated growth of industry, with large factories replacing homes and small workshops as work centers. The lives of people changed drastically, and a largely agricultural society changed to an industrial one. In Western Europe, the period of colonialism began. The industrialized nations seized and claimed parts of Africa and Asia in an effort to control and provide the raw materials needed to feed the industries and machines in the "mother country." Later developments included power based on electricity and internal combustion, replacing coal and steam.

The first phase of the Industrial Revolution (1750-1830) saw the mechanization of the textile industry; vast improvements in mining with the invention of the steam engine; and numerous improvements in transportation with the development and improvement of turnpikes, canals, and the invention of the railroad.

The second phase (1830-1910) resulted in improvements in a number of industries that had already been mechanized through such inventions as the Bessemer steel process and steam ships. New industries arose as a result of the new technological advances, including photography, electricity, and chemical processes. New sources of power were harnessed and applied, including petroleum and hydroelectric power. Precision instruments were developed and engineering was launched. It was during this second phase that the Industrial Revolution spread to other European countries, Japan, and the United States.

The direct results of the Industrial Revolution, particularly as they affected industry, commerce, and agriculture, included:

- Enormous increases in productivity
- Huge increases in world trade
- Specialization and division of labor
- Standardization of parts
- Mass production
- Growth of giant business conglomerates and monopolies
- A new revolution in agriculture facilitated by the steam engine, machinery, chemical fertilizers, processing, canning, and refrigeration

The political results included:

- Growth of complex government by technical experts
- Centralization of government, including regulatory administrative agencies
- Advantages to democratic development, including the extension of franchise to the middle class (and later to all elements of the population), mass education to meet the needs of an industrial society, and the development of media of public communication, including radio, television, and cheap newspapers
- Dangers to democracy, including the risk of media manipulation, the facilitation of dictatorial centralization and totalitarian control, the subordination of the legislative function to administrative directives, greater efforts to achieve uniformity and conformity, and social impersonalization.

The economic results included:

- The conflict between free trade and low tariffs and protectionism
- The issue of free enterprise against government regulation
- Struggles between labor and capital, including the trade-union movement
- The rise of socialism
- The rise of the utopian socialists
- The rise of Marxian or scientific socialism

The social results of the Industrial Revolution included:

- Increase of population, especially in industrial centers
- Advances in science applied to agriculture, sanitation, and medicine
- Growth of great cities
- Disappearance of the difference between city dwellers and farmers
- Faster tempo of life and increased stress from the monotony of the work routine
- The emancipation of women
- The decline of religion
- The rise of scientific materialism
- Darwin's theory of evolution

1920s America

Many refer to the decade of the 1920s as the *Jazz Age*. The decade was a time of optimism and of exploring new boundaries. In many ways, it was a clear movement away from conventionalism. Jazz music, uniquely American, was the country's popular music at the time. Jazz is essentially free-flowing improvisation on a simple theme with a four-beat rhythm; this musical style perfectly typified the mood of society. Jazz originated in the poor districts of New Orleans as an outgrowth of the Blues. The leading jazz musicians of the time included: Buddy Bolden, Joseph "King" Oliver, Duke Ellington, Louis Armstrong, and Jelly Roll Morton.

As jazz grew in popularity and in intricacy of the music, it gave birth to swing and the era of big band jazz. Some of the most notable musicians of the Big Band era were: Bing Crosby, Frank Sinatra, Don Redman, Fletcher Henderson, Count Basie, Benny Goodman, Billie Holiday, Ella Fitzgerald, and the Dorsey Brothers.

Information Revolution

The *Information Revolution* refers to the sweeping changes during the latter half of the twentieth century as a result of technological advances and a new respect for the knowledge provided by trained, skilled, and experienced professionals in a variety of fields. This approach to understanding a number of social and economic changes in global society arose from the ability to make computer technology both accessible and affordable. In particular, the development of the computer chip led to such technological advances as the Internet, the cell phone, Cybernetics, wireless communication, and the related ability to disseminate and access a massive amount of information quite readily.

In providing rapid access to massive amounts of information through wireless means, the Information Revolution has transcended national and cultural boundaries and affected the lives of people all over the world. It is not only the highly paid computer AI (artificial intelligence) experts who access this information. It is school children worldwide, women using back room computers in countries that deny women access to school, budding young scientists and designers in remote parts of the world who can now chat about their designs and share information on a daily basis. It has been said that you can find *anything*, good or bad, on the internet (e.g., formula for a bomb, symptoms of thrombosis, child rearing advice, childhood photos of presidents and stars, economic predictions, and **jobs**).

The evolution of *e-commerce* and internet job hunting and online jobs has begun what many consider an extension of the information revolution into economics. In terms of economic theory and segmentation, it is now very much the norm to think of three basic economic sectors: agriculture and mining, manufacturing, and "services." Indeed, labor is now often divided between manual labor and informational labor. The fact that businesses are involved in the production, distribution, processing, and transmission of **information** has, according to some, created a new business sector.

The *Information Revolution* has clearly changed modern life in many ways, including by creating devices and processes that actually control much of the world as it is experienced by the average person. It has most certainly revolutionized the entertainment industry, as well as influenced the way people spend their time. In education, new technology has made information on virtually any subject instantly accessible. It has also thoroughly altered the minute-to-minute knowledge persons have of world events. Sixty years ago, news from the war front became available by radio for the first time. Visual images, however, were primarily available through the weekly newsreels shown in motion picture theaters. Today, live pictures from the battlefield are instantly available to people, no matter where they are.

[s47]
EXAMPLES OF NATIONS

As mentioned earlier, "nations" here refers to the broader civilizations and groups with common culture and political/social boundaries, rather than modern nation states. History can be understood in terms of the ongoing influence of ancient civilizations, cultures, and nations whose achievements and actions still impact the world today. Although the specific list of such nations might vary from one source to another, most lists would include the following sixteen civilizations and their accomplishments:

Egypt made numerous significant contributions, including constructing the Great Pyramids; developing hieroglyphic writing; preserving bodies after death; making paper from papyrus; contributing to developments in arithmetic and geometry; inventing the method of counting in groups of 1-10 (the base ten or decimal system); completing a solar calendar; and laying the foundation for science and astronomy.

The ancient civilization of the **Sumerians** invented the wheel; developed irrigation through use of canals, dikes, and devices for raising water; devised the system of cuneiform writing; learned to divide time; and built large boats that allowed trade to expand into a global enterprise, incidentally spreading culture, technology, and language. The Babylonians devised the famous *Code of Hammurabi*, a code of laws that is considered to be an embryonic form of a constitution, listing offences and punishments as well as reparations and economic structures.

The ancient **Assyrians** were warlike and aggressive due to a highly organized military. They achieved an unprecedented degree of military power over their part of the world. They were experts in both the tactics (including the use of horse drawn chariots) and psychology of war. They were also specialists in architecture and sculpture. One of their libraries of 30,000 fire hardened clay documents survives today, providing invaluable information about civilizations of the period.

The **Hebrews**, also known as the ancient Israelites, instituted "monotheism," which is the worship of one God, Yahweh.

The **Minoans** had a system of writing using symbols to represent syllables in words. They built palaces with multiple levels that contained many rooms, water and sewage systems with flush toilets, bathtubs, hot and cold running water, and bright paintings on the walls.

The **Mycenaeans** changed the Minoan writing system to aid their own language and used symbols to represent syllables.

The **Phoenicians** were sea traders well-known for their manufacturing skills in glass and metals. They also developed their famous purple dye. They became so proficient in the skill of navigation that they were able to sail by the stars at night. Further, they devised an alphabet using symbols to represent single sounds, which was an improved extension of the Egyptian principle and writing system. Their wide ranging trade explorations are responsible for spreading many cultural elements around the world.

In **India**, the caste system was developed, the principle of zero in mathematics was discovered, and the major religion of Hinduism began. Industry and commerce developed along with extensive trading with the Near East. Outstanding advances in the fields of science and medicine were made, and the civilization was one of the first to be active in navigation and maritime enterprises.

China began building the Great Wall, practiced crop rotation and terrace farming, increased the importance of the silk industry, and developed caravan routes across Central Asia for extensive trade. Also, they increased proficiency in rice cultivation and developed a written language based on drawings or pictographs (no alphabet symbolizing sounds, as each word or character had a form different from all others). China is considered by some historians to be the oldest, uninterrupted civilization in the world; it was in existence around the same time as the ancient civilizations founded in *Egypt, Mesopotamia*, and the *Indus Valley*. The Chinese studied nature and weather; stressed the importance of education, family, and a strong central government; followed the religions of Buddhism, Confucianism, and Taoism; and invented such things as gunpowder, paper, printing, and the magnetic compass.

The ancient **Persians** developed an alphabet; contributed the religions/ philosophies of *Zoroastrianism, Mithraism,* and *Gnosticism*; and allowed conquered peoples to retain their own customs, laws, and religions. The classical civilization of **Greece** reached the highest levels in mankind's achievements based on the foundations already laid by such ancient groups as the *Egyptians, Phoenicians, Minoans*, and *Mycenaeans*.

Among the more important contributions of Greece were the Greek alphabet derived from the Phoenician letters. The Greek alphabet formed the basis for the Roman alphabet and our present-day alphabet. Extensive trading and colonizing resulted in the spread of the Greek civilization. The love of sports, with emphasis on a sound body, led to the tradition of the Olympic Games. Greece was responsible for the rise of strong, independent city-states.

Other important areas that the Greeks are credited with influencing include drama, epic and lyric poetry, fables, myths centered on their many gods and goddesses, science, astronomy, medicine, mathematics, philosophy, art, architecture, and records of historical events. The conquests of Alexander the Great spread Greek ideas and brought to the Greek world many ideas from Asia. Some of these ideas included the values of wisdom and curiosity as well as the desire to learn as much about the world as possible.

A most interesting and significant characteristic of the Greek, Hellenic, and Roman civilizations was "secularism," in which emphasis shifted away from religion to the state. Men were not absorbed in or dominated by religion as had been the case in Egypt and the nations located in Mesopotamia.

The civilization in **Japan** appeared around the same time as the Greeks, having borrowed much of its culture from China. It was the last of the classical civilizations to develop. Although they used, accepted, and copied Chinese art, law, architecture, dress, and writing, the Japanese refined these into their own unique way of life, including incorporating the religion of Buddhism into their culture.

The nations in **Africa** south of the Sahara developed systems of refining and using iron, especially for farm implements (and later for weapons). Trading was done by land using camels as well as overseas from important seaports. The Arab influence was extremely important, as was the Arabs' later contact with Indians, Christian Nubians, and Persians. In fact, their trading activities were probably the most important factor in the spread of and assimilation of different ideas and stimulation of cultural growth in Africa.

The **Vikings** had a lot of influence at this time through spreading their ideas and their knowledge of trade routes and sailing. Most of this was accomplished first through their conquests and later through trade.

In other parts of the world were the **Byzantine** and **Saracenic** (or Islamic) civilizations, both dominated by religion. The major contributions of the Saracens were in the areas of science and philosophy. Included were accomplishments in astronomy, mathematics, physics, chemistry, medicine, literature, art, trade and manufacturing, agriculture, and a marked influence on the Renaissance period of history. The Byzantines (Christians) made important contributions in art and in the preservation of Greek and Roman achievements, including architecture (especially in Eastern Europe and Russia) as well as the Code of Justinian and Roman law.

The ancient empire of **Ghana** occupied an area that is now known as Northern Senegal and Southern Mauritania. There is no absolute certainty regarding the origin of this empire. Oral history dates the rise of the empire to the seventh century BCE (Before Common Era). Most believe, however, that the date should be placed much later. Many believe that the nomads who were herding animals on the fringes of the desert posed a threat to the early *Soninke* people, who were an agricultural community. In times of drought, it is believed that the nomads raided the agricultural villages for water and places to pasture their herds. To protect themselves, these farming communities formed a loose confederation that eventually became the empire of ancient Ghana.

The empire's economic vitality was determined by geographic location. It was situated midway between the desert, which was a major source of salt, and the gold fields. This location along the trade routes of the camel caravans provided exceptional opportunities for economic development. The caravans brought copper, salt, dried fruit, clothing, and manufactured goods. For these goods, the people of Ghana traded kola nuts, leather products, gold, hides, ivory, and slaves. In addition, the empire collected taxes on every trade item that entered its boundaries. With the revenue from the trade goods tax, the empire supported a government, an army that protected the trade routes and the borders, and maintained the capital and primary market centers.

However, it was control of the gold fields that gave the empire political power and economic prosperity. The location of the gold fields was a carefully guarded secret. By the tenth century, Ghana was very rich and controlled an area about the size of the state of Texas. Demand for this gold sharply increased in the ninth and tenth centuries as the Islamic states of Northern Africa began to mint coins. As the gold trade expanded, so did the empire. The availability of local iron ore enabled the early people of the Ghana kingdom to make more efficient farm implements and effective weapons.

EXAMPLES OF SPECIALIZED TOPICS

In addition to organizing the study of history into time periods and nations, it is often organized into specialized topics, usually related to a particular field of study or endeavor:

- History of Art
- History of Education
- History of Medicine
- History of Library Science
- History of Economics
- History of Aircraft Design
- Social History
- History of any specialized field, science, technology, etc.

0012.03 **Demonstrating knowledge of the importance and lasting influence of diverse people, events, issues, and developments in Georgia, U.S., and world history (e.g., slavery, roots of democracy, the Civil War, women's suffrage, World War I, the Great Depression, World War II, the Cold War, the civil rights movement)**

Please refer to Skill 12.01 for information on the History of Georgia

THE ROOTS OF DEMOCRACY

Please refer to Skill 13.02 for more on this topic

Ancient Greece

The term, *democracy,* comes from the Greek word meaning "popular government" or "government by the people." Although there are a variety of forms of Democracy, the primary criterion includes rule by the people or their elected representatives, basically majority rule. In 510BCE Athens' great general Pericles stated, "It is true that we (Athenians) are called a democracy, for the administration is in the hands of the many...with equal justice to all alike in their private disputes." Ancient Greece, particularly Athens and Sparta, provided a model for democratic principles, some of which are still found in our government today. The Framers of the U.S. Constitution were classically educated men, many of who were very familiar with ancient Greek democratic models.

The Iroquois Confederacy

As mentioned earlier, the Iroquois Confederacy of 1142 united independent Iroquois groups into one nation, allowing autonomy for each groups under a united government; election by both men and women, and voting for treaties and laws, and separate councils for civil, military, and religious affairs. Two Framers of the Constitution, Thomas Jefferson and Ben Franklin, were familiar with this government and recommended it to the colonists at various points in time.

The Magna Carta

The Magna Carta was established in 1215 in an effort to limit the powers of the King of England. Though it was repealed later, it spelled out both the rights and responsibilities of citizens, and specifically stated that the King was subject to the *rule of law.* The Writ of Habeas Corpus was a key element. Its provisions led to the concept of constitutional law, and have directly influenced many constitutions, including that of the United States.

English Bill of Rights

Although the Colonists fought Great Britain for independence, many of their ideas about citizens' rights and freedoms come from British history and government. The English Bill of Rights of 1689 outlined such citizen rights as petition for grievances, bearing arms, and habeas corpus.

The Articles of Confederation

The Articles of Confederation were drafted in 1776 right after the Declaration of Independence, were ratified in 1777, and took effect in 1781. This was the first attempt to provide a system of government for the U.S. The articles established a fairly weak federal government while leaving a lot of autonomy to the loosely organized body of states. Congress had the power to declare war, appoint the military, and coin money. However, states had to approve laws, as well as agree to provide money to Congress. In addition, there was no significant power in the chief executive, so there was no one to oversee the implementation of laws.

OVERVIEW OF KEY ELEMENTS IN US HISTORY IN 19TH AND 20TH CENTURIES

The *Industrial Revolution* (see Skills 12.02 and 13.01 for more) had spread from Great Britain to the United States. Before 1800, most manufacturing activities were done in small shops or in homes. However, starting in the early 1800s, factories with modern machines were built to make it easier to produce goods faster. The eastern part of the country became a major industrial area (although some developed in the west as well). At about the same time, improvements began to be made in building roads, railroads, canals, and steamboats. The increased ease of travel facilitated the westward movement; it also boosted the economy with a faster and cheaper shipment of goods and products. One of the notable innovations of the time was the construction of the Erie Canal, which connected the interior of the country and the Great Lakes with the Hudson River and the coastal port of New York.

Westward expansion occurred for a number of reasons, most notably those reasons founded in economics. Cotton had become the most important crop to most of the people who lived in the southern states. With the invention of power-driven machines, the demand for cotton fibers was greatly increased along with the need for the yarn for spinning and weaving. Eli Whitney's cotton gin made the separation of the seeds from the cotton much more efficient and faster. This, in turn, increased the demand for cotton; more and more farmers became involved in raising and selling cotton plants.

The innovations and developments of better methods of long-distance transportation moved the cotton in greater quantities to textile mills in England (as well as the areas of New England and the Middle Atlantic States in the United States). As prices increased along with increased demand, southern farmers began expanding by clearing increasingly more land to grow cotton. Movement, settlement, and farming headed west to utilize the fertile soils. This, in turn, demanded increased need for a large supply of cheap labor. The system of slavery expanded, both in numbers and in the movement to lands "west" of the South.

Cotton farmers and slave owners were not the only ones heading west. Many individuals in other fields of economic endeavor also began the migration: trappers, miners, merchants, and ranchers were among those seeking their fortunes. The Lewis and Clark expedition stimulated the westward push. Fur companies hired men, known as "Mountain Men," to go westward, searching for animal pelts to supply the market and meet the demands of the East and Europe. These men, in their own way, explored and discovered the many passes and trails that would eventually be used by settlers in their trek to the west. The California Gold Rush also had a very large influence on the westward movement.

In the American Southwest, expansion also took place.. Spain had claimed this area since the 1540s, had spread northward from Mexico City and, in the 1700s, had established missions, forts, villages, towns, and very large ranches. After the purchase of the *Louisiana Territory in 1803*, Americans began moving into Spanish territory. A few hundred American families in what is now Texas were allowed to live there but had to agree to become loyal subjects to Spain. In 1821, Mexico successfully revolted against Spanish rule, won independence, and chose to be more tolerant toward the American settlers and traders. The Mexican government encouraged and allowed extensive trade and settlement, especially in Texas. Many of the new settlers were Southerners who brought their slaves with them. Slavery was outlawed in Mexico and was technically illegal in Texas; however, the Mexican government adopted a system of "looking the other way."

The *Red River Cession* was the next acquisition of land; it came about as part of a treaty with Great Britain in 1818. It included parts of North and South Dakota and Minnesota. In 1819, Florida was ceded to the United States by Spain, along with parts of Alabama, Mississippi, and Louisiana. Texas was annexed in 1845, and after the war with Mexico in 1848, the government paid $15 million for what would become the states of California, Utah, Nevada, and parts of four other states. In 1846, the Oregon Country was ceded to the United States, which effectively extended the western border to the Pacific Ocean. The northern U.S. boundary was established at the 49th parallel. The states of Idaho, Oregon, and Washington were formed from this territory. In 1853, the *Gadsden Purchase* rounded out the present boundary of the forty-eight contiguous states through a payment to Mexico of $10 million for land that makes up the present states of New Mexico and Arizona.

The election of Andrew Jackson as president signaled a swing of the political pendulum from government influence of the wealthy, aristocratic Easterners to the interests of the Western farmers and pioneers—a time also known as the era of the "common man." Jacksonian democracy was a policy of equal political power for all. Many of his policies dealt with making changes to policies created after the War of 1812, when Henry Clay and supporters favored economic measures that came to be known as the *American System*. This system involved creating tariffs that protected American farmers and manufacturers from having to compete with foreign products, stimulating industrial growth, and increasing employment opportunities. The goal was that with more people working, more farm products would be consumed, prosperous farmers would be able to buy more manufactured goods, and the additional monies from tariffs would make it possible for the government to make the needed internal improvements. To get this going, Congress not only passed a high tariff in 1816, but it also chartered a second Bank of the United States. Upon becoming president, Jackson fought to get rid of the bank.

Many *social reform movements* began during this period, including those dealing with education, women's rights, working conditions, temperance, prisons, and insane asylums. Among the most intense and controversial was the abolitionists' efforts to end slavery, an effort that alienated and split the country, hardening the Southern defense of slavery and leading to four years of bloody civil war. The abolitionist movement had political fallout, affecting the admittance of states into the Union and the government's continued efforts to keep a balance between the total number of free and slave states. Congressional legislation after 1820 reflected this.

Robert Fulton's "*Clermont*," the first commercially successful steamboat, led the way in developing an efficient method to ship goods. Later, steam-powered railroads became the biggest rival of the steamboat as a means of shipping, eventually becoming the most important transportation method (also effectively opening the West). With expansion into the interior of the country, the United States became the leading agricultural nation in the world. The hardy pioneer farmers produced a vast surplus of goods, and emphasis went to producing products with a high-sale value. New implements, such as the cotton gin and reaper, improved production. Travel and shipping were greatly assisted in areas not yet touched by railroad or by improved or new roads, such as the National Road in the eastern portions of the United States and the Oregon and Santa Fe Trails in the West.

With better communication and travel, people were exposed to greater numbers of works of literature, art, newspapers, drama, live entertainment, and political rallies. In addition, more information was desired about previously unknown areas of the country, especially the West. The discovery of gold and other mineral wealth resulted in a literal surge of settlers and even greater interest. *Public schools* were established in many of the states, allowing more and more children to become educated. With greater literacy and more participation in literature and the arts, the young nation was developing its own unique culture— becoming less and less influenced by and dependent on Europe.

More industries and factories required more labor. Women, children, and, at times, entire families worked incredibly long hours and days to make ends meet until the 1830s. By that time, factories were getting even larger and employers began hiring the immigrants who were coming to America in huge numbers. Before then, efforts were made to organize a labor movement to improve working conditions and increase wages. It never really caught on until after the Civil War, but the seed had been sown in these early years.

As 1860 began, the nation had extended its borders north, south, and west. Industry and agriculture were flourishing. Although the United States did not involve itself actively in European affairs, the relationship with Great Britain was much improved, and other nations that dealt with the young nation accorded it more respect and admiration. Nevertheless, war was on the horizon. The country was deeply divided along political lines concerning slavery and the election of *Abraham Lincoln.*

Civil War

In 1833, Congress lowered tariffs at a level acceptable to South Carolina. Although President Jackson believed in states' rights, he also firmly believed in and was determined to keep the preservation of the Union. A constitutional crisis had been averted, but sectional divisions were getting deeper and more pronounced. The abolition movement was growing rapidly, becoming an important issue in the North. The slavery issue was at the root of almost every problem, crisis, event, decision, and struggle from then on.

For example, the next major crisis involved Texas. By 1836, Texas was an independent republic with its own constitution. During its fight for independence, Americans were sympathetic to and supportive of the Texans, and some recruited volunteers who crossed into Texas to help the struggle. Problems arose when the state petitioned Congress for statehood. Texas wanted to allow slavery, but Northerners in Congress opposed admission to the Union because it would disrupt the balance between free and slave states and give Southerners in Congress increased influence.

A few years later, Congress took up consideration of new territories between Missouri and present-day Idaho. Again, a heated debate over permitting slavery in these areas flared up. Those opposed to slavery used the *Missouri Compromise* to prove their point by demonstrating that the land being considered for territories had already been designated as banned to slavery. On May 25, 1854, Congress passed the infamous *Kansas-Nebraska Act,* which nullified the provision creating the territories of Kansas and Nebraska. This provided for the people of these two territories to decide for themselves whether or not to permit slavery to exist there. Feelings were so deep and divided that any further attempts to compromise met with little, if any, success.

Political and social turmoil swirled everywhere. Kansas was called "Bleeding Kansas" because of the extreme violence and bloodshed due to the two governments that existed there—one pro-slavery and the other anti-slavery. In 1857, the Supreme Court handed down a decision guaranteed to cause explosions throughout the country. Dred Scott was a slave whose owner had taken him from the slave state of Missouri, to free-state Illinois, into Minnesota Territory (a free territory under the provisions of the Missouri Compromise), and finally back to slave-state Missouri. Abolitionists pursued the dilemma by presenting a court case stating that because Scott had lived in a free state and free territory, he was in actuality a free man. Two lower courts ruled before the Supreme Court became involved, one ruling in favor and one against. The Supreme Court decided that residing in a free state and free territory did not make Scott a free man because Scott (and all other slaves) was not a U.S. citizen or a state citizen of Missouri. Therefore, he did not have the right to sue in state or federal courts.

The Court went a step further and ruled that the old Missouri Compromise was now unconstitutional because Congress did not have the power to prohibit slavery in the Territories.

In 1858, Abraham Lincoln and Stephen A. Douglas were both running for the office of U.S. Senator from Illinois. They participated in a series of debates that directly affected the outcome of the 1860 Presidential election. Douglas, a Democrat, was up for re-election and knew that if he won this race, he had a good chance of becoming President in 1860. Lincoln, a Republican, was not an abolitionist but he believed that slavery was morally wrong; he also firmly believed in and supported the Republican Party principle that slavery must not be allowed to extend any further.

The final straw came with the election of Lincoln to the Presidency the next year. Due to a split in the Democratic Party, there were four candidates from four political parties. With Lincoln receiving a minority of the popular vote and a majority of electoral votes, the Southern states, one by one, voted to secede from the Union, as they had promised they would do if Lincoln and the Republicans were victorious. The die was cast.

South Carolina was the first state to secede from the Union, and the first shots of the war were fired on Fort Sumter in Charleston Harbor. Both sides quickly prepared for war. The North had quite a bit in its favor: a larger population; superiority in finances and transportation facilities; and more manufacturing, agricultural, and natural resources. The North possessed most of the nation's gold, had about 92 percent of all industries, and almost all known supplies of copper, coal, iron, and various other minerals. Most of the nation's railroads were in the North and mid-West, men and supplies could be moved wherever needed, and food could be transported from the farms of the mid-West to workers in the East and soldiers on the battlefields. Trade with nations overseas could go on as usual due to the North's control of the navy and the merchant fleet. The Northern states numbered twenty-four and included western (California and Oregon) and border (Maryland, Delaware, Kentucky, Missouri, and West Virginia) states.

The Southern states numbered eleven and included South Carolina, Georgia, Florida, Alabama, Mississippi, Louisiana, Texas, Virginia, North Carolina, Tennessee, and Arkansas, making up the Confederacy. Although outnumbered in population, the South was completely confident of victory. They knew that all they had to do was to fight a defensive war and protect their own territory; the North had to invade and defeat an area almost the size of Western Europe.

Another advantage of the South was that a number of its best officers had graduated from the U.S. Military Academy at West Point and had had long years of army experience. Many had exercised varying degrees of command in the Indian Wars and the war with Mexico. Men from the South were conditioned to living outdoors and were more familiar with horses and firearms than men from northeastern cities. Since cotton was such an important crop, Southerners felt that British and French textile mills were so dependent on them that they would be forced to help the Confederacy in the war.

The South won decisively until the Battle of Gettysburg, July 1 - 3, 1863. Until Gettysburg, Lincoln's main commanders, McDowell and McClellan, were less than desirable, and Burnside and Hooker were not what was needed. Lee, on the other hand, had many able officers; Stonewall Jackson and J.E.B. Stuart were depended on heavily by him. Jackson died at Chancellorsville and was replaced by Longstreet. Lee decided to invade the North and depended on Stuart and his cavalry to keep him informed of the location of Union troops and their strengths.

The day after Gettysburg, on July 4, Vicksburg, Mississippi surrendered to Union General Ulysses Grant, thus severing the western Confederacy from the eastern part. In September 1863, the Confederacy won its last important victory at Chickamauga. In November, the Union victory at Chattanooga made it possible for Union troops to go into Alabama and Georgia, splitting the eastern Confederacy in two. Lincoln gave Grant command of all Northern armies in March of 1864. Grant led his armies into battles in Virginia while Phil Sheridan and his cavalry did as much damage as possible. In a skirmish at a place called Yellow Tavern, Virginia, Sheridan's and Stuart's forces met; Stuart was fatally wounded.

The Civil War took more American lives than any other war in history, the South losing one-third of its soldiers in battle compared to about one-sixth for the North. More than half of the total deaths were caused by disease and the horrendous conditions of field hospitals. Both sides paid a tremendous economic price, but the South suffered more severely from direct damages. Destruction was pervasive, as towns, farms, trade, industry, and the lives and homes of men, women, and children were all destroyed and an entire Southern way of life was lost.

The South had no voice in the political, social, and cultural affairs of the nation, lessening to a great degree the influence of the more traditional Southern ideals. The Northern Yankee Protestant ideals of hard work, education, and economic freedom became the standard of the United States and helped to influence the development of the nation into a modem, industrial power.

The effects of the Civil War were tremendous. It changed the methods of waging war and has been called the first modern war. It was considered this because of the vast destruction and because it involved the use of all the resources of the opposing sides. There was no way it could have ended other than total defeat and unconditional surrender of one side or the other. It introduced weapons and tactics that, when improved later, were used extensively in the wars of the late 1800s and 1900s. Civil War soldiers were the first to fight in trenches, first to fight under a unified command, and the first to wage a tactic known as the "major cordon defense," a strategy of advance on all fronts. They were also the first to use repeating and breech-loading weapons. Observation balloons were first used during the war along with submarines, ironclad ships, and mines. Telegraphy and railroads were also put to use in the Civil War.

By executive proclamation and constitutional amendment, slavery was officially ended, although deep prejudice and racism remained. The Union was preserved and the states were finally truly united. Sectionalism, especially in the area of politics, remained strong for another 100 years but not to the degree and with the same amount of violence that existed before 1861. It has been noted that the Civil War may have been American democracy's greatest failure because, from 1861 to 1865, calm reason (which is basic to democracy) fell to human passion. Yet, democracy did survive.

The victory of the North established that no state has the right to end or leave the Union. Because of this unity, the United States became a major global power. It is important to remember that Lincoln never proposed to punish the South. He was mostly concerned with restoring the South to the Union in a program that was flexible and practical rather than rigid and unbending. In fact, he never really felt that the states had succeeded in leaving the Union, but that they had left the 'family circle" for a short time.

Economic Upheavals

Between the growing economies, the westward expansion of the population, and improvements in travel and mass communication, the federal government did face periodic financial depressions. Contributing to these downward spirals were land speculations, the availability and soundness of money and currency, failed banks, failing businesses, and unemployment. Sometimes, conditions outside the nation would help to trigger the problems; at other times, domestic politics and presidential elections did.

The Great Depression was the sharpest decline of the American and world economies in the twentieth century. It began with the American stock market crash of 1929. A deflationary spiral caused prices and wages to decline, and those who were in debt face bankruptcy. Unemployment rose to 25% while industrial production fell by 45%. Bank failures were common. The Hoover administration attempted to exclude foreign competition by raising tariffs, but the result was foreign retaliation and decline of US exports. In the presidential election of 1932, Hoover was defeated overwhelmingly by Franklin D. Roosevelt. The new administration's recovery program, the New Deal, provided relief and employment programs. It also extended the role of the federal government into agriculture (Agricultural Adjustment Act), labor relations (National Labor Relations Act), and social security (Social Security Act). Although the economy showed some growth as a result, full employment did not return until the federal government began spending enormous amounts on preparation for and participation in World War II.

Twentieth Century Wars[SAW49]

World War I broke out among European nations in 1914. The major participants were the Central Powers (Germany, Austria-Hungary, and Turkey), opposing the Allied Powers (the United Kingdom, France, and Russia). The United States, following its tradition of noninterference in European affairs, and President Woodrow Wilson was reelected in 1916 on a pledge of neutrality. American public opinion generally favored the Allied Powers. Two incidents led to American involvement: the Zimmermann Telegram of 1917, by which Germany attempted to enlist Mexico as an ally to invade the US, and Germany's decision to conduct unrestricted submarine warfare against neutral shipping to the Allies. At Wilson's request, the US declared war on April 6, 1917.

Some of the domestic effects of the war were hostility to German-Americans, pacifists, and leftists who opposed the war. Under the Espionage Act of 1917 and the Sedition Act of 1918, individuals were harshly punished for expressing opinions that previously had been tolerated. The addition of American forces provided the boost that the Allied Powers needed to defeat the Central Powers. Wilson fought for establishment of the League of Nations to preserve world peace, but the Senate rejected US membership in it.

World War II: After the first World War, America returned to an isolationist stance and tried to follow a policy of non-intervention in foreign affairs. However, this isolationist mood was given a shocking and lasting blow in 1941 with the Japanese attack on Pearl Harbor. The nation arose and forcefully entered the international arena as never before. Declaring itself "the arsenal of democracy," it entered the Second World War and emerged not only victorious, but also as the strongest power on the earth. From that point on, the nation would have a permanent and leading place in world affairs.

In the aftermath of World War II, with the Soviet Union having emerged as the second strongest power on Earth, the United States embarked on a policy known as "Containment" of the communist menace. This involved what came to be known as the "Marshall Plan" and the "Truman Doctrine." The Marshall Plan involved the economic aid that was sent to Europe in the aftermath of the war; it aimed at preventing the spread of communism. To that end, the United States devoted an increasingly large share of its foreign policy making, diplomacy, and economic and military might to combat it.

The Truman Doctrine offered military aid to those countries that were in danger of communist upheaval. This led to the era known as the *Cold War*, in which the United States took the lead (accompanied by the Western European nations) against the Soviet Union and the Eastern Bloc countries. It was also at this time that the United States finally gave up on George Washington's advice against "European entanglements" and joined the North Atlantic Treaty Organization (NATO). This was formed in 1949 and was comprised of the United States and several Western European nations for the purposes of opposing communist aggression.

The United Nations was also formed at this time (1945) to replace the defunct League of Nations for the purposes of ensuring world peace. Even with American involvement, this organization would prove largely ineffective in maintaining world peace. In the 1950s, the United States embarked on what was called the "Eisenhower Doctrine," named after the then president, Dwight D. Eisenhower. This policy aimed at trying to maintain peace in a troubled area of the world, the Middle East. However, unlike the Truman Doctrine in Europe, it would have little success.

The United States became involved in a number of world conflicts in the ensuing years. At the core, each was a struggle against communist expansion. Among these were the *Korean War* (1950-1953), *the Vietnam War* (1965-1975), and various continuing entanglements in Central and South America and the Middle East. By the early 1970s, under the leadership of then Secretary of State Henry Kissinger, the United States and its allies embarked on a policy that came to be known as "Détente." This was aimed at easing the tensions between the United States and its allies as well as between the Soviet Union and its allies.

By the 1980s, the United States embarked on what some saw as a renewal of the Cold War. This was owed to the fact that the United States was becoming more involved in trying to prevent communist insurgency in Central America. A massive expansion of its armed forces and the development of space-based weapons systems were undertaken at this time. As this occurred, the Soviet Union, with a failing economic system and a risky adventure in Afghanistan, found itself unable to compete. By 1989, events had come to a head; they ended with the breakdown of the Communist Bloc, the virtual end of the monolithic Soviet Union, and the collapse of the communist system by the early 1990s.

Women's Suffrage[SAW50]

The term *women's suffrage* refers to the struggle of women to gain the right to vote and to acquire rights equal to those of men. During U.S. Colonial times, only white men who owned property could vote. The issue of women's rights began as soon as planning for the new U.S. government did. In 1176, Abigail Adams wrote her husband, John Adams as he met with other Founding Fathers at the Continental Congress, asking him and the other "gentlemen" to "remember the ladies" as they drew up guidelines for the new government. In spite of this request, the Declaration of Independence states only that "all men are created equal." It was some years before any organized movement to correct this omission began.

The roots of the women's suffrage movement lie in both educational and political movements of the time. In the early to mid 1800's women were becoming better educated. In 1821 the Troy Female Seminary, a fully funded school for girls, opened, followed by the first coed college (Oberlin College) in 1833, and Mount Holyoke College in 1837. As more women became educated, they demanded more rights.

Political and social movements demanding rights for African Americans also influenced the origins of women's suffrage. Famous Underground Railroad Conductor, Harriet Tubman not only led black slaves to freedom for more than a decade (1849-1860), she also fought for women's rights. In 1851 the equally famous Sojourner Truth made her famous "Ain't I a Woman" speech and continued to press for women's right to vote. Other leaders in the anti-slavery and Black rights movement also supported women's rights. In 1870, Black men were granted the vote, further encouraging the women's suffrage movement.

The Seneca Fall Convention of 1848 is generally seen as the formal start of the women's suffrage movement. This Convention, called by Cady Stanton, Lucretia Mott, Martha C. Wright, and May Ann McClintock, met in Seneca Falls, NY in July of 1848 and produced a *Declaration of Principles* similar to the *Declaration of Independence*. It began with the statement that "all men and women are created equal..." and demanded the rights of women to vote, be educated, teach, and earn a living independently. There followed years of struggle against fierce, often violent opposition from both men and women in the United States. Women (and men who supported the movement) were jailed, beaten, and killed. At one point, women involved in a hunger strike to protest their lack of rights were force fed in jails. Such treatment, along with the addition of the Women's Christian Temperance Union (WCTU-a women's organization opposed to alcohol) served to lend both support the movement and garner support from outside agencies.

As support for women's rights increased, some states began extending voting rights to women. Wyoming was the first. Having extended full voting rights to women when it was a territory in 1869, it came into the Union in 1890 as the first state with that right enshrined in its constitution. It was followed by other states, including Colorado (1893), Utah and Idaho (1896), Washington (1910),and California (1911). Prior to the passing of the 19th Amendment, more than half the states had given women the vote within the state.

The final push for women's right to vote was provided by the work of women supporting the war effort in WWI. Finally, a modified version of the amendment first introduced in Congress in 1878, was passed: the 19th Amendment gave women the right to vote.

Diverse Populations in the United States

For over four centuries tens of millions of people have been coming to what is now the U.S. from countries all over the world. The impact of the breadth of their diversity alone is incalculable. Their individual and group contributions have literally made the United States what it is today. Immigrants came (and are still coming) from virtually every part of the globe. They had German, French, Spanish, Polish, Irish, Italian, Dutch, English, Asian, Scandinavian, and African backgrounds, cultures, and languages. The flow of immigrants was relatively slow until the 1820's, but from 1820 to 1880, fifteen million immigrants arrived in the U.S.

This influx continues today. As of 2006, the USA has more legal immigrants as permanent residents than any other country in the world. In 2008 alone, a record 1,046,539 people became naturalized citizens of the U.S. These diverse groups of people provide a wide range of ideas and contributions to the American way of life. The diversity of these groups is so great there is not room to mention more than a tiny fraction of them here.

African Americans: Not all the people who came to this country from other places came willingly. The slave trade brought many against their will, but both before and after their emancipation, they helped build this country. For example, as African Americans left the rural South and migrated to the North in search of opportunities, many settled in Harlem in New York City. By the 1920s, Harlem had become a center of life and activity for people of color. The music, art, and literature of this community gave birth to a cultural movement known as the *Harlem Renaissance*. The artistic expressions that emerged from this community in the 1920s and 1930s celebrated the Black experience, Black traditions, and the voices of Black America. Major writers and works of this movement included: Langston Hughes (The Weary Blues), Nella Larsen (Passing), Zora Neale Hurston (Their Eyes Were Watching God), Claude McKay, Countee Cullen, and Jean Toomer.

Hispanic Americans have contributed to American life and culture since before the Civil War. Hispanics have distinguished themselves in every area of society and culture. Mexicans taught Californians to pan for gold and introduced the technique of using mercury to separate silver from worthless ores. Six state names are of Hispanic origin.

Native Americans have made major contributions to the development of the nation and have been contributors, either directly or indirectly, in almost every area of political and cultural life. In the early years of European settlement, Native Americans were both teachers and neighbors. Even during periods of extermination and relocation, their influence was profound. Native American support through Navajo code talkers in WWII was a key component in eventual US victory.

Numerous conflicts, often called the *Indian Wars*, broke out between the U.S. army and many different Native peoples during the nineteenth century. Many treaties were signed with the various tribes, but most were broken by the government for a variety of reasons. Two of the most notable battles were the Battle of Little Bighorn in 1876, in which the Native people defeated General Custer and his forces, and the massacre of Native Americans in 1890 at Wounded Knee. In 1876, the U.S. government ordered all surviving Native Americans to move to reservations.

Asian Americans, particularly in the West and in large cities, have made significant contributions despite immigration bans, mistreatment, and confinement. Asians were particularly important in constructing the trans-continental railroad, mining metals, and providing other kinds of labor and services.

U.S. Civil Rights

The Civil Rights Movement is a long and complex series of events involving a great many people from all walks of life and it has been critical to fundamental changes in the way American society works. In many ways it began with the anti-slavery movement and is still going on today. A very brief list of some of the most influential events is provided here. It should be noted that although the civil rights struggle focused on the rights of African Americans, its results had a profound impact on members of all minorities, including not only ethnic minorities, but Americans with disabilities, students with special needs, and the gay and lesbian community.

1948: President Truman signs the Executive order 9981 requiring equality of treatment and opportunity for everyone in the armed forces regardless of race.

1954: In landmark legislation, **Brown v. Board of Education of Topeka, Kansas**, the Supreme Court ruled unanimously that school segregation was unconstitutional.

1955: NAACP member, Rosa Parks was arrested for refusing to give up her seat on a public bus for a white passenger in Montgomery, Alabama. In response, the Montgomery community (both Blacks and Whites) rallied together for a bus boycott that lasted for more than a year, until the buses were desegregated in December of 1956.

1957: The *Southern Christian Leadership Conference* was formed by Rev. Martin Luther King, Jr., John Duffy, Rev. C. K. Steele, Rev. T. J. Jemison, Rev. Fred Shuttlesworth, Ella Baker, A. Philip Randolph, Bayard Rustin, and Stanley Levison and began providing training and assistance to local efforts to fight segregation. Non-violence was its central doctrine as well as its major method of fighting segregation and racism.

1960's: This decade was characterized by widespread civil rights activities and conflicts. Student volunteers crisscrossed the country soliciting support for various civil rights issues. "Freedom Riders" volunteered to test bus segregation on lines throughout the country by trying to ride interstate buses with white passengers. Many protest marches, sit-ins, and demonstrations were held throughout the nation. Martin Luther King, himself was jailed in 1962 and wrote his famous *Letter From Birmingham jail.* 200,000 people marched on Washington in 1963 and heard his "I Have a Dream" speech. Black protesters, civil rights workers (both Black and White), and church going children were murdered and these events fueled further conflict.

In **1965** Congress passed the Voting Rights Act, making it easier for Blacks in the South (who still did not have the de facto right to vote) to register to vote. The same year saw race riots in Los Angeles and Affirmative Action Legislation signed by President Johnson.

In **1967** the Supreme Court ruled that prohibiting interracial marriage was unconstitutional and the 16 states that still forbade interracial marriage had to drop those laws.

1967: Martin Luther King, Jr. was assassinated by James Earl Ray, a career criminal and committed racist.

In **1968** President Johnson signed the Civil Rights Act of 1968, which prohibited discrimination in a range of business and housing areas.

1988: Congress (overriding President Reagan's veto) passes the Civil Rights Restoration Act and extends anti-discrimination laws to private enterprise.

2003: Edgar Ray Lillen, the organizer of the *Mississippi Civil Rights Murders* of 1964 was finally convicted (of manslaughter) in the killing of two white and one black civil rights workers. It was the 41st anniversary of the murders.

2008: On November 4, Barack Obama was elected President of the United States.

OBJECTIVE 0013 UNDERSTAND IMPORTANT CONCEPTS AND METHODS OF INQUIRY RELATED TO GEOGRAPHY, U.S. GOVERNMENT AND CIVICS, AND ECONOMICS.

0013.01   Applying knowledge of basic concepts of geography (e.g., location, movement of people, interaction among peoples); major physical and human-constructed features of the earth; the interactions between physical systems and human systems (e.g., economic, cultural, political); and applying knowledge of maps (e.g., political, physical, topographic, resource), globes, and other geographic tools (e.g., compass rose, legend, map scale)

Geography involves studying location and how living things and the earth's features are distributed. It includes where animals, people, and plants live as well as the effects of their relationships with earth's physical features. Geographers also explore the locations of earth's features, how they got there, and why they are so important.

Geographical studies tend to be divided into:

- **Regional**: Elements and characteristics of a place or region
- **Spatial Analysis**: The distribution of natural and human features worldwide
- **Physical**: Earth's physical features, what creates and changes them, and their relationships to each other as well as to human activities
- **Human-Land Relationships**: Human activity patterns and how they relate to the environment including political, cultural, historical, urban, and social geographical fields of study

As with any field of study, there are a variety of ways of organizing the topics studied in the discipline. In geography there are usually said to be either five or six *themes,* some of which may overlap:

Location: This includes relative and absolute location. A relative location refers to the surrounding geography, such as "on the banks of the Mississippi River," and absolute location refers to a specific point, such as 41 degrees North latitude, 90 degrees West longitude, or 123 Main Street. Map study (below) is critical to this theme.

Spatial Organization: This is a description of how things are grouped in a given space. In geographical terms, this can describe people, places, and environments anywhere and everywhere on Earth. The most basic form of spatial organization for people is where they live. This branch of geography involves studying the relationship between where people live and the topography (physical features) of the location.

An example of this theme would include study of the spatial distribution of water and its relationship to human settlement and civilization. The vast majority of people live near other people, in villages, towns, cities, or settlements. Oftentimes, these people live near others in order to take advantage of the goods and services that naturally arise from cooperation.

Villages, towns, cities, and settlements are, to varying degrees, near bodies of water. Water is a staple of survival for every person on the planet, is a good source of energy for factories and other industries, and is a form of transportation for people and goods. For example, in a city, where are the factories and heavy industry buildings? Are they near airports or train stations? Are they on the edge of town, near major roads? What about housing developments? Are they near these industries, or are they far away? Where are the other industry buildings? Where are the schools and hospitals and parks? What about the police and fire stations? How close are homes to each of these things? Towns, and especially cities, are routinely organized into neighborhoods so that each house or home is near to most things that its residents might need on a regular basis. This means that large cities have multiple schools, hospitals, grocery stores, fire stations, etc.

Other studies related to this theme might include the distribution of natural resources and their relationship to economic needs of communities.

Place: A place has both human and physical characteristics. Physical characteristics include features such as mountains, rivers, deserts, etc. Human characteristics might include demographic variables such as size, growth, age, various vital statistics. Places can be described in terms of these characteristics, and in terms of the interaction of these sets of characteristics. For example, what is the relationship between mountain characteristics such as altitude and climate and the size or density of the human population, and so forth.

Human-Environmental Interaction: The theme of human-environmental interaction has three main concepts: humans depend on the environment (for food, water, and raw materials), humans adapt to the environment (wearing warm clothing in a cold climate), and humans modify the environment (planting trees to block a prevailing wind). The latter (ways humans modify the environment) is a major focus of modern geographic study. Human interaction with the environment can change geographic variables in significant ways, which in turn affects and changes human demographics. Humans cut down rain forests, producing a landscape more seriously affected by erosion; humans build the Eerie or Panama Canal, affecting movement of people and supplies; humans build dams, restructuring habitats; humans produce greenhouse gases that change the climate, and so forth.

Movement: The theme of movement includes movement of populations, products, or ideas, and how this movement is affected by topography and other geographic variables, as well as how that movement affects topography. It covers how humans interact with one another through trade, communications, emigration, and other forms of contact. An example of this area is the study of the impact of the Mountains of the Hindu Kush on the campaigns of Alexander the Great, or the expansion of the British Empire due to their mastery of seafaring skills.

Region: A region is an area that has some kind of unifying characteristic, such as a common language, a common government, or common topographical features that powerfully impact life in the area. There are three main types of regions: **formal regions** are areas defined by actual political boundaries, such as a city, county, or state; **functional regions** are defined by a common function, such as the area covered by a telephone service; and **vernacular regions** are less formally defined areas that are formed by people's perceptions (e.g., the Middle East or the South).

Sometimes one or more of these themes are treated jointly, but most are addressed in any geography curriculum.

More on **Human Geography: Interactions between Physical Environmental Systems and Human Systems**

One way to describe where people live is by the **topography** around them. The vast majority of people on the planet live in areas that are very hospitable. It is true that people live in the Himalayas and in the Sahara, but the populations in those areas are very small when compared to the plains of China, India, Europe, and the United States. People naturally want to live where they won't have to work really hard just to survive, and world population patterns reflect this. However, it is important to remember that these patterns of human distribution took many thousands of years to develop.

Initially, human communities subsisted as gatherers collecting berries, leaves, and other food items. With the invention of tools, it became possible for people to dig for roots, hunt small animals, and catch fish from rivers and oceans. Humans observed their environments and eventually learned to plant seeds and harvest crops. As people migrated to areas in which game and fertile soil were abundant, communities began to develop.

As habitats attracted larger numbers of people, environments became crowded and there was competition for resources (See Skill 10.03). The concept of dividing labor and sharing food began to be realized in more heavily populated areas. Some groups of people focused on growing crops, while others concentrated on hunting. Individual experiences led to the development of skills and of knowledge that made the work easier. Farmers began to develop new plant species, and hunters began to protect animal species from other predators for their own use. This ability to manage the environment led people to settle down and to guard and manage their resources.

Camps soon became villages, and villages became year-round settlements. Animals were domesticated and gathered into herds that met the needs of the village. Along with settled life came a decrease in the need to "travel light"; pottery was developed for storing and cooking food.

By 8000 BCE, civilization was beginning to evolve in these villages. Agriculture was developed for the production of grain crops, which led to a decreased reliance on wild plants. Domesticating animals for various purposes decreased the need to hunt wild game. Life became more settled. It was then possible to turn attention to such matters as managing water supplies, producing tools, and making cloth.

From here, there was an increase in both social interaction and the opportunity to reflect upon existence. Mythologies arose alongside various kinds of belief systems. Rituals that re-enacted the mythologies that gave meaning to life were developed.

As farming and animal husbandry skills increased, the dependence upon wild game and food gathering declined. With this change came the realization that a larger number of people could be supported on the produce of farming and animal husbandry.

Two things seem to have come together to produce *cultures* and *civilizations*: a society based on agriculture, and centers of the community with literate social and religious structures. The members of the community hierarchies began to manage water supply and irrigation, develop ritual and religious life, and exert their own right to use a portion of the goods produced by the community for their own subsistence in return for their management.

Sharpened skills, the development of more sophisticated tools, commerce with other communities, increasing knowledge of their environment, greater resources available to them, responses to the needs to share an ordered community life, and the protection of their possessions from outsiders led to further division of labor and community development.

As trade routes developed and travel between cities became easier, trade led to specialization. Trade enables a people to obtain the goods they desire in exchange for the goods they are able to produce. This, in turn, leads to increased attention to refinements of technique and the sharing of ideas. As each community learned the value of the goods they produced and improved its ability to produce the goods in greater quantity, industry was born. These concepts continue to prevail in the economic world of today.

The **Agricultural Revolution** (See Skill 12.02 for details) initiated by the invention of the plow, led to a thorough transformation of human society by making large-scale agricultural production possible and facilitating the development of agrarian societies

The **Industrial Revolution** of the eighteenth and nineteenth centuries resulted in even greater changes in human civilization, and its geographic context, as it created opportunities for trade, increased production, and the exchange of ideas and knowledge. (See Skill 12.02 for more details).

MAPS

Physical locations of the earth's surface features include the four major hemispheres and the parts of the earth's continents in them. Political locations are the political divisions, if any, within each continent. Both physical and political locations are precisely determined in two ways: 1) surveying is done to determine boundary lines and distance from other features, and 2) exact locations are determined by imaginary lines of **latitude** (parallels) and **longitude** (meridians). The intersection of these lines at right angles forms a grid, making it possible to pinpoint an exact location of any place using two grid coordinates.

The process of putting the features of the earth onto a flat surface is called **projection**. All maps are really map projections. There are many different types—each one deals in a different way with the problem of distortion. All flat projections or maps are distorted, of course, because the Earth is NOT flat. Map projections are made in a number of ways; some, for example, are done using complicated mathematics. However, the basic ideas behind map projections can be understood by looking at the three most common types:

Cylindrical Projections - These are done by taking a cylinder of paper and wrapping it around a globe. A light is used to project the globe's features onto the paper. Distortion is least where the paper touches the globe. For example, suppose that the paper was wrapped so that it touched the globe at the equator, the map from this projection would have just a little distortion near the equator. However, in moving north or south of the equator, the distortion would increase. In general, small objects or objects near the Equator are accurately sized, but the size of large objects are more and more distorted as you get further from the Equator. The accuracy of direction, however, is preserved, so this projection is very useful to sailors and those trying to get somewhere. Most world maps hanging in classrooms are Mercator Projections. The best known and most widely used cylindrical projection is the

Mercator projection - It was first developed in 1569 by Gerardus Mercator, a Flemish mapmaker.

Conical Projections - The name for these maps comes from the fact that the projection is made onto a cone of paper. The cone is made so that it touches a globe at the base of the cone only. It can also be made so that it cuts through part of the globe in two different places. Again, there is the least distortion where the paper touches the globe. If the cone touches at two different points, there is some distortion at both of them. Conical projections are most often used to map areas in the middle latitudes. Maps of the United States are most often conical projections (because most of the country lies within the middle latitudes).

Flat-Plane Projections - These are made with a flat piece of paper. It touches the globe at one point only. Areas near this point show little distortion. Flat-plane projections are often used to show the areas of the north and south poles. One such flat projection is called a **Gnomonic Projection**. On this kind of map, all meridians appear as straight lines. Gnomonic projections are useful because any straight line drawn between points on it forms a **Great-Circle Route**.

Great-Circle Routes can best be described by thinking of a globe. When using a globe, the shortest route between two points can be found by simply stretching a string from one point to the other. However, if the string were extended in reality, so that it took into effect the globe's curvature, it would then make a great-circle. A great-circle is any circle that cuts a sphere (or spheroid), such as the globe, into two equal parts. Because of distortion, most maps do not show great-circle routes as straight lines. Gnomonic projections, however, do show the shortest distance between the two places as a straight line; because of this, they are valuable for navigation. They are also called Great-Circle Sailing Maps.

Reading a Map

To properly analyze a given map, it is important to be familiar with the various parts and symbols that most modern maps use. For the most part, this is standardized and there are a number of common features:

Title - All maps should have a title, just like all books should. The title tells you what information is to be found on the map: e.g., *Population Density of the United States,* or *Topographical Map of Chile*, or *Atlanta City Road Map.*

Legend - Most maps have a legend. The legend tells the reader about the various symbols that are used on that particular map as well as what the symbols represent. (It is also called a **map key**.)

Grid - A grid is a series of lines that are used to find exact places and locations on the map. There are several different kinds of grid systems in use; however, most maps do use the longitude and latitude system, known as the *Geographic Grid System*.

Directions - Most maps have some directional system to show which way the map is being presented. Usually, a small compass will be present with arrows showing the four cardinal directions: north, south, east, and west. A more elaborate compass will show intermediate directions (e.g., northeast, southwest) as well. This is called a *compass rose*. Direction is usually measured relative to the location of the north or South Pole. Directions determined from these locations are said to be relative to "true north" or "true south." The magnetic poles can also be used to measure direction. However, these points on the earth are located in spatially different spots from the geographic north and south poles. The north magnetic pole is located near 78.3° north, 104.0° west. In the southern hemisphere, the south magnetic pole is located in or near Antarctica and has a geographical location near 65° south, 139° east. However, the magnetic poles are not fixed; over time, they shift their spatial position and move 10-25 miles per year.

Scale - This is used to show the relationship between a unit of measurement on the map versus the real world measurement on the earth. Maps are drawn to many different scales. Some maps show a lot of detail for a small area. Others show a greater span of distance. It is important to be cognizant of the scale. For example, the scale might be something like 1 inch = 10 miles for a small area or, for a map showing the whole world; it might have a scale in which 1 inch = 1,000 miles.

Maps have four main properties. They are:

1) The size of the areas shown on the map
2) The shapes of the areas
3) Consistent scales
4) Straight line directions

A map can be drawn so that it is correct in one or more of these properties. No map can be correct in all of them.

Equal Areas - One property that maps often have is that of equal areas. In an equal area map, the meridians and parallels are drawn so that the areas shown have the same proportions as they do on the earth. For example, Greenland is about 118th the size of South America; thus, it will show as 118th the size on an equal area map. The **Mercator projection** is an example of a map that does not have equal areas. In it, Greenland appears to be about the same size of South America. This is because the distortion is worst at the poles (see above), and Greenland lies near the North Pole.

Conformal Maps Conformal Maps show features such as land and water in shapes that are as close as possible their true shapes. There are no maps that can show very large areas of the earth in their exact shapes; only globes can do that.. The United States is often shown by a Lambert Conformal Conic Projection Map.

Consistent Scales - Many maps attempt to use the same scale on all parts of the map. Generally, this is easier when maps show a relatively small part of the earth's surface. For example, a map of just Florida could be a Consistent Scale Map. Maps showing large areas are typically not Consistent Scale Maps. This is due to distortion. Often, large area maps will have two scales noted in the key. One scale, for example, might be accurate to measure distances between points along the equator. Another might be then used to measure distances between the north and south poles.

Relief Maps - Maps showing physical features often try to show information about the elevation or **relief** of the land. **Elevation** is the distance above or below the sea level. The elevation is usually shown with colors; for instance, all areas on a map that are at a certain level may be shown in the same color.

Relief Maps specifically show the shape of the land surface: flat, rugged, or steep. They usually give more detail than simply showing the overall elevation of the land's surface. Land shape is also sometimes shown with colors, but another way to show this type of relief is by using **contour lines**. These lines connect all points of a land surface that are the same height surrounding the particular area of land.

Thematic Maps - These are used to show more specific information, often on a single theme or topic. Thematic Maps show the distribution or amount of something over a certain given area. This can include things such as population density, climate, economic information, cultural, political information, etc.

Other Geographic Tools

An **atlas** is a collection of maps (usually bound into a book) that contain geographic features, political boundaries, and perhaps social, religious, and economic statistics. Atlases can be found at most libraries, but they are also widely available on the Internet. The United States Library of Congress holds more than 53,000 atlases; it is most likely the largest and most comprehensive collection in the world.

Surveying : the American Congress on Surveying and Mapping (ACSM), defines surveying as "the science and art of making all essential measurements to determine the relative position of points and/or physical and cultural details above, on, or beneath the surface of the Earth, and to depict them in a usable form, or to establish the position of points and/or details." This skill and the equipment used in its employ are critical to drawing accurate and precise maps.

Illustrations: Many maps use illustrations of various sorts to make their theme or topic clearer and easier to read. Maps depicting natural resources, for example, might use pictures of trees for lumber, cows for beef, etc., inserted onto the map at the relevant locations. Such illustrations can make a map easier to read at a glance.

Aerial photography: Aerial photography is extremely useful in cartography (drawing of maps). Prior to the invention of modern aircraft, hot air balloons were used to provide an aerial view of the land to be mapped. Modern cartography often begins with an aerial photograph and uses computer programs to produce a map.

Opisometer: This is a mechanical device used to measure curvilinear map distances. It uses a small rotating wheel that records the distance traveled. The recorded distance is measured by this device either in centimeters or inches.

0013.02   **Demonstrating knowledge of the functions of government and the basic principles of the U.S. government as a republic; and the roles and interrelationships of national, state, and local governments in the United States**

Many of the core values in the U.S. democratic system can be found in the opening words of the Declaration of Independence. This includes the important beliefs in equality and the rights of citizens to "life, liberty and the pursuit of happiness."

The Declaration was a condemnation of the British King's tyrannical government, and these words emphasized the American colonists' belief that a government received its authority to rule from the people, and its function should not be to suppress the governed, but to protect the rights of the governed, including protection from the government itself. These two ideals, popular sovereignty and the rule of law, are basic core values of democracy.

Popular sovereignty grants citizens the ability to directly participate in their own government by voting and running for public office. This ideal is based on a belief of equality that holds that all citizens have an equal right to engage in their own governance. The ideal of equality has changed over the years, as women and non-white citizens were not always allowed to vote or bring suit in court. Now, all U.S. citizens above the age of 18 are allowed to vote. This expansion of rights since the adoption of the Constitution demonstrates an American value of *respect for minority rights*.

The democratic system of election and representation is based on majority rule. In the case of most public elections, the candidate who receives the most votes is awarded the office. Majority rule is also used to pass legislation in Congress. Majority rule is meant to ensure that authority cannot be concentrated in one small group of people.

The *rule of law* is the principle that states that the law applies not only to the governed, but to the government as well. This core value gives authority to the justice system, which grants citizens protection from the government by requiring that any accusation of a crime be proved by the government before a person is punished. This is called *due process,* and it ensures that any accused person will have an opportunity to confront his accusers and provide a defense. Due process follows from the core value of a right to liberty. The government cannot take away a citizen's liberty without reason or without proof. The correlating ideal is also a core value—that someone who does harm to another or breaks a law will receive justice under the democratic system. The ideal of justice holds that a punishment will fit the crime, and that any citizen can appeal to the judicial system if he feels he has been wronged.

Central to the ideal of justice is an expectation that citizens will act in a way that promotes the common good, meaning that they will treat one another with honesty and respect and will exercise self-discipline in their interactions with others. These are among the basic responsibilities of a citizen of a democracy.

National, State, and Local Governments in the United States

Powers delegated to the Federal government:

1. To tax.
2. To borrow and coin money
3. To establish postal service.
4. To grant patents and copyrights.
5. To regulate interstate & foreign commerce.
6. To establish courts.
7. To declare war.
8. To raise and support the armed forces.
9. To govern territories.
10. To define and punish felonies and piracy on the high seas.
11. To fix standards of weights and measures.
12. To conduct foreign affairs.

Powers reserved to the states:

1. To regulate intrastate trade.
2. To establish local governments.
3. To protect general welfare.
4. To protect life and property.
5. To ratify amendments.
6. To conduct elections.
7. To make state and local laws.

Concurrent powers of the Federal government and states.

1. Both Congress and the states may tax.
2. Both may borrow money.
3. Both may charter banks and corporations.
4. Both may establish courts.
5. Both may make and enforce laws.
6. Both may take property for public purposes.
7. Both may spend money to provide for the public welfare.

Implied powers of the Federal government.

1. To establish banks or other corporations to tax, borrow, and regulate commerce.
2. To spend money for roads, schools, health, insurance, etc., to establish post roads, to tax to provide for general welfare and defense, and to regulate commerce.
3. To create military academies to raise and support an armed force.
4. To locate and generate sources of power and sell surplus to dispose of government property, commerce, and war powers.
5. To assist and regulate agriculture to tax and spend for general welfare and to regulate commerce.

0013.03   Recognizing the roles and powers of the executive, legislative, and judicial branches of government; demonstrating knowledge of the Declaration of Independence, the U.S. Constitution, and the Bill of Rights; and identifying the rights and responsibilities of U.S. citizenship

The blueprint for federal government of the United States, including the branches, their powers, their duties, their selection (election or appointment), and the way in which they check and balance each other, as well as basic rights and laws at the federal level are provided by the Constitution of the United States.

Branches of Federal Government

Legislative – Article I of the Constitution established the legislative, or law-making, branch of the government called the Congress. It is made up of two houses, the House of Representatives and the Senate. Voters in all states elect the members who serve in each respective House of Congress. The legislative branch is responsible for making laws, raising and printing money, regulating trade, establishing the postal service and federal courts, approving the president's appointments, declaring war, and supporting the armed forces. The Congress also has the power to change the Constitution itself, and to *impeach* (bring charges against) the president. Charges for impeachment are brought by the House of Representatives, and are then tried in the Senate.

Executive – Article II of the Constitution created the executive branch of the government, headed by the president, who leads the country. This branch recommends new laws and can veto bills passed by the legislative branch. As the chief of state, the president is responsible for carrying out the laws of the country as well as the treaties and declarations of war passed by the legislative branch. The president also appoints federal judges and is commander-in-chief of the military when it is called into service. Other members of the executive branch include the vice-president, also elected, and various cabinet members as the president might appoint: ambassadors, presidential advisors, members of the armed forces, and other appointed and civil servants of government agencies, departments, and bureaus. Though the president appoints them, they must be approved by the legislative branch.

Judicial – Article III of the Constitution established the judicial branch of government headed by the Supreme Court. The Supreme Court has the power to rule that a law passed by the legislature (Federal, state or local), or an act of the executive branch, is illegal and unconstitutional. Citizens, businesses, and government officials can, in an appeal capacity, ask the Supreme Court to review a decision made in a lower court if they believe that the ruling by a judge is unconstitutional. The judicial branch also includes lower federal courts known as federal district courts that have been established by the Congress. These courts try lawbreakers and review cases referred from other courts.

Declaration of Independence

The beginnings of civil liberties and the idea of civil rights in the United States go back to the ideas of the ancient Greeks. This same concept of civil rights was illustrated by the early struggle for civil rights against the British and by the very philosophies that led people to come to the New World in the first place. Religious freedom, political freedom, and the right to live one's life as one sees fit are basic to the American ideal. These were embodied in the ideas expressed in the Declaration of Independence and the Constitution.

The Declaration of Independence was adopted on July 4, 1776. It laid out the reasons and justifications for separating from Britain, but was also used as a founding document to later form the United States of America. It was a joint work created by some of America's most important founding fathers, including John Adams, Benjamin Franklin, Roger Sherman, Robert Livingston, and Thomas Jefferson.

Influences for the Declaration of Independence included the Dutch Oath of Abjuration and philosophies of the Enlightenment period in addition to those of early Greek democratic processes.

U.S. Constitution

The United States Constitution is the supreme law of the United States of America. Its first draft was written in 1787 by the Constitutional Convention in Philadelphia, Pennsylvania. It was adopted on September 17, 1787. (see Skills 12.03 and 13.01 for more).

It is composed of a preamble (a statement of purpose), seven articles, and twenty-seven amendments. The seven articles include information on the following:

Article One: Legislative power   Article Five: Process of Amendments
Article Two: Executive power   Article Six: Federal power
Article Three: Judicial power   Article Seven: Ratification
Article Four: States' powers and limits

Bill Of Rights

The first ten of the twenty-seven amendments to the United States Constitution are known as the Bill of Rights. They outline information on civil liberties and civil rights. They were ratified in 1789. James Madison was credited with writing a majority of them. Part of the purpose of the Bill of Rights was to specifically enumerate certain rights as part of the Constitution, so that these rights would be guaranteed and clear to all:

- **First** Amendment: Freedom of speech, the press, religion, peaceable assembly, and petition the government
- **Second** Amendment: Right to keep and bear arms
- **Third** Amendment: Protection from unwanted quartering of troops in private homes
- **Fourth** Amendment: Protection from unreasonable search and seizure
- **Fifth** Amendment: Guaranteed due process, no double jeopardy, protection from self incrimination, no eminent domain without due cause and reparation
- **Sixth** Amendment: Trial by Jury, rights of the accused, right to confront accuser, right to counsel, etc.
- **Seventh** Amendment: Right to civil trial by jury
- **Eighth** Amendment: Prohibition of excessive bail and cruel or unusual punishment
- **Ninth** Amendment: Protection of other rights not specifically stated in Constitution
- **Tenth** Amendment: Powers reserved to the states and people.

The cause of human rights has been advanced significantly, both in theory and in fact, since the eighteenth century, when these rights were ratified as part of the US Constitution. The concepts of rights of citizens expressed in these amendments have been reflected in a number of significant statements of expanded human rights throughout the world. Such statements have extended and established human rights worldwide.

The Declaration of the Rights of Man and of the Citizen is a document created by the French National Assembly and issued at about the same time and the US Bill of Rights, in 1789. It sets forth the "natural, inalienable and sacred rights of man." It[SAW52] proclaims a number of rights very similar to those in the US Bill of rights, including the right to liberty, property and security, due process, and freedom of the press.

The United Nations Declaration of Universal Human Rights (1948) extends many of these concepts beyond national borders. It opens with these words: "Whereas recognition of the inherent dignity and of the equal and inalienable rights of all members of the human family is the foundation of freedom, justice and peace in the world. Whereas disregard and contempt for human rights have resulted in barbarous acts which have outraged the conscience of mankind, and the advent of a world in which human beings shall enjoy freedom of speech and belief and freedom from fear and want has been proclaimed as the highest aspiration of the common people." It then sets out numerous rights regarding equality before the law, basic freedoms such as speech and religion, right to trial and freedom from arbitrary arrest, and the abolition of slavery worldwide.

The United Nations Convention on the Rights of the Child brings together the rights of children as they are enumerated in other international documents. In this document, those rights are clearly and completely stated, along with the explanation of the guiding principles that define the way society views children. The goal of the document is to clarify the environment that is necessary to enable every human being to develop to his or her full potential.

Responsibilities of U.S. Citizenship

Since the US Constitution is a design for "government by the people," it follows that the people must have certain responsibilities if the government is to function properly[SAW53]. Although those who are Americans by birth do not need to sign a pledge or oath of citizenship, it is assumed that they will carry out their responsibilities as citizens. When immigrants to the United States apply to become citizens, they must take an oath to conscientiously perform the same responsibilities natural born American citizens have:

- Serve on a jury if called upon to do so (can't have a right to a jury trial if there is no jury...)
- Obey the legally established laws of the land
- Pay taxes legally established by Congress
- Defend the country (e.g., register for Selective Service, comply with civilian defense needs)
- Vote one's conscience
- Support the Constitution

0013.04   Recognizing basic economic concepts (e.g., scarcity, supply and demand, needs and wants, opportunity cost, trade) and the purposes and functions of currency, the basic structure of the U.S. economy, and ways in which the U.S. economy relates to and interacts with the economies of other nations

BASIC ECONOMIC CONCEPTS

The fact that resources are scarce is the basis for the existence of economics. Economics is defined as a study of how scarce resources are allocated to satisfy unlimited wants. **Resources** refer to the four factors of production: labor, capital, land, and entrepreneurship. The individual has the right to supply whatever resources he or she wants to the market. The fact that the supply of these resources is finite means that society cannot have as much of everything as it wants. There is a constraint on production and consumption, and on the kinds of goods and services that can be produced and consumed. **Scarcity** means that choices have to be made. If society decides to produce more of one good, this means that there are fewer resources available for the production of other goods.

Assume a society can produce two goods: good A and good B. The society uses resources in the production of each good. If producing one unit of good A results in a reduction of the same amount of resources used to produce three units of good B, then producing one more unit of good A results in a decrease in three units of good B. In effect, one unit of good A "costs" three units of good B. This cost is referred to as opportunity cost. **Opportunity cost** is the value of the sacrificed alternative (the value of what had to be given up in order to have the output of good A). Opportunity cost does not just refer to production. Your opportunity cost of studying with this guide is the value of what you are not doing because you are studying, whether that cost is watching TV, spending time with family, or working. *Every choice has an opportunity cost.*

The **supply curve** represents the selling and production decisions of the seller; it is based on the costs of production. The costs of production of a product are based on the costs of the resources used in its production. The costs of resources are based on the scarcity of the resource. The scarcer a resource is, relatively speaking, the higher its price. A diamond costs more than paper because diamonds are scarcer than paper is. All of these concepts are embodied in the seller's supply curve. The same thing is true on the buying side of the market. The buyer's preferences, tastes, income—all of his buying decisions— are embodied in the **demand curve**. Where the demand and supply curves intersect is where the buying decisions of buyers are equal to the selling decisions of sellers. At this point, the quantity that buyers want to buy at a particular price is equal to the quantity that sellers want to sell at that particular price. When this occurs, the market is in equilibrium.

What happens when there is a change? Suppose a new big oil field is found. Also suppose there is a technology that allows its recovery and refining at a fraction of the present costs. The result is a big increase in the supply of oil at lower costs. When supply and demand curves are shown on a graph, such an increase will be reflected by a rightward shifting oil supply curve. Oil is used as an input into almost all production. Firms now have lower costs. This means that the firm can produce the same amount of output at a lower cost, or they can produce a larger amount of output at the same cost. The result is a rightward shift of the firm's, and therefore, the industry's supply curve. This means that sellers are willing and able to offer for sale larger quantities of output at each price. Assuming buyers' buying decisions stay the same, there is a new market equilibrium, or new point of intersection of the shifted supply curve with the buyers' demand curve. The result is a lower price with a larger quantity of output. The market has achieved a new equilibrium based on the increase in the quantity of a resource. The opposite shift would, of course, occur if the change *reduced* the amount of oil available (been there, done that).

Firms in markets tend to grow over time. If there is a market for the firm's product, it experiences economies of scale (lower per unit costs) as it grows. As firms grow, they tend to become larger relative to the market, and the smaller, more inefficient firms tend to go out of business. Larger firms have more market power and are able to influence their price and output. They can become monopolistic. Government counters this reduction in competition in a market by enacting anti-trust legislation to protect the competitive nature of the market.

THE U.S. ECONOMY AND THE ECONOMIES OF OTHER NATIONS

The **traditional economy** is one based on custom. This term usually describes the situation that exists in many less developed countries, where people tend to do things the way their ancestors did. Since their whole mindset is directed toward tradition, they are typically not very interested in technology, equipment, and new ways of doing things. Technology and equipment are viewed as a threat to the old way and to their traditions; there is usually very little upward mobility. A **market economy** is an economy in which production and price are based on supply and demand.

Capitalism is a market economy based on the private ownership of the means of production. It operates on the basis of free markets, on both the input and output sides. The free markets function to coordinate market activity (see above) and to achieve an efficient allocation of resources. Capitalist economies tend to occur under democratic forms of government because the system is based on competition and individual freedoms.

Laissez-faire capitalism is based on the premise of no government intervention in the economy. According to this approach, the market will eliminate any unemployment or inflation that occurs. Government needs only to provide the framework for the functioning of the economy and to protect private property. The role of financial incentives is crucial, as they result in risk-taking and research and development.

A **command economy** is almost the exact opposite of a market economy. A command economy is based on government ownership of the means of production; it also uses planning to take the place of the market. Instead of the market determining the output mix and the allocation of resources, the bureaucracy fulfills this role by determining the output mix and establishing production targets for the enterprises, which are publicly owned. The result is usually inefficiency. There is little interest in innovation and research because there is no financial reward for the innovator. A command economy tends to occur under an authoritarian form of government because a planning mechanism that replaces the market requires a planning authority to make decisions, reducing any freedom of choice of consumers and workers.

A **mixed economy** uses a combination of markets and planning, with the degree of each varying according to country. The real world can be described as a series of mixed economies, each with varying degrees of planning. The use of markets in a mixed economy results in the greatest efficiency because markets direct resources in and out of industries according to changing profit conditions. However, government is needed to perform various functions. The degree of government involvement in the economy can vary in mixed economies. Government is needed to keep the economy stable during periods of inflation and unemployment.

Most of the *major* economies of the world are mixed economies. They use markets but have different degrees of government involvement in the functioning of the markets and in the provision of public goods. For example, in some countries, health care and education are provided by government and are not a part of the private sector. In the United States, most health care and higher education organizations are private at the expense of the consumer.

The US economy relates to other nations' economies through trade, investment, and foreign aid. The US is the world's largest importer of foreign-made goods and the third-largest exporter. Canada and Mexico are the nation's leading trade partners; with the US, they are members of the North American Free Trade Agreement, which eliminates barriers to trade and investment. Other trading partners are Japan, the United Kingdom, Germany, and China. Investments by Americans in foreign countries provide capital and skills that are not available locally. Foreign investments in the US return some of the dollars that foreigners receive for their exports to the US. Foreign aid helps to reduce poverty, promote development, and strengthen military allies.

Currency is the money that is generally accepted in a particular country or place. Until the nineteenth century, precious metals filled that role nearly exclusively; gold and silver coins circulated, and banks issued notes that could be redeemed for gold or silver. In the nineteenth century, governments entered the picture, setting up central banks that controlled the issuance of paper money. The Federal Reserve System, established in 1913, is the central bank of the United States. Although the members of its Board of Governors are appointed by the President of the US, it can act independently of the legislative and executive branches, using its own judgment concerning the need for money in the banking system. It uses various policies to influence the money supply. It can simply create deposits and invest them in treasury bonds, then sell those bonds and wipe out the deposits. It can regulate the percentage of their deposits the banks must keep as reserve. It can raise or lower the interest rates it charges on loans to banks. The dollar and other currencies are not backed by gold and silver deposits, but by public faith in the banking system.

0013.05 **Identifying the roles and interactions of consumers and producers in the U.S. economy; the functions of private business, banks, and the government in the U.S. economy; and the knowledge and skills necessary to make reasoned and responsible financial decisions as a consumer, producer, saver, and borrower in a market economy**

The U.S. economy consists of the **household** or consumer sector, the **business** sector, and the **government** sector. Households earn their incomes by selling their factors of production in the *input market*. Businesses hire their inputs in the *factor market* and use them to produce *outputs*. Households use their incomes earned in the factor market to purchase the output of businesses. A *factor of production* can be a product or a service. For example, say Mr. Smith earns an income as a plumber. His factor of production is his skill as a plumber. A business, the Atlanta Braves Organization, hires his input to repair the plumbing at the ballpark, thus allowing them to produce an output (a baseball game, or tickets to the game). Other households purchase this output (the tickets to the game). Both households and businesses are active participants in both the input and output market. Households do not spend all of their income; they save some of it in banks. A well-organized, smoothly functioning banking system is required for the operation of the economy.

Sometimes, labor is organized into **labor unions** in the input market. The function of **organized labor** is to help obtain a higher factor income for workers. Organized labor negotiates the work agreement, or contract, for their union members. This collective bargaining agreement is a contract between the worker and the employer; it states the terms and conditions of employment for the length of the contract. It can also establish a procedure for grievances.

Macroeconomics is the study of the functioning of the economy on the national level as well as the functioning of the aggregate units that comprise the national economy. Macroeconomics is concerned with the economy's overall economic performance, or what is called the **Gross Domestic Product** (GDP). The GDP is a measure of the economy's output during a specified time period. Tabulating the economy's output can be measured in two ways, both of which give the same result: the expenditures approach and the incomes approach. Basically, what is spent on the national output by each sector of the economy is equal to what is earned producing the national output by each of the factors of production.

The macroeconomy consists of four broad sectors: *consumers, businesses, government,* and the *foreign* sector. In the expenditures approach, GDP is determined by the amount of spending in each sector. GDP is equal to the consumption expenditures of consumers, plus the investment expenditures of businesses, plus the spending of all three levels of government, plus the net export spending in the foreign sector. It can be determined by the equation below:

$$GDP = C + I + G + (X-M)$$

When the economy is functioning smoothly, the amount of national output produced, or the aggregate supply, is just equal to the amount of national output purchased, or aggregate demand. It is at this point that we have an economy in a period of prosperity without economic instability. However, market economies experience the fluctuations of the business cycle (the ups and downs in the level of economic activity). There are four phases: **boom** (period of prosperity), **recession** (a period of declining GDP and rising unemployment), **trough** (the low point of the recession), and **recovery** (a period of lessening unemployment and rising prices). There are no rules pertaining to the duration or severity of any of the phases.

The phases result in periods of unemployment and periods of inflation. **Inflation** results from too much spending in the economy; it occurs when buyers want to buy more than sellers can produce and bid up prices for the available output. **Unemployment** occurs when there is not enough spending in the economy; sellers have produced more output than buyers are buying, and the result is a surplus situation. Firms faced with surplus merchandise then lower their production levels and lay off workers. The result is unemployment. These are situations that result in government policy actions.

The U.S. economy is based on the concepts of individual freedom of choice and competition. Economic agents are free to pursue their own interests. They can choose their occupation and undertake entrepreneurial ventures. If they are successful, they gain in the form of profits. The profit incentive is very important because people and businesses are willing to take risks for the possibility of gaining profit. The U.S. economy is one of the most successful economies in the world, with the highest total GDP. Like any market economy, it is subject to the business cycle and temporary bouts of inflation and/or unemployment. When they do occur, appropriate policies are typically implemented in time to counteract them.

Private Business, Banks, and the Government in the U.S. Economy

Households, businesses, and government are related through the **circular flow diagram**. They are all integral parts of the macroeconomy, and they contain two markets. The **input market** exists when factor owners sell their factors and employers hire their inputs. The **output market** exists when firms sell the output they produce with their inputs. It is where factors owners spend their incomes on goods and services.

There are two sectors of the macroeconomy: households and businesses. Households sell their factors in the input market and use their income to purchase goods and services in the output market. Therefore, wages, interest, rents, and profits flow from the business sector to the household sector. Because factor incomes are based on the scarcity of the factor as well as the contribution of the factor, there is often an unequal distribution of income; not all factors are equal.

Households that earn their factor incomes in the factor market spend their incomes on goods and services produced by businesses and sold in the output market. Receipts for goods and services flow from households to businesses. The government receives tax payments from households and businesses, and then provides services to businesses and households. Each of these three exchanges of factors is a component of the aggregate sectors of the economy; as such, they all make a contribution to the GDP.

Adding financial institutions to the picture demonstrates how the Federal Reserve implements monetary policy. There are three components of monetary policy: the *reserve ratio, the discount rate, and open market operations*. Changes in any of these three components affect the amount of money in the banking system and thus, the level of spending in the economy. The **reserve ratio** refers to the portion of deposits that banks are required to hold as vault cash or on deposit with the Federal Reserve. The purpose of this reserve ratio is to give the Federal Reserve a way to control the money supply. These funds can't be used for any other purpose. When the Federal Reserve changes the reserve ratio, it changes the money creation and lending ability of the banking system. When the Federal Reserve wants to expand the money supply, it lowers the reserve ratio, leaving banks with more money to loan. This is one aspect of **expansionary** monetary policy. When the reserve ratio is increased, the result is that banks have less money to use for loans, which is considered a form of **contractionary** monetary policy. This type of policy leads to a lower level of spending in the economy.

Another way in which monetary policy is implemented is by changing the discount rate. When banks have temporary cash shortages, they can borrow from the Federal Reserve. The interest rate on the funds they borrow is called the discount rate. Raising and lowering the discount rate is a way of controlling the money supply. Lowering the discount rate encourages banks to borrow from the Federal Reserve, instead of restricting their lending to deal with the temporary cash shortage. By encouraging banks to borrow, their lending ability is increased; this results in a higher level of spending in the economy. Lowering the discount rate is another form of expansionary monetary policy. Discouraging bank lending by raising the discount rate is another form of contractionary monetary policy. In this way, a well-developed banking system is necessary for capital formation and investment purposes.

Responsible Financial Decisions

Economics is the study of how a society allocates its scare resources to satisfy what are basically unlimited and competing wants. Economics can also be defined as a study of the production, consumption, and distribution of goods and services. Both of these definitions are the same. A fundamental fact of economics is that resources are scarce and that wants are infinite. The fact that scarce resources have to satisfy unlimited wants means that choices have to be made, whether the entity is a consumer, producer, saver, or investor. As mentioned in Skill 13.04, if society uses its resources to produce good A, then it doesn't have those resources to produce good B. More of good A means less of good B. Producers must make an informed decision about which products and how much of each to produce.

On the consumption side of the market, consumers buy the goods and services that give them satisfaction, or utility. They want to obtain the most utility they can for their dollar. The quantity of goods and services that consumers are willing and able to purchase at different prices during a given period of time is referred to as demand. Since consumers buy the goods and services that give them satisfaction, this means that, for the most part, they don't buy the goods and services that they don't want or that don't give them satisfaction. Consumers are, in effect, voting for the goods and services that they want with their dollars, or what is called **dollar voting**. Consumers are basically signaling firms about how they want society's scarce resources used with their dollar votes. A good that society wants acquires enough dollar votes for the producer to experience **profits**—a situation in which the firm's revenues exceed the firm's costs. The existence of profits indicates to the firm that it is producing the goods and services that consumers want, and that society's scarce resources are being used in accordance with consumer preferences.

This process through which consumers vote with their dollars is called **consumer sovereignty**. Consumers are directing the allocation of scarce resources in the economy with their dollar spending. Firms, who are in business to earn profit, then hire resources, or inputs, in accordance with consumer preferences. This is the way in which resources are allocated in a market economy, with consumers basing their decisions on the utility or satisfaction they receive from buying goods.

Supply is based on production costs. The supply of a good or service is defined as the quantities of a good or service that a producer is willing and able to sell at different prices during a given period of time. Remember, market equilibrium occurs when the buying decisions of buyers are equal to the selling decision of sellers, or where the demand and supply curves intersect. At this point, the quantity that sellers want to sell at a price is equal to the quantity the buyers want to buy at that same price. This is the market equilibrium price.

The price of an input or output allocates that input or output to those who are willing and able to transact at the market price. Those who can transact at the market price or better are included in the market; those that can't or won't transact at the market price are excluded from the market.

The fundamental characteristics of the U.S. economic system are the uses of competition and markets. Profit and competition all go together in the U.S. economic system. Competition is determined by market structure. Since the cost curves are the same for all the firms, the only difference comes from the revenue side. Each firm maximizes profit by producing at the point where marginal cost equals marginal revenue. The existence of economic profits, an above normal rate of return, attracts capital to an industry and results in expansion.

Whether or not new firms can enter the market depends on barriers to entry. Firms can enter easily in perfect competition, and the expansion will continue until economic profits are eliminated and firms earn a normal rate of return. A **monopoly**, however, exists when there is only one seller of a good or service. The significant barriers to entry in monopoly serve to keep firms out, so the monopolist continues to earn an above normal rate of return. Some firms will be able to enter in monopolistic competition but won't have a monopoly over the existing firm's brand name. The competitiveness of the market structure determines whether new firms or capital can enter in response to profits.

Profit functions as a financial incentive for individuals and firms. The possibility of earning profit is why individuals are willing to undertake entrepreneurial ventures and why firms are willing to spend money on research and development and innovation. Without these kinds of financial incentives, there wouldn't be new product development or technological advancement.

Savings represents delayed consumption. Savers must be paid a price for delaying consumption. Typically, this price is paid through the interest rates. Savers will save more money at higher interest rates than at lower interest rates. The interest rate is the price of borrowing to the investor. Investors will borrow more funds at lower interest rates than at higher interest rates. The equilibrium rate of interest is the rate at which the amount savers want to save is equal to the amount borrowers want to borrow for investment purposes.

0013.06   Demonstrating knowledge of strategies (e.g., interpreting graphs and tables) and resources (e.g., Internet, mass communication) for inquiry related to history, geography, government, civics, and economics

Primary sources are works, records, etc. that were created during the period being studied or immediately after it. Secondary sources are works written significantly after the period being studied; they are based upon primary sources. Suppose an individual is preparing for a presentation on the Civil War and intends to focus on causes, an issue that has often been debated. If examining the matter of slavery as a cause, a graph of the increase in the number of slaves by area of the country for the previous 100 years would be very useful in the discussion. If focusing on the economic conditions that were driving the politics of the age, graphs of GDP, distribution of wealth geographically and individually, and relationship of wealth to ownership of slaves would be useful.

In that same manner, if discussing the war in Iraq, detailed maps with geopolitical elements would help to clarify not only the day-to-day happenings, but also the historical features that led up to it. A map showing the number of oil fields and where they are situated with regard to the various political factions, and charts showing output of those fields historically, would be useful.

As another example, when teaching the history of space travel, photos of the most famous astronauts can add interest to the discussion. Graphs showing the growth of the industry, and charts showing discoveries and their relationship to the lives of everyday Americans might also be helpful.

Geography and history classes are often labeled as "dull" by students. With all the visual resources available today, however, those classes have the potential for being the most exciting courses in the curriculum.

OBJECTIVE 0014 UNDERSTAND BASIC PRINCIPLES AND PRACTICES RELATED TO HEALTH, SAFETY, AND PHYSICAL EDUCATION

0014.01 **Demonstrating knowledge of the primary functions of the human body systems; the processes of human growth and development; the basic principles of human nutrition; and the differences between communicable and noncommunicable diseases and strategies for prevention (e.g., hand washing, regular exercise, and proper diet)**

The major systems of the human body consist of organs working together to perform important physiological tasks. To understand how all of these systems work together, it is important to have a grasp of several major body systems, including the musculoskeletal system, the cardiovascular system, the respiratory/excretory system, the nervous system, the endocrine system, the reproductive system, and the immune system. In addition, it is valuable to know how these systems adapt to physical activity, produce movement, and contribute to fitness.

MUSCULOSKELETAL SYSTEM

Structures, Locations, and Functions of Muscular Tissue

The main function of the muscular system is movement. There are three types of muscle tissue: skeletal, cardiac, and smooth.

Skeletal muscle is voluntary. These muscles are attached to bones and are responsible for their movement. Skeletal muscle consists of long fibers and is striated due to the repeating patterns of the myofilaments (made of the proteins actin and myosin) that make up the fibers.

Cardiac muscle is found in the heart. Cardiac muscle is striated like skeletal muscle, but differs in that the plasma membrane of the cardiac muscle causes the muscle to beat even when away from the heart. The action potentials of cardiac and skeletal muscles also differ.

Smooth muscle is involuntary. It is found in organs and enables functions such as digestion and respiration. Unlike skeletal and cardiac muscle, smooth muscle is not striated. Smooth muscle has less myosin and does not generate as much tension as skeletal muscle.

Mechanism of Skeletal Muscle Contraction

To begin, a nerve impulse strikes a muscle fiber. This causes calcium ions to flood the sarcomere (the muscle's filaments). These calcium ions allow adenosine triphosphate (ATP), which is basically the "gasoline" of the human body, to expend energy. The myosin fibers then creep along the actin, causing the muscle to contract. Once the nerve impulse has passed, calcium is pumped out and the contraction ends.

Skeletal System

The axial skeleton consists of the bones of the skull and vertebrae. The appendicular skeleton consists of the bones of the legs, arms and tail, and shoulder girdle.

Bone is actually a specialized form of connective tissue. Parts of the bone include compact bone, which gives strength; spongy bone, which contains red marrow to make blood cells and yellow marrow in the center of long bones to store fat cells; and the periosteum, which is the protective covering on the outside of the bone.

Movement of Body Joints

A **joint** is a place where two bones meet; enabling movement. Within the joint, ligaments attach bone to bone, and tendons attach bone to muscle. Ligaments and tendons are also forms of connective tissue. All of these parts work together to allow the joint to move. There are three types of joints:

1. **Ball and socket** – allows for rotational movement. An example is the joint between the shoulder and the humerus. Ball and socket joints allow humans to move their arms and legs in many different ways.
2. **Hinge** – movement is restricted to a single plane. An example is the joint between the humerus and the ulna.
3. **Pivot** – allows for the rotation of the forearm at the elbow and the hands at the wrist.

HUMAN NERVOUS AND ENDOCRINE SYSTEMS

The **central nervous system** (CNS) consists of the *brain* and *spinal cord*. The CNS is responsible for the body's response to environmental stimuli. The **spinal cord** is located inside the spine. It sends out motor commands for movement in response to stimuli. The **brain** is where responses to more complex stimuli occur.

The meninges are the connective tissues that protect the CNS. The CNS also contains fluid filled spaces called ventricles. These ventricles are filled with cerebrospinal fluid, which is formed in the brain. This fluid cushions the brain and circulates nutrients, white blood cells, and hormones. The CNS's response to stimuli is a reflex, an unconscious, automatic response.

The **peripheral nervous system** (PNS) consists of the nerves that connect the CNS to the rest of the body. The **sensory division** of the PNS brings information to the CNS from sensory receptors, and the motor division sends signals from the CNS to effector cells. The **motor division** consists of the somatic nervous system and the autonomic nervous system. The body consciously controls the somatic nervous system in response to external stimuli. The hypothalamus in the brain unconsciously controls the autonomic nervous system to regulate the internal environment. This system is responsible for the movement of smooth muscles, cardiac muscles, and the muscles of other organ systems.

Role of Nerve Impulses and Neurons

The **neuron** is the basic unit of the nervous system. It consists of an **axon**, which carries impulses away from the cell body to the tip of the neuron; the **dendrite**, which carries impulses toward the cell body; and the **cell body**, which contains the nucleus. Synapses are the spaces between neurons. Chemicals called neurotransmitters are found close to the synapses. The myelin sheath, composed of Schwann cells, covers the neurons and provides insulation.

Nerve action depends on depolarization and an imbalance of electrical charges across the neuron. A polarized nerve has a positive charge outside the neuron. A depolarized nerve has a negative charge outside the neuron.

Neurotransmitters turn off the sodium pump, which results in depolarization of the membrane. This wave of depolarization (as it moves from neuron to neuron) carries an electrical impulse. This is actually a wave of opening and closing gates that allows for the flow of ions across the synapse.

All nerves have an action potential. There is a threshold of the level of chemicals that must be met or exceeded in order for muscles to respond. This is the "all or nothing" response.

ENDOCRINE SYSTEM

Major Endocrine Glands and the Function of their Hormones
The function of the **endocrine system** is to manufacture proteins called hormones. **Hormones** circulate in the bloodstream and stimulate actions when they interact with target tissue. There are two classes of hormones: steroid and peptide. Steroid hormones come from cholesterol and include the sex hormones. Amino acids are the source of peptide hormones.

Hormones are specific; they fit receptors on the target tissue cell surface. The receptor activates an enzyme that converts ATP to cyclic AMP. Cyclic AMP (cAMP) is a second messenger from the cell membrane to the nucleus. The genes found in the nucleus turn on or off to cause a specific response. Endocrine cells, which make up endocrine glands, secrete hormones. The major endocrine glands and their hormones include:

Hypothalamus – located in the lower brain, it signals the pituitary gland.

Pituitary gland – located at the base of the hypothalamus, it releases growth hormones and antidiuretic hormone (retention of water in kidneys).

Thyroid gland – located on the trachea, it lowers blood calcium levels (calcitonin) and maintains metabolic processes (thyroxine).

Gonads – located in the testes of the male and the ovaries of the female, the testes release androgens to support sperm formation, and ovaries release estrogens to stimulate uterine lining growth and progesterone to promote uterine lining growth.

Pancreas – secretes insulin in order to lower blood glucose levels and glucagon to raise blood glucose levels.

INTEGUMENTARY SYSTEM

The primary organ of the integumentary system is the external covering of the body. Its primary organ, and the largest organ in the human body, is skin.
Structure and Function of the Skin

The skin consists of two distinct layers: the **epidermis** and the **dermis**. The epidermis is the thinner outer layer, and the dermis is the thicker inner layer. Layers of tightly packed epithelial cells make up the epidermis. The tight packaging of the epithelial cells supports the skin's function as a protective barrier against infection.

The top layer of the epidermis consists of dead skin cells and contains keratin, a waterproofing protein. The dermis layer consists of connective tissue. It contains blood vessels, hair follicles, sweat glands, and sebaceous glands. The body releases an oily secretion called sebum, produced by the sebaceous gland, to the outer epidermis through the hair follicles. Sebum maintains the pH of the skin between three and five, which inhibits most microorganism growth.

The skin also plays a role in thermoregulation. Increased body temperature causes skin blood vessels to dilate, which then causes heat to radiate from the skin's surface. Increased temperature also activates sweat glands, increasing evaporative cooling. Decreased body temperature causes skin blood vessels to constrict. This results in blood from the skin diverting to deeper tissues, thereby reducing heat loss from the surface of the skin.

HUMAN RESPIRATORY AND EXCRETORY SYSTEMS

Function of the Respiratory and Excretory Systems

The **lungs** are the respiratory surface of the human respiratory system. A dense net of capillaries contained just beneath the epithelium form the respiratory surface. The surface area of the epithelium is about $100m^2$ in humans.

Based on the surface area, the volume of air inhaled and exhaled is known as the tidal volume. This is normally about 500mL in adults. Vital capacity is the maximum volume the lungs can inhale and exhale. This is usually around 3400mL.

The function of the **excretory system** is to rid the body of nitrogenous wastes in the form of urea. The **kidneys** are the primary organ in the excretory system. Each of the two kidneys in humans is about 10cm long. Despite their small size, they receive about 20 percent of the blood pumped with each heartbeat.

The Process of Breathing and Gas Exchange

The respiratory system functions in the gas exchange of oxygen and carbon dioxide waste. It delivers oxygen to the bloodstream and picks up carbon dioxide for release from the body. Air enters the mouth and nose, where it is warmed, moistened, and filtered of dust and particles. Cilia in the trachea trap and expel unwanted material in mucus. The trachea splits into two bronchial tubes, and the bronchial tubes divide into smaller and smaller bronchioles in the lungs. The internal surface of the lung is composed of alveoli, which are thin walled air sacs. These allow for a large surface area for gas exchange. Capillaries line the alveoli.

Oxygen diffuses into the bloodstream and carbon dioxide diffuses out of the capillaries. It is then exhaled from the lungs due to partial pressure. Hemoglobin, a protein containing iron, carries the oxygenated blood to the heart and all parts of the body.

The thoracic cavity holds the lungs. The diaphragm muscle below the lungs is an adaptation that makes inhalation possible. As the volume of the thoracic cavity increases, the diaphragm muscle flattens out and inhalation occurs. When the diaphragm relaxes, exhalation occurs.

HUMAN CIRCULATORY AND IMMUNE SYSTEMS

Structure, Function, and Regulation of the Heart

The function of the closed circulatory system (**cardiovascular system**) is to carry oxygenated blood and nutrients to all cells of the body and to return carbon dioxide waste to the lungs for expulsion. The heart, blood vessels, and blood make up the cardiovascular system. The following diagram shows the structure of the heart:

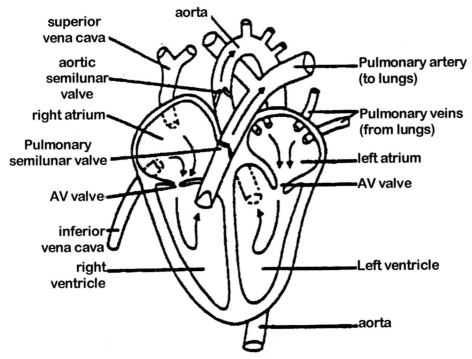

The atria are the chambers that receive blood returning to the heart, and the ventricles are the chambers that pump blood out of the heart. There are four valves, two atrioventricular (AV) valves and two semilunar valves. The AV valves are located between each atrium and ventricle. The contraction of the ventricles closes the AV valve to keep blood from flowing back into the atria. The semilunar valves are located where the aorta leaves the left ventricle and the pulmonary artery leaves the right ventricle. Ventricular contraction opens the semilunar valves, pumping blood out into the arteries, and ventricular relaxation closes the valves.

Cardiac output is the volume of blood per minute that the left ventricle pumps. This output depends on the heart rate and stroke volume. The **heart rate** is the number of times the heart beats per minute, and the **stroke volume** is the amount of blood pumped by the left ventricle each time it contracts. Humans have an average cardiac output of about 5.25 L/min. Heavy exercise can increase cardiac output up to five times. Epinephrine and increased body temperature can also increase heart rate and, thus, the cardiac output.

Cardiac muscle can contract without any signal from the nervous system. The sinoatrial node is the pacemaker of the heart. It is located on the wall of the right atrium; it generates electrical impulses that make the cardiac muscle cells contract in unison. The atrioventricular node briefly delays the electrical impulse to ensure the atria are empty before the ventricles contract.

Structure, Function, and Regulation of the Immune System

The immune system is responsible for defending the body against foreign invaders. There are two defense mechanisms: non-specific and specific. The **non-specific** immune mechanism has two lines of defense. The first line of defense involves the physical barriers of the body. These include the skin and mucous membranes. The skin prevents the penetration of bacteria and viruses as long as there are no abrasions on the skin. Mucous membranes form a protective barrier around the digestive, respiratory, and genitourinary tracts. In addition, the pH of the skin and mucous membranes inhibit the growth of many microbes. Mucous secretions (tears and saliva) wash away many microbes; they also contain lysozyme, which kills microbes.

The second line of defense includes white blood cells and the inflammatory response. **Phagocytosis** is the ingestion of foreign particles such as bacteria to remove them from the body. It is a defensive reaction to invasion. Neutrophils make up about 70 percent of all white blood cells. Monocytes mature to become macrophages, which are the largest phagocytic cells. Eosinophils are also phagocytic. Natural killer cells destroy the body's own infected cells instead of invading the microbe directly.

The other second line of defense is the inflammatory response. When this occurs, the blood supply to the injured area increases, causing redness and heat. Swelling also typically occurs with inflammation. Delivering more blood to the injured area brings more white blood cells to defend the body. Basophils and mast cells release histamine in response to cell injury. This triggers the inflammatory response.

The **specific** immune mechanism recognizes specific foreign material and responds by destroying the invader. These mechanisms are specific and diverse. They are able to recognize individual pathogens. An **antigen** is any foreign particle that elicits an immune response. The body manufactures **antibodies** that recognize and latch onto antigens, hopefully destroying them. They also discriminate between foreign materials versus self material. Memory of the invaders provides immunity upon further exposure.

Immunity is the body's ability to recognize and destroy an antigen before it causes harm. Active immunity develops after recovery from an infectious disease (e.g., chickenpox) or after a vaccination (e.g., mumps, measles, and rubella). Passive immunity may be passed from one individual to another and is not permanent. Good examples of passive immunities are those passed from mother to nursing child. A baby's immune system is not well-developed, so the passive immunity they receive through nursing keeps them healthier.

There are two main responses made by the body after exposure to an antigen:

- **Humoral response**: Free antigens activate this response. During the humoral response, B-cells (lymphocytes from bone marrow) give rise to plasma cells that secrete antibodies as well as memory cells that will recognize future exposures to the same antigen. The antibodies defend against extracellular pathogens by binding to the antigen and making them an easy target for phagocytes to engulf and destroy. Antibodies are in a class of proteins called **immunoglobulins**. There are five major classes of immunoglobulins (Ig) involved in the humoral response: IgM, IgG, IgA, IgD, and IgE.

- **Cell mediated response**: Infected cells activate T-cells (lymphocytes from the thymus) in this response. These activated T-cells defend against pathogens in the body cells or cancer cells by binding to the infected cells and destroying them along with the antigen. T-cell receptors on the T helper cells recognize antigens bound to the body's own cells. T helper cells release IL-2, which stimulates other lymphocytes (cytotoxic T-cells and B-cells). Cytotoxic T-cells kill infected host cells by recognizing specific antigens.

Vaccines are antigens given in very small amounts. They stimulate both humoral and cell mediated responses. After vaccination, memory cells recognize future exposure to the antigen so that the body can produce antibodies much faster.

HUMAN DIGESTIVE SYSTEM

Roles of Basic Nutrients Found in Foods

The function of the digestive system is to break food down into nutrients, to absorb them into the blood stream, and to deliver them to all cells of the body for use in cellular respiration.

Essential nutrients are those nutrients that the body needs but cannot make. There are four groups of essential nutrients: essential amino acids, essential fatty acids, vitamins, and minerals.

There are eight essential amino acids humans need. A lack of these amino acids results in protein deficiency. There are only a few essential fatty acids. Vitamins are organic molecules essential for a nutritionally adequate diet. Scientists have identified thirteen vitamins essential to humans. There are two groups of vitamins: water-soluble (includes the vitamin B complex and vitamin C) and water insoluble (vitamins A, D, and K). Vitamin deficiencies can cause severe health problems.

Unlike vitamins, minerals are inorganic molecules. Calcium is important in bone construction and maintenance. Iron is important in cellular respiration and is a major component of hemoglobin.

Carbohydrates, fats, and proteins are fuel for the generation of ATP. Water is necessary to keep the body hydrated.

Essential Amino Acids	Essential Vitamins
<ul><li>Arginine</li><li>Histidine</li><li>Isoleucine</li><li>Leucine</li><li>Lysine</li><li>Methionine</li><li>Phenylalanine</li><li>Threonine</li><li>Tryptophan</li><li>Valine</li></ul>	<ul><li>Vitamin A</li><li>Vitamin B complex (8 vitamins)</li><li>Vitamin C</li><li>Vitamin D</li><li>Vitamin E</li><li>Vitamin K</li></ul>

Mechanical and Chemical Digestion

The function of the excretory system is to rid the body of nitrogenous wastes in the form of urea. The teeth and saliva begin digestion by breaking food down into smaller pieces and lubricating it to allow swallowing. The lips, cheeks, and tongue form a bolus, or ball of food. The process of **peristalsis** (wave-like contractions) carries the food down the pharynx, where it enters the stomach through the sphincter. Once through, the sphincter closes to keep food from going back up.

In the stomach, pepsinogen and hydrochloric acid form pepsin, the enzyme that hydrolyzes proteins. This chemical action breaks the food down further and churns it into a semifluid mass called acid chyme.

The pyloric sphincter muscle opens to allow the food to enter the small intestine. Most nutrient absorption occurs in the small intestine. Its large surface area, resulting from its length and protrusions called villi and microvilli, allow for a great absorptive surface into the bloodstream. Neutralization of the chyme after arrival from the acidic stomach allows the local enzymes to function. Accessory organs function in the production of necessary enzymes and bile. The pancreas makes many enzymes necessary to break down food in the small intestine. The liver makes bile, which breaks down and emulsifies fatty acids. Any food left after the trip through the small intestine enters the large intestine. The large intestine functions to reabsorb water and produce vitamin K. The feces, or remaining waste, pass out through the anus.

HUMAN REPRODUCTIVE SYSTEM

The Function of Male and Female Reproductive Systems

Hormones regulate sexual maturation in humans. Humans cannot reproduce until puberty, about the age of eight to fourteen, depending on the individual. Prior to puberty, the hypothalamus begins secreting hormones that help to mature the reproductive system and to develop the secondary sex characteristics. Reproductive maturity in girls occurs with the first menstruation; it occurs in boys with the first ejaculation of viable sperm.

Hormones also regulate reproduction. In males, the primary sex hormones are the androgens, testosterone being the most important. The testes produce androgens that dictate the primary and secondary sex characteristics of the male.

Female hormone patterns are cyclic and complex. Most women have a reproductive cycle length of about twenty-eight days. The menstrual cycle is specific to the changes in the uterus. The ovarian cycle results in ovulation; it occurs in parallel with the menstrual cycle. Hormones regulate this parallelism. Five hormones participate in this regulation, most notably estrogen and progesterone. Estrogen and progesterone play an important role in sending signals to the uterus and in developing and maintaining the endometrium. Estrogen also dictates the secondary sex characteristics of females.

Gametogenesis, Fertilization, and Birth control

Gametogenesis is the production of the sperm (spermatogenesis) and egg cells (oogenesis). **Spermatogenesis** begins at puberty in the male. One spermatogonia, the diploid precursor of sperm, produces four sperm. The sperm mature in the seminiferous tubules, which are located in the testes. **Oogenesis**, the production of egg cells (ova), is usually complete by the birth of a female. Females do not release egg cells until menstruation begins at puberty. Meiosis forms one ovum with all the cytoplasm, and three polar bodies that the body reabsorbs. The ovaries store the ovum and release them each month from puberty to menopause.

Seminiferous tubules in the testes house sperm, where they mature. The epididymis, located on top of the testes, contains mature sperm. After ejaculation, the sperm travel up the vas deferens where they mix with semen made in the prostate and seminal vesicles; they then travel out the urethra. Ovulation releases the egg into the fallopian tubes, where cilia move the egg along the length of the tubes. Fertilization of the egg by the sperm normally occurs in the fallopian tube. If pregnancy does not occur, the egg passes through the uterus and is expelled through the vagina during menstruation. Levels of progesterone and estrogen stimulate menstruation. Implantation of a fertilized egg down-regulates the levels, stopping menstruation.

STAGES AND CHARACTERISTICS OF PHYSICAL, COGNITIVE, SOCIAL, AND EMOTIONAL GROWTH AND DEVELOPMENT

Please refer to skill 16.01 for more detail on these issues.

Physical development – Small children (ages three to five) have a propensity for engaging in periods of a great deal of physical activity, punctuated by a need for a lot of rest. Children at this stage lack fine motor skills and cannot focus on small objects for very long. Their bones are still developing. At this age, girls tend to be better coordinated, and boys tend to be stronger.

The lag in fine motor skills continues during the early elementary school years (ages six to eight).

Pre-adolescent children (ages nine to eleven) become stronger, leaner, and taller. Their motor skills improve, and they are able to sit still and focus for longer periods. Growth during this period is constant. This is also the time when gender-related physical predispositions will begin to show. Pre-adolescents are at risk of obesity without proper nutrition or adequate activity.

Young adolescents (ages twelve to fourteen) experience drastic physical growth (girls earlier than boys), and are highly preoccupied with their physical appearance.

As children proceed to the later stages of adolescence (ages fifteen to seventeen), girls will reach their full height, while boys will still have some growth remaining. The increase in hormone levels will cause acne, which coincides with a slight decrease of preoccupation with physical appearance. At this age, children may begin to initiate sexual activity (boys generally are more motivated by hormones and girls more by peer pressure). There is a risk of teen pregnancy and sexually transmitted diseases.

Cognitive development – Language development is the most important aspect of cognitive development in small children (ages three to five). Acknowledging successes, rewarding mature behavior, and allowing the child to explore can improve confidence and self-esteem at this age.

Early elementary school children (ages six to eight) are eager to learn and love to talk. Children at this age have a very literal understanding of rules and verbal instructions, and must develop strong listening skills.

Pre-adolescent children (ages nine to eleven) display increased logical thought, but their knowledge or beliefs may be unusual or surprising. Differences in cognitive styles develop at this age (e.g., field dependant or independent preferences).

In early adolescence (ages twelve to fourteen), boys tend to score higher on mechanical/spatial reasoning, and girls on spelling and language tasks. Boys are better with mental imagery, and girls have better access and retrieval of information from memory. Self-efficacy (the ability to self-evaluate) becomes very important at this stage.

In later adolescence (ages fifteen to seventeen), children are capable of formal thought, but don't always apply it. Conflicts between teenagers' and parents' opinions and worldviews will arise. Children at this age may become interested in advanced political thinking.

Social development – Small children (ages three to five) are socially flexible. Different children will prefer solitary play, parallel play, or cooperative play. Frequent minor quarrels will occur between children, and boys will tend to be more aggressive (children at these ages are already aware of gender roles). Early elementary school children (ages six to eight) are increasingly selective of friends (usually of the same sex). Children at this age enjoy playing games, but are excessively preoccupied by the rules. Verbal aggression becomes more common than physical aggression, and children of this age begin learning how to solve their own conflicts.

Pre-adolescent children (ages nine to eleven) place great importance on the (perceived) opinions of their peers and on their social stature, and will go to great lengths to "fit in." Friendships at this age are very selective, and usually of the same sex.

Young adolescents (ages twelve to fourteen) develop a greater understanding of the emotions of others, which results in increased emotional sensitivity and impacts peer relationships. Children at this age develop an increased need to perform.

In the later stages of adolescence (ages fifteen to seventeen), peers are still the primary influence on day-to-day decisions, but parents will have increasing influence on long-term goals. Girls' friendships tend to be close and intimate, whereas boys' friendships are based on competition and similar interests. Many children this age will work part-time, and educators should be alert to signs of potential school dropouts.

Emotional development – Small children (ages three to five) express emotion freely and have a limited ability to learn how emotions influence behavior. Jealousy at this age is common.

Early elementary school children (ages six to eight) have easily bruised feelings and are just beginning to recognize the feelings of others. Children this age will want to please teachers and other adults.

Pre-adolescent children (ages nine to eleven) develop a global and stable self-image (self-concept and self-esteem). Comparisons to their peers and the opinions of their peers are important. An unstable home environment at this age contributes to an increased risk of delinquency.

Young adolescence (ages twelve to fourteen) can be a stormy and stressful time for children, but, in reality, this is only the case for roughly 20 percent of teens. Boys may have trouble controlling their anger and display impulsive behavior. Girls may suffer depression. Young adolescents are very egocentric and concerned with appearance; they often feel very strongly that "adults don't understand."

In later stages of adolescence (ages fifteen to seventeen), educators should be alert to signs of surfacing mental health problems (e.g., eating disorders, substance abuse, schizophrenia, depression, and suicide).

NUTRITION AND WEIGHT CONTROL

Identifying the Components of Nutrition

The components of nutrition are carbohydrates, proteins, fats, vitamins, minerals, and water.

Carbohydrates are the main source of energy (glucose) in the human diet. The two types of carbohydrates are simple and complex. Complex carbohydrates have greater nutritional value because they take longer to digest, contain dietary fiber, and do not excessively elevate blood sugar levels. Common sources of carbohydrates are fruits, vegetables, grains, dairy products, and legumes.

Proteins are necessary for growth, development, and cellular function. The body breaks down consumed protein into component amino acids for future use. Major sources of protein are meat, poultry, fish, legumes, eggs, dairy products, grains, and legumes.

Fats are a concentrated energy source and important component of the human body. The different types of fats are saturated, monounsaturated, and polyunsaturated. Polyunsaturated fats are the healthiest because they may lower cholesterol levels, while saturated fats increase cholesterol levels. Common sources of saturated fats include dairy products, meat, coconut oil, and palm oil. Common sources of unsaturated fats include nuts, most vegetable oils, and fish.

Vitamins and minerals are organic substances that the body requires in small quantities for proper functioning. People acquire vitamins and minerals in their diets and in supplements. Important vitamins include A, B, C, D, E, and K. Important minerals include calcium, phosphorus, magnesium, potassium, sodium, chlorine, and sulfur.

Water makes up 55 to 75 percent of the human body. It is essential for most bodily functions and obtained through foods and liquids.

Determining the Adequacy of Diets in Meeting the Nutritional Needs of Students

Nutritional requirements vary from person-to-person. General guidelines for meeting adequate nutritional needs are no more than 30 percent total caloric intake from fats (preferably 10 percent from saturated fats, 10% percent from monounsaturated fats, and 10 percent from polyunsaturated fats); no more than 15 percent total caloric intake from proteins (complete); and <u>at least</u> 55 percent of caloric intake from carbohydrates (mainly complex carbohydrates). Exercise and diet help to maintain proper body weight by equalizing caloric intake and caloric output.

Choosing a Healthy Diet

A healthy diet is essential for achieving and maintaining optimum mental and physical health. Making the decision to eat well is a powerful investment. Selecting foods that encompass a variety of healthy nutrients will help to reduce the risk of developing common medical conditions; it will also boost one's immune system while increasing energy level.

Experts agree that the key to healthy eating is balance, variety, and moderation. Other tips include:

- Enjoy plenty of whole grains, fruits, and vegetables
- Maintain a healthy weight
- Eat moderate portions
- Eat regular meals
- Reduce but don't eliminate certain foods
- Balance your food choices over time
- Know your diet pitfalls
- Make changes gradually—remember, foods are not good or bad.
- Select foods based on your total eating patterns, not whether any individual food is "good" or "bad."

Food Guide Pyramid and Dietary Guidelines

The Food Guide Pyramid illustrates the different components of a healthy diet and number of servings of each food group people should consume. Specifically, people should consume the greatest number of servings of carbohydrate-based products like cereals, breads, and pasta; a large number of vitamin- and mineral-rich carbohydrates like fruits and vegetables; a number of protein-rich foods; and very few foods with higher fat content.

The Dietary Guidelines for Americans is a document published by the United States Department of Health and Human Services and the United States Department of Agriculture. It is a primary source of dietary health information for policymakers, nutrition educators, and health providers so they can help direct the individuals that they represent, teach, and care for to make informed and healthy decisions regarding their diets.

Regulations related to food labels and packaging ensure that consumers receive accurate information about the products they buy. Food labels include the breakdown of ingredients, nonfood components, nutritional values, and accuracy of claims relating to the food product.

DISEASES: CAUSES, CHARACTERISTICS, AND PREVENTION

Pathogens that enter the body through direct or indirect contact cause communicable, or infectious, diseases. A **pathogen** is a disease-causing organism. Familiar communicable diseases include influenza, the common cold, chickenpox, pneumonia, measles, mumps, and mononucleosis. To minimize the circulation of pathogens that cause these illnesses, people must follow simple precautions. Individuals who are ill with these diseases should stay away from others during the contagious period of the infection. All people should avoid sharing items such as towels, toothbrushes, and silverware.

At home, thorough clothes washing, dishwashing, and frequent hand washing can decrease pathogen transmission. Keeping immunizations up-to-date is also important in reducing the spread of communicable diseases.

Sexual activity is the source of transmission for many other communicable diseases. The commonly used term for these types of diseases is **sexually transmitted disease** (STD) or **sexually transmitted infection** (STI). Common STIs include chlamydia, gonorrhea, syphilis, genital herpes, genital warts, bacterial vaginosis, human papillomavirus (HPV), pediculosis pubis (pubic lice), hepatitis B, and HIV. Certain STIs can result in infertility. HPV can result in a deadly form of cervical cancer. HIV may result in acquired immunodeficiency syndrome (AIDS), which can be fatal. Some of these diseases, such as genital herpes, last a lifetime.

A **chronic disease** is a disease that is long-lasting; it typically continues for more than three months. Examples of chronic conditions include diseases such as heart disease, cancer, and diabetes. These diseases are currently the leading causes of death and disability in the United States. Many forms of these widespread and expensive diseases are preventable. Choosing nutritious foods, participating in physical activity, and avoiding tobacco use can prevent or control these illnesses.

A **degenerative disease** is a condition in which diseased tissues or organs steadily deteriorate. The deterioration may be due to ordinary wear and tear, or lifestyle choices such as lack of exercise or poor nutrition. In addition, many degenerative diseases are of questionable origin, and may be linked to heredity and environmental factors. Some examples of degenerative diseases include: osteoporosis, Alzheimer's disease, ALS (Lou Gehrig's disease), osteoarthritis, inflammatory bowel disease (IBD), and Parkinson's disease.

Primary Prevention activities are the most cost-effective in health care, as they help to avoid the suffering, cost, and burden associated with a particular disease or condition. These precautions promote health by targeting specific health care concerns.

Examples of primary prevention include both active and passive immunization against disease. **Passive immunization** is treatment that provides immunity through the transfer of antibodies obtained from an immune individual. **Active immunization** is treatment that provides immunity by challenging an individual's own immune system to produce an antibody against a particular organism. Recently developed vaccines include the ones for hepatitis A and chicken pox. Education to promote health protection is also a primary prevention strategy. Advising automobile drivers and passengers to use seat belts while in transit illustrates an action of primary prevention, as does advocating the use of helmets while riding a bicycle or motorcycle.

Secondary Prevention is early detection using accepted screening technologies. The intent is to identify patients with an increased risk, since many conditions do not show symptoms until the disease is well established, significantly reducing chances of recovery. Finding problems early in the development of diseases such as hyperlipidemia, hypertension, and breast and prostate cancer can frequently curb or eliminate the damage and reduce pain and suffering (U.S. Preventative Services Task Force (1996) Guide to Clinical Preventative Services (2d edition) Baltimore: Williams & Wilkins).

Children who are disruptive, inattentive, hyperactive, impulsive, or aggressive may be at heightened risk for the development of antisocial behavior, substance abuse, and school dropout in later years (Barkley, Fischer, Edelbrock, & Smallish, 1990). Secondary prevention in these cases includes skill-building interventions such as teaching children problem-solving strategies and educating parents to use these techniques at home. Instructors can create environments that allow children to work together with their peers, their parents, and school personnel to channel their energy into positive outcomes (Weissberg, Caplan, & Sivo, 1989).

Relationship between Diet and the Prevention of Disease

Diet plays an important role in the prevention of disease. Consuming a healthy diet that is rich in polyunsaturated fats, whole grains, fish, fruits, vegetables, and lean protein, and low in saturated fat and sugar, reduces the risk of many chronic diseases. Proper nutrition can help to prevent heart disease, strokes, osteoporosis, and many types of cancers. In addition, good nutrition helps to boost the body's immune system, lowering the risk of infectious disease.

Issues Related to Ideal Weight and Body Composition

Nutrition and exercise are closely related concepts that are important to student health. A primary responsibility of health instructors is to teach students about proper nutrition and exercise, as well as how they relate to each other.

The two key components of a healthy lifestyle are the consumption of a balanced diet and regular physical activity. Exercise and diet maintain proper body weight by equalizing caloric intake to caloric output. Nutrition can affect physical performance. Proper nutrition produces high energy levels and allows for peak performance. Inadequate or improper nutrition can impair physical performance and lead to short-term and long-term health problems (e.g., depressed immune system and heart disease, respectively). Regular exercise improves overall health. The benefits of regular exercise include a stronger immune system, weight management, a reduced risk of premature death, a reduced risk of heart disease, improved psychological well-being, and stronger muscles, bones, and joints.

Body Composition Management

It is vital to analyze procedures, activities, resources, and benefits involved in developing and maintaining healthy levels of body composition. Maintaining a healthy body composition allows an individual to move freely and to obtain a certain pattern necessary for activity. Furthermore, maintaining a healthy body composition is positively related to long-term health and resistance to disease and sickness.

The total weight of an individual is a combination of bones, ligaments, tendons, organs, fluids, muscles, and fat. Because muscle weighs three times more than fat per unit of volume, a person who exercises often gains muscle. This could cause an individual to be smaller physically, but weigh more than he or she appears to weigh.

The only proven method for maintaining a healthy body composition is following a healthy diet and engaging in regular exercise. A healthy program of nutrition and exercise helps to balance caloric intake and output, thus preventing excessive body fat production.

0014.02   **RECOGNIZING CHARACTERISTICS OF INTERPERSONAL RELATIONSHIPS (E.G., WITHIN FAMILIES, AMONG PEERS) AND STRATEGIES FOR MAINTAINING HEALTHY INTERPERSONAL RELATIONSHIPS (E.G., USING CONFLICT RESOLUTION AND POSITIVE CHARACTER DEVELOPMENT SKILLS)**

Families and Changing Family Structures

Today's family is often quite different from the traditional mom, dad, and biological children. While from two thirds to three quarters of school age children do live with two biological parents, divorce, stepfamilies, and adoption have changed the typical American family. Studies show that children suffer the most with divorce, remarriage, and stepfamily situations. They are particularly at risk if their biological parents are in conflict. Divorce takes a long time, and unhappy parents, who are focused on severing ties with the ex-spouse and starting over, often overlook their children. Relationships with the absent parent change as well (*Family Relations* (Vol. 52, No. 4, pages 352–362) by Emery of UVA and Joan B. Kelly, PhD). A child's adjustment to divorce is heavily dependent on the degree of conflict between the parents and the degree to which they are able to put the needs of the children ahead of their own personal pain and agendas.

The adjustment of children of divorce is also dependent on the child's resiliency. Contributing factors include the child's age during the divorce; the amount of time elapsed, parenting style, financial security, and parental conflict. For example, 50 percent of adjustment problems for children of divorce are due to economic problems faced by divorced households.

Adoptions of international children and those of ethnicities that are different from the parents are creating multicultural families and communities. Attachment disorder is often a problem in these types of adoptions—often due to lack of nurturing early in a child's life. More same-sex couples and single parents adopt, and grandparents often adopt their grandchildren following parental abuse or neglect. The twenty-first century American family is very different from what was common thirty years ago (Adam Pertman, "Adoption Nation: How the Adoption Revolution is Transforming America", Basic Books, 2001).

The demographics of stepfamilies are complex, with nearly 25 percent of the parents unmarried. Both heterosexual parents and gay, lesbian, or bisexual partners may head families. Stepfamilies are a blend of parents, their respective children, the nonresidential parents of those children, grandparents, and other members of the extended family, as well as children born to remarried ex-spouses.

The blended family's challenges include parenting, disciplining, developing new relationships between the stepparent and other spouse's children, strengthening the marital relationship, and working to include nonresidential family (divorced spouses and children not living with the stepfamily).

Many Americans are part of a stepfamily, each with its own character. The stepchildren rarely see a new stepparent as a "real parent," and years may pass before they gain acceptance. It is also difficult for parents in second marriages to treat their stepchildren the same as their biological children. Children are often given too much power in the new family, and may try to create conflict between their biological parent and the stepparent in an attempt to make the stepparent leave.

Creating family stability requires the same steps, whether the situation is a first-marriage, stepfamily, or a single-parent family. What really matters is that parents maintain a routine that fosters security. How families resolve conflicts is also important. Children need an anchor when it seems that everything in their lives is changing. This could be a special friend, neighbor, or relative outside the immediate family. Consistency in school settings helps to predict positive adjustment in children, especially when their home lives are chaotic.

Strategies recommended for parents of second marriages include:

- Discussing and deciding on finances before getting married.
- Building a strong marital bond that will benefit everybody.
- Developing a parenting plan, which likely will involve having the stepparent play a secondary, non-disciplinary role for the first year or two. Letting the children adjust slowly prepares for a successful transition.
- Taking the time to process each change.
- Making sure that big changes are communicated adult-to-adult, not via the children.
- Working with therapists who are specially trained in stepfamily dynamics.

Key factors that contribute to healthy adjustments post-divorce include appropriate parenting, access to the non-residential parent, custody arrangements, and low parental conflict. Appropriate parenting includes providing emotional support, monitoring children's activities, disciplining authoritatively, and maintaining age-appropriate expectations. Finally, the research demonstrates that the best predictor of child's adjustment following divorce is the parents' psychological health and the quality of the parent-child relationship.

Maintaining Healthy Relationships

Regardless of the type of relationship, mutual respect, shared values and interests, and a mutually felt ability to trust and depend on each other all characterize a healthy relationship. Genuine respect for one's friends and family members is vital for the creation of a positive and responsible interpersonal life. It is much easier to dismiss commitments towards and the needs of those we do not respect. Shared values are the foundation for mutual respect, and shared interests are necessary for the exploration and development of a friendship. Trust and dependability are the cement that holds relationships together. Many of these concepts are learned at home when families have healthy relationships and teach principles of mutual respect and value.

Individuals can develop positive interpersonal relationships by devoting time to character-building activities that strengthen the traits listed above. They can work to become people who espouse the values that they would like to see in their friends, and they can make efforts toward becoming trustworthy and dependable. Specific techniques that can be applied to develop positive interpersonal relationships with others include active listening and considerate respect for the things others value. These principles are particularly important when the individuals come from diverse backgrounds.

Active listening is the process of repeating back what was said in the form of a question or restatement without making a value judgment about it.(e.g., if someone tells you, "I'm thinking of taking a vacation, maybe to Florida", you might repeat back, "You're saying that you want to take a vacation to Florida"). These exercises should not be performed mechanically (i.e., parroting); they should be done as a personal reminder to listen to the concerns and interests of others.

Considerate respect for others can be developed by actively asking ourselves what about the current scenario that we are facing would others see as significant. It is an exercise aimed at placing value and emphasis on the priorities of others.

Social support systems are the networks that students develop with their peers and others that provide support when students experience challenges and difficulties. The support offered by these systems is often emotional and sometimes logistical. Financial support in these relationships is generally inappropriate. Social support systems are vital to students (and individuals in general), especially students who don't have other support mechanisms in place.

The benefits of maintaining healthy peer relationships include having a social support system to assist in difficult times as well as having knowledge of the existence of that system. This means that students can feel confident to take greater risks (within reason) and achieve more because they know the support system is there if they need it.

Conflict Management

Interpersonal conflict is a major source of stress and worry. Common sources of interpersonal conflict include problems with family relationships, competition, and disagreement over values or decisions. Teaching students to manage conflict will help them to reduce stress levels throughout their lives, thereby limiting the adverse health effects of stress. The following is a list of conflict resolution principles and techniques.

1. Think before reacting – In a conflict situation, it is important to resist the temptation to react immediately. You should step back, consider the situation, and plan an appropriate response. Do not react to petty situations with anger.
2. Listen – Be sure to listen carefully to the opposing party. Try to understand the other person's point of view.
3. Find common ground – Try to find some common ground as soon as possible. Early compromise can help to ease the tension.
4. Accept responsibility – In every conflict there is plenty of blame to go around. Admitting when you are wrong shows you are committed to resolving the conflict.
5. Attack the problem, not the person – Personal attacks are never beneficial and usually lead to greater conflicts and hard feelings.
6. Focus on the future – Instead of trying to assign blame for past events, focus on what needs to be done differently to avoid future conflict.

0014.03   Recognizing the effects of substance abuse; factors contributing to substance abuse (e.g., media advertising, peer pressure); strategies for resisting pressure to use alcohol, tobacco products, and other drugs; safety practices to avoid accidents and injuries; and strategies for maintaining personal emotional and physical health (e.g., stress management, sleep, proper diet)

Contributing Factors to Substance Abuse

Factors that contribute to the misuse and abuse of tobacco, alcohol, and other drugs include modeling at home, mental health problems, stress, difficult life circumstances, and peer pressure. Identifying alternatives to substance abuse is an important preventative and coping strategy. It is important that children learn to recognize factors that might lead to substance abuse so that they can be proactive in seeking alternative solutions to the problems.

Alternatives to substance use and abuse include regular participation in stress-relieving activities like meditation, exercise, and therapy, all of which can have a relaxing effect. More importantly, the acquisition of longer-term coping strategies (for example, self-empowerment through the practice of problem-solving techniques) is key to maintaining a commitment to alternatives to substance use and abuse. Again, a healthy social support network can also be helpful.

Aspects of substance abuse treatment that must be considered include the processes of physical and psychological withdrawal from the addictive substance, acquisition of coping strategies and replacement techniques to fill the void left by the addictive substance, limiting access to the addictive substance, and acquiring self-control strategies.

Withdrawal from an addictive substance has both psychological and physical symptoms. The psychological symptoms include depression, anxiety, and strong cravings for the substance. Physical withdrawal symptoms stem from the body, which is adapted to a steady intake of the addictive substance. When removed, the body must adapt to accommodate the no-longer-available substance. Depending on the substance, medical intervention may be necessary. Coping strategies and replacement techniques, as discussed earlier, center around providing the individual with an effective alternative to the addictive substance as a solution to the situations that they feel would necessitate the substance.

Limiting access to the addictive substance (opportunities for use) is important, because the symptoms of withdrawal and the experiences associated with the substance can provide a strong impetus to return to using it. Recovering addicts should learn strategies of self-control and self-discipline to help them stay off the addictive substance.

Implications of Substance Abuse

Disease and substance abuse issues have significant implications for both individuals and for society as a whole. Specific implications, though, will depend greatly on the perception of the disease or substance abuse problem (defined by the Surgeon General as a disease) in the society. Education that gives the individuals in a society a clear understanding of the nature of diseases—what they are and are not linked to, how they can and cannot be transmitted, and what effects they will and will not exert on the afflicted individuals—will positively impact both the afflicted individual and society as a whole.

This same education is often the deciding factor that dictates the willingness of the community to allocate resources to programs for treatment and prevention. It is this willingness to "get involved" on a societal level that plays a central role in the likelihood of improved resources for substance abuse issues.

On the individual level, one very important implication of disease and substance abuse problems relate to responsible behavior. This is not a simple matter, as both disease and substance abuse problems will often lead to highly impaired judgment, making the choice to act responsibly and seek out help on an individual level much harder to do. Individuals in a society must act responsibly to help those around them who are diseased or in the throes of a substance abuse problem to seek appropriate treatment.

Safety Practices

Basic healthy behaviors in and out of school reduce the risk of injuries, illness, disease, and other health problems.

Injuries are usually a result of unforeseen accidents. Falls are the leading cause of death among home accidents. Falls occur most frequently among the elderly and young children. The most common location of falls is in bathtubs and showers. Examples of precautions that can help to decrease the risk of falls include using rubber mats in bathtubs and showers, using safety gates to block young children from stairs, wearing appropriate safety equipment during physical activity, and promptly removing ice and snow from steps and sidewalks.

At a more cognitive level, rules, discipline, cooperation, etiquette, and safety practices play a vital role in staying safe during personal performance and other movement-based activities. These activities, by their very nature, will often challenge individuals to push their limitations, both in terms of their current physical and psychological limitations, and in terms of what they might consider to be behaviorally acceptable in competitive situations. Rules and discipline are critical in competitive situations where there is a strong drive to "achieve at any cost" (at least in terms of personal sacrifice and dedication).

Rules and self-discipline are the lines that divide healthy athletes from those who engage in unsportsmanlike behavior and training practices that do not fit into a balanced lifestyle. Similarly, cooperation is the element that allows athletes in a hard-training situation, who are both physically and mentally exhausted, to rely on each other for support. This is a critical factor to healthy training practices. Etiquette is the formalization of these cooperative practices. In situations where individuals might try to push their personal limits beyond what they know they are capable of, safety practices are critical to prevent injuries and accidents.

General Safety Concerns

Safety education related to outdoor pursuits and recreation should emphasize the importance of planning and research. Students should consider in advance what the potential dangers of an activity might be; they should prepare accordingly (for example, students and instructors should examine weather forecasts). Of course, educator supervision is required; first-aid equipment and properly trained educators must be present for all outdoor education activities. Students should use proper safety gear when appropriate (e.g., helmets, harnesses, etc.). Parental consent is also generally required for these types of scenarios.

Actions that Promote Safety and Injury Prevention

The following is a list of practices that promote safety in all types of physical education and athletic activities.

- Having an instructor who is properly trained and qualified.
- Organizing the class by size, activity, and conditions of the class.
- Inspecting buildings and other facilities regularly, and immediately giving notice of any hazards.
- Avoiding overcrowding.
- Using adequate lighting.
- Ensuring that students dress in appropriate clothing and shoes.
- Presenting organized activities.
- Inspecting all equipment regularly.
- Adhering to building codes and fire regulations.
- Using protective equipment.
- Using spotters.
- Eliminating hazards.
- Teaching students correct ways of performing skills and activities.
- Teaching students how to use the equipment properly and safely.

Strategies for Injury Prevention

- Participant screenings – evaluate injury history, anticipate and prevent potential injuries, watch for hidden injuries and the reoccurrence of an injury, and maintain communication.
- Standards and discipline – ensure that athletes obey rules of sportsmanship, supervision, and biomechanics.
- Education and knowledge – stay current in knowledge of first aid, sports medicine, sport technique, and injury prevention through clinics, workshops, and communication with staff and trainers.
- Conditioning – programs should be year-long and participants should have access to conditioning facilities in and out of season to produce more fit and knowledgeable athletes who are less prone to injury.
- Equipment – perform regular inspections; ensure proper fit and proper use.
- Facilities – maintain standards and use safe equipment.
- Field care – establish emergency procedures for serious injury.
- Rehabilitation – use objective measures such as power output on an isokinetic dynamometer.

Prevention of Common Athletic Injuries

- Foot – start with good footwear, foot exercises.
- Ankle – use high top shoes and tape support; strengthen plantar (calf), dorsiflexor (shin), and ankle eversion (ankle outward).
- Shin splints – strengthen ankle dorsiflexors.
- Achilles tendon – stretch dorsiflexion and strengthen plantar flexion (heel raises).
- Knee – increase strength and flexibility of calf and thigh muscles.
- Back – use proper body mechanics.
- Tennis elbow – avoid lateral epicondylitis caused by bent elbow, hitting late, not stepping into the ball, heavy rackets, and rackets with strings that are too tight.
- Head and neck injuries – avoid dangerous techniques (e.g., grabbing a facemask) and carefully supervise dangerous activities like the trampoline.

Physical activity and inactivity greatly affect many aspects of a person's life, including physical fitness abilities, general health, physical resilience, physical self-confidence, psychological well-being, and cognitive function. Regular physical activity can improve or increase these elements, while inactivity can damage or decrease these elements.

The most obvious and direct benefit of physical activity is the physical dimension, which includes fitness and general health. Regular physical activity leads to improved physical fitness, improved strength and endurance of the muscular and cardio-respiratory systems, and improved function of the circulatory system. Improved function of all these systems means that the body expends far less energy on day-to-day activities, significantly increasing overall energy levels. Conversely, a lifestyle of physical inactivity will gradually lead to a deterioration of the muscular, cardio-respiratory, and circulatory systems, which leads to decreased energy levels.

Regular physical activity also contributes to increased physical resilience. When coupled with sufficient rest and a healthy diet, physical activity strengthens the musculoskeletal system, which makes the individual less susceptible to injury. Physical activity also tends to improve reflexes and balance, reducing the likelihood of injury. Conversely and as previously mentioned, a lifestyle of physical inactivity leads to a deterioration of the same physical systems that regular exercise strengthens; it also contributes to a gradual "de-sharpening" of reflexes and balance. In sum, these changes increase the likelihood and susceptibility of the individual to injury.

The bridge between physical and psychological benefits is the physical self-confidence derived from regular physical activity. The individual's increased ability to perform physical tasks leads to the growth of their sense of ability to perform any physical activity (for example, you don't have to actually climb ten flights of stairs to know that you could if you wanted to—this is very liberating, as it creates options). Conversely, a lifestyle of physical inactivity, which implies a decreased fitness level, will often eat away at an individual's physical self-confidence.

Regarding psychological well-being, physical activity causes the brain to release **endorphins**, which function to reduce stress levels (prolonged physical endurance activities can produce levels of endorphins that induce a pleasant and healthy "runner's high"). Most physical activities also mix a degree of repetitive motion and action that require directed attention. In combination, this can function as a sort of meditative activity. For all of these reasons, regular physical activity contributes to psychological balance and well-being as well as reduced stress levels. Conversely, a lifestyle of physical inactivity allows physical confidence to deteriorate and removes alternatives of stress-relief, which can contribute negatively to the individual's psychological well-being.

Finally, regular physical activity benefits the circulatory system, which improves blood flow to the brain. This, in turn, leads to increased cognitive function and mental acuity. Those who are physically inactive do not experience these benefits.

Benefits of Sleep

Sleep gives the body a break from the normal tasks of daily living. During sleep, the body performs many important cleansing and restorative tasks. The immune and excretory systems clear waste and repair cellular damage that accumulates in the body each day. Similarly, the body requires adequate rest and sleep to build and repair muscles. Without adequate rest, even the most strenuous exercise program will not produce muscular development. A lack of rest and sleep leaves the body vulnerable to infection and disease.

Adequate sleep in school children is particularly important. Elementary and middle school age children need from ten to eleven hours of sleep per night and teenagers need nine to ten hours per night. Many students do not get that many hours of sleep. Even short term loss of sleep can cause many problems:

- sleepiness in school
- difficulty concentrating
- reduced working and short term memory
- reduced reaction time
- difficulty with routine decision making
- reduced creativity
- anxiety and irritability
- depression and moodiness
- hyperactivity

It can be seen that many of these effects of inadequate sleep will have a direct impact on school achievement. In addition to these, long term sleep deprivation can include such things as obesity, diabetes, delay of recovery from illness or injury, and a less effective immune system.

Stress management and good nutrition are among the cornerstones of healthy living. Physical education instructors can introduce students to these important concepts through the development of individualized fitness and wellness plans. Fitness and wellness plans should include a concrete exercise plan and a detailed nutritional plan.

0014.04   Demonstrating knowledge of health-related fitness (e.g., cardiovascular endurance, muscular strength, flexibility) and appropriate activities for promoting them; activities that promote the development of locomotor, nonlocomotor, manipulative, and perceptual awareness skills in children; basic rules and strategies for developmentally appropriate physical activities, cooperative and competitive games, and sports; and the role that participation in physical activities can play in promoting positive personal and social behaviors

There are five health-related components of physical fitness: cardio-respiratory or cardiovascular endurance, muscle strength, muscle endurance, flexibility, and body composition.

Cardiovascular endurance – the ability of the body to sustain aerobic activities (activities requiring oxygen utilization) for extended periods.

Muscle strength – the ability of muscle groups to contract and support a given amount of weight.

Muscle endurance – the ability of muscle groups to contract continually over a period of time and to support a given amount of weight.

Flexibility – the ability of muscle groups to stretch and bend.

Body composition – an essential measure of health and fitness. The most important aspects of body composition are body fat percentage and ratio of body fat to muscle.

Physical activity improves each of the components of physical fitness. Aerobic training improves cardiovascular endurance. Weight training, body support activities, and calisthenics increase muscular strength and endurance. Stretching improves flexibility. All types of physical activity improve body composition by increasing muscle and decreasing body fat.

Activities for Various Objectives, Situations, and Developmental Levels

The following is a list of physical activities that may reduce specific health risks, improve overall health, and develop skill-related components of physical activity. Some of these activities, such as walking and calisthenics, are more suitable to students at beginning developmental levels, while others, such as circuit training and rowing, are best suited for students at more advanced levels of development.

1. Aerobic Dance: Health-related components of fitness = *cardio-respiratory, body composition.* Skill-related components of fitness = *agility, coordination.*
2. Bicycling: Health-related components of fitness = *cardio-respiratory, muscle strength, muscle endurance, body composition.* Skill-related components of fitness = *balance.*
3. Calisthenics: Health-related components of fitness = *cardio-respiratory, muscle strength, muscle endurance, flexibility, body composition.* Skill-related components of fitness = *agility.*
4. Circuit Training: Health-related components of fitness = *cardio-respiratory, muscle strength, muscle endurance, body composition.* Skill-related components of fitness = *power.*
5. Cross Country Skiing: Health-related component of fitness = *cardio-respiratory, muscle strength, muscle endurance, body composition.* Skill-related components of fitness = *agility, coordination, power.*
6. Jogging/Running: Health-related components of fitness = *cardio-respiratory, body composition.*
7. Rope Jumping: Health-related components of fitness = *cardio-respiratory, body composition.* Skill-related components of fitness = agility, coordination, reaction time, speed.
8. Rowing: Health-related components of fitness = *cardio-respiratory, muscle strength, muscle endurance, body composition.* Skill-related components of fitness = *agility, coordination, power.*
9. Skating: Health-related components of fitness = *cardio-respiratory, body composition.* Skill-related components of fitness = *agility, balance, coordination, speed.*
10. Swimming/Water Exercises: Health-related components of fitness = *cardio-respiratory, muscle strength, muscle endurance, flexibility, body composition.* Skill-related components of fitness = *agility, coordination.*
11. Walking (brisk): Health-related components of fitness = *cardio-respiratory, body composition.*

Cardiovascular Activities

Walking is a good generic cardio-respiratory activity for promoting basic fitness. Instructors can incorporate it into a variety of class settings (not only physical education instructors—for example, a Biology class might include a field trip to a natural setting that would involve a great deal of walking). Walking is appropriate for practically all age groups, but can only serve as noteworthy exercise for students who lead a fairly sedentary lifestyle (athletic students who train regularly or participate in some sport will not benefit greatly from walking).

Jogging or **Running** is a classic cardio-respiratory activity in which instructors can adjust the difficulty level by modifying the running speed or the incline of the track. It is important to stress proper footwear and the gradual increase of intensity to prevent overuse injuries (e.g., stress fractures or shin splints).

Bicycling is another good cardio-respiratory activity that is appropriate for most age groups. Obviously, knowing how to ride a bicycle is a prerequisite, and it is important to follow safety procedures (e.g., ensuring that students wear helmets). An additional benefit of bicycle riding is that it places less strain on the knee joints than walking or running.

Swimming is an excellent cardio-respiratory activity that has the added benefit of working more of the body's muscles more evenly than most other exercises, without excessive resistance to any one part of the body that could result in an overuse injury. To use swimming as an educational cardio-respiratory activity, there must be qualified lifeguards present, and all students must have passed basic tests of swimming ability.

There are many alternatives for cardio-respiratory activities, like **inline skating** and **cross-country skiing**. More importantly, instructors should modify the above exercises to match the developmental needs of the students—for example, younger students should receive most of their exercise in the form of games. An instructor could incorporate running in the form of a game of tag, soccer, or a relay race.

Flexibility Training
Flexibility is the range of motion around a joint or muscle. Flexibility has two major components: static and dynamic. **Static flexibility** is the range of motion without a consideration for speed of movement. **Dynamic flexibility** is the use of the desired range of motion at a desired velocity. These movements are useful for most athletes. **Static active flexibility** refers to the ability to stretch an antagonist muscle using only the tension in the antagonist muscle. **Static-passive flexibility** is the ability to hold a stretch using body weight or some other external force.

Good flexibility can help to prevent injuries during all stages of life and can keep an athlete safe. To improve flexibility, you can lengthen muscles through activities such as swimming, a basic stretching program, or Pilates. These activities all improve the muscles' range of motion. While joints also consist of ligaments and tendons, muscles are the main target of flexibility training. Muscles are the most elastic component of joints, while ligaments and tendons are less elastic and resist elongation. Overstretching tendons and ligaments can weaken joint stability and lead to injury.

Coaches, athletes, and sports medicine personnel should always use stretching methods as part of their training routine for athletes. They help the body to relax and to warm-up for more intense fitness activities.

The following is an example of a flexibility program design:

- **mode:** stretching
- **frequency:** 3 to 7 days/week
- **intensity:** just below individual's threshold of pain
- **time:** 3 sets with 3 reps holding stretches 15 to 30 seconds, with a 60 rest interval between sets

Dynamic stretching is generally very safe and very effective for warming up muscle groups and moderately improving flexibility. When performing dynamic stretches, participants must be careful to avoid sudden, jerky movements.

Static stretching is also safe, if the participant warms up the muscles prior to stretching. Because cold muscles are less elastic, static stretching without adequate warm-up time can lead to injury. Static stretching is very effective in increasing muscle flexibility.

Isometric, PNF, and ballistic stretching are more advanced techniques that require extreme caution and supervision. Most physical trainers believe ballistic stretching (bouncing into stretches) is ineffective and dangerous. Most trainers do not recommend ballistic stretching. PNF and isometric stretching are effective in certain situations such as rehabilitation and advanced training, but require close supervision.

Muscular Strength and Endurance Activities
Possessing the strength and ability to overcome any resistance in one single effort or in repeated efforts over a period of time is known as muscular strength and endurance. They represent the ability to complete a heavy task in a single effort. Muscular strength and endurance not only help in keeping body ailments in check, but also in enabling better performance in any sporting event.

Most fitness experts regard calisthenics as the best form of exercise to increase muscular development and strength. Although calisthenics are good beginning exercises, participants should complement them with progressive resistance training later on so that there will be an increase in bone mass and connective tissue strength. Such a combination also helps in minimizing any damages or injuries that are apt to occur at the beginning or initial training stages.

Besides calisthenics and progressive resistance training, aerobics can also help in maintaining muscular strength and endurance.

Muscular strength is the maximum amount of force that one can generate in an isolated movement. **Muscular endurance** is the ability of the muscles to perform a sub-maximal task repeatedly or to maintain a sub-maximal muscle contraction for extended periods. Body-support activities (e.g., push-ups and sit-ups) and callisthenic activities (e.g., rope jumping) are good exercises for young students or beginners of all ages. Such exercises use multiple muscle groups and have minimal risk of injury. At more advanced levels of development, and for those students interested in developing higher levels of strength and muscle mass, weight lifting is the optimal activity.

To improve muscular strength and endurance a student can:

- Train with free weights
- Perform exercises that use an individual's body weight for resistance (e.g., push-ups, sit-ups, dips, etc.)
- Do strength training exercises that incorporate all major muscle groups two times per week

Development of Locomotor, Nonlocomotor, Manipulative, and Perceptual Awareness Skills in Children

Motor-development learning theories that pertain to a general skill, activity, or age level are important and necessary background details for effective lesson planning. Motor-skill learning is unique to each individual but does follow a general sequential skill pattern, starting with general gross motor movements and ending with specific or fine motor skills. Teachers must begin instruction at a level where all children are successful and proceed through the activity only to the point where frustration for the majority is hindering performance. In addition, it is important to differentiate the activity so that all students can participate regardless of the inevitable differences in ability and development.

Students must learn the fundamentals of a skill, or subsequent learning of more advanced skills becomes extremely difficult. Instructors must spend enough time on beginning skills to enable them to become second nature. Teaching in small groups with enough equipment for everyone is essential. Practice sessions that are too long or too demanding can cause physical and/or mental burnout.

Teaching skills over a longer period of time, but with slightly different approaches, helps to keep students attentive and involved as they internalize the skill. The instructor can then teach more difficult skills while continuing to review the basics. If the skill is challenging for most students, allow plenty of practice time so they retain it before having to use it in a game situation.

Visualizing and breaking the skill down mentally are other ways to enhance the learning of motor movements. Instructors can teach students to "picture" the steps involved and to see themselves executing the skill. An example is teaching dribbling in basketball. Start teaching the skill with a demonstration of the steps involved in dribbling. Starting with the first skill, introduce key language terms, and have students visualize themselves performing the skill. A sample-progression lesson plan to teach dribbling could begin with students practicing while standing still. Next, add movement while dribbling. Finally, introduce how to control dribbling while being guarded by another student.

Sequential Development and Activities for Locomotor Skills Acquisition

Sequential Development = crawl, creep, walk, run, jump, hop, gallop, slide, leap, skip, step-hop.

- **Activities to develop walking skills** include walking slower and faster in place; walking forward, backward, and sideways with slower and faster paces in straight, curving, and zigzag pathways with various lengths of steps; pausing between steps; and changing the height of the body.
- **Activities to develop running skills** include having students pretend they are playing basketball, trying to score a touchdown, trying to catch a bus, finishing a lengthy race, or running on a hot surface.
- **Activities to develop jumping skills** include alternating jumping with feet together and feet apart, taking off and landing on the balls of the feet, clicking the heels together while airborne, and landing with a foot forward and a foot backward.
- **Activities to develop galloping skills** include having students play a game of Fox and Hound, with the lead foot representing the fox and the back foot the hound trying to catch the fox (alternate the lead foot).
- **Activities to develop sliding skills** include having students hold hands in a circle and sliding in one direction, then sliding in the other direction.
- **Activities to develop hopping skills** include having students hop all the way around a hoop and hopping in and out of a hoop, reversing direction. Students can also place ropes in straight lines and hop side-to-side over the rope from one end to the other and change (reverse) the direction.
- **Activities to develop skipping skills** include having students combine walking and hopping activities leading up to skipping.
- **Activities to develop step-hopping skills** include having students practice stepping and hopping activities while clapping hands to an uneven beat.

Sequential Development and Activities for Nonlocomotor Skill Acquisition

Sequential Development = stretch, bend, sit, shake, turn, rock and sway, swing, twist, dodge, and fall.

- **Activities to develop stretching** include lying on the back and stomach and stretching as far as possible; stretching as though one is reaching for a star, picking fruit off of a tree, climbing a ladder, shooting a basketball, placing an item on a high self, and yawning.
- **Activities to develop bending** include touching knees and toes then straightening the entire body and straightening the body halfway, bending as though picking up a coin, tying shoes, picking flowers/vegetables, and petting animals of different sizes.
- **Activities to develop sitting** include practicing sitting up from standing, kneeling, and lying positions without the use of hands.
- **Activities to develop falling skills** include first collapsing in one's own space and then pretending to fall like bowling pins, raindrops, snowflakes, a rag doll, or Humpty Dumpty.

Manipulative Skill Development

Sequential Development = striking, throwing, kicking, ball rolling, volleying, bouncing, catching, and trapping.

- **Activities to develop striking** begin with the striking of stationary objects by a participant in a stationary position. Next, the person remains still while trying to strike a moving object. Then, both the object and the participant are in motion as the participant attempts to strike the moving object.
- **Activities to develop throwing** include throwing yarn/foam balls against a wall, then at a big target, and finally at targets decreasing in size.
- **Activities to develop kicking** include alternating feet to kick balloons/beach balls, then kicking them under and over ropes. Change the type of ball as proficiency develops.
- **Activities to develop ball rolling** include rolling different size balls to a wall, then to targets decreasing in size.
- **Activities to develop volleying** include using a large balloon and hitting it with both hands, then hitting it with one hand (alternating hands), and then hitting it using different parts of the body. Change the object as students progress (balloon, beach ball, foam ball, etc.)
- **Activities to develop bouncing** include starting with large balls and using both hands to bounce, then using one hand (alternate hands).

- **Activities to develop catching** include using various objects (balloons, beanbags, balls, etc.) to catch, first catching the object the participant has thrown him/herself, then catching objects someone else threw, and finally increasing the distance between the catcher and the thrower.
- **Activities to develop trapping** include trapping slow and fast rolling balls; trapping balls (or other objects such as beanbags) that are lightly thrown at waist, chest, and stomach levels; and trapping different size balls.

Rhythmic Skill Development

Dancing is an excellent activity for the development of rhythmic skills. In addition, any activity that involves moving the body to music can promote rhythmic skill development.

Rules for Individual and Dual Sports

Archery:
- Arrows that bounce off the target or go through the target count as 7 points.
- Arrows landing on lines between two rings receive the higher score of the two rings.
- Arrows hitting the petticoat receive no score.

Badminton:
- Intentionally balking the opponent or making preliminary feints results in a fault (side in = loss of serve; side out = point awarded to side in).
- When a shuttlecock falls on a line, it is in play (i.e., a fair play).
- If the striking team hits a shuttlecock before it crosses net, it is a fault.
- Touching the net when the shuttlecock is in play is a fault.
- The same player hitting the shuttlecock twice is a fault.
- The shuttlecock going through the net is a fault.

Bowling:
- There is no score for a pin knocked down by a pinsetter (human or mechanical).
- There is no score for the pins knocked down when any part of the foot, hand, or arm extends or crosses over the foul line (even after the ball leaves the hand) or if any part of the body contacts the division boards, walls, or uprights that are beyond the foul line.
- There is no count for pins displaced or knocked down by a ball leaving the lane before it reaches the pins.
- There is no count when balls rebound from the rear cushion.

Racquetball/Handball:

- A server stepping outside the service area when serving faults.
- The server is out (relinquishes serve) if he or she steps outside of the serving zone twice in succession while serving.
- A server is out if he or she fails to hit the ball rebounding off the floor during the serve.
- The opponent must have a chance to take a position or the referee must call for play before the server can serve the ball.
- The server re-serves the ball if the receiver is not behind the short line at the time of the serve.
- A served ball that hits the front line and does not land back of the short line is "short"; therefore, it is a fault. The ball is also short when it hits the front wall and two sidewalls before it lands on the floor back of the short line.
- A serve is a fault when the ball touches the ceiling from rebounding off the front wall.
- A fault occurs when any part of the foot steps over the outer edges of the service or the short line while serving.
- A hinder (dead ball) is called when a returned ball hits an opponent on its way to the front wall—even if the ball continues to the front wall.
- A hinder is any intentional or unintentional interference of an opponent's opportunity to return the ball.

Tennis:
A player loses a point when:

- The ball bounces twice on his or her side of the net.
- The player returns the ball to any place outside of designated areas.
- The player stops or touches the ball in the air before it lands out-of-bounds.
- The player intentionally strikes the ball twice with the racket.
- The ball strikes any part of a player or racket after the initial attempt to hit the ball.
- A player reaches over the net to hit the ball.
- A player throws his or her racket at the ball.
- The ball strikes any permanent fixture that is out-of-bounds (other than the net).
- A ball touching the net and landing inside the boundary lines is in play (except on the serve, where a ball contacting the net results in a "let" or replay of the point).
- A player fails, on two consecutive attempts, to serve the ball into the designated area (i.e., a double fault).

Appropriate Behavior in Physical Education Activities

Appropriate Student Etiquette/Behaviors: following the rules and accepting the consequences of unfair action, good sportsmanship, respecting the rights of other students, reporting accidents and mishaps, not engaging in inappropriate behavior under peer pressure encouragement, cooperation, paying attention to instructions and demonstrations, moving to assigned places and remaining in the designated space, complying with directions, practicing as instructed to do so, properly using equipment, and not interfering with the practice of others.

Appropriate Content Etiquette/Behaviors: the teacher describing the performance of tasks and students engaging in the task, the teacher assisting students with task performance, and the teacher modifying and developing tasks.

Appropriate Management Etiquette/Behaviors: the teacher directing the management of equipment, students, and space prior to practicing tasks; students getting equipment and partners; the teacher requesting that students stop "fooling around."

Rules of Team Sports

Basketball:
- A player touching the floor on or outside the boundary line is out-of-bounds.
- The ball is out of bounds if it touches anything (a player, the floor, an object, or any person) that is on or outside the boundary line.
- An offensive player remaining in the three-second zone of the free-throw lane for more than three seconds is a violation.
- A ball firmly held by two opposing players results in a jump ball.
- A throw-in is awarded to the opposing team of the last player touching a ball that goes out-of-bounds.

Soccer:
The following are direct free-kick offenses:
- There is hand or arm contact with the ball.
- A player uses his or her hands to hold an opponent.
- A player pushes an opponent.
- The player engages in striking/kicking/tripping or attempting to strike/kick/trip an opponent.
- The goalie uses the ball to intentionally strike an opponent.
- A player jumps at or charges an opponent.
- The player knees an opponent.
- There are any contact fouls.

The following are indirect free-kick offenses:

- The same player plays the ball twice at the kickoff, on a throw-in, on a goal kick, on a free kick, or on a corner kick.
- The goalie delays the game by holding the ball or carrying the ball more than four steps.
- There is a failure to notify the referee of substitutions/re-substitutions, and that player then handles the ball in the penalty area.
- Any person who is not a player enters the playing field without a referee's permission.
- There are unsportsmanlike actions or words following a referee's decision.
- A player dangerously lowers his or her head or raises his or her foot too high to make a play.
- A player resumes play after being ordered off the field.
- Offsides occurs (offensive players must have at least one defender between themselves and the goal when a teammate passes the ball).
- Players attempt to kick the ball when the goalkeeper has possession or they interfere with the goalkeeper to hinder the release of the ball.
- Illegal charging occurs.
- Players leave the playing field without the referee's permission while the ball is in play.

Softball:
- Each team plays nine players in the field (sometimes ten for slow pitch).
- Field positions are one pitcher, one catcher, four infielders, and three outfielders (four outfielders in ten player formats).
- The four bases are 60 feet apart.
- Any ball hit outside of the first or third base line is a foul ball (i.e., runners cannot advance and the pitch counts as a strike against the batter).
- If a batter receives three strikes (i.e., failed attempts at hitting the ball) in a single at bat, he or she strikes out.
- The pitcher must start with both feet on the pitcher's rubber and can only take one step forward when delivering the underhand pitch.
- A team must maintain the same batting order throughout the game.
- Runners cannot lead off.
- Runners may overrun first base, but they can be tagged out if they run off any other base.

A base runner is out if:
- The opposition tags the runner with the ball before he or she reaches a base.
- The ball reaches first base before the runner does.
- The runner runs outside of the base path to avoid a tag.
- A batted ball strikes him or her in fair territory.

Volleyball:
The following infractions by the receiving team result in a point awarded to the serving side and an infraction by the serving team results in a side-out:

- Illegal serves or serving out of turn occurs.
- Illegal returns, catching, or holding the ball occurs.
- Dribbling occurs or a player touches the ball twice in succession.
- There is contact with the net (two opposing players making contact with the net at the same time results in a replay of the point).
- The ball is touched after it has been played three times without passing over the net.
- A player's foot completely touches the floor over the centerline.
- A player reaches under the net and touches another player or the ball while the ball is in play.
- The players change positions prior to the serve.

Applying Appropriate Strategies to Game and Sport Situations

Basketball Strategies:

Use a zone defense
- To prevent drive-ins for easy lay-up shots.
- When the playing area is small.
- When the team is in foul trouble.
- To keep an excellent rebounder near the opponent's basket.
- When the opponents' outside shooting is weak.
- When opponents have an advantage in height.
- When opponents have an exceptional offensive player, or when the best defenders cannot handle one-on-one defense.

Offensive strategies against zone defense
- Use quick, sharp passing to penetrate the zone, forcing the opposing player out of assigned position.
- Use overloading and mismatching.

Offensive strategies for one-on-one defense
- Use the "pick-and-roll" and the "give-and-go" to screen defensive players to open up offensive players for shot attempts.
- Teams may use free-lancing (spontaneous one-one-one offense), but more commonly they use "sets" of plays.

Soccer Strategies:
- Heading – use the head to pass, to shoot, or to clear the ball.
- Tackling – the objective is to take possession of the ball from an opponent.
- Successful play requires knowledgeable utilization of space.

Badminton Strategies:
Strategies for return of service
- Return serves with shots that are straight ahead.
- Return service so that opponent must move out of his or her starting position.
- Return long serves with an overhead clear or drop shot to the near corner.
- Return short serves with an underhand clear or a net drop to the near corner.

Strategies for serving
- Serve long to the backcourt near the centerline.
- Serve short when the opponent is standing too deep in his or her receiving court to return the serve
- Use a short serve to eliminate a smash return if the opponent has a powerful smash from the backcourt.

Handball or Racquetball Strategies:
- Identify the opponent's strengths and weaknesses.
- Make the opponent use his or her less dominant hand or backhand shots if they are weaker.
- Frequently alternate fastballs and lobs to change the pace (changing the pace is particularly effective for serving).
- Maintain a position near the middle of the court (the well), close enough to play low balls and corner shots.
- Place shots that keep the opponent's position at a disadvantage to return cross-court and angle shots.
- Use high lob shots that go overhead but do not hit the back wall with enough force to rebound and drive an opponent out of position when he or she persistently plays close to the front wall.

Tennis Strategies:
- Lobbing – use a high, lob shot for defense, giving one more time to get back into position.
- Identify the opponent's weaknesses, attack them, and recognize and protect one's own weaknesses.
- Outrun and out-think the opponent.
- Use a change of pace, lobs, spins, approaching the net, and deception at the correct time.

- Hit cross-court (from corner to corner of the court) for maximum safety and an opportunity to regain position.
- Direct the ball where the opponent is not.

Volleyball Strategies:
- Use forearm passes (bumps, digs, or passes) to play balls below the waist, to play hard driven balls, to pass the serve, and to contact balls distant from a player.

The Role of Participation in Physical Activities in Promoting Positive Personal and Social Behaviors

For most people, the development of social roles and appropriate social behaviors occurs during childhood. Physical play between parents and children, as well as between siblings and peers, serves as a strong regulator in the developmental process. Chasing games, roughhousing, wrestling, or practicing sport skills such as jumping, throwing, catching, and striking, are some examples of childhood play. These activities may be competitive or non-competitive; they are important for promoting the social and moral development of both boys and girls. Unfortunately, fathers often engage in this sort of activity more with their sons than their daughters. Regardless of the sex of the child, both boys and girls enjoy these types of activities.

Physical play during infancy and early childhood is central to the development of social and emotional competence. Research shows that children who engage in play that is more physical with their parents, particularly with parents who are sensitive and responsive to the child, exhibited greater enjoyment during the play sessions and were more popular with their peers. Likewise, these early interactions with parents, siblings, and peers are important in helping children to become more aware of their emotions and to learn to monitor and regulate their own emotional responses. Children learn quickly through watching the responses of their parents which behaviors make their parents smile and laugh as well as which behaviors cause their parents to frown and disengage from the activity.

If children want the fun to continue, they engage in the behaviors that please others. As children near adolescence, they learn through rough-and-tumble play that there are limits to how far they can go before hurting someone (physically or emotionally), which results in a termination of the activity or later rejection of the child by peers. These early interactions with parents and siblings are important in helping children learn appropriate behavior in the social situations of sports and physical activities. Such principles may need to be taught in school, however, as not every child will have learned them at home.

Children learn to assess their social competence (e.g., their ability to get along with peers as well as acceptance by peers, family members, teachers, and coaches) in sports through the feedback received from parents and coaches. Initially, authority figures teach children, "You can't do that because I said so." As children approach school age, parents begin the process of explaining why a behavior is right or wrong because children continuously ask, "Why?" In school, it is important to explain why certain behaviors are not appropriate because you want the child to begin to self regulate behavior.

Similarly, when children engage in sports, they learn about taking turns with their teammates, sharing playing time, and valuing rules. They understand that rules are important for everyone, and that without these regulations, the game would become unfair. Learning social competence is continuous as we expand our social arena and learn about different cultures. A constant in the learning process is the role of feedback as we assess the responses of others to our behaviors and comments. Teachers can reinforce correct responses and help guide students away from inappropriate ones.

In addition to the development of social competence, sports participation can help youth to develop other forms of self-competence. Most important among these self-competencies is self-esteem. Self-esteem is how we judge our worth; it indicates the extent to which an individual believes he or she is capable, significant, successful, and worthy. Educators have suggested that one of the biggest barriers to success in the classroom today is low self-esteem.

Children develop self-esteem by evaluating abilities and by evaluating the responses of others. Children actively observe parents' and coaches' responses to their performances, looking for signs of approval or disapproval of their behavior. Children often interpret feedback and criticism as either a negative or a positive response to the behavior. In sports, research shows that the coach is a critical source of information that influences the self-esteem of children.

Little League baseball players whose coaches use a "positive approach" to coaching (e.g., more frequent encouragement, positive reinforcement for efforts, and corrective, instructional feedback) had significantly higher self-esteem ratings over the course of a season than children whose coaches used these techniques less frequently. The most compelling evidence supporting the importance of coaches' feedback was found for those children who started with the lowest self-esteem ratings and considerably increased their self-assessment and self-worth throughout the season. In addition to evaluating themselves more positively, low self-esteem children evaluated their coaches more positively than did children with higher self-esteem who played for coaches who used the "positive approach." Moreover, studies show that 95 percent of children who played for coaches trained to use the positive approach signed up to play baseball the next year, compared with 75 percent of the youth who played for untrained adult coaches.

We cannot overlook the importance of enhanced self-esteem on future participation. A major part of the development of high self-esteem is the pride and joy that children experience as their physical skills improve. Children will feel good about themselves as long as their skills are improving. If children feel that their performance during a game or practice is not as good as that of others, or as good as they think mom and dad would want, they often experience shame and disappointment. It is important to remember that children will vary greatly in their athletic capacity. Their self esteem should be based not upon how their performance compares to that of others, but to how their performance improves with practice. This can be difficult to teacher in team sports unless the coach or teacher takes care to do so.

Some children will view mistakes made during a game as a failure and will look for ways to avoid participating in the task if they receive no encouragement to continue. At this point, it is critical that adults (e.g., teachers and coaches) intervene to help children to interpret the mistake or "failure." We must teach children that a mistake is not synonymous with failure. Rather, a mistake shows us that we need a new strategy, more practice, and/or greater effort to succeed at the task.

Fairness is another trait that physical activities, especially rules-based sports, can foster and strengthen. Children are by nature very rules-oriented, and have a keen sense of what they believe is and isn't fair. Fair play, teamwork, and sportsmanship are all values that stem from proper practice of the spirit of physical education classes. Of course, a pleasurable physical education experience goes a long way towards promoting an understanding of the innate value of physical activity throughout the life cycle.

Social Development

Physical education activities can promote positive social behaviors and traits in a number of different ways. Instructors can foster improved relations with adults and peers by making students active partners in the learning process and delegating responsibilities within the class environment to students. Giving students leadership positions (e.g., team captain) can give them a heightened understanding of the responsibilities and challenges facing educators.

Team-based physical activities like team sports promote collaboration and cooperation. In such activities, students learn to work together, both pooling their talents and minimizing the weaknesses of different team members in order to achieve a common goal. The experience of functioning as a team can be very productive for the development of loyalty between children, and seeing their peers in stressful situations that they can relate to can promote a more compassionate and considerate attitude among students. Similarly, the need to maximize the strengths of each student on a team (who can complement each other and compensate for weaknesses) is a powerful lesson about valuing and respecting diversity and individual differences. Varying students between leading and following positions in a team hierarchy is a good way to help students gain comfort levels being both followers and leaders.

Physical fitness activities incorporate group processes, group dynamics, and a wide range of cooperation and competition issues. Ranging from team sports (which are both competitive and cooperative in nature) to individual competitive sports (like racing), to cooperative team activities without a winner and loser (like a gymnastics team working together to create a human pyramid), there is a great deal of room for the development of mutual respect and support among the students, safe cooperative participation, and analytical, problem-solving, teamwork, and leadership skills.

Teamwork situations are beneficial to students because they create opportunities for them to see classmates with whom they might not generally socialize, and with whom they may not even get along, in a new light. It also creates opportunities for students to develop reliance on each other and to practice interdependence. Cooperation and competition can also offer opportunities for children to practice group work. These situations provide good opportunities to practice analytical thinking and problem-solving in a practical setting.

The social skills and values gained from participation in physical activities include:
- The ability to make adjustments to both self and others by an integration of the individual to society and the environment.
- The ability to make judgments in a group situation.
- Learning to communicate with others and to be cooperative.
- The development of the social phases of personality, attitudes, and values in order to become a functioning member of society (such as being considerate).
- The development of a sense of belonging and acceptance by society.
- The development of positive personality traits.
- Learning for constructive use of leisure time.
- A development of attitude that reflects good moral character.
- Respect of school rules and property.

The above list represents a sample of the socio-cultural benefits of participating in physical activity with others. Physical activity serves as a very important part of the socialization process. Physical activity during the socialization process creates an opportunity for children to define personal comfort levels with different types of physical interaction, as well as to establish guidelines for what is (and is not) acceptable physical behavior as related to their relationship with other individuals.

Participating in physical activity with others is also a step away from the trend of "playground to PlayStation," where students are less and less physically active, and spend less and less time engaging in outdoor physical activity. Physical activity on a socio-cultural level is an important aspect of the struggle against rising obesity levels in the United States, as well as related problems (e.g., heart disease).

OBJECTIVE 0015 UNDERSTAND BASIC ELEMENTS, CONCEPTS, AND TECHNIQUES ASSOCIATED WITH THE ARTS

0015.01   **Identifying the basic elements, concepts, and terms associated with dance, music, drama, and the visual arts (e.g., pathways, rhythm, plot, perspective)**

Elements of Music

- **Accent** - Stress of one tone over others, making it stand out; often it is the first beat of a measure.
- **Accompaniment** - Music that goes along with a more important part; often it is harmony or rhythmic patterns accompanying a melody.
- **Adagio** - Slow, leisurely
- **Allegro** - Lively, brisk, rapid
- **Cadence** - A closing of a phrase or section of music.
- **Chord** - Three or more tones combined and sounded simultaneously.
- **Crescendo** - Gradually growing louder
- **Dissonance** - A simultaneous sounding of tones that produce a feeling of tension or unrest and a feeling that further resolution is needed.
- **Harmony** - The sound resulting from the simultaneous sounding of two or more tones consonant with each other.
- **Interval** - The distance between two tones.
- **Melody** - An arrangement of single tones in a meaningful sequence.
- **Phrase** - A small section of a composition comprising a musical thought.
- **Rhythm** - The regular occurrence of accented beats that shape the character of music or dance.
- **Scale** - A graduated series of tones arranged in a specified order.
- **Staccato** - Separate; sounded in a short, detached manner
- **Syncopation** - The rhythmic result produced when a regularly accented beat is displaced onto an unaccented beat.
- **Tempo** - The rate of speed at which a musical composition is performed.
- **Theme** - A short musical passage that states an idea. It often provides the basis for variations, development, etc.
- **Timbre** - The quality of a musical tone that distinguishes voices.

Elements of Theater

It is vital that teachers be trained in critical areas that focus on important principles of theater education. The basic course of study should include state-mandated topics in arts education, instructional materials, products in arts, both affective and cognitive processes of art, world and traditional cultures, and the most recent teaching tools: media and technology.

Areas that should be included:

- **Acting** - Acting requires the student to demonstrate the ability to effectively communicate using skillful speaking, movement, rhythm, and sensory awareness.
- **Directing** - Direction requires management skills to produce and perform an onstage activity. This requires guiding and inspiring students as well as script and stage supervision.
- **Designing** - Designing involves creating and initiating the onsite management of the art of acting.
- **Scriptwriting** - Scriptwriting demands that a leader be able to produce original material and staging for an entire production. It includes writing and designing a story that has performance value.

Each of the above mentioned skills should be incorporated into daily activities with young children. It is important that children are exposed to character development through stories, role-play, and modeling through various teacher guided experiences. Some of these experiences that are age appropriate for early childhood level include puppet theater, paper dolls, character sketches, storytelling, and re-telling of stories in a student's own words.

Elements of Dance

Dance is an artistic form of self expression that uses the various elements of physical movement such as use of space, time, levels, and force—all of which form a composition.

The primary grades have a gross understanding of their motor movements, whereas older children are apt to have a more refined concept of their bodies. Individual movements should be developed by the instructor with attention to various aspects such as:

1. The **range** of movement or gestures through space.
2. The **direction** of the action or imaginary lines that the body flows through space.
3. The timing of when movements form the dramatic effects.
4. Students being made aware of the **planes** formed by any two areas, such as height and width or width and depth.
5. The introduction of **levels** so that the composition incorporates sitting, standing, and kneeling, etc.
6. Using **elevation**—the degree of lift, as in leaping, and movements that are done under that allusion of suspension.
7. The force and energy of dance can be a reflection of the music, such as adagio (slow music) or allegro (quickening steps).

The various *styles* of dance can be explained as follows.

Creative dance is the type of dance that is most natural to a young child. Creative dance depicts feelings through movement. It is the initial reaction to sound and movement. Older elementary students will often incorporate mood and expressiveness. Stories can be told to release the dancer into imagination. Isadora Duncan is credited with being the mother of modern dance. **Modern dance** today refers to a concept of dance where the expressions of opposites are developed—for example, concepts of fast-slow, contract-release, varying heights, and levels to fall and recover. Modern dance is based on four principles: substance, dynamism, metakinesis, and form.

Social dance requires a steadier capability than the previous levels. Social dances refer to a cooperative form of dance with respect for sharing the dance floor with others and for one's partner. The social aspect of dance, rather than romantic aspect, represents a variety of customs and pastimes. Changing partners frequently within the dance is something that is subtly important to maintain. Social dance may be in the form of marches, the waltz, or the two-step.

Upper level elementary students can learn dance in connection with historical **cultures** (such as the minuet). The minuet was introduced to the court in Paris in 1650, and it dominated the ballroom until the end of the eighteenth century. The waltz was introduced around 1775; it was an occasion of fashion and courtship. The pomp and ceremony of it all makes for fun classroom experiences. Dance is central to many cultures, and the interrelatedness of teaching history and dance (such as a Native American dance, the Mexican hat dance, or Japanese theater) can be highly beneficial to the students.

Structured dances are recognized by particular patterns, such as the tango. They were made popular in dance studios and gym classes alike.

Ritual dances are often of a religious nature; they may celebrate a significant life event such as a harvest season, the rain season, the gods, or ask for favors in hunting, birth, and death. Many of these themes are carried out in movies and theaters today, but they have their roots in Africa.

Dancing at weddings in some cultural groups today is a prime example of ritual dance. The father dances with the bride, then the husband dances with the bride. The two families then dance with one other.

Basic **ballet** uses a barre (a specialized, usually waist high handrail or series of handrails) to practice the five basic positions used in ballet. Alignment is the way in which various parts of the dancer's body are in line with one another while the dancer is moving. It is a very precise dance that is executed with grace and form. The mood and expressions of the music are very important to ballet, as they form the canvas upon which the dance is performed.

0015.02 **Recognizing the basic techniques, processes, tools, and materials for creating, performing, and producing works in the various arts**

Please refer to Skill 15.01 for more on music and the performing arts.

Visual arts

The components and strands of visual art encompass many areas. Students are expected to fine tune observation skills and be able to identify and recreate the experiences that teachers provide for them as learning tools. For example, students may walk as a group on a nature hike, taking in the surrounding elements, and then begin to discuss the repetition found in the leaves of trees, the bricks of the sidewalk, or the size and shapes of the buildings. They may also use such an experience to describe lines, colors, shapes, forms, and textures. Beginning elements of perspective are noticed at an early age. The questions of why buildings look smaller when they are at a far distance and bigger when they are closer are sure to spark the imagination of early childhood students.

Students can also take their inquiries to a higher level of learning with some hands-on activities, such as building three-dimensional buildings using paper and geometric shapes. Eventually, students should acquire higher level thinking skills, such as analysis, in which they will begin to question artists and art work and analyze many different aspects of visual art.

It is vital that students learn to identify the characteristics of visual arts that include materials, techniques, and those processes necessary to establish a connection between art and daily life. Early ages should begin to experience art in a variety of forms. Students should be introduced to the recognition of simple patterns found in the art environment. They must also identify art materials such as clay, paint, and crayons. Each of these types of materials should be introduced and explained for use in daily lessons with young children. Young students may need to be introduced to items that are developmentally appropriate for their age and for their fine motor skills.

Many pre-kindergarten and kindergarten students use oversized pencils and crayons for their first semester. Typically, after this first semester, development occurs enough to enable children to start using smaller sized materials. Students should begin to explore artistic expression at this age using colors and mixing. The color wheel is a vital lesson for young children, as they can begin to learn the uses of primary colors and secondary colors. By the middle of the school year, students should be able to explain the process of mixing. For example, a student may need orange paint but only has a few colors. He or she should be able to determine that by mixing red and yellow, orange is then created.

Teachers should also use variation in lines, shapes, textures, and many different principles of design. By using common environmental figures such as people, animals, and buildings, teachers can base many art lessons on characteristics of readily available examples.

Students should be introduced to as many techniques as possible to ensure that all strands of the visual arts and materials are experienced at a variety of levels. By using original works of art, students should be able to identify visual and actual textures of art and to base their judgments of objects found in everyday scenes. Other examples that can be included as subjects are landscapes, portraits, and still life. The major areas that young students should experience should consist of the following:

- Painting, using tempera or watercolors
- Sculpture, typically using clay or play-dough
- Architecture, performing building or structuring design with 3D materials such as cardboard or poster-board
- Ceramics, using a hollow clay sculpture and pots made from clay and fired in a kiln
- Engraving (cutting design or letters into some medium such as wood or metal); this might involve the use of a stylus and clay tablets in early elementary school and move to sharper cutting tools at upper grade levels.
- Printmaking or Lithography, drawing a design on a surface and lifting the print from the surface

An excellent opportunity for teachers is to create an "art sample book" with the students. These books can include a different variety of textured materials, including sandpaper and cotton balls. Samples of pieces of construction paper designed into various shapes can be used to represent shapes. String samples can represent the element of lines. The sampling of art should also focus clearly on basic colors. Color can be introduced more in-depth when discussing intensity, the strength, and the lightness or darkness of the colors.

0015.03   Recognizing the connections among the arts as well as between the arts and other areas of the curriculum and everyday life

The field of the humanities is overflowing with examples of works of art that reflect common themes, motifs, and symbols. The representation of various themes, motifs, and symbols crosses the lines between the visual arts, literature, music, theater, and dance. Listed below are a few examples culled from the immense heritage of the arts.

Examples of Works that Share Thematic and Symbolic Motifs

A popular symbol or motif of the fifteenth, sixteenth, and seventeenth centuries was David, the heroic second king of the Hebrews. The richness of the stories pertaining to David and the opportunities for visual interpretation made him a favorite among artists, all of whom cast him in different lights. Donatello's bronze statue of *David* is a classically proportioned nude, portrayed with Goliath's head between his feet. His *David* is not gloating over his kill, but instead seems to be viewing his own, sensuous body with a Renaissance air of self-awareness. Verrocchio's bronze sculpture of *David*, also with the severed head of Goliath, represents a confident young man, proud of his accomplishment, and seemingly basking in praise. Michelangelo, always original, gives us a universal interpretation of the David theme. Weapon in hand, Michelangelo's marble *David* tenses muscles as he summons up the power to deal with his colossal enemy, symbolizing as he does so, every person or community who has had to do battle against overwhelming odds. Bernini's marble *David*, created as it was during the Baroque era, explodes with energy as it captures forever the most dramatic moment of David's action, the throwing of the stone that kills Goliath.

Caravaggio's painting, *David and Goliath*, treats the theme in yet another way. Here David is shown as if in the glare of a spotlight, looking with revulsion at the bloodied, grotesque head of Goliath, leaving the viewer to speculate about the reason for disgust. Is David revolted at the ungodliness of Goliath, or is he sickened at his own murderous action?

Symbols related to the David theme include David, Goliath's head, and the stone and slingshot.

Another popular religious motif, especially during the Medieval and Renaissance periods, was the Annunciation. This event was the announcement by the archangel Gabriel to the Virgin Mary that she would bear a son and name him Jesus. It is also believed that this signified the moment of Incarnation.

Anonymous medieval artists treated this theme in altarpieces, murals, and illuminated manuscripts. During the thirteenth century, both Nicola Pisano and his son, Giovanni, carved reliefs of the Annunciation theme. Both men included the Annunciation and the Nativity theme in a single panel. Martini's painted rendition of *The Annunciation* owes something to the court etiquette of the day in the use of the heraldic devises of the symbolic colorings and stilted manner of the Virgin. Della Francesca's fresco of the Annunciation borders on the abstract, with its simplified gestures, its lack of emotion, and the ionic column providing a barrier between Gabriel and Mary. Fra Angelico's *Annunciation* is a lyrical painting, combining soft, harmonious coloring with simplicity of form and gesture.

Symbols related to the Annunciation theme are Gabriel, Mary, the dove of the Holy Spirit, the lily, an olive branch, a garden, a basket of wool, a closed book, and various inscriptions.

During the 1800s, a new viewpoint surfaced in Europe. Intellectuals from several countries became painfully aware of the consequences of social conditions and abuses of the day and set out to expose them.

The English social satirist Hogarth created a series of paintings entitled *Marriage a-la-Mode*, which honed in on the absurdity of arranged marriages. Other works by Hogarth explored conditions that led to prostitution and the poor-house. In France, Voltaire was working on the play *Candide*, which recounted the misfortunes of a young man while providing biting commentary on the social abuses of the period.

In the field of music, Mozart's *Marriage of Figaro*, based on a play by Beaumarchais, explores the emotion of love as experienced by people from all ages and walks of life. At the same time, it portrays the follies of convention in society.

The Effect of a Particular Work upon Another

The history of the humanities is replete with examples of artists in every field being influenced and inspired by specific works of others. Influence and inspiration continuously cross the lines between the various disciplines in the humanities.

Examples of Artistic Works that Influence Another

A) Michelangelo's painting of the Sistine Chapel ceiling (1508-1512) had a profound effect on Raphael, as evidenced by his fresco *The School of Athens* (1509-1511). The influence can be seen by the treatment of the human figures, particularly in the gestures and chiaroscuro.

B) Virgil's epic, the *Aeneid* (29-19) was a source of inspiration to Dante Alighieri, the renowned Florentine writer who claimed to have memorized the lengthy piece. When Dante wrote *The Divine Comedy* (1308-1321), he included Virgil as his (Dante's) guide through hell and purgatory, a character who represents the highest pinnacle of human reason. In addition, his poetry imitates the form of the *Aeneid* in several places.

C) Dante's *The Divine Comedy* (1308-1321), in turn, served as inspiration for many devotees of the Romantic school in the 1800s. In 1822, the French painter Eugene Delacroix painted a canvas entitled *Dante and Virgil in Hell*, an emotional painting illustrating the anguish of tormented souls drowning in the river Styx, as Dante and Virgil pass over them in a capsizing bark. One of Delacroix's companions read the "Inferno" (the first book of *The Divine Comedy*) to him as he painted. Later, Delacroix claimed that the section that most electrified him was the eighth canto of the "Inferno." Also during the mid-1800s, the French author, Victor Hugo, wrote a poem entitled *After Reading Dante*, a Romantic piece full of melancholy ruminations. This poem was later used as the basis for a piano program by the Hungarian composer, Franz Liszt (1811-1886); inspired by *The Divine Comedy* and dedicated to the Romantic notion that the arts be related, Liszt wrote the *Dante Symphony*, reflecting the pathos he found in Dante's work.

D) Homer's *Odyssey* (ca 950-ca 800 BCE) has influenced many of the classical writers, but it is surprising to discover that it also influenced the writing of *Ulysses* (1922) by James Joyce. Because the "stream-of-consciousness" technique is so confusing to readers, Joyce used the classical allusions of the *Odyssey* as a sort of map to help guide readers through his work.

Recognizing Connections between the Arts and Other Disciplines

Whether we express ourselves creatively from the theatrical stage, visually through fine art and dance, or musically, appreciating and recognizing the interrelationships of various art forms are essential to an understanding of ourselves and our diverse society.

By studying and experiencing works of fine art and literature, and by understanding their place in cultural and intellectual history, we can develop an appreciation of the human significance of the arts and humanities through history and across cultures.

Through art projects, field trips, and theatrical productions, students can learn that all forms of art are a way for cultures to communicate with each other and the world at large. By understanding the concepts, techniques, and various materials used in the visual arts, music, dance, and written word, students can begin to appreciate the concept of using art to express oneself. Perhaps they can begin by writing a short story, which can then be transformed into a play with costumes, music, and movement to experience the relationship between different art forms.

In recent years, more and more emphasis has been placed on the need to *differentiate* instruction and to offer students a variety of ways to respond to literature as well as to other areas of instruction. Art can provide another means by which students can respond to their learning. An artistic rendering of their feelings in response to a literature selection can be a literal drawing of some scene or an abstract use of color or lines to represent a feeling evoked by the piece. Some children may be better able to "retell" the main events in a story (a frequent comprehension requirement) through drawings of these events. A child studying the conditions in Europe that led people to choose to come to the new world to colonize it, might use art to demonstrate their knowledge (e.g., a crown depicted negatively, portrayal of poverty or hunger or persecution, etc.), and so forth. It is important to remember that art is a form of expression and can be used to access a child's knowledge and thoughts.

The arts have played a significant role throughout history. The communicative power of the arts is notable. Cultures use the arts to impart specific emotions and feelings, to tell stories, to imitate nature, and to persuade others. The arts bring meaning to ceremonies, rituals, celebrations, and recreation. By creating their own art and by examining art made by others, children can learn to make sense of and communicate ideas. This can be accomplished through dance, verbal communication, music, and other visual arts.

Through the arts and humanities, students will realize that although people are different, they share common experiences and attitudes. They will also learn that the use of nonverbal communication can be a strong adjunct to verbal communication.

0015.04   **Recognizing how the arts can be used as a form of communication, self-expression, and social expression; the role and function of the arts in various cultures and throughout history; and diverse strategies for promoting critical analysis, cultural perspectives, and aesthetic understanding of the arts**

Music

When we listen to certain music styles, they often connect us to a memory, a time in the past, or even an entire historical period. Very often, classical pieces, such as Bach or Beethoven, create a picture in our minds of the Baroque Period. The historical perspective of music can deepen one's understanding both of the music and of the historical period.

Throughout history, different cultures have developed different styles of music. Music characteristic of a particular culture can help students better understand that culture.

Music styles varied across cultures and throughout periods in history. As in the opening discussion, classical music, although still popular and being created today, is often associated with traditional classical periods in history such as the Renaissance.

As world contact merged more and more as civilizations developed and prospered, increased influence from various cultural styles emerged across music styles. For example, African drums emerged in some Contemporary and Hip Hop music. Also, the Bluegrass music in the United States developed from the "melting pot" contributions from Irish, Scottish, German, and African-American instrumental and vocal traditions.

In addition, the purposes for music changed throughout cultures and times. Music has been used for entertainment, but also for instruction, propaganda, worship, ceremony, and communication.

Common Musical Styles

Medieval
Classical Music (loosely encompassing Renaissance and Baroque)
Gospel Music
Jazz
Latin Music
Rhythm and Blues
Funk
Rock
Country
Folk
Bluegrass
Electronic (Techno)
Melodic
Island (Ska, Reggae, and other)
Hip Hop
Pop
African
Contemporary

Visual Art

Teachers should be able to utilize and teach various techniques when analyzing works of art. Students will learn and then begin to apply what they have learned in the arts to all subjects across the curriculum. By using problem-solving techniques and creative skills, students will begin to master the techniques necessary to derive meaning from both visual and sensory aspects of art.

Students should be asked to review, respond, and analyze various types of art. They must learn to be critical, and it is necessary that students relate art in terms of life and human aspects of life. Students should be introduced to the wide range of opportunities to explore such art. Examples may include exhibits, galleries, museums, libraries, and personal art collections. It is imperative that students learn to research and locate artistic opportunities that are common in today's society. Some opportunities for research include reproductions, art slides, films, print materials, and electronic media.

Once students are taught how to effectively research and use sources, they should be expected to graduate to higher level thinking skills. Students should be able to begin to reflect on, interpret, evaluate, and explain how works of art and various styles of art work explain social, psychological, cultural, and environmental aspects of life.

Theater and Dance

Students are expected to be able to meet a variety of standards set forth for performing arts and dance. It is necessary for young students to master skills such as walking, running, galloping, jumping, hopping, and balance. Students must also learn to discriminate between opposites used to describe performance activities such a high/low, forward/backward, and move/freeze. Creative movements and expressions are necessary tools for dance as well. Students must be able to recall a feeling or personal experience they have had and perform accordingly. Students must learn to discern between different types of dance and dance experiences as well as learn what to expect from performances regarding staging, costume, setting, and music.

THE ARTS THROUGHOUT HISTORY[SAW54]

The greatest works in art, literature, music, theater, and dance all mirror universal themes. **Universal themes** are themes that reflect the human experience, regardless of time period, location, or socioeconomic standing. Universal themes tend to fall into broad categories, such as Man vs. Society, Man vs. Himself, Man vs. God, Man vs. Nature, and Good vs. Evil, to name the most obvious. The general themes listed below all fall into one of these broad categories.

Prehistoric Arts (ca 1,000,000-ca 8,000 BCE)
Major themes of this vast period appear to center around religious fertility rites and sympathetic magic, consisting of the imagery of pregnant animals and faceless, pregnant women.

Mesopotamian Arts (ca 8,000-400 BCE)
The prayer statues and cult deities of the period point to the theme of polytheism in religious worship.

Egyptian Arts (ca 3,000-100 BCE)

The predominance of funerary art from ancient Egypt illustrates the theme of preparation for the afterlife and polytheistic worship. Another dominant theme, reflected by artistic convention, is the divinity of the pharaohs. In architecture, the themes are monumentality and adherence to ritual.

Greek Arts (800-100 BCE)

The sculptures of ancient Greece are replete with human figures—most nude and some draped. The majority of these sculptures represent athletes and various gods and goddesses. The predominant theme is that of the ideal human, in both mind and body. In architecture, the theme is scale based on the ideal human proportions.

Roman Arts (ca 480 BCE- 476 CE)

Judging from Roman arts, the predominant themes of the period deal with the realistic depiction of human beings and how they relate to Greek classical ideals. The emphasis is on practical realism. Another major theme is the glory in serving the Roman state. In architecture, the theme is rugged practicality mixed with Greek proportions and elements.

Western Art

Middle Ages Arts (300-1400 CE): Although the time span is expansive, the major themes remain relatively constant. Since the Roman Catholic Church was the primary patron of the time, most work is religious in nature. The purpose of much of the art is to educate. Specific themes vary from the illustration of Bible stories to interpretations of theological allegory, and the lives of the saints to consequences of good and evil. Depictions of the Holy Family are popular. Themes found in secular art and literature center on chivalric love and warfare. In architecture, the theme is the glorification of God and the education of the congregation to religious principles.

Renaissance Arts (ca 1400-1630 CE): Renaissance themes include Christian religious depiction (see Middle Ages), but they tend to reflect a renewed interest in all things classical. Specific themes include Greek and Roman mythological and philosophic figures, ancient battles, and legends. Dominant themes mirror the philosophic beliefs of Humanism, emphasizing individuality and human reason, such as those of the High Renaissance, which center around the psychological attributes of individuals. In architecture, the theme is scale based on human proportions.

Baroque Arts (1630-1700 CE): The predominant themes found in the arts of the Baroque period include the dramatic climaxes of well-known stories, legends, and battles and the grand spectacle of mythology. Religious themes are found frequently, but it is drama and insight that are emphasized, and not the medieval "salvation factor." Baroque artists and authors incorporated various types of characters into their works, often being careful to include minute details. Portraiture focuses on the psychology of the sitters. In architecture, the theme is large scale grandeur and splendor.

Eighteenth Century Arts (1700-1800 CE): Rococo themes of this century focus on religion, light mythology, portraiture of aristocrats, pleasure, and escapism (and occasionally satire). In architecture, the theme is artifice and gaiety, combined with an organic quality of form. Neo-classical themes center on examples of virtue and heroism, usually in classical settings and historical stories. In architecture, classical simplicity and utility of design is regained.

Nineteenth Century Arts (1800-1900 CE): Romantic themes include human freedom, equality, civil rights, a love for nature, and a tendency toward the melancholic and mystic. The underlying theme is that the most important discoveries are made within the self, and not in the exterior world. In architecture, the theme is fantasy and whimsy, known as "picturesque." Realistic themes include social awareness and a focus on society victimizing individuals. The themes behind Impressionism demonstrate the constant flux of the universe and the immediacy of the moment. In architecture, the themes are strength, simplicity, and upward thrust as skyscrapers entered the scene.

Twentieth Century Arts (1900-2000 CE)

Diverse artistic themes of the century reflect a parting with traditional religious values and a painful awareness of man's inhumanity to man. Themes also illustrate a growing reliance on science, while simultaneously expressing disillusionment with man's failure to adequately control science. A constant theme is the quest for originality and self-expression, while seeking to express the universal in human experience. In architecture, "form follows function."

Genres by Historical Periods

Ancient Greek Art (ca 800-323 BCE)

Dominant genres from this period are vase paintings, both black-figure and red-figure, and classical sculpture.

Roman Art (ca 480 BCE- 476 CE)

Major genres from the Romans include frescoes (murals done in fresh plaster to affix the paint), classical sculpture, funerary art, state propaganda art, and relief work on cameos.

Middle Ages Art (ca 300-1400 CE)
Significant genres during the Middle Ages include Byzantine mosaics, illuminated manuscripts, ivory relief, altarpieces, cathedral sculpture, and fresco paintings in various styles.

Renaissance Art (1400-1630 CE)
Important genres from the Renaissance include Florentine fresco painting (mostly religious), High Renaissance painting and sculpture, Northern oil painting, Flemish miniature painting, and Northern printmaking.

Baroque Art (1630-1700 CE)
Pivotal genres during the Baroque era include Mannerism, Italian Baroque painting and sculpture, Spanish Baroque, Flemish Baroque, and Dutch portraiture. Genre paintings in still-life and landscape appear prominently in this period.

Eighteenth Century Art (1700-1800 CE)
Predominant genres of the century include Rococo painting, portraiture, social satire, Romantic painting, and Neoclassic painting and sculpture.

Nineteenth Century Art (1800-1900 CE)
Important genres include Romantic painting, academic painting and sculpture, landscape painting of many varieties, realistic painting of many varieties, impressionism, and many varieties of post-impressionism.

Twentieth Century Art (1900-2000 CE)
Major genres of the twentieth century include symbolism, art nouveau, fauvism, expressionism, cubism (both analytical and synthetic), futurism, non-objective art, abstract art, surrealism, social realism, constructivism in sculpture, Pop and Op art, and conceptual art.

Strategies for Promoting Critical Analysis, Cultural Perspectives, and Aesthetic Understandings of the Arts

Although the elements of design have remained consistent throughout history, the emphasis on specific aesthetic principles has periodically shifted. Aesthetic standards or principles vary from time period to time period and from society to society.

East and West

An obvious difference in aesthetic principles occurs between works created by eastern and western cultures. Eastern works of art are more often based on spiritual considerations, while much Western art is secular in nature. In attempting to convey reality, Eastern artists generally prefer to use line, local color, and a simplistic view. Western artists tend toward a literal use of line, shape, color, and texture to convey a concise, detailed, complicated view. Eastern artists portray the human figure with symbolic meanings and little regard for muscle structure, resulting in a mystical view of the human experience. Western artists use the "principle of ponderation," which requires the knowledge of both human anatomy and an expression of the human spirit.

In attempts to convey the illusion of depth or visual space in a work of art, Eastern and Western artists use different techniques. Eastern artists generally prefer a diagonal projection of eye movement into the picture plane, and they often leave large areas of the surface untouched by detail. The result is the illusion of vast space, an infinite view that coincides with the spiritual philosophies of the Orient. Western artists rely on several techniques, such as overlapping planes, variation of object size, object position on the picture plane, linear and aerial perspective, color change, and various points of perspective to convey the illusion of depth. The result is space that is limited and closed.

In the application of color, Eastern artists use arbitrary choices of color. Western artists generally rely on literal color usage or emotional choices of color. The end result is that Eastern art tends to be more universal in nature, while Western art is more individualized.

Renaissance and Baroque

An interesting change in aesthetic principles occurred between the Renaissance period (1400-1630 CE) and the Baroque period (1630-1700 CE) in Europe.

The Renaissance period was concerned with the rediscovery of the works of classical Greece and Rome. The art, literature, and architecture were inspired by classical orders, which tended to be formal, simple, and concerned with the ideal human proportions. This means that the paintings, sculptures, and architecture were of a closed nature, composed of forms that were restrained and compact. For example, consider the visual masterpieces of the period: Raphael's painting *The School of Athens*, with its precise use of space; Michelangelo's sculpture *David*, with its compact mass; and the facade of the *Palazzo Strozzi*, with its defined use of the rectangle, arches, and rustication of the masonry.

Compare the Renaissance characteristics to those of the Baroque period. The word "baroque" means "grotesque," which was the contemporary criticism of the new style. In comparison to the styles of the Renaissance, the Baroque was concerned with the imaginative flights of human fancy. The paintings, sculptures, and architecture were of an open nature, composed of forms that were whimsical and free-flowing. Consider again the masterpieces of the period: Ruben's painting *The Elevation of the Cross*, with its turbulent forms of light and dark tumbling diagonally through space; Puget's sculpture *Milo of Crotona*, with its use of open space and twisted forms; and Borromini's *Chapel of St. Ivo*, with a facade that plays convex forms against concave ones.

In the 1920s and 30s, the German art historian, Professor Wolfflin, outlined these shifts in aesthetic principles in his influential book *Principles of Art History*. He arranged these changes into five categories of "visual analysis," sometimes referred to as the "categories of stylistic development." Wolfflin was careful to point out that no style is inherently superior to any other; they are simply indicators of the phase of development of that particular time or society. However, Wolfflin goes on to state, correctly or not, that once the evolution occurs, it is impossible to regress. These modes of perception apply to drawing, painting, sculpture, and architecture. They are as follows:

From a linear mode to a painterly mode

This shift refers to stylistic changes that occur when perception or expression evolves from a linear form that is concerned with the contours and boundaries of objects to a perception or expression that stresses the masses and volumes of objects. To move from viewing objects in isolation to seeing the relationships between objects is an important change in perception. Linear mode implies that objects are stationary and unchanging, while the painterly mode implies that objects and their relationships to other objects are always in a state of flux.

From plane to recession

This shift refers to the perception or expression that evolves from a planar style, wherein the artist views movement in the work in an "up and down" and "side to side" manner, to a recessional style, wherein the artist views the balance of a work in an "in and out" manner. The illusion of depth may be achieved through either style, but only the recessional style uses an angular movement forward and backward through the visual plane.

From closed to open form

This shift refers to the perception or expression that evolves from a sense of enclosure, or limited space in "closed form," to a sense of freedom in "open form." The concept is obvious in architecture, as in buildings that clearly differentiate between "outside" and "inside" space, and buildings that open up the space to allow the outside to interact with the inside.

From multiplicity to unity

This shift refers to an evolution from expressing unity through the use of balancing many individual parts to expressing unity by subordinating some individual parts to others. Multiplicity stresses the balance between existing elements, whereas unity stresses emphasis, domination, and the accent of some elements over other elements.

From absolute to relative clarity

This shift refers to an evolution from works that clearly and thoroughly express everything there is to know about the object to works that express only part of what there is to know, and leave the viewer to fill in the rest from his or her own experiences. Relative clarity, then, is a sophisticated mode, because it requires the viewer to actively participate in the "artistic dialogue." Each of the previous four categories is reflected in this, as linearity is considered to be concise, while painterliness is more subject to interpretation. Planarity is more factual, while recessional movement is an illusion, and so on.

REFERENCES

Ager, C. L. & Cole, C. L. (1991). A review of cognitive-behavioral interventions for children and adolescents with behavioral disorders. *Behavioral Disorders, 16,* 260-275.

Aiken, L. R. (1985). *Psychological testing and assessment* (5th ed.). Boston: Allyn and Bacon.

Alberto, P. A. & Trouthman, A. C. (1990). *Applied behavior analysis for teachers: influencing student performance.* Columbus, Ohio: Charles E. Merrill.

Algozzine, B. (1990). *Behavior problem management: Educator's resource service.* Gaithersburg, MD: Aspen Publishers.

Algozzine, B., Ruhl, K., & Ramsey, R. (1991). *Behaviorally disordered: assessment for identification and instruction: CED mini-library.* Renson, VA: The Council for Exceptional Children.

Ambron, S. R. (1981). *Child development* (3rd ed.). New York: Holt, Rinehart and Winston.

Anders, P. L., & Bos, C. S. (1986). Semantic feature analysis: An interactive strategy for vocabulary development and text comprehension. *Journal of Reading, 29,* 610-16.

Anerson, V., & Black, L. (Eds.). (1987, Winter). National news: US Department of Education releases special report (editorial). *GLRS Journal* [Georgia Learning Resources System].

Anguili, R. (1987, Winter). The 1986 amendment to the Education of the Handicapped Act. *Confederation* [Georgia Federation Council for Exceptional Children].

Ashlock, R. B. (1976). *Error patterns in computation: A semi-programmed approach* (2nd ed.). Columbus, Ohio: Charles E. Merrill.

Association of Retarded Citizens of Georgia (1987). *1986-87 Government report.* College Park, GA: Author.

Ausubel, D. P. & Sullivan, E. V. (1970). *Theory and problems of child development.* New York: Grune & Stratton.

Banks, J. A., & McGee Banks, C. A. (1993). *Multicultural education* (2nd ed.). Boston: Allyn and Bacon.

Baratta-Lorton, M. (1978). *Mathematics their way: An activity-centered mathematics program for early childhood education*. Menlo Park, CA: Addison-Wesley.

Barrett, T. C. (1985). The relationship between measures of prereading visual discrimination and first grade reading achievement: A review of the literature. *Reading Research Quarterly,* 1, 51-76.

Barrett, T. C. (ed.) (1967). *The evaluation of children's reading achievement in perspectives in reading, No. 8*. Newark, Delaware: International Reading Association.

Bartoli, J. S. (1989). An ecological response to Cole's interactivity alternative. *Journal of Learning Disabilities*, 22, 292-297.

Bauer, A. M., & Shea, T. M. (1989). *Teaching exceptional students in your classroom*. Boston: Allyn and Bacon.

Bentley, E. L. (1980). *Questioning skills* (Videocassette & Manual Series). Northbrook, IL: Hubbard Scientific Company. (Project STRETCH [Strategies to Train Regular Educators to Teach Children with Handicaps], Module 1.

Berdine, W. H., & Blackhurst, A. E. (1985). *An introduction to special education*. (2nd ed.) Boston: Little, Brown and Company.

Bialo, E., & Sivin, J. (1990). *Report on the effectiveness of microcomputers in schools*. Washington, DC: Software Publishers Association.

Biemiller, A. (2003). Oral comprehension sets the ceiling on reading comprehension. *American Educator,* 27, 23-44.

Blake, K. (1976). *The mentally retarded: An educational psychology*. Englewood Cliff, NJ: Prentice-Hall.

Blevins, W. (1997). *Phonemic awareness activities for early reading success: Easy, playful activities that prepare children for phonics instruction*. New York: Scholastic.

Bley, N. S., Thornton, C. A., & Bley, N. S. (2001). *Teaching mathematics to students with learning disabilities*. Austin, Tex: Pro-Ed.

Bloom, B. S. (1956). *Taxonomy of educational objectives, handbook I: The cognitive domain*. New York: David McKay Co.

Bohline, D. S. (1985). Intellectual and affective characteristics of attention deficit disordered children. *Journal of Learning Disabilities*, 18, 604-608.

Boone, R. (1983). Legislation and litigation. In R. E. Schmid, & L. Negata (Eds.). *Contemporary Issues in Special Education*. New York: McGraw Hill.

Brantlinger, E. A., & Guskin, S. L. (1988). Implications of Social and Cultural Differences for Special Education. In Meten, E. L. Vergason, G. A., & Whelan, R. J. *Effective instructional strategies for exceptional children*. Denver, CO: Love Publishing.

Brolin, D. E. (Ed). (1989). *Life centered career education: A competency based approach*. Reston, VA: The Council for Exceptional Children.

Brolin, D. E., & Kokaska, C. J. (1979). *Career education for handicapped children and youth*. Renton, VA: The Council for Exceptional Children.

Brown, J. W., Lewis, R. B., & Harcleroad, F. F. (1983). *AV instruction: technology, media, and methods* (6th ed.). New York: McGraw-Hill.

Bryan, T. H., & Bryan, J. H. (1986). *Understanding learning disabilities* (3rd ed.). Palo Alto, CA: Mayfield.

Bryen, D. N. (1982). *Inquiries into child language*. Boston: Allyn & Bacon.

Bucher, B. D. (1987). *Winning them over*. New York: Times Books.

Burns, P. C., Roe, B. D., & Smith, S. H. (2002). *Teaching reading in today's elementary schools*. (8th ed.). Boston: Houghton Mifflin.

Bush, W. L., & Waugh, K. W. (1982). *Diagnosing learning problems* (3rd ed.). Columbus, OH: Charles E. Merrill.

Carbo, M., & Dunn, K. (1986). *teaching students to read through their individual learning styles*. Englewood Cliffs, NJ: Prentice Hall.

Carlyon, W. D. (1997). Attribution retraining: implications for its integration into prescriptive social skills training. *School Psychology Review*. 26 (1), 61.

Cartwright, G. P., & Cartwright, C. A., & Ward, M. E. (1984). *Educating special learners* (2nd ed.). Belmont, CA: Wadsworth.

Cejka, J. M., & Needham, F. (1976). *Approaches to mainstreaming*. (Filmstrip and cassette kit, units 1 & 2). Boston: Teaching Resources Corporation.

Chalfant, J. C. (1985). Identifying learning disabled students: A summary of the National Task Force Report. *Learning Disabilities Focus,* 1, 9-20.

Chaney, C. (1994). Language development, metalinguistic awareness, and emergent literacy skills of 3-year-old children in relation to social class. *Applied Psycholinguistics,* 15, 371.

Chard, D. J., & Osborn, J. 1999. Phonics and word recognition instruction in early reading programs: Guidelines for accessibility". *Learning Disabilities Research and Practice,* 14, 107-17.

Charles, C. M. (1976). *Individualizing instruction.* St Louis: The C. V. Mosby Company.

Chrispeels, J. H. (1991). District leadership in parent involvement: Policies and actions in San Diego. *Phi Delta Kappan,* 71, 367-371.

Clarizio, H. F. & McCoy, G. F. (1983). *Behavior disorders in children* (3rd ed.). New York: Harper & Row.

Clay, M. M. (1967). The reading behavior of five-year-old children. *New Zealand Journal of Educational Studies,* 2, 11-31.

Coles, G. S. (1989). Excerpts from the learning mystique: A critical look at disabilities. *Journal of Learning Disabilities*, 22, 267-278.

Collins, E. (1980). *Grouping and special students.* (Videocassette & manual series). Northbrook, IL: Hubbard Scientific Company. (Project STRETCH [Strategies to Train Regular Educators to Teach Children with Handicaps], Module 17.

Compton, C., (1984). *A guide to 75 tests for special education.* Belmont, CA., Pitman Learning.

Cooper, J. D., & Kiger, N. D. (2009). *Literacy: Helping students construct meaning.* Boston: Houghton Mifflin.

Council for Exceptional Children (1983). *Council for exceptional children code of ethics* (Adopted April 1983). Reston, VA: Author.

Council for Exceptional Children. (1976). *Introducing P. L. 94-142.* [Filmstrip-cassette kit manual]. Reston, VA: Author.

Council for Exceptional Children. (1987). *The council for exceptional children's fall 1987 catalog of products and services.* Renton, VA: Author.

Craig, E., & Craig, L. (1990). *Reading in the content areas.* (Videocassette & manual series). Northbrook, IL: Hubbard Scientific Company. (Project STRETCH [Strategies to Train Regular Educators to Teach Children with Handicaps], Module 13.

Czajka, J. L. (1984). *Digest of data on persons with disabilities* (Mathematics Policy Research, Inc.). Washington, D. C.: U. S. Government Printing Office.

Dell, H. D. (1972). *Individualizing instruction: Materials and classroom procedures.* Chicago: Science Research Associates.

Demonbreun, C., & Morris, J. *Classroom management* [Videocassette & Manual series]. Northbrook, IL: Hubbard Scientific Company. Project STRETCH (Strategies to Train Regular Educators to Teach Children with Handicaps]. Module 5.

Department of Health, Education, and Welfare, Office of Education. (1977, August 23). Education of handicapped children. *Federal Register, 42,* 163.

Digangi, S. A., Perryman, P., & Rutherford, R. B., Jr. (1990). Juvenile offenders in the 90's: A descriptive analysis. *Perceptions,* 25, 5-8.

Division of Educational Services, Special Education Programs (1986). *Fifteenth annual report to congress on implementation of the Education of the Handicapped Act.* Washington, D.C.: U.S. Government Printing Office.

Doyle, B. A. (1978). Math readiness skills. Paper presented at National Association of School Psychologists, New York. In Dunn, R. S. and Dunn, K. J. (1978). *Teaching students through their individual learning styles.* Reston, Va.: Reston Publishing.

Duke, N. K, Bennett-Armistead, V.S., & Roberts, E. M. (2003). Filling the nonfiction void. *American Educator, 27,* 30.

Dunn, R. S., & Dunn, K. J. (1978). *Teaching students through their individual learning styles: A practical approach.* Reston, VA: Reston Publishing.

Ekwall, E. E., & Shanker, J. L. 1983). *Diagnosis and remediation of the disabled reader* (2nd ed.) Boston: Allyn and Bacon.

Epstein, M. H., Patton, J. R., Polloway, E. A., & Foley, R. (1989). Mild retardation: student characteristics and services. *Education and Training of the Mentally Retarded,* 24, 7-16.

Ezell, H. K., & Justice, L. M. (2000). Increasing the print focus of adult-child shared book reading through observational learning". *American Journal of Speech Language Pathology,* 9, 36-47.

Firth, E. E. & Reynolds, I. (1983). Slide tape shows: A creative activity for the gifted students. *Teaching Exceptional Children,* 15, 151-153.

Flippo, R. F. (2002). *Reading assessment and instruction: A qualitative approach to diagnosis.* Portsmouth, NH: Heinemann.

Flippo, R. F. (2003). *Assessing readers: Qualitative diagnosis and instruction.* Portsmouth, NH: Heinemann.

Frith, U. (1985). Beneath the surface of developmental dyslexia. In Patterson, K., Marshall, J. C., & Coltheart, M. *Surface dyslexia: Neuropsychological and cognitive studies of phonological reading*. London: L. Erlbaum Associates, 1985.

Frymier, J., & Gansneder, B. (1989). The Phi Delta Kappa study of students at risk. *Phi Delta Kappan, 71*, 142-146.

Fuchs, D., & Deno, S. L. 1992). Effects of curriculum within curriculum-based measurement. *Exceptional Children, 58*, 232-42.

Fuchs, D., & Fuchs, L. S. (1989). Effects of examiner familiarity on Black, Caucasian, and Hispanic Children: A meta-analysis. *Exceptional Children, 55*, 303-308.

Fuchs, L. S., & Shinn, M. R. (1989). Writing CBM IEP Objectives. In M. R. Shinn, *Curriculum-based measurement: assessing special students*. New York: Guilford Press.

Gage, N. L. (1990). Dealing with the dropout problems? *Phi Delta Kappan, 72*, 280-85.

Gallagher, P. A. (1988). *Teaching students with behavior disorders: Techniques and activities for classroom instruction* (2nd ed.). Denver, CO: Love Publishing.

Gearheart, B. R. & Weishahn, M. W. (1986). *The handicapped student in the regular classroom* (2nd ed.). St Louis, MO: The C. V. Mosby Company.

Gearheart, B. R. (1980). *Special education for the 80s*. St. Louis, MO: The C. V. Mosby Company.

Gearheart, B. R. (1985). *Learning disabilities: Educational strategies* (4th ed.). St. Louis: C. V. Mosby Company.

Georgia Department of Education. Program for Exceptional Children (1986). *Mild mentally handicapped* (Vol. II), Atlanta, GA: Office of Instructional Services, Division of Special Programs, and Program for Exceptional Children. Resource Manuals for Program for Exceptional Children.

Geren, K. (1979). *Complete special education handbook*. West Nyack, NY: Parker.

Gillet, P. K. (1988). Career development. In Robinson, G. A., Patton, J. R., Polloway, E. A., & Sargent, L. R. (eds.). *Best practices in mild mental disabilities*. Reston, VA: The Division on Mental Retardation of the Council for Exceptional Children.

Gillingham, A., & Stillman, B. W. (1997). *The Gillingham manual: Remedial training for students with specific disability in reading, spelling, and penmanship.* Cambridge, MA: Educators Pub. Service.

Glass, G. G. (1967). The strange world of syllabication. *Elementary School Journal,* 67, 403-05.

Gleason, J. B. (1993). *The development of language* (3rd ed.). New York: Macmillan Publishing.

Good, T. L., & Brophy, J. E. (1978). *Looking into classrooms* (2nd Ed.). New York: Harper & Row.

Goodman, K. S. (1985). Growing into Literacy. *Prospects: Quarterly Review of Education,* 15, 57-65.

Gresham, F. (1995). Best practices in social skills training. In Thomas & Grimes (eds.) *Best practices in school psychology* (pp. 1021-1030). Washington, DC: National Association of School Psychologists.

Hall, M. A. (1979). Language-centered reading: Premises and recommendations. *Language Arts,* 56, 664-670.

Hallahan, D. P. & Kauffman, J. M. (1994). *Exceptional children: Introduction to special education* (6th ed.). Boston: Allyn and Bacon.

Halllahan, D. P. & Kauffman, J. M. (1988). *Exceptional children: Introduction to special education.* (4th ed.). Englewood Cliffs, NJ; Prentice-Hall.

Hamill, D. D., & Brown, L. & Bryant, B. (1989) *A consumer's guide to tests in print.* Austin, TX: Pro-Ed.

Hammill, D. D., & Bartel, N. R. (1982). *Teaching children with learning and behavior problems* (3rd ed.). Boston: Allyn and Bacon.

Hammill, D. D., & Bartel, N. R. (1986). *Teaching students with learning and behavior problems* (4th ed.). Boston and Bacon.

Haney, J. B. & Ullmer, E. J. (1970). *Educational media and the teacher.* Dubuque, IA: Wm. C. Brown Company.

Hardman, M. L., Drew, C. J., Egan, M. W., & Wolf, B. (1984). *Human exceptionality: Society, school, and family.* Boston: Allyn and Bacon.

Hardman, M. L., Drew, C. J., Egan, M. W., & Worlf, B. (1990). *Human exceptionality* (3rd ed.). Boston: Allyn and Bacon.

Hargrove, L. J., & Poteet, J. A. (1984). *Assessment in special education.* Englewood Cliffs, NJ: Prentice-Hall.

Haring, N. G., & Bateman, B. (1977). *Teaching the learning disabled child.* Englewood Cliffs, NJ: Prentice-Hall.

Harris, K. R., & Pressley, M. (1991). The nature of cognitive strategy instruction: Interactive strategy instruction. *Exceptional Children*, 57, 392-401.

Hart, T., & Cadora, M. J. (1980). The exceptional child: Label the behavior. [Videocassette & manual series], Northbrook, IL: Hubbard Scientific Company. (Project STRETCH [Strategies to Train Regular Educators to Teach Children with Handicaps], Module 12.

Hart, V. (1981) *Mainstreaming children with special needs.* New York: Longman.

Hatfield, M. M., Edwards, N. T., Bitter, G. G., & Morrow, J. (2005). *Mathematics methods for elementary and middle school teachers.* (5th ed.). New York: Wiley.

Henley, M., Ramsey, R. S., & Algozzine, B. (1993). *Characteristics of and strategies for teaching students with mild disabilities.* Boston: Allyn and Bacon.

Henry, F., Reed, V. & McAllister, L. (1995). Adolescents' perceptions of the relative importance of selected communications skills in their positive peer relationships. *Language, speech, and hearing services in schools.* 26, 263-272.

Hewett, F. M., & Forness, S. R. (1984). *Education of exceptional learners.* (3rd ed.). Boston: Allyn and Bacon.

Hoban, T. (1987) *26 letters and 99 cents.* New York: Greenwillow Books.

Hook, P., & Jones, S. (2002). The importance of automaticity and fluency for efficient reading comprehension. *Perspectives: The International Dyslexia Association,* 28, 9-14.

Howe, C. E. (1981) *Administration of special education.* Denver: Love.

Human Services Research Institute (1985). *Summary of data on handicapped children and youth.* Washington, D.C.: U.S. Government Printing Office.

International Reading Association. (1981). *Resolution on misuse of grade equivalents.* Newark, DE: Author.

International Reading Association. (1997). *The role of phonics in reading instruction: A position statement of the International Reading Association.* Newark, Del: International Reading Association.

Johnson, D. D., & Pearson, P. D. (1984). *Teaching reading vocabulary.* New York: Holt, Rinehart and Winston.

Johnson, D. W. (1972) *Reaching out: Interpersonal effectiveness and self-actualization.* Englewood Cliffs, NJ: Prentice-Hall.

Johnson, D. W. (1978) *Human relations and your career: A guide to interpersonal skills.* Englewood Cliffs, NJ: Prentice-Hall.

Johnson, D. W., & Johnson, F. P. (1975). *Joining together.* Englewood Cliffs, N.J.: Prentice-Hall, 1975.

Johnson, D. W., & Johnson, R. T. (1990). Social skills for successful group work. *Educational Leadership,* 47, 29-33.

Johnson, S. W., & Morasky, R. L. (1977). *Learning disabilities.* Boston: Allyn and Bacon.

Johnson, S. W., & Morasky, R. L. (1980). *Learning disabilities* (2nd ed.) Boston: Allyn and Bacon.

Jones, F. H. (1987). *Positive classroom discipline.* New York: McGraw-Hill Book Company.

Jones, V. F. & Jones, L. S. (1981). *Responsible classroom discipline: Creating positive learning environments and solving problems.* Boston: Allyn and Bacon.

Jones, V. F., & Jones, L. S. (1986). *Comprehensive classroom management: Creating positive learning environments.* (2nd ed.). Boston: Allyn and Bacon.

Justice, L. M., & Ezell, H. K. (2000). "Enhancing children's print and word awareness through home-based parent intervention". *American Journal of Speech Language Pathology,* 9, 257-269.

Justice, L., & Ezell, H. (2001). Written language awareness in preschool children from low-income households." *Communication Disorders Quarterly,* 22, 123-134.

Kauffman, J. M. (1981) *Characteristics of children's behavior disorders.* (2nd ed.). Columbus, OH: Charles E. Merrill.

Kauffman, J. M. (1989). *Characteristics of behavior disorders of children and youth.* (4th ed.). Columbus, OH: Merrill Publishing.

Kem, M., & Nelson, M. (1983). *Strategies for managing behavior problems in the classroom.* Columbus, OH: Charles E. Merrill.

Kerr, M. M., & Nelson, M. (1983) *Strategies for managing behavior problems in the classroom.* Columbus, OH: Charles E. Merrill.

Kirk, S. A., & Gallagher, J. J. (1986). *Educating exceptional children* (5th ed.). Boston: Houghton Mifflin.

Kohfeldt, J. (1976). Blueprints for Construction. *Focus on Exceptional Children,* 8, 1-14.

Kokaska, C. J., & Brolin, D. E. (1985). *Career education for handicapped individuals* (2nd ed.). Columbus, OH: Charles E. Merrill.

Lambie, R. A. (1980). A systematic approach for changing materials, instruction, and assignments to meet individual needs. *Focus on Exceptional Children,* 13, 1-12.

Landau, S. & Moore, L. (1991). Social skills deficits in children with attention-deficit hyperactivity disorder. *School Psychology Review* 20, 235-251.

Larson, S. C., & Poplin, M. S. (1980). *Methods for educating the handicapped: An individualized education program approach.* Boston: Allyn and Bacon.

Lerner, J. (1976) *Children with learning disabilities.* (2nd ed.). Boston: Houghton Mifflin.

Lerner, J. (1989). *Learning disabilities,: Theories, diagnosis and teaching strategies* (3rd ed.). Boston: Houghton Mifflin.

Levenkron, S. (1991). *Obsessive-compulsive disorders.* New York: Warner Books.

Lewis, R. B., & Doorlag, D. H. (1991). *Teaching special students in the mainstream.* (3rd ed.). New York: Merrill.

Lindberg, L., & Swedlow, R. (1985). *Young children exploring and learning.* Boston: Allyn and Bacon.

Lindsley, O. R. (1990). Precision teaching: By teachers for children. *Teaching Exceptional Children,* 22, 10-15.

Long, N. J., Morse, W. C., & Newman, R. G. (1980). *Conflict in the classroom: The education of emotionally disturbed children.* Belmont, CA: Wadsworth.

Lonigan, C. J., Bloomfield, B. G., Anthony, J. L. & Bacon, K. D. (1999). Relations among emergent literacy skills, behavior problems, and social competence in preschool children from low- and middle-income backgrounds. *Topics in Early Childhood Special Education,* 19, 40.

Losen, S. M., & Losen, J. G. (1985). *The special education team.* Boston: Allyn and Bacon.

Lovitt, T. C. (1989). *Introduction to learning disabilities.* Boston: Allyn and Bacon.

Lund, N. J., & Duchan, J. F. (1988) *Assessing children's language in naturalist contexts.* Englewood Cliffs, NJ: Prentice Hall

Male, M. (1994) *Technology for inclusion: Meeting the special needs of all children.* (2nd ed.). Boston: Allyn and Bacon.

Mandelbaum, L. H. (1989). Reading. In G. A. Robinson, J. R., Patton, E. A., Polloway, & L. R. Sargent (eds*.). Best practices in mild mental retardation.* Reston, VA: The Division of Mental Retardation, Council for Exceptional Children.

Mannix. D. (1993). *Social skills for special children.* West Nyack, NY: The Center for Applied Research in Education.

Marshall, E. K., Kurtz, P. D., & Associates. *Interpersonal helping skills.* San Francisco, CA: Jossey-Bass Publications.

Marshall, et al. vs. Georgia. U.S. District Court for the Southern District of Georgia. C.V. 482-233. June 28, 1984.

Marston, D. B. (1989) A Curriculum-based measurement approach to assessing academic performance: What it is and why do it. In M. Shinn (Ed.). *Curriculum-based measurement: Assessing special children.* New York: Guilford Press.

Mastropieri, M. A., Leinart, A., & Scruggs, T. E. (1999). Strategies to increase reading fluency. *Intervention in School and Clinic,* 34, 278-83, 92.

McDowell, R. L., Adamson, G. W., & Wood, F. H. (1982). *Teaching emotionally disturbed children.* Boston: Little, Brown and Company.

McGinnis, E., Goldstein, A. P. (1990). *Skill streaming in early childhood: teaching prosocial skills to the preschool and kindergarten child.* Champaign, IL: Research Press.

McLoughlin, J. A., & Lewis, R. B. (1986). *Assessing special students* (3rd ed.). Columbus, OH: Charles E. Merrill.

Mercer, C. D. (1987). *Students with learning disabilities.* (3rd. ed.). Merrill Publishing.

Mercer, C. D., & Mercer, A. R. (1985). *Teaching children with learning problems* (2nd ed.). Columbus, OH: Charles E. Merrill.

Meyen, E. L., Vergason, G. A., & Whelan, R. J. (Eds.). (1988). *Effective instructional strategies for exceptional children.* Denver, CO: Love Publishing.

Miller, L. K. (1980). *Principles of everyday behavior analysis* (2nd ed.). Monterey, CA: Brooks/Cole Publishing Company.

Mills v. Board of Education of the District of Columbia. 348 F. Supp. 866 (D.C. 1972).

Montierth, J. (2009). The C-V-C game. Retrieved from http://edweb.sdsu.edu/Courses/EDTEC670/Cardboard/Card/C/c-v-c_game.html]

Mopsik, S. L. & Agard, J. A. (Eds.) (1980). *An education handbook for parents of handicapped children.* Cambridge, MA: Abt Books.

Morris, C. G. (1985). *Psychology: An introduction* (5th ed.). Englewood Cliffs, NJ: Prentice-Hall.

Morris, J. & Demonbreun, C. (1980). *Learning styles* [Videocassettes & Manual series]. Northbrook, IL: Hubbard Scientific Company. (Project STRETCH [Strategies to Train Regular Educators to Teach Children with Handicaps], Module 15.

Morris, J. (1980). *Behavior modification.* [Videocassette and manual series]. Northbrook, IL: Hubbard Scientific Company. (Project STRETCH [Strategies to Train Regular Educators to Teach Children with Handicaps,] Module 16, Metropolitan Cooperative Educational Service Agency.).

Morris, R. J. (1985). *Behavior modification with exceptional children: Principles and practices.* Glenview, IL: Scott, Foresman and Company.

Morsink, C. V. (1984). *Teaching Special needs students in regular classrooms.* Boston: Little, Brown and Company.

Morsink, C. V., Thomas, C. C., & Correa, V. L. (1991). *Interactive teaming, consultation and collaboration in special programs.* New York: MacMillan Publishing.

Musselwhite, C. R. (1986). *Adaptive play for special needs children: strategies to enhance communication and learning.* San Diego: College Hill Press.

National Council of Teachers of Mathematics. (2000). *Principles and standards for school mathematics*. Reston, VA: National Council of Teachers of Mathematics.

National Reading Panel (2000). *Teaching children to read: An evidence-based assessment of the scientific research literature on reading and its implications for reading instruction : Reports of the subgroups*. Washington, D.C.: National Institute of Child Health and Human Development, National Institutes of Health.

North Central Georgia Learning Resources System/Child Serve. (1985). *Strategies handbook for classroom teachers*. Ellijay, GA.

Patton, J. R., Cronin, M. E., Polloway, E. A., Hutchinson, D., & Robinson, G. A. (1988). Curricular Considerations: A Life Skills Orientation. In Robinson, G. A., Patton, J. R., Polloway, E. A., & Sargent, L. R. (Eds.). *Best practices in mental disabilities*. Des Moines, IA: Iowa Department of Education, Bureau of Special Education.

Patton, J. R., Kauggman, J. M., Blackbourn, J. M., & Brown, B. G. (1991). *Exceptional children in focus* (5th ed.). New York: Macmillan.

Paul, J. L. & Epanchin, B. C. (1991). *Educating emotionally disturbed children and youth: Theories and practices for teachers*. (2nd ed.). New York: MacMillan.

Paul, J. L. (Ed.). (1981). *Understanding and working with parents of children with special needs*. New York: Holt, Rinehart and Winston.

Pellegrini, L. & Rooney Moreau, M. (1995). Pragmatics: The social uses of language. Professional development presentation, June 27, 1995.

Pennsylvania Association for Retarded Children v. Commonwealth of Pennsylvania, 343 F. Supp. 279 (E.D. Pa., 1972).

Phillips, V., & McCullough, L. (1990). Consultation based programming: Instituting the collaborative work ethic. *Exceptional Children, 56*, 291-304.

Pierangelo, R., & Giuliani, G. A. (2007). *EDM: The educator's diagnostic manual of disabilities and disorders*. San Francisco, CA: Jossey-Bass.

Podemski, R. S., Price, B. K., Smith, T. E. C., & Marsh, G. E., IL (1984). *Comprehensive administration of special education*. Rockville, MD: Aspen Systems Corporation.

Polloway, E. A., & Patton, J. R. (1989). *Strategies for teaching learners with special needs*. (5th ed.). New York: Merrill.

Polloway, E. A., Patton, J. R., Payne, J. S., & Payne, R. A. 1989). *Strategies for teaching learners with special needs* (4th ed.). Columbus, OH: Merrill Publishing.

Pugach, M. C., & Johnson, L. J. (1989a). The challenge of implementing collaboration between general and special education. *Exceptional children,* 56, 232-235.

Pugach, M. C., & Johnson, L. J. (1989b). Pre-referral interventions: Progress, problems, and challenges. *Exceptional Children,* 56, 217-226.

Radabaugh, M. T., & Yukish, J. F. (1982). *Curriculum and methods for the mildly handicapped.* Boston: Allyn and Bacon.

Ramsey R. W., & Ramsey, R. S. (1978). Educating the emotionally handicapped child in the public school setting. *Journal of Adolescence,* 13, 537-541.

Ramsey, R. S. (1981). Perceptions of disturbed and disturbing behavioral characteristics by school personnel. (Doctoral Dissertation, University of Florida) Dissertation Abstracts International, 42 (49), DA8203709.

Ramsey, R. S. (1986). Taking the practicum beyond the public school door. *Journal of Adolescence,* 21, 547-552.

Ramsey, R. S., (1988). *Preparatory guide for special education teacher competency tests.* Boston: Allyn and Bacon, Inc.

Ramsey, R. S., Dixon, M. J., & Smith, G. G.B. (1986) *Eyes on the special education: Professional knowledge teacher competency test.* Albany, GA: Southwest Georgia Learning Resources System Center.

Reinert, H. R. (1980). *Children in conflict: Educational strategies for the emotionally disturbed and behaviorally disordered.* (2nd ed.). St Louis, MO: The C. V. Mosby Company.

Robinson, F. P. (1961). *Effective study.* New York: Harper.

Robinson, G. A., Patton, J. R., Polloway, E. A., & Sargent, L. R. (Eds.) (1989a). *Best practices in mental disabilities.* Des Moines, IA: Iowa Department of Education, Bureau of Special Education.

Robinson, G. A., Patton, J. R., Polloway, E. A., & Sargent, L. R. (Eds.) (1989b). *Best practices in mental disabilities.* Renton, VA: The Division on Mental Retardation of the Council for Exceptional Children.

Rothstein, L. F. (1995). *Special education law* (2nd ed.). New York: Longman Publishers.

Sabatino, D. A., Sabatino, A. C., & Mann, L. (1983). *Discipline and behavioral management: A handbook of tactics, strategies, and programs.* Aspen Systems Corporation.

Salvia J., & Ysseldyke, J. E. (1991). *Assessment* (5th ed.). Boston: Houghton Mifflin.

Salvia, J. & Ysseldyke, J. E. (1995) *Assessment* (6th ed.). Boston: Houghton Mifflin.

Salvia, J., & Ysseldyke, J. E. (1985). *Assessment in special education (3rd. ed.).* Boston: Houghton Mifflin.

Sattler, J. M. (1982). *Assessment of children's intelligence and special abilities* (2nd ed.). Boston: Allyn and Bacon.

Schloss, P. J., & Sedlak, R. A.(1986). *Instructional methods for students with learning and behavior problems.* Boston: Allyn and Bacon.

Schloss, P. J., Harriman, N., & Pfiefer, K. (1985). Application of a sequential prompt reduction technique to the independent composition performance of behaviorally disordered youth. *Behavioral Disorders,* 11, 17-23.

Schmuck, R. A., & Schmuck, P. A. (1971). *Group processes in the classroom.* Dubuque, IA: William C. Brown Company.

Schubert, D. G. (1978). Your teaching - the tape recorder. *Reading improvement,* 15, 78-80.

Schulz, J. B., Carpenter, C. D., & Turnbull, A. P. (1991). *Mainstreaming exceptional students: A guide for classroom teachers.* Boston: Allyn and Bacon.

Semmel, M. I., Abernathy, T. V., Butera G., & Lesar, S. (1991). Teacher perception of the regular education initiative. *Exceptional Children,* 58, 3-23.

Shea, T. M., & Bauer, A. M. (1985). *Parents and teachers of exceptional students: A handbook for involvement.* Boston: Allyn and Bacon.

Simeonsson, R. J. (1986). *Psychological and development assessment of special children.* Boston: Allyn and Bacon.

Smith, C. R. (1991). *Learning disabilities: The interaction of learner, task, and setting.* Boston: Little, Brown, and Company.

Smith, D. D., & Luckasson, R. (1992). *Introduction to special education: Teaching in an age of challenge.* Boston: Allyn and Bacon.

Smith, J. E., & Patton, J. M. (1989). *A resource module on adverse causes of mild mental retardation.*

Smith, T. E.C., Finn, D. M., & Dowdy, C. A. (1993). *Teaching students with mild disabilities.* Fort Worth, TX: Harcourt Brace Jovanovich College Publishers.

Smith-Davis, J. (1989). *A national perspective on special education.* Keynote presentation at the GLRS/College/University Forum, Macon, GA.

Spafford, C., & Grosser, G. (1993). The social misperception syndrome in children with learning disabilities. *Journal of Learning Disabilities.* 26 (3), 178-189.

Stephens, T. M. (1976). *directive teaching of children with learning and behavioral disorders.* Columbus, OH Charles E. Merrill.

Sternberg, R. J. (1990). Thinking styles: Key to understanding Performance. *Phi Delta Kappan,* 71, 366-371.

Strickland, D. S., & Riley, S. (2006). *Early literacy: Policy and practice in the preschool years.* NIEER policy brief. New Brunswick, NJ: National Institute for Early Education Research.

Sulzer, B., & Mayer, G. R. (1972). *Behavior modification procedures for school personnel.* Hinsdale, IL: Dryden.

Swanson, H. L., & Malone, S. (1992). Social skills and learning disabilities: A meta-analysis of the literature. *School Psychology Review.* 21, 427.

Taberski, S. (2000). *On solid ground: Strategies for teaching reading K-3.* Portsmouth, NH: Heinemann.

Tateyama-Sniezek, K. M. (1990.) Cooperative Learning: Does it improve the academic achievement of students with handicaps? *Exceptional Children,* 57, 426-427.

Thiagarajan, S. (1976). Designing instructional games for handicapped learners. *Focus on Exceptional Children,* 7, 1-11.

Thomas, O. (1980). *Individualized instruction* [Videocassette & manual series]. Northbrook, IL: Hubbard Scientific Company. (Project STRETCH [Strategies to Train Regular Educators to Teach Children with Handicaps]. Module 14.

Thomas, O. (1980). *Spelling* [Videocassette & manual series]. (Project STRETCH [Strategies to Train Regular Educators to Teach Children with Handicaps]. Module 10.

Thornton, C. A., Tucker, B. F., Dossey, J. A., & Bazik, E. F. (1983). *Teaching mathematics to children with special needs.* Menlo Park, CA: Addison-Wesley.

Turkel, S. R., & Podel, D. M. (1984). Computer-assisted learning for mildly handicapped students. *Teaching Exceptional Children, 16,* 258-262.

Turnbull, A. P., Strickland, B. B., & Brantley, J. C. (1978). *Developing individualized education programs.* Columbus, OH: Charles E. Merrill.

U.S. Department of Education. (1993). *To assure the free appropriate public education of all children with disabilities: Fifteenth annual report to Congress on the implementation of the Individuals with Disabilities Education Act.* Washington, D. C.: U.S. Government Printing Office.

Walker, J. E., & Shea, T. M. (1991). *Behavior management: A practical approach for educators.* New York: Macmillan.

Wallace, G., & Kauffman, J. M. (1978). *Teaching children with learning problems.* Columbus, OH: Charles E. Merrill.

Wehman, P., & Mclaughlin, P. J. (1981). *Program development in special education.* New York: McGraw-Hill.

Wesson, C. L. (1991). Curriculum-based measurement and two models of follow-up consultation. *Exceptional Children, 57,* 246-256.

West, R. P., Young, K. R., & Spooner, F. (1990). Precision Teaching: An Introduction. *Teaching Exceptional Children, 22,* 4-9.

Wheeler, J. (1987). *Transitioning persons with moderate and severe disabilities from school to adulthood: What makes it work?* Materials Development Center, School of Education, and Human Services. University of Wisconsin-Stout.

Whiting, J., & Aultman, L. (1990). *Workshop for parents.* (Workshop materials). Albany, GA: Southwest Georgia Learning Resources System Center.

Wiederholt, J. L., Hammill, D. D., & Brown, V. L. (1983). *The resource room teacher: A guide to effective practices* (2nd ed.). Boston: Allyn and Bacon.

Wiig, E. H., & Semel, E. M. (1984). *Language assessment and intervention for the learning disabled.* (2nd ed.). Columbus, OH: Charles E. Merrill.

Willis, J. (2008). "Building a bridge from neuroscience to the classroom". *Phi Delta Kappan, 89,* 424-427.

Wolfgang, C. H., & Glickman, C. D.(1986). *Solving discipline problems: Strategies for classroom teachers* (2nd ed.). Boston: Allyn and Bacon.

Yssedlyke, J. E., Thurlow, M. L., Wotruba, J. W., Nania, Pa. A (1990). Instructional arrangements: Perceptions from general education. *Teaching Exceptional Children, 22,* 4-8.

Ysseldyke, J. E., Algozzine, B., & Thurlow, M. L. (1992). *Critical issues in special education* (2nd ed.). Boston: Houghton Mifflin Company.

Ysselkyke, J. E., Algozzine, B., (1990). *Introduction to special education* (2nd ed.). Boston: Houghton Mifflin.

Zargona, N., Vaughn, S., & Mcintosh, R. (1991). Social skills interventions and children with behavior problems: A review. *Behavior Disorders,* 16, 260-275.

Zigmond, N., & Baker, J. (1990). Mainstream experiences for learning disabled students (Project Meld): Preliminary report. *Exceptional Children,* 57, 176-185.

Zirpoli, T. J., & Melloy, K. J. (1993). *Behavior management.* New York: Merrill.

SAMPLE TEST

1. **All of the following are true about phonological awareness EXCEPT:**
    (0001.03 and 1.05)

    A. It may involve print.
    B. It is a prerequisite for spelling and phonics.
    C. Activities can be done by the children with their eyes closed.
    D. It starts before letter recognition is taught.

2. **How do children make the transition from letter forms to invented spelling?**
    (0004.01)

    A. Write strings of letters
    B. Organize groups of letters
    C. Leave spaces
    D. All of the above

3. **Which of the following explains a significant difference between phonics and phonemic awareness?**
    (0001.05)

    A. Phonics involves print, while phonemic awareness involves language.
    B. Phonics is harder than phonemic awareness.
    C. Phonics involves sounds, while phonemic awareness involves letters.
    D. Phonics is the application of sounds to print, while phonemic awareness is oral.

4. **John is having difficulty reading the word *reach*. In isolation, he pronounces each sound as /r/ /ee/ /sh/. Which of the following is a possible instructional technique which could help solve John's reading difficulty?**
    (0001.04)

    A. Additional phonemic awareness instruction
    B. Additional phonics instruction
    C. Additional skill and drill practice
    D. Additional minimal pair practice

5. **Students are about to read a text that contains words that will need to be understood for the students to understand the text. When should the vocabulary be introduced to students?**
    (0002.02)

    A. Before reading
    B. During reading
    C. After reading
    D. It should not be introduced.

6. Ms. Chomski is presenting a new story to her class of first graders. In the story, a family visits the children's grandparents where they all gather around a record player and listen to music. Many students do not understand what a record player is, especially some children for whom English is not their first language. Which of the following would Ms. Chomski be best to do?
(0002.02)

A. Discuss what a record player is with her students
B. Compare a record player with a CD player
C. Have students look up record player in a dictionary
D. Show the students a picture of a record player

7. Contextual redefinition is a strategy that encourages children to use the context more effectively by presenting them with sufficient vocabulary _____ the reading of a text.
(0002.03)

A. After
B. Before
C. During
D. None of the above

8. What is the best place for students to find appropriate synonyms, antonyms, and other related words to enhance their writing?
(002.04)

A. Dictionary
B. Spell check
C. Encyclopedia
D. Thesaurus

9. Which of the following indicates that a student is a fluent reader? (Easy)
(0003.01)

A. Reads texts with expression or prosody
B. Reads word-to-word and haltingly
C. Must intentionally decode a majority of the words
D. In a writing assignment, sentences are poorly organized structurally.

10. Exposition occurs within a story:
(0003.04)

A. After the rising action
B. After the denouement
C. Before the rising action
D. Before the setting

11. A sixth-grade science teacher has given her class a paper to read on the relationship between food and weight gain. The writing contains signal words such as "because," "consequently," "this is how," and "due to." This paper has which text structure?
(0003.05)

A. Cause and effect
B. Compare and contrast
C. Description
D. Sequencing

12. Which of the following is not a technique of prewriting?
(0004.01)

A. Clustering
B. Listing
C. Brainstorming
D. Proofreading

13. Which is not a true statement concerning an author's literary tone? (Rigorous)
(0004.03)

A. Tone is partly revealed through the selection of details.
B. Tone is the expression of the author's attitude toward his/her subject.
C. Tone in literature is usually satiric or angry[rwag69][SAW70].
D. Tone in literature is analogous to the tone of voice a speaker uses.

14. Which of the following are good choices for supporting a thesis?
(0004.04)

A. Reasons
B. Examples
C. Answer to the question why
D. All of the above.

15. Which of the following contains an error in possessive inflection? (Rigorous)
(0004.06)

A. Doris's shawl
B. Mother's-in-law frown
C. Children's lunches
D. Ambassador's briefcase

16. An item that sells for $375 is put on sale at $120. What is the percent of decrease?
(0006.02)

A. 25%
B. 28%
C. 68%
D. 34%

17. $(5.6) \times (-0.11) =$
(0006.04)

A. -0.616
B. 0.616
C. -6.110
D. 6.110

18. A boat travels 30 miles upstream in three hours. It makes the return trip in one and a half hours. What is the speed of the boat in still water?
(0006.06)

A. 10 mph
B. 15 mph
C. 20 mph
D. 30 mph

19. 3 km is equivalent to:
(0006.07)

A. 300 cm
B. 300 m
C. 3000 cm
D. 3000 m

20. What is the area of a square whose side is 13 feet?
(0007.01)

A. 169 feet
B. 169 square feet
C. 52 feet
D. 52 square feet

21. In similar polygons, if the perimeters are in a ratio of x:y, the sides are in a ratio of:
(0007.04)

A. x : y
B. x2: y2
C. 2x : y
D. 1/2 x : y

22[SAW71]. Given segment AC with B as its midpoint, find the coordinates of C if A = (5,7) and B = (3, 6.5).
(0007.05)

A. (4, 6.5)
B. (1, 6)
C. (2, 0.5)
D. (16, 1)

23. Which of the following is an irrational number?
(0008.01)

A. .362626262...
B. 4
C. $\sqrt{5}$
D. - $\sqrt{16}$ [rwag72][SAW73]

24. Which statement is true about George's budget?
(0008.03)

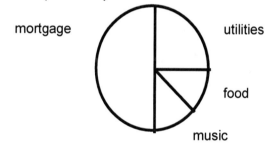

A. George spends the greatest portion of his income on food.
B. George spends twice as much on utilities as he does on his mortgage.
C. George spends twice as much on utilities as he does on food.
D. George spends the same amount on food and utilities as he does on mortgage.

25. Solve for x: $|2x +3| > 4$
(0008.04)

A. $-\frac{7}{2} > x > \frac{1}{2}$

B.. $-\frac{1}{2} > x > \frac{7}{2}$

C. $x < \frac{7}{2}$ or $x < -\frac{1}{2}$

D. $x < -\frac{7}{2}$ or $x > \frac{1}{2}$ [SAW74]

[rwag75]26.   The following chart[rwag76] shows[SAW77] the yearly average number of international tourists visiting Palm Beach for 1990-1994. How many more international tourists visited Palm Beach in 1994 than in 1991? (0009.01)

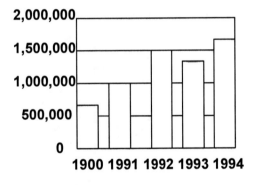

```
2,000,000
1,500,000
1,000,000
  500,000
        0
            1900 1991 1992 1993 1994
```

A.   100,000
B.   600,000
C. 1,600,000
D. 8,000,000

27. What number comes next in this pattern?

3, 8, 13, 18, _____
(0009.02)

A. 21
B. 26
C. 23

D.   5

28. Corporate salaries are listed for several employees. Which would be the best measure of central tendency?

$24,000 $24,000 $26,000
$28,000 $30,000 $120,000
(0009.03)

A. Mean
B. Median
C. Mode
D. No difference

29. What is the last step in the scientific method?
(00010.01)

A. Pose a question
B. Draw a conclusion
C. Conduct a test
D. Record data

30. Accepted procedures for preparing solutions should be made with ____.
(0010.02)

A. alcohol
B. hydrochloric acid
C. distilled water
D. tap water

31. Identify the correct sequence of organization of living things from lower to higher order:
(0010.03)

    A. Cell, Organelle, Organ, Tissue, System, Organism
    B. Cell, Tissue, Organ, Organelle, System, Organism
    C. Organelle, Cell, Tissue, Organ, System, Organism
    D. Organelle, Tissue, Cell, Organ, System, Organism

32. Which of the following is the most accurate definition of a non-renewable resource?
(0010.03)

    A. A nonrenewable resource is never replaced once used.
    B. A nonrenewable resource is replaced on a timescale that is very long relative to human life spans.
    C. A nonrenewable resource is a resource that can only be manufactured by humans.
    D. A nonrenewable resource is a species that has already become extinct.

33. The transfer of heat by electromagnetic waves is called _____.
(0011.02)

    A. conduction
    B. convection
    C. phase change
    D. radiation

34. The Doppler Effect is associated most closely with which property of waves?
(0011.02

    A. Amplitude
    B. Wavelength
    C. Frequency
    D. Intensity

35. What is the most accurate description of the Water Cycle?   (Average Rigor)
(0011.03)

    A. Rain comes from clouds, filling the ocean. The water then evaporates and becomes clouds again.
    B. Water circulates from rivers into groundwater and back, while water vapor circulates in the atmosphere.
    C. Water is conserved, except as a result of chemical or nuclear reactions, and any drop of water could circulate through clouds, rain, ground water, and surface water.
    D. Weather systems cause chemical reactions to break water into its atoms.

36. The mass of an Oreo cookie [rwag78][SAW79]is closest to:
(0011.02)

    A. 0.5 kg[rwag80]
    B. 0.5 grams
    C. 15 grams
    D. 1.5 grams

37. Which one of the following is not a reason why the first Europeans came to the New World?
(0012.01)

A. To find resources in order to increase wealth
B. To establish trade
C. To increase a ruler's power and importance
D. To spread Christianity

38. The Westward expansion occurred for a number of reasons, however, the most important reason was:
(0012.03)

A. Colonization
B. Slavery
C. Independence
D. Economics

39. What does geography include the study of?
(0013.01)

A. Location
B. Distribution of living things
C. Distribution of the earth's features
D. All of the above

40. Who has the power to veto a bill that has passed the House of Representatives and the Senate?
(0013.02)

A. The President
B. The Vice President
C. The Speaker of the House
D. Any member of Congress

41. Capitalism and communism are alike in that they are both:
(0013.04)

A. Organic systems
B. Political systems
C. Centrally planned systems
D. Economic systems

42. An economist might engage in which of the following activities?
(0013.05)

A. An observation of the historical effects of a nation's banking practices.
B. The application of a statistical test to a series of data.
C. Introduction of an experimental factor into a specified sample of a population[rwag81] to measure its effect[SAW82].
D. An economist might engage in all of these.

43. Which of the following is not a type of muscle tissue?
(0014.01)

A. Skeletal
B. Cardiac
C. Smooth
D. Fiber

44. **Through physical activities**[rwag83] **shared with others**[SAW84]**, John has developed self-discipline, fairness, respect for others, and new friends. John has experienced which of the following?**
(0014.02)

A. Positive cooperation psycho-social influences
B. Positive group psycho-social influences
C. Positive individual psycho-social influences
D. Positive accomplishment psycho-social influences

45. **A physical education instructor anticipates and prevents potential injuries, watches for hidden injuries, and takes an injury evaluation of the entire class. Which of the following strategies to prevent injuries is the teacher demonstrating?**
(0014.03)

A. Maintaining hiring standards
B. Proper use of equipment
C. Proper procedures for emergencies
D. Participant screening

46. **The affective domain of physical education contributes to all of the following except:**
(0014.04)

A. Knowledge of exercise, health, and disease
B. Self-actualization
C. An appreciation of beauty
D. Good sportsmanship

47. **Creating movements in response to music helps students to connect music and dance in which of the following ways?**
(0015.01)

A. Rhythm
B. Costuming
C. Speed
D. Vocabulary skills

48. **What should the arts curriculum for early childhood avoid?**
(0015.02)

A. Judgment
B. Open expression
C. Experimentation
D. Discovery

49. **What would the viewing of a dance company performance be most likely to promote?**
(0015.04)

A. Critical-thinking skills
B. Appreciation of the arts
C. Improvisation skills
D. Music vocabulary

50. Mark is a 6th grader. The teacher has noticed that he doesn't respond to simple requests like the other students in the class. If asked to erase the board, he may look, shake his head, and say no, but then he will clean the board. When the children gather together for recess, he joins them. Yet, the teacher observes that it takes him much longer to understand the rules to a game. Mark retains what he reads. Mark most likely has:
(005.01)

A. Autism
B. Tourette's syndrome
C. Mental retardation
D. A pragmatic language disability

SAMPLE ESSAY QUESTIONS[SAW91]

TEST I: ELEMENTARY EDUCATION

Question 1: Recent research has highlighted the importance of reading fluency in improving overall reading comprehension. Describe the nature of reading fluency, its relationship to reading comprehension, and methods you would use to promote it in an early elementary class.

SAMPLE ANSWER:

In its report on teaching children to read (2000), the National Reading Panel defined fluency; the ability to read with speed, accuracy and proper expression without conscious attention and to handle both word recognition and comprehension simultaneously. A fluent reader reads accurately at a speed appropriate to the text, and with expression and phrasing that show an understanding of what is being read. Readers who are not fluent read slowly, often one word at a time or sounding out individual words haltingly, without expression or comprehension. They often leave out words or substitute other words for what is in the text. Measures of fluency typically include accuracy, speed, and prosody, or expression. Running records are frequently used to assess fluency.

Fluency is an important skill when learning to read because it helps readers to progress from the word recognition stage to one where they can understand what they read. When readers don't have to spend time focusing on reading individual words, they can group words together to form ideas, which leads to comprehension. Not only can they grasp the main idea of the text, but they can also make connections between the text and their prior knowledge and events in their own lives.

In order to improve reading fluency, students need practice reading connected text that has been chosen to be consistent with their reading level. I would give students repeated opportunities to read aloud to the teacher, to aides, and to one another. Arranging for the class to read to students at a lower grade level (say, reading to Kindergarten buddies, etc) can provide fun practice of this sort. I would provide ample adult modeling of appropriate oral reading. I would first describe the skills they should practice in a short mini-lesson. I would read a passage inappropriately, demonstrating common mistakes as well as appropriate prosody, etc. I would be sure to read aloud to students frequently. Other techniques I might use would include:

Arranging for students to listen to stories on tape or CD, then having them read the same story to a teacher

Holding whole class or small group choral reading—choral reading provides struggling readers with lots of external cues to help them read fluently.

I would arrange reader's theatre activities with stories like *Anansi and the Talking Melon*, a story with lots of dialogue. Students enjoy theatre and will be practicing their oral fluency skills every time they read.

I would arrange for a "radio" time when children could practice reading text like a news or weather announcer, anything to let them practice reading aloud.

Question #2: You are an elementary teacher of math. Other teachers notice that your students are not spending much time at their desks writing down problems. They are playing with all sorts of blocks, chips, and objects, arranging and rearranging them, talking about them and it's all actually rather noisy. They ask why your kids spend so much time playing. How do you justify the way you run your math class?

SAMPLE ANSWER:

I would point out that the NCTM standards state that children should spend lots of time actively exploring math concepts and *doing* math things. There should be lots of hands-on math at the first stage of math learning, the *concept stage.* At this level, children need lots of interaction with manipulatives. They need to interact intensively with a variety of objects, to see patterns, combinations and relationships among the objects before they can internalize concepts. When introducing new concepts, this is the level at which the child will spend the most time. I know that it is not enough for the teacher to use the objects to demonstrate concepts; the child needs to *discover* concepts and relationships. My role is to ask questions that trigger higher order thinking and learning from the child.

I would point out that all this "playing" IS actually learning math. Not only are they internalizing math concepts, but they are learning how to solve problems together. I have some groups looking for patterns and others making patterns for them to find. I have some groups counting objects into cups that will only hold a specified number, then transferring them all to another level of cup when they reach a certain amount as they explore different base number systems. They work together to find out how to get 45 chips can be put into 8 cups, and how many will be left over, etc.

I would point out that I try to keep the math activities as close to the real uses for which they will need math as possible. Once they are confident in the concrete concepts, I will introduce connections to the more symbolic math that is familiar to adults. We will begin by drawing pictures or using symbols with the objects present (the *connecting level* of instruction). They will begin to write down problems and solutions, design ways to draw and explain what they are doing in symbols and words.

This foundation in concrete manipulation of concepts followed by an increasing use of symbols will provide a strong foundation for later math concepts and work.

Test II Special Education Sample Essay Questions[SAW92]:

Question #3: You are a special education teacher in an elementary school. One of your students, who has autism, is receiving academic instruction in a general education class. The general education teacher approaches you for information regarding strategies for working with this student.

Identify at least two characteristics of autism. Identify strategies to address those characteristics of autism within the general classroom setting.

Sample Response:

Characteristics of Autism:

- Apparent sensory deficit
- Severe affect isolation
- Self-stimulation
- Tantrums and self-injurious behavior
- Echolalia
- Severe deficits in behavior and self-care skills

In working with a student with autism within the general education classroom, the teacher must be aware of the student's sensory deficits and often the need for sensory stimulation. Strategies such as allowing for movement are helpful. Some teachers allow the student to be out of his/her seat or to sit on the floor, or define a specific "space" for the student. Students might be allowed to use "squeeze balls" or other items.

Teachers should also be aware that many students with autism are highly sensitive to sound. Loud noises, such as the fire alarm can be particularly stressful. If possible, warn the student ahead of time. If a warning is not possible, provide reassurance and explanation about what is happening. For general classroom noises, some students are allowed to wear headphones to "tune out" noises.

Students with autism need structure. A classroom schedule, preferably a picture schedule works well and an individual schedule for the student is ideal. If the teacher must deviate from the regular schedule for an assembly or special event, warn the student with autism about the schedule change. It can be helpful to have a visual signal to use when transitions are necessary.

For the higher functioning student with autism, it is important to establish clear rules and expectations for behavior. The teacher needs to provide the student with a means of "escape" if he/she senses that he/she is experiencing stress or sensory overload. This could mean a trip to the restroom or to get a drink or water or a visit to the counselor if the student feels the need.

Many students with autism are highly visual. Use pictures or actual objects as much as possible.

Question #4: Lamar is an eighth grade student who has been identified as having ADD. He has been having behavioral difficulties in school. The IEP team has conducted a Functional Behavioral Assessment (FBA) and has targeted these behaviors: Blurts out in class, talks without permission

The team determines that the antecedents to these behaviors are:

- Independent work
- Teacher directive
- Teacher correction
- During unstructured time.

The behaviors occur an average of 15 to 20 times a day throughout the school day.

Develop a Behavior Intervention Plan for this student, following this format:

I.   Target Behaviors and Definitions
II.   Functional Behavioral Assessment and Identified Function of the Target Behavior
III. Intervention Strategies (Positive Behavioral Supports)
      A. Modifications to the Identified Antecedents
      B. Alternative Behaviors (meet the same function as the target behavior)
IV.   Reinforcers and Consequences
      A. Reinforcers
      B. Consequences
V.   Action Plan for Data Collection and Monitoring of BIP

Sample Response:

I.   Target Behavior and Definitions: Lamar talks out in class without permission.

II. Identified Function of the Behavior: gain attention, gain power & control

III. Intervention Strategies: Staff will remind Lamar to raise his hand before speaking. Staff will only acknowledge Lamar when he raises his hand. Staff will reinforce class rules. Staff will praise or reward Lamar for following the steps.

    A. Modifications to the Identified Antecedents: Lamar will raise his hand to talk to the teacher or class. He will start assignments immediately after they are given. He will ignore other things going on around him.

    B. Alternative Behaviors: Lamar will raise his hand and wait to be acknowledged before speaking. He will write things down that he would normally shout out in class. He can tell the teacher later and does not need to worry about forgetting to say whatever it is he needs to say.

IV. Reinforcers and Consequences:

    A. Reinforcers: Reminders, positive reinforcement, positive attention when on task, reward chart to be submitted for game time on computer

    B. Consequences: Redirection, reminders, private conference with student, loss of computer game time, call parents, office referral.

V. Action Plan: Data will be collected by each teacher on a daily basis using an interval time checklist. Special education teacher will compile weekly report.

ANSWER KEY

1.	A	18.	B	35.	C
2.	D	19.	D	36.	C
3.	D	20.	B	37.	B
4.	A	21.	A	38.	D
5.	A	22.	B	39.	D
6.	D	23.	C	40.	A
7.	B	24.	C	41	D
8.	D	25.	D	42.	D
9.	A	26.	B	43.	D
10.	C	27.	C	44.	B
11.	A	28.	B	45.	D
12.	D	29.	B	46.	A
13.	C	30.	C	47.	A
14.	D	31.	C	48.	A
15.	B	32.	B	49.	B
16.	C	33.	D	50.	D
17.	A	34.	C		

SAMPLE TEST WITH RATIONALES

1. **All of the following are true about phonological awareness EXCEPT: (0001.03 and 1.05)**

   A. It may involve print.
   B. It is a prerequisite for spelling and phonics.
   C. Activities can be done by the children with their eyes closed.
   D. It starts before letter recognition is taught.

   Answer: A. It may involve print.

   All of the options are correct aspects of phonological awareness except the first one, A, because phonological awareness DOES NOT involve print.

2. **How do children make the transition from letter forms to invented spelling? (0004.01)**

   A. Write strings of letters
   B. Organize groups of letters
   C. Leave spaces
   D. All of the above

   Answer: D. All of the above.

   Young children write strings of letters, organize them into groups, and then leave spaces between the groups. These are important steps in a child's early developmental stages of learning to read and write.

3. **Which of the following explains a significant difference between phonics and phonemic awareness? (0001.05)**

   A. Phonics involves print, while phonemic awareness involves language.
   B. Phonics is harder than phonemic awareness.
   C. Phonics involves sounds, while phonemic awareness involves letters.
   D. Phonics is the application of sounds to print, while phonemic awareness is oral.

   Answer: D. Phonics is the application of sounds to print, while phonemic awareness is oral.

   Both phonics and phonemic awareness activities involve sounds, but it is with phonics that the application of these sounds is applied to print. Phonemic awareness is an oral activity.

4. John is having difficulty reading the word *reach*. In isolation, he pronounces each sound as /r/ /ee/ /sh/. Which of the following is a possible instructional technique which could help solve John's reading difficulty?
(0001.04)

A. Additional phonemic awareness instruction
B. Additional phonics instruction
C. Additional skill and drill practice
D. Additional minimal pair practice

Answer A: Additional phonemic awareness instruction

John is having difficulty with the sound symbol relationship between the /ch/ and /sh/. While it may appear at first that this is a phonics problem, it is important to begin with the earlier skill of phonemic awareness to ensure the student has a solid foundational understanding of the oral portions before moving totally into the sound symbol arena. If John is able to distinguish between the two sounds orally, it is obvious that more phonics instruction is needed. However, proceeding directly to phonics instruction may be pointless and frustrating for John if he is unable to hear the distinctions.

5. Students are about to read a text that contains words that will need to be understood for the students to understand the text. When should the vocabulary be introduced to students?
(0002.02)

A. Before reading
B. During reading
C. After reading
D. It should not be introduced.

Answer A: Before reading

Vocabulary should be introduced before reading if there are words within the text that are definitely keys necessary for reading comprehension.

6. Ms. Chomski is presenting a new story to her class of first graders. In the story, a family visits the children's grandparents where they all gather around a record player and listen to music. Many students do not understand what a record player is, especially some children for whom English is not their first language. Which of the following would Ms. Chomski be best to do?
(0002.02)

    A. Discuss what a record player is with her students
    B. Compare a record player with a CD player
    C. Have students look up record player in a dictionary
    D. Show the students a picture of a record player

Answer D: Show the students a picture of a record player

The most effective method for ensuring adequate comprehension is through direct experience. Sometimes this cannot be completed and therefore it is necessary to utilize pictures or other visual aids to provide the students with experience in another mode besides oral language.

7. Contextual redefinition is a strategy that encourages children to use the context more effectively by presenting them with sufficient vocabulary _____ the reading of a text.
(0002.03)

    A. After
    B. Before
    C. During
    D. None of the above

Answer: B. Before

Contextual redefinition is a strategy that encourages children to use the context more effectively by presenting them with sufficient context BEFORE they begin reading. To apply this strategy, the teacher should first select unfamiliar words for teaching. No more than two or three words should be selected for direct teaching.

8. **What is the best place for students to find appropriate synonyms, antonyms, and other related words to enhance their writing? (002.04)**

   A. Dictionary
   B. Spell check
   C. Encyclopedia
   D. Thesaurus

   Answer: D. Thesaurus

   Students need plenty of exposure to the new words. A thesaurus is an excellent resource to use when writing. Students can use a thesaurus to find appropriate synonyms, antonyms, and other related words to enhance their writing.

9. **Which of the following indicates that a student is a fluent reader? (Easy) (0003.01)**

   A. Reads texts with expression or prosody
   B. Reads word-to-word and haltingly
   C. Must intentionally decode a majority of the words
   D. In a writing assignment, sentences are poorly organized structurally.

   Answer: A. Reads texts with expression or prosody.

   The teacher should listen to the children read aloud, but there are also clues to reading levels in their writing.

10. **Exposition occurs within a story: (0003.04)**

    A. After the rising action
    B. After the denouement
    C. Before the rising action
    D. Before the setting

    Answer C. Before the rising action

    Exposition is where characters and their situations are introduced. *Rising action* is the point at which conflict starts to occur and is often a turning point. *Denouement* is the final resolution of the plot.

11. A sixth-grade science teacher has given her class a paper to read on the relationship between food and weight gain. The writing contains signal words such as "because," "consequently," "this is how," and "due to." This paper has which text structure?
(0003.05)

   A. Cause and effect
   B. Compare and contrast
   C. Description
   D. Sequencing

Answer: A. Cause and effect

Cause and effect is the relationship between two things when one thing makes something else happen. Writers use this text structure to show order, inform, speculate, and change behavior. This text structure uses the process of identifying potential causes of a problem or issue in an orderly way.

12. Which of the following is not a technique of prewriting?
(0004.01)

   A. Clustering
   B. Listing
   C. Brainstorming
   D. Proofreading

Answer: D. Proofreading

Proofreading cannot be a method of prewriting, since it is done on already written texts only.

13. Which is not a true statement concerning an author's literary tone?
(Rigorous)
(0004.03)

   A. Tone is partly revealed through the selection of details.
   B. Tone is the expression of the author's attitude toward his/her subject.
   C. Tone in literature is usually satiric or angry[rwag93][SAW94].
   D. Tone in literature is analogous to the tone of voice a speaker uses.

Answer: C. Tone in literature is usually satiric or angry.

Tone in literature conveys a mood and can be as varied as the tone of voice of a speaker (e.g., sad, nostalgic, whimsical, angry, formal, intimate, satirical, sentimental, loving, etc).

14. **Which of the following are good choices for supporting a thesis?
(0004.04)**

   A. Reasons
   B. Examples
   C. Answer to the question why
   D. All of the above.

   Answer: D. All of the above

   All are good ways to support a thesis. When answering "why," you are
   giving reasons, but those reasons are best supported with examples.

15. **Which of the following contains an error in possessive inflection?
(Rigorous)
(0004.06)**

   A. Doris's shawl
   B. Mother's-in-law frown
   C. Children's lunches
   D. Ambassador's briefcase

   Answer: B. Mother's-in-law frown

   Mother-in-Law is a compound common noun and the inflection should be at
   the end of the word, according to the rule: Mother-in-law's frown.

16. **An item that sells for $375 is put on sale at $120. What is the percent
of decrease?
(0006.02)**

   A. 25%
   B. 28%
   C. 68%
   D. 34%

   Answer: C. 68%

   Use 375 – 120 = 255 as the discount. Divide 255 by 375 to get the percent:
   68%, which is answer C.

17. **(5.6) X (-0.11) =**
    (0006.04)

    A. -0.616
    B. 0.616
    C. -6.110
    D. 6.110

    Answer: A. -0.616

    This is simple multiplication. The answer will be negative because a positive times a negative is a negative number, which is answer A.

18. **A boat travels 30 miles upstream in three hours. It makes the return trip in one and a half hours. What is the speed of the boat in still water?**
    (0006.06)

    A. 10 mph
    B. 15 mph
    C. 20 mph
    D. 30 mph

    Answer: B. 15 mph

    Let x = the speed of the boat in still water and c = the speed of the current.

	rate	time	distance
upstream	$x - c$	3	30
downstream	$x + c$	1.5	30[rwag95]

    Solve the system:
    3x - 3c = 30
    1 .5x + 1 .5c = 30

19. **3 km is equivalent to:**
    (0006.07)

    A. 300 cm
    B. 300 m
    C. 3000 cm
    D. 3000 m

    Answer: D. 3000 m

    To change kilometers to meters, move the decimal 3 places to the right.

20. **What is the area of a square whose side is 13 feet?**
(0007.01)

A. 169 feet
B. 169 square feet
C. 52 feet
D. 52 square feet

Answer: B. 169 square feet

Area = length times width (l x w)
Length = 13 feet
Width = 13 feet (square, so length and width are the same)
Area = 13 x 13 = 169 square [rwag96]feet[SAW97]
Area is measured in square feet. The answer is B.

21. **In similar polygons, if the perimeters are in a ratio of x:y, the sides are in a ratio of:**
(0007.04)

A. x : y
B. x2: y2
C. 2x : y
D. 1/2 x : y

Answer: A. x : y

The sides are in the same ratio.

22[SAW98]. **Given segment AC with B as its midpoint, find the coordinates of C if A = (5,7) and B = (3, 6.5).**
(0007.05)

A. (4, 6.5)
B. (1, 6)
C. (2, 0.5)
D. (16, 1)

Answer: B. (1, 6)

23. **Which of the following is an irrational number?**
    (0008.01)

    A. .362626262...
    B. 4
    C. $\sqrt{5}$
    D. $-\sqrt{16}$ [rwag99][SAW100]

    Answer: C

    Irrational numbers are real numbers that cannot be written as the ratio of two integers, such as infinite non-repeating decimals. $\sqrt{5}$ fits this description; the others do not.

24. **Which statement is true about George's budget?**
    (0008.03)

    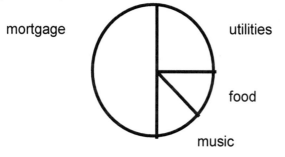

    A. George spends the greatest portion of his income on food.
    B. George spends twice as much on utilities as he does on his mortgage.
    C. George spends twice as much on utilities as he does on food.
    D. George spends the same amount on food and utilities as he does on mortgage.

    Answer: C. George spends twice as much on utilities as he does on food.

25. Solve for x: $|2x + 3| > 4$
   (0008.04)

   A. $-\frac{7}{2} > x > \frac{1}{2}$

   B.. $-\frac{1}{2} > x > \frac{7}{2}$

   C. $x < \frac{7}{2}$ or $x < -\frac{1}{2}$

   D. $x < -\frac{7}{2}$ or $x > \frac{1}{2}$ [SAW101]

   [rwag102]**Answer: D**

   The quantity within the absolute value symbols must be either > 4 or < -4. Solve the two inequalities $2x + 3 > 4$ or $2x + 3 < -4$.

26. **The following chart**[rwag103] **shows**[SAW104] **the yearly average number of international tourists visiting Palm Beach for 1990-1994. How many more international tourists visited Palm Beach in 1994 than in 1991? (0009.01)**

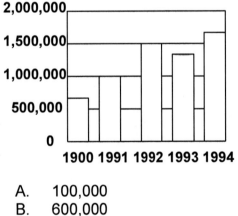

   A. 100,000
   B. 600,000
   C. 1,600,000
   D. 8,000,000

   Answer: B. 600,000

   The number of tourists in 1991 was 1,000,000 and the number in 1994 was 1,600,000. Subtract to get a difference of 600,000, which is answer B.

27. **What number comes next in this pattern?**
3, 8, 13, 18, _____
(0009.02)

A. 21
B. 26
C. 23
D. 5

Answer C: 23

This pattern is made by adding five to the preceding number. The next number is found by adding 5 to 18, which gives the answer 23.

28. **Corporate salaries are listed for several employees. Which would be the best measure of central tendency?**
$24,000 $24,000 $26,000 $28,000 $30,000 $120,000
(0009.03)

A. Mean
B. Median
C. Mode
D. No difference

Answer: B. Median

The median provides the best measure of central tendency in this case, as the mode is the lowest number and the mean would be disproportionately skewed by the outlier $120,000.

29. **What is the last step in the scientific method?**
(0010.01)

A. Pose a question
B. Draw a conclusion
C. Conduct a test
D. Record data

Answer B: Draw a conclusion

The steps in the scientific method, in order, are: pose a question, form a hypothesis, conduct a test, observe and record data, and draw a conclusion.

30. **Accepted procedures for preparing solutions should be made with
____.**
(0010.02)

A. alcohol
B. hydrochloric acid
C. distilled water
D. tap water

Answer: C. Distilled water.

Alcohol and hydrochloric acid should never be used to make solutions
unless one is instructed to do so. All solutions should be made with distilled
water as tap water contains dissolved particles that may affect the results of
an experiment. The correct answer is (C).

31. **Identify the correct sequence of organization of living things from
lower to higher order:**
(0010.03)

A. Cell, Organelle, Organ, Tissue, System, Organism
B. Cell, Tissue, Organ, Organelle, System, Organism
C. Organelle, Cell, Tissue, Organ, System, Organism
D. Organelle, Tissue, Cell, Organ, System, Organism

Answer: C. Organelle, Cell, Tissue, Organ, System, Organism

Organelles are parts of the cell; cells make up tissue, which makes up
organs. Organs work together in systems (e.g., the respiratory system), and
the organism is the living thing as a whole. Therefore, the answer must be
(C).

32. **Which of the following is the most accurate definition of a non-renewable resource?**
    (0010.03)

    A. A nonrenewable resource is never replaced once used.
    B. A nonrenewable resource is replaced on a timescale that is very long relative to human life spans.
    C. A nonrenewable resource is a resource that can only be manufactured by humans.
    D. A nonrenewable resource is a species that has already become extinct.

    Answer: B. A nonrenewable resource is replaced on a timescale that is very long relative to human life-spans.

    Renewable resources are those that are renewed, or replaced, in time for humans to use more of them. Examples include fast-growing plants, animals, or oxygen gas. (Note that while sunlight is often considered a renewable resource, it is actually a nonrenewable but extremely abundant resource[SAW105].)[rwag106] Nonrenewable resources are those that renew themselves only on very long timescales, usually geologic timescales. Examples include minerals, metals, or fossil fuels. Therefore, the correct answer is (B).

33. **The transfer of heat by electromagnetic waves is called _____.**
    (0011.02)

    A. conduction
    B. convection
    C. phase change
    D. radiation

    Answer: D. Radiation

    Heat transfer via electromagnetic waves (which can occur even in a vacuum) is called radiation. Heat can also be transferred by direct contact (conduction), by fluid current (convection), and by matter changing phase, but these are not relevant here. The answer to this question is therefore (D).

34. **The Doppler Effect is associated most closely with which property of waves?**
(0011.02)

    A. Amplitude.
    B. Wavelength.
    C. Frequency.
    D. Intensity.

    Answer: C. Frequency.

The Doppler Effect accounts for an apparent increase in frequency when a wave source moves toward a wave receiver or apparent decrease in frequency when a wave source moves away from a wave receiver. (Note that the receiver could also be moving toward or away from the source.) As the wave fronts are released, motion toward the receiver mimics more frequent wave fronts, while motion away from the receiver mimics less frequent wave fronts. Meanwhile, the amplitude, wavelength, and intensity of the wave are not as relevant to this process (although moving closer to a wave source makes it seem more intense). The answer to this question is therefore (C).

35. **What is the most accurate description of the Water Cycle? (Average Rigor)**
(0011.03)

    A. Rain comes from clouds, filling the ocean. The water then evaporates and becomes clouds again.
    B. Water circulates from rivers into groundwater and back, while water vapor circulates in the atmosphere.
    C. Water is conserved, except as a result of chemical or nuclear reactions, and any drop of water could circulate through clouds, rain, ground water, and surface water.
    D. Weather systems cause chemical reactions to break water into its atoms.

    Answer: C. Water is conserved, except a a result of chemical or nuclear reactions, and any drop of water could circulate through clouds, rain, ground water, and surface water.

All natural chemical cycles, including the Water Cycle, depend on the principle of Conservation of Mass. Any drop of water may circulate through the hydrologic system, ending up in a cloud, as rain, or as surface- or ground-water. Although answers (A) and (B) describe parts of the water cycle, the most comprehensive answer is (C).

36. **The mass of an Oreo cookie** [rwag107][SAW108]**is closest to:**
(0011.02)

   A. 0.5 kg[rwag109]
   B. 0.5 grams
   C. 15 grams
   D. 1.5 grams

Answer: C. 15 grams

Science utilizes the metric system, and the unit of grams is used when measuring mass (the amount of matter in an object). A common estimation of mass used in elementary schools is that a paperclip has a mass of approximately one gram, which eliminates choices B and D as they are very close to 1 gram. A common estimation of one kilogram is equal to one liter of water. Half of one liter of water is still much more than one Oreo cookie, eliminating choice A. Therefore, the best estimation for one Oreo cookie is narrowed to 15 grams, or choice C. Note, also, that it is necessary to be specific about the cookie. Many bakeries now sell cookies the size of large cakes, so simply asking about a cookie would not work.

37. **Which one of the following is not a reason why the first Europeans came to the New World?**
(0012.01)

   A. To find resources in order to increase wealth
   B. To establish trade
   C. To increase a ruler's power and importance
   D. To spread Christianity

Answer: B. To establish trade[rwag110][SAW111]

The Europeans came to the New World for a number of reasons; they often came to find new natural resources to extract for manufacturing. The Portuguese, Spanish, and English were sent over to increase the monarch's power and to spread influences such as religion (Christianity) and culture. Since they were establishing colonies, they assumed that the resources found would *belong to them*. Therefore, the only reason given that Europeans didn't come to the New World was to establish trade. However, Columbus did, in fact, trade with the locals when he found them, even though it was not his major goal. In addition, as time passed, trade (based on resources acquired in various countries' new colonies) did become a major reason for continued European expansion.

38. **The Westward expansion occurred for a number of reasons, however, the most important reason was:**
    (0012.03)

    A. Colonization
    B. Slavery
    C. Independence
    D. Economics

    Answer D. Economics

    Westward expansion occurred for a number of reasons, the most important being economic.

39. **What does geography include the study of?**
    (0013.01)

    A. Location
    B. Distribution of living things
    C. Distribution of the earth's features
    D. All of the above

    Answer D: All of the above

    Geography involves studying location and how living things and earth's features are distributed throughout the earth. It includes where animals, people, and plants live and the effects of their relationship with earth's physical features.

40. **Who has the power to veto a bill that has passed the House of Representatives and the Senate?**
(0013.02)

A. The President
B. The Vice President
C. The Speaker of the House
D. Any member of Congress

Answer A: The President

Once a bill receives final approval from both houses of Congress, it is sent to the President for consideration. The President may either sign the bill or veto it. If he vetoes the bill, his veto may be overridden if two-thirds of both the Senate and the House vote to do so. Once the President signs it the bill becomes a law. If a bill has different versions in the House and Senate, a conference committee[rwag112] meets[SAW113] to resolve the issues and hammer out a single bill to be sent to the President. Any bill approved by the Senate is formally signed by the Vice President, who is President of the Senate and any bill approved by the house of Representatives is formally signed by the Speaker of the House; these signatures are, however, mere formalities, as they must sign on behalf of their respective houses regardless of whether they agree with the bill or not..

41. **Capitalism and communism are alike in that they are both:**
(0013.04)

A. Organic systems
B. Political systems
C. Centrally planned systems
D. Economic systems

Answer: D. Economic systems

While economic and (B) political systems are often closely connected, capitalism and communism are primarily (D) economic systems. Capitalism is a system of economics that allows the open market to determine the relative value of goods and services. Communism is an economic system where the market is planned by a central state. While communism is a (C) centrally planned system, this is not true of capitalism. (A) Organic systems are studied in biology, a natural science.

42. **An economist might engage in which of the following activities?**
    (0013.05)

    A. An observation of the historical effects of a nation's banking practices.
    B. The application of a statistical test to a series of data.
    C. Introduction of an experimental factor into a specified sample of a population[rwag114] to measure its effect[SAW115]..
    D. An economist might engage in all of these.

    Answer: D. An economist might engage in all of these

    Economists use statistical analysis of economic data, controlled experimentation, and historical research in their field of social science.

43. **Which of the following is not a type of muscle tissue?**
    (0014.01)

    A. Skeletal
    B. Cardiac
    C. Smooth
    D. Fiber

    Answer: D. Fiber

    The main function of the muscular system is movement. There are three types of muscle tissue: skeletal, cardiac, and smooth.

44. **Through physical activities[rwag116] shared with others[SAW117], John has developed self-discipline, fairness, respect for others, and new friends. John has experienced which of the following?**
    (0014.02)

    A. Positive cooperation psycho-social influences
    B. Positive group psycho-social influences
    C. Positive individual psycho-social influences
    D. Positive accomplishment psycho-social influences

    Answer: B. Positive group psycho-social influences

    Through physical activities shared with others, whether informal play one on one or in groups, or more formalized sports, John developed his social interaction skills. Social interaction is the sequence of social actions between individuals (or groups) that modify their actions and reactions due to the actions of their interaction partner(s). In other words, they are events in which people attach meaning to a situation, interpret what others mean, and respond accordingly. Through socialization with other people, John feels the influence of the people around him.

45. **A physical education instructor anticipates and prevents potential injuries, watches for hidden injuries, and takes an injury evaluation of the entire class. Which of the following strategies to prevent injuries is the teacher demonstrating?**
(0014.03)

A. Maintaining hiring standards
B. Proper use of equipment
C. Proper procedures for emergencies
D. Participant screening

Answer: D. Participant screening

In order for the instructor to know each student's physical status, he or she takes an injury evaluation. Such surveys are one way to know the physical status of an individual. It chronicles past injuries, tattoos, activities, and diseases the individual may have or had. It helps the instructor to know the limitations of each individual. Participant screening covers all forms of surveying and anticipation of injuries.

46. **The affective domain of physical education contributes to all of the following except:**
(0014.04)

A. Knowledge of exercise, health, and disease
B. Self-actualization
C. An appreciation of beauty
D. Good sportsmanship

Answer: A. Knowledge of exercise, health, and disease

The affective domain encompasses emotions, thoughts, and feelings related to physical education. Knowledge of exercise, health, and disease is part of the cognitive domain.

47. Creating movements in response to music helps students to connect music and dance in which of the following ways?
(0015.01)

A. Rhythm
B. Costuming
C. Speed
D. Vocabulary skills

Answer A. Rhythm

Students should be able to understand the connections made between movement and music is related by rhythm.

48. What should the arts curriculum for early childhood avoid?
(0015.02)

A. Judgment
B. Open expression
C. Experimentation
D. Discovery

Answer A: Judgment

The arts curriculum for early childhood should focus on the experimental and discovery aspects of the arts. The emphasis should be on creative processes with little judgment, and criticism should be minimal.

49. What would the viewing of a dance company performance be most likely to promote?
(0015.04)

A. Critical-thinking skills
B. Appreciation of the arts
C. Improvisation skills
D. Music vocabulary

Answer B: Appreciation of the arts

Live performances are an important part of learning arts and they help to develop aesthetic appreciation of the arts. A dance company performance is one example of a live performance that students could attend.

50. **Mark is a 6th grader. The teacher has noticed that he doesn't respond to simple requests like the other students in the class. If asked to erase the board, he may look, shake his head, and say no, but then he will clean the board. When the children gather together for recess, he joins them. Yet, the teacher observes that it takes him much longer to understand the rules to a game. Mark retains what he reads. Mark most likely has:**
(005.01)

A. Autism
B. Tourette's syndrome
C. Mental retardation
D. A pragmatic language disability

Answer D: A pragmatic language disability

Pragmatics is the basic understanding of a communicator's intent, particularly when nonverbal cues and body language are involved. The issue here is Mark's ability to respond correctly to another person.

XAMonline, Inc.
25 First Street, Suite 106
Cambridge, MA 02141
P. 1-800-509-4128
F. 617-583-5552
www.XAMonline.com

2010

Georgia Assessments for the Certification of Educators (GACE)

PO#:	Store/School:
Address 1:	
Address 2:	
City, State, Zip:	
Credit Card #:	Exp:
Phone:	Fax:
Email	

Titles	Paperback Information				eBook Information				
Titles	Paperback ISBN	Retail	Qty.	Paperback Subtotal	eISBN	Retail	Qty.	eBook Subtotal	Title Subtotal
Art Education Sample Test 109, 110	978-1-58197-531-4	$15.00			978-1-60787-783-7	$12.00			
Basic Skills 200, 201, 202	978-1-58197-257-3	$28.95			978-1-60787-777-6	$25.95			
Biology 026, 027	978-1-58197-773-8	$59.95			978-160787-778-3	$56.95			
Chemistry 028, 029	978-1-58197-540-6	$59.95			978-1-60787-786-8	$56.95			
Early Childhood Education 001, 002 (Available May 1st)	978-1-60787-064-7	$39.95			978-1-60787-679-3	$36.95			
Early Childhood Special Education 003 (Available May 1st)	978-1-60787-065-4	$39.95			978-1-60787-677-9	$36.95			
Early Childhood Special Education 004	978-1-60787-061-6	$59.95			978-1-60787-692-2	$56.95			
Educational Leadership 173, 174	978-1-60787-060-9	$59.95			978-1-60787-781-3	$56.95			
English 020, 021 (Available May 1st)	978-1-60787-062-3	$59.95			978-1-60787-680-9	$56.95			
English to Speakers of Other Languages (ESOL) 119, 120	978-1-60787-063-0	$59.95			978-1-60787-693-9	$56.95			
French Sample Test 143, 144	978-1-58197-530-7	$15.00			978-1-60787-802-5	$12.00			
Health and Physical Education 115, 116	978-1-58197-774-5	$59.95			978-1-60787-785-1	$56.95			
History 034, 035	978-1-58197-685-4	$59.95			978-1-60787-784-4	$56.95			
Mathematics 022, 023	978-1-58197-346-4	$59.95			978-1-60787-794-3	$56.95			
Media Specialist 101, 102	978-1-58197-724-0	$59.95			978-1-60787-788-2	$56.95			
Middle Grades Language Arts 011	978-1-58197-598-7	$59.95			978-1-60787-793-6	$56.95			
Middle Grades Mathematics 013	978-1-58197-345-7	$59.95			978-1-60787-791-2	$56.95			
Middle Grades Reading 012	978-1-58197-535-2	$59.95			978-1-60787-789-9	$56.95			
Middle Grades Science 014	978-1-58197-591-8	$59.95			978-1-60787-790-5	$56.95			
Middle Grades Social Science 015	978-1-58197-686-1	$59.95			978-1-60787-792-9	$56.95			
Paraprofessional Assessment 177	978-1-58197-588-8	$59.95			978-1-60787-796-7	$56.95			
Physics 030, 031	978-1-58197-569-7	$59.95			978-1-60787-782-0	$56.95			
Political Science 032, 033	978-1-58197-549-9	$59.95			978-1-60787-795-0	$56.95			
Professional Pedagogy Assessment 171, 172	978-1-58197-589-5	$28.95			978-1-60787-797-4	$25.95			
Reading 117, 118	978-1-58197-534-5	$59.95			978-1-60787-787-5	$56.95			
School Counseling 103, 104	978-1-58197-587-1	$59.95			978-1-60787-799-8	$56.95			
Science 024, 025	978-1-58197-584-0	$59.95			978-1-60787-779-0	$56.95			
Spanish 141, 142	978-1-58197-720-2	$59.95			978-1-60787-800-1	$56.95			
Special Education General Curriculum 081, 082	978-1-58197-610-6	$73.50			978-1-60787-801-8	$70.50			

Order Subtotal

Discount

1 book $8.70, 2 books $11.00. 3+ books $15.00   Shipping

TOTAL